Passion for Skiing

This aerial photo of the Dartmouth Skiway shows the snow filled ski slopes of the Winslow and Holt's Ledge sides of the ski area layout (Adrian Bouchard, 1979).

Passion for Skiing

*The story of how one small college, Dartmouth College,
has been the dominant institution in the development of modern skiing.*

By Stephen L. Waterhouse

*With James C. Collins, Richard Durrance II, H. Roger Hansen, Stuart J. Keiller, Jeffrey R. Leich,
Douglas C. Leitch, James W. Page, Charles J. Sanders, Nicholas B. Stevens (Editor),
Thomas G. Washing and many others.*

Forewords by Warren Miller and Chiharu "Chick" Igaya

Book design by A Mind 4 Design, Claremont, New Hampshire
Printed by Whitman Communications, Lebanon, New Hampshire

ISBN 0-9758820-1-5

Photographs courtesy of the Dartmouth College Library, the Hood Museum, Dartmouth College Photographer Joe Mehling, Richard Durrance II and the Durrance Trust, Jeff Leitch and the New England Ski Museum, Judy Holmes, Ned Jacoby, Steve Bradley, Sachele Burns, and Stephen Waterhouse.

Front cover: Paul Starrett Sample, American, 1896-1974; Title: Winter Holiday, c.1954, oil on canvas, 30-1/4" x 40". Gift from Springville High School Junior and Senior Class 1954, Springville Museum of Art collection 1954.002. Sample is a 1920 graduate of Dartmouth College and a former artist-in-residence at Dartmouth (1938-1962)

Back cover: The Dartmouth Skiway at the End of the Season (April, 2009) by Felix de la Concha, American (born Leon, Spain 1962). Oil on canvas, 18 in. by 29 in. The artist is a former resident of Hanover, NH.

First Edition; First Published in February, 2010

I dedicate this book to all the members of the Dartmouth family who have been leaders on the ski slopes, cross country courses, and in all the other ways of sliding over snow. We also salute those innovators in the various related ski industry careers we outline in this book for, in Robert Frost's words, they have often taken "The road less traveled by and that has made all the difference…"

And

The several Dartmouth family members who have left us in the past year, or even earlier, but still managed to make important contributions to the written words in this book… Blair Wood '30, Herman Nunnemacher '36, Budd Schulberg '36, Dave Bradley '38, Sarge Brown, William Stark '50, Edward Lathem '51 and many, many more…….

Stephen L. Waterhouse
February, 2010

UNDERWRITERS

We wish to express our sincere thank-you to all the many alumni and friends of this project who have stepped up with gifts to underwrite the publication of Passion for Skiing. We particularly wish to thank the following Dartmouth Classes and Clubs, individuals and organizations for their support at our medal award levels.

MULTI-GOLD MEDALS

Dartmouth Class of 1965

GOLD MEDAL

Stephen L. Waterhouse '65, Tu '67

SILVER MEDAL

Dartmouth Class of 1958
Dartmouth Class of 1963
Dartmouth Class of 1964
Dartmouth Class of 1981

Trygve E. Myhren '58, Tu '59
Thomas G. Washing '63
Fritz W. Corrigan '64

Byrne Foundation
and John J. Byrne III '81

BRONZE MEDAL

Dartmouth Class of 1957
Dartmouth Class of 1962
Dartmouth Class of 1966
Dartmouth Class of 1967
Dartmouth Class of 1971
Dartmouth Class of 1985
Dartmouth Club of the Vail Region

Marvin '32, Carmen & Thomas '63 Chandler
Norman E. "Sandy" McCulloch Jr.'50 H '00
Clark A. Griffiths '57, Th '58
Josiah Stevenson IV '57, Tu'58
Arthur M. Kelton, Jr. '61
Mimi & Carl Boe '65
Theodore L. Bracken '65
James W. Griffiths '65
H. Roger Hansen '65
Ronald H. "Ron" Riley '65
Marshall F. Wallach '65
R. Stephen Cheheyl, Jr. '67
Peter M. Fahey '68, Th'69, Th'70
Peter S. Pratt '71

Hohliebi School's "Winter Term in Switzerland"
and Peter Harvey '90

Dartmouth Images LLC/Dartmouth Coop and
Gene Kohn '60

Hanover Inn and Carl Pratt, General Manager

NOTE: Michael Gonnerman '65, Jim Griffiths '65, Robert Murphy '65 and John Walters '62 have organized the financial underwriting. The Class of 1965 has provided the administration for the financial activities to complete this book.

CONTENTS

PASSION FOR SKIING

BUILDING THE FOUNDATION

SKI RESORT DEVELOPMENTS IN THE UNITED STATES

THE INDIVIDUAL INFLUENCERS AND CONTRIBUTORS

Looking Back, Looking Forward

Conclusion

Appendices

Abbreviations frequently used in this book:

A-K	Arlberg Kandahar Ski Race	NESM	New England Ski Museum
AMC	Appalachian Mountain Club	NSP	National Ski Patrol
AIAW	Association of Intercollegiate Athletics for Women	NSSHF	National Ski and Snowboard Hall of Fame
CCC	Civilian Conservation Corps	NSA	National Ski Association
D	Dartmouth College	ROTC	Reserve Officers Training Corps
DMS	Dartmouth Medical School	Th	Dartmouth's Thayer School of Engineering
DOC	Dartmouth Outing Club		
D-Plan	Dartmouth's four-quarter academic calendar	Tu	Dartmouth's Amos Tuck School of Business Administration
FIS	Federation Internationale de Ski	USOC	U.S. Olympic Committee
H	Honorary degree from Dartmouth College	USSA	U.S. Ski and Snowboard Association
ISHA	International Skiing History Association	USEASA	U.S. Eastern Amateur Ski Association
ISU	Intercollegiate Ski Union	UNH	University of New Hampshire
IWSU	Intercollegiate Winter Sports Union	UVM	University of Vermont
NCAA	National Collegiate Athletic Association	WC	Winter Carnival

FOREWORD

DARTMOUTH'S CONTINUING LEGACY

By Warren Miller (San Juan Islands, Washington)

Thawed out and then forged from the freezing-cold New England winters came the Dartmouth graduates who changed the face of American mountains more than did those of any other college or university.

On Hanover's nearby Oak Hill was built the first overhead cable ski lift in the country. Prior to that lift being built, men such as Charlie Proctor had to climb snow-covered mountains to ski and to preach the gospel of freedom on a pair of skis from the mountainside. That freedom was not easily earned in the 1920's and thirties because the skis were at least seven-foot six-inches long and without metal edges. It was impossible to hang on to the ice on the side of a hill. There were no safety bindings and the bindings that did exist were very dangerous. However the boots were low, soft and comfortable.

Warren Miller with his camera in front of Webster Hall at Dartmouth where he first showed his ski movies

Students still get off the train in White River Junction and travel on to Hanover. Just as I did the first time I showed my feature length ski film, and filmed the already famous Dartmouth Winter Carnival in the early 1950s. It was during the worst thaw on record and the expected magnificent ice sculptures had already melted away in the hot winter sun.

Even the thaws and deep freezes familiar to everyone who lives in that part of the world did not deter early skiers from flocking to Dartmouth like moths to a candle. Graduates such as Charlie Proctor, who competed in the 1928 Olympics in St. Moritz, Switzerland, left to carry the gospel west to Omaha, Nebraska where he helped invent the world's first chairlift. It was designed for the Union Pacific Railroad in their then experimental ski resort, Sun Valley, Idaho. Charlie's ski lift knowledge, together with his knowing the engineer who built an offshore banana-loading overhead cable rig, helped to get Sun Valley's revolutionary chairlift running on Dollar Mountain within six months. I first met Charlie Proctor in Yosemite in 1944 when he was the General Manager of Badger Pass and he was still a formidable skier almost twenty years after he graduated from Dartmouth.

Another exceptional alumnus, Dick Durance, was farther ahead of other ski racers of the 1930s than any other American ski racer has been since that time. As such, he did more to further the marriage of ski racing and his college than any other Dartmouth student before or after him. Three-time winner of the Harriman Cup at Sun Valley, he was America's top skier in the 1936 Olympics in Germany.

If you wanted a college education and to be a ski racer at the same time, Dartmouth was the only place to go. In recent years ski academies designed specifically to train ski racers, such as the Burke Academy in Vermont, have taken over the ski racing side of winning but not the educational side to the same extent. So far, no graduate of the Burke Academy or the other dozen or so ski academies has gone on to develop ski resorts such as Dartmouth alumnus Tom Corcoran did when he developed Waterville Valley, New Hampshire.

The list of accomplishments of Dartmouth alumni and staff reads like the Who's Who of skiing in North America.

There is Sarge Brown who worked tirelessly for many years on the trails, safety aspects and innovative snow grooming procedures at Vail, Colorado.

Jim Branch developed Alyeska, Alaska, the only ski resort in America where you can go night skiing all day long.

Roger Brown and Barry Corbet, working as a team, revolutionized short ski film production with their 1960s Mobius Flip movie.

Steve Bradley developed and patented an early snow grooming machine that a skier with a low IQ could tow down the hill hoping he never fell under the almost half-ton roller that he was racing down in front of and securely attached to.

Walter Prager who coached Dartmouth racers through the 1950s and helped produce such outstanding Olympic skiers as Silver medalist Chick Igaya and North American Downhill Champion Ralph Miller, the first man in the world to be clocked at over 100 miles an hour on a pair of skis.

The list of Dartmouth alumni who have contributed to your enjoyment of skiing is virtually endless and continues to this day. A sampling of them and their contributions over the last 100 years, whether great or small, is documented within these pages as testimony to their on-going legacy.

Background on Warren Miller: *The most prolific of all the ski movie makers, Warren is a legend in too many ways to be recounted here, and a member of the US National Ski Hall of Fame (1978). He has spent his adult life, over 60 years, traveling around the ski industry, meeting practically every important figure in the business since WW II.*

***

MY DARTMOUTH YEARS

By Chick Igaya '57 (Tokyo, Japan)

Simply stated, my four years at Dartmouth College were the highlight of my life. They were absolutely wonderful, and I am honored to be asked to provide a few words to introduce this epic story of Dartmouth's worldwide, historic impact on the development of modern skiing.

The smooth skiing style of Ski Team Captain Chick Igaya '57 is on display at Winter Carnival.

My own skiing story begins with the luck of having a skiing father and mother who taught me. They got me started, but it was Dartmouth that contributed so much to my future development, and what I have achieved in life. I was mentored by a wonderful person, CV Starr (founder of AIU, the developer of the Stowe, Vermont ski area, and a strong admirer of what he felt was the most renowned school in skiing, Dartmouth College). CV introduced me to Dartmouth where he said I would get an excellent education, and experience skiing in new ways. My matchless College President, John Sloane-Dickey, our legendary ski coach and world champion racer, Walter Prager, and some outstanding ski teammates and classmates did the rest.

During my Dartmouth undergraduate years, Coach Prager encouraged me, as my father Kunio had done, to develop my own style. Despite going to Dartmouth shortly after WW II, I was treated by my classmates and ski mates just like everybody else. The only time I thought of myself as Japanese was when I woke up in the morning and washed my face in front of the mirror. I learned that Dartmouth men, and today women as well, treat people for who they are, not where they have come from. And I received a superb education in addition to my skiing experiences.

The 1950ties were a golden age for the Dartmouth ski team so the competition for the positions on the first team was fierce. Dartmouth had many great skiers in the past like the first Olympian John Carleton '22, the precocious Charlie Proctor '28, legendary racer Dick Durrance I '39, the whole Olympic team in '36 and '40 was mainly Dartmouth boys, and others… And since my day, the school continues to turn out more Winter Olympic athletes than any other institution. However, I am partial to the racers from my era like Brooks Dodge '51 Th '54, Bill Beck '53, Tom Corcoran '54, Ralph Miller '55, Tony Spiess '56 from Austria, Egil Stigum '56 from Norway, Bill Smith '58, and many more who challenged me to a level of skiing that I never expected to reach. It was an incredible personal honor to be awarded a Dartmouth "letter", and to be elected Captain of the Dartmouth Ski Team.

As I look at the history of skiing at Dartmouth, I am constantly amazed at the diversity of the contributions by racers and non-racers alike; and how they have made great use of the marvelous Dartmouth education. This book is a wonderful compilation of data on how skiing developed, and the ever present contribution of the Dartmouth family. It is more than a ski racing story, and it is an extreme personal pleasure to be part of it in some small way. It is also very special to share this activity with Warren Miller who has done so much to build the excitement for skiing around the world thru his lifetime of making ski movies.

Background on Chick Igaya '57: *Silver Medalist, 1956 Olympics; member of 3 Japanese Olympic teams (1952, 1956, 1960); Japanese National Champion; 5 time US National Alpine Champion; 6 time NCAA Champion; member of US National Ski Hall of Fame (1971); current Vice-President, IOC; Chairman Emeritus, AIU Japan (See full summary in Chapter XIV).*

Steve Waterhouse (standing) first outlines his concept on the impact of Dartmouth skiers to the Dartmouth Ski Weekend (DSW) group gathered in Keystone, February 2008

Knowledgeable historians of skiing; (l. to r.) Densmore '83, Waterhouse '65, Leich '71 and Leitch '65 lead discussions on the implications of Dartmouth's skiing history in Hanover, August 2008.

Hayes '65 (near right), Densmore '83, Leich '71 and Orr '58 (far right) listen as Jacoby '40 (near left) tells his story of cutting trails in Sun Valley in 1939 (70+ years ago!) with many future legends of skiing, August 2008.

ACKNOWLEDGEMENTS

FIRST, I am greatly indebted to the many alumni, staff, and family members of Dartmouth College who provided information and financial contributions to support this book. I believe the information shows that modern skiing would not exist in the form it does today if it were not for the efforts of members of the greater Dartmouth family over the past 120 years. Over 500 people have been helpful in one way or another to aid our research process that has taken almost five years to bring to fruition. We hope this book will properly honor these contributions.

There are many individuals who deserve to be singled out. First, our steady, ever-present editor and researcher, Nick Stevens, has read and massaged almost as many words as I have and provided countless valuable suggestions. Ned Jacoby has contributed amazingly to our photo collection and with his first-hand accounts of trail cutting in Sun Valley in 1939 and printing the first view in 1938 of possibly the most famous skiing action photo ever, i.e., Dick Durance skiing across a slope in New Zealand. Then, our group of guest chapter writers—Jim Collins, Dick Durrance II, Roger Hansen, Stu Keiller, Jeff Leich, Doug Leitch, Jim Page, Charlie Sanders and Tom Washing—have contributed immensely to the overall process. Leitch, Page and Washing have been involved in many aspects of this project other than just their chapters. Durrance, Leich and Sanders have added significantly by making available photo images in their possession.

Warren Miller and Chick Igaya took the time to comment in their own words on their personal Dartmouth impressions in their respective Forewords. And our many other article writers or contributors—Monk Bancroft, Mary Kendall Brown, Roger Brown, Bill Cantlin, Tom Corcoran, Lisa Feinberg Densmore, Nate Dougall, David Durrance, Newc Eldredge, Cartter Frierson, Peter Graves, Clark Griffiths, Fred Hart, Henry Hof, Pam Crisafulli Hommeyer, David Hooke, Gerry Huttrer, Rick Isaacson, Ned Jacoby, Valerie Chiyo Jaffee, Alan Kouns, Eric Lambert, Larry Langford, Chelsea Little, Jean Nunnemacher Lindemann, Phil Livingston, Morten Lund, Jamie Meiselman, Tony Morse, Rick Moulton, Chik Onodera, Phil Peck, Chip Richards, Max Saenger, Heidi Nunnemacher Schulz, Meredith Scott, Peter Stark, Jan Stearns, Joe Stephenson, Nick Stevens, Bill Smith, Curt Synnes, Doug Tengdin, Cami Thompson, Bradley Wall, Joe Walsh, Kevin Whitcher, Ed Williams, George Wood, Roger Urban, Johannes von Trapp and Sam von Trapp—have often added a personal context to the story because they were involved in some way.

John Walters, Mike Gonnerman, Bob Murphy, Jim Griffiths and the leaders of the Dartmouth Classes of 1957, 1958, 1962, 1963, 1964, 1965, 1966, 1967, 1971, 1981 and 1985 bought in to our ambitious goal and helped organize all the generous "Underwriters" (listed on a separate page) and the many other contributors. The Class of 1965 provided extra help by taking an administrative role, controlling the inflow/outflow of underwriter funds. For all the contributors, their support here is an example of their personal love for skiing and Dartmouth.

We had great help from the Rauner Special Collections Library, now based in Webster Hall where many of us first saw Warren Miller's ski movies during his early trips to Hanover. Dartmouth College is fortunate to have this outstanding resource in the building, named after the great alumnus Daniel Webster, with interesting background notes, pictures, and historical documents on Dartmouth's alumni/others going back over 250 years. Senior Archival Specialist Barbara Krieger was invaluable in tracking down historical facts. Photographic Records Specialist Pat Cope spent long hours finding and scanning many of the images we have included. Special Collections Librarian Jay Satterfield, Archivist Peter Carini, Joshua Shaw '95, Phyllis Gilbert, and the rest of the Special Collections staff, were always very helpful in providing details that have been included in this book.

We obtained many unusual images through the efforts of Mint Dole (Minnie Dole's son), Bob Downey and his Keystone team, Art Kelton and many others. We benefitted from exceptional photographers like Joe Mehling, Judy Holmes, Dick and Meg Durrance, Steve Bradley, Sachele Burns and Ned Jacoby. The Hood Museum's Barbara MacAdam researched Paul Sample's ski paintings for us. Tim Sample (Paul's son), Vern Swanson (Director of the Springville Museum in Springville, Utah), and artist Felix de la Concha helped with specific skiing art. Some older images are not as viewable as we might like, but they provide a wonderful historical reference.

Dartmouth President Jim Wright and his then assistant Dan Nelson (now the new head of Dartmouth's Outdoor Programs) regularly supported our project in useful ways. The folks in Dartmouth's Alumni Affairs area, particularly Sue Young, helped secure background information for us; Bob Donin (Dartmouth's General Counsel) worked on legal issues with us; and Sean Plotner (and his staff at the Dartmouth Alumni Magazine) did some early advertising for us.

We have been privileged to have the involvement of many leading ski history writers, including John Allen, Morten Lund and John Fry, who have supplemented our history team of Jeff Leich (Director, New England Skiing Museum "NESM"), Meredith Scott (Director, Vermont Ski Museum), Dean Ericson (President of International Skiing History Association "ISHA"), Rick Moulton (Board Member of ISHA and NESM; leading authority on ski films), Lisa Densmore (Emmy-winning producer/presenter of ski and outdoor programs) and others. All shared their expertise openly, and with no personal gain, to help highlight this amazing history.

My 35 years in London, Great Britain, and Europe produced some other helpful contacts, including the family of Britain's ski legend, Sir Arnold Lunn. We had input from Herbert Scheider (son of ski legend Hannes Schneider); Elisabeth Hussey (leader of the British Ski Journal after Sir Arnold retired and the FIS timeline team); Philippa Hussey (who helped Sir Arnold with the Arlberg-Kandahar races); and John Collard who supplied data from his own ski research. The British Ski Club (Maggie Colpus and Bridget Cassey) and Ski Library in Wimbledon, England, and Austrian historian Anneliese Gidl supplied useful information.

We appreciated the great help from the USOC Olympic Library, Tom Kelley at US Ski and Snowboard, David Orr (Dartmouth's Wearers of the Green award program), Joe Walsh at US Paralympics, Max Cobb at US Biathlon Association, Dick Needham at ISHA, the New England Ski Museum and Peter Dodge/Cami Thompson (current Dartmouth ski team coaches).

Several hundred Dartmouth alumni came through with information not previously known. I was particularly pleased to have the input from older Dartmouth alumni who have had an amazing range of experiences (ski racing in the 1930/40s, service in the 10th Mtn Div in WW II, founding ski areas, and lots of other ski related activities) that impact on our story, including, Bill Rotch '37, John Litchfield '39, Percy Rideout '40, Gary Allen '40, Phil Puchner '44, Newc Eldredge '50, John Caldwell '50, Bill Briggs '54, Tom Corcoran '54 and Ralph Miller '55. As I indicated in the Dedication, certain individuals (Blair Wood '30, Herman Nunnemacher '36, Budd Schulberg '36, Dave Bradley '38, Sarge Brown, and William Stark '50) have contributed greatly to the writing despite not being with us as we wrap up. Kari Prager '69 (son of ski legend Walter Prager) provided input on his father that was very valuable in finally sorting out Walter's personal life at Dartmouth. There are many, many other alumni who provided insights, but I will miss some if I tried to list them all so I won't do that. Just know that we thank you for your help.

I deeply regret that I could no longer rely on the unerring editorial advice of my great friend Edward Lathem '51 on the final preparation of this book. Ed has been the master of Dartmouth's history books and the most prolific editor/writer ever about the college's history. Unfortunately, he is not around at the end as he left us just a few months ago while hard at work in his office. While he lived, he provided us with some very useful historical information. One does not expect to see another Edward Connery Lathem, former Librarian of the College, Bezaleel Woodward Fellow, and an able Counselor to several Dartmouth Presidents.

AND A COMMENT -

This has been a fascinating project with more unexpected results than I could have possibly imagined. With nearly 70 volunteer writers and hundreds of cooperative researchers, interview facilitators, interested alumni, and far-flung friends of skiing across the country and around the world contributing almost entirely via e-mail and Skype, the information flow became constant, diverse, and voluminous.

What began as a simple exploration five years ago, with no expectation that a documentary book of any respectable size would be produced, snowballed into near avalanche proportions when I introduced my basic premise to the February 2008 gathering of Dartmouth skiers at the Dartmouth Ski Weekend event in Keystone and then at CarniVAIL. One comment led to another and another and then another. A stone tossed loosely in to our spontaneous network created ripples that turned in to more new information flowing in than we had ever expected.

A team of like-minded individuals grew up around the idea that something special was being uncovered. Meetings in August 2008 first in Vail, led by Tom Washing '63, and then in Hanover, assisted by Dan Nelson '75 and the President's Office, generated momentum and more ideas. I asked others to join me in the research and writing process, and the historical results of this book show that the response has been overwhelming and extremely productive. Nick Stevens '58, a former ski instructor, English major at Dartmouth, retired Army Intelligence officer and now part time editor, offered his expertise to work with all writers during the editing process which has been very helpful. Similarly, Ned Jacoby '40, a lifelong graphics artist since his days of working in Professor Proctor's photo lab in the late 1930s, provided consistent help in massaging or supplying many of our image needs. Doug Leitch '65 did great research on the early DOC history, and provided some excellent writing based on this research and his life time in skiing. Tom Washing '63 and Jim Page '63 spent long hours finding the detailed notes that appear in our Appendix, and this now provides as accurate a summary of Dartmouth ski facts as exists.

The Project benefited greatly from having access to the new media of the Internet, online search programs like Google, and advanced mobile computer systems. These combined to provide nearly instantaneous electronic transfer of original texts, archival documents, photographs and other images needed to illustrate my original contention. The information was never lost, bent, torn, or delayed in the mail. All of it could be filed without using any physical space and most could be retrieved with relative ease. That kind of efficiency would have required a sizable dedicated indoor area and a couple of staffers on 24-hour shifts in pre-computer times, making the project next to impossible to complete in an earlier day. My original concept of exposing examples of Dartmouth's leadership in skiing has developed into a final product that, by continual e-mail exchanges of questions, discussions and decisions among a few key people, has, we think, highlighted what has to be a one of a kind institutional leadership role in developing a major multi-faceted sport that no other institution can claim in any other sport.

Even in the last 3 days before going to print, access to rapid fire responses via the Internet allowed us to find and place several interesting photographs and make other appropriate text corrections. And the exchange between the Book Designer (KB Miller), the Printer (Steve Whitman Tu '67) and his staff, the Indexer (Christine Hoskin), my helpmates at the Rauner Special Collections Library (Pat Cope and Barbara Krieger) and individual members of the team was seamless and extremely productive.

As the hub of this group effort for the past two years—and for five years when I include my earlier research—I functioned with my trusty laptop, average computer skills, and occasional use of my Blackberry to coordinate research and other necessary activities while on the move in a busy life. My daily digital link with the hundreds of participants in this project was critical to keeping the momentum going and meeting my self-imposed deadline for getting this work into print. This may be one of the first publications of a non-commercial nature—that is, I do not have the dedicated resources of even the most modest magazine, newspaper, or book publisher at my disposal nor do I have a profit motive as my incentive—to collect such a massive quantity of data on a single historical subject and compile it into a comprehensive reference document. I believe this is a unique situation and may not be the forerunner of others to follow. On the other hand, the technical approach remains open to anyone to complete a similar odyssey with some other subject, so just maybe there will be more to come.

Finally, I want to express not only my heartfelt appreciation to everyone who showed up online or in person to contribute in a material way to the content of this book, but also my pride and delight in the enthusiastic spirit of shared enterprise so many people have displayed in wanting to help make the overall story richer—more complete, more accurate, and more interesting—and to play a part in preserving the abundant, but sometimes perishable, evidence that ensures Dartmouth College is accorded its rightful place in the history of the sport it helped to launch and popularize in this country over 100 years ago. This legacy is the foundation for a new century of Dartmouth influence and leadership in the wider world of skiing, a sport that is almost synonymous with the 240-year-old institution so aptly nicknamed "the college on the hill."

Stephen L. Waterhouse
February, 2010

The Dartmouth Winter Carnival has contributed greatly to building enthusiasm amongst individual skiers, and providing a starting place for many developments in skiing; these colorful posters have been a highlight of each Winter Carnival.

CHAPTER I

INTRODUCTION

By Stephen L. Waterhouse '65, Tu '67
Businessman, Author of *Dartmouth's Dedicated Alumni* (2004)

The institution at the heart of this tale began over two centuries ago when Eleazar Wheelock obtained permission from King George III of England to start a new college in the "Colonies." Eleazar had been trying to find a "place" and to get permission for his college for many years. He was finally offered some land in the middle of New Hampshire by the State's leader, Governor Wentworth, and had the good fortune to have a prior connection with the 2nd Earl of Dartmouth who, as the British Government Secretary for the Colonies, was able to request a Royal Charter from the king. In 1769, George III authorized the ninth—and final—Royal Charter for an American college. And thus was born Dartmouth College, smack dab in the middle of a mountainous region of New England where the winters were cold and snow- filled. Over the next 230 years, Eleazar and his successors developed an outstanding academic institution, always thought of as one of the top ten schools of higher education in the United States. And it still is!

In the 19th Century and earlier, skiing was practiced in a rudimentary form in many parts of the world. Skiing was originally used simply as a utilitarian means to get around in snowy conditions. As the 20th Century began, more organized skiing activities started taking place around the world leading to ski lifts, ski resorts, special racing approaches and many elements of skiing never before seen. This is what we will refer to as "modern skiing". In North America, Dartmouth College, its alumni, students, staff, and their families have taken on a leadership role in developing modern skiing that continues to this day. This book will highlight the most relevant activities the greater Dartmouth community has undertaken, and is still doing, and how these activities have uniquely influenced the development of skiing. As one reviews these areas of participation in skiing and their results, we believe it will become clear to the reader, as it has to the many members of the very large team involved with gathering this information, that the greater Dartmouth family has been *the single greatest force in the development of skiing in North America*, and to a lesser extent, a very positive stimulant to skiing developments in other parts of the world. Although the Dartmouth influence on winter activities is broader than skiing, it is in the skiing area that this one small institution, Dartmouth College, based in Hanover, New Hampshire, USA, is preeminent. In the course of perusing this story, the reader will find many examples of this group's enthusiastic and irrepressible "passion for skiing."

Skiing did not start in New Hampshire, and almost certainly did not have an early start on the North American Continent. A recent historical analysis by a study team led by British ski historian Elisabeth Hussey for the Fédération International de Ski (FIS), and involving many ski historians from around the world, has created a timeline of how skiing developed. This study reports that ski artifacts were found as early as 6,000 B.C. in Russia, and many other early relics of skiing have been found in the Scandinavian countries. It is also recognized that Europeans were sliding around on early skies in the Alps long before any similar activities were noted in North America. In the United States, skiing activities started in the Midwest when Scandinavian immigrants settled there long before the time period on which this book focuses. However, much of what passed as skiing in those earlier days was of a different nature than what we now describe as modern skiing which involves special equipment to groom the slopes, ski lifts to move people effortlessly up the mountains, refined racing techniques and supervisory organizations, specially constructed ski areas, a variety of clothing options, real estate developments mainly for skiing, and a myriad of other features that exist today and which only came about in the 20th Century.

Skiing for sport and recreation started in New Hampshire, and at Dartmouth College, sometime late in the 19th Century. Organized group skiing was first noted by the 1880s. Some members of the Dartmouth Class of 1897 wrote extensively about their college ski activities (1893-1897) in a story told at their 50th Class Reunion. This is a similar time frame to when a celebrity British skier brought skiing to nearby Vermont. That skier, Sherlock Holmes creator Sir Arthur Conan Doyle, visited his author friend Rudyard Kipling at his home near Brattleboro in 1894, bringing along a pair of skis that Doyle had obtained from one of his earlier ski trips to Switzerland. Doyle's visit was probably not the earliest ski adventure in Vermont as some have suggested, but it would have been one of the first by a visiting foreigner for recreational purposes. At this early date, none of the key elements of what we have defined as modern skiing existed. To ski down a hill, an individual had to first climb up the hill. No one was organizing slalom races or the like since the concept did not yet exist. The creation of a major industry dedicated to facilitating pleasurable ski adventures was several decades away. What existed as ski equipment was elemental at best. All these aspects of skiing were to dramatically change as the sport evolved in the 20th Century.

"PASSION" AND SKIING

We allot considerable space to detailing the facts of our story which are many, varied, and truly fascinating; but the subject of "passion" and why skiers do what they do is an important ingredient. Webster's dictionary assigns terms like "compelling emotion, a strong fondness, an enthusiasm, or a great desire" to define passion. We include many personal histories involving magical lifelong experiences to illustrate how this **"Passion for Skiing"**—for simply sliding over snow—became expressed in exciting alpine runs, challenging cross-country trekking, aggressive snowboarding, thrilling extreme skiing, purpose-made ski clothing and specialized skis, innovative ways to stabilize and repair a broken leg, and new methods for instructing novice skiers in the best techniques for learning quickly and safely, or a myriad of other activities and products.

For many people, this simple activity of sliding over snow seems quite peculiar and not something to stir much enthusiasm. And yet, as you will see, this sport has so stirred the inner soul of thousands that it has led them to pursue a lifelong involvement in this particular act. It is this passionate enthusiasm that has been the driving force to cause so many of Dartmouth's bright, energetic graduates, as well as the college's staff and their families, to play a major role in the making of a great industry. Lest you think this is some small collection of people involving a few true believers, a recent study team of students and faculty at The Amos Tuck School of Business Administration at Dartmouth, one of the leading graduate schools of business in the world according to the various surveys of *The Wall Street Journal* and London's *Financial Times*, has analyzed the financial contribution of the greater ski industry in the United States and concluded that the size of this industry is roughly equivalent to two companies the size of the computer giant Microsoft or three companies the size of the world's largest purveyor of coffee, Starbucks. Annually, the greater ski industry in the U.S. alone generates some $ 25-30 *billion* in Gross Domestic Product. To anyone, that should indicate how significant the financial contribution of the simple act of skiing has become to the US economy! And if one took in to account the economic activity of this industry in the many other countries around the world where skiing is organized, the worldwide impact of skiing-related businesses is very significant.

Dartmouth College, its alumni, students, family and friends can rightfully claim the lead role in the development of skiing in the past, present and future. As Robert Frost, Class of 1896, has famously written: "I shall be telling this with a sigh somewhere ages and ages hence: Two roads diverged in the wood, and I -- I took the one less traveled by, And that has made all the difference." Dartmouth alumni, students, and friends have taken the road less traveled by, and that has made all the difference in the amazing development of skiing in North America and other parts of the world! Individual passions take many different forms. This book has outlined many examples of how the lives of numerous members of the greater Dartmouth family have been impacted by this sport and their "road taken." To provide a sense of this, here are comments on the lives of four individuals who are mentioned in chapters of this book.

David J. Bradley '38 is one of the people who played a central role in the development of ski jumping in the United States and is one of three member of his family to be elected to the National Ski and Snowboard Hall of Fame (NSSHF). His passion for skiing led him to many other activities that we refer to in different chapters, but his greatest enthusiasm was for the soaring leap. His excitement for this activity is captured in a story on jumping called "The Big Jump" that David wrote in 2001 for *Skiing Heritage*, the journal published by the International Ski History Association (ISHA). He vividly describes what it was like to make a real leap of faith when jumping at Dartmouth's Vale de Tempe ski jump, once the biggest in the East.

"Memory steps out on a platform higher than the golf course pines. Once on top the worst is over: you've quit the doubting and fretting, you've lugged your boards up 127 steps while other skiers clattered down. Now you deposit your skis on the icy planks, clean off the snow, pant a moment, then snug your boots into the iron toe plates and feel the heel springs tighten down solidly.

The view from the jump at Dartmouth's Vale of Tempe

You step in line. The next rider gets the signal from someone down on the knoll. He crosses himself three times, once more just in case. "Make it good," he says, banging off the top onto icy tracks. He crouches, accelerating from 0 to 35 mph in three seconds. The curve to the takeoff lofts him into space. He twists, flails, drops in a clatter of skis, and disappears.

Wait then while someone down there fixes a hole in the hill. You check your bindings, take some deep breaths, and look around over the white peace of the hills—seeing almost nothing. Your job is down there, straight down, down and up and out and down where you cannot see and up again—all in one motion.

At last the signal comes. "Make it good," you say, to yourself as much as to the next jumper, and slide over the edge. Gravity hauls you down, incredible acceleration, a crescendo of roaring, the takeoff rushes up toward you. Every cell of your body is shouting: "Hit it right, right at the lip, between the spruce boughs. Up and forward and out over your tips." Centrifugal force glad hands you into streaming air. The knoll flashes under, then the whole giddy panorama bursts open: the scarred hill, the upturned faces, the exact spot where you will land. Float. Float. Jolt! Catch your balance, strain to hold it through the dip, cheeks pulling down, colors going gray—then you're up and out and gliding to a stop, all the bells ringing." [1]

Murray W. Thurston '43 founded the Sunday River ski area in Maine. Sometimes it takes unusual actions to make your dreams come true. Murray was faced with an early challenge to find a source of money to finance the start of the ski area. He had to raise $90,000 to build the facilities to start ski slope operations. First, he sold lifetime and five-year passes as well as stock in his Bethel Area Development Corp. Then, still needing more money, the corporation applied for a $40,000 Small Business Association loan to bridge the gap in funding needed to open up the area. No one had ever obtained such a loan for this purpose before, and none are known to have been granted one later, so it was an unusual move. Murray passed away in 2008, and his son, **David P. "Fuzzy" Thurston '72**, reported the "real story" to the Bethel Citizen newspaper: "This [loan given to Sunday River] was the first, and probably only, SBA loan to start a ski area. One of the first big investors, which means he probably had $250 [invested] in [Sunday River], hid a bottle of Scotch next to a brook on the way up the mountain. He poured the SBA guy three glasses [when he came to visit], and that's how they got the loan. That's fact." Passions can lead one to organizing strange ways to get things done[2] (see Chapter VII).

Ralph E. Miller, Jr. '55, DMS '59, J. Brooks Dodge '51, Th '54, and Buddy Werner, the US's leading racer of the day, were in St. Anton in 1954 to train for the World Championships in Are, Sweden. Brooks had some regular ski pants made by a local tailor. It occurred to Ralph and Buddy that they could escape the use of ties around the knees to tighten the pants for downhill racing, the then common way to cut down on wind resistance, by getting this tailor to create a very tight ski pant for their use. The three implemented the proposal via Brooks' tailor, enabling them to out-race the Austrians in a trial race, which was a highly unusual result. The Austrians found out about this tactic and created their own tight racing pants. They won the next race, firmly cementing this style of ski pant as a feature of ski racing. A passion for winning ski races was the motivation for all these skiers. They all wanted to go faster.[3] There is more to this story so look for it later in the book (see Chapter XIII).

John Byrne, III '81's personal history has been, as has that of so many other people in our story, not only a result of his own "passions" but is yet another thread of Dartmouth green weaving along in ways not often recognized, but all very real, through the history of modern skiing. As an illustration of this, consider the involvement of other Dartmouth family members in John's short lifetime of ski adventures, including his instructor days at Okemo in Vermont, his love for the unique elements of Alta's operations, and his current ownership of Alyeska, Alaska's most significant ski area. Factually, the green tread is entwined everywhere as we show later when highlighting **Donald Cutter '45 (**the early manager of Okemo, Copper Mountain and the Dartmouth Skiway,); **Dick Durrance '39** (the early developer of Alta and other areas); **Jim Branch '52** (the early mountain manager of Alyeska and later a leader of Sno-Engineering, now called the SE Group); and **Sel Hannah '35** (the original founder of the SE Group that is peppered full of Dartmouth connections). John's ski area recently hosted the 2009 National Slalom Championship, won by **David Chodounsky '08**. John's life shows how the green thread of past, present, and future Dartmouth skiers is alive.... and still winding a path through yon hills and plains covered in snow (see Chapter IX and XIV).

The enthusiasm for skiing binds thousands of individuals together in pursuit of a common interest. Skiing is something that has been enjoyed and fostered by the underlying efforts of this one institution for over 100 years. Dartmouth's leading role in the development of the basic activity of sliding over snow has been an important tenant of life for all skiers whether they are aware of this or not. For many Dartmouth-connected skiers, these passions have been, and continue to be, very important to follow whenever and wherever they can.

THE EARLY DAYS OF DARTMOUTH SKIING

If a college were to be established for the purpose of becoming a "fountainhead of the skiing spirit"[4], it would certainly make sense to locate it where the climate favored long snowy winters and the topography offered varied terrain, from rolling hills and plains to the proximity of high mountains, the kind of place that would move Dartmouth poet **Richard Hovey, Class of 1885,** to describe as "Daughter of the woods and hills, Dartmouth, my... sybil of the snows."[5] Such was the geography of Hanover, New Hampshire, when Eleazar Wheelock ventured up the Connecticut River Valley in 1770 to inaugurate activities at Dartmouth College. His institution, sited on a hill above the river, was founded, not to become a fountainhead of skiing spirit, but with the mission to bring spiritual enlightenment and scholarship to the inhabitants of the wilderness far north of the colonial civilization of coastal Connecticut. Young men would enroll and earn their degrees at Dartmouth for more than a century before even the word "ski" was ever spoken on campus, yet a fountainhead of the skiing spirit it did become.

When and where the first parallel ski tracks sliced through New Hampshire snowfields are difficult questions to answer. The first ski club in America was organized in the 1870s east of Hanover in Berlin, NH. The earliest records of local Hanoverians using skis suggest that they appeared in that part of the state in the 1880s. Being the site of a college campus, Hanover benefited from a regular influx of new people with ideas often more adventurous than those in the mostly rural surrounding communities. Ski tracks began to cross the snows covering the Hanover Plain at least as early as that decade. **Edwin B. Frost, 1886,** whose father was a doctor on the Dartmouth Medical School faculty, attended the college and later became a noted astronomer. In his book, *An Astronomer's Life*, Frost reminisced about growing up in Hanover: "Skis did not begin to come into use in Hanover until the end of the [eighteen-] eighties. I inherited a pair from **Arthur Fairbanks**, my classmate, who shared them with **C. [Charles] S. Cook**…These skis were so long that a pair of old shoes had been attached to the rear for a second person. The situation got very painful for the man riding behind when the leader began to toe in and the skis spread in the rear."[6]

Arthur Fairbanks, Class of 1886, was another Hanover boy who became a Dartmouth student and skier, marking the beginning of a familiar pattern of local Hanover children taking a serious interest in skiing that became significant as skiing subsequently developed. Where those early skis originated is not mentioned, but soon other pairs of skis began arriving as students came to Dartmouth. However, the presence of skis was such a rarity in the late 19th century that individuals, who proudly owned and used them, would later recognize their historic significance by making a record of their early skiing experiences. **William R. Jarvis, 1893**, a student from just down the river in Claremont, NH, recalled that he was "in the proud possession of a pair of eleven-foot skis which originally belonged to a cousin and which were in his room when [he] was a freshman [1889] in Dartmouth Hall."[7] A Dartmouth Trustee and friend of Mr. Jarvis wrote about Jarvis's interest in presenting those venerable skis to the College. "Mr. Jarvis is anxious to present these skis to the College for their historic interest, and I thought that perhaps you or John Rand of the Outing Club…might cook up some pleasant occasion or make appropriate arrangements to bring about Mr. Jarvis's presentation of the skis to the College with suitable ceremonies."[8] No record exists of whether they were ever presented following his expressed intentions in 1952.

Soon after Jarvis was storing his skis in Dartmouth Hall, **John B. Thomes, DMS 1894,** enrolled at the Dartmouth Medical School bringing along another pair of skis. He noted, "[He] purchased them from a Swede living in my old home town in Cumberland, Maine, in 1887."[9] Like Mr. Jarvis, Dr. Thomes later offered his skis to the College after reading an account in the *Dartmouth Alumni Magazine* that led him to consider his as perhaps the first skis used in Hanover. Dr. Thomes shipped his old skis back to Dartmouth in 1935. By then, skiing had become quite the dominant winter sport on campus, and Dartmouth Outing Club Director, **Daniel P. Hatch, Jr. '28**, was thinking of converting one of the rooms at the Outing Club House into a Trophy Room and the skis would be among the exhibits there.

In 1893, a bunch of Dartmouth undergraduates came to town ready for some winter fun. They left a story and more detailed comments on skiing than any prior group or individual. **Herman Holt, 1897,** was the instigator and record keeper of this class group, noting in his diary in the winter of 1896:

The enthusiastic skiers of the Dartmouth Class of 1897. Composit photograph shows Herman Holt (center) jumping over the prone form of Weld Rollins. Clockwise from upper left, Weld Rollins, Herman Holt, Paul Clay, George Tent, George Lewis, W.H. Ham, Joseph Simpson, Edward Woodworth, Albert Morrill and Horace Pender.

15 Jan – [At Dartmouth] tried to get some skees [sic], but in vain.

16 Jan – Horace found that the skees [sic] Paul Clay ordered from Portland [Maine] had come. They cost 75 cents per pair and 17 cents express. I practiced some before supper and succeeded in loosing a foot piece. Sup. Pender, Clay and I found the foot piece I practiced some more skeeing.

27 Jan – At four the six of us went skiing down Mink Brook way. It was fine, I only had one fall.

28 Jan – Put on skiing togs, and went up with Al [Morrill], Auty, Stodie [Hodie?] and Pa [Weld Rollins] to the observatory seeing a star through transit. Then we went skiing toward Mink Brook. An elegant moonlight night, and almost as light as day. We had an out of sight good time.

31 Jan – Pa, Auty, Horace and I

went skiing toward the Connecticut. Snow just right. I had two disastrous falls. Horace broke part of one of the ends of his skis, the ski escaping from him and going down river bank.

Early Dartmouth skiers checking out their equipment.-

The snow for a Winter Carnival statue gets used for a ski run.

19 Feb – Horace, Pa and I went skiing, built jump at bottom of "long" hill and jumped all over ourselves. Nearly broke my neck. Good fun. Jerry, Rounds and I went skiing in Vale of Tempe. Elegant.[10]

Winters on the Dartmouth campus were on the brink of radical change. Holt and his pals were discovering the fun of ski outings, the excitement of learning this new skill, the "out of sight good times," and the elegance of "jumping all over" themselves. But after a winter or two of their whoops and hollers echoing through the pine-studded Hanover winterscape, Holt and company all just graduated and left town, taking their skis with them. They had gotten some notice with a small item in the student newspaper, *The Dartmouth*, where the following appeared on January 31, 1896: "Lewis, Clay, Morrill, Rollins, and Holt of the junior class have formed a skee club. Trips into the surrounding country will be taken every week."[11] But skiing had yet to find its promoter at Dartmouth, so by the first bloom of pussy willows in the spring of 1897, Holt's ski tracks were nothing but memories. The written record of skiing faded for the next few years, too.

After the turn of the century, skis and skiing became a more frequent sight around the Hanover area. However, finding skis was a problem. Some brought them to Hanover from distant parts. Some students bought them from the carpenter at the College carpentry shop. Fred Garvey, a Dartmouth carpenter from just across the river in Thetford, Vermont, would take raw planks home, steam the ends to bend the tips and fix a leather strap. They sold well. And some students figured out how to make skis themselves. **John Ash** and **Ralph Wilder**, **Class of 1899**, may have been the first students to make a real pair of skies in 1896, but others followed as the years rolled on. The New Hampshire hills were still white and cold in the winter, and students were learning to make some use of them. However, the inauguration of the real force behind the development of skiing, not just at Dartmouth and in the Hanover area, but across the US and to some degree around the world, was just about to be started; and with it came the development of modern skiing.

MODERN SKIING

The purpose of our story is to explain the impact of this one institution, Dartmouth College, on the development of modern skiing. Early on, we began to recognize that it went far beyond starting the first outing club, having some early racing successes, leading many aspects of the 10th Mountain Division in World War II, and founding the occasional ski area. We did not expect the depth and diversity of the contributions we discovered, and neither did the experts in the history of skiing. To present this information, we have created a series of chapters that present the Dartmouth contributions by topic. The chapters are then organized in four groups to show the evolving elements of the greater ski industry and how each has been affected by the expansive Dartmouth family:

1. Building the Foundations – The History of the DOC and its many Contributions, Ski Racing at all Levels, US Ski Clubs, and the 10th Mountain Division
2. Ski Resort Developments in the United States – East, West, and Other Regions
3. The Legendary Influencers who Popularized Skiing, organized Support Industries, created Technical Innovations, and made International Contributions

4. Looking Forward, Looking Back – Profiles of People who have made an Impact and some interesting Elements of Skiing Today

Within each chapter, you will read about the exploits of the people who have contributed to that topic. A number of individuals will have contributed to more than one topic and so will be mentioned in more than one chapter. For each chapter, we have organized special articles on relevant subjects within the main story of that chapter, highlighting special issues of interest. Where possible, these articles have been written by individuals with their own personal knowledge of the subject. In Chapter XIV, we highlight a wide range of individuals who have made contributions to skiing, providing the reader with another way to gain a sense of the amazing diversity of contributions by the Dartmouth family. We briefly mention some highlights below.

BUILDING THE FOUNDATIONS

As will be shown thru the comments in several chapters, the start of organized skiing activities at Dartmouth, and essentially in the United States, began with the founding of the **Dartmouth Outing Club (DOC)** during the winter of 1909-1910 by **Fred Harris '11**. Throughout the past 100 years, the DOC has influenced the skiing interests of thousands of Dartmouth graduates, and the DOC participants have been at the heart of all of skiing developments. These men and women have gone on to both enthusiastically spread the word on skiing and creatively help evolve various aspects of the sport. It all started with Harris who will be featured throughout this book and who was one of the first people elected to the National Ski Hall of Fame (later the National Ski and Snowboarding Hall of Fame) where Dartmouth-connected members are by far the largest group from any institution, representing some 13% or more of the total (see Appendix 1).

Fred Harris '11 continued to give advice to succeeding heads of the DOC. Here he is advising Fred Hart '58 at the 1958 Winter Carnival.

Real changes in skiing were taking shape as the Dartmouth students and professors began to find ways to explore new mountain terrain, to use recreational skiing for specific events, and to organize ways to race against each other. The first ski exploration of note by Dartmouth students or staff was an ascent (and descent) of Mt. Moosilauke on January 31, 1912, according to **Carl Shumway '13** in his story "Cross Country on Skis to Mt. Moosilauke" for a book, *Dartmouth Out O' Doors,* published by Fred Haris in 1913. He made the trip with his classmate **G. S. "Eric" Foster '13**. Other trips like this were to occur regularly over the years, from Mt. Moosilauke to Tuckerman Ravine to Mt. Mansfield to mountains right across the country and the world as the adventurous Dartmouth family spread out to explore new skiing territory.

In 1910 (Winter Sports Day) and 1911 (by adding entertainment), the DOC created the first, and still greatest, Winter Carnival. This became a very big deal, attracting coverage by *Life* magazine, *The New York Times*, *The Boston Globe*, *Playboy* magazine, and used as a theme in some major motion pictures. In 1938, Norwegian skater Sonja Henie starred in *My Lucky Star*, a musical, which was her fourth and possibly best movie. Norway's "Ice Queen," who won Olympic Gold Medals in 1928, 1932 and 1936, was joined by stars of the day like Richard Green, Cesar Romero, Joan Davis, Arthur Treacher and Buddy Ebsen in a take-off on Dartmouth's Winter Carnival skating events. Then, in 1939, the Dartmouth Winter Carnival was immortalized in a movie aptly titled *Winter Carnival* that featured Ann Sheridan, Richard Carlson, Helen Parish, and James Corner. In a footnote, F. Scott Fitzgerald was hired to write the script, but he was fired after he found the refreshments of the Dartmouth campus and the parties at the fraternity houses to be more motivating than spending time creating the desired script (see Chapter III).

The first "collegiate ski race" was held February 1, 1914, at McGill University in Montreal when **Professor Charles Proctor, 1900,** led a party of 12 from Dartmouth, including faculty and students, to engage a group of skiers at McGill. Later, Professor Procter helped organize the first US Slalom (Hanover, 1925) and Downhill races (Mt. Moosilauke, 1927), and became known to many as the Father of American Skiing. He helped start a variety of collegiate racing activities in the 1920s and '30s. He led the effort to put together the Lake Placid Olympics in 1932. He and his son, **Charlie Proctor '28** (a Dartmouth racer, 1928 Olympic skier, and US ski industry leader), are both in the National Skiing and Snowboard Hall of Fame (NSSHF). In one contribution, Charlie Jr. helped to design the first chair lift in Sun Valley, Idaho, for millionaire Averell Harriman, which was based partly on the first overhead cable lift J-bar built at Dartmouth's Oak Hill in 1935-36. We provide new details on the background of the Oak Hill lift that shows how this first in North America lift was created and how this concept was spread around by enthusiastic ski innovators like Proctor and another member of the Hall of Fame and the greater Dartmouth family, Fred Pabst.

As ski racing evolved in the US and elsewhere, the personal connections between members of the Dartmouth family and leading ski enthusiasts in Europe was an important element. Up through the 1930s, European racing techniques were far advanced over those in North America. Initially in cross-country running, the Lilienfeld technique in the high Alps and the Norwegian technique in the lower mountains were the most common. In 1913, a new technique of Telemarking began to gain supporters in the high mountains using long skis and short sticks. Finally, the Christiania approach gained in popularity. In the 1920s, German writer and filmmaker Arnold Fanck wrote a book that outlined the best ski technique of the day, the Stem-Christiana, exemplified best by photo images of the skiing of Austrian Hannes Schneider, often called the Father of Modern Skiing.

Sir Arnold Lunn pictured at the first winter ascent of the Eiger in 1924.

Arnold Lunn organizng the Arlberg-Kandahar races with his A-K administrator, Philippa Hussey, FIS historian Elisabeth Hussey's sister.

Largely thru the Dartmouth connection, New England had become the initial hot bed of Alpine skiing and the legendary Schneider came to Mount Cranmore, NH, in 1939, after escaping imprisonment in his native St. Anton. Schneider lived in NH and established a successful Ski School at Mount Cranmore until he passed away in 1955. His son carried on running this ski school for decades and has shared his insights for this history. Europeans Sepp Ruschp, Toni Matt, and Benno Rybizka also set up shop in New England. Dartmouth skiers who joined the 10th Mountain Division in World War II met other great European skiers who moved west like Friedl Pfeifer, Otto Lang and Luggi Foeger. Many of these men contributed to the growth of skiing through North American, often in partnership with the skiers from Dartmouth.

Some of these international relationships started as a consequence of Dartmouth ski racers participating in European races. And this was also the genesis of the connection with another great ski legend, Sir Arnold Lunn of Great Britain, one which would prove particularly fruitful. The connection of the first American-born Olympic skier, John Carleton '22, to Sir Arnold led to connections in Hanover with Professor Proctor and with Dartmouth's skiing Librarian, Nathaniel Goodrich. Carleton and Goodrich are also members of the NSSHF. It was Sir Arnold who developed the Arlberg Kandahar race with Hannes Schneider in 1928 and Charlie Proctor was a participant in the first such race. Dartmouth ski coach Walter Prager was an early race winner. Sir Arnold also started the British Ski Club, initiated perhaps the most complete periodical ski journal of the early decades of skiing, and was a visitor to Hanover on numerous occasions.

These technical changes in Europe were to influence the ski lessons of a young American, **Richard "Dick" Durrance, I '39,** who spent his formative skiing years in the Austrian and German Alps before matriculating in 1935 at Dartmouth

College. At the US Olympic trials on Mt. Rainier, Washington, in 1935, the first to involve Alpine racing, Durrance's skills and experience from his days of skiing in Europe would help give the Dartmouth team a leadership role in the 1936 Olympics. Dick Durrance used his European racing techniques to become one of the greatest American skiers of his day and a principal in many ski developments in this country. He was involved early in the resort developments at Sun Valley, Alta, and Aspen Mountain, and later a creator of many of the early ski movies that encouraged a wider public interest in skiing. He was also involved in the training of the early members of the 10th Mountain Division and an advisor to those alumni of that unit, like Peter Seibert who founded Vail, on the development of their mountains.

At the urging of Fred Harris and other early DOC skiers, several well thought of European skiers were hired from 1923-1957 to help develop the Dartmouth ski racing team. Several were legends in skiing, particularly Walter Prager, possibly the world's greatest ski racer in the early 1930s; he, along with Otto Schniebs, was a developer of several great US ski racers. In 1956, Sir Arnold Lunn awarded Prager the A-K Diamond Pin for his racing prowess in the 1930s at the famous Arlberg-Kandahar race in Europe which was as close to a World Championship as any race of the time. Prager was one of only four males to have received this honor. One of the others, Otto Furrer, had a son Charles who served as a Dartmouth Assistant Ski Coach in 1953-54.

Prager's career involved many outstanding achievements as he became one of Dartmouth's greatest ski coaches (1936-1957), helped train the 10th Mountain Division skiers (as did many of his fellow European skiers along with skiers from Dartmouth and other Eastern colleges), and encouraged many others in the development of skiing. Prager also was a man of many mysteries whose tale has yet to be fully told. We, and many of his very loyal ski team members, were amazed by some of the revelations we turned up in our research about Prager, such as his being credited as an Assistant Director for perhaps the most widely known of Nazi propaganda movies, *Triumph of the Will*, which featured all the leaders of Nazi Germany from Adolph Hitler on down. Further research showed that the role had more to do with his then romance with the German moviemaker and lead director of this film, Leni Riefenstahl, than his own moviemaking skills or any interest in Nazi propaganda. And certainly his future role as a heroic leader in the US 10th Mountain division showed where his true feelings lay. Our research also uncovered the lingering

Europeans Benno Rybizka, Hannes Schneider, Arnold Lunn, Toni Matt, and Herbert Schneider gather at Hannes's home in NH.

Carl Ringer (Capt, German team) with Coach Schniebs.

Walter Prager with Leni Riefenstahl on top of the Alps, mid 1930s.

mystery behind his departure from Dartmouth in 1957 and the degree of loyal support from his former ski team members in later life after coaching.

The legendary Dartmouth Winter Carnival has spawned some interesting off-shoots, including the largest annual alumni event outside of Hanover: a ski weekend in Vail, Colorado, called Dartmouth-Tuck Winter CarniVAIL, an event that brings together alumni from the undergraduate school and the three graduate schools (The Tuck School of Business Administration, the Thayer Engineering School, and the Dartmouth Medical School—abbreviated later in this work as Tu, Th, and DMS). As is outlined in this story, the alumni of each of the three graduate programs have also been instrumental in various developments in the ski world and continue to be so. Many of the early businesses supporting the ski industry involved Tuck graduates; the Thayer School alumni and faculty have contributed much to the technical side of skiing; and large numbers of Dartmouth's medical alumni can be found serving the local communities of most leading ski areas.

In addition, we highlight the impact of several specific foundation blocks that have enhanced the Dartmouth impact on recreational skiing and ski racing, the formation of US Ski Clubs, and the aftermath of the 10th Mountain Division's formation.

DARTMOUTH SKI RACING

The Dartmouth contribution to intercollegiate skiing has always been significant. We have already mentioned the early role in developing US ski racing techniques, holding the first collegiate ski races, and the early use of the most experienced ski racing coaches from Europe. Since the National Collegiate Athletic Association (NCAA) initiated an annual college ski championship in 1957, Dartmouth has won or tied for the Championship three times, 1958, 1976, and most recently in 2007. Shortly after the adoption of coeducation in 1972, Dartmouth's women skiers became a significant force in college racing with an early victory in the Association of Intercollegiate Athletics for Women (AIAW) Championships in 1977, its first official year, before they were combined with the men racers in the NCAA championships from1983. Dartmouth's impact on Winter Sports has been felt everywhere. In the 2006 Winter Olympics in Utah, Dartmouth contributed 14 Olympians and many staff members to the Olympics program, more than any other US college. The Dartmouth Olympians and Paralympians added three Gold and two Bronze medals to the total US results. Throughout the history of the Winter Olympic and Paralympic Games, from Dartmouth's first Olympic skier, John Carleton '22, a participant on the American team at the first Winter Olympics in 1924, to the latest Winter Olympics in Vancouver, Dartmouth has contributed more skiers, coaches and staff than any other institution (see Chapter IV).

SKI CLUBS, AND THE GROWTH OF ENTHUSIASTIC US SKIERS

As a sign of local enthusiasm and support, The Hanover Inn had Winter Carnival posters hanging in the coffee shop.

The pervasive Dartmouth influence goes far beyond simply running businesses or racing or DOC activities in Hanover, NH. It has been an instrumental part of creating the enthusiasm for skiing throughout the US. Perhaps nothing illustrates that better than its imprint on the founding and growth of ski clubs in every part of this country. We have outlined the background of clubs in the East, South, Midwest and Far North. We detail some of the early founders as well as the leaders of today. It is these clubs that often stimulated the early enthusiasm for trips to the mountains or formed shared cabin schemes to provide places to stay. Dartmouth folks wanted to continue to enjoy the sport they had experienced as members of the Dartmouth Outing Club or with some of the sub-groups like the Carcajou Club that provided an off-campus home for skiers in Hanover. This was true in 1910 and it is still true today in 2010 (see Chapter V).

WORLD WAR II 10TH MOUNTAIN DIVISION

Dartmouth's skiing exploits have played a role in two world wars. We have focused our story on World War II, but skis came in to play in World War I in a minor way. **Charles Dabney Horton '15** was a participant in the first college race of Dartmouth vs. McGill in 1914. In a historical aside, he later married Helen Wheelock Hubbard, a direct descendant of Dartmouth's founder, Eleazar Wheelock. In the winter of 1915-16, Dabney became the first Dartmouth alumnus to answer the call for volunteer mountain rescue work on skis in support of the Allied Forces in World War I; he may have been the first American to use skis to carry out this type of aid during a military conflict. His job was to provide medical assistance to wounded soldiers in the Alps where normal transport was difficult. At the end of the ski season in 1916, Horton became a member of the Lafayette Escadrille and flew missions for the French Air Force. He was awarded a Croix de Guerre by the French Government.

Dartmouth's 1942 Ski Team Captain, Jake Nunnemacher '42

Whether Dabney's early work on skis was a true military service may be questioned by some. However, if these volunteers were killed, like **Richard Hall '15** who died in France on Christmas Day in 1915 when he was hit by a bomb while driving an ambulance, their burial (in France) often included military honors. Hall had a Croix de Guerre medal pinned on his French Tri-Color-draped casket by the French Commanding General of the 66th Division to which Hall's ambulance company was attached. He was buried next to a French major who served in the same "military" unit. In the interim between Spring 1916 and the entry of the U.S. a year later, many of the American men serving in the ambulance corps rotated into the new Lafayette Escadrille to fly for the French Air Force, just like Dabney Horton. Once the U.S. entered the war, those ambulance corps units became the US Army Ambulance Corps and were duly "militarized."

Nunnemacher becomes a 10th Mountain Division soldier at Camp Hale and eventual WWII hero.

The key point for our story is that when the call came for help from the front for experienced skiers to assist with medical evacuation from the snow-covered mountains, Dartmouth was the first place they went to find such volunteers, and one Dartmouth alum answered the call without the availability of a US military unit to join. This precedent of Dartmouth skiers answering the call to duty was repeated again 25 years later when **Charles McLane '41** became the first enlistee of the 10th Mountain Division in World War II.

Besides being the first mountain ski troops ever developed by the US Military, the 10th Mountain veterans went on after World War II to become among the first to build up ski resorts across the US and beyond. Many of these ski resort pioneers were Dartmouth grads or their close friends, influenced by Dartmouth-connected folks from the 10th—people like **Larry Jump '36, Percy Rideout '40, Charles McLane '41, John Litchfield '39, Newc Eldredge '50, William "Sarge" Bill Brown,** Walter Prager, and many others. Other World War II vets not in the 10th, like **Malcolm McLane '46,** also contributed much to the post-war development of skiing. Places like Arapahoe Basin, Aspen, Vail, Sugarbush, Crystal Mountain, and Whiteface Mountain are but a few of the ski resorts built by the veterans of the 10th. These men

Dartmouth's legendary ski coach becomes role model: Sergeant Prager in the mountain troops.

also started ski magazines, opened ski schools, and got involved in all aspects of the relatively new ski industry. No 10th Mountain soldier was more impressed with the Dartmouth folks than Sarge Bill Brown. He became one of our nation's most decorated soldiers, a heroic participant in the Korean War as well as WW II, a member of the 10th Mountain Divison who went on to achieve the highest enlisted rank in the US Army, that of Command Master Sergeant- Major. In the mid 50s, with his Dartmouth friends in mind, he took on a role as the Reserve Officer Training Corp Instructor for a special mountain climbing military unit at Dartmouth. This lasted until the mid-60s and allowed him to participate in developing the early skiing activities at the Dartmouth Skiway that started in 1957 under the leadership of **John Meck '33**. At the urging of Peter Seibert, Bob Parker, and other 10th Division alumni who were building Vail Mountain, he moved to Vail in 1967 to spend roughly 25 years creating this great North American ski resort. Sarge Brown shared his views on, and his pleasure in being part of, the Dartmouth connection for this book, as did a number of other 10th Division members (see Chapter VI).

SKI RESORTS AND OTHER RELATED SKI ACTIVITIES IN THE UNITED STATES

In the ski resort industry, Dartmouth's impact has been the longest, strongest, and most enduring of any institution, affecting ski area operations, financing of ski resorts, ski area real estate developments, ski shop retail, ski clothing and equipment design/manufacture, etc. It is hard to imagine any institution that can claim as much involvement in starting or managing ski areas, and participating so significantly in other aspects of the life of ski communities. The Dartmouth-connected group has played a role in major ski areas including Wildcat, Mad River Glen, Mt. Attitash, Mt. Cranmore, Stowe, Saddle River, Shawnee Peak and Sugarloaf Mountain in the East; Sun Valley, Alta, Arapahoe, Aspen, Vail, Keystone, Copper Mountain, Winter Park and Teluride in the West; Alyeska in Alaska; and in every place in between, like Seven Springs in Pennsylvania and Buck Hill in Minnesota. We document the activities of a never-ending list of Dartmouth-connected folks like Sherman Adams '20, Murray Thurston '43, Sandy McCulloch '50, Joe Dodge '51, Tom Corcoran '54, Johannes Trapp '63 and Sam von Trapp '94, Warren Cook '67, Bill Cantlin '70, Chet Homer '73, Charlie Proctor '28, Hal Leich '29, Chuck Stone '53, John Byrne, III '81, Herman Dupre, Blair Wood '30, Larry Jump '36, Dick Durrance '39, John Litchfield '39, Steve Bradley '39, "Sarge" Bill Brown, Chuck Lewis '58, Ed Callaway '77, John Norton '77 and many more who have played important roles. We also discuss Dartmouth activities in associated hospitality and other business in the West and the wilderness skiing activities practiced in places like Alaska by a large contingent of the Dartmouth family. Our three chapters on the greater Dartmouth family's involvement in the ski areas of the East, West, and other parts of the U.S. should be as much of a revelation to you as it was to us (see Chapters VII, VIII and IX).

SUPPORT INDUSTRIES, TECHNICAL DEVELOPMENTS AND INTERNATIONAL CONTRIBUTORS

But this book is about more than ski areas. To our knowledge, no one has made a comprehensive review of these activities beyond chronicling the early history of skiing and the primitive ski resorts that were the foundation of US skiing but which are only part of the big picture of modern skiing. In the technical developments, the support industries, international activities, and other facets of the greater ski industry, Dartmouth alumni have played equally important roles,...people like Harold Hirsch '29, the founder of White Stag, Sel Hannah '35, the founder of Sno-Engineering, and many other Dartmouth alumni who designed and created ski areas; Larry Jump '36 and Steve Bradley '39, leaders in establishing adaptive skiing techniques; Chick Igaya '57, probably the leading Japanese racer of all time and a senior officer in the Olympics movement; Phil Livingston '58, setting up a ski development program for severely injured vets returning from Iraq and Afghanistan; Stu Keiller '65 of Profile and AMF Head Sports Wear companies; Diane Boyer '80 of Skea Ski Clothes; John Stahler Tu '69 of leading ski equipment makers Technica and Volkl; Dean Ericson '67, a leader at ISHA (and *Skiing Heritage* magazine); Jeff Leich '71 and Meredith Scott '96 heading up separate New England ski museums; movies made by Jack McCrillis '19 (*Moosilauke Downhill*, 1932), Dick Durrance '39 and Steve Bradley '39 (*Sun Valley Ski Chase*, 1941), Roger Brown '57 (of Vail Ski Films), Rick Moulton (*Skiing Legends* and others); doctors in ski areas like Freeman '66, DMS '67 (Aspen),Veralli '71, Cooliton DMS '90 and Lloyd DMS '93 (Breckenridge), Johnson '70, Andrea '79, DMS '86, Nickelsen '86, Kitson DMS '91 and Chauhuri DMS '95 (Durango), Compton '69, and Hopperstead '87 (Park City), Bennum '76, James '88, Rueschemeyer DMS '97 and Collins DMS '99 (Stowe), Millett DMS '95 (Vail); and many, many others. This broad involvement across the entire business landscape of skiing helps to explain why Dartmouth has contributed more honored members to the National Ski Hall of Fame than any other source and why Dartmouth as an institution has made such a significant impact on the development of skiing.

LOOKING BACK, LOOKING FORWARD

At the end of our book, we provide profiles of some 40 individuals or family groups that make up the greater Dartmouth family and summarize their past contributions. Most of these alumni are mentioned in one or more of the earlier chapters. There are so many more that we could mention but so little space to say it in that this part can be but a survey of the possible. Therefore we cannot present "the" list of Dartmouth folks who have influenced the development of skiing, but rather provide a sampling of the wide range of these contributions through comments about individual members and several significant families. The chapter will, in total, comprise a composite of the Dartmouth contribution to skiing

The Dartmouth passion for skiing did not end decades ago when early accomplishments had solidified the industry as a major part of many lives. Instead, there are probably more alumni and Dartmouth ski families involved today than ever. Ski towns, ski racing, ski prep schools, various ski mountains, the Olympics/ Paralympics/other racing are all heavily colored in green. This chapter offers a view of Dartmouth skiing activities today and highlights the enthusiasm still being shown in class mini-reunions and special gatherings of Dartmouth skiers taking place all over the world.

OTHER DARTMOUTH WINTER ACTIVITIES

In assessing the impact of the winter snow and cold on Dartmouth and the world, we have focused on skiing and all things related to skiing. But there are many other elements of the winter story that we do not have time to describe in full, elements which relate in a tangential way to an appreciation for the season of ice and snow. Just to provide some sense of these, we have outlined a few examples here of the Dartmouth involvement in things with a winter theme. For example, Hanover has been blessed with many skating opportunities over the years. We have briefly mentioned the importance of skating to Dartmouth's famous Winter Carnival where special programs were presented in years past, often with elaborate skating routines and scenery that today are usually seen only in televised extravaganzas or major events that play at big arenas around the US and elsewhere. And these led to several movies with a Winter-Carnival-like theme or setting. But skating in Hanover has also been in play in other ways than just the presence of competitions during Winter Carnival weekends and on the early Dartmouth Winter Sports teams. Skating has distanced itself from skiing into its own realm with highly competitive men's and women's hockey teams creating one aspect and figure skating for both individuals and teams being another.

Although Dartmouth has always been a strong competitor in collegiate hockey championships and has sent its skaters to both Olympic and professional hockey teams, it has established an even stronger presence in the sport of figure skating. A few will recall that **Mike McGean '49** and his wife, **Lois McGean '84,** were National Pairs Figure Skating champs in the early 1950s. Mike later became one of Dartmouth's greatest Alumni Affairs administrators and was the leader of the local Hanover Skating Club for close to 50 years. Over a decade ago, Mike was approached by undergraduates to help put together and coach a skating team to represent Dartmouth College in inter-

Lois '84 and Mike '49 McGean, World and Olympic skaters.

collegiate figure skating competitions. The skating team blossomed under the direction of Mike and his daughter, **Loren McGean '92**. Mike and Loren recently completed a record run as coaches, leading Dartmouth's amazing figure skating team to an unprecedented five straight National College Figure Skating Championships from 2004 through 2008. This is a feat unmatched in any of Dartmouth's other major or minor sports programs over the decades. It is only fitting that it was a winter sports team!

A Portrait of Dr. Seuss (Ted Geisel '25) hangs in the 1965 Galleries in Webster Hall.

Rudolph the Red Nosed Reindeer, Bob May 26's classic character, in the Rauner Special Collections Library.

Dancers with skis in Momix directed by Moses Pendleton '71.

Another result of the influence of winter on Dartmouth alumni has been the Christmas storybooks that have been favorably received by our greater society. For example, Dr. Seuss (**Theodor Seuss Geisel '25,** the recipient of an honorary doctorate in 1955) has used winter themes in his wonderfully creative children's stories like ***The Grinch Who Stole Christmas.*** Then there is the most wonderful reindeer of them all, Rudolph, who sports that bright and shiny red nose. ***Rudolph, The Red Nosed Reindeer*** was created by **Robert L. May '26** as an assignment while at Montgomery Ward in 1939. The retailer had been buying and giving away coloring books at Christmas every year and it was decided that creating their own book would save money. The task of developing such a book was given to Bob May. Millions of copies of Rudolph's story were distributed by Montgomery Ward in its first year, and it has remained a long-term legend of Christmas. May's brother-in-law, Johnny Marks, made a song adaptation of Rudolph. Though the song was turned down by popular vocalists such as Bing Crosby and Dinah Shore, it was eventually recorded by "the singing cowboy", Gene Autry. "Rudolph the Red-Nosed Reindeer*"* was released in 1949 and became a phenomenal success, selling more records than any other Christmas song with the exception of "White Christmas." And in recent years, **Robert Sullivan '75** created a unique story, ***Flight of the Reindeer,*** in 1996 about an imaginary flight of Santa's reindeer and the scientific evidence turned up on the flight. The book is full of references to Hanover and the people at Dartmouth or in the Hanover community. Artist Glenn Wolff illustrated the book and created a *Chart of Evidence.* The "evidence" collected involves the fictional contributions of several people mentioned in ***Passion for Skiing***, including **Joe Mehling '69**, the photographer of many of our images, and **Ned Gillette '67**, the famed adventure and Olympic skier.

Many people do not know that students from Dartmouth left the Hanover Plain to create two of today's most unique modern dance companies, Pilobolus and Momix. One individual, **Moses Pendleton '71**, played a key role in the formation of both. Moses's early personal life revolved around top-level ski racing. As a recognized downhill skier of considerable talent, he spent every summer in special camps at places like Mt. Hood in Oregon, completing race training on glaciers with members of the Austrian ski team. These camps featured racing legends like Pepi Gramshammer, Anderl Molterer and Erich Sailer who also show up later in our story. In high school, Moses broke his leg twice and this caused a change in his skiing specialization to cross-country, but not in his competitive drive.

As a leading competitive skier in Vermont, Moses was a highly desirable recruit to the ski college of the time, Dartmouth. He was interested in benefiting from the personal instruction of Dartmouth's Al Merrill and was influenced by Dartmouth's cross-country legend, **John Caldwell '50**. Unfortunately, on his second day in Hanover, a ski team exercise game of soccer led to another broken leg. Two years later, in the fall of 1970, with no significant ski results to his name and a declining enthusiasm, he took a modern dance class with instructor Alison Chase, and the rest is dance history. He, Alison, and a few other Dartmouth modern dance students formed Pilobolus, a very original modern dance company. It still thrills audiences around the world with its unusual dance routines. Years later,

Moses left to form another dance venture called Momix. He still skis and, unique to the dance world, he uses skis in his dance work, having created choreography centered around skiing, and by using skis and boots regularly in his dances to enable dancers to form unusual angles for body shapes. In 1982, a documentary was created to summarize his dance life at the time. It was entered in the Sundance Film Festival, and won Best Picture.

Not only have Dartmouth alumni been affected by the ski bug and winter themes; sometimes the impact spreads to other recognized legends. For example, clothing designer Emilio Pucci, or Marchese Emilio di Barsento as he might be more formally titled, enjoyed an early ski racing career that led to an association with **Harold Hirsch '29**, the originator of stylish ski clothing. This in turn led to Pucci establishing a clothing design business that still functions under that name today although owned by LVMH. Pucci, a dedicated member of the Italian Olympic team, went to Reed College in Oregon where Hirsch became a life Trustee. His first venture involved designing uniforms for the Reed ski team, and after WW II, he and Hirsch hooked up on a joint venture to produce ski clothing for White Stag. They maintained that relationship thru the 1960s. At one point, Pucci designed the entire White Stag collection (1962), some of which was featured in *Vogue* magazine.

The theme of winter and snow plays through many other activities at Dartmouth. It is a fundamental part of life in Hanover in the cold months of the year. And although skiing is a major manifestation of this combination of bright, active students and their winter environment, there are many others, and varied ones as well.

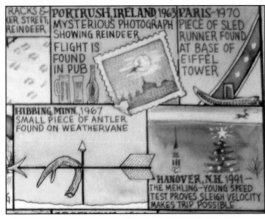

Hanover, NH: Flight of Reindeer photographic speed evidence gathered by Mehling '69 and Young is noted in this portion of the Chart of Evidence.

Artist Glenn Wolff's depiction of The Flight of the Reindeer written by Bob Sullivan '75.

SUMMARY

The research effort for this book turned up hundreds of stories of how a passion for skiing has expressed itself in the lives of Dartmouth-connected folks. All the stories are fascinating, some are close to unreal, and many clearly show the impact of past generations as the green thread of Dartmouth winds through our lives and our contemporary activities, often in ways people do not yet understand. Our story highlights the activities of folks who have created what is now the biggest ski jump in New England; helped develop the first rope tow, overhead cable lift and chair lift; designed most of the ski mountain layouts in the United States; initiated modern extreme skiing; led skiing activities in the Olympics; been leaders of skiing in foreign countries; promoted the design of wheelchairs for snow conditions; been lifelong ski instructors; innovated new forms of sliding over snow such as freestyle skiing and snowboarding; been leaders in adaptive and paralymic skiing; become national ski racing champions; and much, much more..

Dartmouth's famed alumnus, **Daniel Webster** of the **Class of 1801**, spoke immortal words before the Supreme Court of the United States in 1818 to defend the college from an undesired take-over by the State of New Hampshire: "It is sir, as I have said, a small college. And, yet there are those who love it!" This led to a remarkable legal decision that established the principal of private institutions having property rights that states could not take away which is still the law of the land today. A similar comment could be said about Dartmouth skiers and the development of their sport. It is a small college with a limited number of skiers and winter sports advocates, but yet their love for, and contributions to, skiing and other winter themes have been truly remarkable, and this has lasted from the 19th century to this day!

Leading Finishers, First Dartmouth Winter Sports Day 1910 (First row l to r) Day '14, Hastings '14, Harris '11 (D on sweater), Dick Bowler, Cobb '12, White '12; (Stndg l to r) Jack Bowler, Watts '13, Holway '12, Schellenberg '13, Weston Jr. '11, Miller '12, Griffin '12, Shumway '13, Lyons '12. (Names per A. S. Holway '12 in letter February 15, 1938).

Notes Chapter I

1. *Skiing Heritage,* **Third Issue 2001, September, Vol 13 #3.** 2. Obituary, The Bethel Citizen.Com after Murray's death on November 25, 2008. 3. Based on and email message from Ralph Miller on August 30, 2009. 4. From Patricia Peterson's Phd thesis on Competitive Skiing for Women, p. 28-29, Univ of California, 1967. 5. Hovey, Richard, "Dartmouth Ode," Along the Trail: A Book of Lyrics, 1899. 6. Frost, Edwin B., An Astronomer's Life, Houghton Mifflin, 1933. 48. 7. Memorandum, Robert Allen to Rand, Jan 21, 1952, quoting a letter from Trustee William Andrus, Rauner DOC Collection, Box 3, File 23. 8. Ibid. 9. Letter, Thomes to Hatch, Apr 7, 1935, Rauner DOC Collection, Box 14, File 20. 10. Holt diary entries transcribed by E. John B. Allen, Apr 7, 1983 from originals in possession of Barbara J. Holt, a descendant of Henry Holt. 11. The Dartmouth, January 31, 1896.

CHAPTER II

THE DARTMOUTH OUTING CLUB: PUTTING DARTMOUTH ON SKIS

By Douglas C. Leitch '65
Former President of the New England Ski Museum

With James W. Page '63

THE EARLY YEARS OF THE DOC

In Brattleboro, Vermont, in 1904, an ambitious 16-year-old fellow named Fred Harris had a solution to outfitting himself with skis. He made his own, and – he began keeping a diary. For eight winters he would record his exploits on "skees" beginning with this entry on January 1, 1904: "R. Frost and I took skees down to F. Lawton's"[1] Over that month and the rest of that winter Harris jotted sparsely worded notes about his early efforts at making his own equipment – bending skis, experimenting with binding designs, trying different woods for use as poles. He commented on snow conditions and his results from trying various techniques. When spring came, he continued working on skis, talking about skiing with friends, scouting good locations to ski. The next fall he wrote on September 24: "Worked on a skee brake. [went hiking] looking for good ski hills"[2] His patience and curiosity in trying new ski designs were reflected in the entry for February 14, 1905, when he wrote:

> "My idea of a skee now is between 8 and 9 ft long, at least 5 ½ in wide. Today cut my shoes because my feet project out over the sides. As stiff as possible in back and still have it balance down. Wider at the front than at the back. Quite thin and bendy at front. Grooved of course nearly to the back end, am not sure about the front end. I wonder what my idea will be a year from now!?!"

By 1907 Fred Harris's passion was clear, as he wrote on January 27 after skiing all day: "Have got skeeing on the brain evidently."[4] No one could have imagined how much impact Fred Harris would have on the sport he so dearly enjoyed when he entered Dartmouth College as a freshman that fall. He had already taken his skis and his dog to Hanover that spring, and on March 8 he wrote in his diary: "Tried skeeing a little south of Hanover."[5] During that same winter he experimented with photographing himself jumping on skis by attaching a silk thread to the camera shutter. He also tried out new designs for his ski pole. By the time his first winter as a Dartmouth student began, he had already scouted places to ski and noted on December 4 that he'd seen some fellows "skee a little in distance."[6] A week later, he "Tried skeeing before chapel, 'es war nicht gut'" and the next day, "Went skeeing in the afternoon up through park to golf links and back."[7]

Fred was not only passionate about his own skiing, he was also an organizer extraordinaire. On December 17, 1908, his sophomore year, he visited the dean to talk about skiing and organizing a shooting club. That winter he found a few other friends on campus to join him in skiing expeditions to Wilder, Vermont, across the river from Dartmouth and up onto Balch Hill east of campus. He and his father made a trip to Montreal, Canada, in February 1909, giving him a chance to witness skiing events at the winter festival there. Before winter ended, he stopped by to show the dean some

Fred Harris '11 flys off his jump.

pictures of skiing he had taken and he also showed them to a friend on the faculty. Among other activities, he was busy estimating the grade of a hill where he intended to build a jump and making skis for sale. On March 26 he wrote: "Tried to get orders for skis with success on two."[8]

It wasn't until the fall of Harris's junior year that he forever changed student life for generations of Dartmouth students. After skiing on Balch Hill on November 30, Fred returned to his dormitory to write a letter to the student newspaper, *The Dartmouth*. As he noted in his diary that evening, he "sent an article to the Dartmouth on the formation of an outing club."[9] His letter, printed in *The Dartmouth* on December 7, 1909, read:

> ".... The question 'What is there to do at Dartmouth in the winter?' gives rise to the thought that we might take better advantage of the opportunities which the admirable situation of our college offers.
>
> Winter sports are fast growing in popularity as is testified by the Carnivals at Montreal and the big ski jump contests at the northern and middle western cities, where thousands of people assemble to watch the contestants.
>
> The writer suggests that a ski and snow-shoe club be formed, the purposes of which would be:
>
> 1. To stimulate interest in out-of-door winter sports.
> 2. To have short cross-country runs weekly and one long excursion each season (say, to Moose lac)...
>
> By taking the initiative in this matter Dartmouth might well become the originator of a branch of college organized sport hitherto undeveloped by American Colleges. . . .
>
> Respectfully submitted, F. H. Harris '11" [10]

The response to his invitation resulted in a meeting in his dormitory room on December 14 attended by several students and faculty to officially organize the Dartmouth Outing Club. Harris noted in his diary that day: "Had an Outing meeting **Prof Hull, Dick Lane, Prof Clark, Walt Greenwood, Bob Barstow, Sid Clark** and I talked over the question. **T. Miller** came in and I gave him the dope."[11] Fred continued to ski and publicize the new club on campus and he started work on building a new ski jump. Soon after the new year, the Dartmouth Outing Club held another meeting, January 10, 1910, and signed up 55 new members. They organized regular winter outings, traveling around the surrounding towns on skis and snowshoes. *The Dartmouth* urged the Outing Club to consider holding a special winter event.[12] In February, Harris returned again to Montreal to compete in the ski jumping events. While there, he prevailed on two of the Canadian experts to give him some ski jumping pointers. Once back at Dartmouth, he and his Outing Club friends organized a winter "Field Day" of intramural competitions on snow and ice on March 1. His dormitory had suffered a fire the night before, and, distracted by the

The Snowshoe Race at the first Winter Sports Day in 1910.

emergency, Harris expressed disappointment that the best he could do was gain second place in two events. But *The Dartmouth* enthusiastically cheered, "It is not impossible that Dartmouth, in initiating this movement, is setting an example that will later find devotees among other New England and northern colleges.î[13]

As winter approached in Harris's senior year, he was "writing a ski-story for some magazine"[14] and continued to cultivate interest in the Outing Club among both students and faculty. Before the Christmas break, he asked a professor to proofread his ski-story and got another student to design the seal for the Outing Club. As soon as they returned to campus in January 1911, Harris and his fellow club members began work on a "winter carnival." He had attended the Montreal winter festival twice and had also met James Taylor, the Assistant Headmaster at Vermont Academy where a winter carnival had been held in 1909. Harris and his Dartmouth friends were intent on expanding their earlier "field day" to a Winter Carnival combining the outdoor winter sports events with a schedule of social activities and an Outing Club Ball. Harris wrote in his diary about the many new concerns of planning a winter sports event, running from a dance committee meeting to the Outing Club executive committee meeting on the same evening, worrying about enough snow ("woke up to find it snowing AT LAST!!!)[15] and rounding up officials for the athletic contests. The first Dartmouth Winter Carnival took place on the weekend of February 10-11, 1911. Harris went to the Outing Club dance Friday evening and competed in the cross-country race, ski dashes, and jumping events on Saturday. A week later, he went to the nearby village of Etna, New Hampshire, to give a talk on skiing to the boys club. Before the ski season ended, the Dartmouth Outing Club (DOC) had also held a ski jumping tournament and conducted a day trip by train to Thetford, Vermont, and skied back to Hanover.

Harris graduated from Dartmouth that June, not only as the founder of a very successful outing club that has lasted one hundred years but having lettered in tennis as an intercollegiate champion. By the fall of 1911 he was writing skiing articles for several publications including *Country Life in America, Springfield* [Mass.] *Republican,* and *The Yearbook of the Ski Club of Great Britain.* His legacy at Dartmouth was a growing student organization which, over the next few decades, came to dominate the policies and structure of the emerging ski-sport in North America. Although Fred Harris had completed his college education, he would remain a key figure in the early development of the sport he loved so much.

W. Lee White '13 and Harris's successor as president of the Outing Club, wrote to fellow alumnus John Carleton in 1934 recounting Harris's work in founding the club:

> "The Club was founded by Fred Harris, and while a small group of us assisted him in various details of organization and maintenance, he is the one who started skiing as a sport at Dartmouth. He is the one who conceived the idea, who organized the club, who shouldered the major part of the expense of advertising the club, buying badges, prizes, etc. during the early days, who wrote much of the publicity himself; who even published, at his own expense, a book on the Club; who built with his own hands, with some assistance, the first ski-jump in Hanover and was the first man over the jump; who conceived of the idea of the first Carnival; who planned the first Carnival dance and was one of those who hauled spruce boughs from Velvet Rocks for the decoration of the dining room in College Hall. ...he brought the first real ski equipment to Hanover and was instrumental in getting the stores in Hanover, Boston, and New York to stock real skis and real ski harnesses. I know this because I helped him make the arrangements with the stores. I think it can be said without exaggeration that Fred Harris had more to do with initiating and developing winter sports in the northeastern part of the United States than any other one man."[16]

The Outing Club was not universally appreciated at first, but there were two things working in its favor that enabled the idea to succeed despite this reaction. One was the toughness of the early members of the club who found exhilaration in challenging environments. The other was the strong support Harris was able to gain from the faculty. He approached professors and deans alike with self-assured maturity to promote his idea of a student-run outdoor organization and found in them a receptive audience. He gained their immediate and enthusiastic support as evidenced by remarks from Charles F. Emerson, Dean of the College, which Harris published in a small book titled *Dartmouth Out 'O Doors* in 1913:

"I am convinced that there is a demand for such a club as the Outing Club in Hanover. The place and the times call for something of this nature in the winter to induce the young men to enjoy to the full the scenery of this part of the country. If rightly conducted, outdoor sports would be an advantage to all concerned. The opportunities in this region for skiing, tobogganing, snowshoeing and other winter sports can hardly be surpassed."[17]

This kind of support from the administration, combined with active faculty participation in the club's activities, would become part of the solid foundation on which the Dartmouth Outing Club would grow and thrive. The students themselves even recognized the benefits of an aspect of student life that brought them into closer relationships with their professors outside the classroom.

Early Ski Outings

Those who had signed up with Harris to join the new Outing Club paid little heed to any campus critics or doubters. Instead, they packed their rucksacks and strapped on their skis for adventures across the snow-covered New Hampshire hills. It did not take long to begin a lengthy list of accomplishments credited to Dartmouth Outing Club members. In late January 1912, **Carl E. Shumway '13** and classmate **G. S. ("Eric") Foster '13** took off from Hanover on the first ski ascent of Mount Moosilauke, at an elevation of 4,802 feet and a distance of over 40 miles from campus. They skied the entire way, made the ascent to Moosilauke's summit, and returned to Hanover–all on skis in two days, an amazing feat of "extreme skiing" for a couple of students, especially considering the distance traveled on skis and the primitive equipment available in 1912. Shumway wrote about this ski trip for Harris's *Dartmouth Out O'Doors* in an article titled "Cross-country on Skis to Mt. Moosilauke":

Carl Shumway '13 at Tuckerman Ravine in later years.

".... After I had long wished for an opportunity to climb Mt. Moosilauke on skis, the chance came when G.S. ("Eric") Foster '13 and I found that we were to have nearly a week off after finishing our mid-year examinations. As the time drew near, we worked out the route which we expected to take, carefully examined our skis for any defects in straps or wood, and then loaded up a pack bag with all the necessaries. At last our exams were over, and on the last day of January 1912 we strapped on our skis for the start. We had our supper at Warren, and covered the five miles on skis to Mr. Eastman's at the foot of Mt. Moosilauke...The next morning we got away early, and at quarter after one we reached the Tip Top House, and rested. We commenced to stiffen up on account of the intense cold, and accordingly decided to start back, sliding down the mountain side through the inability of our skis to cling to the icy crust."[18]

He later wrote to the DOC Director **John Rand '38** in 1954 reminiscing about this trip:

"For many years after I graduated, I used to come up [to Hanover] & judge the Winter Carnivals or ski miles across with them. In 1952, 40 years after Eric Foster and I skied at mid-year's from Crosby Hall to Moosilauke, climbed the mountain and skied back to Hanover, I have wanted to do it again, or even half of it in twice as much time."[19]

A month after Shumway and Foster climbed Mount Moosilauke in 1912, Harris would rally some of his DOC pals to make a ski trip to Mount Washington, the highest peak in the northeastern United States (6,288 ft), in hopes of being the first to climb it on skis. They ascended as far as they could up the carriage road but were unsuccessful in attaining the summit. The winter following their 1912 ascent of Mt Moosilauke, a group of DOC skiers, including Carl Shumway, were the first to reach the summit of Mount Washington on skis. **Jeff Leich '71** described the accomplishment in the New England Ski Museum's journal and in Chapter VII:

"Led by Shumway, now a senior and president of the club, a DOC group returned [to Mt. Washington]… The group accessed the ravine by climbing the carriage road for two miles, then turning off on the Raymond Path, the standard footpath to Tuckerman in those days. Accompanying Shumway on skis were **C. M. Rundlett ['16]**, **Eric Foster ['13]**, **F. H. Weed ['14]**, **E. S. Bidwell ['13]**, and **Joseph Cheney ['13]**….. The venture into the ravine was not the main event for the DOC group, who had their eyes on the prize of the summit. The following day, March 10, Shumway, Fred Harris, and Joseph Cheney succeeded in reaching the summit of the mountain on skis in good weather with 19-degree temperatures…"[20]

The DOC skiers trying out Tuckerman Ravine in the early days.

Joe Cheney from Orlando, Florida, and a self-described "Southern Man," had never seen snow until he attended Dartmouth. Like many students who followed him, it did not take him long to develop an interest in and ability on skis. He wrote a brief article in Harris's *Dartmouth Out O' Doors*: "The Club has been formed only three years, but its growth and influence have been very great, owing to the fact that it fills a much needed want; it is hoped that it will not be long before its membership will include nearly the whole student body as well as the faculty, and that, through its power, Dartmouth will become even more than it is now, the "College of Winter Sports."[21]

Shumway's father Franklin, owner of the Franklin P. Shumway Company (an advertising, merchandising and business counselors in Boston, Massachusetts), was quite favorably impressed with the work of the Outing Club. In 1913 he wrote letters to other Dartmouth parents in an effort to raise funds to provide cabins for the Outing Club, saying, "I found [Dartmouth] **President [Ernest Fox] Nichols** intensely interested in the matter and, in writing me about the Outing Club, he says: 'It breeds in the minds of the students a love for out-of-doors, and contributes, in my judgment, more to well-balanced, normal physical development than do the more specialized forms of athletics.'"[22]

Franklin Shumway subsequently backed his pitch to other parents by making the first philanthropic gift to the fledgling Outing Club to fund construction of cabins at Moose Mountain east of Hanover and Cube Mountain to the northeast in the town of Lyme, NH. Dartmouth President Ernest Fox Nichols would later consider the development of the Dartmouth Outing Club and the construction of a line of cabins for use of students' enjoyment of the outdoors to be the outstanding achievements of his administration.[23]

The timing could not have been better for skiing to take hold on this northern college campus. Skiing's long history of utilitarian purpose was undergoing a rapid transition to becoming a sport. All skiing needed was a few organizers like Fred Harris to stir the embers and light the torch. **David Bradley '38**, a Dartmouth skier of great acclaim in the 1930s, wrote: "There was already [a] small but lively tradition of winter sports at Dartmouth - What the tradition needed most was a dominant figure, an organizer, and this was Fred Harris."[24] College men at Dartmouth had the time to enjoy sport and were situated in an ideal location to take advantage of the winter environment in a robust way.

Dartmouth skiers ready to go up the mountain; what Harris started had blossomed!

The Skiing Librarian

The longest-serving Dartmouth College Librarian, **Nathaniel L. Goodrich**, was another of the faculty who took a quick interest in the Outing Club. With his own experience as a mountaineer, it was an interest he would maintain for the remainder of his life. In recounting his pioneering first ski ascent of Mt. Mansfield in Stowe, Vermont, at the age of 34 in 1914, Goodrich described his introduction to skis upon arriving in Hanover two years earlier:

Budd Schulberg '36 suggested that this shows Dartmouth skiers from his day shortly after arriving at the old Norwich, Vt, RR Station, ready to go skiing.

"When I came to Dartmouth College as Librarian in 1912, I had for many years been an enthusiastic snowshoer, but never even seen a pair of skis, I found a small number of students engaged in that form of sport and two or three members of the faculty were experimenting with it. I tried the game in the winter of 1912-13, and the following season felt like tackling something more interesting than the pasture hills around Hanover."[25]

On February 1, 1914, Goodrich became the first person to ascend Mt. Mansfield, Vermont's highest peak at an elevation of 4,395 feet, after only one year of skiing experience: "There were no ski instructors in those days, and we had to try and teach ourselves from a book or by watching the students. I think at the time I had not got beyond a snowplow and a rudimentary telemark which I could not execute at any great speed."[26] He would remain not only an active member of the Dartmouth Outing Club, but also an influential participant in the larger development of skiing organizations yet to come. Mr. Goodrich became the first editor of the *American/Eastern Ski Annual* in 1934, author of many skiing articles, a noted trail builder in the White Mountains of New Hampshire, and compiler of an outstanding collection of skiing titles (notable for the quantity of European works he acquired on the subject) in the Dartmouth Library. "He saw Dartmouth as a leader in the growth of skiing in the United States, so what was more natural than for the Dartmouth Library to have an outstanding collection on the subject? ...he made an excellent selection as is evidenced by a look at the stack shelves."[27] Goodrich even contributed a piece of his own work, a small 16-page booklet he authored in 1917, *The D.O.C. Equipment Manual* with advice on the types and uses of equipment available for skiing and mountaineering.

An Unexpected Benefactor

When Fred Harris graduated from Dartmouth in 1911, he was just beginning a lifetime of promoting and developing skiing. He was a dedicated writer and marketer for skiing and for the Dartmouth Outing Club. Through Carl Shumway, Franklin Shumway invited Harris to write an article about the Outing Club and convinced the *Boston Sunday Herald* to print Harris's story titled "Dartmouth Men Plan a Line of Camps in White Mountains" outlining the DOC plans to construct a series of cabins from Hanover northeast to the high peaks of the White Mountains. **Reverend John E. Johnson, Class of 1866**, a Civil War veteran, read of this event and it motivated him to attend the dedication of the first of these cabins. Before the ceremonies, he met with Dartmouth President Nichols and asked to be introduced to the president of the Dartmouth Outing Club, requesting that he be permitted to make a few brief remarks during the dedication. Johnson's remarks were reportedly far from brief, but when he concluded, he withdrew a document from his coat pocket and presented to President Nichols a deed to his 100-acre "Sky Line" farm in Littleton, NH, serve as the northern terminus of the planned line of DOC cabins.[28] Over the ensuing years, "Johnny" Johnson would become the DOC's leading benefactor and an alumnus much beloved by the Heelers who benefited from his generosity.

The second and third Winter Carnivals in 1912 and 1913 were popular social events that quickly caught on with most students. *The Dartmouth* offered its positive outlook on the 1912 weekend: "The Winter Carnival is yet young, and guests of this week will witness the beginnings of an institution which seems destined to a promising career..."[29] Harris's multiple visits to Montreal produced an invitation for Dartmouth Outing Club men to compete against skiers from McGill University at the 1914 Montreal winter festival. Although there was yet to be a formal ski team at Dartmouth, the Outing Club had no trouble finding willing competitors to make the trip north. They were soundly beaten on February 22, 1914, in Quebec's Laurentian Mountains by the more experienced Canadian skiers, but the event marked the first intercollegiate ski competition in North America.

A year later, Dartmouth returned the favor by inviting McGill and three other colleges to compete in the first intercollegiate ski competition in the United States. The *New York Times* announced: "Skiing as an intercollegiate sport in this country will make its debut at the annual Winter Carnival of the Outing Club of Dartmouth College at Hanover the week of Feb. 8. Entries have been received from four colleges – Yale, New Hampshire, Williams, and McGill – in addition to the many men who will represent Dartmouth."[30] Dartmouth won the carnival ski events which included a 10-mile ski relay, ski dashes, and ski jumping. Their success was assured when they out-pointed McGill in ski jumping on style points using rules from the Montreal Ski Club. In addition to intercollegiate skiing competition, the 1915 Dartmouth Winter Carnival included a dramatic play, a concert, sports events (basketball, ice hockey), a glee club competition with Harvard and Yale, and fraternity house parties. After a short history of five years, Winter Carnival was rapidly developing into a seasonal social and athletic event that would dominate collegiate calendars for decades.

John E. Johnson, by then enjoying the honorific students had given him as "Founder of the Dartmouth Outing Club" (much to the dismay of Fred Harris), attended that 1915 Winter Carnival. At the conclusion of the weekend, a handwritten note on Hanover Inn stationery was presented to the Treasurer of the Dartmouth Outing Club. The note, in Johnson's aging hand, read: "J. E. Johnson of the Class of '66' has been so much pleased by the phenomenal success of 'The Carnival' that he has handed a check for One Thousand Dollars to the Treasurer of the Outing Club..."[31]

Winter Carnival had barely concluded when Johnny wrote to President Nichols to express his concern about a notice that a "White Mt. Trip" [meaning Mt. Washington] for which only the fittest [Johnson's underlining] would be permitted to make. He asked President Nichols if it would be "practicable to have the 'weaklings' try Mt. Moosilauke which is much nearer and easier?"[32] While he considered Moosilauke a very suitable "second" to the more challenging Mt. Washington, he hesitated to recommend the wagon road on Moosilauke as to its skiing suitability. Little did Johnson know that within a decade Dartmouth students would be skiing on that very road. He also wanted the DOC to achieve independence from college control so it could not interfere with the purposes of his future intended gifts to the DOC. To emphasize his point about the importance of the Outing Club to the overall welfare and benefit it presented for Dartmouth, he cited knowing about "five students from one town in the West, who say they were determined largely in the choice of a college by the Dartmouth Outing Club."[33] This DOC impact on Dartmouth admissions would later be confirmed by others even more amply.[34] Johnson felt so strongly about the official resistance and "unco-operative attitude" of the college toward his wish for the DOC to privately incorporate that he threatened to rewrite his will and "leave it all to the New Hampshire State College in Durham."

As a result of Johnson's rapidly emerging close association with and support for the Outing Club, he received a heartening letter from **Ernest Martin Hopkins '01**, former College Secretary and soon to become Nichols' successor as College President. Hopkins wrote, "I have felt now for sometime that the evolution of the Outing Club since you first interested yourself in it had been such as to make it the most significant movement in American undergraduate life....and I believe that no one can realize at the present time what a development of the idea is going to mean to the present day college boys and those of the years to come."[35]

The popularity of the Dartmouth Outing Club grew rapidly on campus with five successful Winter Carnivals and a full program of outdoor activities. Members were responsible from the start for planning and

President Hopkins '01 led Dartmouth from 1916 to 1945 and heavily supported the DOC during the formative years of skiing.

running their own programs, mostly funded on support they were able to gain themselves. They soon began to realize that a program of winter sports competition also demanded a serious commitment to staffing the organization and to executing the many activities required to stage collegiate athletic events like ski races. Fortunately, their new benefactor Johnny Johnson had found great satisfaction in helping these eager young men and began an endowed fund called the Harrison Memorial Fund for support of Winter Carnival and other Outing Club activities.

As plans developed for the 1916 Winter Carnival, Johnson was quick to grasp the significance of an opportunity to help the Dartmouth ski jumpers with some hired coaching. In September 1915 he suggested that he was "willing to pay for Paulson to come to Carnival" and wondered if his [Paulson's] presence in Hanover "would…benefit our boys? Could he teach some of them to do the somersault stunt?"[36] Carl ("Gus") Paulson was a ski jumping expert from Berlin, NH, who was attending New Hampshire State College and widely known for his acrobatic jumps. Johnny's idea of employing an expert to help the Dartmouth ski jumpers is the first record of the idea of hiring a ski coach at Dartmouth. In that same letter, Johnny went on to offer funds for better medals for Canadian competitors (recalling McGill's presence at the 1915 Dartmouth Winter Carnival). He wanted those medals to be inscribed "in such a way as to recognize Dartmouth's colonial origins and common English heritage [with Canada]." Later that spring when he was in Hanover, Johnson left another gift of $500 accompanied by a note directing that $400 of it was to be used for "repair and extension of the ski jumping grounds" as he and Mr. Tibbetts [a DOC faculty advisor] had previously agreed.[37]

For the next few years Johnson would continue to make his gifts and offer his advice. He offered (red jackets) for the winter sports "team," created a "Rum and Molasses" fund to provide Thanksgiving dinners with all the fixings to DOC members remaining in Hanover over that holiday, and for costumes for the Carnival Ball and decorations to make Winter Carnivals more festive.

Johnson perceived disturbing shifts in the college's official attitude toward Winter Carnival. His impression that they wanted to eliminate some of the social aspects and the increasingly popular fraternity parties disturbed him greatly. In a strongly worded letter, he concluded that "the hardships of the winter climate…at Hanover…[result in] a season that needs enlivening. If the Outing Club, by offering opportunities for lovers of 'out-of-doors' to come to Hanover to enjoy its facilities over a considerable period of time and to become better acquainted with the beauties of this country as they actually exist – and not as they may be imagined in front of the fraternity fireplaces – can increase the interest of thoughtful people in the College and its environment, it will have become a real service."[38]

Skis "over there"

In the atmosphere of a war being fought in Europe, combined with the new athletic and social stimulus that the DOC brought to its Winter Carnival, it was probably unsurprising that a philanthropic alumnus who was also a war veteran would find a connection between his generous support of the DOC and the cause for the boys "over there."

The college community returned to campus after New Years Day in 1916 to the news in *The Dartmouth* that their first alumnus, **Richard N. Hall '15**, had been killed on Christmas Day driving an ambulance in France. As this tragic topic wailed with Hanover's winter wolf winds, a headline in the same issue of the newspaper announced "Horton to Go to Front, Dartmouth Man First American to Volunteer for Ski Work." It explained, "C. D. Horton will be the first American to respond to the recent call issued for voluntary ski men to carry on relief work in the Vosges [France] under the direction of the American Relief House of Paris… Horton will leave the country Saturday [January 8, 1916] probably to remain until next spring, his expenses over and back are being paid by the Outing Club and Rev. John E. Johnson."[39]

Johnson wrote to Carl Shumway about an urgent plea for volunteers to serve with the ambulance service in France where skiers were needed to help evacuate wounded from the mountains. He would "advance the money for two Outing Club men $150.00 each."[40] He wrote to "Professor" [most likely DOC faculty advisor **Charles D. Adams, Class of 1877**, Professor of Greek] a day later that, "Horton sails on *La Touraine* on Saturday from New York. The Outing Club contributes $150 towards his expenses which is supposed to be enough to get him to France and back. The French government does the rest. I may go to New York to see him off."[41]

As Dartmouth held its first military drill in Alumni Gymnasium on February 7, 1916, five days before Winter Carnival, Johnson sent a letter to the editor of *The Dartmouth* explaining the need for others like Hall and Horton who could help the rescue efforts in France:

"Knowing the interest that Dartmouth has taken in the work of the American ambulance [corps] in France, culminating in the sacrifice of the life of Richard Hall, while on duty in the mountains of Alsace, I feel sure that the attention of Dartmouth men will be strongly attracted to the word brought to me in two letters I have recently received. In the first, 'They are still crying for men. They want fifteen or twenty more than we have on our books.' This work is doing more than any other agent to build in France a respect for and gratitude to our country, must not be suffered to stop – or even slacken. Secondly: until now the transport of wounded in the Vosges Mountains in Alsace has been done entirely by the American ambulances. But the snowfall has been so heavy that they become inaccessible to motors. For this reason a section of ski-sledges has been formed. And I was asked if I could find five Americans, strong and skillful 'skieurs' who would come, passage one way paid if necessary. Dartmouth is the only college in the East where there is any general practice or considerable skill in the use of snowshoe or ski."[42]

Carl Shumway had considered volunteering along with **Charles "Dabney" Horton '15**, his fellow Dartmouth skier, but his parents had barred him from going to France.

Dabney Horton had won the 220-yard ski dash in the historic 1914 ski meet with McGill. Now he was off to the front in France to put his skiing skills to use evacuating wounded soldiers from the winter mountain battlefields. Horton became a writer, like many of his ambulance corps comrades, who later taught English at Dartmouth and also at Ohio State University. His short stories and poetry were published in magazines like *Atlantic Monthly* and *Scribner's*. In one of his stories, "I Went to Dartmouth," published in *College Stories*, he described his experience learning to ski there: "Skis to me were like the fledgling's first wings. After I learned to get around fast on them, and could do my twenty miles in an afternoon with the best of them, I began to discover Dartmouth."[43]

After his service in the Vosges Mountains in the winter of 1916, Horton remained in France to take flight training and fly in the Lafayette Espadrille of the Franco-American Flying Corps where he was decorated with the *Croix de Guerre*. While living in Paris during World War I, Horton met and married his wife, Helen Wheelock Hubbard, a direct descendant of John Wheelock, second President of Dartmouth and son of the founder. While Horton was the first Dartmouth alumnus known to volunteer for military duty on skis, he would clearly not be the last.

Reverend Johnson's impact on the early growth and stability of the Dartmouth Outing Club was well recognized throughout the college and among the alumni. Carl Shumway noted, "his benefactions came at a time when it meant that the Club grew by leaps and bounds, while if these numerous financial contributions had not been forthcoming, naturally the Club of necessity would not have been able to expand as it did or put on such wonderful Winter Carnivals."[44] In addition to his many financial contributions, Johnson's enthusiasm and philosophical endorsement of the attributes of Dartmouth's physical surroundings supported the tone of outdoor appreciation that became a hallmark not just of the Outing Club but the College itself. As an undergraduate during the Civil War, he wrote an essay about his class's role in choosing the color green for Dartmouth, referring to it as "God Almighty's 'Outing Color.' " Dartmouth awarded him an honorary master's degree in 1916 at his 50th Reunion. Johnson died in 1934 at the age of 92 having made a lasting impact on the future of the Dartmouth Outing Club and skiing even though he had never been on a pair of skis.

Skiing at Dartmouth grew rapidly in its first decade after Fred Harris launched the Outing Club. Harris himself, while not a modest man, "never claimed to be the first man at Dartmouth to use skis."[45] But he did believe that he was "the first to use skis extensively on long as well as short trips and on trips into the mountains...I was the first at Hanover to study skiing intensively, to collect ski pictures from all over the world, to study books of the subject, to make skis, to study the matter of correct bindings, the making of turns, etc. Not until the formation of the Outing Club was there any attempt to put the sport of skiing or snowshoeing on the 'scientific management' basis, nor were the wide opportunities offered by the ideal location at all developed."[46] Historian **William I. Borman '53** would describe the incredibly rapid growth in a survey of the two decades of skiing at Dartmouth from 1910-1930 citing *The Dartmouth* as saying, "Nothing has done so much in the way of boosting Dartmouth's winter sports—and through those, the College itself.[47] Borman also pointed out that the first "team" in 1914 had no coach, no uniforms, no official recognition, no captain and very little experience. "They were in fact nothing more than the four best skiers of a college club devoted to winter sports. This group represented the first step in a process of evolution which was to make the name of their college famous in the skiing areas of the entire world."[48]

Team Spirit and the Need for Professional Instruction

It wasn't long before the competitive exuberance of Dartmouth undergraduates became part of the novel skiing interest Fred Harris had stirred up. The concept of collegiate competitive skiing had yet to develop, but less than two months after their first meeting, Harris had the Dartmouth Outing Club competing among themselves in their first Field Day. For the next three years, Winter Carnival competitions were strictly intramural events for Dartmouth students. Even for their first trip to Montreal to compete against McGill University skiers in 1914, they merely put the four best skiers in the DOC on a train to Montreal. The following year, the first signs of a team appeared when the DOC Council decided to elect a ski captain and make "the men who won points at the last carnival"[49] eligible to vote. In December 1916 the Council formed a committee to look into "costumes for the ski team for carnival,"[50] and so grew the seminal elements of a ski team. By the end of that year, the 1916 edition of the yearbook *Aegis* described Winter Carnival as "assuming intercollegiate proportions." Reverend Johnson's sponsorship of a professional US ski jumper to be engaged prior to that year's carnival was the first attempt to provide coaching, but ski jumping was still being scored using rules from the Montreal Ski Club.

The start of the first North American college ski race at McGill University in 1914.

It was only a matter of time before the early institutional competitors would establish an association to help regulate the new concerns of scheduling meets, scoring, and eligibility rules. Elsewhere in Europe and Canada, ski competitions were sanctioned and held by prominent ski clubs where the members provided the organization, publicity, and officiating. They were designed for individual competitors, not for formal teams in terms of scoring or awards. Ski competition between colleges and universities was a uniquely North American, if not almost entirely American, phenomenon. However, Dartmouth took its skiing quite seriously. In 1916 Johnny Johnson was concerned about the Dartmouth skiers' appearance at Winter Carnivals and purchased red wool jackets for them. They were in use for about a decade until new team uniforms were purchased and Professor **Harold ("Harry") Q. Hillman,** the Dartmouth track coach, was employed to assist the ski team in 1920, mostly in overseeing their conditioning.

Fred Harris continued to push his idea of a getting a "ski man" to help the boys. Harris had been an alumnus for almost ten years, but he held a firm grip on his stewardship of the DOC and never failed to let the boys know his opinions and ideas. He wrote to DOC President **Charles Throop '22** right after the 1921 Winter Carnival with a laundry list of ideas for improving the ski scene at his alma mater adding an animated P.S.: "What do you think would be the chance of hiring Vasesha [a noted ski jumper from Lake Placid] as a ski coach? It would give the sport a big impetus and put DOC ski runners on a higher plane for competition as well as their own pleasure. Vasesha is a marvel on skis, a fine fellow, and is available."[51] A week later he brought up the same point in another letter to Throop. "Do you think the time is ripe for a professional ski coach at Hanover?"[52] Throop replied that poor finances at present prevented hiring a ski coach: "I'm sure it will not be many moons before one will be treading the halls of Robinson [where the DOC offices were located]."[53]

On the management side of the DOC, the relatively simple nature of operations at the start enabled the students to keep things going. But as the list of tasks and decisions increased, the management load for students began to be a burden. The structure of the club did a fine job of preparing new members and training them in the tasks of running Carnival events and outings. Upperclassmen indoctrinated their younger members in the ways of the DOC as committees met, planned, and took action. The presence of interested faculty advisors kept a steady hand ready when needed, but otherwise the college administration allowed the club to function quite well on its own. Two related concerns confronted the DOC after its first years: one was the need for a skilled skier to coach the collection of interested competitors who were forming into a team; the other need was for someone to provide instruction for the incoming students who arrived in Hanover without any skiing experience. The need for a ski instruction program for others in the Hanover community was also clear.

A photograph and roster of six men comprising the "Intercollegiate Ski Team" first appeared in the 1921 *Aegis*. Although "Winter Sports" was officially recognized as a minor sport at Dartmouth in 1922, one of the unique features regarding the development of skiing at the college was its origin and develoment outside the purview of the athletic establishment of the Dartmouth College Athletic Council (DCAC). Football, baseball, basketball, hockey, track, and tennis were all under the DCAC umbrella in 1910 and all enjoyed the services of paid coaching staffs. Faculty members also staffed the physical education program.

Thanks to assistance from their faculty advisor, Professor James Goldthwait, the DOC was able to arrange for gymnasium credit for ski work in 1922. "After several years of good service, the ski classes this winter were given the recognition that they have merited for some time. Through the efforts of some of the faculty members of the Outing Club it was arranged with the management of Freshman Athletics that gymnasium credit would be given for ski work carried out under the supervision of the head instructor of the class, namely Prof. Goldthwait."[54] The 1922 DOC Annual Report noted that 200 students signed up for this program.

Despite implementing student ski instruction, fielding a real team sport, and the continuing interest in DOC activities, there was a lull precipitated by cancellation of Winter Carnival in 1918 plus the loss of Harris and his self-taught contemporaries, all of whom had graduated. However, along came a surprisingly talented skier to restore interest in the sport. Newspaper correspondents happened to be present to record an exhibition of ski jumping skill in February 1919. The account that appeared in *The Boston Post* was titled "The Feat That Made the Crowd Gasp." "Johnny Carleton, a freshman, did it. It was a thriller. He turned a somersault on his long skis as he shot over the 60 feet jump and in landing in good form went tearing up the course to the end of the vale."[55]

If his classmates had only known what **John P. Carleton '22** had yet to accomplish in his own skiing performances or what he would achieve in the wider world of skiing, they would have gasped along with their Carnival guests. He was a hometown boy, born in Hanover where he spent his youth among the skiing men of Dartmouth. Long before entering Dartmouth as a freshman he had already set a New England ski jumping record with a leap of 103 feet in 1914 at Bristol, N.H, at the age of 15. Two years later, Gus Paulson, the ski jumping expert hired by Rev. Johnson, was teaching him to do the somersault off the old ski jump in Hanover. After wowing the crowd with his spectacular somersault performances as a freshman in 1919, the DOC picked Carleton, then a junior, to run the 1921 Children's Carnival. He broke his own New England ski jump record in his senior year just a week before the Dartmouth Winter Carnival. Fred Harris had returned to his hometown of Brattleboro, Vermont, where he had helped organize the Brattleboro Outing Club and build a ski jump in town. 1922 was the first ski jumping tournament at the Brattleboro Winter Carnival. John Carleton was among the competitors on that brand new jump, winning and establishing a new record when he hit a mark of 150 feet.

Carleton was not only a talented skier, but smart, too. Following his graduation from Dartmouth in 1922, he studied at Oxford University in England as a Rhodes Scholar. While there, he skied on the university team and met Arnold Lunn, the British architect of Alpine skiing in Europe. The connection established between Lunn and Carleton was a catalyst for spreading the Alpine discipline from Europe to North America as Lunn was developing it. The main point of contact in this transfer was **Professor Charles A. Proctor '00**, a DOC Advisor who took a great interest in skiing and became connected to Lunn through Carleton.

Carleton was one of the first after Harris to keep skiing a constant part of his world, first in his days at Oxford and later in his professional life. As more and more classes graduated after the DOC began, this steady increase in Dartmouth alumni who skied compounded the interest in this growing snowball as it rolled into the future. Without his skiing talents, Carleton would likely have never met Lunn. And fortunate also was the connection Carleton was able to promote between his old faculty friends back in Hanover and the distant Mr. Lunn.

An Expert Ski Man

If skiing at Dartmouth in the early 1920s still lacked one thing it was the presence of a skilled professional ski instructor or coach. Paulson was only there for a few weeks in 1916 and Track Coach Hillman was not a skier when he helped the "team" in 1920. Thanks to the new links to Arnold Lunn, Professor Proctor and others in the DOC quickly realized that ski-sport, as distinguished from utilitarian Nordic versions of skiing as a way of simply maneuvering over snowy terrain, was taking a more Alpine form of competition. They decided to hire a coach familiar with this emerging Alpine style of ski competition. After another suggestion from Fred Harris early in 1922 urging them again that "an expert ski man be hired to give lessons,"[56] they imported a coach from Europe. In March 1923, the DOC announced that **Colonel Anton Diettrich** would serve as ski coach for the 1923-24 season: "He will be available to the ski team 3 times a week and to the freshman ski classes the same."[57] Anton Diettrich of Budapest, a Lieutenant Colonel in the Austro-Hungarian Army, commander of the Austro-Hungarian Army fencing instructors course and winner of saber championships, arrived early in March to assume his duties as instructor in fencing and skiing.

Col. Diettrich was part of the small group of European skiers who specialized in high alpine skiing and founded the vogue of skiing in Switzerland. He was the first man on skis to ascend various mountains from the Eastern Alps and Carpathians to Norway. For a number of years he served with a regiment of riflemen in the Tyrol and drilled companies in alpine skiing. He was also a writer for the *Annual of the Central European Ski Association.* His experience as an instructor was unquestionable and his credentials of the highest order having been a former pupil of Matthias Zdarsky, one of the leading alpine ski experts in Europe. In addition to embodying the Alpine style of skiing and despite some physical limitations imposed by war wounds, Col. Diettrich brought leadership and discipline to the young American men eager to improve their competitive edge on the slopes, and he brought a new and different perspective to the haphazardly developing ski program.

During his first year on campus, he completed the first of a series of lectures on "Skis and Skiing." Lecture 1 was on equipment and resulted in a 23-page booklet published by the DOC in 1924. No other lectures in the series were published, but Diettrich was to make his presence felt in other ways. He brought to Dartmouth his first-hand knowledge of Alpine ski racing in forms yet to be developed at Hanover. There was great interest in returning Dartmouth to the top of the intercollegiate ski world, and among the talented men Diettrich found on his team was **Charles N. Proctor '28**, son of the physics professor and DOC advisor. Proctor would later say that before he met Col. Diettrich he had no knowledge of Alpine skiing. That would soon change as Diettrich began to propose new ideas for competition based on what he had experienced in the Austrian Alps.

When Col. Diettrich arrived in 1923 a rudimentary form of ski instruction had existed at the college for several years. A formal program of recreational ski instruction for Dartmouth students had been implemented the previous winter of 1921-22 when 198 freshmen enrolled in the ski instruction program. The DOC clearly saw this program's potential as a feeder for talent on the winter sports team.

Col. Diettrich, however, did not agree with the program. He saw competitions only as a means of attracting the public, believed that competition did not develop skiing, felt that the team did not serve to build up skiing in the college, hated the idea of always having to win, and wanted more inter-class rather than inter-collegiate competition[58]–heresy considering the competitive atmosphere that had evolved among the students. To remedy that, he recommended there be a man to run recreational skiing and to have classes by ability. He also implemented ski instruction for the ladies in Hanover, his Continental demeanor making him quite popular with his female students.

The alignment of Diettrich's background—the right talents and ski-world connections— together with the high interest among students in the developing ski-sport produced an opportunity that would be repeated numerous times as skiing took hold at Dartmouth. While John Carleton was studying at Oxford and skiing under the approving eye of Arnold Lunn, Col. Diettrich was stirring some interest on the Hanover Plain for a new kind of ski competition. Until the mid-1920s, ski meets in Hanover consisted of cross-country and ob-stacle races, a few dashes, and ski jumping. Diettrich worked with Professor Charles A. Proctor to introduce the novel idea of skiing down a slope making turns between pairs of pine boughs stuck in the snow—an ersatz Alpine slalom race. Lunn had developed a racing format for slalom competitions in the Alps, and that infor-mation was conveyed back to Professor Proctor. Lunn acknowledged, "In the United States the first group of skiers to adopt our rules were the skiers of Dartmouth College. Professor Proctor was a member of the Ski Club of Great Britain and he did a great work in propagating downhill racing."[59] The first slalom race in the United States using Lunn's scoring format was run at the 1925 Dartmouth Winter Carnival. It was won by the professor's son, Charles N. Proctor. The following February, the DOC Winter Sports Council passed a motion approving the schedule for an intra-mural meet "with the reservation that Col. Diettrich can add a slalom race to the ski events if he sees fit."[60] Slalom was there to stay.

Coach Diettrich was admired by his team and reportedly regaled them with his war stories and skiing escapades in the Alps. His tales of the Austrian down-mountain races inspired the Dartmouth skiers to stage their own version on Mount Moosilauke where a carriage road offered a challenging site for the race. In the winter of 1927, talk began in earnest of holding their own down-the-mountain race. It was held on March 8 and was open only to Dartmouth skiers. Professor Proctor, in charge of timing that 1927 event, was not a nov-ice to either skiing or Mt. Moosilauke. The day of the 1927 race, *The Dartmouth* reported an attempt at such a run 13 years earlier: "The forerunner of the race down Moosilauke was held on February 1, 1914, when an adventurous group of 12 men, members of the Faculty and student body, left Breezy Point to climb Moosi-lauke Summit on skis….Prof. C.A. Proctor was in charge of this group. **Dick Hall '15, R.E. Pritchard '14, Prof. of Physics A.B. Meservey '06, Jess Fenno '14, R.H. Foss '14, Dr. F.P. Lord '98, W.H. Junkins '14, A.P. Richmond '14, a professor in the Thayer School, D.A. Emerson '14, George Dock '16, and Profes-sor Burr** of the Physics Department made up the personnel of this adventuresome party."[61]

The DOC continued to hold this event annually for the next several years as its popularity and reputa-tion grew. Ten years later Dartmouth alumni would still be talking about the history made with that first race in 1927. "The first down-mountain race in this country was run on the Carriage Road on Mt. Moosilauke… [and] was the primer of the pump."[62] Diettrich was the agent who helped to make Dartmouth a pioneer in Alpine skiing, both slalom and downhill, in North America, but his war wounds eventually prevented him from continuing his active role as a ski coach. While he continued to serve in the Physical Education Depart-ment as fencing coach and remained on the Outing Club's Ski Team Committee, the DOC began looking for a replacement to coach the winter sports team in the winter of 1927-28. After the ski season ended in 1927, the Winter Sports Team Committee of the DOC Council recommended that the Outing Club procure a full-time man to handle the downhill, slalom, and cross-country candidates and to lead weekend trips, and another man to coach the beginners' recreational classes.

Dartmouth's next ski coach was a return to the Nordic side. In December 1927, the Winter Sports Com-mittee announced the hiring of **Sig L. Steinwall** as the new coach. Steinwall was a Norwegian ski jumper and a member of the prestigious Norge Ski Club of Chicago. He had won the Fiskatorpet Cup (named for a ski jumping stadium in Stockholm, Sweden) and enjoyed an international reputation as a jumper. His narrow focus on jumping turned out to be not what the Dartmouth ski team needed as it headed into the new world of Alpine skiing. At the same December 1927 meeting, the Winter Sports Team Committee also announced the appointment of **German "Gerry" Raab**, another well-known European skier and graduate of the University of Munich, as recreational ski coach.

The Dartmouth Winter Sports Team had a lackluster season in 1928 despite the outstanding ability of Olympian Charley Proctor (or perhaps more precisely because of his absence from the team while competing at the Olympics in St. Moritz). Nevertheless the blame fell to Steinwall. The season had barely ended when the DOC General Policies Committee recommended that "Mr. Steinwall be not re-engaged next year, and that Gerry Raab be engaged as coach of the Winter Sports Team for next year before he leaves town."[63] They offered Raab the position and he accepted. In January 1929, the committee appointed **Alfred. E. Clarke '29** to fill the recreational ski coach vacancy. By March they were proud to record that 108 men had turned out for recreational skiing. Raab's efforts to consolidate and improve intramural competitions paid off a year later: "The large number of really excellent skiers in College was clearly demonstrated in the highly successful Winter Sports Derby, a combined dormitory, class, and fraternity competition which superseded the old interclass meet."[64] The turnout of over 50 men for the ski team brought about the first cuts to make the squad in the team's history.

Raab returned to coach the Winter Sports Team for the 1929-30 season, and Tom Frost took over as recreational ski coach. Coach Raab outlined his new policy for getting the Winter Sports Team in shape. The DOC agreed that he should train them as he saw fit, including the idea of introducing a second team to compete with high schools and ski clubs.[65]

THE MIDDLE YEARS

DOC officers and their faculty advisors recognized the workload these activities imposed on the students in this traditionally student-run organization. There was no full-time paid staff. In March 1929 the Dartmouth Outing Club Council outlined a proposal for a full-time salaried person who "shall be responsible for the continuance and development of the spirit and ideals of the Club. He shall be Director of Finance."[66] Three months later they nominated **Daniel P. Hatch, Jr. '28** to be appointed to the new position of Comptroller of the DOC for 1929-30 subject to the approval of President Ernest M. Hopkins and the Dartmouth Trustees. Hiring Dan Hatch was one of many fortuitous decisions made in the DOC's successful development. As an undergraduate Dan was an active member of the Winter Sports Council and a proven organizer and manager. He had served as president of the DOC and, on a later alumni questionnaire, listed his undergraduate major as "DOC."[67] That was no doubt a serious response.

Three good friends and legends of skiing: Charlie Proctor '28, Professor Proctor '00, and Dan Hatch '28.

A job description could not adequately address the breadth and depth of responsibilities Hatch would take on for the next seven years. One of his first tasks would be to coordinate the hiring of a new ski coach; that a qualified "ski man" was needed to coach the emerging collegiate powerhouse team was clear to all at Dartmouth. DOC faculty advisor Professor Charles A. Proctor was joined by a growing number of alumni interested in advancing Dartmouth's skiing reputation. One of those alumni was **John W. "Jack" McCrillis '19**. In the foreword of a book he would later publish, McCrillis wrote about his first meeting with a professional ski instructor, **Otto Schniebs**, from the Black Forest in Germany: "I had the privilege of being with Otto…the first time he skied in this country. The first time we saw that man come down a hill we knew he had something we had never seen in fifteen years of skiing…Soon after, Otto began to teach professionally. And we hoped things would work out so that Otto could go to Dartmouth as coach."[68]

At the 1930 Mt. Moosilauke Down Mountain race, the fourth annual running of this quintessential Dartmouth ski event, Dan Hatch, in typical hands-on fashion, was on his skis at the starting line on the top of the mountain talking with Dartmouth skiing alumnus and Appalachian Mountain Club president, **William P. Fowler '21**. As he chatted with Fowler, who was a good friend of Jack McCrillis, the ski coach subject came up. Fowler later recalled, "I recommended…that they should try to get Otto [Schniebs] as ski coach when they were looking for one…It was to Dan Hatch that I recommended Otto on the top of Moosilauke at the start of the downhill race."[69]

Not more than a few days after that 1930 Moosilauke Downhill race, William Fowler wrote to Hatch to confirm their conversation about Schniebs: "I am enclosing a letter from Otto Schniebs who would be the best man for the position at Dartmouth." The enclosed letter to Fowler, written in Schniebs's distinctive and precise hand, read in part: "I send you here my program how to teach skiing successfully to a big crowd…"[70]

William Fowler '21, a leader of the AMC & Dartmouth skiing.

It wasn't long before the DOC launched a recruiting plan to interview Schniebs who had already begun to establish his reputation as a good ski instructor through work with the Harvard Mountaineering Club and the Appalachian Mountain Club in Boston. Professor Proctor, wisely invited a student, **Morrison G. Tucker '32**, to accompany him on a train to Boston to meet with Otto Schniebs; liking what he saw, Proctor offered him a position. Professor Proctor's plan to augment Schniebs's salary with off-season work in his physics laboratory never quite worked out as Proctor had hoped. Otto did, however, dedicate himself to his ski coaching responsibilities with all the fervor of his own infamous heavily accented and often repeated saying, "Schkiing iss not a schport, it iss a vay of life." His other well-quoted expression summed up his style of Alpine skiing: "Schtem! Schtem like hell!"

Schniebs's success continued to build as he made his distinctive mark on the team. Skiing was clearly his way of life. In his second season (1931-32), the DOC Winter Sports Committee voted to drop snowshoeing and speed skating from the Winter Sports Team making it now purely a Ski Team. When he was not coaching, Schniebs was busy arranging lessons and traveling to the women's colleges in the Northeast to make them "ski conscious."[71] "We have over fifty girls skiing at Bennington College... 'Otto' was over there February 22nd [1934] and did a wonderful job of making them ski conscious." He also made visits to Skidmore College in 1936 with some of his star skiers, including **Dick Durrance '39**, for a day of skiing lessons and demonstrations as well as to a number of ski clubs throughout New England and New York.[72]

Otto reflected on the growth and popularity of winter sports as a result of Dartmouth's leadership and its "suggestive help to other organizations, colleges, clubs, and individuals." He took great pride in his third season of sponsoring and leading the first United States Eastern Amateur Ski Association (USEASA) ski school. The success of the skiers led them to boast that they had "grown to be one of the [few] successful teams that Dartmouth has produced in the last few years and we feel that we should be given a fair chance to retain that position as befitting a championship team."[73]

Dartmouth Coach Otto Schniebs

Skiing was still a relatively new activity at Dartmouth and at the other colleges and universities in North America. Dartmouth's intercollegiate skiing fortunes had run the gamut during that time. They had won the President Harding Cup at the Lake Placid Club's College Weekend ski competitions for three consecutive years from 1923-25 and in the first years of winter carnival competitions dominating their rivals. But not all the years prior to Schniebs's arrival were total success for the Dartmouth ski team. However, many graduating members of the early winter sports teams left Hanover after graduation to spread the word about skiing and Dartmouth's relative prominence in the sport. The word of mouth from skiing alumni and the ample press coverage Dartmouth skiing enjoyed helped to attract new skiers and to promote a healthy interest in skiing among the incoming classes.

Otto Schniebs's success as a coach at Dartmouth was assisted greatly by the high quality of talent that entered his program. During the five winters he coached, he made a significant impact on varsity skiers in eight Dartmouth classes from 1931-38, accounting for a total of at least 200 students. Through his initiatives in organizing ski schools and making visits to other colleges, he expanded his local influence in Hanover to several hundred more skiers directly and to thousands indirectly. The combination of his own efforts to create "ski consciousness" and get people skiing produced the fortuitous results of strong admissions success in bringing talented skiers to Dartmouth which, in turn, made his instructional outcomes even more dramatic. He ended up having coached eight members of the United States Olympic ski team and winners of many other skiing honors while he was employed by Dartmouth.

For nearly two decades, Dartmouth had already been attracting an increasing number of talented skiers. Some were local boys like John Carleton, Charley Proctor, **Thurston ("Ted") Frost '25** and **Colin Campbell**

(L to R) Professor Proctor '00 of Dartmouth and four others - "Jack Rabbit" Johannsen, W. Thompson (President, CASA), R.D. Forster and Harry Pangman (front).

The D ski team at first ISWU races in 1930s: (l. to r.) Coach Schniebs, Lingly, Washburn, Hunter, D. Bradley, W. Chivers, Capt. Hannah with the Cup, Titcomb, Durrance, Woods, Richardson and Mgr. Saunders.

'40, many of whom came from Dartmouth faculty and alumni families. Others came in response to the widening reputation of Dartmouth as the place to go for a good education and the opportunity to ski competitively. The arrival of Coach Schniebs simply added to the allure of making a mark in big-time collegiate skiing. In his first seasons in Hanover, Schniebs began to assemble an impressive roster of talent. Hanover boys **A. Lincoln Washburn '35, Henry "Bem" Woods '36, Edgar "Ted" Hunter '38, Roy Chamberlin '38**, and the **Chivers brothers Warren '38 and Howard '39,** plus others like **Sel Hannah '35, Dick '33** and **Lawrence "Pug" Goldthwait '36, Larry Jump '36, Dave '38** and **Steve Bradley '39, Edward B. Meservey '38, John '38** and **Charlie McLane '41, Eddie Wells '39,** and **Dick Durrance '39.** Many of those and other names of Schniebs's protégés would become linked to skiing long after their few years of wearing the Dartmouth "D" on their ski sweaters. It was an amazing confluence of talent, leadership, and opportunity. Even after Otto left his coaching position at Dartmouth, his legacy continued to draw new talent up to World War II with many subsequent skiers following older brothers or friends to Dartmouth (like more Durrance, Bradley, and McLane siblings and faculty offspring like Harry Hillman) – all of whom had grown up hearing about Schniebs.

At the conclusion of his third season (1932-33), Schniebs filed a report that captured many of the successes he helped to bring about: "People realize more and more the magic relaxation one gets from a day spent out of doors in winter either on skies, or skates, snowshoes, or toboggan, or even a little hike in the snowy hills."[74]

Before Otto was hired by Dartmouth, he and Jack McCrillis had become friends and business associates. Jack had continued to pursue his own skiing interests after graduating, first in the Pacific Northwest where he introduced skiing to boys at a private school and helped start some regional ski clubs; but now back in New Hampshire, he was active in his hometown ski club in Newport. He and Otto started combining their talents for the benefit of skiing. McCrillis filmed the early downhill races on Mount Moosilauke and used some of his shots to illustrate a book, *Modern Ski Technique*, written by the *Meisterskier* Schniebs. Their films and book were instant hits and drew customers from across the country. Their efforts together resulted in a new race and a trophy they donated to create greater interest among Dartmouth skiers. Jack was sensitive to Otto's need to support his family and did what he could to help Otto through their business ventures. To the dismay of the DOC, Schniebs's primary employer at the time, the coach began marketing his name in other ski-related businesses through product promotions and appearances. Otto was dedicated to his boys on the ski team—and to promoting the sport that was to him "a way of life."

Seeing the tension unfolding between employer and employee, Fred Harris proposed that the DOC make Otto Schniebs a full time Outing Club employee "so he could devote his full energy to his coaching work."[75] That did not happen, and not long after Harris's proposal, Dan Hatch reported that Otto Schniebs had "decided definitely to put his full time into his ski supply business next year and not to coach for the Club."[76] Among the many related endeavors that had lured Schniebs away from his coaching was his work as an agent for selling White Stag skiwear, a new business founded by Dartmouth alumnus **Harold S. Hirsch '29** (another McCrillis protégé). Schniebs would later head to Lake Placid and eventually finish his coaching career at St. Lawrence University in Canton, New York. Even there his memories of Dartmouth remained fond. He wrote to John Rand at the DOC in 1954, "Here it is still Dartmouth which has the magic word in skiing. Four years as an Outing Clubber has opened many boys and girls eyes to let them see the true values of life."[77]

Among his many other contributions to the sport, Otto designed a slalom ski that was manufactured and sold by the Northland Ski Company and he designed the silver snowflake pin for the Dartmouth ski team that has remained a distinctive insignia for Dartmouth skiers for well over half a century.

His would be tough ski boots to fill. Schniebs left behind a strong ski team and four members of the 1936 US Winter Olympic ski team: Link Washburn, Ted Hunter, Warren Chivers, and Dick Durrance. Coach Schniebs was not one to abandon the team or his boys and suggested as his replacement **Winston Durgin '30** of Lewiston, Maine, and Fritz Steuri, a Swiss skier who had been at Woodstock, Vermont. While neither of Otto's recommendations became candidates for the position, he was not the only scout available; there were a number of alumni who had contact with key ski personnel worldwide. One of these, **Dr. Ralph Miller '24**, happened to be in Germany studying pathology. Miller was among the many who had skied at Dartmouth and sustained his skiing interest beyond graduation. Even before the DOC Trustees had accepted Schniebs's resignation, Dan Hatch had requested in mid-March 1936 that they ask Dr. Miller to "look around for us [in Europe] and to give us a report on any good prospects."[78] Then he wrote to Miller requesting his assistance and attached a list of eight top European skiers to be considered.[79]

Hatch also wrote to Dick Durrance who was training in the Alps that spring and asked if he would coordinate with Dr. Miller on finding prospects for a new coach as Durrance would know many of the names of fellow competitors and he also spoke German. The DOC Trustees agreed that "the selection of a successor for Otto should be made with the utmost care and that every effort ought to be made to bring a personality to Hanover who would be able to enthuse the community for the sport in somewhere near the degree that Otto has done it."[80] They also debated the issue of cost for obtaining a top quality person from Europe, finally deciding it would be "both desirable and necessary." It is likely that few deans or department heads in the rest of the College were selected with as much care and diligence as the DOC applied to the search for such a critical position as ski coach.

Dr. Miller reported that Anton Seelos, Otto Furrer, and many other good men were available within the estimated salary budget. Miller expected to be in Hanover by early June and would report further. At about the same time, Hatch received a letter from Alfred Lindley, a former teammate on the 1936 United States Olympic Ski Team, of the other Dartmouth skiers competing at Garmisch, Germany; he had evaluated two of Dartmouth's top prospects and gave reasons why they were not best suited for the job. Lindley went on to promote a new candidate whose name had not even been on the Dartmouth short list, but was subsequently penciled in under a list of eight of Europe's best skiers: "...it seems to me that your needs at Dartmouth would be better filled by a younger man who is more of an all round skier. I have in mind particularly **Walter Prager** of Arosa, Switzerland, one of the outstanding skiers of Europe. He spoke to me once about wishing to come to America and get a job skiing and particularly getting a job coaching all around skiing."[81]

In the early 1930s, Walter Prager was arguably the leading racer in the world, and he brought that skill to Dartmouth.

Dan Hatch and Al Lindley continued to discuss the prospect of hiring Prager for the next week by correspondence and phone. Hatch encouraged Lindley to contact Prager about the coaching job. They brought in others of the skiing world familiar with Prager, like Bob Livermore of Harvard, to review his skiing ability. Prager showed interest, and on June 9, 1936, he wrote to Hatch requesting clarification and negotiation of the terms of employment. Hatch replied with details. Prager accepted, and after a few more reference checks, Hatch sent Prager a contract. Three days later John Carleton, by then a lawyer practicing in New Hampshire, wrote to congratulate Hatch on securing Prager as coach: "You could do no better."[82] They went on to discuss the immigration requirements which Carleton then helped negotiate to bring Prager to Hanover.

Hatch went to pro-active lengths to prevent some of the product endorsement conflicts that had formerly plagued the employer-employee relationship with Schniebs by writing a letter to local ski equipment purveyors **John Piane '14** (Dartmouth Co-operative Society), **James W. Campion '28** (Campion's clothing store), Otto Schniebs, and Carl Shumway (ski advertising business in Boston).[83] Despite that effort, Prager had been in Hanover only a few months when Carpenter Metal Products of Cleveland, Ohio, shipped him a pair of aluminum poles to try out and then endorse. Hatch interceded by politely acknowledging receipt of the poles and offering to provide a generic DOC report of their use. The cachet of the Dartmouth name combined with that of a European racing star was so powerful that ski equipment companies could not resist trying to obtain the advantage such endorsements offered no matter how hard the DOC tried to avoid these conflicts. Four years later Prager was pictured in a Burton skiwear advertisement under the caption "a tribute to Dartmouth's skiers, the pioneers of American skiing."[84]

Over the course of the next several years, in addition to his numerous other responsibilities in running an increasingly complex organization like the DOC, Dan Hatch faced a succession of challenges to satisfy and sustain good employee morale with his successful new ski coach. There was no denying Dartmouth's being at the top of the intercollegiate ski world. Among the many relationships that had developed between the DOC and the ski world far beyond Hanover was a growing connection with the Union Pacific Railroad (UPRR). The railroad was actively sponsoring new ski facilities in the west. In 1937 Sun Valley (a Union Pacific property) was ready to host the Harriman Cup. Hatch wrote a reply to an officer of the railroad and provided the requested publicity photos that the Union Pacific wanted to use of Durrance and Prager, both of whom would be racing in that event. Hatch copied that letter to UPRR President Averill Harriman.[85]

At the same time, Hatch was busily attempting to line up summer work for Prager, hoping that Dartmouth's efforts would demonstrate good faith and interest in retaining such a qualified employee. Hatch wrote to the Ski Club of Victoria in Melbourne, Australia as well as to the Australian National Ski Federation and the Victorian Railways in Melbourne inquiring about the possibilities for summer employment for Prager.[86] That same summer Dick Durrance and David and Steve Bradley, two more up and coming Dartmouth skiers, had arranged on their own to travel to Australia and New Zealand to train on Southern Hemisphere snow. It would have made great sense to have their coach along with them, or at least nearby. In the Western Hemisphere in 1937, another contingent of Dartmouth skiers was making plans for summer training and to compete in Chile. Despite Hatch's efforts, Prager ended up back in Switzerland where he endeavored to get Dartmouth to send skiers to a future Christmas race there. Hatch replied that it depended on the approvals of Dartmouth's Dean and President.[87]

By the end of that summer, Hatch resigned to accept a job in the private sector. But before he left, he advised Prager that **Ford K. Sayre '33**, a noted ski instructor in town and the new manager of the Hanover Inn, had offered to provide Prager room and board at the Hanover Inn for the coming season. Sayre felt it would be good for the Hanover Inn's promotion of their winter ski packages to have a star like Prager among their residents and to have Walter mingle with the guests at mealtime.[88]

For the next several seasons under Prager's leadership, Dartmouth skiing thrived. The pipeline of skiing talent continued class after class. On the management side, **John Wilcox ("Will") Brown '37** took over the reins from Dan Hatch who had departed with the legacy of a new ski facility and a first of its kind in North America J-Bar ski lift (tramway, they called it) on Oak Hill, not to mention the hiring of two of Dartmouth's all-time great ski coaches in Schniebs and Prager. He had also established a close personal relationship with Dartmouth President Ernest Martin Hopkins. That was essential to the pervasive support throughout the institution for skiing and its steady forward momentum at Dartmouth. Will Brown's watch at the DOC saw the growth of popularity for skiing by others than just the varsity ski team at places like Mt. Moosilauke plus the creation of a ski patrol and a new race format, the giant slalom. Brown was also the man in charge when Hollywood came to Hanover in 1939 to film the movie *Winter Carnival*, produced by **Walter Wanger '15**.

Walter Prager skiing in the American West.

While Prager's boys were winning ski races, their coach was offering ski lessons to the rest of Hanover under the sponsorship of the Hanover Inn. *The Dartmouth* announced in the winter of 1938 that Prager's night school had opened "under Golf Course floodlights."[89] In December that year, Prager wrote to Harry Hicks, president of the Lake Placid Club and an officer with the National Ski Association, in response to a query regarding the status of cross-country at Dartmouth. Prager noted that he felt it was an important component for conditioning and the making of all-round four-event skiers.[90] Coming from a fellow whose early ski experience was from the heart of Alpine ski country, this was a strong testimonial for the Nordic side of the sport. Again, Prager complained to the Winter Sports Committee that nobody showed any interest for two types of competition, jumpers and *langlaufers*, as they required expensive special types of skis.[91] The DOC Trustees authorized him to spend up to $50 to purchase jumping and cross-country skis. Walter's coaching philosophy produced a fine record of meet skimeisters for the Dartmouth team during his tenure by stressing both Alpine and Nordic training.

In 1941 World War II began to impact not only the United States, but also Dartmouth skiing. Even before Pearl Harbor, Prager was drafted into military service soon after the ski season concluded that year. On Christmas Day 1941, only weeks after Pearl Harbor, he wrote to DOC General Manager **Hans Paschen, Tu '28,** to express his regrets that he would not be returning to Hanover but had a new offer as an Army ski instructor with a commission.[92] He was in Alta, Utah, with Dick Durrance teaching paratroopers how to ski. He concluded the letter raving about western skiing. Prager ended up serving with the Army's elite 10th Mountain Division along with many of his Dartmouth skiers. **Percy Rideout '40** filled in as the Dartmouth ski coach for the 1941-42 season. The intercollegiate ski competition circuit, along with many other elements of day-to-day life in America, slowed measurably during the war years from the combined loss of talent to the armed services and the inability to travel due to gas rationing.

By 1942 Winter Carnival had operated at a loss after many seasons of net gains. At the start of the 1942-43 ski season, Dartmouth faced the same shortages of rationed gasoline that all Americans were dealing with at the time; and just as the public was limited in driving their vehicles, so too was the DOC limited in running the Oak Hill lift.[93] Consequently, they decided not to operate the lift that season. Although there were still collegiate ski competitions each February during the war years, the social aspects of Winter Carnival were put on hold until 1945. Even so, a short list of Dartmouth ski team alumni picked up the slack on the coaching end; after Rideout, **Bob Meservey '43** took a turn in 1942-43, **W. H. Ashley '45** in 1943-44, while **Sel Hannah '35** and **Ed Blood** (University of New Hampshire) shared the job in 1944-45.

David Lawrence '51, Olympian and husband of Hall of Fame skier Andrea Mead Lawrence.

Walter Prager returned to his coaching position at Dartmouth for the winter of 1945-46. At the end of that winter, his fellow 10th Mountain Division veteran and now boss at the DOC, John Rand, received a glowing testimonial letter from Alec Bright (Harvard skier and a founder of the prestigious Ski Club Hochgebirge in Boston) about Prager's skill and sportsmanship: "I wish to express...how tremendously vital his greatness as a competitor and as a man have affected the sport and a great many of the sport's competitors."[94] A year later, when Prager took leave of absence to coach the 1948 US Olympic Ski Team, he was replaced by **Ja Densmore** as the interim ski coach at Dartmouth for 1947-48.

During this second Prager hiatus as the college's active professional coach, Fred Harris wrote to DOC Director Rand with a nine-point list of concerns for the future of skiing at Dartmouth. Among his points, Harris urged the DOC to hire enough coaches to take care of all students not good enough to make the varsity or freshman squads. He exhorted Rand to "Groom freshmen so they can make the squad." Harris also presciently observed: "It is evident that competition will be even harder as the years go by. More and more colleges are getting good material and good coaching. Good skiers are just as apt to come from the Stowe, Vermont high school and similar places whose graduates may not be able to pass our high scholastic tests. It behooves us to do everything possible to retain our supremacy."[95]

He also put a high value on the long-term benefits of skiing when he encouraged Rand that the DOC "must do everything for the boy who will never be varsity material but who will like to improve and who will enjoy skiing all his life. Must broaden the base. Accent intercollegiate competition, Yes! But also accent recreational skiing. Make him proud to say 'I learned in the Dartmouth school.' "[96]

These observations and recommendations from the progenitor of Dartmouth skiing were received with due respect and notice. The result was a meeting promptly called by **Virgil Poling,** Chairman of the DOC Board of Trustees. Poling produced a three-page summary of that meeting that included recommendations to keep the ski team under the control of the DOC, asked the question, "What is Dartmouth's position in the ski world?" with the added emphasis of saying, "A new post-war period is starting." To Harris's nine points, Poling also implored the DOC to "make skiing a lifetime sport. This spreading out of a knowledge of skiing will make for a happy alumni body in this respect."[97]

Olympian and National Champion Ralph Miller '55 racing for Dartmouth.

Coaches Merrill and Prager watching the race.

When he returned to Hanover, Prager found post-war Dartmouth, like the rest of the country, to be quite different from when he had left for military service. The ski team that had thrived under his direction and dominated the collegiate circuit in the late 1930s was decimated by the departure of those classes and the call to arms of so many of this country's able-bodied young men. He began rebuilding his program with top-notch Vermont skiers like **John Caldwell '50** from Putney and **Fred Springer-Miller '49** from Stowe, and New Hampshire boys like **Brooks Dodge '51** from North Conway and **Charlie Tremblay '52** from Lebanon, together with **David Lawrence '51** from France, **Tor Arneberg '50** from Norway, three skiers from nearby Kimball Union Academy, and two more from Hanover High School making a potent mix of locally developed talent with others from far away. As always, Prager continued to promote the development of all aspects of skiing–Caldwell in cross-country, Tremblay in jumping, Dodge in slalom, and soon-to-arrive **Bill Beck '53** and a Hanover boy, **Ralph E. Miller '55**, in downhill. In an article for *Sports Illustrated* in 1955 about the Dartmouth Winter Carnival, author and screenwriter **Budd Schulberg '36** remarked about this ability of Prager to push his skiers' ability to excel in both Alpine and Nordic skiing. Dartmouth's skiing star from Japan, **Chiharu "Chick" Igaya '57**, was a slalom skier par excellence, yet was also able to perform with style in the ski jump. As Schulberg noted on his return to Winter Carnival in 1955, "It was a rare aesthetic thrill to stand below the imposing 95-foot superstructure of the [ski jump] in-run and watch the elegant Igaya address himself to this unfamiliar event as if it were as much a part of him as the slalom."[98]

Other members of the Prager squad regularly competed in multiple events across both Nordic and Alpine disciplines. Over the next several years his Dartmouth skiers would rise again to the highest levels of ski competition and take on other roles within skiing. These Prager skiers, like many who preceded them in the pre-war years of the 1930s, were Walter Prager's rich legacy to skiing and to Dartmouth. However, his time at the college would soon come to an abrupt end. In the summer of 1957, Prager returned to Switzerland to visit with an old friend to seek his advice. Just a few months before the next ski season would begin for his Dartmouth skiers, Prager sent a tersely worded telegram of resignation to John Rand at the DOC that he could not return for another season as coach. "IMPOSSIBLE TO CONTINUE COACHING ANOTHER YEAR..."[99] was the way he began his short message to his former 10th Mountain Division buddy Rand. Like the rest of the Dartmouth Outing Club and the college in general, Rand was stunned and upset by the suddenness of Prager's decision not to return. Rand had thought the arrangements for Prager's next coaching contract were quite generous. After a brief phone call to Walter in Zurich, he learned that the real problem was a matter of Walter's personal marital relationship, compounded by a deteriorating hip condition, and not due to any dissatisfaction with his Dartmouth situation. Walter felt he could no longer live in Hanover. Rand and the DOC recognized Walter truly was not coming back and moved quickly to fill this gaping hole in their vaunted ski program.

Prager did eventually return to the United States, moving first to Mt. Snow in Vermont to run a ski shop there and later to open one near Whiteface Mountain in Wilmington, NY. He remained there as his personal life began to come apart. After a few years, some of his former skier alumni sensed that all was not well with their beloved coach. **Tom Corcoran '54** visited Prager in New York. The condition and frame of mind he found Prager to be in disturbed him. Corcoran contacted other Dartmouth friends and former ski team comrades who together conducted a discrete appeal among themselves to help Prager out and lift his low spirits.[100] Their effort to solicit over 500 alumni and friends of Prager resulted in 232 contributions totaling over $31,000—a generous sum back in the 1980s. With the help of **Paul Paganucci '53**, then CFO of the college, Dartmouth added another $2,000 and presented Prager with the gift, disguised as a belated "pension," and also bestowed on him the unique honorific title of "Head Ski Coach Emeritus." Such was the bittersweet but strong testimony to the respect and camaraderie that had developed on the ski team during Prager's years at Dartmouth that these appreciative alumni came together once again to make a heartfelt response to help a friend in difficult times and to organize it in such a way that it would not cause further heartache or harm to a man who is, in reality, one of skiing's greatest legends.

The need to find a qualified replacement for Prager only a few months before the next ski season put pressure on the DOC. Once again, good fortune shined on the Dartmouth ski world since the successor, **Al Merrill**, was right there at hand. DOC Director John Rand had sent a memo to College Treasurer **John F. Meck '33** two years earlier recommending Merrill to manage the new Dartmouth Skiway at Holt's Ledge with a glowing recommendation that Merrill was "well-known, had a strong skiing background, a knowledge of forestry, and was likeable." However, these facts were counterintuitive to some, like Meck, still of the mind that the best coaches could only be found in Europe and that having a German or French accent would be an asset for Dartmouth. Meck expressed this attitude in a letter to Dr. Ralph Miller, who had been recruited to help in the previous search that had hired Prager: "In addition to the teaching and performance abilities of a top-notch Austrian, would not the foreign association have other advantages for Dartmouth?" Meck told Miller that a foreign coach "would continue to attract good boys from Europe to Dartmouth. Also it is good publicity and adds color and flavor to our program."[101]

The accent Dartmouth got was not European, but Maine. Despite Meck's focus on finding another European to add "color and flavor to our program," he, along with the Outing Club Board and several ski team members who were polled on their opinions, unanimously agreed to select Al Merrill as the head coach. Merrill had been coaching very successfully at nearby Lebanon, NH, high school and had also assisted Prager the previous year. John Rand noted to the selection committee that Merrill was sought after by at least three other of the top skiing colleges and universities and two municipal areas as well: "We were fortunate in getting hold of Al who, at the time, was on the West Coast laying out the cross-country trails for the 1960 Olympics."[102] Merrill's coaching record included two terms as US Nordic Team Coach for FIS meets (1950 and 1954) and also the US Olympic Nordic Team Coach (1956).

Al was a native of Andover, Maine–an early hotbed of accomplished Nordic skiers. Al knew how to run on skis but was not the kind of Alpine high performer in slalom and downhill that Meck felt was essential for Dartmouth. Merrill had attended Hebron Academy in Maine and then skied for the University of New Hampshire (UNH), captaining the team for three years when the UNH Wildcats won successive Dartmouth Winter Carnivals. When he came to Hanover, he established himself as a coach with a reputation for being tough and demanding while still being understanding and able to foster and develop hidden talent on his teams. One of his protégés, **Ed Williams '64**, would go on to become an Olympic Biathlon skier after graduation. Ed described his coach by saying, "He was a man who never mentioned his many accomplishments or the honors he had received. He saw no need to do that; his world was here and now. He was a coach who respected the fact that athletics, while important, were subsidiary to the demanding academic environment at Dartmouth. Al was a role model for us, a true teacher, and a gentleman; someone for us to strive to emulate."[103]

Merrill would accomplish much as the Dartmouth ski coach. He started with a bang taking the talent he inherited from Prager all the way to the NCAA Championship in 1958. In his 15-year tenure leading the Dartmouth Ski team, Merrill's boys would win eight Dartmouth Winter Carnivals and never finish lower than fifth in the NCAAs. In addition, he coached two more Olympic Nordic teams (1964 and 1968), served as President of the USEASA (1964), and was a member of the US Olympic Ski Games Committee and of the Cross-Country Ski Committee of the FIS. He was elected to the US Ski and Snowboard Hall of Fame in 1974.

Al's tenure as ski coach came to an end in 1972. After having been promoted to the DOC's newly created position of Director of Outdoor Affairs in 1970, he came to realize he could not oversee all the operations of the Outing Club—which involved active management of the Dartmouth Skiway, the Oak Hill ski area, and the recreational ski programs plus all the college lands including the property at Mt. Moosilauke and the College Grant–and continue to coach Dartmouth's ski teams. As Al was leaving his ski coach position, Dartmouth was going through its own major transition of becoming a coeducational institution and accepting its first class of women. As part of this transition, the college adopted the Dartmouth Plan (D-Plan) that created very flexible attendance patterns–a boon for elite skiers who could now take time off during the fall and winter and chase their Olympic dreams—but an additional challenge for the ski team, which often had to compete without its best talent.

THE LATER YEARS
by James W. Page '63

With the departure of Al Merrill in 1972, Dartmouth needed to find a new men's head coach and, for the first time, a women's coach. A search committee headed by DOC board member **Gordie DeWitt** hired Dartmouth graduate **James W. "Jim" Page '63** as Head Coach. Page, from Lake Placid, NY, was a star skier for the Big Green in the early sixties where he was a three-time NCAA All-American, a three-time NCAA individual champion, and following graduation from Dartmouth, a 1964 Nordic Skiing Olympian.

Jim Page '63 conversing with the man he replaces, Al Merrill.

Perhaps the most profound change in Al Merrill's career at Dartmouth came in the form of a memo from Dartmouth Athletic Director **Sever Peters '54** in May 1972. Women would soon be coming to Dartmouth to study and to ski. Peters urged Merrill to "consider adding women's competition to the Dartmouth Winter Carnival". How could Al imagine that this memo would lead him to his future wife. Al took on the challenge of hiring a Women's Coach himself and decided on Middlebury College graduate **Pam Reed**.

Good news traveled fast as evidenced by this note in the Class of 1966 Newsletter just before the start of the 1972-1973 ski season: "Dartmouth has named its first woman ski coach. **Pam Reed**, Middlebury '72, has been named an assistant ski coach. Ms. Reed, a native of Meredith, N.H., will have responsibility for development of a competitive ski program for the College's women students. She is one of the nation's leading women ski racers."

A young Pam (Reed) Merrill was Dartmouth's first women's ski coach.

Not only did Pam succeed in her position as another successful Dartmouth ski coach and as the first to coach the Dartmouth women, but she would soon become Mrs. Merrill. Not surprisingly, Al found time during the winters to take on the duties of Women's Cross-Country coach. In 1975, women were indeed added to the Winter Carnival Ski Program as Sever Peters had foreseen, and the Dartmouth women competed successfully against teams from Middlebury, University of Vermont, Johnson State College, University of New Hampshire, New England College, Williams College, St. Lawrence University, Plymouth State College and Colby College of New Hampshire.

A year later the first national women's intercollegiate races were held. Dartmouth finished a very respectable third. In the second American Intercollegiate Athletic Association for Women (AIAW) National Women's Championship in 1977, Dartmouth won, achieving only its fourth national championship in a major sport. The team finished third in both 1978 and 1979. All in all, it was a great start for a brand new program and a brand new coach.

Jim Page's team of male skiers enjoyed success as well, winning the Dartmouth Carnival and Eastern Intercollegiate Championships in 1974 and 1975 and the NCAA Men's Ski Championships in 1976. In 1974 Page hired **Dave Durrance**, son of alumnus Dick Durrance '39 and brother of **Dick Durrance II '65**, to coach the Dartmouth Alpine Teams. Dave quickly became the third Durrance to make a major contribution to Dartmouth Skiing, recruiting national level Alpine skiers and establishing a reputation as one of the nation's best coaches. The combination of Page, Durrance, and former US National Team ski jumper **Peter Robes** gave Dartmouth a very strong staff.

Page also reorganized the Development Team racing program hiring **Colby Bent** and **Put Blodgett '53** to provide a high-level competitive skiing experience for aspiring racers in both Alpine and Cross-Country ski disciplines. While this program had grown and experienced significant athletic success under Al and Pam Merrill and Jim Page, it also continued a strong commitment to those undergrads who wanted to learn to race and to develop individually.

Page and Durrance resigned from Dartmouth Skiing in 1978 to take positions with the US Ski Team. Page left to become Director of the Nordic Programs and Durrance, noted for his ability to relate to and improve young skiers, became the Alpine Ski Team's Development Coach. Page went on to coach the Olympic Nordic Combined Team at the 1980 Olympics and was Team Leader of the Nordic team in 1984 in Sarajevo, Yugoslavia.

Dartmouth has always had an ability to attract great coaches. The turnover in staff for the men's program was quickly and efficiently accomplished. Two-time Biathlon Olympian and Middlebury graduate **John Morton** was hired as Head Men's Coach and he moved quickly to bring in **Tim Beck** as Alpine Coach and local great ski jumper **Don Cutter '73** as Ski Jumping Coach. Cutter coached ski jumping for its final three-year run at Dartmouth; in 1981, the NCAA dropped ski jumping from the championship program. Don continued on at the college and for many years managing and improving the Dartmouth Skiway. Beck left after two years and was replaced by another successful Alpine ski racer, **Mark Ford**.

John Morton was a great fit for the college. He was passionate about his athletes, his program, and the out-of-doors. He is famous for insisting that his athletes show up on time for every workout. **Erich Wilbrecht '84** recalls that Morty stopped him and a friend in the middle of a workout one time as they were "socializing" and exclaimed, "I give 120% and I expect you to give 120% each and every day you're out here."[104] Though somewhat a taskmaster, all the athletes loved skiing for him and with him. "He was funny, a terrific story-teller, and a wonderful coach."[105] When John discovered that several of his skiers had an interest in Biathlon, he helped them form a Biathlon Club as part of the DOC. Five of his skiers made Olympic Teams in Biathlon. John himself coached the Olympic Biathlon teams in 1988, 1992 and 1994.

Another very significant transition occurred in Robinson Hall in 1978. John Rand, who had guided the DOC for 34 years, retired from the position of Executive Director. His sure and gentle hand had guided and supported DOC staff and Dartmouth students from the end of World War II through all the various institutional changes brought about by the D-Plan and coeducation and during the time of Dartmouth's greatest collegiate and international skiing successes.

Earl Jette, who had been hired by Al Merrill back in the summer of 1970 as Assistant to the Executive Director, took over as the new Executive Director. He was to become the "rock" of the DOC. Not only did he replace John Rand, the longest tenured Executive Director, in 1984 he replaced Al Merrill when he stepped down from his 27-year career with the Outing Club. Earl moved up to the newly reorganized position of Director of the Office of Outdoor Programs, a position which he held until 2001. Then he was "brought back" for two interim terms, in 2001 and in 2008, to give the club time to find replacements. Earl was a true Dartmouth character. His office was known to DOC members as the "World of Earl", with its mobile made of a flattened chainsaw, several plants in the final stages of dehydration (kept alive with coffee, mostly), and his big file cabinet with four drawers labeled 'misc', 'this', 'that' and 'the other'. You were in a place where you got listened to, all the way. If your idea had merit, he'd give you all the support you'd ever need."[106]

From 1945, when John Rand took over as Executive Director of the DOC, until Earl Jette retired in 2001, the Outing Club had only these three remarkable senior leaders—and 56 years of calm and effective management of all the subordinate clubs, all the ski teams, and all of the college's various forest properties and their appurtenances.

Martha Rockwell, Dartmouth coach & National Ski Hall of Fame member.

Pam Merrill retired as Women's Ski Coach in 1979 giving way to **Martha Rockwell**, a native of Putney, Vermont, protégé of John Caldwell, and one of the most successful American cross-country skiers ever. Martha was a gentle but effective coach who made hard training fun and whose competitive drive inspired her skiers to perform to the best of their ability. She brought in **Tim Fisher** as Alpine Coach and together they continued the Women's Team tradition of top finishes at the AIAW Championships each year.

In 1983 the NCAA, bowing to national pressure to develop strong athletic programs for women all over the country, made the decision to begin hosting National Championship competitions for women. Skiing became the first sport to combine men and women in a single championship event, the NCAA Men's and Women's Ski Championships. Not wholly coincidentally, Dartmouth skiing was reorganized concurrently. John Morton became Director of Skiing and Martha Rockwell, who was much more comfortable on the snow with her athletes than managing the business of skiing in Robinson Hall, became the Women's Cross-country Coach. Tim Fisher continued as Women's Alpine Coach and Mark Ford ably managed and coached the Men's Alpine Team.

During the 1987-1990 period, Dartmouth Skiing went through yet another major transition. Martha Rockwell left in 1987 and was replaced for two years by **Tim Gibbons**. In 1989 John Morton, Mark Ford and Tim Fisher departed with Gibbons following shortly thereafter in 1990. It was the second major departure of Dartmouth ski coaches in 12 years.

Fortunately, as has always been the case, Dartmouth was able to quickly find excellent replacements. The program brought in three outstanding young coaches who heralded the current era of Dartmouth skiing. First to sign on, and immediately appointed as the Director of Skiing, was **Ruff Patterson**, a US National Team and three-time Olympic cross-country ski coach. Ruff was a very popular and respected coach who brought instant credibility to the Dartmouth Nordic program. He had worked with all the top cross-country skiers at a time when the US was a very competitive nation in the sport and he knew all the top junior coaches and skiers. This was a nice advantage for Dartmouth.

He was joined by Dartmouth grad **Peter Dodge '78** as Alpine Coach and **Cami Thompson**, a National Team cross-country skier, as Women's Cross-country Coach. Thompson's sister, **Leslie Thompson Hall '86**, has been a great Dartmouth skier and became a three-time Olympic racer. All three of these—Patterson, Dodge and Thompson—are currently starting their twentieth year coaching at Dartmouth, a most unusual record of stability for ski coaches anywhere. It took a little longer to find a Women's Alpine Ski Coach who would stay longer term with this group, but in 2004, **Christine Booker** joined the coaching staff. After five years, Christine seems to have stabilized that position as well.

Peter Dodge provided the following explanation of the ski team coaching structure today:

"In 2006 the four 'varsity' coaching positions were all re-titled Head Coaches. The Director of Skiing responsibilities became supplemental to be added to one of the head coach positions on a rotating basis. Cami Thompson is currently serving in that capacity and Peter Dodge will take over in 2010.

In 2004 the NCAA required that the Development Team be separated from and coached independently from the Varsity program, due to the NCAA limitation that each skiing gender can only have two paid coaches. It is still called the Development Team but technically it is a club program. At this point the development coaches can only serve as "managers" for the varsity teams but can coach those skiers which were designated as club skiers.

Since 1990 Dartmouth Skiing has carried up to 20 skiers on each team; men's Alpine, women's Alpine, men's x-c and women's x-c. Today there are 10 varsity skiers on each of the four teams, with 10 junior varsity x-c and 5 junior varsity Alpine skiers on each squad, all coached by the head coaches. In 2008, given increased demand for Alpine racing, a DOC Alpine Club was formed and currently has about 30 members. The club is student run, coached by the "Managers" with Alpine head coaches acting as advisers." [107]

Dan Nelson '75, Dartmouth's new Director of Outdoor Programs.

The new structure and coaching staff appear to be working well. After winning only one Dartmouth Carnival and EISA Championships between 1975 and 2007, the ski teams have won the Dartmouth Carnival in 2007, 2008 and 2009; the EISA Championships in 2007 and 2009; and impressively the NCAA Men's and Women's NCAA National Ski Championships in 2007!

Following Earl Jette's departure in 2001, the Outing Club Outdoor Program Office was led by three different leaders (Kathleen Doherty, Geoffrey Brown and **Andy Harvard '71**) each with a brief tenure for a total of eight years. Today, the Office is headed by a new leader, **Dan Nelson '75** who is has substantial experience in the affairs of the college. Nelson returned to the college in 1987, and has held various positions in the Dean's office and Presidents office since, moving to the Outing Club in September, 2009 from the position of Senior Assistant to former **college president James Wright**. Continuing the tradition of the very small and select group of former Outing Club leaders, he is an avid outdoor enthusiast, skier, biker, canoeist, hiker, fisherman and climber, who has the advantage of having participated actively in advising the Outing Club over his many years at Dartmouth. Dan's latest adventure was not on skis, but involved riding his bike across the United States from the Pacific Ocean to the Atlantic Ocean in the summer of 2009. His experience and interests seem to be a perfect background for the Outdoor Program leadership role, and an ideal position for Dan who exclaims that his "own life and Dartmouth education have been enriched by the opportunities for friendship, learning and adventure in the out of doors"[108]

SUMMARY

The DOC is really quite a club! Formed and run by students for one hundred years, it continues to introduce each new class of freshmen to the special beauty of Hanover and New Hampshire in all four seasons; it has nurtured arguably the nation's best intercollegiate ski racing program, sent hundreds of students on to other racing venues at all levels of competition, and encouraged literally thousands of its undergraduates and alumni to engage in skiing worldwide. It succeeded in putting Dartmouth on skis before most of the country knew what skis were, and in developing physical fitness, improving skiing competence, and not only fostering an enjoyment of the out-of-doors but incorporating it into a central part of a life well lived.

Notes

1. Harris, F. H. Diaries 1904-1911, transcribed by E. John B. Allen from originals with permission from Mrs. Helen C. Harris, Brattleboro, VT, Jan 1, 1904. 2. Ibid., Sep 24, 1904. 3. Ibid., Feb 14, 1905. 4. Ibid,. Jan 27, 1907. 5. Ibid., Mar 8, 1907. 6. Ibid., Dec 4, 1907. 7. Ibid., Dec 16 and 17, 1907. 8. Ibid., Mar 26, 1909. 9. Ibid., Nov 30, 1909. 10. Harris, F. H., Letter, The Dartmouth, Dec 7, 1909. 11. Op cit., Dec 14, 1909. 12. The Dartmouth, Jan 1910. 13. Ibid., Feb 1910. 14. Harris, F. H., Diaries 1904-1911, Nov 27, 1910. 15. Ibid., Feb 2, 1911. 16. Letter, White to Carleton, Dec 6, 1934, Rauner DOC Collection, Box 2, File 34. 17. Emerson, Charles F., Letter, Jul 12, 1912, Dartmouth Out O' Doors, 1913. 18. Shumway, C. E., "Cross Country on Skis to Mt. Moosilauke," Dartmouth Out O' Doors, 1913. 19. Letter, Shumway to Rand, Nov 8, 1954, Rauner DOC Collection, Box 3, File 27. 20. Leich, Jeff, "First on Skis in Tuckerman's Ravine," New England Ski Museum On-line Journal, Jan 23, 2008. 21. Cheney, J. Y., "What Winter Sports Have Done for Me," Dartmouth Out O' Doors, 1913. 22. Letter, Shumway to Weston, Mar 12, 1913, Rauner DOC Collection, Box 3, File 28. 23. Ibid., Nichols quoted in Shumway to Weston letter. 24. Bradley, David, "Dartmouth in the Old Days," SKI Magazine, Jan 1959. 25. Goodrich, Nathaniel L., "A Pioneer Ski Ascent," Mt Mansfield Skiing, V9, N1, May 1, 1943. 26. Ibid. 27. Adams, Ellen F., Baker Bulletin, V 4, N 5, February 1960. 28. Chase, Henry Jay, "Dartmouth – A Winter College," Outing, Jan 1914. 29. The Dartmouth, Feb 15, 1912. 30. "Collegians on Skiis," New York Times, Jan 24, 1915. 31. Johnson, J. E., handwritten note, Feb 13, 1915, Rauner DOC Collection, Box 64, File 12. 32. Letter, Johnson to Nichols, Feb 20, 1915, Rauner DOC Collection, Box 64, File 12. 33. Letter, Johnson to "Professor" [C.D. Adams?], Aug 10, 1915, Rauner DOC Collection, Box 64, File 12. 34. Secretary of Dartmouth College confirmed to Harris that admission application counts increased from 824 in 1920 to 2,625 in 1921. 35. Op cit., Johnson quoted Hopkins from a letter dated Aug 3, 1915. 36. Letter, Johnson to DOC, Sep 22, 1915, Rauner DOC Collection, Box 64, File 13. 37. Note, Johnson to Treasurer of the DOC, May 2, 1916, Rauner DOC Collection, Box 64, File 12. 38. Letter, Johnson to Prof. Adams, Mar 21, 1919, Rauner DOC Collection, Box 64, File 17. 39. The Dartmouth, Jan 6, 1916. 40. Letter, Johnson to Shumway, Jan 4, 1916, Rauner DOC Collection, Box 64, File 19. 41. Letter, Johnson to "Prof" [Adams], Jan 5, 1916, Rauner DOC Collection, Box 64, File 19. 42. The Dartmouth, Feb 7, 1916. 43. Horton, Dabney, "I Went to Dartmouth," College Stories, Jun 1931. 44. Letter, Shumway to Hatch, Nov 2, 1934, Rauner DOC Collection, Box 64, File 19. 45. Letter, Harris to H. Beardsley, Jan 9, 1937, Collection of E. John B. Allen. 46. Harris, F. H., "The Dartmouth Outing Club," Dartmouth Out O' Doors, 1913. 47. The Dartmouth, Dec 11, 1919. 48. Borman, William, "The Birth and Development of Competitive Skiing at Dartmouth, 1910-1930," Rauner DOC Collection, Box 55, File 16. 49. DOC Council Minutes, May 28, 1915, Rauner DOC Collection, Box 50, File 1. 50. Ibid., Dec 18, 1916. 51. Letter

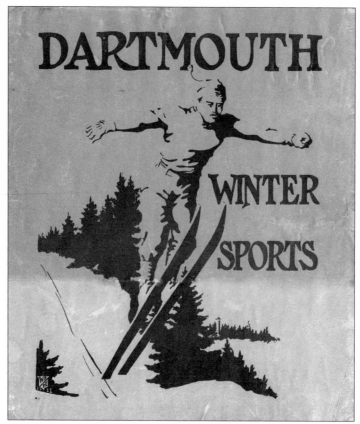

The first Dartmouth Winter Carnival poster by Walter Beech Humphrey '14 in 1911.

Chapter II Notes Continued...

Harris to Throop, Feb 27, 1921, Rauner DOC Collection, Box 2, File 33. 52. Letter Harris to Throop, Mar 3, 1921, Rauner DOC Collection, Box 2, File 33. 53. Letter Throop to Harris, Mar 18, 1921, Rauner DOC Collection, Box 2, File 33. 54. DOC 1922 Annual Report, Rauner DOC Collection, Box 3, File 41. 55. The Boston Post, Feb 23, 1919. 56. Letter, Harris to DOC (Throop?), Jan 5, 1922, Rauner DOC Collection, Box 2, File 33. 57. DOC Council minutes 1923, Rauner DOC Collection, Box 50, File 1. 58. DOC Winter Sports Council Minutes Mar 29, 1927, Rauner DOC Collection, Box 7, File 2. 59. Lunn, Arnold, "Downhill Racing, The Atlantic, February 1949. 60. DOC Winter Sports Council Minutes Feb 16, 1926, Rauner DOC Collection, Box 7, File 2. 61. The Dartmouth, March 8, 1927. 62. Letter, C. Parker Paul to Ned Moss, Nov 6, 1937, Rauner DOC Collection, Box 3, File 41. 63. DOC Council Minutes Feb 21 and Dec 4, 1928, Rauner DOC Collection, Box 7, File 2. 64. The Aegis 1929, p.359. 65. DOC Council Minutes, Dec 9, 1929, Rauner DOC Collection, Box 7, File 2. 66. Ibid., Mar 1929, Rauner DOC Collection, Box 7, File 2. 67. Hatch, Daniel P., Alumni File [renumber UP one from here to 73]. 68. McCrillis, J. W., Foreword, Modern Ski Technique, 1933. 69. Fowler, William P., A Way of Life, p.14. 70. Winter Sports Comm Reports, 3 Dec 1931, Rauner DOC Collection, Box 7, File 2. 71. The Ski Bulletin, 16 Mar 1934. 72. Skidmore Scope, Spring 2001. 73. Winter Sports Div Reports, Schniebs 1932-33, Rauner Box 15, File 9. 74. Ibid. 75. DOC Trustees Minutes, 13 Jan 1936, Rauner, Box 50, File 4. 76. Ibid., 16 Mar 1936, Rauner, Box 50, File 4. 77. Letter, Schniebs to Rand, 5 Oct 1954, Rauner, Box 3, File 25. 78. DOC Trustee Minutes, 16 Mar 1936, Rauner, Box 50, File 4. 79. Letter, Hatch to Miller, 14 Apr 1936, Rauner, Box 3, File 1. 80. Op. cit. 81. Letter, Lindley to Hatch, 28 May 1936, Rauner, Box 3, File 20. 82. Letter, Carleton to Hatch, 24 Jul 1936, Rauner Box 3, File 20. 83. Letter, Hatch to named recipients, 3 Sep 1936, Rauner, Box 3, File 20. 84. Rauner DOC Collection, Box 3, File 27. 85. Letter, Hatch to Basinger [UPRR], Mar 5, 1937, Rauner DOC Collection, Box3, File 20. 86. Letters, Hatch to Gibson, Jan 28, 1937; Hatch to Hall, Mar 25, 1937; Hatch to Keown, Apr 1, 1937, Rauner DOC Collection, Box 3, File 20. 87. Letter, Hatch to Prager, Apr 23, 1937, Rauner DOC Collection, Box 3, File 20. 88. Letter, Hatch to Prager, Jul 29, 1937, Rauner DOC Collection, Box 3, File 20. 89. The Dartmouth, Jan 12, 1938. 90. Letter, Prager to Hicks, Dec 7, 1938, Rauner DOC Collection, Box 2, File 38. 91. Winter Sports Comm Minutes, Jan 16, 1940, Rauner DOC Collection. Box 7, File 4. 92. Letter, Prager to Paschen, Dec 25, 1941, Rauner DOC Collection, Box 3, File 21. 93. Winter Sports Comm Minutes, 1942, Rauner DOC Collection, Box 7, File 4. 94. Letter, Bright to Rand, Mar 11, 1946, Rauner DOC Collection, Box 3, File 21. 95. Letter, Harris to Rand, Mar 12, 1947, Rauner DOC Collection, Box 2, File 35. 96. Ibid. 97. Poling, V., "Thoughts in Regard to the Dartmouth Outing Club," undated but in response to Mar 12, 1947 DOC Trustees meeting, Rauner DOC Collection, Box 2, File 35. 98. Schulberg, Budd, "The Dartmouth Winter Carnival," Sports Illustrated, 21 Feb 1955. 99. Telegram, Prager to Rand, undated [summer 1957?], Rauner DOC Collection, Box 3, File 20. 100. Letter, Corcoran to Friends of Walter Prager, May 18, 1982, copy loaned by Fred Barstow '52. 101. Letter, Meck to Miller, Sep 18, 1957, Rauner DOC Collection, Box 16, File 4. 102. Letter, Rand to Harris, Oct 9, 1957, Rauner DOC Collection, Box 2, File 35. 103. Williams, Edward G., "I'll Teach You How to Ski," Sports: A Generation's Common Bond, Schram, 2007. 104. Wilbrecht, Erich, "Reflections on Dartmouth Skiing," e-mail correspondence with Jim Page, June 2009. 105. Ibid., Wilbrecht, "Reflections on Dartmouth Skiing". 106. Hooke, David, Speech on the Occasion of Earl Jette's Retirement, Woodsmoke 2001, p.2. 107. Dodge, Peter, e-mail correspondence with Jim Page, September 17, 2009. 108. Nelson, Dan, interview, "VOX of Dartmouth," April 27, 2009, p.3. 109. Names confirmed in letter from A. S. Holway '12, participant, to Dartmouth Alumni Magazine February 15, 1938).

CHAPTER III

OTHER DOC DEVELOPMENTS -
HANOVER CLUBS; WINTER CARNIVAL; SKI FACILITIES,
INSTRUCTION & PATROL; PREP SCHOOLS INTERACTIONS

By Stephen Waterhouse '65, Tu 67, and Douglas C. Leitch '65

With Michael Choukas '51, Clark Griffiths '57, Th '58, Ned Jacoby '40, Stearns A. ("Tony") Morse '52,
R. Phillip Peck '77 and Nicholas B. Stevens '58

Dartmouth College and the town of Hanover, New Hampshire, were in many ways one and the same thing when it came to skiing. The sport took on a special role in the community and various skiing activities mixed students, faculty, and townspeople in unique and instrumental ways to create a feeling of common objectives and a shared enthusiasm. This common interest in skiing engendered the establishing of new ski clubs, the participation in Winter carnival of more than Dartmouth students and their male counterparts, the broad promotion of Winter Carnival through movies and posters, the beginning of ski instruction and ski patrol activities that were of service to all, the creation of ski facilities open to locals as well as college personnel, and interactions with local area preparatory schools that were both cordial and mutually supportive.

First, we will discuss the creation of local ski clubs that provided vehicles for organizing many of the local ski activities and added new competitive racing opportunities. **Doug Leitch '65** provides some history on how and why the ski club phenomena got started. **Tony Morse '52** shares a personal comment on one of the most important ski clubs, the Carcajou Club, which still plays a role today.

The highly successful introduction of the most famous of all college Winter Carnivals had an impact on much more than the social lives of the male students of Dartmouth. These effects were not anticipated at the beginning and are still not fully appreciated today except by a few ski historians with long memories. We provide comments on the activities of Winter Carnival for children and women to show that the impact of this aspect of the Dartmouth ski world was much greater than the revels of a boisterous group of men in the back woods of New England. In an extensive article, written by Doug Leitch with **Steve Waterhouse '65** and **Nick Stevens '58** for the 2009 International Ski History Association (ISHA) Congress on Skiing, we highlight a little known facet of the college's early all-male history: that the Dartmouth Winter Carnival played an important role in the early development of Alpine ski racing for women in the 1930s and 1940s.

Nick Stevens will briefly outline the history of the infamous *Winter Carnival* ski movie, involving the legendary F. Scott Fitzgerald and his equally legendary sidekick, **Budd Schulberg '36**. **Ned Jacoby '40** will highlight the unique contribution of Winter Carnival ski posters. These promotional items stirred up more interest in Dartmouth's Winter Carnival and brought outsiders in to the Hanover area to share the excitement of skiing felt by the local college and town residents.

We follow this with brief discussions of the critical importance of local Ski Instruction and Ski Patrol work in the Dartmouth–Hanover ski world, a basic reason why Dartmouth personnel and Hanover locals featured so prominently in early ski racing activities across the United States. Local ski instruction programs and safety patrol activities were cutting edge for their time.

Dartmouth's ski facilities were used by all in the local community and have greatly changed over the past 100 years to keep up with the ever-evolving requirements of Alpine skiing. Doug Leitch will outline how the Dartmouth/Hanover area ski facilities have modernized and provide some insights in to the challenging financial decisions that Dartmouth College's Trustees have long faced to maintain skiing in the community at a level consistent with its historical importance. **Clark Griffiths '57, Th'58,** provides very important historical details on the revolutionary innovation of the first overhead cable lift in the U.S. constructed at Dartmouth's Oak Hill ski area in 1935-6. This first J-bar was the forerunner and conceptual model for the first chair lift built at Sun Valley a year later and accelerated the early expansion of ski areas across North America, an enterprise promoted most aggressively by men like Fred Pabst, heir to the Pabst Beer Company and brother of **Harold "Shorty" Pabst '38.**

Finally, **Mike Choukas '51** will highlight the interactions between Dartmouth and several of the leading Eastern ski prep schools. In addition to those student skiers and racers matriculating at our legendary ski college, Dartmouth skiers often accepted positions at the prep schools after college. As an example, **Phil Peck '77** will show how a number of Dartmouth grads found careers at Holderness School as ski coaches, teachers, administrators and even as a Headmaster.

Dartmouth's ski relationships and enthusiasm for skiing impacted many people everywhere, but particularly in Hanover and Northern New England. Why this happened, how this happened, and what it meant to the development of skiing generally are the issues of this chapter.

LOCAL SKI CLUBS

The stories of ski clubs that developed across the country are addressed in Chapter V. This discussion focuses on the development of ski clubs at Dartmouth College itself with the desire to find additional opportunities for ski racing amongst Dartmouth's large skiing population. Doug Leitch outlines the early development of ski clubs and the organized racing associations formed to oversee this activity in the East. Tony Morse provides a personal summary of his experience with the Carcajou Club, which was a unique organization that provided one of the best insights in to the thinking of the college people and the Hanover locals on the sport of skiing. The history of the Carcajou is still somewhat of a mystery, but Tony weaves an interesting tale of community and college involvement that is rare at any institution. And as Tony points out, the principals of the Carcajou are still in play today, not only at Dartmouth, but in ski areas around the world where the club's alumni still wear the famous Carcajou pin as a symbol of the unique society to which they belong.

***

1,700 PAIRS OF SKIS
DOC FINDS A WAY TO GET MORE SKIERS IN THE RACE

By Douglas C. Leitch '65

Less than a decade after **Fred Harris '11** had introduced the scientific management of skiing and the thrills of ski competition to his fellow Dartmouth students, there was a marked increase in ski competition not only in Hanover but also around the northern parts of the country. Intercollegiate ski meets had been held since Dartmouth and McGill University first competed against each other in Montreal in 1914. Prior to that, ski competitions in the United States consisted mainly of ski jumping, a sport whose rules were set by the Midwestern-based National Ski Association. The increasing interest in ski competitions, especially among colleges and universities, created a need for organization and rules to govern entrant eligibility and competition formats to keep things fair. In the eastern US, spurred by Harris and executed by Professor Charles A. Proctor and others, Dartmouth took the lead in developing and implementing these standards.

Fred Harris offered his own encouragement for such organization in a letter to Dartmouth Outing Club (DOC) Secretary **Ellis Briggs '21** in 1920:

"I am keen to see a United States Amateur Ski Association formed, and I think the D.O.C. could well take the lead in it."[1] In 1923 Harris represented the DOC at the first meeting of the United States Eastern Amateur Ski Association (USEASA), together with the Lake Placid Ski Club and Saranac [NY] Ski Club, and was elected its first president. The USEASA, affiliated with the National Ski Association in Chicago, served as the governing body for ski racing in the Northeast. It sanctioned races and coordinated club memberships with its national parent.

Interest in skiing grew over the next decade and through the Great Depression. Races were blessed by the USEASA, which kept official records and published results in its bulletin, the "Eastern Ski Annual", first edited by Dartmouth Librarian Nathaniel Goodrich. As the Dartmouth Ski Team gained in stature and popularity on campus and beyond, the number of students who became official ski team members increased from 40 in 1933 to 70 in 1934, and of those, seven Dartmouth men lettered in skiing in 1933 and nine in 1934. In the meantime, it was estimated that there were 1,700 pairs of skis in Hanover. With that many skiers, it was obvious that most of them would not have the opportunity to race for the Dartmouth Outing Club, the only official USEASA-sanctioned entity in Hanover.

DOC General Manager **Dan Hatch '28** was quite sensitive at that time to differences in the social structure of North American skiing versus the situation in Europe, particularly in Great Britain. There, much of the skiing was conducted under the auspices of private clubs which assumed the atmosphere of similar private sporting groups (golf, tennis, yachting, and hunt) in imposing a notable degree of exclusivity for "the right people" who could afford the steep dues and who fit the social class membership image. With the preponderance of interest in skiing in North America during the Great Depression based in colleges and universities instead of in exclusive private clubs, Hatch wrote to Harry Wade Hicks, President of the USEASA (and also of the Lake Placid Club, one of the few American examples of the selective private ski clubs found in Great Britain), to predict that the increase in club dues proposed by the mostly genteel directors of the USEASA would result in a decreasing membership. Hatch argued that most skiers in the US came from the ranks of "country boys and mill-town boys...membership drawn largely from men who work with their hands." He argued that a 50-cent increase in dues to $1.50 would risk diminishing the base of members from USEASA clubs (including the DOC), especially then during the Depression. He concluded that growth within the organization's member clubs could be accomplished "without upsetting the element [of skiers] who do not qualify under the 'white collar' part of the popular definition of 'gentleman'." [2]

While Dartmouth may have been comparatively immune to the exclusivity associated with some other Ivy League schools, the DOC was even more egalitarian. Skiing, especially, was open to anyone who was interested, and the DOC often endeavored to provide equipment for those who could not afford it. The Faculty Committee of the DOC reported their support for the idea that the [DOC] "fosters competition with the conviction that they will be an inspiration for more general skiing." The faculty qualified their endorsement of competition with the understanding that they "encouraged a strong varsity squad only in the hope of raising the general level of skill and enthusiasm among the bulk of Club members." [3] Competition, in the view of the faculty, was the means to the end of greater student participation in skiing. Along with the element of such institutional endorsement of skiing was the role of fraternities in the College's social life.

Those two factors converged in the early 1930s with the development of small independent ski clubs on campus that accepted members from the student body as well as the local community. These functioned first as early provisioners of what would come to be known as the "après ski" camaraderie of skiing, or as the Dartmouth Glee Club often sang, "a skoal by the fire in the pledge of fellowship." But the presence of these new ski clubs also drew the attention of observant people like Dan Hatch. In early 1936 he described the "task of finding a sufficiently broad basis of organization to enlist the active interests of all students who ski...The Outing Club is the vehicle, but the present form of the organization is too tight, too restrictive." [4] He cited the example of the newly formed Ski Club Carcajou as an indication of broader campus interest.

Seeing an opportunity to resolve the two problems of how to increase membership in the USEASA clubs without raising the dues of current members and how to provide greater opportunities for Dartmouth students to compete in ski meets without qualifying for the small number of openings on the official Dartmouth Ski Team, Hatch began to pitch his new idea. He first proposed it in a 1936 letter to R. S. "Doc" Elmer, the new president of the USEASA. His suggestion was designed to "enable more skiers to be eligible for USEASA-sanctioned competition through club affiliation. Such clubs [at Dartmouth] would be sub-divisions of the Dartmouth Outing Club, but would not be representing the College in competition." He continued, "With about 1,700 skiers here in Dartmouth, it seems almost impossible to establish the hold of Eastern [USEASA] on all these men through the existing one connection, and it would seem worthwhile to establish five or six sub-divisions in the manner described...and so to enlist the support of these groups both financially and otherwise directly in behalf of Eastern. We believe earnestly that the system would be good for the sport...and worthwhile to Eastern." [5] Hatch argued that such a plan would provide natural units for individual competition and rivalry as well as training for Dartmouth's varsity ski team. Two days later, Harry Hicks, still at Lake Placid, wrote to Doc Elmer endorsing Hatch's sub-division club plan, [6] and it was soon implemented.

While Dartmouth's well-established fraternal instincts may have inspired the creation of such clubs, their emergence presented a timely opportunity to address the need for more avenues for student ski competition. They also presented a neat solution to the broader organizational needs of sanctioned ski meets that someone like Dan Hatch could envision. The editors of the 1939 *Aegis* yearbook recognized this evolution:

"The Ski Club Carcajou was founded in the winter of 1935 by a body of Dartmouth undergraduates who felt that the need for such an institution existed in the College. Designed primarily as an instrument through which the alumni members could be kept informed concerning skiing throughout the season, and could continue ski competition together after graduation, the spirit of the club is one of good fellowship extending beyond the trails and slopes into all walks of life. ... The management of club activities rests in the hands of the undergraduate section composed of officers and members who conduct the competitions sponsored by the club and arrange for the annual Carcajou Gluhwein Party during Winter Carnival."[7]

Its early members included some of the most illustrious skiers of the time in Hanover, among whom were students, faculty, local business people, and ski instructors. It was accepted as an affiliate DOC ski club on November 30, 1937. The following February, Ski Club Carcajou began a tradition of running the Women's Eastern Slalom race.[8]

Preceding Carcajou as an official DOC affiliated club was the **Sahara Ski Club**, organized on March 2, 1937 [and approved as an affiliate club of the DOC on that date]. In 1939, Sahara held the USEASA-sanctioned New Hampshire Class C Downhill Championships on Moose Mountain east of Hanover. The 1939 *Aegis* chronicled the emergence of these new ski clubs:

"Along with the tremendous growth of interest in skiing that has been obvious on this campus in the last few years, there became evident a need for some sort of organization within the Dartmouth Outing Club to organize this interest, to bring the skiers together in the good fellowship and companionship that skiing breeds, and to give those men not on the Dartmouth ski team a chance to enter competition. The Sahara Ski Club was one of the first of numerous ski clubs organized to take care of this need. Now at the end of its second year, it has become an important cog in the skiing fraternity at Dartmouth with its major aim to provide recreation and good fellowship to its members."[9]

Others included the **Hell Divers Ski Club** (approved as a DOC affiliate club in February 1937) which sponsored the New Hampshire Slalom Championships in 1939, the **Stem Twisters Ski Club** (approved by the DOC in April 1937)[10] and the **Valkmeister Ski Club**. Dan Hatch summarized the advancements of Dartmouth skiing up to 1937 by noting that, "our approach to the sport has always been as a recreation for the average club member as well...as a medium for competition between this and other clubs...The membership policy of the Eastern and the provision for open races...are accomplishments that would not have become fact without the work of Dartmouth men."[11]

Of all the new ski clubs on the Dartmouth campus, the one that stood out from the 1930s to the 1960s as the leading player was the Carcajou. Tony Morse provides some insights in to the activities of this club from his lifelong involvement with and knowledge of the Carcajou as a member, a Hanover native, a Dartmouth student, and an interested alumnus.

```
                Here's To the Ski Club Carcajou

Here's to the Ski Club Carcajou, the social skiing bums,
We can wiggle 'round those turns, take anything that comes.
With a timber, track, and long ski heil, we'll jump right
    to the gun,
We drink...and then we have another...

    Hurrah! Hurrah! We're schussing down the trails.
    Hurrah! Hurrah! We're landing on our tails.
    Here's to the Ski Club Carcajou, we're rough and
        tough as nails,
    We drink...and then we have another.

Let us raise a lusty cheer to the schuss-boom Carcajou.
He skis with ease o'er rocks and trees, who would dare pursue.
He climbs up on the mountain top, and don't know what to do,
So, he drinks...and then he has another....

    Chorus.

There is no moral to this tale, why make a poor excuse?
To be a loyal Carcajou you only have to schuss.
For telemarks and christies we really have no use,
So, let's drink...and then let's have another.

    Chorus.
```

"Here's to the Ski Club Carcajou."

***

SKI CLUB CARCAJOU

By Stearns A. ("Tony") Morse '52

Born and bred in Hanover, New Hampshire, this ski club survived ups and downs over the years but still has a tenuous hold on life. I have no idea who started this club or just when, but the club's official beginning has been noted as late 1937, and information received from **Don Page '47** indicates that it was a going concern in 1939 and that young **Ben Ames Williams, Jr. '39** may have been its president. By 1946 it was in full swing again after the war. It was a remarkable institution, with members from the community at large, business people, parents, doctors, as well as college students and faculty, and especially many members of the Dartmouth Ski Team. Among this diverse group were the overseers of the Ford Sayre Ski Program, including, for a while, the management of the Hanover Inn.

*The original Carcajou Songbook
is still in demand.*

At the time, the Inn maintained a small frame building out back called the Ski Hut where they sponsored occasional gatherings, and for some years this was the main venue for Carcajou meetings. There was often food as well as beer and liquor. There were showings of slides and movies. There was song, and a songbook—a few original copies of which are still extant. Other Carcajou songs made it into the pages of "Crud and Corruption," the songbook of **Bill Briggs '54**. The club's most famous song was about skiing the Headwall with "No Falls at All," set to the tune of a very similar but very coarse title and refrain. It

ramified to all the famous and later infamous locals, starting with a verse about the very accomplished Neidlinger twins and ending with an awkward leg fracture by your reporter. Songwriting bloomed in the talents of **Jay Larmon '47** and **Alan Hall '47**, who dreamed up the counter-cultural parody of ski instruction, *The Elliptical Technique*, sung to the tune of "The Man on the Flying Trapeze." Our lives were also graced by the multicultural song bag and guitar of the late Mary Craig McLane.

There were Carcajou picnics as well, fall and spring. The fall picnic gathered everybody together, including new students and guests, to get started right before ski season. In the spring, the picnics celebrated the close of skiing and the arrival of other interests, such as **Tom Corcoran's ['43]** vigorous application of slalom agility to the speedy maneuvers of lacrosse.

The Carcajou pin was a stroke of genius; I have no idea who designed it. I do recall that Art and Eleanor Bennett kept it going. It is a very simple, spare design in an enamel rectangle with a middle block of white flanked by black ends with brass vertical dividers. Running across the whole in brass is the single word CARCAJOU. The name refers to the Algonquian name for the wolverine, largest member of the weasel family and a very formidable denizen of the snowy North. We as members never aspired to the rougher reputation of the animal. Hallmarks on the back of two pins contain the union labels and other references, and a shield with the letters M.P.B over a line with P.T.U. The clearest and freshest of these carries the mark of Bastian Bros. Co. Rochester N. Y. Other pins, however, came stamped "Japan."

The Carcajou Pin is worn with pride!

As Tom Corcoran has remarked, the mix in the Club of locals and students, professionals and athletes, older and younger people, was an enlivening experience for all concerned. As young people, we got to know as "just plain folks" the surgeons who might put us back together, even before they had the chance. We got to know the people in town who made things work as they did, and to enjoy the cross-cultural experiences of those Norwich people from across the river and those friends who dwelt for a time in the cradle of skiing in Norway. We met generations of great names in skiing: the Chivers brothers and the Stewarts and the Neidlingers from Hanover, the Densmores from Lebanon, the Fitzgeralds from Norwich, the storekeepers upon whom we relied, the college administrators who guided the Outing Club and built ski lifts, their wives who contributed as teachers in the children's ski program, and ourselves as social skiers and racing competitors.

The Club also acted as sponsor for social skiers who wanted to race in sanctioned meets but who were not otherwise affiliated with an approved group; even college ski team racers who were not selected for a given meet could enter as individuals under the auspices of Club Carcajou. This happened sporadically over the years, but as recently as 2009 at the Hannes Schneider Meisters Race in North Conway, NH.

Carcajou also coordinated with the Dartmouth Outing Club to offer a Glühwein Party to participants in the Dartmouth Winter Carnival. At one time this event was held in the Ski Hut, with the piping hot Glühwein mixed in the Inn kitchen's vast steam kettles and lifted in their vacuum kegs out back to the Ski Hut. Later, the event was moved to the DOC House (The Outing Club House) at the end of Occom Pond and next to the Golf Course, which afforded a larger, more dignified, and more elegant venue. During this time, the recipe for the Glühwein was refined and perfected by your correspondent and the late and sorely lamented **Michael Marx '54**, to abjure any foreign infusion of liquor and to keep close to the Alpine version of the drink. The mix calls for 2 wine (e.g., claret) to one water, and for each gallon of wine, ½ gallon water, 1.5 oranges cut in half and squeezed by hand, 1.5 lemons same, 3 sticks of cinnamon, 1 teaspoon of cloves (best bagged to remove before they overdo their duty), and <2 cups of sugar.

There came a time in the late 1950s when the DOC management decided that the extracurricular activities of Carcajou were inimical to the purity and innocence of competitive sports, and so banned the teams from membership in this ecumenical society of skiing and non-skiing friends. Nevertheless, a straw poll in 2009 revealed many formerly active racing and social members from the late recent century still had their Carcajou pins — and many fond memories.

Carcajou remains a ghost of a productive era of interplay among town and gown, old and young, serious and social racers. But its heritage is still there and it might yet rise again, like the sunken Mary Ellen Carter of the ballad, rise again...rise again.

WINTER CARNIVAL: THE INSPIRATIONAL SOURCE OF MUCH SKIING

In the history of Dartmouth skiing, perhaps no other single event has contributed so significantly to the enthusiasm of individual skiers as the Dartmouth Winter Carnival. This event was first introduced in 1911 as the follow-on to a successful Winter Sports Day created in 1910 by Fred Harris '11. Earlier comments have outlined how this event was started. There are four subjects of interest that have added to the Winter Carnival story in ways that may be long forgotten by most if they ever knew of them: Posters, The Children's Carnival, Women's Racing and *Winter Carnival*, the movie. However, to appreciate the significance of Dartmouth's impact on the world of skiing, these contributions are important to know about. More than anything else, the enthusiasm spread around the universe of potential skiers may be

Enthusiastic skiers arrive by train at the local station.

the single most important contribution of the Dartmouth community to the development of skiing in the United States and elsewhere. The Dartmouth Winter Carnival has played—and continues to play— a major role by inspiring much of that enthusiasm.

Posters: The Winter Carnival poster is a simple device used to advertise the annual event and is still a factor in the annual process for putting on these weekends. In the collecting conscious world of today, the old posters are avidly sought by collectors. **Ned Jacoby '40** was an early Dartmouth skier and spent his career in the graphic arts. He brings to his brief comments some 70+ years of exposure to this medium and to Winter Carnival posters. Ned is the same individual who worked in Professor Charles Proctor's photo development lab in 1938 to bring alive one of the most famous ski images of all time, the marvelous **Dick Durrance '39** in full flight across a ski slope in New Zealand, a subject he comments on later in this book. And Ned has provided invaluable help in all the graphic representations you will find throughout this book. As a non-skiing side point, it may intrigue those with an interest in the history of Dartmouth College that the very first poster of the initial Winter Carnival in 1911 was created by **Walter Beach Humphrey '14**. This is the very same artist who painted the now "out of view" murals formerly on display in the Hovey Grill at Dartmouth's student dining facility, Thayer Hall. These murals depict a view of Native Americans that was perceived by some to be uncomplimentary and they were quietly taken down some time after the college increased its opportunities for Native American students in the 1970s. The future for these murals is unclear, but what is clear is that this particular artist has played a leading role in at least two very unique artistic components of the history of Dartmouth College.

Skijoring races were an important event in early Winter Carnivals (1932).

A special honor guard with ski poles during performance (1931).

Winter Evening venue: ice rink and exhibition ski slope (1935).

Skating Spectacular (1947).

Richard Kurts '56, winner of 1956
WC sculpture design contest.

1956 Winter Carnival sculpture
of Ullr, Norse God of Skiing.

Fred Harris '11 crowns Winter Carnival
Queen Geraldine Parkhurst (1961).

***

THE STORY OF DARTMOUTH'S WINTER CARNIVAL POSTER

By Ned Jacoby '40

It was in 1910 that Dartmouth Outing Club (DOC) president **Fred Harris '11** created an event to celebrate the fast growing popularity of winter sports and invited students from nearby colleges to compete against Dartmouth skiers. The event was so successful that the following year it was officially called Winter Carnival and rapidly became one of the nation's most popular college weekends. In an article he wrote for *National Geographic* magazine, Harris described the event as the "Mardi Gras of the North."

Asked to help publicize that first weekend, Hovey Muralist **Walter Beach Humphrey '14** designed Dartmouth's first Winter Carnival poster; it pictured a ski jumper flying high over the trees and the jump tower itself. Popular as they became, the early Carnival posters were not produced every year, and an annual poster design competition didn't begin until 1937 when the poster competition that we have today was first instituted.

The winning poster was usually chosen by that year's DOC Carnival Committee, but in 1961 the Student Activities Office & Programming Board took over. Before then, voluntary poster designs came from many talented painters, designers, local artists and students–some of whom found it their

1953 Winter Carnival poster
by Len Clark '56, a future graphic artist.

entry into future art and design careers. New York's Parson's School of Art and Design made it a student project for a number of years after the First World War. Among the many Dartmouth students who submitted entries for consideration was **Len Clark '56**, who won the poster contest while an undergraduate and went on to a career as a graphic artist.

The Winter Carnival posters were a huge success from the start. The new European alpine ski resorts had already started using posters to popularize the attractions of outdoor winter sports but this was an idea still relatively unknown in America. Perhaps the biggest reason for the Carnival posters' instant success was that they sparked an instinctive recognition that our winters were going to become at least as important and popular as our summers as a season for sport and recreation.

Especially in the early years, Carnival poster designs ran the full range of renderings from amusing student kitsch to the most sophisticated American, European, and Bauhaus influenced graphic design and illustration. And because of the event itself, almost every approach seemed to work in celebrating a snowy Mardi Gras of fun and skiing.

When it comes to Winter Carnival posters everybody has their favorites, but records indicate that the 1938 poster is the all-time winner. Looking upwards in exaggerated perspective at a skier flying overhead out of the sun, it makes his huge left ski tip look like it's shooting right off the poster into thin air. Acquiring these posters has become increasingly popular over the years and the good news for collectors is that now it's possible to choose excellent well-priced reprints in original or smaller sizes. Meanwhile originals from past years often sell for hundreds of dollars while a few rare posters in perfect condition have brought over $5,000 apiece at auction.

Happily, the Dartmouth Co-op makes quality reprints both more affordable and easily available. A computer web search will produce

The most expensive Dartmouth WC poster (1938) in past ski poster auctions

many sources for Winter Carnival posters, but the preferred site is www.DartmouthImages.com run by the Co-op. You can browse their full collection of posters and frames there and make purchases online. Current year Carnival posters are available from the DOC or the Co-op during the week of Carnival as well as the week before.

Even better news for those interested in Dartmouth's Carnival posters and their history should be the definitive coffee-table book planned for the late fall of 2010 to commemorate the Dartmouth Outing Club's Centennial. This book will show every Winter Carnival poster since the event began in 1911 along with a rich history about the artists and the poster design selections.

The Children's Carnival: After the excitement of the first few Winter Carnivals, the war-time lack of coal cancelled Winter Carnival in 1918. Dartmouth paused to catch its winter breath, but the town of Hanover and the surrounding area had already picked up the skiing fever. It was evident that the youngsters in town were copying their older role models at Dartmouth and learning to become good skiers themselves. "It is claimed by the real Hanoverians," boasted *The Hanover Gazette*, "that the best thing about winter is the way the little children…take to skis and snowshoes as soon as they can walk. There are many of the town boys, some of them sons of faculty families, and some girls as well, who can out-ski and out-snowshoe the most expert members of the Dartmouth student body."

The Hanover Inn, with help from Dartmouth students, began a long tradition of holding Children's Carnivals. The town newspaper remarked on the success of the first such event in 1917 and the promise it held for the future. "The children's carnival of last week was a gratifying success, especially for a first attempt and the interest shown offers much encouragement for making the event an annual occurrence." Not only was it a popular winter sports event for boys and girls, but also among

A children's ski jump event at an early Winter Carnival.

the youthful competitors in the early years of this annual February event were many future stars of the Dartmouth ski team and the world of skiing beyond – **Charles Dudley**, the **Chivers** brothers, **Bob Meservey, Harry Hillman, Charley Proctor, Ted Hunter, Fred Chamberlain, John Carleton.** This early involvement of Hanover area children in skiing was relatively unique for the time, and when combined with Dartmouth's taking the lead in ski racing, provides a very simple reason for so many Dartmouth students and Hanover area residents becoming the early leaders in ski racing and the ski industry. They were in at the beginning of the development of this new and eventually bustling modern recreational and competitive version of a very old winter physical activity.

By 1925 it was clear to Dartmouth that there was a benefit to helping to host these events where the kids in town took the opportunity to show their potential as future Dartmouth skiers. It also made sense for the DOC to assign a member from the junior class each year to chair the club's group helping to run the children's event as one of a growing number of opportunities for DOC members to perform public service; besides, it was understood to have value as a subtle recruitment program for the ski team. The Children's Carnival also benefited from the repeated financial support of alumnus **Johnny Johnson, Class of 1866**. The trophy engraved with his name was awarded to the winner of the Children's Carnival. This was the first of several examples of the DOC reaching out to the community to spread enthusiasm for winter sports, a step that had a lasting influence on the perennial strength of the region's interscholastic skiers.

Important to the subject of the story that follows, "The Origins of Women's Collegiate Ski Racing", the Children's Carnival provided an equal opportunity for girls to perform in the competitive events as well as boys. And there were some great lady ski competitors, like the twin daughters, Susan and Sally, of **Lloyd Neidlinger '23**, Dean of the College, who would develop in Hanover just like their great male competitors. Some of those ladies had siblings who helped achieve great fame for Dartmouth skiing. One of the Children's Carnival winners was **Beth Miller**, daughter of **Dr. Ralph Miller '24**, who greatly helped in the selection of some of Dartmouth's ski coaches and other Dartmouth ski decisions. Beth also had a rather active brother, **Ralph Miller '55**, of whom much is written in this book, particularly about the amazing world speed record on skis that he set in Chile in 1955, and as a leading American racer and Olympian.

Women Racing at Winter Carnival: In the course of early research for this book, we came across a long forgotten facet of the history of the Winter Carnival events. This led to more research in order to prepare a separate write-up on this subject for submission to the International Skiing History Congress ("From Skiing to Snow-Sport: Cultures, Images, and Adventures") at Mammoth Lakes, California, March 29 – April 3, 2009. We are pleased to present this information here as it highlights a very special achievement in Dartmouth skiing long before women represented part of the college's student body. Before coeducation at Dartmouth and very early in the development of racing venues for women, they were invited to the Dartmouth Winter Carnival to show off their racing skills and enhance their reputations for fast skiing. As you will find in the next chapter, on the history of Dartmouth racing, the women students of later years have measured up very well to these early female racers on the Hanover hills.

***

Dartmouth's Impact on the Origins of Women's Collegiate Ski Racing

By Douglas C. Leitch '65 with Nicholas B. Stevens '58 and Stephen L. Waterhouse '65

Dartmouth and the DOC's involvement with women's racing started somewhat innocently in May 1935 when the only skiing-related reminder in evidence on campus was a notice in the student newspaper that "All skis being stored in Robinson Hall [the DOC offices] must be removed this week."[12] And yet, Dave Putnam, the new Winter Carnival Director, headed for Robinson Hall with skiing very much on his mind. Soon, five other students joined him there for the first meeting of the committee to plan the 1936 Winter Carnival, the crown jewel of their hibernal social life.

Dartmouth's annual Winter Carnival had gained a wide reputation over the quarter century since its inception as a hearty celebration of outdoor winter sports in the midst of equally robust conviviality. By 1935, this so-called "Mardi Gras of the North" was the must-attend seasonal social event for college women in the Northeast and the premier competition venue for men's intercollegiate skiing. It celebrated its Silver Anniversary that same year, which was also the first year ski competitions were held under new rules: The Intercollegiate Winter Sports Union (IWSU), recently reconfigured as the Intercollegiate Ski Union (ISU), had dropped snowshoeing and speed skating from competition scoring. Skiing was now "the" winter sport. Dartmouth was instrumental both in creating the IWSU and in its subsequent transformation to the ISU, and it was the perennial team to beat on the collegiate skiing circuit.

In Dartmouth's vibrant spirit of inter-class rivalry, the 1936 Winter Carnival Committee wanted to outdo all past Carnivals while still adhering to 25 years of tradition. Discussions got underway to plan the spectacular Outdoor Evening program, the elaborately staged and choreographed production of figure skating, fireworks, and torch-lit ski processions that kicked off each Carnival. The 1936 committee launched into some brainstorming and someone suggested that:

"...the Queen be selected [from] a group of girls who had to show they could ski by entering a girls' slalom during these festivities.... Then it was suggested that the fraternities send teams of girls and boys into competition, this later being cut to a girls' slalom alone, and the winning fraternity be allowed to appoint the queen from among its guests. This would emphasize the winter sports angle, girls skiing, keep the people on the golf course after the program, have fraternities participate and yet allow...the possibility of getting some good girl skiers like Mary and Alma Byrd [sic] here to add to the charm as well."[13]

Despite Dartmouth's all-male enrollment, the planners were certainly familiar with the notion of women skiing: they had been competing in the US and Canada since the early 1920s. The Dartmouth men were also aware that women skiers had been competing in growing numbers during that decade. The Lake Placid College Week competitions first offered women's skiing events in 1925: a cross-country race and a "ski efficiency" test. That year, the Dartmouth Winter Sports Team won the President Harding Trophy at Lake Placid for the third consecutive time. Soon, other colleges began holding their own winter carnivals and including ladies' sports in their festivities. Michigan College of Mining and Technology held its first Queen's competition in 1928, during which participants were judged not only on their beauty but on their ice skating and skiing skills.[14] The inclusion of women in the 1930 Moosilauke Down-Mountain Race prompted a DOC member to observe that "a delegation from the Appalachian Mountain Club also tried the course, and some of the women members showed that skiing isn't a sport for men only."[15]

Skiing was definitely gaining in popularity at the women's colleges, too. J. Dwight Francis, promoting Woodstock, Vermont, skiing in 1932, wrote to Natalie Hoyt at Smith College: "This is a sport for the ladies certainly, and there is every reason why they should play an important part in this country just as they do in the Alps. I leave it to you to stir up an interest at Smith...."[16] That winter, the Summit Camp on Mt. Moosilauke opened on weekends for the first time: "The first ski party was composed of about thirty undergraduates and members of the Holcomb Ski Club of Smith College. They ascended the mountain on the afternoon of January 9...It was a success from every point of view."[17]

Skiing began taking hold at other women's colleges too. Robert Billings, a ski instructor from Brattleboro, Vermont, commented: "Bennington College...is taking up skiing with a vengeance. I am going to give them instructions two days a week...one third of the student body expressed their desire to attend these classes...A few of these girls have skied at Lake Placid, in the White Mountains, or in Europe"[18] "We have over 50 girls skiing at Bennington College....'Otto' [Schniebs, Dartmouth ski coach] was over there February 22nd and did a wonderful job of making them ski conscious."[19]

Dartmouth's 1934 Alumni Carnival at Mt. Moosilauke had included a Women's Slalom with seven entrants. The Nansen Ski Club's Mount Washington Snow Fest fielded 20 competitors in a ladies' downhill ski race, plus a married women's race with seven entrants, including two Dartmouth alumni wives who finished first and second. In the challenging 1934 USEASA Downhill Championship Race at Cannon Mountain, Mary Bird finished 22nd out of 58 entrants, most of them male.[20] A year later, at Mount Rainier, WA, Mary Bird qualified for the 1936 US Women's Olympic Ski Team while Dartmouth skiers **Dick Durrance, Ted Hunter, Linc Washburn,** and **Warren Chivers** earned berths on the US Men's Team.

In Hanover, the high interest in undergraduate skiing exerted strong influence on the local community. In 1917, the DOC and the Hanover Inn combined to organize an annual Children's Carnival.[21] Dartmouth coaches shared their expertise through community ski schools and positive results began to show. By 1932, Children's Carnival included ski jumping for girls. "The last, run simultaneously with boys on the old jump, will give a girl a better than even chance to win the Cup." The very next year "a girl won the cup....Mary Beetle was the winner."[22] The 1933 Dartmouth yearbook, *Aegis,* enthused that it was "the first time a girl had won."

By the time Dave Putnam and his Carnival Committee held their first meeting in May 1935, they knew that their 1936 Carnival would run simultaneously with the 4th Winter Olympics in Garmisch-Partenkirchen, Germany, the first to include women's Alpine ski races. They realized that Mary Bird, one of the "good girl skiers" who might "add some charm" to their Outdoor Evening festivities, had made the US team and couldn't attend the Hanover events. Mary's success notwithstanding, they also realized that no one had yet seen women competing at college winter carnivals.

As the Carnival Committee deliberated its method of selecting a Queen, a girls' slalom race did not initially surface as a pioneering venture into women's intercollegiate ski competition. However, by autumn, the minutes of its meeting noted: "Girl's Ski Race. Department to take charge and when to have, part of the Outdoor Evening program? Competitions Friday afternoon during skating." This was sparse on details, yet it showed that some thought was being given to how such a race might fit into Carnival activities. Subsequently, "Girls' Ski Race Friday 3:30 p.m." appeared on a schedule compiled at the December 11th meeting.

The Hanover Gazette summarized this new addition to Winter Carnival: "The program this year includes a downhill ski race exclusively for girls. The D.O.C. feels that in the past not enough participation has been encouraged on the part of undergraduate guests, and therefore takes this opportunity to give them a chance to enter into winter sports activities and get a taste of the thrill of competition. The prize...will be given to the first girl to reach the bottom of the Golf Course hill." [23]

Looking back to Feb 9, 1936, and the image of a happy Patty McLane, winner of the first Dartmouth Winter Carnival "Girl's Ski Race"

Before Carnival, *The Dartmouth* (the college's daily newspaper) ran a story entitled "Ski Clothes Replace Formals as Official Carnivaltide Attire," written **by Bill Rotch '37**. His future wife, **Patty McLane** from a prominent New Hampshire family of skiers, would soon arrive from Smith College and win that first race. Friday morning, the lead story in *The Dartmouth* was an overview of the weekend events: "...at the golf course the female of the species will have its rugged moment...on skis, in the Girls' Slalom Race. The half-hour postponement... was made...to allow the unusually large number of expected entries unofficially representing Wellesley, Smith, Vassar and a host of New England colleges, ample time to prepare for the test."[24]

Bill Rotch corresponded with our team in this past year to say that, " yes, Patty did win the first girl's ski race at the Dartmouth Winter Carnival of 1937 and that perhaps because it was a first and perhaps because it was a Friday afternoon and the news people were waiting for something to happen, it got more publicity than a coast down a golf course hill within sight of the Outing Club House deserved. No matter. There was some publicity: newspaper pictures in the Boston papers and one, I believe, in the *New York Herald Tribune*. The prize for winning the race was an 18-inch hickory ridge-top ski with a plaque instead of a binding. Patty was in the Class of 1937 at Smith, and her brother Peter and I were Dartmouth '37. I don't think she was my Carnival date that year but we were good friends. I was on the carnival committee that year and both Peter and I were active in the Outing Club and its various boards and committees." [25]

And as Bill remarked, on Saturday morning, *The Dartmouth* reported: "A Smith girl...chairman of the Smith Outing Club, Patty McLane...swished to victory in the girls' downhill race yesterday afternoon on the Hanover golf course. Her time was a full second faster than Dody Stevens...in 2nd place, followed by 16 others representing eight colleges....A ski-suited throng of more than a thousand braved the late afternoon chill to watch the field careen down the same brief slope that Rec skiers use on less festive occasions.... Smith College anchored the unofficial team championship...by garnering 1st, 3rd, 6th, 8th, and 10th places. No other college placed more than one girl among the select first eleven."[26]

Referring to the new Winter Carnival event, the 1936 *Aegis* noted, "Femininity had finally entered Carnival competition, permanently we hope."[27] And even though some confusion persisted as to whether it was a "downhill" or a "slalom," the 1936 "girls' slalom race" was a success.

Reviews of the 1936 Winter Carnival were mostly favorable; criticism was limited to the Outdoor Evening pageant, variously described as "dull," "very boring," and "terrible." So much for the Carnival Committee's creative planning. The majority sentiment, however, was distinctly positive. Under the headline "Faculty and Visiting Students United in Praising 26th Carnival," Dean Chamberlain commented: "...another feature of the weekend was the number of students who displayed fine skiing talents." He declared that Dartmouth students and guests from men's and women's colleges had never shown such personal enthusiasm for winter sports by actually skiing themselves—rather than simply being race spectators—as during the 1936 Carnival.[28]

The decidedly high approval rating of the newly introduced girls' ski race demonstrated the committee's understanding of such interest. Although they had discussed whether it should be part of the pageantry or a race unto itself, their decision to separate it from the Outdoor Evening program was sound. The addition of a women's race to the premier men's collegiate race weekend was unquestionably instrumental in promoting women's intercollegiate racing. The underlying motivation to increase participation in Carnival was but another example of Dartmouth's efforts to excite a wider public interest in skiing.

The success of the 1936 girls' ski race was great enough to assure its reconsideration in 1937. Although more women were taking up skiing and opportunities for them to compete in races were increasing, there were few alternative possibilities for college women to ski competitively with their peers. Dartmouth opened that door; its men had embraced skiing with a rousing fervor, and they recognized it was in their interest to encourage the women they dated to take up the sport with similar passion.

The 1937 Carnival Committee announced the second girls' ski race, thereby carrying forward their predecessors' initiative. Clearly they had higher expectations than the 1936 Committee and expressed pleasant surprise that the women in the opening race did much better than merely "reach the bottom of the Golf Course hill." Their announcement showed growing awareness of the unique nature of this event: "The girls' ski races, initiated last year in an effort to encourage participation for as many Carnival guests as possible, has again attracted interest in New Eng-

land women's colleges. Sponsored by the Hanover Inn on the golf course Friday afternoon, the race will see real skiing ability."[29]

The announcement noted that the Dartmouth Outing Club was setting the pace in girls' ski competitions in New England. "Elizabeth Durrance, sister of Dick Durrance, Dartmouth ski star, proved herself worthy of her famous brother, as she took first place in the girls' slalom race run off on the golf course yesterday afternoon."[30] Other finishers included Betty McLane (sister of Dartmouth skier Charles McLane), Peggy Johannsen (sister of a McGill University skier), plus skiers from Bennington and Radcliffe, and the 1936 winner Patty McLane.

After two successful seasons, the 1938 Carnival Committee pressed on, taking the girls' ski race to the more challenging Oak Hill. That race was won by Peggy Johannsen of McGill; Blanch McLane, wife of Johnny McLane of the notable skiing McLane family, was second. Again the results exceeded the committee's expectations: "The times this year were of an unusually high standard and evidenced the fact that much interest has been taken in the event," said Hank Merrill, DOC director of the event. "The favorable reception and the fine times recorded this year insure this event a permanent place on the Carnival program."[31]

The 1939 Winter Carnival women's slalom returned to the golf course with a short course set by Dartmouth's National Slalom Champion **Ed Meservey '43**. The names on the entry list were becoming familiar – Elizabeth Durrance, now at Skidmore, along with Peggy Johannsen of McGill, and undergraduates from Smith, Bennington, Middlebury Colleges, all places where skiing was becoming a popular activity, but mostly institutions that didn't support intercollegiate competition or organized ski teams for women. Three of the top finishers were sisters of Dartmouth varsity skiers – Elizabeth Durrance, Sally Litchfield, and Elizabeth McLane. Their attraction to competition resulted partly from family ties, but other women raced for other reasons: a top finish in a Dartmouth Winter Carnival race was an asset for their ski resumés.

But Dartmouth was beginning to question the direction its Carnival was taking. The increasing popularity of the parties and outdoor events drew ever-larger crowds from far beyond the circle of women's colleges from which Dartmouth men found their Carnival dates. This growth strained college resources and its "town & gown" relationships. While the 1936 race was simply a way of increasing participation among Carnival guests, its reputation had grown sufficiently to attract serious competitors. The girls' ski race, which had now acquired a more prestigious identity as the "Women's Slalom," was only one part of the overall situation, but it reflected how the biggest and oldest collegiate winter carnival had expanded far beyond its intended local focus on students and their guests and on men's intercollegiate skiing competition.

Despite such concerns, the 1940 Carnival Committee planned to return the women's slalom to Oak Hill. They rescheduled it from Friday afternoon to Saturday morning, setting it within a ticketed event, the Men's Slalom, a departure from the casual atmosphere of the first four girls' races. Again, Ed Meservey set the course, described as "somewhat less difficult than the men's course."[32] The results were hardly surprising, given the level of competition the event was now attracting. Marilyn Shaw, a 15-year old from Stowe, VT and winner of the New Hampshire Women's Slalom Championship earlier that winter, won the race in a strong field of 37. The Carnival Committee again questioned the direction of the "girls' race" after the fact: "The Girls' Slalom Race… proved to be somewhat of a farce, with the first three places going to a skier of almost Olympic standing and two girls from St. Mary's in the Mountains. None of the three were guests of the Carnival."[33]

The week after the 1940 Winter Carnival, *The Dartmouth* ran a story mentioning this vexing situation: "Another question which must be decided in future Carnivals is the nature of the girls' slalom race… the first three places in the race this year were taken by girls who were not the guests of Dartmouth men but…who competed in championship races all over New England…the committee was in favor of excluding all girls…who were not the dates of students."[34]

The Girls' Ski Race had become too successful. Dartmouth dates were being outraced by outsiders. The only ones with college connections were relatives of the Dartmouth ski team. This led to a rules change, but weather and war provided a solution the Carnival Committees never envisioned.

The 1941 Carnival schedule showed a new stipulation for the event: "With a field limited strictly to Carnival dates, the…Girls' Slalom Race on Oak Hill will be held… between the divisions of the men's slalom."[35] However, heavy rains required busing the men to Suicide Six in Woodstock, VT. The girls were

left behind—their race a washout. There would be no more girls' ski races at Winter Carnival for half a dozen years.

After unsuccessful attempts to reinstate the event in 1946 and 1947, it reappeared on the 1948 Carnival schedule: "…the traditional girls' ski race, following a lapse of six years, will add to this year's athletic and social calendar. All dates and wives of Dartmouth men are eligible"[36] That race, with a field of 40, was run by Ski Club Carcajou, a local club of students and townspeople; the DOC was too stretched for manpower to do so itself. The following year, Carcajou again organized this event; but with other venues becoming available for women's racing and with Winter Carnival assuming an ever fuller schedule, this would be the last "Girls' Race" until Dartmouth began admitting women.

Ever since Fred Harris's exhortation in 1909 to rally students outdoors and onto skis, Dartmouth has remained in skiing's vanguard. An all-male tradition of over 166 years was no obstacle to the 1936 Carnival Committee's "taking opportunity to give [female Carnival guests] a chance to enter into winter sports activities and get a taste of the thrill of competition." By then, Dartmouth men had reached the pinnacle of intercollegiate and Olympic skiing, but their sisters, wives and girlfriends still lacked the same range of opportunities to experience the exhilaration of organized ski competition.

Among the New England women's colleges where skiing was popular, there was scant motivation to provide competition for students. Smith College, where skiing enjoyed substantial interest, resisted the notion of forming an intercollegiate ski team even though they started holding informal intramural "ski meets" by 1938. Harriette Auell, Smith's Physical Education head, explained, "We feel that, without the added complication of developing a ski team, many more girls are learning to ski than if the coaching had to be concentrated on a few."[37] Dartmouth students seized the idea to provide women an early opportunity to race on skis when few other academic institutions had the resources or the inclination to do so.

Dartmouth's initial idea of including girls on skis only in a pageant role quickly shifted to their participation in organized ski races such as had been afforded to its men for over a decade. This filled a conspicuous void for women who wanted to ski competitively. Racing at Winter Carnival became an attractive proposition for women skiers when few other opportunities existed. Long before its admission of women undergraduates in 1972, Dartmouth had engendered a level of acceptance for women's racing that contributed immeasurably to the growth of women's intercollegiate skiing and stimulated countless young women to take an enthusiastic interest in recreational skiing that helped spur the development of a billion-dollar-a-year industry.

Winter Carnival, **the movie.** As a sign of the public acceptance of winter carnivals, movies with a Winter-Carnival-like theme have been made over the decades, and two specific examples stand out. One, *Lucky Star* (1938) with Sonja Henie, is special because it did not happen in Hanover, and yet many people believe it did. Many alumni who are old enough to have been around in those days have given vivid descriptions of Sonja skating her routines in the specially prepared ice arena on the Hanover Golf Course next to Occom Pond. Those skating events did occur but other star skaters of the time were the participants, not Miss Henie. This was a highly successful film and is often referred to as Sonja Henie's greatest movie. But a second movie, called *Winter Carnival* (1939) and produced by Dartmouth alumnus **Walter Wanger '15**, did take place partly in Hanover and involved celebrities F. Scott Fitzgerald and **Budd Schulberg '36**, many Dartmouth skiers, and some leading actors of the time. Nick Stevens describes the backstory for the movie below. The film still lives on as a very special adventure in movie making and a highlight of Dartmouth's Winter Carnival history. It is the hijinks of Fitzgerald that gets much play in the later stories about this event, but another culpable participant was Schulberg. Before Budd passed away in 2009, he was a helpful contributor to our project and we were able to gain his personal comments on this particular slice of his very productive life.

Skier gets ready to start.

Waiting at the Finish Line.

Dartmouth student extras getting in position.

***

WINTER CARNIVAL MOVIE – THE PREQUEL

By Nicholas B. Stevens '58

In 1939, Walter Wanger '15 produced two extraordinary movies: one was Director John Ford's *Stagecoach*, considered one of the year's "ten best pictures on lists compiled by 33 leading critics and [accorded] general recognition as 'The finest Western character drama ever made.'"[38] The other was *Winter Carnival*, which the *New York Times* put on its irreverent list of the ten worst movies of 1939. Despite this Jekyll & Hyde discontinuity, Wanger was elected president of The Academy of Motion Picture Arts and Sciences the very next year.

Here was a man of obvious ambition and talent, but also one whose business acumen could fall prey to his emotions. Such was the case with two of his famous-women films, *Joan of Arc* in 1951, which was "a financial disaster"[39], and his 1965 final production, *Cleopatra*, starring Claudette Colbert, "a $37-million-dollar failure that almost ruined 20th Century Fox."[40] Although a far less damaging box-office failure than either of those, *Winter Carnival* had its own attendant drama.

The stimulus for the movie derived from a romantically themed 1937 short story in *The Saturday Evening Post* by popular author of the day Corey Ford [41], who in the early 1950s adopted Hanover as his home. He soon forged close bonds with a cross-section of the student body, not only by dint of his sociability, literary popularity, and man-to-man conversational style, but also because he organized, trained, and managed an off-campus student boxing team at his own expense. He would later also lend considerable personal and financial support to Dartmouth's newly established rugby team.[42]

Corey's article eventually came to the attention

of Walter Wanger in Hollywood. Being an enthusiastic and nostalgic alumnus, as well as a man who recognized the potential for free advance publicity, he decided that his studio should turn the short story into a feature film. Adding to the project's appeal was the fact that Dartmouth's Winter Carnival was already the most renowned of such cold-weather college festivals and no one had yet used it as the setting for a movie.

Wanger now needed to engage a scriptwriter, someone to turn a leisurely 10-minute read into a 100-minute cinematic experience. Initially, he gave the task to **Budd Schulberg '36** who was already a movie-savvy script writer having grown up in Hollywood as the son of the head of Paramount Studios. Budd seemed tailor-made for the job. He had been encouraged to attend Dartmouth by alumnus **Gene Markey '18** who would eventually retire from the Navy as a Rear Admiral but who, in the early 1930s, was also a screenwriter for 20th Century Fox. (His eventual wives would include movie stars Joan Bennett, Heddy Lamarr, and Myrna Loy, as well as the widow of the owner of Calumet Farms.) It was he who convinced Budd that Dartmouth was a good place for an aspiring writer and, eventually, that choice proved Markey correct.

But Wanger disliked the product Budd had produced (as did Budd). He then reasoned: who better to craft a solid story of unrequited love among the academically privileged sons and daughters of the middle and upper classes than the celebrated creator of *The Great Gadsby*. Yes, the famous (albeit fading) F. Scott Fitzgerald himself!

But there was a problem: sending the alcoholically inclined Fitzgerald off alone to imbibe nothing more than the celebratory atmosphere of a campus-wide party and expect him to return with a serious script was rather like sending a fox into the hen house to inventory eggs. Clearly, a responsible and companionable chaperone had to be found.

That choice was obvious: send Schulberg.

Budd's job would ostensibly be to act as Fitzgerald's guide in Hanover and to fill him in on campus life generally and on the traditions of Winter Carnival in particular. He was also expected "to help out" with the script, that is, to amplify where detail was sparse, to revise if the scenario strayed too far from the plausible, and to motivate the great writer if he slackened—and to keep him sober.

Leaving the Southern California warmth behind, the two writers finally arrived by train in Norwich, Vermont, across the Connecticut River from Hanover, aboard the Carnival Special from New York City, and then perfunctorily set about their collaborative writing mission, each with an opposing personal agenda: the one to join in the spirit of the festivities, the other to keep bottled spirits out of reach. To be brief and blunt about the outcome, the needed script did not materialize because neither writer had a taste for the project, much preferring to discuss any other topic that came to mind. That they slept little, wrote even less, and imbibed congenially and often is well known—and Wanger fired them both from the project. It then fell to Budd's childhood friend and fellow alumnus, **Maurice Rapf '37** to develop the unfinished screenplay. Unfortunately, Rapf could not turn the thin plot into a suitably substantial vehicle for actress Ann Sheridan, and despite her considerable popularity at the time, the film did poorly.

However, there was something positive to eventually emerge from this fiasco: in 1950, Budd's insightful novel about the incident, *The Disenchanted*, was published. A best-seller, it related the full story in all its essential details. It is still very readable today—and far more absorbing than the movie whose genesis begat the book. Schulberg is remembered not only for this and other socially disturbing novels, but for his Oscar-winning screenplay for *On the Waterfront*, starring Marlon Brando and Eva Marie Saint, a film awarded a total of eight Oscars in 1954 and whose title might almost as aptly have been that of his revelatory 1950 novel of a different tragic character, F. Scott Fitzgerald.

The curious who might view *Winter Carnival* on their video screens today are likely to react not so differently from those who watched it on "the silver screen" 70 years ago: with a mix of amusement and disappointment. Those expecting to see extended scenes of Olympic caliber ski racing, daring leaps off what was then one of New England's most important jumps, and exciting outdoor skating competitions, might feel short-changed. And those who hope for more than a glimpse of the imaginative snow sculptures built by fraternity men and dormitory residents, or of the towering thematic statue in the center of campus erected by Outing Club members with shovels and pails from the huge mounds of trucked-in snow, would be denied most of these staples of the typical Dartmouth mid-winter gala of the period. Happily, this movie endures neither as a documentary nor as a good example of art imitating life; if it did, the event would already have imploded. The *real* Winter Carnival has yet to be filmed.

There are many other elements that made up the Winter Carnival weekend and added to its luster. For example, we comment in other chapters on the significance of the ski racing and jumping events to the reputations of competitors and on the appearance in the racing activities of many leading international skiers. This all added to the glamour of what has become "the" Winter Carnival. All of these things caused thousands, if not millions, of Dartmouth students, their guests, and many others who never came to a Dartmouth Winter Carnival but heard about them from friends or the media, to get enthused at the prospects of fun and glamour in the snow mountain climes of this and other countries. There is no way to measure the full impact of the Dartmouth Winter Carnival on the development of a broad public interest in skiing, but it was to bring the excitement and joy of this spectacular event to his audiences that the great ski moviemaker Warren Miller decided to film Winter Carnival as part of his ski film presentations long ago. Today, Winter Carnival may not be the event of old, but it still is the biggest and the best. And as commented on in the next to last chapter, the impact of this subject is still being spread around the world by alumni reviving versions of the Dartmouth Winter Carnival in other locations.

Lunch at Mt Moosilauke was a special Ski School experience.

High up the trail on Moosilauke looking down at the Lodge.

Many of us started our skiing right here on the Hanover Golf Course.

Climbing up the trail to ski down at Moosilauke.

SKI INSTRUCTION: THE GROWTH ENGINE OF SKIING

Instruction is central to the operation of any ski area. Without a way to educate individuals in how to ski, the sport would not go far. Initially, there was little Hanover ski instruction as everything was new and there were no ski instructors in Hanover. When Fred Harris visited Montreal's Winter Carnival, he made a point of taking photographs and talking with local experts about how to jump and do a Telemark turn. That served as his ski training.

However, ski instruction started fairly soon thereafter in Hanover as something done for both students and the community. A ski school program of sorts operated on the Hanover Golf Club course for students from the early years after Fred Harris's founding of the Dartmouth Outing Club in 1909-10. The local community shared in the ski instruction process with many Dartmouth students, coaches, and faculty participating as instructors. Early on, the program was sponsored by the Hanover Inn. This ultimately led to the Ford Sayre program after **Sayre '33** took over management of the Inn and played a lead role in evolving the local ski instruction.

A well-organized group of children head home from ski lessons.

George Ostler demonstrating his turns for his ski school.

At various points in the history of the area, ski schools for locals and visitors were operating at Mt. Moosilauke, Moose Mountain, and Oak Hill in addition to the long time activity at the Hanover golf course. By 1935, the menu of activities at Moosilauke included a "standing-room only" ski school operated by Coach Otto Schniebs and Swiss skier Florian Haemmerle, a Hanover Inn employee. Photographs from this time show that there were many, many participants in these ski schools.

An important addition to local ski instruction for area children was the evolution of an instruction program started by the Hanover Inn into the Ford Sayre Program that still exist today. Many members of the Hanover community have learned to ski thru this program. Key leaders in the early days of this program were Peggy and Ford Sayre '33. And over the decades, many leaders of Hanover skiing activities have participated in this program, people like Rosalie Cutter, wife of **Don Cutter '45** and mother of **Don Cutter '73**, who chaired the Ford Sayre Program for many years. The Cutter family has played many roles in the evolution of local skiing from managing ski areas like Okemo and the Dartmouth Skiway to running the Art Bennett Ski Shop to ski instruction. They have been instrumental in much of what has made Hanover a hotbed of skiing.

After World War II ended, the Dartmouth ski instruction was handled by the recreation program, but this foundered. When the new Skiway was started in 1957, the DOC took control of the ski instruction program. The then Vice President of Winter Sports, **Sam Silverstein '58**, took charge as the point person to get this critical area of skiing re-energized. One of his early tasks was to find a lead instructor. Various names were suggested, but Don Cutter '45 suggested the eventual choice, **George Ostler**. Don knew George from their days in Austria after the close of WW II when Don ran a military ski school and George worked for him. With no official backing, pay was a problem at first, but Winter Sports got together with Hanover High School and the Ford Sayre Ski Program for grade-school children and managed to scrape together enough money to offer an acceptable salary. The next winter, George Ostler was also hired as the assistant Alpine Ski Coach; performing both functions provided him with a livable wage.[43]

George turned out to be great head of the ski instruction program and many alumni remember fondly working with him. By the 1960s, the DOC Ski School program, now fully headed by Ostler, had 800 students with 50 instructors and was one of the all- time most successful programs run by the DOC. The student ski instructors initiative became one of the first activities at the college to feature students training other students. The program was also especially popular because, much like the advent of multiple ski clubs at Dartmouth discussed earlier, the Ostler-run ski school offered a racing option and sanctioned Eastern Region ski races every Wednesday. Thus, would-be racers had an alternative to being on the ski team and still have the opportunity to race.

In other chapters, the story is told of Dartmouth alumni leading ski instruction programs in many locations in the U.S. and elsewhere in the world. **Blair Wood '30** was the first American ski instructor at Puckets Ski program in Franconia Notch, NH. **"Bunny" Bertram '33** was leading a ski school effort in Woodstock, VT. **Dick Durrance '39** was involved with a ski school in Sun Valley and Alta before WW II. **John Litchfield '39** was involved with **Friedl Pfeifer** in starting the Aspen Ski School just after WW II. Thousands of Dartmouth alumni have served as ski instructors in US ski areas over the decades since and still do. And on it went around the world with Dartmouth alumni leading ski instruction in Australia, New Zealand, Chile, Japan, and many other countries.

Over the years the ski instruction program in Hanover has changed, but there are still many students that take a bus out to the Skiway during the "Season" and learn to ski or learn to teach. And many carry on as ski instructors, part time or full time, for much of their lives. The greater Dartmouth/Hanover community has benefitted greatly from local ski instruction and helped make this activity a basic component in the engine driving the growth of skiing.

Dartmouth's Safety Patrol and the National Ski Patrol

From the beginning, a concern for safety was one of the factors guiding the work of the DOC. In the late 1930s, **John Rand '38** became a leader in this area and was very conscious of the need for ski safety. He constantly sought to organize better ski patrol approaches. He was one of the first 50 participants in the National Ski Patrol (NSP) set up by C. Minot ("Minnie") Dole just before WWII. He not only did his own thing at Dartmouth, but also was in regular touch with Dole to review safety procedures being recommended by the NSP.

Minnie Dole (seated) and Dick Durrance '39 in discussion about skiing issues of interest to both. (Photo by Meg Durrance).

Numerous other important Dartmouth ski figures advised Dole on the structure and set-up of the NSP. Amongst the first 125 members of the National Ski Patrol formed were **Dick Durrance '39** (#7), **Marvin Chandler '32** (#8) (see image of Marvin's certificate on page 62), **John Rand '38** (#49), **Henry Perkins '23** (# 73), **Charlie Proctor '28** (# 93), **Joe Dodge H '55** (#99), **Richard Rocker '33** (#108, and a member of the National Committee of the National Ski Patrol System), and **Sel Hannah '35** (#124). There were no doubt more members of the Dartmouth family within the early NSP membership and many, many more over the years since, such as Mary Jaffee (#131 of the first 170 women in the NSP, and the mother of **Valerie Jaffee '78**), but the records are spotty and it is a challenge to identify them all.

Before World War II, John Rand and the Dartmouth group had its own ski patrol operation that provided support for races at Tuckerman Ravine, Oak Hill and other venues. Rand and the Dartmouth patrol often operated as a stand-in for the NSP when most of the NSP that existed was Minnie Dole himself. In 1946, after the conclusion of the 10th Mountain Division's efforts in Europe, many former 10th Division members brought some of their military ski patrol work into play on behalf of the National Ski Patrol and Dartmouth. **Richard Bredenberg '48**, with help from John Rand, reorganized the patrol team at Dartmouth during the fall of 1946. All men were required to have knowledge of first aid and have good skiing ability. Some 18 qualified for the Dartmouth patrol in this first rebirth year. They provided patrol cover at various local areas like Pico Peak and Stowe in Vermont and Tuckerman Ravine in NH that first year, with 17 qualifying at the end to joining the NSP. [44]

One of the more amusing tales we encountered in our research was a ski patrol story shortly after the Dartmouth Skiway opened in 1957. Many members of the Dartmouth ski fraternities were involved as Ski Patrollers, including Happy Griffiths, wife of **Clark Griffiths '57, Th '58,** and **Joe McHugh '60, Tu '61**. Happy was also one of the first two female instructors in the Dartmouth recreation ski program. As Joe has related, this memory has stayed with him for over 50 years. He and Happy were partnered up one day on the Dartmouth Skiway Patrol and were faced with the task of getting a lady with a broken leg down the mountain. Joe took the front of the sled and Happy took the tail. Joe has always wondered what the lady in

The Original #8 NSP Certificate for Marvin Chandler '32 (1939).

the sled was thinking as she looked back at one of her saviors, Happy, guiding the tail when she was an obvious over six months pregnant and carrying a then 18-month-old second child, papoose style, on her back! It must have been quite a sight, and an exemplary feat by Happy, and it certainly left a lasting impression on Joe McHugh—as well as, we suspect, on the lady with the broken leg!

In addition to the ski patrol work on campus, there are many alumni stories of special patrol activities that developed elsewhere in the world. Many Dartmouth- trained patrollers have worked, or are currently working, at ski areas throughout mainland U.S., East, West, North and even South. Dartmouth folks have also taken on NSP leadership roles, like **Dick Rosston '73,** a lawyer in Anchorage, Alaska, who learned his initial ski patrol skills at the Dartmouth Skiway and was patrol leader in 1972-73. He has worked as a professional patroller in Bozeman, Montana, Alpine Meadows, Lake Tahoe, and is now the Alaskan Division NSP Ski and Toboggan Advisor based at Alyeska Ski Resort where he is also the resort's lawyer. Dartmouth trained patrollers are also working in other countries. **Norwell Coquillard '74** learned patrol skills in Hanover, and when he was transferred to Korea in 1984, he joined a US Military foreign ski patrol that worked at the various ski hills in that country.

Such were the adventures of the Dartmouth Ski Patrollers. They were active on the slopes of the Hanover area as undergraduates and often continued this activity wherever they traveled in life. This is just one more important example of the Dartmouth factor playing a role in the expansive mosaic that makes up the greater ski world.

FACILITIES DEVELOPMENTS AT DARTMOUTH/HANOVER

Important to the Dartmouth ski history has been the evolving facilities used in and around Hanover NH to provide a place for skiers to develop their skills or simply to enjoy the skiing sport. The following two articles provide an historical review of these facilities and some information on one particular creation that adds to Dartmouth's reputation for leadership in this sport.

First, Doug Leitch explores the sequence of developments which have taken place in the Hanover area since the beginning to provide ski opportunities for students and other area residents. As Doug identifies, the process has often been a struggle because of the cost of maintaining suitable facilities to support the most important college ski program in the U.S. Any institution is faced with spending priority decisions, and not every leader in later years has been as enthusiastic about skiing as the earlier leaders of the college. Historical continuity is an important component in the way any institution or country is viewed over the long term. Fortunately, the key decision- makers at Dartmouth have continued to support the sport of skiing in ways that have enabled Dartmouth to maintain its leadership role. And as the premise of this book is built around the idea that Dartmouth has a unique position in developing this sport and is able to make a rare claim to being "the" prime institutional leader in something worldwide, it is a wise leadership that has made the decisions to continue this role.

The second article is a case study review by Clark Griffiths of the creation of the first overhead cable ski lift designed and built in the United States for the specific use of skiers. This article is an important contribution to the history of skiing as it puts to rest much of the confusion over the role played by Dan Hatch '28, the Dartmouth Outing Club, Split Ballbearing, American Steel and Wire Company, American Wire & Cable Company, and the Constam group of Switzerland in the creation of the first such lift in the U.S. This single lift served as a forerunner design for early lifts in Sun Valley, whose creation was assisted by Charlie Proctor '28, and for the many early lifts installed around North America by ski area entrepreneur and Dartmouth family member Fred Pabst who will also be discussed in Chapter V as the first President of the Heiliger Hugel Ski Club founded in the 1930s with many other Dartmouth skiers in Wisconsin.

**

EVER EVOLVING SKI FACILITIES

By Douglas C. Leitch '65

At the beginning of the Twentieth Century, not only were there only a handful of skiers in the Hanover, New Hampshire area, there were also no designated places to ski. In the days of Fred Harris, skiing was pretty much a do-it-yourself sport. You made and repaired your own equipment and discovered places suitable for your own level of self-taught skiing. If you wanted to ski down a slope, you had to either start from the top or climb up first. Harris and a few of his cohorts had to construct their own small ski jumps to enjoy that aspect of early skiing styles. His diary entries during his student years at Dartmouth recorded his early efforts to construct ski jumps near campus. "I walked up to the Davison Hill and constructed framework of ski jump." (15 December 1909), then after diligently practicing on his new jump for the next week, Harris enthusiastically recorded, "Went skiing. Tried jump several times, and at last made it. Hurrah! Twice oh! ye! gods!" (16 January 1910)[45]

The jump event at Winter Carnival always drew a big crowd.

While Harris and his friends were enjoying the newfound thrills of ski-sport, there was little time, organization, or funding to make improvements on any facilities for skiing. In addition to the decisions members of the DOC had to consider in creating a winter sports team, there was this question of facilities. In the spring of his sophomore year Fred Harris "took pictures of prospective ski-hill, estimated grade and measured slide." As the next winter began he "walked up to the Davison Hill and constructed framework of ski jump." That was undoubtedly the jump they used in the first Field Day in February 1910. The DOC members managed to build a substantial wooden ski jump trestle in the woods off the golf course, "a level platform fifty feet long, with a 'take-off' eight feet above the slope."[44] The big attraction at each of those early Winter Carnivals was the ski jump. The new spectacle of young daredevils jumping off a raised trestle to soar out over a steep landing hill was a real crowd-pleaser and a draw for shivering hordes of spectators. The jumping event was always the grand finale of Carnival, but there was demand for something better.

Five years later Dartmouth skiers and their competition had outgrown that early jump. The College loaned the Dartmouth Outing Club $7,000 with an additional $1,000 gift from Johnson to build a new 40-meter steel trestle ski jump in a steep ravine on the golf course known as the Vale of Tempe.[47] Its steel trestle, which would become a town landmark for seven decades, would also become an early test of town-gown relations. Some of the neighbors, from whose homes the top of the ski jump trestle was visible, complained that it was unsightly. The college wisely decided to paint the jump an "inconspicuous color".... dark green. It first saw use for the 1922 Winter Carnival and was also the first capital investment Dartmouth made in ski facilities. Of course, the college expected the loan to be repaid by receipts from ski jump ticket sales. No other facility for Dartmouth athletes during that period was paid for by the athletes or the club to which they belonged–neither the tennis nor the basketball courts, nor the football field or track were funded by any other sources than the college treasury. Nor did the college expect to be repaid for building any of those athletic facilities. With skiing, it has always been different.

The nature of ski competition in those pioneer days was limited to what might be called Nordic events, cross-country races and ski-jumping, along with some novelty events like obstacle races often including snowshoe runners, and eventually "proficiency tests" consisting of demonstrations of a variety of turns and maneuvers. None of these demanded special facilities with the exception of ski jumping. Even though members of the DOC had brainstormed

Dartmouth Winter Carnival Directors review the remodeled ski jump in the Vale of Tempe.

the notion of a mechanical lift to hoist ski jumpers to the top of the trestle, no mechanisms were devised or built to eliminate the need to climb.

Since Shumway and Foster first climbed Mount Moosilauke on skis in 1912, that mountain has been a part of Dartmouth skiing. Only three years later, alumnus John Johnson proposed in a letter to Dartmouth President Ernest Nichols that Dartmouth students be encouraged to try a ski trip to Moosilauke in lieu of the one planned for Mount Washington, citing Moosilauke's relative closeness to Hanover and easier terrain. He knew the mountain from his involvement with the Society for the Preservation of New Hampshire Forests and thus suggested what he imagined might be a skiable route, a portion of which included the Carriage Road. He offered gold medals to be awarded to those who made the trip. The DOC politely declined the idea of medals to avoid making it a competitive undertaking which they feared would compromise its safety. There is no record of whether such a trip, with or without Johnson's medals, was undertaken. A decade later however, still well before the days of mechanical uphill assistance, the Moosilauke Carriage Road would begin to attract more Dartmouth skiers. That was chosen as the route for the first down-the-mountain races that Col. Anton Diettrich and Professor Charles A. Proctor promoted in 1927. Subsequent improvements to the Carriage Road by Coach Otto Schniebs and alteration of the exact course to eliminate flat sections, along with shrewd promotion of films made of earlier such races by John McCrillis '19, made it the course for the first sanctioned national downhill race in 1933, still before the advent of lifts.

Dartmouth had acquired ownership of large sections of Mt. Moosilauke and began to develop some rudimentary facilities to promote its use as a ski destination and site for competition. Ford Sayre '33 and his wife Peggy started opening up the summit camp on Moosilauke weekends in the winter of 1932 to accommodate Dartmouth students and alumni as well as guests from other college outing clubs.[48] Soon after that first national race, Otto Schniebs and Dan Hatch began laying out trails to be cut using student labor as soon after the 1933 Commencement as possible.[49] After cruising the area with Hatch, Schniebs wrote to his partner Jack McCrillis that, "now I know what a beautiful [sic] Mt. it is and what a great possibility it has as a real recreation center." He raved about the suitability of the slopes for racing and the fact that there was still 1-3 feet of snow on the northeast and east sides in late May. "…it is the place where Dartmouth men and their families will find a real recreation throughout the year."[50]

Not until skiing downhill began to take precedence over cross-country and jumping was there any concerted effort to address the uphill chore that was accepted as part of early skiing. Dartmouth skiers were masters at learning the herringbone and side-stepping methods of gaining elevation in order to descend. The first mechanical lift in the United States was a rope tow installed at nearby Woodstock, Vermont in 1934, and run for many years by Bunny Bertram '31. Before the next ski season began, Dan Hatch, assisted by Otto Schniebs and others, submitted an ambitious 13-page proposal to the Society for Protection of New Hampshire Forests, owner of sections of Mt. Blue, part of the Moosilauke summit area, to build a tramway ski lift that would have greatly enhanced Dartmouth's usage of Moosilauke's skiing potential. In part it argued, "The Moosilauke proposal involves a longer line up a larger and higher range [compared to the competing proposal for a tram at Cannon Mountain in Franconia Notch] – a genuine mountain tramway, offering opportunities to develop new and significant year around recreational use of the high mountain country."[51] Later, the Trustees would withdraw that proposal, not, according to Hatch, because they were in support of the proposal for Franconia Notch just to the east where a tram was later successfully installed, but because it was simply too expensive for the College to consider. However, Hatch would continue to beat the drum for expanded use of Moosilauke as a ski facility for Dartmouth for two key reasons. It was the reserve, or as Hatch asserted, "the snow insurance policy for anything we may wish to do in Hanover, Moosilauke

is the foundation." He was also in favor of developing Moosilauke because it was "home grounds" for alumni skiing. "Alumni skiing organizations are going to flourish…they could well grow to such stature in both recreational and competitive skiing, that Dartmouth will be known as much for its alumni as for its undergraduate teams." Recognizing that skiing was then the "fad and fashion sensation of the country," he concluded with the fanfare, "our Dartmouth clientele are not the dilettantes in the sport."[52]

Still, before American ski lifts reached higher than a long rope, Dartmouth would expand ski activity on Mount Moosilauke. They built a Ravine Camp to offer more lodging for skiers, and soon formed "Dartmouth at Moosilauke" with a Parkhurst Hall office (the main administration building at Dartmouth, as opposed to Robinson Hall which housed DOC offices) and a list of directors from the who's who of early Dartmouth skiers.[53] They promoted activities of the Dartmouth Alumni Outing Club and informal ski racing on Moosilauke. In 1935 the Dartmouth at Moosilauke committee met with President Hopkins and convinced him that the out-of-door interests of the College had become so extensive and so involved that their entire direction should be put in the hands of one central organization. The menu of activities at Moosilauke now included "standing-room only" ski schools operated by Schniebs, and Swiss skier Florian Haemmerle, a Hanover Inn employee, as well as the annual alumni ski race and the Moosilauke Downhill race run for undergraduates. Still no lifts, and after a fire in September 1935, they had no Ravine Camp, either. This elite organization of skiers pushed for the construction of a new lodge, and Hatch's drumbeat was given a trustee's timbre when Judge John R. McLane, a frequent skier at Moosilauke with his progeny of future Dartmouth skiers, began to lobby for better facilities like central heating. An optimistic prospectus with architect's renderings of the proposed new lodge was signed by Natt Emerson Class of 1900, chairman of the committee, boasting of this as "the most comprehensive outdoor project yet undertaken by an American college." At the DOC Trustees meeting on February 5, 1938, Professor Proctor emphasized the need to set aside funds out of the Ravine Camp improvement budget to provide better skiing facilities.[54]

Not satisfied with the amount of vertical drop or the length of the run the rope tow on the golf course offered – even though it had been lighted for night skiing since 1931 well before the advent of the tow itself, ever more proficient Dartmouth skiers now demanded improved "facilities." Pressure to expand local ski facilities was also coming from the community with numerous alumni including Hanover business owners like John Piane '14 at the Dartmouth Co-operative Society, who had offered to underwrite such construction in 1934.[55] Piane and other members of the Hanover Community Council were considering a plan to work with the DOC and have Otto Schniebs lay out trails on Balch Hill. They tabled their plans once they became aware of the Dartmouth at Moosilauke effort to centralize DOC and College outdoor facilities management. Fortunately for skiing and the DOC, Dan Hatch had established himself as a successful spokesman and business manager for the Outing Club. Support for his initiative came in a Report of the Faculty Committee on the Outing Club 1934-35, which noted that "the explosive growth of winter sports in New England…deals largely with the story of an undergraduate club to keep on the crest of a movement which is no longer collegiate but public and general, and to promote in a field in which keen commercial promotion is already providing heavyweight competition."[56] Hatch also prudently opened a direct line of communication on the subjects of ski facilities and DOC management with College President Ernest Martin Hopkins.

Hopkins replied to Hatch's concerns in two lengthy letters addressing the subject of DOC reorganization and how to protect its student-run status as well as the community pressure to expand ski facilities. "We have reached a stage where a great void in the provisions made for the interest in winter sports must be filled either under Dartmouth auspices or outside of those…to ignore that fact would simply be to relinquish its leadership in the field of winter sports, becloud the fact that the origin of winter sports began at Dartmouth in the Outing Club, and preclude the possibility that ever again we could get the public recognition, to say nothing of the preeminence, which we hold at present."[57]

Recognizing the impact of increased expenses that such expansion would incur for the DOC and the College and sensitive to the potential of increased obligations placed on students and DOC management, Hopkins also wrote: "I should hope [expenses] should be taken over by the College and provided for through the Alumni Fund or elsewhere, and thus we might preserve to Dartmouth the prestige of her historical connection with the whole development of winter sports and Outing Club activities, while in the meantime we should not make any individual at any point the scapegoat of our enlarged effort."[58]

Two months later Hopkins wrote again to Hatch to convey the Trustees authorization at their June 13, 1935 meeting "not to exceed $7,000 for developing a ski terrain with ski tows at Hanover."[59] They had hopes during the Great Depression that federal funds might be available to help offset that expense. Named to a Trustees' Ski Tow Committee with Adelbert Ames, Albert Dickerson, Halsey Edgerton, Ralph Miller, and Max Norton, Dan Hatch began a full-steam project of completing a new ski facility in Hanover by the next season. He had already engaged Otto Schniebs to layout and cut the trails on nearby Oak Hill, east of the Hanover Country Club in anticipation of the Trustees' approval. Now he busied himself with a new design for an overhead lift similar to one he had seen in a brochure from Davos, Switzerland. The choice of this new ski terrain was determined mostly by its skiable distance from campus and unfortunately not for its qualifications as ski terrain. It lacked the elevation, snow depth and suitable exposure that benefit good ski slopes.

Although Oak Hill hosted Dartmouth Winter Carnival events for almost the next two decades, its shortcomings as a ski facility would soon become obvious. Immediately after the first season at Oak Hill, Dan Hatch was pulling for a second ski tow. Professor Charles Proctor, faculty advisor to the DOC, appointed Hatch to chair a committee to consider the advisability of constructing further ski facilities near Hanover and methods of financing such developments.[60] Along with Hatch, Proctor appointed Ames and Edgerton from the previous ski tow committee and added Trustee John R. McLane. Hatch had already done his homework and presented a study of ski hills within ten miles of Hanover, showing comparisons of them in terms of elevation above sea level, length of run, exposure, and skier capacity. He proposed that such a new tow could be built at a cost of $4,000 and retire its investment over a ten-year period. The rest of that summer Hatch would be occupied with hiring a new ski coach, but the seed for a better mountain had been planted based on those general criteria.

Dan Hatch was not one to rest on his laurels. Knowing that the jumping events were the revenue producing element of tournaments, and aware of the shortcomings of the 40-meter ski jump then in its 15th season, Hatch, fresh from the success of building an overhead lift facility at Oak Hill, entertained the idea of a bigger ski jump. In May 1936, he wrote to Harry Wade Hicks at Lake Placid to request a profile of the 60-meter jump at Lake Placid. "We are contemplating the construction of a larger jump here at Dartmouth." But Dartmouth's appetite for new ski facilities had been sated for almost another two decades. Student and community skiers would have to be happy with Oak Hill despite weaknesses already documented in Hatch's thorough memorandum at the end of the first Oak Hill season. Oak Hill needed lift equipment upgrades, support in the form of food services and a warming hut, an electrical timing system, and floodlights similar to the ones that had been in use on the golf course for several seasons, and the need for another ski tow.[61]

Oak Hill's low elevation, inadequate natural snow depths, and the southwestern exposure made for tenuous skiing conditions. At the 1941 Winter Carnival it poured rain on Saturday, washing out the varsity alpine races and the newly added girls' slalom scheduled for Oak Hill. The DOC had a contingency plan which they implemented to bus the men to Suicide Six in Woodstock, Vermont. For the next decade, Suicide Six would be the backup for training and last minute displacements due to poor conditions at Oak Hill. Right after World War II, the DOC Board of Trustees appointed a committee "to make a careful study and investigation of skiing and ski facilities in and about Hanover and to make a report."[62] For the interim, they planted pine trees on the south side of the lift line to shade the snow and keep that critical area covered and skiable.

The change of DOC directors when **John Rand '38** returned from active duty with the 10th Mountain Division to fill that position and the return of fellow 10th Mountain veteran **Walter Prager** as coach were key to stimulating interest in a better ski facility of the caliber Dartmouth skiers deserved. Their ally in the College Administration was College Vice President and **Treasurer John F. Meck, Jr. '33**, a recent convert to skiing and among the Trustees of the College, **John R. "Judge" McLane '07**. In 1953 the College formed a "Search Committee" of Prager, Rand, and the College Forester **Robert S. Monahan '29** charged to find a site for a new ski facility within 25 miles of Hanover. They were further advised to consider requirements of slope exposure, base elevation and vertical drop, skiable terrain, access, and price.[63]

A very tall order.

This time they would approach the search for new ski terrain with a full understanding of the requirements. Over the next year the committee, with the expertise of a skier, a forester, and a DOC director/alumnus who had spent considerable time in the neighboring out-of-doors, would pore over topographic maps and aerial photographs seeking that desired mix of characteristics, high enough, snowy enough, and still accessible to Hanover. The following year they added two more locals to the Search Committee, Harry Sanborn of Lyme Center and Allison Catheron, a local woodsman, plus Dr. Ralph Miller, not only a skier but also a pilot who could fly them over potential new ski terrain. No peak in the Upper Connecticut River Valley went unexamined, although most were eliminated from the list for lacking in one or more qualities. Time was moving on and pressure was building. The cover of the February 1955 issue of the Dartmouth Alumni Magazine depicted the dejected mood of two Dartmouth skiers viewing the ski condition report of "poor" at their own facility while "good to excellent" at several other nearby slopes. Some questioned whether Meck had an inside hand in staging this not-so-subtle propaganda. The committee, feeling those students' pain (with justifiable basis, whether or not staged), not only examined nearby mountains for possible development, but also visited existing ski areas to see what was working for others. Committee member Meck, accompanied by Middlebury alumnus Louis Menard, visited Middlebury College's Snowbowl in early March 1955. Meck reported to the committee that "the general level of skiing was very good – much higher than the level of student skiing at Oak Hill." Then he threw down the gauntlet adding that the new Middlebury ski facility was providing "a tremendous impetus to their skiing, and within a few years would make Middlebury the prominent skiing college."[64]

With that added incentive, Prager, Rand, Meck, and Sanborn piled into a jeep for a second look at Holt's Ledge in Lyme Center on March 24, 1955. They sent Prager scrambling up the slope for a look. When he returned he exclaimed, "Gentlemen, I think the search ends here." A second review of aerial photos comparing Holt's Ledge and Moose Mountain confirmed that opinion and concluded that Holt's Ledge offered more favorable conditions. The decision on where gave a tremendous lift and surge of enthusiasm and urgency to how. They promptly submitted a memo to the Trustees' Planning Committee on April 8 titled "Development of Adequate Skiing Facilities for Dartmouth Students in the Hanover Area."[65]

The preamble of that memo made an impassioned case for the priority of this project to save Dartmouth's skiing preeminence with an opening salvo, "The Place of Skiing at Dartmouth."[66]

"In terms of winter sports, Dartmouth and skiing have been virtually synonymous for over thirty years. This has been true both in terms of competitive skiing at the ski team level and in…recreational winter sports as part of the College's general program. Since World War II, however, despite outstanding Dartmouth ski teams, Dartmouth's preeminence has been seriously threatened. Two other Eastern institutions, Middlebury College and Norwich University, have made great strides this year in developing first class ski areas adjacent to their campuses. Time is running out so far as Dartmouth's clear-cut superior reputation in skiing is concerned.

"Oak Hill is a symbol of what has happened to Dartmouth skiing. When Oak Hill was developed in 1935 with an uphill lift other than a rope tow, it represented a tremendous advance for Dartmouth skiing. The winter of 1955, however, marked the twentieth year of operation of the Oak Hill facility. It is startling to realize that in twenty years there has not been any improvement whatever in the skiing facilities available to Dartmouth students. The only minor development – a small investment by Dartmouth and the Hanover Inn in the Suicide Six Poma lift in 1954 [John Rand subsequently served on the Suicide Six board of directors in 1955-56] and a short-lived rope tow at Moosilauke, no longer operating."

The basic premises of the memo were clearly spelled out to highlight Dartmouth's preeminence in skiing has been beneficial to the school; to continue that preeminence requires having its own ski facilities; snow cover could be a problem with a base elevation of 1000'; and the bottom line was that to maintain Dartmouth's lead role in skiing would require a substantial capital investment, and the underwriting of operating deficits.

The memo boldly concluded with the caveat that if the Trustee Planning Committee did not accept the validity of those premises, the balance of the report "need not be considered." It also appended a note about Holt's Ledge observing that opposite the site lay the steep westerly exposure of Winslow Hill,

"a possibility for subsequent development." Meck, appreciating the way things worked at Dartmouth especially when an impending project of this scope would demand significant resources on short notice, asked Rand, Prager, and College Secretary Sid Hayward for strong arguments why such a ski facility should be available in the coming 1955-56 season. He reminded them to, "please remember the strong argument against going ahead is that Dartmouth has gone along without this ski facility for many years and therefore, why is it so important that it be done this winter. At the same time, perhaps we have been 'asleep at the switch.' Any arguments you can give me will be helpful."[67]

Rand responded with the observation that since the war he and Prager had been running the competitive program on a shoestring budget, citing the lack of a coordinated Dartmouth ski facility on the final results of ski team meets (i.e. inability to improve existing conditions). He also commented on safety concerns arising from absenteeism at ski instruction classes when students opted to drive to Stowe, Franconia, Pico, or Sunapee where better snow conditions prevailed and the lack of facilities for freshman and others without cars or transportation. The amount of travel time ski team members needed to spend to get adequate training had a negative impact on their studies. He tersely concluded that the lack of facilities placed Dartmouth's reputation as a winter sports college in jeopardy "if historical fact is, today, at all important. Frankly, any reference to Dartmouth's preeminence in winter sports in any vein of public relations except historical is today an insertion of false information."[68]

Sepp Ruschp (front left) leads the team to inspect the site for the Skiway (1955).

He suggested that if Dartmouth did not build a new ski area there would be a lack of participation in the development of a 'carry over' sport, an increase in student ski accidents, a lack of a focal point for Dartmouth ski activity, and the unavailability of a stimulating therapeutic facility for the Dartmouth family. As a counter to the pushback that an immediate restricted summer fundraising campaign would conflict with that fall's broader alumni fund results, Rand added his optimism that a small group of interested persons could accomplish the necessary fundraising.[69]

Armed with the strong argument he sought from his allies, Meck succeeded in making the pitch at the June Trustees meeting a few days later. He issued a memo recapping the Trustees' executive committee vote to approve Holt's Ledge as the site and to acquire the land, to authorize the Dartmouth Development Council to launch a fundraising program with a goal of $100.000 to be completed by March 1, 1956, and to authorize $5,000 for an engineering study for trail design.[70] Discussions continued over the ensuing weeks about the best way to develop Holt's Ledge. Rand consulted with Stowe and Cannon Mountain as to their planning experience in developing their ski areas, and was advised neither of those mountains had formal plans in place before construction began. Influential ski instructor Sepp Ruschp came from Stowe for an inspection of the site in the fall of 1955. His letter and report back to Meck ended with the encouragement that he hoped the new ski area would go through, "after all, Dartmouth is the leading ski college in the East."[71] Howard Chivers was appointed as manager/supervisor in November 1955.

In true Dartmouth style, the fundraising campaign began and the old Dartmouth ski alumni were solicited often by their peers. Bob Monahan wrote a warm and collegial letter to his old classmate Harold Hirsch, by then the successful founder of White Stag skiwear. "Well, Hal," went Monahan's pitch, "the College is going all out to assure a satisfactory area for developing a higher degree of ski-proficiency among its undergraduates, who represent a continuing source of skiers for the world's ski centers – and customers for the best manufacturers of ski apparel in the country."[72] Those kinds of appeals went to many who had skied at Dartmouth.

But the college was also well aware of the community interest and pressure for Dartmouth to provide a public benefit when it came to skiing, as Dartmouth had so generously done for decades. The pitch to the community was packaged in a professionally designed prospectus title "The Long White Afternoons," borrowing an apt and familiar lyric from one of Dartmouth's favorite songs. Inside was a listing of some of Dartmouth's outstanding skiers who had come from the community: **Colin Stewart '48**, 1948 Olympian, the **Chivers brothers – Warren '38, Howard '39,** and **John '45** (among them four national titles and one Olympian), **Ed Meservey '38** and **Bob Meservey '43** (both national champions), **Ed Wells '39** (national champion) and his brother **Bob Wells '43, Ralph Miller '55, Ted Hunter '38** and **Linc Washburn '35** (all Olympians) and **Henry "Bem" Woods '36** (national champion). Dartmouth knew how to appeal to the town when it needed to, as well. The solicitation to Hanoverites concluded with: "Skiing today is linked inextricably with Dartmouth. Four undergraduate years at Hanover have opened up to many the delights of recreational skiing. Later, as alumni, these men discover that skiing is a sport for wives and children as well…Dartmouth families and friends who have turned to skiing as an activity in which the whole family can participate."[73]

Hanover resident, Polly Case, was the winner of the naming contest for the Skiway, and her prize was to be the first person to go up the lift.

Fundraising efforts successfully exceeded their goal with a total of $150,000, and the Skiway was built in the summer of 1956. **Francis "Dan" Drury '26**, a Thayer School of Engineering professor at Dartmouth, oversaw the installation of the Poma lift with assistance from the French lift inventor himself, Bernard Pomagalsky. Drury had previous lift installation experience with the construction of Mount Sunapee ski area. The original base lodge was named for **Peter Brundage '45**, a former Director of the DOC Winter Sports Council and a World War II casualty. The lifts opened for skiing on December 15, 1956. They were subsequently dedicated on January 12, 1957 with a grand party of skiing and Dartmouth celebrities which included **Dartmouth President John Sloan Dickey '29, Trustee John R. McLane '07, Fred Harris '11, DOC Director John Rand '38, Dartmouth Olympians Chick Igaya '57, Tom Corcoran '54, Brooks Dodge '50,** and **Ralph Miller, Jr. '55** and the new Dartmouth Skiway manager **Howard Chivers '39**. All was well in the Dartmouth ski world – briefly.

Opening Day at the Dartmouth Skiway: (l. to r.) Meck '33, Harris '11, President Dickey '29, Rand '38 and Tobey '27 (1957)

During the preliminary jockeying for trustee approval and the rush of planning that ensued with the go-ahead, John Rand wrote a letter to fellow alumnus **Robert Brace '52** about the future of Dartmouth skiing. "I would be the last in the world to predict that this is or will be the final step in the Dartmouth ski program. I hope that we do not become that static."[74] Static it would not be. Only a month into operations, the Skiway was suffering from a lack of snow with the added insult of lift problems. The mechanical lift problems were overcome; the lack of snow would intermittently plague Skiway operations for years.

Al Merrill, the new ski coach for 1958, enjoyed a national championship year in his first season, but it wasn't long before he was chafing at the bit for more development at the Skiway. He submitted a report at the end of the 1961 season recommending development of Winslow Hill. His idea sat on the backburners of Parkhurst Hall for several years until John Meck

presented the College Trustees with a proposal to complete the development of the Skiway by adding skiable terrain on Winslow Hill in March 1967.[75] It went nowhere. Ever forward-looking, Meck inquired about snowmaking that same year, inspired perhaps by Merrill's recommendation for Skiway snowmaking in his Report of the Competitive Skiing Program at Dartmouth.[76] In the meantime Chivers and the Skiway crews did their best with lean years of snowfall. 1973-74 was one of those winters lacking natural snowfall. The impact on Dartmouth was widespread. Day after day that winter *The Dartmouth* ran a display ad that read simply "THINK SNOW." When it came time for Winter Carnival, the unskiable Skiway conditions forced the DOC to move all of the ski events to Waterville Valley, New Hampshire, where there was snowmaking.[77] This would not be the last time Carnival skiing would have to relocate for lack of snow at the Skiway. This was just one of the costs associated with not installing snowmaking. The Hanover Inn, for one, complained of the impact poor ski conditions had on their winter business.[78] Grooming could not make up for that skiing essential, and in the 1979-80 season they were only able to operate four days, even after the College had finally hired consultants to conduct a feasibility study of snowmaking. Of course cost was the key limitation for overcoming this natural handicap. Meck had already quietly set aside a fund for when the time came to add snowmaking at the Skiway.

Such help couldn't come fast enough when **Earl Jette** passed along a New Hampshire Alpine Racing Association ruling at the start of the 1978-79 season that refused to schedule USSA Class A or B races at any area without snowmaking. That news "came as a shock" to Merrill, who replied, "considering Dartmouth's rich heritage in the sport of skiing, it is somewhat humiliating to be told that we can no longer sponsor races for the better skiers."[79] **John Morton** had replaced Merrill as the head ski coach when Merrill moved up to the new position of Director of Outdoor Affairs overseeing all of the College's outdoor programs. They continued discussing the lack of snowmaking with each other and their frustration with the college's refusal of an offer from ski team parents to fund snowmaking. Newly arrived, Morton was in disbelief at the College turning down such an offer, of such a failure to cooperate.

Morton's frustration festered until surfacing again two years later in a report to Professor **Jere**

Daniell '55, chairman of the Dartmouth College Athletic Council Facilities Study Committee, in which Morton commented, "the one aspect that separates Dartmouth from the other Ivy League institutions is its traditional ties to the Northland…only Dartmouth has its own ski area, incomparable cross-country skiing within walking distance of campus, and a historic ski jump. It seems obvious to me that we should concentrate on and emphasize what we do best, namely skiing. There should be no educational institution in the world equal to Dartmouth in its ability to combine top notch academics with national and international class ski racing."[80] By 1984, Middlebury, Morton's alma mater had installed snowmaking at the Snow Bowl.

The 1984-85 season was the year the ski team had no home. The need for snowmaking at the Skiway was critical. With the College about to build a new multi-million dollar gymnasium, skiers were confounded at the lack of administrative enthusiasm for snowmaking. To the unthinkable prospect of giving up control of the Skiway by leasing it, those closest to the skiing program could now think of such a travesty. Morton dared say: "philosophically it strikes me as an erosion of Dartmouth's once famous reputation as a leader and innovator in the skiing world. However, if the only feasible method of installing snowmaking is leasing the Skiway, then it must be leased, because there is no future for the Skiway without snowmaking."[81]

At the 1985 Men's Ski Team banquet held at Pierce's Inn, a nostalgic little '40s vintage ski hill in Etna, New Hampshire, ski team parent and ski area developer George Macomber presented a check for $100,000 to **Dartmouth President David McLaughlin '54** as a first pledge toward Skiway snowmaking. The Trustees' Budget Committee quickly approved a proposal from **College Vice President Paul Paganucci '53** to "invest in the Skiway or close it. While closing the Skiway is an option, we are influenced by our difficulty to imagine Dartmouth without it."[82] Assignments were issued for the

President McLaughlin led the charge to add snowmaking to the Skiway.

fundraising necessary. Al Merrill took the Friends of Dartmouth Skiers as his assignment, while Jane Chivers, Howard's widow, took the local community pool of donors. Just weeks before the deadline, they were still short of the goal by almost $170,000. A phone call from Alaska to the Development Office was soon followed by a check for the balance from **Lowell Thomas, Jr. '46**. Snowmaking was installed in December 1985 at the Dartmouth Skiway, one of the last New England ski areas to add what had become as essential as lifts for successful operation.

Paul Paganucci proposed that the Trustees provide further support for the Skiway.

The 1955 note to the Trustees Planning Committee that the slope opposite Holt's Ledge, known as Winslow Hill presented "a possibility for subsequent development" was finally revisited after the installation of snowmaking assured the area's future. In 1993 Dartmouth cut new slopes and installed a quad lift on Winslow to mirror the original layout across the valley floor on Holt's Ledge. In 1999, Dartmouth undertook another major renovation by upgrading the original base lodge with a complete new rebuild that quadrupled the size of the former Brundage base lodge. That project captured the attention of one of Dartmouth's historic skiing dynasties, the McLane family. **Andy McLane '69**, son of **Peter McLane '37** and member of the McLane family that included **Charles '41** and **Malcolm '46** as well as Dartmouth Trustee and early Skiway advocate **John R. McLane, Class of 1907**, along with numerous other third generation McLanes of Dartmouth skiing note, made a generous gift to lead the new base lodge construction. At its completion in the winter of 2000-2001, it included a tribute to all of the Dartmouth veterans of the 10th Mountain Division. And now a fourth generation of the McLane family are competing at the Skiway.

Finally, nearly another quarter century after the long struggle to add the first snowmaking system to the Skiway, another Dartmouth family's philanthropy made a significant expansion of that system possible. Four Dartmouth sisters from **the Dupré family– Denise '80, Rosi '82, Anni '83,** and **Michele '88**

Dupré–made a gift in honor of their father Herman Dupré, an early entrepreneur and pioneer in snow-making technology. Their gift provided expansion that effectively tripled the capacity the original snow-making installation at the Skiway while also improving its efficiency. In tribute Dartmouth named one of the trails on the Winslow side of the Skiway as Herman's Highway. Dartmouth President James Wright acknowledged their gift by saying that it would "not only recognize Herman Dupré's groundbreaking contributions to the ski industry but will benefit skiers at Dartmouth and in our surrounding communities for years to come."[83]

The long discussions over the development of ski facilities at Dartmouth have always involved the community as well as the college. It has always been the college's role to take the lead and to manage the process, but the many contributing members of the community were needed to make things happen. And the results of the efforts have always provided benefits to both.

In the history of facility improvements, one change stands out not for its long-term success at Dartmouth but as a very important step in the development process for skiing in the United States. This was the creation of the first overhead cable J-bar ski lift in the United States at Oak Hill. As has been outlined before, Oak Hill did not work out as the best of ski areas, and it no longer functions as one. However, this first lift was to be the beginning of rapid lift developments across the United States as it served the important purpose of showing the days of climbing up a mountain as opposed to being assisted up the hill mechanically were on their way out. And importantly, it was achieved at Dartmouth where the students and alumni would quickly spread the word across the ski world that this was the new way to go.

***

OAK HILL: THE FIRST NORTH AMERICAN OVERHEAD CABLE SKI LIFT

By Clark Griffiths '57, Th '58

The Rauner Special Collections Library has an amazing collection of historical information on almost any topic associated with Dartmouth. A search for Oak Hill information yielded a full carton of files, some not looked at for decades, and I was able to scan around 75 useful documents in trying to verify some of the rumors that exist about the origin and history of Oak Hill's ski lift.

The January 7, 1955 issue of *The Dartmouth*, a student-published newspaper, highlighted many of the key points in the evolution of this lift which was in operation from 1936 through 1977. The design of the "J-Bar" hangers as noted in the article were modeled after those of a banana-sack conveyer but replacing the sharp hooks with smooth padded ash bars. While the Oak Hill lift was the first to use this technology in the U.S., a photo with a very minimal view of a similar lift in Davos, Switzerland, built prior to the Oak Hill lift, is in these documents

THE DARTMOUTH, Jan. 7, 1955

Oak Hill Observes 20 Years As The Nation's First Tow

OAK HILL, the nation's first ski tow, celebrates its twentieth anniversary with its opening this week. The tow services four trails and three slopes of moderate difficulty.

This 1955 news story in The Dartmouth recounts the Oak Hill achievement.

and was seen by **Dan Hatch**, Director of the DOC, who reasoned that the concept should work just as well here.

Having arrived at Dartmouth in 1953, I can recall riding on this lift many times –much easier than hanging on to a rope tow. The basic J-bar design was used for the entire life of the lift and is shown below.

By the mid-forties, other lift designs were already in operation elsewhere, but the only other uphill transportation Dartmouth had at that time was the rope tow on the golf course ski area.

After graduating from Thayer Engineering School in 1958, I elected to join what was then a small plant in Lebanon called Split Ballbearing. I had the pleasure of working there for 35 years and retired as Head of Engineering with just under 900 employees. What I never knew was that Split Ballbearing received the contract to build—and either obtained or fabricated the components for—the Oak Hill lift and constructed it for the Outing Club in 1935 according to agreed upon specifications. The specific contract called for a payment of $2,298 to cover the cost of creating something no one had made in this country before. How inexpensive can you get??

Split Ballbearing, over the next five years or so, did additional maintenance work on the lift, replaced the motor and gearbox, and suggested safety improvements, including adding extra towers at the top to prevent injury should the cable derail from the single wheel.

Another interesting facet of the project is that on October 29, 1935, Dan Hatch, sent a letter to Constam, the firm that had designed the lift in Davos, to ask for possible support of the design that was to be built by Split Ballbearing. At the time, it was not known by Hatch that Constam held a Swiss patent (issued August 17, 1934) that incorporated a number of key design features including the "J bar." Constam filed this patent in the US Patent Office on February 21, 1935, and it was eventually issued as US patent #2,087,232 on July 20, 1937.

Constam responded to Hatch informing him that a patent did exist and had been submitted for approval in the U.S. Hatch replied that he did not want to duplicate the lift but only to adapt some of its features, presumably hoping that the issue would go away. Receiving no further response from Constam, Hatch went ahead with his plans to build the Oak Hill ski lift. Subsequently, a partner of Constam visited the U.S. and sent a letter to **J. Wilcox Brown**

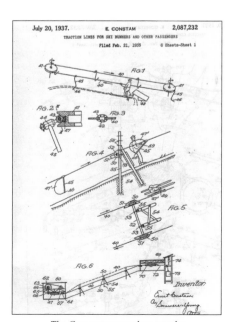
The Constam patent lays out the overhead cable system (1937).

(then Director of the DOC) dated April 8, 1939, which describes this sequence of correspondence and requested a one-time payment of either $500 (with no technical support being provided to Dartmouth) or $1000 (to include further design support) to resolve the potential patent infringement issue.

Following receipt of this letter, Wilcox Brown solicited support from **Judge John McLane '07** in Manchester and also from American Steel and Wire Co. who supplied the cable for the Oak Hill lift. The issue was finally settled on January 27, 1941, when the DOC agreed on a $450 payment to Constam. By this time, Ernst Constam was visiting the U.S. and selling his technology to other ski areas including Pico Peak, Vermont, which used the same basic design but replaced the J bar with a T. However, there was never any question that Oak Hill was this nation's first overhead lift.

A rider beginning the trip on the J-bar.

In 1958, five of the ten original wood towers were replaced and 60 new J-bars were added with new cable clamps. Oak Hill never did change to a double-occupancy T-bar design.

Significantly, a Poma Lift was installed at the new Dartmouth Skiway in 1955-56. This facility attracted the better skiers by offering greater vertical and trail length as well as faster uphill speed. Over the next 20 years

The main drive for the Oak Hill Lift.

attendance at Oak Hill declined. As a result, **Rod Morgan**, Vice President for Administration of the College, issued a long note in July of 1977 advising that due to high annual losses (as high as $8000), the lift would be closed down and the savings would be used to help replace the Skiway Poma with a new double chair.

The early creation of an important ski jump; the use of rope tow and lights on the early golf course hill; the creation of major downhill facilities at Mt. Moosilauke; the creation of the first overhead cable lift at Oak Hill; and finally the slow development of the Dartmouth Skiway to be a modestly significant ski area have been a sequence of important developments that added to the image of Dartmouth College as a leader in skiing developments. Time will tell what the next significant facility change is to be.

THE SKI BULLETIN

HANOVER'S SKI TRAMWAY

Probably of greatest general interest to skiers is the new ski tramway that nears completion on Oak Hill, Hanover, N. H. The new tramway is a remarkable achievement and represents a considerable investment that called for enthusiastic faith in the sport on the part of the Dartmouth Outing Club, and on the part of the Trustees of the College who have backed the project. It is the result of much earnest spade work by Professor Ames, by John Piane '14, other members of the community, and the Club officers.

And on January 1 Dartmouth and Hanover will have not the usual ski tow, but a ski TRAMWAY. It is the distinction between a ski tow and a ski tramway that makes the Oak Hill development significant. For although there are going to be eight or more ski tows in New England, the Outing Club has constructed the only ski tramway on the North American continent, in fact, one of the two ski tramways in the entire ski world.

The D. O. C.'s new tramway is dependable, mechanically well designed and well powered. At the bottom of the tramway a 1,600 pound drive-wheel powered by an 80 H. P. Ford V-8 motor gives the steel cable motion. Some of the more interesting facts about the tramway are: from top to bottom the difference in elevation is 350 feet. It takes approximately one-half a mile of cable to complete the loop. It will only take two minutes to travel from bottom to top at an average speed of six or seven miles an hour. At the top a 7000 pound counterweight holds the half mile of cable taut and compensates for the weight of 600 skiers per hour that the tramway is capable of conveying. The ride you will get measures 1200 feet and all you have to do is hold onto safe, convenient handles that will hang waist high down from the steel cable itself. It will be possible to leave the tramway at any desired height.

· Hanover Gazette.

Ski Bulletin outlines Oak Hill Tramway in Hanover.

INTERACTIONS WITH THE SKIING PREP SCHOOLS

One of the great sources of skiers for Dartmouth and other New England ski colleges has been the prep school community in the region. They have enjoyed the same outdoor activities that Dartmouth students have for many decades. As academic centers as well as sports oriented institutions, a number of them share the same basic interests as Dartmouth College. This has led to many interesting interactions. The story below by Mike Choukas, Jr. will provide a summary of these interactions. The second story, by Phil Peck, will provide further details to highlight Dartmouth's continuing involvement with one of these schools, the Holderness School.

***

THE PREP SCHOOLS: CRADLES OF SKIING EXCELLENCE

By Michael Choukas, Jr '51

Dartmouth's impact on the North American ski world was helped considerably by the infusion of accomplished skiers who flowed in from the preparatory schools of northern New England. In particular, in the order of their founding, Kimball Union Academy, Proctor Academy, The Holderness School, and Vermont Academy provided a steady stream of young men already honed by four-event tournament competition. And as each school became coeducational in the 1970s young women joined that stream. In addition, the Putney School was a perennial power in cross-country skiing due exclusively to the tutelage of **John Caldwell '50**.

Those first mentioned were the Big Four of the New England skiing secondary Independent School world, and it was no accident that they were well versed in the sport of skiing. They were uniquely located near the relatively few ski areas in the Twin States. Three of their headmasters were Dartmouth alumni: **Fred Carver '27** (Kimball Union), **Don Hagerman '35** (Holderness), and **Larry Leavitt '25** (Vermont Academy), and they needed no convincing of the value of skiing to their respective campuses.

Kimball Union Academy (KUA) had a flow of students go on to ski for Dartmouth and, in return, a long line of Dartmouth alumni helped coach skiing at KUA. Olympic skier and jumping judge **Dave Bradley '38** helped coach jumpers a couple of years, and the captain of Dartmouth's 1959 team, **Dick Taylor '59**, helped coach in 1963. Additionally, **John Clough '45, John Donaghy '75, Jonathan Davie '76, Anne Donaghy '85, Tove Stigum '88, Richard Nichols '89, Kimberly Lewis '90, Cary Roseth '94**, and **Marilyn (Morano) Lord '95** all coached for varying lengths of time. There were also a number of KUA skiers who skied for Dartmouth starting with **Ja Densmore '44** who not only skied for Dartmouth but coached there for a couple of years while Walter Prager was in the Army. **Wilbur Bull '46, John Fairbanks '46, Seward "Pat" Brewster '50, Ed Post '51, Jim Cooke '52, Jim Branch '52, Jim Oberlander '53, Phil Cooke '54, Roger Brown '57**, and **John Stowell '61** all skied for Dartmouth.

Proctor Academy also began its ski program in the 1930s. **Roland "Ro" Burbank '33**, joined the Proctor faculty as a science instructor right out of college. He had learned his skiing under Otto Schniebs at Dartmouth and he started Proctor's ski program not only coaching the team but also developing ski hills, building a jump and building and installing a rope tow. "Ro" went on to be Headmaster at Cardigan Mountain School where he continued his lifelong love of outdoor activities. And Bob Beattie, former head of the US Alpine Team, a driving force behind the pro circuit and later a longtime ski racing television commentator, honed his own skiing skills as a student at Proctor in 1951.

Holderness, meanwhile, was quickly becoming a prep ski power under Don Hagerman's administration. He hired Don Henderson, a Middlebury great, to coach the ski team and Don turned out lots of top skiers, many of whom skied for Dartmouth and some who went on to be Olympic skiers. In turn, a number of Dartmouth alumni coached at Holderness following graduation. **Don Hagen '41, Jim Page '63, George Perry '72, Donnie Cutter '73, John**

Mott '75, Belle Traver '83, and **Kevin Omland '86** all skied for Dartmouth and coached at Holderness. And the current Headmaster, **Phil Peck '77**, Assistant Headmaster **Jory Macomber '85**, and **Academic Dean Peter Durnan '85** are former Dartmouth skiers. Some of the Holderness skiers who went on to ski at Dartmouth are **Dick Taylor '59, Charlie Kellogg '62, Harold Welch '63, Chris Palmer '64, Adrian "Skip" Bryan '66, Ned Gillette '67, Peter Anderson '76, Walter Malmquist '78, Kirk Siegle '82, Nancy Lane '87, Peggy Lamb '87, Kathleen Corcoran '87, Eva Pfosi '88, Ian Harvey '91, Carl Swenson '92, Christopher "Chip" Martin '92**, and **Andy Martin '92**.

Vermont Academy lays claim to holding the first school Winter Carnival. Their Assistant Headmaster, James Taylor, who later started Vermont's Long Trail, organized a winter sports competition on Lincoln's Birthday in 1909. **Fred Harris '11** and a couple of other Dartmouth students later came down to the VA campus to find out more about the event prior to starting Dartmouth's famed Carnival the next year.

Larry Leavitt became Headmaster of Vermont Academy in the fall of 1934 and immediately hired a Dartmouth graduate, **Ted Gregory '34**, to coach the ski team. Two brothers on his teams, **Amos "Bud" Little '39** and **Edward "Spif" Little '41**, skied for Dartmouth. Bud, a physician, later gained fame as "The Flying Doctor of the Rockies" for his daring parachute rescues of stranded skiers in need of medical attention. Ted Gregory was followed later in the decade by **Warren Chivers '38**, an Olympian and national champion, who coached skiing from 1939 to 1975 and continued as Director of Skiing until his retirement in 1996. Another Dartmouth skier who coached skiing at Vermont Academy in the years following Warren's retirement was **Tim Caldwell '76**, the son of Putney's John Caldwell. **Don Cutter '45**, who later managed Okemo and was instrumental in the design of The Dartmouth Skiway, skied for Warren. There were other skiers developed by Chivers who later skied for Dartmouth. **Ray Colby '43, Phil Booth '47, Bob Burton '57, Mal Hibbard '58, Peter Burton '59**, and **Jay Pedley '59** all wore the Green.

Other notable Vermont Academy skiers coached by Warren were Olympians Mike Gallagher (Nordic), Wayne Fleming (Biathlon), Dick Leatherbee (a Chilean national champion and member of the Chile Olympic team in Grenoble in 1968), and

Marty Hall who coached both US and Canadian Nordic teams. Another, C. B. Vaughan, was holder of the world's fastest skier title (after **Ralph Miller '55**). Others were Harry Brown who was Director of the Eastern Nordic Program, and Hank Tauber, President of Marker International, of ski binding fame.

Various other New England prep schools also benefited from the coaching of Dartmouth alumni and, in turn, sent their skiers to Dartmouth as the sport expanded and its most dedicated athletes proliferated over the ensuing years.

***

THE DARTMOUTH/HOLDERNESS COACHING CONNECTION

By By R. Phillip Peck '77

Looking at Holderness School today, the Dartmouth skiing connection is a behind-the-scenes leadership story. Academic Dean, **Peter Durnan '85**, the Assistant Headmaster, **Jory Macomber '85**, and the Headmaster, **Phil Peck '77**, are all former Dartmouth skiers. For all of us, especially Jory and Phil, skiing was the hook that brought us to Holderness. We were looking to work with motivated kids in the classroom who were also national caliber skiers.

That said, Jory, Peter, and I were merely emulating a long line of role models, mentors, and friends who followed a similar trajectory from Dartmouth to Holderness. This pattern started with **Jim Page '63** (Captain, All-American, and Olympian), who came to Holderness in 1966 and stayed through 1972. He taught history, coached skiing, and ran a dorm. Page went from Holderness to be the head coach at Dartmouth and then Nordic Director for the US program. Coincidentally, he taught and coached the same courses that **John Mott '81** (Captain and All American) did at Holderness. In 1984, Phil Peck left his position as the Assistant Men's World Cup and Olympics coach to come to Holderness to replace John Mott.

While Jim Page was at Holderness, he mentored two young Dartmouth graduates, **George Perry '72** and **Don Cutter '73**, both of whom taught and coached at Holderness for a few years in the early 1970s. Then in the 1980s we enjoyed having **Belle Traver '83** and **Kevin Omland '86**, both for two years each. Jory Macomber, a three-time All-American and Captain of the Dartmouth Team, arrived at Holderness the first time in 1985 for three years. He returned in 1992 with his wife, **Martha Macomber '86**, and has been teaching history and coaching skiing since then. In 2007, still teaching and coaching, he became the Assistant Headmaster. In that same year, Holderness alumna **Sophia Schwarz '13** placed second at the US Freestyle Championships. Peter Durnan, now our Academic Dean, rekindled his love for skiing while at Holderness and continues to coach the Nordic program. The school's most recent promising prospect for skiing glory is Julia Ford, who was named to the US Women's Alpine Development Team in June 2009.

The school remains thankful to a Middlebury graduate, Don Henderson, who was brought to Holderness by **Don Hagerman '35** in 1951 to teach history and to create a national caliber ski program. In

Holderness Headmaster Phil Peck '77 (top) and Asst Headmaster George "Jory" Macomber '85 (bottom) in their racing days when both were D Ski Team Captains.

addition to mentoring generations of teachers and coaches, several of whom are still at Holderness today, Don also directly and indirectly nurtured and inspired generations of students who went on to achieve great success at Dartmouth and beyond. Most of these Holderness skiers noted here, and in the article above, achieved All America, national team, or captain of team status; their assorted successes as skiers and as students are relevant measures of the quality of teaching both on and off the slopes, both at Holderness and at Dartmouth.

SUMMARY

Throughout this review of DOC-related influences on others in Hanover, the New England Region, and elsewhere, we see the constant enthusiastic interactions—of Dartmouth as an institution with its students, its staff and their families, and with many others having an interest in skiing—that have ended up improving skiing both in this region and elsewhere. The Dartmouth/Hanover ski clubs, Winter Carnival posters and movies, the competitive activities for children and women, the early availability of ski instruction and the existence of a Safety Patrol, the evolving ski facilities, and the interactions with the nearby prep schools all played a role… and they continue to play a role in the development of skiing. Central to all of this is the Dartmouth Outing Club, its many supporters, and the enthusiasm they generate for all things involving skiing. This enthusiasm for skiing is the key reason for Dartmouth-connected individuals having contributed so much over the past 100 years to the development of modern skiing. As long as this enthusiasm continues to permeate so many from this community, Dartmouth will remain as the institutional leader for this sport.

Notes

1. Letter, Harris to Briggs, 27 Apr 1920, Rauner, DOC Collection, Box 2, File 38. 2. Letter, Hatch to Hicks, 3 Jun 1935, Rauner, DOC Collection, Box 2, File 38. 3. Report of the Faculty Committee of the DOC 1932-33, Rauner, DOC Collection, Box 3, File 43. 4. Hatch, Memo, Dartmouth Ski Development, 27 Mar 1936, Rauner, DOC Collection, Box 3, File 5. 5. Letter, Hatch to Elmer, Rauner, DOC Collection, Box 2, File 36, 19 Sep 1936. 6. Ibid, Box 2, File 26, 21 Sep 1936. 7. *The Aegis 1939*, p 85. 8. Winter Sports Committee Minutes, 15 Feb 1938, Rauner, DOC Collection, Box 7, File 3. 9. *Op. cit.* p 86. 10. *Op. cit.*, 20 Apr 1937, Rauner, DOC Collection, Box 7, File 3. 11. Letter, Hatch to C.N. Proctor, 25 Jun 1937, Rauner, DOC Collection, Box 55, File 34. 12. *The Dartmouth,* 27 May 1935, 6. 13. Rauner Special Collections, DO-1, Outing Club, Box 6, File 14, "Minutes of the Meetings of the Carnival Committee of the 26ᵗʰ Annual Carnival," 23 May 1935. 14. http://www.mtu.edu/carnival/history. 15. *Dartmouth Outing Club Annual Report*, June 1930, 23. 16. Letter, J. Dwight Francis to Natalie Hoyt, 28 Oct 1931, copy from collection of E. John B. Allen. 17. *Dartmouth Out O'Doors 1932*, 10. 18. *The Ski Bulletin*, 5 Jan 1934, 5. 19. Ibid, 16 Mar 1934, 6. 20. Rauner Special Collections, DO-1, Outing Club, Box 53, File 43. Ski Meet Results 1933-1934. 21. *The Hanover Gazette*, 1 Mar 1917, 1. 22. Ibid, 18 February 1933, 1. 23. *The Hanover Gazette,* 16 Jan 1936, 1. 24. *The Dartmouth*, 7 Feb 1936, 1. 25. Letter from Bill Rotch to Andy McLane, 2008. 26. Ibid, 8 Feb 1936, 1. 27. *Aegis 1936*, 84. 28. Op. cit., 10 Feb 1936, 1. 29. Ibid, 5 Feb 1937, 1. 30. Ibid, 6 Feb 1937, 1. 31. Ibid, 12 Feb 1938, 1. 32. Ibid, 10 Feb 1940, 1. 33. *Aegis 1940*, 69. 34. Op. cit., 12 Feb 1940, 1. 35. Ibid, 8 Feb 1941, 9. 36. Ibid, 29 Jan 1948, 1. 37. *American Ski Annual, 1939-1940,* Auell, Harriette, "Smith College 'Shees'," 77. 38. Johnston, John LeRoy, Profile: Looking at Walter Wanger Film Producer, February 15, 1940, pp. 2-8. 39. Univ of Delaware Library, Special Collections Dept, Walter Wanger Papers, home page, http://www.lib.udel.edu/ud/spec/findaids/wanger.htm. 40. Ibid. 41. Ford, Corey, "Echoes that Old Refrain", Saturday Evening Post, 5/29/1937, Vol. 209, Issue 48, pp 10-11, 86, 88, & 90. 42. In 2005, a magnificent and mostly privately funded clubhouse for the men's and women's rugby teams, built on property Corey Ford bequeathed to the college, was formally dedicated and named for him. 43. Reach the Peak by David Hooke P. 269. 44. Ibid, P. 261. 45. Fred Harris Diaries, 1904-1911, entries for 15 Dec 1909 and 16 Jan 1910. 46. Skiing Over the New Hampshire Hills," Fred H. Harris, *National Geographic*, February 1920. 47. DOC Council Minutes, 19 Apr 1922, Rauner, DOC Collection, Box 50, File 1. 48. Dartmouth Out O' Doors 1932, 10. 49. Letter, Schniebs to McCrillis, 16 May 1933, NESM, L1999.14.3a. 50. Ibid, 29 May 1933, NESM, L1999.14.3a. 51. "An Argument for the Installation of an Aerial Tramway at Kinsman Notch, NH," Prepared by the DOC, July 1934, 13, Rauner, DOC Collection, Box 1, File 22. 52. "The Dartmouth Ski Development," Memorandum, D.P. Hatch, 27 Mar 1936, Rauner, DOC Collection, Box 2, File 36. 53. "Dartmouth at Moosilauke", prospectus, 30 Jan 1936, accompanying letter, N. Emerson to McCrillis, 8 Aug 1936, NESM, L1999.14.1.5. 54. DOC Trustees Minutes, 5 Feb 1938, Rauner, DOC Collection, Box 7, File 3. 55. "A Plan for Developing Ski Terrain with Ski Tows at Hanover," Rauner, DOC Collection, Box 16, File 16. 56. "Report of the Faculty Committee on the Outing Club," 1935, Rauner, DOC Collection, Box 2, File 36. 57. Letter, Hopkins to Hatch, 3 May 1935, Rauner, DOC Collection, Box 16, File 16. 58. Ibid, Box 2, File 42. 59. Ibid, 18 July 1935, Box 2, File 42. 60. DOC Trustees Minutes, 11 Jun 1936, Rauner, DOC Collection, Box 50, File 4. 61. "The Dartmouth Ski Development," Memorandum, D.P. Hatch, 27 Mar 1936, Rauner, DOC Collection, Box 2, File 36. 62. DOC Trustees Minutes, 19 Feb 1946, Rauner, DOC Collection, Box 6, File 34. 63. "Development of Adequate Skiing Facilities for Dartmouth Students in Hanover Area," Memorandum, 8 April 1955, Subcommittee on Skiing to Trustees Planning Comm, Rauner, DOC Collection, Box 16, File 17. 64. "Middlebury and Mad River Skiing Facilities," Memo, Meck to Subcommittee on Skiing, 22 Mar 1955, Rauner, DOC Collection, Box 16, File 17. 65. Op. cit. 66. "Development of Adequate Skiing Facilities for Dartmouth Students in Hanover Area," Memorandum, 8 April 1955, Subcommittee on Skiing to Trustees Planning Comm, Rauner, DOC Collection, Box 16, File 17 (Op. cit.?). 67. "Proposed Ski Facilities." Memo, Meck to Rand, Prager, and Hayward, 6 Jun 1955, Rauner, DOC Collection, Box 16, File 17. 68. Letter, Rand to Meck, 7 Jun 1955, Rauner, DOC Collection, Box 16, File 17. 69. Ibid. 70. Ski Facility, Memo, Meck to Rand, Prager, Hayward, et. al., 11 Jun 1955, Rauner, DOC Collection, Box 16, File 17. 71. Letter, Ruschp to Meck, 18 Nov 1955, Rauner, DOC Collection, Box 16, File 17. 72. Letter, Monahan to Hirsch, 8 Dec 1955, Rauner, DOC Collection, Box 16, File 17. 73. "The Long White Afternoons…," undated fundraising brochure (1955?), Rauner, DOC Collection, Box 16, File 18. 74. Letter, Rand to Brace, 13 June 1955, Rauner, DOC Collection, Box 16,

THE DARTMOUTH SKIING WALL OF FAME
AT THE McLANE LODGE, DARTMOUTH SKIWAY

Dartmouth's commitment to and support for individual excellence is well represented by the accomplishments of its skiers in national championship competitions. On this Wall of Fame are the names of many of the Big Green skiers who have won 34 NCAA, 18 Biathlon, more than 60 Paralympic and some 110 USSA National Championships.

Chapter III Notes Continued...
File 17. 75. "Dartmouth Skiway, Completion of Winslow Hill Development," Report to Trustees Executive Comm, 28 Mar 1967, Al Merrill, in *Skiway, A Dartmouth Winter Tale*, Everett W. Wood, Dartmouth College, 1977. (check publication date). 76. "Report on The Competitive Skiing Program at Dartmouth," 1967, C. Allison Merrill, Rauner, DOC Collection, Box 55, File 23. 77. *The Dartmouth*, Feb 1974. 78. Ibid. 79. "Sponsoring Alpine Ski Races," Memo, Jette to Merrill. 20 Jan 1979, Rauner, DOC Collection, Box 55, File 7. 80. Memo, Morton to Daniell, 9 Feb 1982, Rauner, DOC Collection, Box 55, File 7. 81. quoted in *Skiway*, Wood. 82. Ibid. 83. "Dupre gift funds major snowmaking upgrade," *Dartmouth News*, 5 Dec 2008.

CHAPTER IV

SKI RACING – COLLEGIATE, OLYMPICS, PARALYMPICS, OTHER

By Jim Page '63

Former Dartmouth Ski Team Captain & Coach, Olympic Skier, Coach and Administrator

With William E. Smith, M.D. '58, R. Phillip Peck '77, Mary Kendall Brown '78, Stephen L. Waterhouse,
Morten Lund, Tom Corcoran '54

The Dartmouth Outing Club (DOC) was not founded to provide a home for the college's ski racing program but that was certainly one of the fortunate outcomes. The club's social and philosophical orientation, which embraced individual initiative and commitment, allowed the ski team to adopt a broad program of ski racing that, on the one hand, produced highly competitive Nordic and Alpine teams and, on the other, inspired individual excellence at all levels of recreational skiing as well as developmental programs for would-be competitors.

Racing over snow and ice began almost immediately as one of the first organized activities of the DOC. Intercollegiate ski competition got its start in 1914 when Dartmouth accepted an invitation to participate in the McGill University Winter Festival; subsequently, the first intercollegiate ski team competition in the US was run at Dartmouth in 1915. Ever since, the Dartmouth Ski Team has been the college's most successful athletic program.

DARTMOUTH SKI TEAM PERFORMANCES

The Winter Carnival Cup, presented for the first time in 1922, has been awarded every year since then—a total of 87 times. Dartmouth has etched its name on that coveted silver vase on 37 of those occasions.[1] Hundreds of Dartmouth skiers have donned their forest green winter skiing uniform to race between the flags on Oak Hill and the Skiway, to ski across the trails on the Hanover golf course and behind Oak Hill, or to launch themselves off the ski jump at Vale de Tempe to represent the college in this granddaddy of the Eastern Winter Carnival circuit. And no group of skiers from any other college has ever done it better. An equally prestigious trophy, The Dartmouth Winter Cup, is presented after the Eastern Intercollegiate Ski Championships each year, usually at the Middlebury College Carnival, and has been won by Dartmouth 29 times in its 82-year history, leading the list of the winners of that competition as well.[2]

At the NCAA Championships, the traditional measure of top athletic programs in every collegiate sport, the Big Green team has achieved an amazing record. Dartmouth has competed in 54 of the 56 NCAA ski championships, more than any other college. The ski team won the event three times (1958, 1976 and 2007) and has finished in the top five 33 times, nearly two out of every three times it has entered the competition. D Skiers have only finished below eighth place twice since the first official championship in 1954.[3]

The Women's Ski Team, which began in 1972 with the admission of the first class of women at Dartmouth, has been as successful as the men, winning the Association of Intercollegiate Athletics for Women (AIAW) Championships in 1977, its first official year, and finishing among the top five women's programs every year until the program merged into the joint Men's and Women's NCAA Skiing Championship in 1983.

For each of the four National Championship teams mentioned above, a detailed summary has been provided at the end of this chapter which offers a look at the skiers, the coaches, and the times--an interesting window into team skiing at Dartmouth. Each championship team had its own special character, whether because of its differing mix of events and genders, whether because of being considered the favorite or the underdog, or whether because of its rare concentration of exceptional individual skiers or a concerted effort by every member of the team to peak when it counted most. Written largely by those who actually participated, these accounts chronicle the emotion and the excellence of all those involved and allow us to see the excitement of each event through their eyes. But to better appreciate how these teams worked their way to the top, it helps to understand the legacy they wanted to live up to and the program that helped them do so.

DARTMOUTH'S NATIONAL CHAMPIONS

Over the past 76 years or so, Dartmouth College has provided a long list of National Champions starting with the first Downhill Champion in 1933.

The first ever US National Downhill Ski Champion, "Bem" Woods '36 (National Downhill run on Mt. Moosilauke, 1933).

Dick Durrance '39, winner of 21 National Championship-style races in Slalom, Downhill, Alpine, Alpine Combined, X-C and Ski Jumping (1937-39)

Colin Stewart '48, ISU National Alpine Champ (1948).

Bill Smith '58, National Downhill Champion (1958).

Ed Williams '64, National Cross Country Champion (1963).

Tim Caldwell '76 trained tirelessly to achieve his 8 National X-C Championships (1973-82).

Liz McIntyre '87 Free Style Moguls National Champion (1998).

Carl Swenson '92, 11-time National X-C Champion (1994-2004).

David Chodounsky '08, National Slalom Champion (2009).

DARTMOUTH SKIERS

Dartmouth College ski racing is far more than a summary of its intercollegiate record. It is just as much a look at a unique philosophy of skiing that attracted neophytes and national teamers to the same program, at the same time, under the aegis of an exceptionally supportive Outing Club. It's the compelling story of young men and women who came to Hanover, trained and competed together, found companionship on the team and individual excellence on the ski slopes, and gave back to the college an amazing record of success.

The stated mission of the Dartmouth College Ski Team is "…to enable Dartmouth student-athletes to develop as individuals and achieve excellence in ski racing at all levels…(and) to maintain a position of pre-eminence in intercollegiate, national and international skiing."[4] If we look just at participation in the Olympic and Paralympic Games, that mission is certainly being accomplished. Sixty-six Dartmouth men and women have represented the United States–and the college–at those Games, a third more than the number from any other college or university in the country. Over the course of 20 Olympic Games, Dartmouth skiers have qualified for 109 Olympic Team spots and competed in 202 Olympic events.[5] Dartmouth has had skiers, coaches and officials at literally every Winter Olympic Games since the first Winter Games in 1924—an unbroken and unparalleled record of excellence and accomplishment in the skiing sports.

The 1925-26 Winter Sports Team (l to r): Cogan '26, Mooney '27, Mann '26, Proctor '28, Capt. Farwell '26,
Mgr. Millard '26, Coach Diettrich, Conant '26, Hadlock '26.

DICK DURRANCE AND THE 1936 OLYMPICS

John Carleton '22, the first US-born Winter Olympian**, and Charles Proctor '28** competed in the 1924 and 1928 Olympic Games respectively, and **Fred Harris '11** and **Charles Proctor '00** helped organize and run the 1932 Olympic Games in Lake Placid, NY. But those early Games were small and relatively insignificant in the development of skiing in North America. Perhaps the greatest challenge was just to find ski jumpers and cross-country skiers who could take the time to actually attend the Games in Europe. Alpine skiing was not yet included in those early Games.

Things were looking a whole lot better for the Winter Olympic movement in 1936. Alpine skiing had been accepted on the program and women were to be included for the first time. It looked like the Olympics that year were going to be spectacular! "It had Adolf Hitler, it had the first nationwide Olympic effort [in Germany] and the first huge central Olympic ski stadium. There was worldwide media coverage in press and film–even the first Olympic TV. The Fourth Winter Olympic Games were going to be an international spectacle."[6]

In the US, the National Ski Association and the National Olympic Committee had finally figured out how to work together to fund and field a full team. The organizations raised the money needed to properly prepare and support the team and they adopted a scheme to select athletes through trials, the first such events to be conducted in the history of skiing in North America.

Noted ski historian Morten Lund has summarized the times and the challenge, as well as the major contributions played by Dartmouth skiers, coaches and officials, in this first Olympic skiing selection event.

The 1934-35 Dartmouth Ski Team (l. to r.): Coach Schniebs, Team Manager, Warren Chivers '38, Dick Durrance '39, Sel Hannah '35, Bem Woods '36, Ted Hunter '38. Durrance was attending Newport, NH High School at the time, but had been accepted by Dartmouth.

***

THE FIRST AMERICAN OLYMPIC ALPINE TRIALS IN 1935: AMERICAN SKI RACING BEGINS AN INTERNATIONAL COURSE

By Morten Lund

The era of great American western downhills got underway in the mid-1930s with races on the three Northwestern volcanic cones—Mt. Baker, Mt. Hood and Mt. Rainier—high peaks with reliable snow through spring and skiable verticals that met international race standards. In 1934, the Seattle Post Intelligencer put up the first great American down-mountain race trophy, the Silver Skis, which was won by Don Fraser of the University of Washington. On the national level, the National Ski Association (NSA) had barely become "national" by holding its first meeting of regional ski associations representing all regions in 1930.

There had yet to be a national US Alpine championship race meet that gave awards for slalom, downhill and combined, but on the other side of the Atlantic the Fédération International de Ski, the FIS, had already held four such successful alpine combined world championships. While Americans did

occasionally race in Europe, including in the 1933 FIS world championship and in the all-important international open, the Arlberg-Kandahar, the American racers were not part of an officially chosen US national team.

Even though American Alpine national championships that included the slalom, downhill, and combined had not yet come into existence—nor even been suggested—the NSA had already certified two early single-race events in the form of two downhill national championships. The first of these was the 1933 downhill national championship held by the Dartmouth Outing Club on Mt. Moosilauke, New Hampshire. Nineteen Eastern racers skiers entered that race. The first American National Downhill Champion, Dartmouth's **Henry "Bem" Woods '36** had enjoyed the benefit of two seasons of coaching by Otto Schniebs, the first European certified instructor to coach an American team. In 1934, the National Ski

Association equalized things by certifying a Western downhill run at Estes Park, Colorado, as the national title race. It was won by an Estes Park boy, J. J. "Junior" Duncan. Three Eastern racers did show up—one of them, **Lincoln Washburn '35** of Dartmouth, took third out of 16 racers.

But the magic words "Winter Olympics" were being discussed abroad, and when the 1936 Winter Games were assigned to Germany they included, for the first time, a single Alpine category, the Alpine Combined, with winners to be awarded the first Olympic Alpine skiing medals. Austria's Toni Seelos, 1933 World Alpine Champion and inventor of the revolutionary "tempo turn," had been hired for a season as Germany's national coach. To meet the challenge, the NSA US National Ski Association decided to mount both the Olympic alpine trials and the national championship races in April 1935. The Washington Ski Club of Seattle and Tacoma, which offered deep April snow on the slopes of Mt. Rainier, and bagged both events—the national championship and the Olympic trials—to be held concurrently. The Seattle Post-Intelligencer immediately offered its 1935 Silver Skis trophy to the winner of the downhill.

Durrance '39 Winning 1932 German Junior National Championship.

The Seattle Times reported that the pre-race betting favored Dick Durrance of Dartmouth College, Hannes Schroll of Austria, and Hjalmar Hvam of Portland. Each was an extraordinary racer. Durrance was a freshman at Dartmouth who had spent six years as a schoolboy in Garmisch, Germany, and at 17 he had become the fastest young skier in the 1932 Bavarian championship races, placing 16th in downhill and 35th in slalom out of 80 racers in the 1933 Arlberg-Kandahar, essentially the open world championship race. Durrance had made good use of

several opportunities in Europe to watch Seelos do his tempo turn and adopted the technique, one that eliminated the small stem everyone had previously thought necessary even for a high-speed turn.

Durrance had become an immediate American hero in 1934, his first year back in the U.S., by winning the Mt. Washington Inferno, a hair-raising race down the 60-degree Tuckerman Headwall, while still a senior at Newport High School in NH by an awesome six-minute margin. That fall, he entered Dartmouth in the class of 1939. Dartmouth's racers soon improved considerably simply by studying Durrance's imported tempo turn.

The second pre-race favorite, Austrian Hannes Schroll, had arrived just three weeks before the NSA's Olympic trials and was easily one of Austria's top ten. He had also learned the tempo turn from watching Seelos and had won the 1934 Marmolada down-mountain race and placed 7th or better in each of the 1934 Arlberg-Kandahar's downhill, slalom and combined rankings. The third pre-race favorite, Hjalmar Hvam, later became the inventor of the first practical safety-release binding. He had immigrated to Portland, OR from Norway in 1927 and had won the 1932 national Nordic combined championship at Lake Tahoe. Even with no Alpine training other than normal Norwegian turns, Hvam had won the 1934 Oregon slalom championship on Mt. Hood. He learned fast and came to Rainier as the Pacific Northwest Downhill and Alpine Combined champion. The other western racers rated highly by newspapers were John Woodward, Damrosch Crookes, and slalom specialist Hans Grage (all from the Washington University Ski Club) and a dark horse, Jack Taylor, a top Western Canadian racer. Don Fraser, considered the best in the Northwest, had torn a ligament in downhill practice on Rainier a few days before the races and missed them all.

There were 59 entrants for the downhill race at Rainier coming from all over American snow country. The race ran over a two-mile course and turned out to be a very strange experience. **Charley Proctor**, Dartmouth's former intercollegiate champion, 1928 Olympian and an official for the race, reported that "When it came to the race, the weather did bad things. The clouds came down over more than half the total length of the course, making visibility almost zero… [so it was] very difficult to find the proper line… impossible to judge speed…. One had no idea which way the hill might slope... Many good men reported sudden spills... with [little] momentum [thereafter] to carry them … over the gradual terrain at any but a snail's pace… All runners spent …time feeling about in the clouds trying to find the flags. It was remarkable that more runners did not get completely lost and fail to finish… as Warren Chivers [did]… Many were temporarily lost."[7]

Hannes Schroll had evidently skied through enough high mountain fog in his native Alps to have mastered the spooky skill of running straight regardless of visibility. Starting fifty-first, he passed so many fallen skiers along the course that he was sure he had won. He burst over the last ridge airborne, letting out a triumphant yodel. At times, Schroll must have averaged close to sixty miles an hour and his total time was two minutes and ten seconds, a minute and seven seconds ahead of Dick Durrance in second. Schroll, though not eligible for a berth on the US team, received the giant Silver Skis trophy as winner of the national downhill. So Schroll got all the glory. Durrance had to be satisfied with second place and the fact that his team placed four men in the top seven in the downhill. Behind Durrance came Dartmouth's Washburn who took 3rd, Livermore taking 6th, and Hunter taking 7th.

The national slalom the next day would decide the top ten in combined. Charley Proctor's reported that the course was "on the easy side… but if a racer cut close to the pole…he could find the flag wrapped around an ankle, [and carry] it downhill, [making it] extremely difficult for the flag keepers." (Not to mention the racers.) Durrance fell in his first run, giving the win to Schroll. Dick lost to Livermore as well, taking but took third in the slalom. The final Alpine Combined score put Schroll first and the four Dartmouth easterners next—Durrance, Livermore, Hunter, and Washburn. With Schroll not eligible, this amounted to a clean sweep of the first four places for the Eastern skiers—all but one of them from Dartmouth—in the concurrent Olympic trials.

The meet notched a row of important firsts into American ski history. As Kirby Gilbert wrote, "The 1935 Tryouts brought together ski leaders and top alpine competitors for the first time … [and] led to increased demand for better skiing facilities across the country"[8]. They had learned that an annual national championship alpine race could be funded and organized and this gave American alpine racing a new importance in the national ski picture.

The idea of a national alpine team had been firmly established and national championships would continue to be held every year thereafter—with the exception of the World War II years. Realistic evaluations of American racing technique led to a quick modification of the old low-stance Arlberg technique in favor of Dartmouth's tempo turn with its more erect stance on skis. Today, the US national team almost routinely—happily—takes home World Cup medals every year and at least a few of the semi-annual array of either World Championship or Olympic medals. Toward this outcome, the Dartmouth skiers, and the 1935 Olympic trials as a whole, made a significant contribution.

There were four Dartmouth students and grads on the 1936 Olympic Team. **Dick Durrance '39, Lincoln Washburn '35** and **Ted Hunter '38** competed in Alpine events and **Warren Chivers '38** in cross-country. The Games were very significant for the US in many important ways. The Olympic Association named a Ski Games Committee to oversee preparations and to raise money to fund the team. The trials events described above were held to choose the

Warren Chivers '38.

squad, and then final trials were held in Europe just before the Games to name the participants in each event. The teams were "professionally" prepared, funded reasonably well, and selected properly for the first time. The athletes themselves got to participate in the first Winter Olympics that was really a great international event on a grand scale. It was by most measures a great success.[9]

And Dick Durrance was widely heralded as the first truly competitive skier to represent the United States at the Olympic Games. It seemed that we were finally ready to compete with the best in the world.

But the Olympics are sometimes unkind to even the greatest of athletes. When the most important event only happens once every four years, things can go wrong that allow no time for recovery. Illness, injury, and the vagaries of fate can negate the best of preparation. Dick injured an ankle four days before the first Alpine event and it was weak enough on competition days to require taping. On the day of the downhill, responding to difficult conditions with new snow on rough ice, the organizers "set extra control flags."[10] Many years later, Dick told his sons **Dick**

Dick Durrance I '39 skiing in the Olympic Slalom (1936).

Durrance, Jr. '65 and **Dave**, outstanding Alpine ski competitors in their own right, about that day. He had prepared a special strategy: on one of the steep sections in the middle of the course, to ski a section straight where all others were making turns to control speed. Dick had skied it many times and knew he could handle it – but on this race day extra flags were put on that face requiring him to make turns and thereby lose his planned advantage.[11]

In addition, during the race, the bottom of the course turned very warm "causing racers to stand up and pole desperately across a third-of-a-mile flat toward the end." Durrance missed the wax and finished 11th. "I had to pole and pole and pole," he recalls. "I poled my heart out. All my preparation and work, knowing how to take every hill and corner, had gone to waste. I knew that none of the other people had done that much preparation. It was awful. I was terribly, terribly disappointed." [12]

In the slalom he skied well, was in third place near the end of the race, but knocked over a pole in the last gate and was assessed a 6-second penalty (in 1936 skiers were given time penalties for missed or straddled gates). Although he and the entire US team were convinced he had passed through the gate, the manager at the time declined to issue a protest. Dick said, "I was totally amazed that I'd gotten a penalty. I asked Frosty [Manager Joel Hildebrand] to protest the thing…He said, 'Oh, I don't' think we'd better get in an argument'"[13] Dick wound up in 10th place in the Alpine Combined, the only official Olympic Alpine ski event at those Games,…not such a bad result given the circumstances.

The good news was he was just 21, rounding into top form and approaching the best ski years of his career. The bad news was that WWII would cause the cancellation of the next two Olympic Games and deny Dick a chance to demonstrate his greatness on an Olympic stage.

THE 1940 OLYMPIC SKI TEAM – THE TEAM THAT DIDN'T COMPETE

Ironically, the aftermath of the highly successful Garmisch Games was that there were no more Olympics for 14 years.[14] Unfortunately, it denied the greatest group of Dartmouth ski athletes ever assembled at the school up to that time their opportunity to compete as Olympians. Happily, the United States Olympic Committee and the National Ski Association decided to honor all those who would have made that team with official Olympian status anyway. The result was that nine Dartmouth athletes were named to that Olympic squad. The Downhill and Slalom team included the aforementioned Dick Durrance and Ted Hunter plus **Edward Well '39** and **Harold Hillman '40**. The Ski Jumping Team included **John Litchfield '39,** and the Cross- Country and Nordic Combined team included Warren Chivers and John Litchfield (both mentioned previously) plus **Selden Hannah '35, David Bradley '38**, and **Howard Chivers '39**.

As it had been in 1936, America was organized to prepare and field an Olympic team in 1940. Trials were held in good conditions for all disciplines. Money had been raised to support the team activities. The Ski Association and the Olympic Committee had figured out how to work together to prepare a team environment at the Olympic Games which would benefit athletes and support their competitive dreams. The American Ski Association and the American Olympic Association had come of age, finally prepared to participate in the international competitive experience of athletes and coaches. "The winter of 1940 was to have been a red-letter one in the history of American competitive skiing," and Dartmouth had an incredible nine members ready to be part of those events. [15]

It is interesting to note that John Litchfield was named to both the Ski Jumping and the Cross-Country/Nordic Combined squads. He was also an outstanding Alpine skiing competitor and was a member of the US Alpine "A" Team in 1937. He, like many of his Dartmouth teammates, pretty much excelled at anything that involved strapping long skinny board on his feet and heading down a hill or across the snow covered countryside. John's roommate, Dick Durrance, was also universally good on skis, with a record of winning in all four skiing disciplines. In fact, he is reputed to have won all four events all four years at the collegiate championships. Dartmouth always encouraged, needed, and was blessed with strong "four-way" skiers. Pre-WWII was the era of the generalist, of the guys who did all the events and did them well. The best, like Durrance, Litchfield, David Bradley and Warren Chivers, adhered to the **Otto Schniebs** dictum, "Vell, if you must specialize, specialize in four events!"[16] and they were given the title of "Skimeister," in those times the most coveted prize in intercollegiate and national competitions.

The Golden Years of Dartmouth Alpine Skiing – 1948-1960

When the Olympic Winter Games returned to St. Moritz, Switzerland, in 1948, Alpine Skiing had become fully established around the world, including in the US and at Dartmouth. Alpine Combined had been added to the program in 1936, a concession of sorts by the Scandinavians to the Europeans and Americans who were pushing hard for inclusion of gate skiing. More Alpine events were scheduled in 1940, but a raging debate on "amateurism" had threatened the International Olympic Association's support for these events; but then WWII forced cancellation of the Games. In 1948 Alpine skiing made its true Olympic debut with three events each for both the men and the women.

The 1948-49 Ski Team (l to r) - Front Row: Asst Coach Densmore, Treat '46, Capt. Bull '46, Lumbard '46, Coach Prager;
Back Row: Mgr. Hotchkiss '50, Caldwell '50, Dodge '51, Stewart '48, Brewater '50, Arneberg '50, Mgr. Hall '47.

By 1948, Alpine skiing was already big in the U.S. Ski lifts had been erected in many areas and top resorts rivaling Europe's best were flourishing in the East and the West. Americans had largely abandoned the herringbone and the *langlauf* in favor of gleefully being carried or pulled uphill and focusing all their attention on the techniques for going down as gracefully or as rapidly as possible.

And the American racers were getting good. The U.S. attracted some excellent ski teachers from Europe, men who were still top racers as well, men such as Walter Prager. "Open" competitions, pitting the teacher/racers against the best American amateur collegians, improved the quality of American skiing.[17] Exemplary races were held, in part the legacy of Professor Proctor, whose insistence on "high standards" led to well organized racing and scoring procedures that generally produced high quality events.[18] Dick Durrance had proven that American skiers could be competitive with the best in the world and the better athletes were attracted to the sport with expectations that they could contend in major events like the Olympic Games.

A disproportionate share of the top skiers was attracted to Dartmouth. The college presented the ideal environment: a great education, a world-class coach in Walter Prager, good ski areas in Woodstock, VT and in Hanover, and a band of skiing brothers who could live and train together and share an inspiration to become champions in the sport. The spirit of the times and the life of Dartmouth ski racers are captured in the following comment by former Olympian **Tom Corcoran '54**.

Steve Bradley '39, Coach of the Colorado University team, handing the Bradley Plate to Tor Arneberg '50, Dartmouth team Captain, for victory in the 6th Sun Valley Intercollegiate Ski Race.

***

THE DARTMOUTH ALPINE SKI TEAM: 1950 - 1960
By Tom Corcoran '54

There were two periods in Dartmouth skiing when the college acted as a particularly strong magnet in pulling talented alpine skiers to the Hanover Plain. The first was in the latter part of the 1930s and coincided with the arrival of Walt Prager, a world-class Swiss skier as coach, and of **Dick Durrance '39**, the foremost American racer of the era. The two were clearly pied pipers, and they attracted fifteen other exceptional racers at or near the top of the national skiing hierarchy. Dick and three other Dartmouth skiers constituted a majority of the 1940 US Olympic Alpine Team that didn't get to compete when the Winter Olympics were cancelled.

An analogous period occurred in the early 1950s when Walt Prager, having returned to Dartmouth as ski coach after serving with the 10th Mountain Division during the war, was once again one of the pied pipers. The others were a trio of Alpine ski racers on campus who had skied for the U.S. in the 1948 Olympics at St. Moritz, Switzerland, or in the 1950 World Championships held at Aspen, Colorado: **Colin Stewart '48, Dave Lawrence '51**, and **Brooks Dodge '51, Th '54**, along **with Bill Beck '53** who would soon appear on the world skiing stage (he placed 5th in the prestigious Arlberg-Kandahar Downhill in 1952, the best finish in that event by any American skier to that time).

I arrived in the fall of 1950 with minimal racing experience, good skiing skills, a strong desire to be coached by Walt and ski for Dartmouth, and to mix with the big boys. By the end of the winter, three freshmen, **Pete Kirby '54, Bill Tibbits '54**, and moi, with Walt's guidance, had developed enough to compete evenly with the best racers in the East and even win a few races.

During the winter of 1951, Brookie Dodge and Bill Beck were picked to be members of the 1952 US Olympic Alpine Team, and Pete Kirby was selected as an alternate for the 1952 Canadian Olympic Alpine Team. Pete subsequently made the 1954 Canadian World Championship Alpine Team, but he won an Olympic gold medal as brakeman on the winning Canadian 4-man bobsled in 1964.

Ralph Miller '55 joined our ranks in the fall of 1951 and was an instant racing success as a freshman, winning the Eastern Downhill Championship. In his sophomore year he won the North American Downhill Championship at Stowe, beating Othmar Schneider who won the silver medal in the 1952 Olympic Downhill; then Ralph went west to Aspen and won the National Downhill title.

In the fall of 1952 **Toni Spiess '56**, a member of the vaunted Austrian Ski Team from St. Anton, came to Dartmouth after placing 3rd in the 1952 Olympic Giant Slalom. He won the Fisk Trophy at Woodstock in February 1953, but did not have great results in the individual races he entered later in the winter. He seemed unable to adjust to campus life or feel at ease, and he left Hanover at the end of the school year.

Also in 1952, after a bitter recruiting competition with archrival Denver University, Walt persuaded **Egil Stigum '56, Tu '59,** from Norway to come to Dartmouth. Egil never skied for Norway in an Olympics, but he was a top contender in national and regional races in this country and a mainstay on the Dartmouth ski teams.

Bill Beck '53 in his racing jacket and holding his skis.

In 1953 Dartmouth landed a huge prize: **Chiharu "Chick" Igaya '57** from Japan, who had just placed 11th in the 1952 Olympic slalom. C.V. Starr, the founder and CEO of the company that became AIG, had a great personal interest in skiing and owned the Mt. Mansfield Company at Stowe as well as skiing investments in St. Anton. He sponsored both Igaya and Spiess to attend Dartmouth. In contrast to Spiess, Igaya was a roaring success, both on and off skis; he was well liked by ski team members and the larger Dartmouth community. He was the most successful male alpine racer ever to ski for Dartmouth. In the 1956 Olympics he earned a silver medal in the slalom, and in the 1958 World Championships he was 3rd in the slalom, 6th in the giant slalom, and 4th in the combined. At the end of his skiing ca-

reer he returned to Japan and has spent the rest of his working life as managing director of AIG's Japanese insurance operations. He was also head of Japan's Olympic organization and was Japan's leading representative with the FIS, the International Ski Federation.

Three of the best performances in the Winter Olympics by American male skiers were turned in by Dartmouth ski team members of the 1950's-era:

- Bill Beck was 5th in the Olympic Downhill in 1952 (the best placing for any American man in that event until Bill Johnson got a Gold medal thirty-two years later in 1984), and he was Captain of the US Men's Olympic Alpine Team in 1956 and then its coach in 1960.

- Brooks Dodge was 4th in the Olympic Slalom in 1956, the best placing for an American man in that event until Billy Kidd got silver and Jimmy Heuga got bronze medals in 1964, eight years later.

- I was 4th in the Olympic Giant Slalom in 1960, the best placing for an American man in that event until Bode Miller got a silver medal in 2002, forty-two years later. Bill Beck was the Men's Alpine coach for our 1960 Olympic team.

One of the best parts of Dartmouth ski competitions was the mix of team skiing on Fridays and Saturdays during the winter carnival season and the individual racing on Sundays. Each college team had four racers in the slalom and in the downhill, with the best three in each event to count for

The 1950-51 D Ski Team: Cox '52, Ashnault '53, Beck '53, Dodge '51, Coach Prager; Kneeling: Branch '52, Tremblay '52, Capt. Blake '51, Barstow '52, Mgr Terry '51.

points. Walt would be a wreck until he knew that he had three racers at or near the top of the leader board in each event. He drilled into us that consistency in team skiing was much more important than brilliance. And he really did instill a strong team spirit into the carnival teams. They were great fun. After partying on Saturday night, we'd get up and head for an individual race where it was every man for himself, and often the principal rivalries were among ourselves. Those weekends of racing are the fondest memories I have of my Dartmouth years.

The best Dartmouth downhill racers in that era were Miller, Beck, Kirby, Tibbits and Dodge, and the best slalom/giant slalom racers were Igaya, Dodge, Tibbits, Miller,

Stigum and myself. We had the talent to win any alpine ski race in North America on any given day. In fact, this group of Dartmouth ski racers provided the winner at least once, and often multiple times, in every major alpine ski meet in North America from 1950 through 1960.

Somewhat surprisingly, we all got along well despite the internal competition. Among us was a bond of friendship, sportsmanship and pride in the Dartmouth Ski Team. We were all so close in ability that there was no room for swelled heads or cliques. And Walt was the glue that held it all together and made it so special. He was very even-tempered and treated every team member the same. There was no favoritism. He always had a little smile and was upbeat, but not boastful or full of superlatives. If we skied well he told us so. If we skied poorly and were down in the dumps, he'd try to pick us up.

We didn't all ski or train the same way, and that was fine with Walt. He was a minimalist coach, usually offering suggestions only if requested, often just reminders of simple things that we had forgotten. And his comments and tips were always spot on. It was a joy and a great privilege to ski for him.

There was great press interest in ski racing in those days, perhaps much more than now. The four major newspapers in Boston and New York had knowledgeable, dedicated ski writers who were all given large amounts of column inches to cover ski racing regionally and nationally, and the winter carnivals, particularly Dartmouth's, got tons of ink. The principal ski writers of the era were Pat Harty of the Boston Globe; Henry Moore of the Boston Herald; Bill Lauder Jr. of the New York Herald Tribune; and Lincoln Werden, Frank Elkins, and later Mike Strauss, all of the New York Times. We knew all of them on a first name basis, and we could not have asked for better press coverage of our sport.

In the 1952-53 school year, nine team members signed up for three 3-person bedrooms on the top floor of College Hall. It was a raucous year with a lot of pranks that caught the attention of the campus police and college administration. Several of us at one time or another were on crutches and the sport of "crutch-humping" was invented: how far you could travel on crutches down the hall with just your crutches touching the ground.

And there were off-campus gatherings, too. Ski Club Carcajou was a truly unique social ski club in Hanover; its membership was half townspeople who liked to ski and half students, made up of ski team members and DOC "chubbers." It was perhaps the most important social outlet for the team. It was an opportunity for us to get to know other DOC members as well as residents of the wider Hanover community. The elected officers came from the student membership in the club. Monthly meetings were conducted in a cabin called the Ski Hut right behind the Hanover Inn; these gatherings were full of fun, kidding, jokes, ski stories, and beer, with the DOC chubbers playing their guitars and everyone singing the classic ski songs, now largely forgotten except by **Bill Briggs '54**. We put on John Jay and Warren Miller ski movies in the fall and raised money for the Ford-Sayre ski program.

Walt was always in attendance, and at some point in the evening he would be toasted with the ballad called "Oh, For the Life of a Skier," and sung to the tune of "O Tannenbaum". It went like this:

> "Oh, for the life of a skier!
> To climb into the Prager's car and shout,
> 'To the next bar, To the next bar!'
> Oh, Walter Lee, oh, Walter Lee,
> Won't you teach me how to ski?
> Won't you really show me how,
> How to schuss and not snowplow?
> Oh, Walter Lee, oh, Walter Lee,
> Here's to you and here's to me.
> Oh, Walter Lee, oh, Walter Lee,
> Here's to you and here's to me,
> And if by chance we disagree,
> The hell with you, and here's to me!"

And there would be a great cheer and lots of laughs, and he would look a little embarrassed, and say, "Cheez, you guys…"

We didn't practice on Oak Hill. I think I only skied there a couple of times in my freshman year when the first ski trials for the freshman team were held. Virtually all of our practice was at Suicide Six in Woodstock, VT, not exactly next door and a pain to get to when most of us didn't have cars. There was no team bus, so it was always a scramble to make practice. Suicide Six, served by the world's longest and steepest rope tow, was owned and run by **Wallace "Bunny" Bertram '31**, a crusty old Dartmouth grad who loved the Dartmouth ski team and would do anything for us. It was a great training area. If you could ski and run gates well on Six, you could do well anywhere. And riding that rope tow sure strengthened the arms.

Leading skiers in the 1950s with Coach Prager: (l. to r.) Igaya '57, Beck '53, Prager, Kirby '54 and Stigum '56.

In the spring of 1951 in our freshman year, Bunny told Bill Tibbits and me that there was a Suicide Six top-to-bottom hill record of 31.8 seconds set in 1947, and he encouraged us to give it a shot. If you broke the record you won a gold "6" pin. Bunny said that it could only be done in the spring on corn snow in the late afternoon, just as it was starting to firm up. The idea was to pick a line down the mogul field, hitting just the tops of selected moguls all the way down the hill to the finish, which was next to Bunny with his hand-held stopwatch. Bill Tibbits went by himself one day at the end of March, lowered the record to 31.4 seconds, and got a gold "6." The next day we both showed up for another try. I won the toss and went first, lowering the record to 30.0 flat. Bill's effort was lower than the day before, but not lower than my run. I went again and

Poster for the 1957 eastern ski championships.

lowered my time to 29.8, and collected two gold "6"s. Bill tried again and fell, lucky to avoid injury because he was traveling about 60 mph, so we called it a day. That was the last time anybody tried for the record and no more gold "6"s were ever awarded.

During the 1950's and spilling over into the early 1960's, there were many fine American Alpine racers on campus who won or placed high in regional and national ski events but who never made an international team representing the US. A number of them raced for Dartmouth on the winter carnival circuit and posted results that led to team victories. Here's a list of who they were: **Tom Agan '54, Wally Ashnault '53, Fred Barstow '52, Art Bookstrom '61, Jim Branch '52, Tu '53, Dave Brew '52, Pete Caldwell '54, Phil Cooke '54, Bob Gebhardt '57, Dave Harwood '58, Pete Johnson '54, Tu '55, Dave Oberlander '55, Jim Page '63, Jack Pierce '54, Jim Porath '53, Tu '54, Bill Smith '58, Jake Stewart '55, Bill Tibbits '54** and **Dave Vorse '57**.

Of all these fine racers, the best was Bill Tibbits. He won more races and had more top-5 finishes in major races than any of them, and he was the National Giant Slalom Champion in 1953. He and I were classmates and fraternity brothers in Sigma Nu, and our skiing career statistics were nearly identical. We both had great racing results in our senior year and knew we had excellent chances of making the 1956 Olympic Team. But at the end of our senior winter we were both in academic trouble, primarily from overindulging in ski racing.

I squeaked through and graduated, but Bill didn't make it. He always had low self-esteem, which we kidded him about, because there was just no reason for it in our minds. And we knew he got depressed, but none of us suspected that he would go home to North River, NY, that summer and take his life.

It makes me sad and tearful every time I think about it, because he was a great guy and a great friend, and a skier as good as any of us from Dartmouth who made the 1956 Olympic Team, and with a much better racing record than four others who also made the team. The four of us from Dartmouth who made the nine-man 1956 Olympic Alpine Team were Beck, Dodge, Miller and myself. But there should have been one more from Dartmouth: Bill Tibbits.

THE SECOND 50 YEARS: 1959 – 2009

But by 1960 collegiate skiing was in the midst of a sea change. Bob Beattie had taken over as coach of the US Alpine Ski Team and had started the first truly national ski program, raising money to hire full-time coaches and support the team, while demanding an unqualified commitment to international competition. He didn't want his skiers in school, but for those just below the team qualification level, he favored Western schools with their access to major resorts and longer on-snow seasons.

At around the same time, ski companies and other sponsors started to endorse and pay athletes to ski race and to use their products. Ski racing at the elite level was becoming a business. College skiers couldn't realistically expect to both pursue their courses of study and to train intensively enough to compete successfully against the pros.

At the ski colleges, athletic scholarships became available to the top American and foreign athletes whose skiing prowess was "hired" rather than nurtured and developed. The challenge for most of these colleges was to win NCAA championships, and program resources were generously expended to get that done. It was a single focus that reduced ski competition to wins and losses as the only measure of success.

Dartmouth could not and would not buy in to that philosophy; and yet, in its second 50 years of skiing, it continued to achieve unusual success in placing undergrads and grads on Olympic teams. During the first 50 years (through the 1960 Games in Squaw Valley, CA), 22 of its skiers qualified for Olympic teams and a remarkable 44 have been named to at least one Olympic or Paralympic Team from 1964 through 2006.[19]

The Dartmouth ski team continued to carry large numbers of athletes and to provide for the full diversity of Olympic ski sports. Undergrads had the opportunity to get a top-quality education in a community that provided ideal training and strong coaching, made accommodations for individual interests and needs, and offered flexible attendance patterns. It was, and is, an extremely attractive option for those who want to ski race at any level.

The man who guided Dartmouth Skiing through this period of change was Al Merrill. Walter Prager had retired in 1957 and Al was named coach. Walter and Al were both four-way skiers, at least on paper, but Walter was most successful and most engaged in Alpine skiing. Al did some Alpine racing but he was primarily a cross-country skier; it must have been quite a sight to watch him negotiate a slope full of gates. He was in every way a dedicated Nordic man.

Since he was the Nordic coach, it is hardly surprising that most of the college skiers who became Olympians during his fifteen-year coaching career were Scandinavian athletes (two-time Olympian **David Currier '74**

Tiger Shaw '85, nine-time National Champion, on the move.

from Madison, NH, being the lone American-born exception). But he, and the Outing Club in general, encouraged and provided at some level for anyone who would commit to train and participate in any of the skiing disciplines. As a result, making sense of the second 50 years of Dartmouth skiing is complex for it involves the whole variety of Olympic and Paralympic skiing options. In fact, 15 of the Dartmouth grads who made Olympic teams during this era qualified in events that are not contested in intercollegiate ski competition.

Skiers who came to Dartmouth during this period ranged from total neophytes looking to join the famous D Ski Team and learn to race, to good ski racers wanting to be part of the college ski team, to those planning to use the flexibility of the D-Plan to take time off to chase their dreams of international skiing and Olympic Games. Following are a few of the success stories.

OLYMPIANS "MADE AT DARTMOUTH"

An important policy of both the Outing Club and the Ski Program was to offer good coaching and a quality skiing experience to all interested and committed undergraduates. Over time, the program has had a "no-cut" policy and has "carried" quite large squads of developing skiers. It has demanded only that those involved be serious enough to participate fully in the training and in the multi-level competition program. It has been a very enriching activity for a large number of aspiring racers and has served the college ski team well as it has been successful at developing athletes who have competed on winter carnival teams. In Olympic terms though, the greatest achievement of this aspect of the program has been the extraordinary success of several athletes who entered Dartmouth with literally no competitive experience and went on to qualify for the Olympic or the Paralympic Games. This just has not happened anywhere else.

One of these success stories is **Edward Williams '64, Tu'69** an Olympic Biathlete. Ed came to Dartmouth Skiing with two Alpine ski competitions under his belt. Actually, he didn't finish either race, so his record was clean. At the freshman ski team orientation meeting he handed in a blank form when asked for information on his skiing career. But he claims he was inspired to try out for the team because his family had some Finnish blood and he had been elected president of his ski club at Kingston High School in southern New York State.[20] This is not your typical Olympian background. However, the entire ski program was so encouraging and accepting that he never felt out of place.

He handled the fall training well enough, but when snow came and real skiing started, he finished next to last in the freshman Alpine team trials. More importantly, he realized for the first time that these other guys could really ski. He thought his Dartmouth skiing career was finished.[21]

But on the return from Holt's Ledge, Coach Al Merrill pulled Ed aside and asked; "Did you ever think of doing cross-country?" He told Ed he needed another Nordic skier and said; "I can teach you to ski cross-country!"[22] Ed jumped at the chance and applied himself ferociously to the task. By sophomore year he was skiing cross-country on the varsity team at some carnivals. As a senior he won a carnival race. He had enough success in open competition that in 1967 he asked for, and was granted, a year off from Tuck Business School to try out for the 1968 Olympic Team. He lived in the house of **Dr. Ralph Miller, Sr. '24,** doing odd jobs and chores for Mrs. Miller to pay for his rent while he trained with **Ned Gillette '67** and the ski team – and with Coach Merrill. He learned, trained, worked hard, planned and eventually qualified for the 1968 Olympic Biathlon team and represented the United States at the Games in Grenoble, France.

Through all this his strategy was simple and efficient. He liked training and skiing because he could calculate exactly "where he stood" vs. his teammates and competitors. He never worried about how much better the winners were than he was: he measured himself against those who were just a little better than him, figured out what he had to do to get to their level, and once he started beating them, he moved on to the next person on the list.[23] His rise in the ranks was a gradual series of small successes and he made it all the way to the highest competition in his sport – the Olympic Games. Coach Merrill asking him if he ever considered cross-country skiing literally changed his life!

Joe Walsh '84 is another "made-at-Dartmouth" success story. Joe developed eyesight problems very early in life. He likes to say; "I can see around the edges, but there is a big black hole in the middle of my vision. If a truck is coming down the road at me I probably wouldn't be able to see it."[24] Nonetheless, he was always active and liked to train as long as he was working out with a guide to avoid the trucks. As a junior at Dartmouth, having never skied in his life, he asked if he could train with the ski team. He had some friends on the team and they encouraged him to become part of the group. **John Morton**, the head coach at the time, welcomed him and Joe spent the fall happily challenging the hills and trails of New Hampshire.

When fall training was over and it was time for the team to start actually skiing, Joe said; "Thanks a lot" and prepared to go his own way. Coach Morton said: "Hey, wait a minute; you're part of the team. You can't leave us now!" Joe was flabbergasted. He had never even been on skis. But he decided to give it a try, learned to balance and move on skinny skis, and loved it.

Needless to say, it was tough. At the beginning he could barely see and barely ski! And there was no prospect the seeing part would get any better. But the skiing did.

Joe was really a Dartmouth Ski Team project. "Morty" and the development coaches provided coaching – and a lot of encouragement. Joe recruited guides to lead him in practices and races from among the college's better racers. Four-time Olympian **Carl Swenson '92** worked with him a lot and **Max Cobb '87**, current Executive Director of USA Biathlon, skied with him as a guide in races.

Joe's brother, **Rob Walsh '88,** was part of this made-at-Dartmouth success story as well. Rob, four years younger, was born with the same sight problem. He came to Dartmouth the year after Joe graduated, also never having skied, but full of enthusiasm to follow in Joe's ski tracks. Joe stayed around to train, eventually buying a house with Rob just off of Lyme Road, and for the next 15 years of their lives they committed to training, skiing, and racing in adaptive skiing competitions. Through it all, the Dartmouth ski team welcomed them in and, even after graduation, worked with them, coached them, acted as guides, and enjoyed their significant successes.

Joe skied in two Paralympic Games ('88 and '92). Rob skied in five!! ('88, '92, '94, '98 and '02). Joe was the first Dartmouth alumnus to win a medal in blind skiing classifications, a Bronze in the 30-km event at Innsbruck, Austria, in 1988. Rob finished fourth in that race just 2.6 seconds behind Joe; and two days later Rob won the first Paralympic Cross-Country Skiing Gold medal in the 15-km Blind Ski Event. Joe was fourth in that event, a scant 0.3 seconds out of third place. Rob went on to compete in nine more Paralympic ski competitions; winning another Bronze medal in 1992 and always finishing near the top. The brothers had gone from new skiers to the podium in the biggest event in their sport.

John Morton, coach at Dartmouth from 1978 to 1989, was one of those special ski team leaders who continued the open program approach and the Ski Team history of producing an occasional national class skiers from athletes with very modest ski beginnings.

During his Dartmouth career, John discovered that many of his skiers had an interest in Biathlon and helped them form a Biathlon Club. The members found a little-used 10-meter pistol range in one of the gymnasiums and used it for indoor rifle practice. They set up an outdoor range at Oak Hill near the ski trails for running/shooting in the fall and skiing/shooting in the winter. They ran races on the golf course and shot at targets in the banks of Occom Pond. It must have been quite a sight with these athletes skiing and running with guns all around Hanover. Clearly this was the pre-9/11 world.

Many national and international class biathletes were made-at-Dartmouth by Morty and by this club. One such was **Erich Wilbrecht '84,** a 1992 Biathlon Olympian. Erich came to Dartmouth from Jackson Hole, WY, where he had been a pretty good runner and had started to cross-country ski. But he was far from a highly sought-after recruit. He was a good student and had some obvious skiing talent, so Morty encouraged him to apply. Erich didn't know anything about Dartmouth or much about the East. But he was excited that someone asked him to consider the school, and even though he says he was "blissfully unaware of the academic standards and his odds of getting in," he applied and was accepted.[25]

It took a couple of years of hard work, but by the end of sophomore year Erich skied in some carnivals and became a regular on the team in his junior year. The quality of coaching and training at Dartmouth, and the inclusive and nurturing year around team program, began to pay off for Erich as he started beating the recruited hot shots from other schools. For his last two years he was one of the best collegiate skiers in the country, a regular top-ten finisher.

He was a total convert. He claims that "fall training was spectacular, with roller skis through the winding New England roads, and running on the gorgeous single track of the Appalachian Trail. Time trials up Mt. Moosilauke were the fitness highlight of the fall!" He loves to point out that "as a westerner I had hated running with wet shoes through mud, but being in New England I developed that perverse satisfaction from returning from a long run through the woods and trails, covered with mud and scarred from crashing through streams and underbrush."[26] It's probably true that any Dartmouth skier who reads Erich's description can identify with the joys and challenges of Ski Training in Hanover. No group ever understood the words from the Dartmouth Alma Mater more personally:

> "They have the still North in their hearts,
> The hill winds in their veins,
> And the granite of New Hampshire
> In their muscles and their brains."

Erich went on to ski seven years for the US Biathlon Team. He was a World Team member first in 1987, then again from 1990 through 1993, and an Olympian in 1992. He won nine National Championships in summer and winter Biathlon. He then launched another seven-year career as a "factory team ski racer" for Fischer Skis on the domestic ski marathon circuit. He is still racing, doing clinics and teaching skiing today.

These are just a few of the many Made-at-Dartmouth stories. They are fascinating in part because they are so unique. Dartmouth's commitment to developing individual talents and abilities and its history of excellence and openness in the ski program have produced some extraordinary results.

Ski Jumper Arne Nielsen '76 shows his form.

THE SKI JUMPERS

It was a difficult challenge for collegiate coaches to find and attract good ski jumpers, and a team had to have several win meets. Many western schools opted to recruit Norwegians who, by and large, were good enough to give their teams big advantages in ski jumping events. And whenever a young American ski jumper came along who could compete with these foreign stars, he was very heavily recruited.

Scott Berry '71 was one of these. Scott came from Deadwood, South Dakota, and a ski jumping program developed by his dad, who built the jump and coached Scott, his brother Paul, and only one other athlete. It would be hard to identify the exact center of ski jumping proficiency in America but it is clearly not Deadwood, SD. Nonetheless, these three ski jumpers were very good and much sought-after since a competent American ski jumper was a real gem for any college ski program.

Landis Arnold '82 jumps out of the trees.

Scott chose Dartmouth to be with Al Merrill, then the recognized leader of the Nordic ski program in the U.S. He knew he could get a great education, improve his skiing, and have the advantage of being with the man who was calling the shots at the national level of the sport.

Interestingly, Al encouraged him to participate in all four skiing events, and to this day, Scott believes his participation in Alpine skiing, with some very good college skiers, taught him a lot about turning and balance and that this training improved his ski skills with those ungainly jumping skis.[27]

But the policy of encouraging individual excellence and participation in open regional and national events can set up some difficult conflicts for Dartmouth's best skiers. In 1972, with Olympic Games in Japan on the horizon, Scott knew he had a chance to make the Olympic team, but probably not if he stayed at Dartmouth. He needed to spend time on the "big hills," i.e., Olympic-sized. But he had skied for Dartmouth for three years, was an important part of the squad, and was excited that the college team was going to be very strong that year; he believed that with him on the team, they probably had a legitimate shot at winning the NCAA championships. Instead, Coach Al Merrill encouraged him to pursue his dream of an Olympic spot and actually helped him get set up for training and competing in Europe, a proposition that impressed him greatly at the time and for which he is thankful to this day. The team did not win the NCAA's that year, but Scott made the Olympic Team and competed in Sapporo. Today, Dartmouth appropriately celebrates his individual accomplishment and the contribution the college made to his becoming an Olympic-caliber competitor.

Several other world-class American ski jumpers have chosen to attend Dartmouth over the years. In fact, the college has produced six Olympic ski jumpers and nine Olympic Nordic Combined competitors. The 45-meter Vale of Tempe jump on the Hanover golf course, a facility **Dave Bradley '38** referred to as "that nightmarish product of a Minneapolis engineer,"[28] was the collegiate training ground for more US Olympic ski jumpers than any other college facility in America.

Walter Malmquist '78 Tu '88 leans for distance.

Dartmouth's most impressive group of ski jumpers was its last. **Walter Malmquist '78**, **Landis Arnold '82** and **Dennis McGrane '84** were members of the US Ski Team at a time when that group was ranked fourth in the world – its highest ranking ever. But unfortunately, they were members of the Dartmouth Ski Team in the final years of collegiate ski jumping; the event was dropped from the NCAA championships in 1981.

It is only appropriate that the facility that produced Charles Proctor and John Carlton (who did back flips off the jump to entertain the Carnival crowds), that developed Litchfield, the Bradleys and the Chivers, and that saw Durrance fly to the bottom of its hill, was used by its most accomplished athletes at the very end of its days. The Vale of Tempe hill was decommissioned in 1983, largely from lack of use (along with liability issues), and was eventually torn down.

DARTMOUTH'S PARALYMPIANS

An unusual number of Paralympians have been also been Dartmouth grads. The college has had no specific program for them, but many had strong skiing backgrounds and had been attracted to Dartmouth in part by the opportunity to benefit from the general ski program. What's more, the ski team supported and included them.

As a group they have been very successful at the Games, winning a total of 21 Paralympic and modified ski competition medals. **Martha Hill Gaskill '82** was the first of the group, winning two Silver medals at the 1984 Paralympic Games Above-the-knee Amputee Alpine ski competitions. She also played a large role in developing training techniques and equipment for adaptive ski racing. The **Walsh brothers, Joe '84 and Rob '88,** added three medals, including a Gold, in blind competitions. **Diana Golden Brosnihan '84** won the first two Alpine skiing Gold medals; **Ramona Hoh '02,** who came to Dartmouth after her Paralympic career having won two medals for Canada in adaptive Alpine events, and then **Sarah Billmeier '82,** also an above-the-knee amputee Alpine skier, won 13 medals in four Paralympic Games, including seven Golds, making her one of our country's most decorated Olympic or Paralympic athletes.[29]

Martha Hill Gaskill '82.

John Morton loves to tell the story of Diana Golden Brosnihan showing up for what turned out to be her first ski team practice at Dartmouth. The entire team—athletes and coaches—was at the football stadium participating in "Ski Team Olympics." One of the many "events" was a two-legged hop competition up the bleacher seats. Morty and Tim Fischer were watching the event together when "a young one-legged amputee woman came bounding across the field towards them" – not "crutching," not walking, but bounding! She came right up to them and asked, "Hey, is this ski team?" and John confirmed that it was; and she asked, "Can I join?" John asked what her "discipline" was and she said, "Alpine." John turned to Women's Alpine Coach **Tim Fischer** who, of course, said, "Sure, why not!" She asked if she could start right then; Tim smiled and directed her over to the stadium steps. She "bounded

Dartmouth Skiers Won 5 NCAA Slalom Championships in a row:

Roger Brown '04 (middle) NCAA Slalom Champ (2002).

Bradley Wall '02 NCAA Slalom Champion (2003).

Paul McDonald '06 NCAA Slalom Champion (2004).

David Chodounsky '08 NCAA Slalom Champion (2005).

Karl Johnson '06 NCAA Slalom Champion (2006).

over to the bleachers, leaned her crutches against the wall, pulled herself up through the railing, climbed on the first step and waited for the whistle to start." Morty says she hopped all the way up on one leg–and she wasn't last!! Then she hopped down and prepared to do it again.[30] So she trained with the team, added great spirit and inspiration to the whole group, and became one of Dartmouth's and America's most successful Paralympic skiers! Dartmouth skiing had not recruited her, didn't have a specific program for her, but found ways to include.

These are a few of the many accomplished young skiers who chose Dartmouth, participated in the ski program, improved as undergraduates, and went on to compete at the national and international levels of the sport. The ability of the coaches at the college to manage and inspire these talented athletes, along with their own commitment to excelling in their sport, have made Dartmouth one of the preeminent ski colleges in America.

THE D-PLAN SKIERS

The D-Plan (Dartmouth's Quarter System) offers four 10-week quarters per year and very flexible attendance patterns. Skiers who want to train and compete with the national team can create their own schedules of attendance that allow them to ski full-time during the winter months and still make progress every year toward a college degree. The excellence of the educational opportunities, the welcoming and supportive attitude of the ski team program, and the D-Plan options have combined to make Dartmouth an ideal place for elite skiers who also desire to earn a meaningful college degree while pursuing intensive physical training and competitive skiing goals.

Since the inception of the D-Plan in the early 1970s, 15 athletes, nearly a quarter of Dartmouth's ski Olympians, have taken advantage of this opportunity. These are a few of their stories.

Scott Macartney '01 entered Dartmouth as a freshman in the fall of 1997, his goals were to complete a college degree program and qualify for the US Ski Team. His dream was to ski on the World Cup circuit and at the Olympic Games. He knew that to reach these goals he was going to have to get out on the national race circuit.

He attended classes for the fall quarter of his freshman year, took a year off, and then attended all spring terms and one summer term until graduation. He completed his degree program in five years and his skiing improved as planned. He made the ski team and qualified for the Olympic teams in 2002 and 2006. His 7th place finish in the Super G at the 2006 Games in Turin, Italy, is one of the best performances ever by a Dartmouth Alpine skier at the Olympics. In fact, he is one of only six Dartmouth skiers to place among the top eight finishers and earn an Olympic Diploma. Despite a spectacular and much publicized fall in the downhill at Kitzbühel, Austria, in 2008 and surgery to repair a torn knee ligament in the spring of 2009, Scott retained his position on the US Ski Alpine "A" Team and, as of this writing, is a strong contender for a spot on the 2010 Vancouver Olympic Ski Team.

Choosing Dartmouth and finding the right plan to mix school and skiing was, like his skiing, part of his strategy of "intelligent risk."[31] In ski racing that meant "living a little on the edge, developing strategies for fast lines down racing courses (the maximum that he felt he could handle), and letting it all go to be the fastest and best on a given day." In school it meant taking off the time he needed to become the best - but knowing he had a great back up plan. If it didn't work out with the ski team and the World Cup he could return to Dartmouth to a great ski team and a great education.

When on campus he did some training under the direction of Alpine Coach **Peter Dodge '78** and was part of whatever group was training at the college during that term. Coach Dodge believes that Scott and many of the D-Plan skiers "make a very positive impact on Dartmouth and Dartmouth Skiing. Elite skiers like Scott are inspiring to live and train with. It's a great tradition that benefits Dartmouth ski team athletes and definitely makes the college special in the world of skiing"[32]

Liz McIntyre '87 grew up in Lyme, NH, and went to school at Hanover High. On the advice of her dad (who apparently thought Alpine skiing was too dangerous) she developed into a talented freestyle (moguls) skier and, like many others, dreamed of a ski career with the US Ski Team and of competing at the Olympic Games. When it was time to go to college she chose Dartmouth because, as she looked around, she realized there was "no place like Dartmouth with both academic excellence and a quarter system."[33]

At Dartmouth she played varsity soccer every fall and, after her freshman year, during which she trained with the Killington Freestyle Team, took all her winters off to go west to participate in US Ski Team programs. She was able to attend school during the spring and summer quarters and stay on track to get her degree.

She is the only freestyle skier from Dartmouth to qualify for the Olympic Team, and she did it three times, competing in 1992, 1994, and 1998. In Lillehammer, Norway, she won a Silver medal, equaling the best performance ever by a Dartmouth skier. During her twelve-year career as a World Cup skier, she won four times and earned 18 other top ten places.[34]

Perhaps her best work though was done as National Freestyle Team Technical Coach from 1999-2006. She coached three Olympic medalists and two overall World Cup season champions. The inscription on her plaque upon induction into the US Ski and Snowboard Hall of Fame reads: "She coached from the heart, challenging the athletes with fresh ideas and new training methods, and dedicated herself to getting the most out of them. She led athletes into a new era in the sport..."[35]

She was never able to participate in the traditional Dartmouth ski team program but she was a varsity athlete at the college, participated in moguls skiing at the highest level, and completed her academic program in a normal period of time.

For cross-country skier **Tim Caldwell '76** the D-Plan was a natural. "By my senior year in high school I had become a pretty serious skier. I had competed in Scandinavia and Japan, competed in the junior nationals three times and the Olympics once. I wanted to go to college and I wanted to ski internationally. Dartmouth had just announced its decision to accept women and go to a year-round calendar. For me the choice was obvious, I had to go to Dartmouth!"[36]

Reflecting back on his career he said, "I never competed for Dartmouth. I will always be a little disappointed by this, but I knew that I couldn't do the racing I wanted to do and keep up with my studies, so I ended up attending Dartmouth for 2 fall quarters, 5 springs and 4 summers."[37]

When on campus though, he was a part of the college program, training with whatever athletes were in attendance that term. He loved his times in Hanover. "Although cross-country skiing is an individual sport, the camaraderie of training and racing with friends and competitors is something I will always value. Learning to live with and appreciate your competitor is a great skill. Dartmouth helped me appreciate this aspect of life."[38]

Dartmouth's men's team won the NCAA collegiate championships in 1976, the year that Tim and several classmates and recent graduates were on the Olympic Ski Team. The opportunity the undergrads had to train with, and to be inspired by, these elite skiers was a big factor in the success of the college team that year.

The D-Plan didn't just take the good skiers away; these athletes, when they were around, raised the training standards and made the program better. **Phil Peck '77**, Dartmouth Ski Team Captain in 1977, commented that "for those of us on the Dartmouth team he was the unelected captain during the off-season. Tim was the instigator behind training. There was a joy that Tim had when he headed off for a workout that was truly contagious."[39]

Tim went on to ski in four Olympic Games, 1972, 1976, 1980 and 1984. He competed in ten Olympic competitions and countless World Cups in a career that spanned nearly thirty years. He is, like his Dartmouth Skiing and Olympian Dad, **John Caldwell '50,** truly an American icon in the sport of cross-country skiing. As you would expect, he is still skiing–mainly with his kids now. It's another generation getting ready to write new chapters in the Caldwell family cross-country ski racing adventure.

Leslie Thompson Hall '86, sister of Dartmouth coach **Cami Thompson,** came to the college as one of the better cross-country skiers in the U.S. She had already had an outstanding career as a junior racer at the national and international level and was highly recruited by the "big ski schools." She chose Dartmouth because "she liked Coach **Martha Rockwell** and the flexibility of the D-Plan," and felt she could develop as a ski racer and accomplish her goal of skiing on World Championship and Olympic Teams.

Leslie's D-Plan adventure was one of the most unique and creative. She was "not ready" to commit full time to cross-country skiing's World Cup circuit, preferring instead to complete her college education and to ski for the college ski team. The World Cup and the Olympics were to be part of the future, but she knew she needed to stay in touch with the "international" level. So after freshman year she took all fall quarters off in order to train with the national team skiers and get a strong base of snow skiing in the late fall. She attended classes all four winters and skied very successfully on the collegiate circuit. At the end of each winter quarter she was able to travel and compete internationally, twice at the World University Games and once at the World Junior Championships.

Her plan worked well, and following college she earned a spot on three Olympic ski teams, in 1988, 1992, and 1994, competing in eleven Olympic events, with a best finish of 25th in the Women's 20-km competitions in Calgary, Canada in 1988. Dartmouth and the D-Plan were a perfect fit for Leslie.

NATIONAL CHAMPIONS

Dartmouth's commitment to and support for individual excellence is well represented by the accomplishments of its skiers in national championship competitions. In fact, Big Green skiers have won 34 NCAA, 18 Biathlon, more than 60 Paralympic and 110 USSA National Championships.

Chick Igaya '57 still holds the record of 6 NCAA Championships.

Chiharu Igaya '57, during his college skiing career, won six NCAA titles, still the record for the most individual titles at these championships. He also won 1-Japan and 5-USSA National Championships in 1954 to 1960. Two-time Olympian **Tiger Shaw '85** won the NCAA Slalom in 1982 and then went on to win nine individual USSA national championships, a record for most wins at the Alpine Skiing nationals he shares with **Dick Durrance '39** and Bode Miller. **Nina Kemppel '92, Tu '05,** won 18 national championships in various cross-country skiing events over her career, also an American record for national championships in that sport. And **Lisa Feinberg Densmore '83** holds the record in Master's Alpine Skiing with an incredible 57 national championship wins. **Ralph Miller '55,** with three NCAA titles and four national Alpine titles, and **Tom Corcoran '54,** with four individual national Alpine titles in the US, two in Canada, two in Argentina, and two in Chile, certainly belong on the list of Dartmouth's most successful skiers as well.

THE JOYS AND PRESSURES OF COLLEGIATE SKIING

But at the end of any discussion on Dartmouth's many ski heroes, it is important to remember that these great skiers, and hundreds of others who made the various teams each winter, skied first and foremost to represent the college in intercollegiate team competition. It's the reason the coaches were hired and the program supported; and for all of those fortunate enough to participate, and ultimately to earn a college letter in skiing, it gives special meaning to the Dartmouth years. Team ski racing is definitely different than individual competition. For one thing, it's fun to be a part of a team, training and racing together; for another, there are different kinds of pressures that make the challenges unique. Skiers who matriculate at Dartmouth, but immediately go on to other, more senior racing venues, may sometimes miss this element of the Dartmouth experience.

For some, like **Eva Pfosi '88**, winner of every slalom race she entered in 1987 including the NCAA Slalom Championship, being part of the team "reignited her love of the sport" after a few years of chasing the US Team circuit. Similarly for **David Viele '98**, two-time NCAA Giant Slalom Champion, who came to the college after several years on the international circuit, "it was redemptive." For many, like Erich Wilbrecht and Ed Williams, mentioned earlier, becoming a good enough racer to qualify for a Carnival team and to win a Dartmouth letter was a dream fulfilled. For most, the camaraderie of training and racing together with friends is one of the most enduring and impactful aspects of the college experience. The shared challenges of the Moosilauke training camps, or the shared excitement and nervousness in the van on the way to the Skiway for a Carnival competition, are unforgettable. Team skiing creates a special bond and it's really fun.

David Viele '98, a two-time NCAA Giant Slalom Champion.

But the pressures of team skiing are significant and different as well. Tom Corcoran noted how nervous Walter Prager got at team events—just hoping all his skiers would stand up. Al Merrill, generally gregarious and upbeat, was almost comatose at a slalom race until he had three "counters" safely down the course. Every Dartmouth Alpine skier has at one time or another undoubtedly been told to "go fast but stay away from the gates and make sure you stand up". It's a difficult concept to execute because it's really not the way you train to win a ski meet.

My own personal most-memorable team skiing moment typified all these challenges. At the 1962 Middlebury Carnival (traditionally The Eastern Intercollegiate Championships), the Dartmouth Team entered the final event, the ski jump, slightly ahead of Middlebury and in first place in the standings. Their team and ours were pretty evenly matched in jumping so our prospects were good. But–as always–it was windy, and a typically raucous anti-Dartmouth-and-anybody-else crowd of several thousand was massed around the outrun at the bottom of the hill.

In the jumping event at that time, each school could enter four athletes–top three to count. Each jumper got three jumps–top two to count. On my first jump, I got blown around by the wind and fell. And the crowd cheered! Al Merrill got very quiet. He didn't have to tell me that I had better find a way to stand up on the next two jumps–but he did. And I got that famous stern, ferocious Al Merrill stare that conveyed the gravity of the moment. I managed a good jump in the second round, and two of our other three guys jumped well and were ahead of Middlebury's second and third competitors, but our first jumper had fallen twice and was out of the scoring.

I vividly remember the final moments in the final round. My teammates had done well and we were obviously going to win–if I had a good jump. Only two jumpers were left on top of the hill: Middlebury's best skier, John Bower, and I. The wind was still blowing and Al Merrill had a pleading look in his eyes. Bower went next and jumped 200 feet—an amazing 25 feet farther than any other jumper to that point. I was watching from behind and saw him blown a good 15 feet off line by the wind, but he held his landing and was greeted by a thunderous cheer from the partying crowd. He had done his part. So I was on top of the jump alone, the last competitor, knowing I needed a good jump. I could see that Al had his back turned, assessing when the wind would be most favorable for me (truly the art of coaching). And all my Dartmouth teammates were up on the knoll of the jump, yelling and screaming encouragement, and from my perspective, believing they were one jump from taking the trophy back to Hanover. Pressure! So I smiled and pushed off. The ski gods were good to me: 185 feet, a solid landing, a delightful groan from the hostile crowd. And for me, relief, satisfaction, and triumph. We got to kiss the trophy. As a team, we won the jump and the meet, and that moment is etched in my soul forever. It is so much more exhilarating and challenging to be a part of a team and to share in the exuberance of victory!

BEYOND TRADITIONAL RACING - SKI FEATS

When you combine the fertile minds, athletic talents, and adventurous spirit of Dartmouth skiers, the results can be very interesting. Dartmouth men and women have figured out about every way you can imagine to strap on skis and challenge snow-covered terrain and the laws of gravity. No history of Dartmouth Skiing would be complete without mention of some of the incredible feats accomplished by members of the Dartmouth skiing family.

Ned Gillette '67, Olympic cross-county skier in 1968, became one of the America's most creative and accomplished wanderers. He came to consider himself a professional adventurer. For a while, after college, he pioneered a cross-country touring program at the Trapp Family Lodge in Stowe, VT, and wrote instructional books on skiing. After discovering that business school was not to be part of his future and that he had the unusual talent to think up, promote, and undertake incredible ski treks, he embarked on an astounding series of expeditions, most on skis, that occupied all his time for nearly twenty-five years. In 1978 he climbed to the top of Mt. McKinley (20,320 feet) in a single day; later that year he led an expedition to ski around its base. He skied around Mt. Everest twice, including one trip above 20,000 ft. He skied down the Mountains of the Moon on the border between Uganda and Zaire, made the first snowboard descent of 22,834-foot Mt. Aconcagua in Argentina (with Pete Patterson, brother of Dartmouth coach **Ruff Patterson**), traversed the Karakoram Range in Russia on skis, and skied off China's 24,757-foot Mt. Muztagata. His have to be the most traveled skis ever! Tragically, in August 1996, while traveling in Northern Kashmir, he was senselessly killed—by bandits.

Nina Kemppel '92 is perhaps the best US woman's cross-country (x-c) ski racer ever. During an international career that spanned 13 years and four Olympic Games (1992, 1994, 1998 and 2002), she won a record 18 national championships and regularly finished among the top 20 in World Cup events – unusual for an American x-c skier. In the last of her 15 Olympic starts she finished 15th in the 30-km classic (traditional diagonal technique) race at the 2002 Games in Salt Lake City, which at the time was the best finish ever by an American woman in an Olympic cross-country ski event.

At home in Anchorage, AK, though, she is also well known as the woman who won the Mountain Marathon an incredible nine times–eight times in a row at one point. This is a race up and down Seward's Mount Marathon. It is a little over one and one half miles in length and 3000 vertical feet up—and then down—complete with cliffs, scree fields, and waterfalls. It's a great tradition for runners and skiers, and typically Nina did it more often and better than any others before.

On a trip home from the World Cup one year, a woman on the plane spotted her and got excited: "You're that woman! You're that woman," the stranger said – "You're that woman who wins the Mount Marathon all the time." Kemppel smiled and said "I actually ski, too."[40]

Carl Swenson '92 is a three-time Olympian cross-country skier (1994, 1998 and 2002). He has the distinction of being named by *Outside Magazine* and the Outdoor Life Network as one of the top ten "Ultimate Bad Boys of the Outdoors." He was, according to their unscientific poll, a "two-sport maniac" and "endurance machine" because of his extraordinary balance of World Cup skiing in the winter and strenuous mountain bike racing in the summer. He was described as "the fittest athlete in the country"[41]

He grew up in North Conway, NH, and was recruited by Coach John Morton to ski cross-country for Dartmouth. While Carl describes himself as "not one of the studs," he skied on the top Carnival teams and continued to improve under Ruff Paterson's guidance after Morty retired.

He started mountain biking after Dartmouth as a way to train during the "off" season and got so good at it he became a pro-racer and almost qualified for the Olympic Games in cycling. For more than ten years he competed at the international level in two grueling winter and summer sports and maintained his position as one of the top Americans in both.

Lisa Feinberg Densmore '83 was an accomplished Alpine ski racer at Dartmouth, but her real ski-racing career started in 1991 when she started racing in "Masters" ski competitions. Since that time she has won an astounding 57 National Masters championship races with one World Masters Championship, the Super G in 2008. She is an author, photographer, avid hiker, businesswoman and mother, living in Hanover, NH. Her busy life does not leave a lot of time for training. She is just one of those gifted athletes who has figured out how to race well. Asked what motivates her, she says, "I still like to go fast."[42]

Lisa is still in her "prime" as a Masters skier and can conceivably add three or four more titles a year if she continues to compete well. Her 57 titles are already unmatched, but this is clearly a case of more is better!

Lisa Densmore winning one of her 57 Masters Championships (2008 SISE Cup Finals at Sugarbush, VT).

Charlotte Moats '03 is a champion freeskier pursing a wild and somewhat undefined sport held on steep mountains with few rules and controls. For eleven years she skied traditional Alpine events and was a nationally top-ranked junior and Junior Olympic Gold medalist. During her Dartmouth years, she was a star on the ski team. Attracted by the unusual challenge, she started freeskiing in 1999 and has had enormous success.

One of her most interesting and daring wins was at the New Zealand "Chinese Downhill" that same year. Chinese Downhill racing is a "gnarly" event where a group of athletes, in this case women on skis, start at the same time at the same place on the top of a snow-covered ridge and race to the bottom of a mountain. First one down wins; there are no other rules or "controls." The New Zealand race was held on remote 7,000-foot Mt. Brewster, "a wind affected, steep and radical peak running into a crevasse-littered glacier." The race was 1½ kilometers long with speeds reaching 70-75 miles an hour. After the race one competitor said, "This event is screwball, totally wild, there were people flying all over the place," and reactions ranged from awe to outright fear. Charlotte won with "great downhill racing skill and smart tactics, blitzing the field with smooth, swooping turns." Charlotte said the strategy was pretty simple: "You just had to get out front. You really wanted to keep away from all the other riders, because you could easily get taken out. It was roller-derby at high speeds."[43]

She continues to be a top freeskier and has appeared in an impressive variety of films, television shows, and magazines, including starring in Warren Miller's film "Off the Grid." Charlotte comes by her love of "off the groomed runs" skiing honestly as her dad, **Alan Moats '70,** is one of the former top racers and innovators in Telemark skiing. He was a member of the US Telemark Ski Team in the mid-nineties competing at World Cups and World Championship events, and is a renowned Telemark ski instructor to whom the experts come for advice and inspiration. In addition, he is a 2009 National Champion Mountain Biker, winner of his age class in the 2009 Jackson Hole Town Downhill, and a part owner of the Mad River Glen ski area.[44]

Dartmouth has had snowboard racers as well - Ann Ojemann '94 boarding. (Photo by Tom Paganucci).

LEADING THE OLYMPIC AND PARALYMPIC MOVEMENT

Every chapter in this book has accounts of Dartmouth leaders and innovators in various aspects of the sport of skiing. Dartmouth grads have also had a significant impact on the Olympic movement itself over the years, helping to establish and guide the organization of Olympic and Paralympic sport in America.

The roles of Fred Harris and Charles A. Proctor in organizing the involvement of the American team

The involvement in the Olympics takes different forms. Former Dartmouth ski team member, Springer- Miller '48 organized the first IBM computer scoring system for the Olympic races (1960s)

at the earliest Winter Games have been mentioned. As have the contributions of Malcolm McClane, Bud Little, Al Merrill and others as members of the Olympic Skiing Committees during the late 1950s, a critical time during which the Olympic Committee and National Sports Organizations figured out how to select, fund, and prepare teams for international competition. It was during these periods, and in no small part due to these Dartmouth icons, that the US Olympic Committee became a professional organization, dedicated to and knowledgeable about how to help athletes and coaches succeed at the Olympic Games.

Ed Williams '64 has played a major role in helping the US Olympic Committee (USOC) learn to protect the athletes' right to compete based on their abilities and their results and not on the whims or prejudices of coaches and sports administrators. His personal accomplishments in skiing encouraged him to apply for and eventually to attend and excel at law school. His involvement with the sport led to membership on the USOC Athlete's Advisory Council, one of the most influential groups advising the USOC on sport related issues. He built a unique legal career by combining his knowledge of athlete eligibility issues and law to create a niche for himself representing athletes. Today he is one of the most effective advocates for athletes in America, often on a *pro bono* basis. Thanks in large part to his efforts, the U.S. has developed fair and unbiased team selection guidelines, increasingly effective anti-doping programs, and guidelines for managing Olympic sport organizations that are the best in the world.

Joe Walsh, Nina Kemppel, Sarah Billmeier and Sarah Konrad '89 have also served as members of the USOC's Athletes' Advisory Council. Nina is still an active member of the Council today and one of the leaders of that group.

Jim Page '63 striding forth in his racing days.

Jim Page '63, after six years as Dartmouth Ski Coach and nine years as US Ski Team Coach and Nordic Team Director, served for 18 years as a senior staff member of the USOC. As one of the few Olympians on the staff, he became the expert on many sport related issues. He led the USOC effort to establish athlete funding and support programs and helped to develop and refine the ways in which the USOC provided sports support services to the National Governing Bodies. Perhaps his most significant contribution was the creation of the Podium Program, a special effort designed to improve American results at the 2002 Winter Olympic Games in Salt Lake City. Under this initiative, the U.S. nearly tripled the number of medals it had ever won before at a Winter Olympics–from a previous high of 13 to a record number of 34. The program has become a model for the USOC for the support of athletes and coaches to achieve improved results at the Olympic Games and other major competitions.

Max Cobb '87, as Executive Director of the US Biathlon Association, has reorganized and fine-tuned the Association to create what the USOC considers a model National Governing Body. Through judicious use of funds and an unrelenting focus on supporting sports performance at all levels, he has built an effective system of recruiting and developing young athletes, has hired excellent coaches and support personnel for his top teams, and started to produce outstanding results. The US Biathlon Olympic Team for 2010 will enter the Games with its first real shot at winning medals in nearly 20 years.

Larry Jump '36 and **Steve Bradley '39** introduced what has long been considered the best amputee ski training program in the U.S. Larry had seen it done and realized what a great opportunity it was for people with disabilities to be able to continue to enjoy ski sports. He introduced the program at Arapahoe Basin, CO. Bradley started a similar program at Keystone, CO. It started as a way to improve the quality of life for wounded World War II veterans and today has grown into highly competitive events for disabled skiers. Colorado, and in particular Winter Park, has become one of the most important centers in the US for these activities and programs.

The thing to understand about disabled athletes is that they are not using sport for therapy or rehabilitation. They are, in most cases, true athletes who happen to have a physical disability. In skiing, they train hard all year around, compete at national and international levels as they qualify for teams and plan for competing at the Paralympic Games. While the U.S., in many cases through the abilities of Dartmouth Paralympic skiers, has done very well in international competitions, it has been a particularly difficult proposition for most of the competitors to find the resources they need to pursue the Athlete lifestyle.

Trygve Myhren '58 has been their "angel," raising funds and helping to organize and support the national program so that America's disabled ski athletes can train and travel to races across the globe. Over the course of fifteen years, Tryg's SkiTAM organization has put on annual fundraisers that provide the base of program financing that enable the U.S. to field competitive Paralympic teams. Tryg has become one of their most trusted supporters and had the honor to serve as Team Leader for the delegation that competed in the 2006 Paralympic Games in Torino, Italy. Today, Tryg's skiers receive on-going support from the US Ski Team and the US Olympic Committee, giving the U.S. one of the strongest teams and best programs in the world in Alpine adaptive skiing.[45]

Joe Walsh '84, Paralympic medalist and Program Director.

Joe Walsh '84, Paralympic medalist in cross-country skiing, is currently serving as Program Director for Paralympic Sports at the USOC. In this position he has been particularly effective at reorganizing the way in which coaching and program support is provided to aspiring Paralympians in both summer and winter sports. Many nations are taking Paralympic sport more seriously and providing funding and program support to win medals at these Games. Joe is responsible for keeping the U.S. competitive and building programs that will attract the best athletes and giving them world-class support.

ON TO THE SECOND 100 YEARS

So in 100 years of organized skiing, Dartmouth can boast 66 Olympians and Paralympians with ties to the school, more than 235 national champions, and an amazingly consistent record of producing excellent skiers, coaches, and officials. The college has had an equally impressive group of creative and enthusiastic ski pioneers who developed new events and pushed the limits of skiing possibilities. Only a few are mentioned in this chapter, but the stories of all the others are every bit as compelling and engaging. A full list of all Dartmouth's Olympians, Paralympians and Olympic coaches can be found in Appendix 2, the list of National Champions in Appendix 3, and members of National Championship Collegiate Teams in Appendix 4.

There are many accomplished and successful Dartmouth alumni in every field and profession. Dartmouth is justly proud of the impact its graduates have had and are having on the quality of recreational and competitive skiing in America and beyond. But it is perhaps its ski teams that best exemplify a program of sustained excellence, innovation, and leadership in a given sport, a program unparalleled in its scope and unrivaled in its success, one which has had a direct transformational effect on the greatest number of under-graduates over the longest period of time.

The environment in Hanover continues to be nearly perfect for those who chose Dartmouth in part to join its successful ski team tradition, for those who want to learn to race, and for those who dream of making Olympic and Paralympic teams. The coaching is world-class and the program standards are high. Training in the Hanover area is ideal. And the D-Plan still offers suitable attendance options for those who need to be away for international events. As Nina Kemppel expressed it so well, "When on-campus, after hours of training and going to school, its inspiring to go back to your dorm at night and realize that literally every young man and woman is working to become really good at something, whether the arts, or an academic field or another sport. It's an environment that creates an expectation of excellence."[46]

Dartmouth can be expected to continue its tradition of placing students and graduates in skiing events in many more Olympics and Paralympics to come. And the ski program is committed to continuing its unique philosophy of supporting and encouraging participants to be engaged at all levels of the sport, even long after they leave the hills of Hanover far behind.

DARTMOUTH'S CURRENT COACHES

Peter Dodge '78, Men's Alpine.   *Christine Booker, Women's Alpine.*   *Ruff Patterson, Men's X-C.*   *Cami Thompson, Women's X-C.*

***

A brief review of Dartmouth's National Championship teams (1958, 1976, 1977 and 2007) in the era since the NCAA started provides the final comment for this chapter. Each year had its own dynamics and mix of participants, but all represent Dartmouth skiing at its best.

MEN'S 1958 NCAA: THE FIRST CHAMPIONSHIP SEASON

By William E. Smith, M.D., '58
Co-Captain, Dartmouth Ski Team and National Downhill Champion, 1958

Hanover, September, 1957. The students have returned for the fall semester. Dry-land training for the ski team has begun--but with a startling announcement: **Walter Prager** has suddenly retired.[47] Our fabled coach and mentor is not coming back. Fortunately, our great Nordic coach, **C. Allison Merrill**, has been moved up to the head coach position, making it a smooth transition. Al had already been with us for two years, but this was still Walt's team; it was composed of five seniors: co-captains, **Dave Harwood '58** and **Bill Smith '58**, **Bob Gebhardt '57**, **Dave Vorse '57**, and **John Ceely '58**, plus three juniors, **Fran Noel '59**, **Dick Taylor '59**, and **Don Peterson '59**. One very important addition to the coaching staff was Olympian **Bill Beck '53**, our new Alpine coach. [Although Gebhardt and Vorse matriculated with the Class of 1957, they graduated with the '58s after taking a year off for traveling or military duties.]

As student athletes, the ski team members had spent their time on campus living together in College Hall and studying, training, racing for four years. During that period, former Dartmouth greats **"Chick" Igaya '57, Egil Stigum '56, Pete Kirby '56**, and **Ralph Miller '55** had been an important part of the mentoring process and added greatly to the team's camaraderie. The pre-snow dry-land training sessions improved our strength, speed, agility and endurance while Igaya's Japanese gymnastics and Stigum's Norwegian soccer workouts brought an international flavor to our training. By the time snow arrived, the team was ready to suit up.

The 1958 intercollegiate ski season started with the 48th Dartmouth Winter Carnival (January 31-February 1). A team must do well in its regional meets to qualify for the NCAA finals—and we started off big. Our complete domination in both the slalom and cross-country (x-c) events allowed the Big Green to get off to an impressive 15-point lead over St. Lawrence University. Middlebury did not compete here because they had to attend a qualification meet elsewhere. Gebhardt, Smith and Ceely took 2nd, 3rd and 4th in slalom. Taylor won the x-c with Smith and Ceely 3rd and 4th.[48] On Saturday at the Skiway, Smith won the downhill with **Dave Britten '59** (substituting for the absent Dave Vorse) coming through for us big by taking 3rd and Harwood placing 10th. In the final event, the jump, the team took 3rd, 4th, and 5th with Peterson, Noel and Taylor. Dartmouth had won by 35 points over runner-up St. Lawrence. Smith won the all-around Skimeister award—the first of several more to come.[49]

Next came the Williams College Winter Carnival (February 8-9). Dartmouth finished second to arch rival Middlebury by 12 points. The Green was missing its top Nordic performers, Taylor, Peterson and Noel, who were in Maine for a national meet; but Gebhardt was brilliant in setting a new record on the famed Thunderbolt downhill course on Mt. Greylock. Smith again won Skimeister honors.[50]

The next week, the team headed to Middlebury and the Eastern Intercollegiate Ski Association (EISA) meet (February 14-15.) In the opening downhill event at the Snowbowl, Smith led a 1-2-3 finish, followed by Gebhardt and Harwood; Dartmouth had a perfect 100 points on the board. The 15-km x-c was run that afternoon. Both Taylor and Noel had been struck by illness the night before the race. Middlebury's Lahdenpera and Kjekshus went 1 and 2. Fine performances by Ceely, Smith and Harwood, 3rd, 6th, and 7th, helped the team to a second place in that event. After day one, the Green trailed Middlebury by a mere 0.36 of a point.[51] Saturday dawned clear and cold, a chill -10° F. The first run of the 55-gate slalom went well for Dartmouth with Smith and Harwood finishing 1st and 3rd; Middlebury's F. Hurt was 2nd. In the second run, Smith went on to win, setting the pace again. Gebhardt finished 2nd and Vorse 4th. Middlebury's two best skiers fell, giving the Big Green a seven-point win. In the 50-meter jump on Saturday afternoon, University of New Hampshire (UNH) star E. Dohlen won his third straight Carnival jumping title. Our own Don Peterson garnered 4th, while Taylor and Noel tied for 8th. Middlebury's Thomas and Manley claimed 3rd and 5th and bested Dartmouth by only 1.5 points. But when the results were posted, Coach Merrill's skiers had amassed 583.13 points to Middlebury's 576.09 to maintain possession of the EISA Championship and capture the Panther's Winter Carnival title. And to make the victory even sweeter, Co-captain Bill Smith won his third straight Skimeister title. He placed first in both the downhill and slalom, took the Alpine combined, added a sixth place finish in x-c and 17th in the jump.[52] The Dartmouth team was totally primed to host the NCAA's.

With the winter carnival season successfully behind us, the team felt realistically optimistic about our chances in the upcoming NCAA championship meet on 1-2 March, which Dartmouth would host. Among those coming to Hanover would be ski powerhouse Denver

1958 NCAA Championship Team:
Robert C. Beghardt '57, David J. Vorse '57, Bernard C. Baehler '58, John A. Ceeley '58, David S. Harwood '58, William E. Smith, MD '58, David D. Britton '59, John R. Capper '59, Francis J. Noel III '59, Hartley B. Paul II '59, Don S. Peterson '59, Richard W. Taylor '59, Thomas J. Brock '60, Roger W. Hackley II '60, Peter M. Ryland '60.

University (DU). Coach Willy Shaeffler's formidable team had already won the first four NCAA crowns and was undefeated in their 1958 Western meets.[53] The University of Colorado (CU), under Tom Jacobs, would also be a strong contender from the West. Middlebury, always a strong team under Bobo Sheehan, Ed Blood's UNH team, St. Lawrence University, and Michigan Tech completed the field.

In the previous two NCAA's held in the West--at Winter Park, CO, in 1956, and Snow Basin, UT, in 1957--Dartmouth had finished 2nd and 3rd respectively. In 1957 the Alpine events were dominated by the Green, with Miller and Igaya starring. The Nordic events, however, were another story; we seemed unable to compete against the strong Western runners, possibly in part because of the altitude.[54] In Hanover, the playing field would be leveled.

The NCAA meet began with the 45-gate slalom at the Dartmouth Skiway. After the first run, Dartmouth skiers were 1st and 2nd with Smith and Gebhardt, and 6th and 10th with D. Vorse and D. Harwood. Middlebury had two skiers in the top ten, but Denver University had only one, and their top skier, Ronnestad, was disqualified. In the second run, Gebhardt and Vorse poured it on to take 1st and 2nd; Harwood made a brilliant recovery and finished a strong 5th. Smith went out of the course and finished 15th. Dartmouth had scored 98.7 points, Middlebury, 94.4, DU, 92.3, and CU, 90.8.[55]

That afternoon the 15-km x-c was held at Oak Hill under cloudy skies and temperatures in the mid 30s. In a very competitive race, Middlebury won (90.7 points), Dartmouth was 2nd (89.8 points) and DU was 3rd (88.4 points), even though DU's Servold won the race. Middlebury placed 2, 6 and 9 with Lahdenpera, Kjekshus and Hurt. Dartmouth placed 4, 7, 8 and 10: Ceely, Smith, Taylor and Harwood. Coach Merrill had hit the wax perfectly for the team! After day one, Dartmouth had a 3-point lead over Middlebury and was ahead of DU by 8 points.[56][57]

The next morning, the Alpine racers traveled to Cannon Mountain at Franconia, NH, for the downhill competition. Coach Beck had prepared the team well for a very fast and steep course, but the race was won by G. Vaughn of Norwich U. But then came the Big Green train: 2nd B. Smith, 3rd D. Vorse, 4th D. Harwood and 5th B. Gebhardt. Dartmouth scored 97.4 points. Middlebury dropped way back with 78.3

points and DU moved up with 92.4 points. Going into the final event, the jump at the Vale of Tempe, Coach Merrill and his team led rival Denver by 18.1 points by virtue of a near perfect performance in the morning's downhill. Willy Shaeffler's DU skiers made a strong attempt at a comeback in the jump with Ronnestad placing 1st, Severson 4th and Lussi 9th. While the Green had no jumpers in the top ten, Noel was 11th, Peterson 16th and Taylor 17th, putting the team second to DU by 6.5 points in that event.

When the results from all the competitions were tallied, Dartmouth was declared the clear winner, thereby ending DU's four-year reign as NCAA skiing champions. The final score was Dartmouth 561.2, Denver 550.6, and Colorado 532.6. Middlebury, St. Lawrence, UNH and Michigan Tech followed in that order. Dartmouth's individual winners were Bob Gebhardt in slalom and Dave Vorse in the Alpine combined. Co-captain Dave Harwood was named Skimeister for the meet by placing 4th in the downhill, 5th in slalom, 10th in x-c, and 19th in the jump.[58]

At the victory banquet held at the Hanover Inn, it was most fitting that the newly commissioned Walter Prager/National Collegiate Ski Champions 1958 trophy was presented to a most deserving coach, Al Merrill, and his team for Dartmouth's first ever NCAA win. Not only had the team defeated the best in the East and the West, but its skiers had also captured almost every individual Alpine honor available: Bob Gebhardt had won the NCAA Slalom, Dave Vorse the NCAA Alpine Combined, and Dave Harwood the NCAA Skimeister title. The only jewel missing from the NCAA Alpine crown was the Downhill title, won by Gary Vaughn of Norwich U. But in mid-March, in a separate race at Snow Basin, UT, Bill Smith took the National Alpine Downhill Championship, arguably an even bigger win, to essentially complete Dartmouth's dominance of collegiate Alpine skiing. 1958 was a ski year to celebrate well and long remember!

***

Men's 1976 NCAA: The Unexpected Championship
By R. Phillip Peck, '77
Men's Nordic Team Captain, 1977

"For the first time in three years, Dartmouth's ski team heads into the NCAA Championship meet without the Eastern title in hand..." read the opening line in the Big Green press release for March 2,

1976. Not an especially auspicious send off for the 1976 team as we headed over to Rumford, Maine for the championships. Nonetheless the reality was that in 1976 we failed to win even one carnival, almost unheard of during the late 60s and 70s. Even if you looked at the previous year, with a team that won the Eastern Championships, we had finished a disappointing eighth place at the NCAA Championships, our top finishes coming from jumper Christian Berggrav and Arne Nielsen, who placed 13th and 16th respectively. On top of that, our team in 1976 was one of the youngest Dartmouth had ever sent to the NCAAs (i.e., five freshmen).

While we knew we were a good team in 1976, I don't think anybody expected us to win in 1977. Even Head Coach **Jim Page '63** told me later, "Phil, I didn't care if we finished fourth as long as Middlebury finished fifth!" If Pagie was thinking that way, his actions didn't reveal any reservations. Pagie and the coaches were pivotal in motivating us towards that victory.

The week of the championships began in a surprising way. Monday following our disappointing show at the Middlebury Carnival, **Tim Kelley '79** remembers:

Pagie and Alpine Coach, Dave Durrance, loaded up two fully-packed vans with Nordies and Alpiners--the Carnival team and the B team--and we headed across the bridge to Norwich. At the bottom of a very long and steep Elm Street hill Pagie and Dave kicked us out of the vans into a driving downpour of cold rain.

Pagie said: "This is going to be a very hard workout. So go hard."

I remember running with Whit (Johnson '77) and Peckah (Phil Peck '77) and we hammered to the top of the hill. I can still remember seeing the little waves of ice cold water coming down the pavement as we splashed to the top of the hill. By then we were totally soaked to the bone. We turned around and started jogging down and saw the van coming up the hill. Pagie drove by and shouted: "Run down and do it again."

No problem we figured. A couple of times up this hill will be okay. The next time up our clothes were so soaked they couldn't hold any more water. But at the top it was the same command: "Run down and do it again!" And same after the third time up: "Do it again!"

At this time we realized that a very epic workout was underway. I remember seeing the faces of my soaked ski team pals as they

*came up the hill. Their expression was of pain, shock and disbelief. I remember looking at the gaunt Stork (**Sverre Caldwell '77**) and saying: "What's going on?!" Stork replied: "I think Pagie's humongously upset!"*

I honestly can't remember if we did 4 or 5 times up that hill. But at the end it didn't matter. We were all thrashed to the max.

I can't speak for the Alpine racers, but I can honestly say that I think that workout definitely kicked the x-c guys into gear and we were ready to notch it up for the NCAAs. It also seemed to bring the team camaraderie back to the days of fall when we would all embark on epic hurt-a-thons as one big team.

Pagie took a gamble by throwing this hard workout in during late season to re-spark us. And it worked. Pagie always seemed to have a unique power to motivate. He is by nature a super-kind and affable guy. So when someone like that gets a bit stern, he gets a lot of attention and action. And that will motivate folks to do things like run endless uphill repeats in a driving cold February rain. Or it can even motivate a bunch of skiers to win the NCAAs.

The effort, grit, and attitude displayed by the entire team (Alpine and Nordic) on that cold and wet Monday was a tribute not only to this young team, but said a lot about the nature of Dartmouth skiing past and present.

1976 NCAA Championship Team:
Douglas S. Hicks '76, Arne H. Nielsen '76, Tu '78, Robert C. Singer '76, Craig T. Stone '76, Christian E. Berggrav '77, R. Phillip Peck, Jr. '77, Whitney L. Johnson '78, Jeffrey K. Kahl '79, Timothy F. Kelley '79, Tim G. Moerlein '79, Bryan N. Wagner '79, Robert E. Zinck, Jr. '79.

The next day **Doug Hicks '76, Rob Singer '76, Arne Nielson '76, Christian Berggrav '77, Dave Cleveland '78, Whit Johnson '78, Phil Peck '77, Tim Kelley '79, Bryan Wagner '79, Bob Zinck '79, Tim Moerlein '79,** and **Jeff Kahl '79** headed off to Rumford with coaches Jim Page, Dave Durrance, and Peter Robes. Just before leaving, Bryan Wagner recalls: "I remember that we had this team meeting before the NCAAs that year. Pagie gave a very motivating 'talk/speech' that really made me realize that this was going to be an important event."

The first event was the Giant Slalom at Sunday River. In addition to Pagie's motivational talk, the team was prepared due to some thoughtful planning. Dave Durrance wrote:

In *late fall 1975, we were looking for a quiet place to have our December training camp; a place that we could afford to stay for a week and some decent snow so that we could be prepared for the early Eastern Cup races. Knowing that the NCAA's were going to be at Sunday River, we made arrangements to go there. What a good choice that turned out to be.*

We stayed at the Bethel Inn, a little B&B on the way out to the ski area, which was like staying at home. We had great training at Sunday River, we were the only people there, and got to know the mountain very well.

When we went back in March for the NCAAs it was like going home. We had the Inn to ourselves and the people who ran it were like family. We knew every twist and turn of the courses, and there is a lot of terrain there so it was very helpful. We even knew all the lift operators. It was like we were the home team. Our familiarity with the area took away a lot of the tension you usually feel at a championship. I know we skied better because of it.

Certainly that planning paid off. On Wednesday, not only was Dave Cleveland an NCAA Champion, but we had placed four skiers in the top twenty: Bryan Wagner 7th, Rob Singer 12th, and Jeff Kahl 19th. Although defending champions Colorado won the overall, we were a relatively close second!

Next was cross-country, where we faced the unexpected challenge of having our wax return to Hanover in the van that was going to pick up the jumping team! Freshmen Nordic skiers Tim Kelley and Tim Moerlein forgot to take the box out of the van, and Pagie had to borrow wax from University of Vermont (UVM) coach Chip LaCasse. As Tim Kelley reflected:

Tim Moerlein and I knew that there was only one way to redeem ourselves at this point. And that was to have our best races of the season. And we did. We were the top two Dartmouth skiers (I was 3rd, Tim Moerlein was 11th). We went from being "stupid 'shmen" to "hero 'shmen" in 15 kilometers. And Pagie was once again our pal!

Those two freshman provided us with enough points to vault us into first place overall after two days: 3 points ahead of UVM, 6 points ahead of Colorado, and 12 ahead of Wyoming. Not to be kept down for long, Wyoming and Colorado came roaring back in Friday's slalom; both teams placed three skiers in the top ten. Dave Cleveland had an impressive 4th, Jeff Kahl was 11th, Bryan Wagner was 16th, and Doug Hicks was 17th. We scored enough points to be third on the day, ahead of UVM, but both Wyoming and Colorado moved ahead of us in the overall--but not by much.

Going into the jump, we were only four points behind first place Wyoming and two behind Colorado. Jumpers Christian Berggrav, Arne Nielson, and Bob Zinck were certainly competitive as they finished 7th, 11th, and 12th; but was it good enough? When the dust settled, four teams were within 5 points of each other. Amazingly, this young, most unlikely, but spirited and inspired Dartmouth team had tied favored University of Colorado for the championship!

Looking back, the 1976 season was one that all involved will remember. From disappointing performances in the Carnivals, to a team and character-building late season workout in Norwich, to a homecoming of sorts at the NCAAs which ended in triumph, it's a great story about inspirational coaching, transformative opportunities, sweet redemption, and--above all–total teamwork.

***

WOMEN'S 1977 AIAW: THE FIRST WOMEN'S CHAMPIONSHIP

By Mary Kendall Brown '78
Women's Alpine Team Captain, 1977, 1978

Since the earliest days of women's intercollegiate ski racing, Dartmouth women have often taken the podium. **Mary Heller '76, Anne Thomas '77, Ann Van Curran '77**, and **Debbie Tarinelli '78** are just a few of the skiers who regularly captured top spots in both the Nordic and Alpine races. Early team victories came mostly at home. In their debut as skiers in their first Dartmouth Winter Carnival in 1974, Ann Van Curan won the slalom, while Annie Thomas and Mary Heller were 1-2 in cross-country (x-c). In 1975, in a repeat performance, Van Curan won both the Carnival's slalom and giant slalom while teammate Thomas captured the x-c.

But in those start-up years, ski meets at traditionally strong Middlebury and the University of Vermont (UVM) frequently found the Dartmouth women scoring second or third as the team still lacked depth, confidence and experience. Even an occasional hot finish by the University of Maine kept the green team from winning on the road.

Mary Kendal Brown '78, Women's Alpine Team Captain (1977, 1978), contributed outstanding runs to Dartmouth's first Women's Championship (1977).

Debbie Tarinelli '78 skied for the US Ski Team before she came to Dartmouth and became an important member of their 1977 AIAW Championship Team.

But by season's end in 1975, the Dartmouth women began to gel. They won the Eastern Women's Division with a point total of 294.81, just ahead of Middlebury, a close second at 291.47. Dartmouth's individual winners were **Chris Simpson '78** in giant slalom and Anne Thomas in x-c. And by the time the first women's National Intercollegiate Skiing Championship took place in 1977, the women's team was ready. The Dartmouth program had developed a core of women skiers who could regularly compete with the best and provide the strength and depth it took to outperform the nation's top teams.

Leading up to the Nationals in the Eastern division, Middlebury regularly dominated the team results. In late January at the University of Maine carnival, Dartmouth scored third behind Middlebury and UVM. At the Williams Carnival in mid-February, Middlebury won the event with Dartmouth coming in third behind Middlebury and Maine. At the Middlebury Carnival, the final weekend of competition before the Nationals, the Dartmouth women placed second behind their hosts. Dartmouth's Tarinelli led the Alpine team, winning both the slalom and giant slalom. Other top ten finishes in the slalom were Chris Simpson's fifth, **Mary Kendall '78** who took seventh, and Ann Van Curan's tenth. In the giant slalom, Kendall was fourth and Simpson sixth. The Middlebury Nordic skiers won the x-c, but Dartmouth skiers Anne Donaghy, **Harriott Meyer '78** and **Wendy Thurber '78** were sixth, seventh and tenth, thereby capturing second place for the team.

With the momentum of the season behind them, the Dartmouth women were fully prepared for the succeeding weekend. Seventeen women's teams arrived in Stowe, VT, from across the country to compete in the first sanctioned Women's Intercollegiate Skiing Nationals. Also attending were the top 24 individual racers whose teams did not qualify for the competition, including skiers like the University of Utah's Toril Forland, a Norwegian native, who finished third in the combined events of the 1972 Olympics and was a five-time champion on the US Women's Pro Ski Tour. But with temperatures in the 60s and skiers donning T-shirts and shorts in mid-March, Stowe was unexpectedly bursting into spring.

The first Alpine event was held at Mt. Mansfield on Friday, March 11th, a giant slalom on the Chin Clip Trail. Deb Tarinelli completed the course as Dartmouth's top finisher in sixth place. Chris Simpson was 23rd and Kendall 28th.

The next event was the 7 1/2 kilometer x-country race at the Trapp Family Lodge. Dartmouth's Harriott Meyer skied to an incredible third place while Middlebury took one and two. With strong finishes by **Caroline Coggeshall '79**, Wendy Thurber, Anne Thomas and **Cate Sprague '78**, Dartmouth women had the lead after the first day of competition.

On Saturday March 12th, the slalom was set on Little Spruce. The sun beat down steadily, softening the course and giving a slight advantage to the Western skiers, but Tarinell raced to fifth with Kendall at 13th and Van Curan 19th.

The final event was the 4x5 kilometer cross-country relay. Supporters lined the course at Trapps. In the words of racer Wendy Thurber, "With adrenaline coming out my ears, I started the first leg of the Nordic relay. It was a beautiful, but unusually warm,

1977 AIAW Championship Team:
Anne Thomas Donaghy '77, Annie Van Curan Johnson '77, Christine Simpson Brent '78, Mary Kendall Brown '78, Cate Sprague Gilbane '78, Wendy Thurber Gross '78, Deborah Tarinelli Purvin '78, Harriott Meyer Shea, MD '78, Dale "Penny" Pennell Breed '79, Caroline E. Coggeshall '80.

spring-like day. In his inimitable style, Al, once again, nailed the wax! I remember coming up a rise out of an open field into a final loop before the tag off for the 2nd leg, with Al, Pam, and every one of the Alpine girls cheering and screaming at the top of their lungs." Wendy's strong effort brought the team in fourth place. Cate Sprague, Caroline Coggeshal and Harriott Meyer kept up the pace and advanced to third.

Tallying the final scores confirmed that the Dartmouth women had captured the national title. It was a heartfelt and hard-earned accomplishment, a true team effort, beating not only the favored Eastern rivals, but the Western schools as well. This was a victory not repeated until 2007. Thurber recalls that while attending an FIS conference with coaches **Jim Page '63**, Al and Pam Merrill and others, that someone noted there were four generations of Dartmouth skiing at the table. She said, "I felt like my teammates and I had earned our place in some corner of the Dartmouth legacy."

***

MEN'S AND WOMEN'S 2007 NCAA CHAMPIONSHIP: A THRILLING FINISH

By Stephen Waterhouse

It was **Lindsay Mann '07**, the last Dartmouth racer down the hill on the final race of her collegiate career, who sealed the deal on Dartmouth's 2007 NCAA Championship. It was an amazing finish to what became Dartmouth's first national team championship since the era of men's and women's teams racing as one, and the first national titles since the women first won in 1977 and men won again in 1976 after not having a championship since their first in 1958.

The championship capped an unprecedented undefeated season in which the Big Green won all six Eastern Intercollegiate Ski Association carnivals, including the Eastern championship at Middlebury. It was also the first time an Eastern school has taken the NCAA ski crown since Vermont won in 1994. It was steady team dominance by the Green that secured the title. They did not win an individual title for the first time in five years. But Dartmouth placed all of its racers in the top 20 of seven of the eight races contested, building up valuable team points and widening the margin against perennial Western powers, the Universities of Denver (DU) and Colorado.

Lindsay Mann '07 in final slashing run down the 2007 NCAA slalom course.

Dartmouth's cross-country team was the foundation for the success. The entire women's team, including **Sara Studebaker '07, Susan Dunklee '08** and **Elsa Sargent '08** placed in the top ten of the women's 5-kilometer race, with Sargent in 7th, Studebaker 8th and Dunklee 10th. In the women's 15-kilometer classical event two days later, Dunklee finished 7th, Studebaker 11th, and Sargent 12th. The men's squad also placed well: in the 10-kilometer freestyle, **Ben True '08** took 8th, **Mike Sinnott '07** was 18th and **Glenn Randall '09** was 23rd. After what they considered a "disappointing" performance in the freestyle, the men really let it all out in the 20-kilometer classical race, with True 4th, Sinnott 8th, and Randall 17th.

In Alpine racing, excellent results were achieved as **Evan Weiss '07** and **Michelanne Shields '08** posted top-ten finishes in giant slalom, with Weiss finishing 2nd in the men's race and Shields 9th in the women's run. Weiss, junior **David Chodounsky '08**, senior Lindsay Mann and Shields all finished in the top ten in slalom with Chodounsky 2nd, Weiss 8th in the men's race, Mann 4th and Shields 10th in the

Lindsay Mann receives congratulations from an excited crowd on her phenomenal final run (2007 NCAA).

women's race.

Not only had Dartmouth not won in three decades, but no one in the East had managed to wrestle the team title away from a block of Western schools in a dozen seasons, not since Vermont claimed it last in 1994. Furthermore, it is generally conceded that Dartmouth is the first school since the NCAA sanctioned the sport in 1954 to win the championship with an entirely American roster. Many of the Western powerhouses have relied heavily on European recruits in recent seasons. Dartmouth often does not win these titles because, in the Dartmouth system, its skiers are encouraged to seek to compete on to the national ski teams whenever they can in order to pursue personal excellence. And Dartmouth's unique year-round, four-term academic system allows these exceptional skiers to be off campus during the winter term. That means that practically every year the best team of skiers that Dartmouth could potentially field is not seen in the college races.

The Big Green of Dartmouth did not win even a single individual event at the 2007 championships, but the team depth proved overpowering with its ability to score well in each discipline. In all, Dartmouth skiers earned a stunning 13 All-America nods. With the top-ten finishers in each event named All America, the Dartmouth tally included Weiss and Shields in slalom and giant slalom, Chodounsky and Mann in slalom, Sinnott in classical cross-country, Studebaker and Sargent in freestyle cross-country, and True and Dunklee in classical and freestyle cross-country,

But the whole championship boiled down to one fantastic race by Lindsey Mann, a senior from Bedford, Mass. She was ninth after the first run and knew it was going to take a big race from her to cement the team title. She was literally the last Dartmouth skier to race in the last race of the championship and in the last race of her college career.

Mann's performance was breathtaking as she outdid all expectations. Knowing that the title was there for the taking, Mann says she felt little pressure as her coach**, Christine Booke**r, had told her to just go out and have fun. **Annie McLane Kuster '78**, a spectator and former Dartmouth skier, commented on the Lindsay's finish: "I was present and watching the NCAA slalom with Lindsay's mother and teammates when she came through the finish victorious! It was a thrilling experience for us all!"[59]

While New Mexico's Malin Hemingsson got the race win, Mann won the second heat with her brilliant run to finish fourth, one place ahead of DU's leading skier Claire Abby. When Michelanne Schield's 10th-best time topped the next-best DU finisher, the title went to Dartmouth. And a great team victory was secured.

The 2007 Dartmouth NCAA Championship Team

Chapter IV Notes:

1. Stats taken from the Winter Carnival Cupacing. 2. Stats taken from the Dartmouth Winter Cup – The Eastern Intercollegiate Ski Championship Trophy. 3. 2009 NCAA Skiing Championships Results and Record – NCAA.org, see All Time Championships and Records. 4. Dartmouth Ski Team Media Guide 2009, p5. 5. Stats from www.Sports-Reference.com, UVM, Middlebury College, University of Colorado and University of Denver Athletic Department web sites. 6. Morton Lund, "The Historic First Four Olympic Games", Skiing Heritage, Volume 13 Number four, p4. 7. In the 1934-35 American Ski Annual. 8. In Gilbert's academic paper for the 2002 International Ski Congress, "The 1935 Olympic Tryouts on Mt. Ranier, a key event in Nationalizing U.S. Skiing." 9. From Dr. Joel Hildebrand, "Report of Manager of 1936 Olympic Ski Team" in the National Olympic Association Commemorative Book on the 1936 Olympic Games. 10. Dave Durrance to Jim Page. 11. Lund, "The Historic First Four Olympic Games", p19. 12. John Jerome, "The Man On The Medal", (Durrance Enterprises, Snowmass Village, Colorado) 1995, p29. 13. Ibid. p30. 14. Lund, "The Historic First Four Olympic Games" p20. 15. Roland Palmedo, "Report of Ski Committee", National Olympic Association Commemorative Book, 1940, p86. 16. Dr. David Bradley, "Dartmouth In The Old Day; The Era Of Prager and Durrance" Ski Magazine, February 1959, p66. 17. From Bradley, "Dartmouth In The Old Days; The Era Of Prager and Durrance" Discussion of Harriman Cup p76-78. 18. Dr. David Bradley, "Dartmouth In The Old Day; Part I" Ski Magazine, January 1959 p 78. 19. See Appendix 2 Dartmouth Olympians, Paralympians, Coaches and Officials: 1924-2006. 20. Ed Williams to Jim Page. 21. Ed Williams '64,, "I'll Teach You To Ski Cross Country" a tribute to Al Merrill p 2. 22. Ibid. p3. 23. Ed Williams to Jim Page. 24. Joe Walsh to Jim Page. 25. Eric Wilbrecht, "Thoughts On Dartmouth Skiing", a paper prepared for Jim Page by Eric Wilbrecht. 26. Ibid. pp2-3. 27. Scott Berry to Jim Page. 28. Bradley, "Dartmouth In The Old Days; Part I" p74. 29. See Appendix 2. 30. John Morton to Jim Page. 31. Scott Macartney to Jim Page. 32. Peter Dodge to Jim Page. 33. Liz McIntyre to Jim Page. 34. United States Ski and Snowboard Association(USSA) press release, "Four Named To Ski Hall Of Fame", www.skiing.teamusa.org/news/article/10954. 35. Ibid. USSA press release 10954. 36. Tim Caldwell to Jim Page. 37. Tim Caldwell to Jim Page. 38. Tim Caldwell to Jim Page. 39. Phil Peck to Jim Page commenting on Tim Caldwell's influence on the Ski Team. 40. From Nina Kemppel interview, www.alaskasportshall.org/inductee_page/9_2_kemppel.html. 41. From "Bad Boys: Bode Miller and Carl Swenson" www.firsttracksonline.com/news/stories/108972335378392.shtm. 42. Lisa Densmore to Jim Page. 43. From http://classicmountainzone.com/ski/99/ripcurl/downhill.html "First to the Bottom Wins". 44. www.snowaffair.com/staffbios.html "Alan Moats – World Renowned skier and instructor". 45. Trygve Myhren to Jim Page. 46. Nina Kemppel to Jim Page. 47. Article, Walter Prager (1910-1984) F.C.Hart, DOC President 1957-58. 48. Dartmouth Outing Club Final Results, 48th Dartmouth Winter Carnival, 1958. 49. The Dartmouth p3 Sat. Feb1, 1958 and The Dartmouth P1, Mon., Feb 3, 1958. 50. The Dartmouth, Feb. 10, 1958. 51. The Dartmouth, Sat., Feb. 15, 1958. 52. From three sources: The Dartmouth, Mon. Feb 15, 1958; New York Times, Mon. Feb 15, Lincoln Werden; Results, Eastern Intercollegiate Ski Association Meet, Middlebury, VT, Feb 13-15, 1958. 53. The Dartmouth, Mon., pg 1, Mar. 3, 1958. 54. NY Times, Sat., Mar. 30, pg 15, and Sun., Mar 31, 1957. 55. The Dartmouth, Mon., Mar 3, 1958, pg. 1. 56. The Dartmouth, Mon., Mar 3, 1958, pg 1. 57. National Collegiate Champsionships Results, March 1-2, 1958, DOC, Dartmouth College. 58. The Dartmouth, March 3, 1958. NCAA results. 59. E-mail AnnieKuster to Waterhouse 1/22/2009.

CHAPTER V

THE BIRTH OF SKI CLUBS: THE SOURCE OF ENTHUSIASTIC SKIERS

By Jim Collins '84
Author, Former Editor of *Yankee* Magazine and *Dartmouth Alumni Magazine*

With Peter Stark '76, Jean Schmidt Nunnemacher Lindemann, Hermann Nunnemacher '36, William F. Stark '50, Blair C. Wood '30, George W. Wood '67, Th '68, Monk Bancroft '57, T. Cartter Frierson '61 and Larry Langford '67

From the beginning, a certain spirit marked the skiing and winter activities of the Dartmouth Outing Club (DOC). Competition was important. Just six weeks after its January 1910 organizational meeting, the club put on a "Field Day" with ski jumping and 100- and 220-yard ski and snowshoe races; and over those first few winters, intramural contests were widely anticipated and fiercely fought. But club members showed an equal interest in building and demonstrating skills. They invited noted jumpers from outside the college to put on exhibitions. They included "proficiency tests" for Telemark and Christiana turns, a curved run, and snowplowing. They made sure technique factored strongly in the judging events. And — perhaps as importantly — they infused their athletic competitions with a friendly, informal, go-for-it brand of fun. In the Winter Carnivals leading up to World War I, snowshoers ran obstacle courses that required climbing over high sawhorses and crawling through barrels. Skiers later faced off in a "Potato Race"; as **David Hooke '84** put it in *Reaching that Peak*, the race "seems to have involved spearing potatoes in the snow while running on skis, and was used in the 1920 Carnival but, alas, not subsequently." But the Outing Club Dance and the Toboggan Party and bonfire and downhill canoe races persisted as hallmarks of Dartmouth's Winter Carnivals, and the members of the DOC became known not only for their skiing prowess but their sense of fellowship and camaraderie.

Increasingly, club members came to view winter sports as a team contest, not just a group of individuals — which was an entirely new way of thinking about competition. Other than against the Montreal Ski Club of McGill University, however, the fledgling DOC had few opportunities for friendly intercollegiate club-to-club competition because there were so few other clubs. That changed as word of the exciting new sports filtered out of Hanover and from across the Atlantic. The Outing Club found itself fielding inquiries from schools around the Northeast and reaching out to others. During the winter of 1914-15, Dartmouth students helped get outing clubs off the ground at Yale, Tufts, Colgate, and the University of Vermont. The 1917 *Aegis* reported that half a dozen similar organizations were looking to Hanover for guidance and advice. Outing clubs would soon sprout at Williams and Middlebury and the University of New Hampshire, and all of them showed genetic material that could be traced to the DOC.

The founding of the University of Wisconsin Hoofers, which would grow into one of the largest and most diverse student outing clubs in the country, serves as an example how this particular part of the Dartmouth Outing Club's legacy — directly and indirectly — helped spread and popularize the sport of skiing in North America. The same story underpinned many other collegiate clubs, with variations only in the details and the names. One of the Hoofers' founders, Porter Butts, described the Dartmouth influence in a 1979 interview for a University of Wisconsin oral-history project:

> "I think I can rightfully say that the Hoofers are noted for the establishment of skiing interest in Wisconsin. This wouldn't seem possible now with skiing universal in Wisconsin and throughout the country, but in the 1920s when the [student] Union came along, there was no such thing as skiing activity except for a few hardy Norwegians and Finns who had brought their ski jumping interests and skills with them and practiced on ski jumps in northern Wisconsin and northern Michigan. Indeed, the Norwegian students had built a wooden ski scaffold on Muir Knoll just a stone's throw from the Union. But this was in the early 1920s, and when most interested Norwegian students left the campus, the wooden scaffold fell into disrepair, and the jumping activity

was not very visible at the time when the Union opened.

In all of Madison you couldn't buy a pair of skis. There was no such thing as a ski with a binding, or boots to fit the bindings, or poles either for downhill or cross-country skiing. One of the first and earliest achievements of the Hoofers was to find a source for proper ski equipment. That came via the Dartmouth Outing Club, which was flourishing already in New Hampshire and which was acquiring its ski equipment from Switzerland. Through the Dartmouth club we were able to come by some twenty sets of hickory skis with leather-thong bindings — it was the only thing available at that time — and boots to fit and poles, and so on. We racked these up, of all places, in the billiard room, for rental. They were checked out and in at the billiard desk by students who wanted to give skiing a try and, of course, with instruction in how to do it. How to use skis was a pioneer program for the Union.

The name "Hoofers" derived from an example of the Dartmouth Outing Club as well, where to be a member you had to first serve as a "heel"; they called them "Heelers." This promoted the idea that the people who graduated from heels ought to be called "Hoofers." Hoofers was appropriate: it signified that you go there under your own power, "on the hoof," so to speak, and it gave us the horseshoe as the emblem for a shoulder patch and all the rest—kind of a symbol of good luck. We had an apprentice system, too, where those who wanted to become Hoofers had to first serve as "heels."

One of the co-founders of the Wisconsin club was an avid skier and biochemistry professor named Harold Bradley. His son William recalls, "My father was a prime mover in the establishment of the Hoofers. The club was patterned after the DOC. Like the DOC, the Hoofers staged an annual Winter Carnival. How father [who had been educated in California and at Yale] knew so much at that time about the DOC I can't say, but I suspect he knew their national reputation, contacted them for information, and ended up with a good working relationship with them."

The working relationship between Bradley and Dartmouth would deepen and expand over the coming years. That story provides a glimpse into how important the web of Dartmouth connections became in the early decades of American skiing — and how formative relationships at the club level often led to other formative relationships on a more personal level.

Dr. Hal Bradley was especially passionate about ski jumping. He helped raise money to reconstruct the Wisconsin jump on Muir Knoll, one of the few outside the Northeast at the time. He staged an annual jumping tournament (which became a life-supporting source of funding for the Hoofers), recruited and housed and paid for foreign-born jumpers to attend Wisconsin, and nurtured the development of four University of Wisconsin Olympians. He also built a back-yard ski jump of his own so his kids could learn the sport. Three of those boys would go on to attend Dartmouth, and two of them, **David Bradley '38** and **Stephen Bradley**

Jumper leaps from Brattleboro Jump on Harris Hill.

'39, would become accomplished skiers at Dartmouth and members of the US Olympic team. David became a major force in ski jumping as an official and judge, and he designed or renovated more than 60 ski jumping hills across the Northeast — greatly expanding the opportunity for young and developing skiers to learn and refine their sport.

While jumping was taking off in Madison and at Dartmouth, now-alumnus **Fred Harris '11** had taken his passion back to his home town of Brattleboro, Vermont, and created the Brattleboro Outing Club to "encourage, develop, and promote family outdoor life and good fellowship." The wording of the mission and the modest membership rates he set — $5 annually for men, $2 for women, $1 for schoolchildren — echoed the spirit and inclusiveness of the outing club Harris had founded at Dartmouth and were emblematic of the kinds of ski clubs that Dartmouth alumni would have a hand in creating throughout New England and beyond. But the impact of the Brattleboro club would be strongest felt in the jumping world. The ski jump Fred Harris built there in 1922 instantly made Brattleboro a national center for jumping, attracting the finest young jumpers from America and Europe. And it did something more for the town; except during World War II and the occasional drought year, the Brattleboro Outing Club hosted a well-attended annual jumping tournament until 2005. Four years after that, *Yankee* Editor Mel Allen wrote on the magazine's web site about the close of that era:

> "There was a time when ski jumping was one of the elite sports at many New England high schools. But school officials grew wary of the potential for lawsuits if a student were hurt. No matter how many football players broke bones, or basketball players took elbows to the face, ski jumping just looked really dangerous, especially if school administrators did not grow up with the sport.
>
> So one by one, ski jumping events all but disappeared from the New England winter landscape. Brattleboro's Harris Hill held on long after it probably should have succumbed. There was just too much history, too many memories; the sport was in the blood of so many local people, and so the competitions continued.
>
> But by 2005 the physical structure of the jump, as important to the safety of the athletes as a runway is to a pilot, had deteriorated beyond what simple goodwill and nostalgia and love could repair. The hill needed real renovation, real funding. So a group of dedicated people took charge. That's the way it has always worked in small communities. A few folks with a lot of drive gather more people, and then a movement is underway. It's how towns keep moving forward, with or without governments propping things up. Over four years, they raised nearly $500,000 —think of that! — to make their ski jump one of the best in the country. They even put in nifty stairs for spectators to use, and from what I could tell looking around, they pretty much spruced up everything — press box, landing zone — just as you would any local landmark that helps define who you are as a town..."

The newly renovated landmark is the only 90-meter jump left standing in New England, and one of only six of its size and caliber in the United States. The annual Fred Harris Memorial Ski Jumping Tournament, now overseen by a nonprofit group split off from the Brattleboro Outing Club, attracted 28 competitors in February 2009 and a record 8,300 spectators looked on.

Dartmouth's role in popularizing recreational jumping and skiing is difficult to measure, but by simply examining the impact of local outing and ski clubs having Dartmouth at their roots, it may be difficult to overstate. The ripples spreading out from the Brattleboro club alone covered decades and far across the winter sports landscape.

The DOC and its newly minted alumni spread the religion of skiing with both missionary zeal and great fun throughout clubs both large and small. And since the DOC had influenced collegiate outing clubs across the land, evangelical alumni from Middlebury and Yale and Harvard and elsewhere were going out into the world on the same mission, with the same belief in healthy competition and sportsmanship and camaraderie. The influence took many forms.

At the large end of the scale, a case in point was the Appalachian Mountain Club (AMC), a venerable mountaineering club dating from 1876. By 1930 the AMC was running annual weekend ski trips to Mt. Moosilauke and had made some attempts at formalized ski instruction. Between 1931 and 1934, some 41,000 skiers rode AMC-sponsored "snow trains" out of Boston on the B&M Railroad north into the mountains of New Hampshire. But the leadership felt the club needed a home base to make the sport more collegial and accessible.

In 1933 the AMC established a skiing committee and hired **William Fowler '21** to lead it. One of Fowler's first priorities was to locate a suitable winter headquarters for the club, one with strong skiing potential within 125 miles of the AMC's home offices on Joy Street in Boston. Fowler enlisted the help of **Johnny Carleton '22**, by then a lawyer in Manchester but still actively skiing. Carleton suggested the eastern slopes of Mount Cardigan, a mountain off the public path but well known to Outing Clubbers some 25 miles east of Hanover in central New Hampshire. Along with Carleton and an eccentric Civilian Conservation Corps trail-building expert named Duke Dimitri von Leuchtenberg (a Russian of reputed noble lineage) who had come to the US by way of Bavaria, Fowler set his sights on the Shem Valley area below the Firescrew, the northernmost of Cardigan's triple peaks, and saw the place he wanted. The new Cardigan Lodge, Fowler decided, would be a renovation of an existing building that, one can imagine, might have daunted someone who hadn't experienced the go-for-it spirit of the Dartmouth Outing Club. (Tellingly, Fowler had briefly held the club record for long-distance walking, covering a rugged 83 miles in one day in 1920.) As Peter Bronski described the site of the future lodge in the Summer/Fall 2009 issue of the AMC journal *Appalachia:*

> "The original farmhouse 'was one of those black, weather-beaten, patched, forsaken New Hampshire farmhouses,' wrote Helen Welch in 1934. The property also had a ramshackle wood-shed, leaky roof, condemned chimney, barn in bad disrepair, and dilapidated carriage sheds. What's more, the main house was occupied by John Yegerman, a hermit with a one-eyed dog (Yegerman peaceably relocated to a nearby shack)…"

Rallying unprecedented volunteer effort, Fowler completed construction by the following season and soon developed a top-notch trail system. The Cardigan Lodge would become a popular focal point for the AMC's winter programs through the post-World War II era until larger, lift-service resorts would take over the winter crowds. Fowler would later become president of the AMC and play key roles in the expansion of skiing in the Northeast, including the early development of the ski area on New Hampshire's Mount Sunapee. Countless other Dartmouth people would foster the work of the AMC in numerous capacities, from students in the huts and on the trail crew to alumni running trips and winter workshops for state chapters. But Fowler's work was typical of the combination of Dartmouth's can-do spirit and alumni connections that improved so much of the New England ski experience.

Still, it was probably at the smaller end of the scale that Dartmouth's influence on clubs and the spread of skiing was most pervasive. **David Austin '04** was among the founders of one of the typical early ski clubs, the Black and Blue Trail Smashers at Waterville Valley. As Tony Chamberlain of *The Boston Globe* wrote on the occasion of the club's 75th anniversary:

> "In its infancy in this country, skiing was pioneering. Long before motor-driven lifts were invented, groups of friends headed to the mountains, climbed up carrying their skis, then skied down the untouched terrain on whatever conditions existed…
>
> As its name suggests, the founders of the Black and Blue Trail Smashers reveled in the very toughness and challenge of the sport in the 1930s. Based in the Boston area, the group would make the long trek in those days and meet at Waterville Valley to blaze trails and ski. Armed with axes and saws, the mountaineers would climb up Mount Tecumseh and create the narrow windy trails that once typified New England skiing. On those same trails, they competed with each other in ski races. Between the climbing, trailblazing, and skiing — so the lore goes — those early founders got so beat up that they adopted the vividly descriptive name for their club."

Much later, **Tom Corcoran '54** would help transform the old Black and Blue Trail Smashers into one of the country's elite racing clubs and training centers for alpine, freestyle, and snowboard competitors.

Ski Team Captain M. McLane '46 joined both the Hochgebirge and Uncanoonuc Clubs.

Wes Blake '24 founded the Downhill Ski Club, one of several early Boston-based clubs such as the Ski Club Hochgebirge, the Altebirge Club, the Schussverein, and the Drifters, the latter all started by Harvard men who had skied (or would ski) on Mt. Moosilauke in the annual Harvard-Dartmouth race in Tuckerman Ravine, or in the Hochgebirge-Dartmouth Slalom on Cannon's Taft Trail, the first downhill trail in the country cut by the Civilian Conservation Corps.

The pollination crossed in all directions. As **Jeff Leich '71** of the New England Ski Museum reported, the legendary 1939 Inferno race on Mt. Washington had its genesis at a Schussverein invitational downhill when a former Harvard hockey-star-turned-skiing-convert named Alec Bright stood with others on Bear Mountain in Bartlett,

NH and looked off toward the snow-covered grandeur of Mt. Washington. In a matter of weeks Bright and his Ski Club Hochgebirge had resurrected its famous club race that **Dick Durrance '39** had won as a high school student five years earlier, but which is more remembered today for Austrian Toni Matt's 1939 hair-raising schuss of the Tuckerman Ravine headwall. The fabric of many, many clubs intertwined, and almost always carried threads of green. Future Hochebirgers, just to pick one club, would later include **Malcolm McLane '46, Brooks Dodge '51, John Strong '57** (whose father was Dean of Admissions at Dartmouth), **Dale Edmunds '75**, and brothers **Johnny '77** and **Jory '85 Macomber,** sons of MIT's Olympian Alpine racer George **Macomber**.

In those pioneering days, organized ski clubs were, in themselves, a sort of fraternity, bonded by difficult travel and a willingness to find their fun in rough skiing terrain and regardless of the weather. Dave Arnold, another Harvard skier in the club Hochgebirge who was still skiing at age 86, recalled driving north with skis strapped to the running boards of his car. "Chances were," he said, "if you saw another car with skis on it, you'd know everyone inside!" On the mountain or high pasture, 10 or 15 skiers would be a crowd.

C. Randall Childs '22 started up the Uncanoonuc Ski Club in Manchester, NH, which many Dartmouth alums would join, including the **Carletons Johnny '22, John '38**, and **Charles '41**, and **Malcolm McLane '46**, and whose home hill featured a cog-railway-style train that carried skiers to the top. **Jack McCrillis '19** was president of the Newport (NH) Ski Club when that club worked closely with the AMC's **Art Fowler '21** to develop the trail system at Mount Sunapee. Dartmouth alumni skied with the Skidaddlers, the S-Kimos, the White Mules, and other clubs in the Mount Washington Valley; others were heavily involved with the Winnipesaukee Ski Club at Gunstock and the Franconia Ski Club at Cannon.

The Franconia Ski Club is a good example of how a single Dartmouth member made a difference. **Sel Hannah '35** forged a strong relationship between the club and Cannon Mountain, where he had been developing trails. The idea of a club formally affiliating with a "home" ski area soon spread to clubs throughout the Northeast. Hannah unified the club's training program — which had been a loose coalition of "ski schools" sponsored by various local inns — under one banner. After World War II, he established a tradition of bringing in outstanding racer-coaches from the Swiss National Team. Paul Pfosi was an early one of them, recruited to coach in the club's junior program. Paul met and married Hannah's daughter, and with her had a daughter of their own: **Eva Pfosi '88**, a future NCAA champion racer and US team member. Eva remembers skiing at Franconia as a pre-schooler, wearing a hat knit by her mother in the club's signature red and blue.

Eva Pfosi '88 on the slopes.

As the sport evolved, personalities and identities of the clubs became distinct. Some, like Franconia, became known for programs that introduced the sport of skiing to local children. Others were mostly social, bachelors only, in it for après ski, and raced just for fun. Others raced seriously and evolved into dedicated racing clubs with world-class instruction. All of them shared a love of speed and friendly competition. Writing in *The Dartmouth* in 1936, **Don MacPhail '32** reported that Dartmouth's alumni, "recent, not-so-recent, and even distant, in astounding numbers, have carried the torch which has lighted much of the way for that lusty Gargantuan addition to our national life — winter sports… Graduates of the College have been in the forefront of the battle from the first."

As alpine racing, in particular, increased in popularity, it became more organized and formalized, and ski clubs multiplied in response. The 1935-36 *American Ski Annual*, published for the National Ski Association listed 135 clubs: 65 belonging to the US Eastern Amateur Ski Association, 39 clubs in the Central US, 10 in the West, 7 in the Pacific Northwest, and 14 in California. These numbers grew rapidly. By 1948 the Eastern Division alone listed 155 member clubs.

Over that same period in New England, recreational skiing was reaching into every hamlet that had a hill high enough to slide down. Jeremy Davis, creator of the New England Lost Ski Areas Project, has documented nearly 600 small, private, and family-run ski areas in the region that are no longer in operation. Little clubs like Uncanoonuc formed around many of them, even the smaller hills with vertical drops of less than several hundred feet. How many of those clubs and schools and communities had some Dartmouth connection is nearly impossible to determine, though it's not hard to guess.

Of course, Big Green influence wasn't confined to New England ski clubs. Alumni often took their passion for skiing back to where they were from, or took it with them when they moved, or married in, or were drafted, or otherwise got involved — even when the purpose of the club was simply to gather like-minded souls and hop a plane to a ski resort in Europe or the mountainous West. Clubs came and come in all flavors.

The old Heiliger Huegel club in Wisconsin is a prime example of how Dartmouth skiers helped lengthen the reach of skiing across the country, first in founding that club and then organizing still others as its members relocated to more challenging ski areas. Clubs bearing a Dartmouth imprint grew up in Waterloo, Iowa, Chattanooga, Tennessee, Aspen, Colorado, and beyond In Anchorage, **Russell Dow '37**, a New Hampshire native, was an active member of south-central Alaska's oldest ski club, the Anchorage Ski Club. During World War II, Dow trained Army ski troops at Anchorage's City Ski Bowl and was part of an illustrious team including Major "Muktuk" Marston and a member of the elite Alaska scouts known as "Castner's Cutthroats" that searched the mountains around Anchorage for an improved ski training area. With the Dow's help, the Army found and developed an Arctic Valley site in the Chugach Mountains, north of the city. In the late 1940s, with civilian skiers crowding the military warm-up building, the Anchorage Ski Club moved up the valley and built its own lodge and rope tows. Recent presidents of the club include four-year Dartmouth Alpine racer **Karen Loeffler '79.**

In the early 1970s, a different Dartmouth connection was set in motion through the Anchorage Nordic Ski Club. **George Moerlein '52** and his wife Judy — along with other club members and parents who had children entering a new school in the Hillside area of the city— helped lead a volunteer effort to build the school a 5-K cross-country trail network. Their work was successful, and the Moerleins' son Tim trained on those trails, joined Dartmouth's class of 1979, and became a member of the 1976 Men's Collegiate National Champion ski team. He later returned to Alaska, married a cross-country ski coach, won "Rookie of the Year" honors in the 1985 Iditarod dogsled race, and sent two strong, outdoorsy daughters of his own back to Dartmouth — thus returning some of the same spirit Dartmouth has been so successful in exporting.

But the story of the first ski area south of the Mason-Dixon Line — built by the Ski Club of Washington, D.C. (SCWDC) — perhaps serves as the best illustration of how the Dartmouth spirit could be introduced to a different region and change the course of ski history.

Hal Leich '29, who skied in the 1927 Moosilauke Down-mountain race, still had skiing in his blood when he moved to Washington, D.C., in the mid-1930s. He took over as president of the SCWDC before the war, and soon after he took a week off, came to Hanover, and got certified as an instructor by **Walter Prager**. The Washington club had cleared a glade off Skyline Drive in the Shenandoah National Park where members skied when there was snow. But following the war and the nearly dry winter of 1949-50, Leich and club member Gorman Young headed to West Virginia looking for reliable snow.

As befits a classic Dartmouth Outing Club story, some mystery surrounds this one. Widely varying published accounts describe how Leich and Young ended up exploring a promising geologic drift formation in the state's northeastern Canaan Valley. But according to **Jeff Leich '71**, the Executive Director of the New England Ski Museum, his "father apparently scoped out potential ski locations from the air with a friend who was in the Naval Reserve and took him up on training flights from D.C. (probably less an infraction of the rules then than now). They found the drift from the air, then went hunting for it."

In any case, Leich and Young found the drift — a narrow stretch of north-facing slope in a large pasture some twenty times longer than it was wide. Nearby residents told Leich that the snow was the real deal. They said it often lasted until July; in fact, sometimes they hauled snow from the drift across the road to cool beer. That was enough for Leich. The club signed a lease from the landowners, found a used rope tow in Maryland and an old truck motor to power it. More than 50 club members spent eight hundred man-hours digging holes for the lift, clearing rocks and stumps, and building a warming hut. The ski area, variously known as Davis Pasture, Davis Drift, Cabin Mountain, Driftland, and Little Tuckerman's, became so popular that special ski trains were arranged to carry loads of skiers out from D.C. The club — more echoes of the Dartmouth spirit — not only provided lessons and a ski patrol, but hosted an annual winter carnival, complete with Snow Ball and the crowning of a carnival queen. **Nick Stevens '58** remembers skiing there with his Explorer troop soon after the area opened:

"The rope tow ran along the upper edge of the drift, just where the slope began to flatten out, resulting in stretches where the sun melted the snow, so one often skied over patches of mud on the way up. But the main problem with Davis was that you spent 90% of your time on the right ski, because the reliable snow cover was only 20 or 30 yards wide, as I remember. So there were no long sweeping turns to the right, just short ones immediately followed by a quick turn to the left (to keep from going into the grass) and then a long traverse. The downhill quads really got a workout. It was a long way from D.C. for marginal skiing — but it was skiing!"

***

Heiliger Huegel: The Small Midwestern Ski Club with a Big Reach

By Peter Stark '76
Based on memories of Jean Schmidt Nunnemacher Lindemann and Hermann Nunnemacher '36, plus A Club History by William F. Stark '50

That's just one story of many, but it's a reminder of how many of them sound so typical of Dartmouth and how often a certain "can-do" adventurous spirit lay behind the spread of the sport. "Little Tuckerman's" introduced skiing to thousands of young people up through the early 1960s and spawned a sizeable ski industry in West Virginia that would grow to include 13 downhill areas. In 2009, the Ski Club of Washington D.C. numbered close to 2,000 members and was an active participant in the Blue Ridge Ski Council, a group of 22 ski clubs in the mid-Atlantic region.

As the decades have slid by, Dartmouth's influence in the formation and evolution of ski clubs has grown less dominant. Perhaps that, in itself, is a testament to how successful Dartmouth missionaries have been in spreading their religion. But Dartmouth skiers and coaches, alumni and parents, and sons and daughters continue to perpetuate a special love of fellowship and hard competition that keeps the sport alive and vital. Dartmouth's spell on them remains and is still just as important to all who have fallen under its infectious blend of physical energy, close personal relationships, and deep appreciation of nature's gifts to skiers.

As participation in downhill skiing spread during the 1930s from its epicenter in Hanover and Upper New England, a small ski club with a strong Dartmouth connection sprang up a thousand miles away

Hermann Nunnemacher '36, discoverer of "Heiliger Huegel" was still skiing in his nineties.

in mountainless Wisconsin. Called Heiliger Huegel, it would exert a disproportionately large influence on American skiing for decades to come.

Skiing was not unknown in Wisconsin at the time. All over the state, Scandinavian ski jumpers had carved their jump sites from hollows in the woods. But purely downhill skiing, imported from the Alps, was new.

Among the alpine skiers scouring the gently rolling farmlands of Wisconsin in the early 1930s for a suitably long and steep hill were the Nunnemacher brothers – Hermann, and his younger sibling, Jacob, sons of a Milwaukee manufacturing family. The entire Nunnemacher family had moved to Germany for two years in the late 1920s and learned to downhill ski using Hannes Schneider's Arlberg Technique while on Christmas holidays in the Alps. Hermann refined his technique further at a Swiss boarding school where his classmate was Rene Roch, son of ski pioneer Andre Roch. From boarding school, Hermann entered Dartmouth in 1931, spending two years there before returning to Wisconsin to complete an engineering degree at Marquette University.

About thirty miles outside Milwaukee, in Washington County, the Nunnemacher brothers discovered their grail in the Kettle Moraine area where two great glaciers had collided during the Wisconsin Ice Age and piled up steep mounds of rock and earth in a region otherwise scraped nearly flat. They knew this hilly area from picnics they'd had there with their relatives, the Zinns.

On the tallest of these knobby hills stood a Carmelite monastery whose two stunning redbrick cathedral spires were visible for many miles; it was known as Holy Hill. The neighboring knob–equally tall at 250 feet–held only a steep pasture where cows from the nearby Hembel farm grazed.

During the winter of 1935-36, known locally as the "Winter of the Big Snows", an invitation went out to sixty-five Milwaukee sporting families and ski enthusiasts to meet on February 21, 1936 and form a club. It began:

Since the heavenly powers have decided to endow Washington County indefinitely with zero weather and six inches of powder snow over unbreakable crust....

Fred Pabst, a diehard skier of the Milwaukee brewing family and brother of **Harold "Shorty" Pabst '38**, was elected the first president. While dairy farmer Walter Hembel milked the cows one evening, three club members negotiated a lease for the hill at $20 per year. **Hermann Nunnemacher '36** used his engineering skills to rig up a 1350-foot-long rope tow powered by Mr. Hembel's tractor. The club cast around for a catchy name, and, after a day of skiing, several members were having drinks with a visiting German skier, Goerz Langfeld, when club member **Bob Niss '40** asked him how one said "Holy Hill" in German. "Heiliger Huegel," he responded, and so the club was named.

Initially open to members of the public, the club soon became so popular it had to go entirely private, eventually adding a log chalet, snowmaking apparatus, and a chairlift to replace the long rope tow. More than just for its facilities, this small Midwestern gem of a ski area founded by Dartmouth skiers–among its earliest and most active members were **Fritz Meyer '33, Bob Manegold '38**, and **John Willetts '40**–has distinguished itself for those who have gone on to larger roles in the ski world.

These include Harold "Shorty" Pabst, who moved to the fledgling resort of Aspen where he helped establish the Aspen Institute and served as Aspen's mayor. Harold Pabst's brother Fred, the first president of HH, but not a Dartmouth alumnus himself, moved east and developed Big Bromley, Vermont, and a broad collection of other ski resorts like Rib Mountain, Wisconsin.

Bob Niss, after competing on the Dartmouth ski team, served during World War II in the 10th Mountain Division. Following the war he founded the Blizzard Ski Club near Milwaukee and modeled it on the Dartmouth Outing Club. This was the first and largest of any ski club in the country that catered to kids up to the age of 18 years, and it traveled around to various ski hills in the area rather than homesteading at just one.

Perhaps the most illustrious and promising of the HH skiers of his era was **Jacob Nunnemacher '42**, who raced on the Dartmouth ski team; much admired for his ski prowess and fun-loving spirit, he served as its captain his senior year. On gradua-

Jacob Nunnemacher '42, and his wife Jean who still visits HH every ski season.

tion in 1942, Jacob joined the 10th Mountain Division and eventually married the former Jean Schmidt, a Milwaukee girl who had skied at Heiliger Huegel since age 13. During training in Camp Hale outside Leadville, CO, he helped survey the initial runs for Aspen–at that time still a vision rather than a ski resort. From racing and from the 10th, Jake knew and learned from many of the famous names in skiing: Hannes Schneider and his son Herb, Toni Matt, Fred and Ellie Iselin, **Walter Prager**, Torger Tokle and others. He was also friends with the Bradley boys (Dartmouth skiers) of Madison, WI.

Sent to Italy with the 10th in late 1944, Sgt. Jake Nunnemacher was on a clearing operation in a small town in the Apennines a month before the end of the war when he was killed by a German sniper who had remained in a house from which Jake had just forced the surrender of several other enemy soldiers. He was the only member of the Dartmouth Ski Team serving in the 10th to give his life during World War II.

[Special thanks in the preparation of this article to Heidi Schulz, daughter of Jacob Nunnemacher and Jean Schmidt Nunnemacher Lindemann, and to Betty Manifold Meyer, Fritz's widow.]

***

THE WATERLOO SKI CLUB (IOWA)

By Blair C. Wood '30 with George W. Wood '67 TH'68
Excerpts from *A World History of Skiing in the United States from Eight to Eighty*
(All excerpts are in quotation marks)

My father, **Blair Wood '30**, began his skiing career in 1916 at age eight in the "bottoms" of Black Hawk Creek in Waterloo, Iowa. I skied with my father on Keystone Mountain in Colorado on the last run of his life in 1988, his eightieth year. This is os-

Wood '30 first on skis at age 8 (1916).

tensibly the story of the Waterloo Ski Club, but it is really my father's story. It was his enthusiasm for skiing at Dartmouth and beyond that created a generation of skiers in Iowa. While the rope tows and flood lights of the Black Hawk County Alps now sit idle and mostly forgotten, many of these Iowa skiing families now populate the slopes of Colorado ski resorts, including my own family: **Mike Wood '60, Blair Wood, Jr. '63, George Wood '67, Th '68** and **John Wood '73**.

This is Blair Wood's account of skiing in Iowa and the Waterloo Ski Club, written at the end of his life …

"I hesitate to write a history of skiing. Even this small beginning is difficult, and the prospect of marshalling words through the three or four volumes required to do justice to the subject is appalling. Hap-

pily, I am spared the burden of research, because I do not intend to do any. I shall simply draw from my failing reservoir of memories which will provide history enough, because fortuitously, the golden age of skiing coincides exactly with my own."

"Dad made my first pair of skis from a pine board *(circa 1916)*. What distinguished this board from others of its kind was the bent ski tip. We boiled the boards in mother's copper wash tub for thirty minutes, then laid them on the basement step nailed down with a cross piece and lifted the rear with an orange crate. The bindings consisted of leather straps tacked to the ski edges. One ski pole was enough in those days, but it was a big one. We skied down the hill at Elmwood Cemetery until we loaned the skis to Gus Helman, who broke one of them. This was probably the high point in Gus' life who ended up in the Reformatory."

After graduating from Dartmouth College and Harvard Law School, Blair returned to Iowa with his wife Eleanor (Vassar & Smith) in 1934:

"The following years in Iowa were good snow years but other than that it was a skiing wasteland. One could not purchase a pair of skis other than the flat ash by Northland or Strand to be found in the hardware stores … There were no ski boots or bindings and no equipment for children. There was no ski clothing. Eleanor fashioned us ski pants out of surplus army khaki … Ski poles reached to the shoulder and had baskets eight inches in diameter … One of the most serious deficiencies in the *(Iowa)* ski world was that we had no one to ski with, that is before I trained my Sunday School class."

"It was later *(1937)* that we discovered the Black Hawk County Alps which did for our skiing everything that the White Mountains did for skiing in New Hampshire. The Alps are a ridge above the flood plain of the Cedar River located in a wooded area be-

The Black Hawk County "Alps" Ski Jump.

*Blair Wood '30 doing a **Geländesprung** (1934).*

tween Waterloo and Cedar Falls. The Waterloo Ski Club was incorporated *(by Blair Wood in 1949)* and employed its treasury to purchase two successive New Sweden portable ski tows. I can remember many evenings when I returned from the office to join my sons where the ski tow was running and the hill illuminated by flood lights."

Mike Wood '60 on the "Back Hill" (circa 1950)
My personal skiing experience (George Wood '67 TH'68) began in 1949 at age four when my family settled into our new home on "The Ridge" of the Black Hawk County Alps. One particularly fond childhood memory is skipping school with my brothers on good snow days to ski on the back hill and having father write "mental" on my excuse card in the little space reserved for "Nature of Illness: _____".

About this time, the Waterloo Ski Club initiated the first of several annual Ski Carnivals. The Carnivals of 1951 through 1953 became the official "Iowa Combined Ski Championships", often drawing over 2,000 spectators with teams from Waterloo, Decorah, Dubuque, Cedar Rapids, Ames and Davenport competing in slalom, cross-country and jumping events. In 1953, Emil Thum (a "ringer" from Germany) soared 70 feet off the trestle ski jump. That's a long jump for Iowa.

The Cedar Rapids group, in spite of their Aspen patches, took one look at our slalom course laid out on the 100 foot vertical with trees for slalom poles and declined to compete … To do the Cedar Rapids

squad justice, this was not a sissy hill. It caused one death and maimed many more including me. Along with the merry shouts of winter echoed the snap and crackle of breaking bones."

Over time, the lure of skiing in Colorado would prove the undoing of the Waterloo Ski Club. Many graduates of the Iowa Ski Championships headed west to the fresh powder slopes of the Rockies and would never return. All four Wood Family sons headed off to Dartmouth and have now settled in Colorado, where we and our families keep up the skiing tradition that our father started so long ago in Iowa with families from other parts, like those of **Hank Paulson '68** from Chicago and **Bob Downey '58** from New York. Blair and Eleanor are buried in Elmwood Cemetery in Waterloo at the base of the gentle hill where Blair first ventured forth on the pine board skis his father made for him.

Mike Wood '60 on the mighty Iowa ski "mountain".

***

THE MONTCLAIR SKI CLUB: PASSION FOR THE MAD RIVER GLEN SINGLE CHAIR

By Monk Bancroft '57

The Montclair Ski Club (MSC) was formed in 1947 so northern New Jersey residents could congregate and ski together on day trips and weekends. Soon after, they were a founding member of the New Jersey Ski Council, along with Watchung, Plainfield, and the Ski Club of New Jersey, which fostered destination trips, instruction, and racing. It didn't take many years before MSC started to focus on Mad River Glen (MRG), VT which opened in 1949 with one single chair. They rented a place in nearby Waitsfield and became regulars at MRG. By 1959 they accumulated enough money to buy land and build a

modest lodge at the foot of one of the MRG trails.

In 1960, when I got out of the Air Force, I heard about the Club. I had raced at MRG while in prep school and always liked it. I decided to join as it was also conveniently near my home. The Club quickly made me their race chairman, and I started building a race team by practice and by recruiting. By the late '60s, I was NJ Council Race Chairman and MSC was state slalom champs in men's, women's, and combined. The Club was also heavily involved with the MRG Ski Patrol, and in 1968, they got me to join. My involvement in racing and the Council waned, but over the years about fifty MSC members have been part of the Patrol. At least three MSC patrol members graduated from Dartmouth, including **Dick Dale '50**, myself, and my son **Coe Bancroft '87**. The MSC members have also included **Steve Conlin '87, Jack Wood '51, Tu/Th '52**, his wife Sue, and the Wood's daughter, **Lauren Wood Schreiner '80**. In the small world of skiing, my son Coe married Dick Dale's daughter. The club is now 62 years old and still going strong. Three years ago, the Vermont Tram Board insisted that the venerable single chair at MRG, our pride and joy for almost 60 years, be replaced. Being co-op owned, the membership discussed and voted on a replacement. By a large majority the choice was a new single as it was an icon and members did not want more crowded trails. Then the fun began. It turned out that singles are not made any more but could be created--at a cost higher than the cost of a new double chair. The membership was determined to "stay single," and with the help of two foundations

Steve Waterhouse & Monk Bancroft '57 in Keystone CO.

used as intermediaries for tax-exempt donations to support historic preservation, they succeeded. The Dartmouth group both contributed to and helped with the fund-raising from other MSC members.

The new single chair has been in use for over a year now. It looks just like the old one, but has modern safety devices and an easier get-off at the top. It is also the fastest fixed-grip chairlift in existence, whisking riders over a mile in length and up over 2000 vertical feet in ten minutes. Mad River Glen has only two large snowmaking guns and the smallest water source imaginable. Two groomer machines touch up the beginner and some intermediate trails, but the rest are quite steep and gnarly. Still, the area consistently ranks very low or lowest for injuries per skier day. It has been called "a particular place for particular skiers" and its motto, as seen on bumper stickers everywhere, is "MAD RIVER GLEN - SKI IT IF YOU CAN." There are many of us who love it, and amongst this group is the core contingent of Dartmouth folks.

***

CHATTANOOGA SKI CLUB: THE SKI CLUB MOVEMENT IN THE SOUTH

By T. Cartter Frierson '61

"You *are* talking about *water skiing*, right?" was what I often heard when we first started chatting up the Chattanooga Ski Club in 1969. Now, a sentimental glance at the wood skis with leather long thongs I used in college, displayed athwart our porch rafters, revives many rich memories connected with skiing, starting with my first face-plant on the Hanover Golf Course harnessed in bear-trap bindings and waving bamboo poles.

After seven years of skiing in New England and Europe during college, army service and graduate school, I settled in Chattanooga in 1966 with my recent bride, Patty Browne Frierson, a Colby Junior College graduate and a beautiful skier. Living in the mid-South made a ski week very expensive. While we were rounding up enough friends to qualify for

airline group affinity fares, I learned that Atlanta had created the largest ski club in the country. Seven ski clubs in the South had already established the Southeastern Ski Club Association (SESCA). This network collaborated in filling charter flights, thus making travel to the best ski areas more affordable. Suddenly the ski resorts and airlines had a new and more accessible target audience: the monthly ski club meeting!

Encouraged by SESCA, I launched the Chattanooga Ski Club in the fall of 1969. We affiliated our club with SESCA, which we soon renamed the Crescent Ski Council because of the expanding array of ski clubs from Texas to Virginia. The airlines recognized the larger Council as the legal affinity group. Soon we could fill several charter flights to the Rockies and Europe from several southern cities each year.

The Crescent Ski Council now has about thirty affiliated ski clubs in the South.

Ski trips attracted new members, as did our monthly dinner meetings. In those days Chattanooga was still a "brown-bag" town: only private clubs could serve mixed drinks. The owner of one of those supper clubs offered to host our meetings in return for the food and corkage revenue. We dined on prime rib and washed it down with booze while watching ski films by Warren Miller. Word of our fun meetings spread rapidly. We recruited the supper club owner as vice president. A born promoter, he soon finagled complimentary round-trip tickets for the two of us on Swissair's inaugural Boeing 747 flight from New York to Geneva so we could evaluate several Swiss ski resorts for future club trips.

Our first club trips, in 1970 and 1971, were to Crested Butte, Colorado, which had just been purchased by Bo Callaway from West Point, Georgia, and his brother-in-law, Ralph Walden. These two men had concocted an ingenious marketing strategy: Crested Butte would target the southern market, where Callaway Gardens was already a prominent resort, and charter an airplane for every weekend of the ski season. Each weekend they would fly one group to Colorado and another back home on the same plane. The breakthrough was that a ski resort could eliminate the extra cost of deadheading, while a single ski club could not. Crested Butte thereby offered an attractive ski week package for any group that could fill an airplane. Delta Air Lines, based in Atlanta, was ideally situated to help the Callaway team go after the southern skier market through the emerging ski clubs.

Crested Butte presented their unique approach at southern ski club meetings, and our club signed on for our first club trip, in March 1970. We learned on arrival that our club was the first to ski Crested Butte under the new package. They spared no effort to insure that we enjoyed our stay. We came home happy, energized, and eager to introduce our friends to a new drink called the "Harvey Wallbanger." Going there again the next year, we discovered that ours was the first four-engine jet ever to land at Gunnison Airport, an event that had engendered considerable speculation there. Parked alongside the runway we noticed a throng of locals settling their bets!

My wife and Beth Callaway were placed in the same expert ski class in 1970 and again in 1971, whereupon Beth invited Patty to stay at the Callaway house and ski with her for another week. Had she been able to accept, she would have met their teenage son Ed who would enroll in Dartmouth three years later. **Ed Callaway '77** became president of Crested Butte in 1987. Thus the Dartmouth connection with Crested Butte began in the fall of 1973 when Bo and Beth Callaway became Dartmouth parents.

In those heydays of the ski club movement it seems anything was possible. Chattanooga Ski Club prompted the development of Cloudmont Ski Area, still the southernmost ski resort in the United States. A man who owned five summer camps in Mentone, Alabama, atop Lookout Mountain, was encouraged to find a thriving club in Chattanooga. Seeing a new way to make money in mid-winter at a summer camp, he joined our club. He scrounged up an old rope tow and six snow guns and cleared a one thousand-foot-long slope with a 225-foot vertical elevation. For press coverage of opening day he recruited the Chattanooga Ski Club to come ski for free so the reporters would observe real skiers, then a rarity in Alabama. Cloudmont Ski Resort is equidistant from Birmingham, Atlanta, Chattanooga and Huntsville. One nearby community college nearby even offers skiing as a physical education elective (I am not making this up). The Huntsville club, with all its rocket scientists, populates the ski patrol. Cloudmont averages thirty days of skiing a year. When we have several freezing nights in a row, we can actually drive south some forty minutes to ski.

It was through Dartmouth skiing connections that I came to know two legendary personalities in skiing, **Sarge Brown** and Warren Miller. I first met the late Sarge Brown, best known for his many years of running Vail Mountain ski operations, when I was Commander of the Army ROTC Drill Team at Dartmouth (1959-1961); Sarge was the Master Sergeant on staff who supervised the team. I treasure the opportunity I had to reminisce with him once again in 2001 when he and two other WW II veterans of the 10th Mountain Division were honored at the museum in Vail. I have Dartmouth classmate **Art Kelton '61** to thank for introducing us to Warren Miller in Vail and for selling us the house there that brought our family and friends so much healthy recreation and fun memories. One of the things that had attracted me to Dartmouth was the chance to ski. Since then my wife and I have skied with our growing family every year but one. We have now skied with six of our nine grandchildren. What other sport can grandparents, parents, children and grandchildren as young as four years of age do together that provides such dramatic scenery, camaraderie, and thrills as skiing?

***

DARTMOUTH AND THE SCHUSSVEREIN

By Larry Langford '67

In the 1930s, if you wanted to join in on the ski racing fad, ski clubs were the way to make it happen. One particular group of Harvard friends had been going up to Hanover to race and ski at Oak Hill. They were mostly friends from the Boston area (many had gone to Milton Academy together) and most were members of Delta Upsilon fraternity. They were excellent and adventurous skiers, and some were members of the earliest Harvard Ski Teams: Bradford Washburn, Charles Lawrence, Andrew Marshall (who later was to marry Ford K. Sayre's widow, Peggy), Herbert S. "Hub" Sise (the Ski Team Captain in 1934), and his brother Albert F. Sise, a New England skiing legend.

Conveniently for them, another schoolmate, Alfred Sawyer, was a part of this group, and his older brother, **George Sawyer '32,** just happened to be President of the DOC. He was therefore able to get his brother the keys to any of the DOC cabins for free lodging. Among the ones the Harvard boys stayed in, the most frequented was Cloudland in Pomfret, Vermont, near Woodstock and the Suicide Six ski hill.

The DOC cabin at Cloudland was either on or adjacent to property owned by William Emmons, Harvard '02. According to Hub Sise, one evening Mr. Emmons paid a visit to the cabin and was well plied by the group's notorious bartenders. It wasn't long before Mr. Emmons said to the group, "Say, you fellows are Harvard guys, and I'm a Harvard guy myself, so you shouldn't be staying in this Dartmouth cabin. I have an old house down the road that I currently use as a chicken house. If you were to fix it up a bit, I'll lease it to you rent free." The boys naturally agreed, and later (after the details were confirmed in a more sober moment) they moved into their first ski house, which is now featured on the mural at the Schussverein clubhouse in Jericho Valley, just north of North Conway, in Bartlett, New Hampshire.

To convert their informal fraternity into a real ski club, in December 1934, the gang formed a Massachusetts corporation they called Schussverein, Inc., "to promote and provide for the enjoyment by its members of skiing and other amateur and competitive and recreational outdoor sports." As the comings and goings to Cloudland increased, "It was strongly suggested that a Register Book be kept in the Schussverein at Woodstock to facilitate recording financial indebtedness for meals, beds, etcetera." These registers today — like the logbooks in the cabins of the Dartmouth Outing Club — are a wonderful source of doggerel and stories and record the hijinks of dozens of young Harvard men. The high-spirited fraternity life they evidently enjoyed is consistent with the description of ski racing, as the President of the Ski Club of Great Britain put it, "...by far the most virile, exacting, and dangerous of all sports yet devised by man."

The newly formed Schussverein traced a direct link to the earliest downhill and slalom races on Moosilauke and Mount Washington by having competed there. For many years the club entered several racers in the Harvard-Dartmouth Slalom in its backyard of Tuckerman Ravine. Susan Proctor, sister of **Charley Proctor '28,** later married Albert Sise, one of the earliest members of the club (and one who raced on Moosilauke in 1928), and Charlie taught many of the Schussvereiners the arts of racing before he moved to Yosemite, California. In 1939, Charlie was made an Honorary Member.

In 1947, **John R. McLane, Jr., '38** was made a member. He was the son of former Dartmouth College Trustee **John "Judge" McLane, Sr. '07,** brother of **Malcolm McLane '46,** a Dartmouth ski team captain, skiing legend, and (among so many other things) co-founder of Wildcat Mountain Ski Area in Pinkham Notch, NH., a locale that is a deep part of the Schussverein's history. Hub Sise recalled climbing up the Fire Trail in the late 1920s with his brother, Albert, in the company of **Joe Dodge H'55**. When Joe died in October 1973, a significant figure in the skiing history of New England and of the Schussverein was lost. He had come to the mountains in 1922 and retired in 1959 after 37 years as manager of the AMC hut in Pinkham Notch. Known to thousands of skiers and hikers as the "Mayor of Porky Gulch," Joe Dodge was made an honorary member of the Schussverein in 1951, four years before being awarded an honorary Master of Arts degree from Dartmouth. Joe's son, **Brooks Dodge '51 TH'54,** became one of Dartmouth's great racers in the '50s and a member of the 1956 Olympic team.

The club's connection to Dartmouth skiing gained a contemporary link through the Lathrop family. Fran Lathrop had been in the 10th Mountain Division and became a member of the Schussverein in 1969; he and his wife Cynthia regularly led their age groups on the Veteran's circuit nationally. Their son Jeff joined the club in 1976, and with his wife, Susie, raised ski-racing daughters, Christin, Abbi, and Jenny, in North Conway. As a family they helped the Schussverein dominate local club races, and later **Christin Lathrop '03**, who became an All-American at Dartmouth, skied for the US Development Team and on the Pro-Am Circuit. As an aside, Abbi and Jenny won All-American honors racing for Colby and University of Denver (alas, not for Dartmouth).

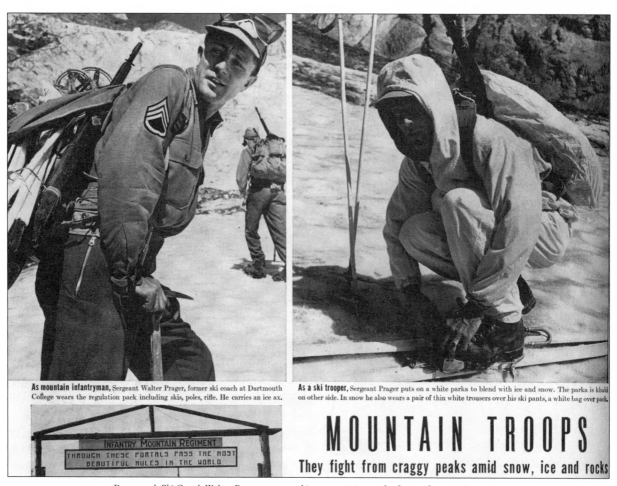

As mountain infantryman, Sergeant Walter Prager, former ski coach at Dartmouth College wears the regulation pack including skis, poles, rifle. He carries an ice ax.

As a ski trooper, Sergeant Prager puts on a white parka to blend with ice and snow. The parka is khaki on other side. In snow he also wears a pair of thin white trousers over his ski pants, a white bag over pack.

INFANTRY MOUNTAIN REGIMENT
THROUGH THESE PORTALS PASS THE MOST BEAUTIFUL MULES IN THE WORLD

MOUNTAIN TROOPS
They fight from craggy peaks amid snow, ice and rocks

Dartmouth Ski Coach Walter Prager was used in news stories as the featured mountain trooper to encourage new recruits to sign up for the adventurous military action in the mountains.

Chapter VI

DARTMOUTH AND THE 10TH MOUNTAIN DIVISION

By Charles J. Sanders
Attorney, Author of *The Boys of Winter* (2004)

As the world once again descended into the madness of total war in the late 1930s, the call went out for American alpinists needed to serve in a new, specialized Army group to be trained in winter mountain warfare. That fighting force, which would soon be designated as the 10th Mountain Division, became one of the most legendary and celebrated in American history, boasting perhaps the most rigorously trained and certainly the most highly educated group of soldiers the US Armed Forces has ever fielded.

Though many groups and localities across the nation and the around the world played key roles in supplying the skilled manpower that comprised the Division during the Second World War –including towns as far ranging as Adams, Massachusetts, Seattle, Washington, Oslo, Norway and St. Anton, Austria—none came close to matching the contribution of Dartmouth College and Hanover, New Hampshire. Over one hundred Dartmouth students, including four ski team captains and their coach, **Walter Prager**, helped to form the nucleus of the Division. This is the story of those Dartmouth contributions, in skill and in blood, to the US Ski Troops during the global war to stop genocidal fascism that the world simply could not afford to lose.

***

10th Mountain Division soldiers on the march in full mountain gear.

It was a bitter cold and blustery night in February 1940 when four friends met at the Orvis Inn near Manchester, Vermont, and had a conversation that would profoundly affect the lives and futures of thousands of the free world's best skiers and mountaineers. National Ski Patrol founder Minot "Minnie" Dole was joined at the fireplace that evening by former Olympic downhiller Robert Livermore, National Ski Association President Roger Langley, and the dean of American ski racers, Alec Bright of Boston, to discuss an idea whose time they believed emphatically had come: the formation of a division of US mountain troops in anticipation of America's entry into the bitter war already devastating Europe and the Pacific.

Conspicuously absent from the fireside chat that evening was one **David J. Bradley '38**, former Dartmouth Ski Team Captain, US National Nordic ski champion, and US Olympic team member. An acquaintance of all four men, young Bradley was at that moment huddled against a similar biting cold some six thousand miles away in Northern Europe observing, as a civilian reporter, what would famously become known as the Russo-Finnish "Winter War" still raging on the Karelian Isthmus of Finland.

A man with many Nordic skiing friends of Finnish descent, Bradley had been incensed by the fact that the Soviet Red Army, emboldened by the Nazi's nearly unopposed invasions of Czechoslovakia and Poland in 1939, had themselves launched a massive attack against tiny but strategically important Finland that November. The Finn defenders, who were severely outnumbered and overwhelmingly out-gunned, fought back against seventy divisions of Soviet infantry and tank groups with guerilla tactics conducted by crudely armed infantry and militia on skis. Against incalculable odds, these hit and run attacks inflicted huge casualties on the Russians, stalling the invasion for months.

Captivated by the success of the Finns, Bradley temporarily abandoned his post-graduate studies at Cambridge University to cover the heroic resistance for the Lee Newspaper Syndicate. It was his dispatches, and those of reporters like him who risked their lives to relay the story of Finland's fierce stand against the might of the Soviet Army, that informed the conversation at the Orvis Inn that night and the actions that followed.

Still nearly two years prior to America's entry into the Second World War, Minnie Dole and the others were already convinced that something had to be done to improve the nation's ability to fight and defend in mountainous regions under winter conditions. In considering whether the US homeland could be adequately protected from invasion, Dole wrote in his memoirs:

The conversation turned to the Russo-Finnish War, and inevitably –because we are skiers- we discussed the amazing job that the Finns were doing. We tried to imagine American troops in a winter environment. 'If foreign troops should attack our northeast coast in winter, can you imagine our Army trying to slug through the sort of weather that is outside tonight?' I asked. 'They'd have a hard enough time getting up the roads, let alone branching off into the woods.' Langley said he thought that he ought to write to the Secretary of War offering the National Ski Association's services. We all agreed that this was a good idea.

It was the irrepressible Dole, however, who took the lead in setting out to convince the US Army that maintaining a division of mountain troops was essential to the welfare and security of the nation. In letter after letter and meeting after meeting throughout early 1940, Dole passionately argued his way up the Army chain of command, asserting that if England fell to the Nazis, an attempted invasion of New England from Canada down through the Champlain and Hudson Valleys (the route used to attack America in colonial times) was not only possible, but likely. He reasoned that such an invasion would have to be met by a counterforce of US alpine troops, pointing to the fact that America's Axis enemies had been training and deploying crack mountain infantry for centuries.

In September, Dole was finally able to arrange for a face-to-face meeting with the one man other than President Franklin Roosevelt who could make the formation of an American mountain division a reality: Commanding General of the Army George C. Marshall. The general listened closely to Dole and was intrigued by his proposal to have the US Ski Patrol help the Army to organize a mountain division, but he was nevertheless non-committal and promised Dole only that he would get back to him in due course. Undeterred, Dole lobbied long and hard throughout the remainder of 1940, but by the onset of winter he still had heard nothing back from the Army and began to despair.

In a very real sense, it was young Dave Bradley who reinvigorated the debate. In a long and historic letter to Dole dated February 18, 1941, Bradley set forth his knowledge and reflections on the Winter War, describing the tactics and equipment that had been utilized so effectively by the Finns. Apologizing for the fact that he and Dole had not had more time to speak at the 1941 Dartmouth Carnival, Bradley noted that "perhaps this written statement will be of more use to you, and to the Army. I'm glad to help in any way that I can, for I feel that the need of preparation for self preservation is no less pressing here now than it was in Oslo a year ago. No one can say when this plague will reach our shores...."

Bradley's in-depth report included thoughts on a proposed training philosophy (that each individual mountain trooper must be totally self-sufficient under the worst weather and combat conditions) and hand-drawn illustrations of proposed tents, ski boots, and bindings. He ended his letter with the prescient opinions:

> "I would urge anyone who is seriously contemplating building up some 'Alpini' in this country to remember that we have several fellows who already know a lot about it and who might well be in at the top of the heap. Specifically, I think Walter Prager and **Jack Durrance [D-'39]** are probably the best men in the country to be at the head of a mountain division. There is little use wasting all the time and energy teaching a bunch of southerners how to ski. I should think that the Army would call in the thousands of experienced skiers, send them to [train] in Colorado, and from them build the nucleus of an expanding winter defense force."

Dole jumped on the opportunity to utilize Bradley's knowledge concerning the practical complexities of winter warfare to impress upon the Army brass that his own proposals were sound. Before long, the Bradley report was circulating among the Army's decision makers, serving to reinforce what had long been Dole's twin mantras: "American desperately needs mountain troops," and "it is easier to teach skiers to soldier than soldiers to ski."

The Army being the Army, however, it had to find out for itself whether learning to ski and mountaineer weren't actually easier than they looked. To do so, the services of yet another former Dartmouth ski team captain, **Dick Durrance '39**, were enlisted. The greatest American skier of his time and a former Olympian, Durrance had left Dartmouth following graduation to race and to teach skiing at Sun Valley, Utah, and later at the renowned Alta Ski School. In the fall of 1941, the Army asked him if he could help establish an "Experimental Winter Survival Training Center" at Alta in steep, avalanche-prone Little Cottonwood Canyon. Durrance agreed and gathered some of the best skiers in the world to assist him, including (just as Bradley had suggested) his brother

10th troops crossing the snow filled slopes of Alta in the sun.

Jack, and Coach Prager (who was re-assigned from Coast Guard duties, having been misdirected there as a draftee despite his reputation as one of the world's greatest ski mountaineers and instructors. **Percy Rideout '40**, a former ski team captain, had taken over coaching duties at Dartmouth in Prager's absence).

The Army, in turn, provided Durrance with about two hundred paratroopers from Fort Benning, Georgia, most of whom had never even seen snow let alone skied on it, and asked only that they be turned into competent military skiers within a few weeks. The stoic Durrance explained the immediate difficulties with the Alta teaching experiment this way: "Their training had been in jumping out of airplanes, and when they hit the ground they had been taught to roll forward. So they applied that same technique to skiing, which didn't work out at all."

Within a few weeks, Durrance had reported his conclusions to the Army that, like Dole and Bradley, he believed that it would be easier to teach skiers to jump from planes than to train paratroopers to ski. Much, much easier. Later, he summed up the Airborne's experience in the snows of Utah more concisely: "They broke a lot of legs."

Apparently in anticipation of the inevitable Alta debacle, by mid-autumn of 1941 General Marshall had already made up his mind regarding Dole's proposals. He wrote to Dole that a mountain infantry unit designated as the 87th Mountain Regiment was to be activated shortly at Fort Lewis near Mount Rainier in

The Mountain troops skiing at Alta in 1941.

Washington State, and that the US National Ski Patrol would immediately need to assist in recruiting skiers and mountaineers to fill its ranks. Each recruit would have to have three letters of recommendation attesting to his skiing and mountaineering proficiencies before being considered for service. This marked the first and only time in American history that a private organization had been enlisted by the US Armed Forces to assist directly in recruitment efforts until well after the advent of the All-Volunteer Force in 1973.

An ecstatic Dole immediately commenced a carefully orchestrated recruitment drive. His job, as he saw it, was simple. He would assemble the greatest skiing and mountaineering club in history, which the US Army would then transform into the world's most formidable mountain fighting force. To do so, he designated the Dartmouth Campus as a major recruitment hub and set out to fill the ranks.

Under Dole's guidance, the National Ski Patrol designed a series of questionnaires which it distributed to its membership and to other likely sources of volunteers such as the Dartmouth Outing Club and the nation's top collegiate ski teams. A publicity outreach campaign to these same groups and individuals was launched that included campus visits by Dole and the careful cultivation of recruitment pieces disguised as articles in the press (of which one particular effort in the erudite *New Yorker* magazine entitled "Minnie's Ski Troops" was particularly effective, despite Dole's objections that it was incorrect to call them *his* troops).

The questionnaires were filled out by the applicants and submitted for processing to the National Ski Patrol with the required three letters of recommendation. As an example of the quality of candidate that Dole was instantly able to attract, the questionnaire of Dartmouth former "B" Ski Team Captain **Larry Jump '36**, included the fact that he spoke four languages fluently, had served as a volunteer ambulance driver with the French Army in 1940, was a globally experienced mountaineer, skier and racer, and had first aid and cartography skills as well as an Ivy League degree in Government and Economics. "I am reasonably sure," Jump wrote in the "remarks" section of his submission, "that my physical condition, training and all around experience together with my love of the open, should qualify me." It did.

Dole, however, chose as his very first recruitment target still another Dartmouth varsity ski team captain, the fun-loving intellectual **Charles McLane '41**. Writing in the 1942-43 American Ski Annual, McLane noted that Dole had reached out to him with the ominous advice that he had better "get in on the ground floor" of the ski troops before he lost his chance. Given authorization by Dole himself to travel on government expense to Fort Lewis, McLane arrived at the camp's gate in November 1941 wearing his green letterman's sweater and carrying a pair of skis. After explaining to the incredulous guards that he really was there on assignment to "the mountain troops," it took hours for a base officer to conclude that McLane's orders were indeed authentic.

The Latrine Quartet of C. Bradley (with 3 Dartmouth brothers),
G. Stanley, C. McLane '41, R. Bromaghin, at Ft. Lewis, WA.

Finally summoned from the gate to report for duty, the young volunteer (in a legendary moment of American ski lore) was informed with some consternation by the officer-in-charge that he had indeed come to the right place; "Son," he was told, "it appears you *are* the mountain infantry." A very surprised Charles McLane was assigned to his own barracks, a one-man regiment waiting for company to arrive. "Ground floor, indeed," he later remarked.

Among the next of Minnie Dole's volunteers who trickled into Fort Lewis were Dave Bradley's younger brother Charles from the University of Wisconsin, Sun Valley skier Glen Stanley, and a tall, lanky local skier and guitarist from

Mountain troops from Ft. Lewis--or "Dartmouth West"--training on Mt. Rainier (1942).

the University of Washington named Ralph Bromaghin. Together, Bradley, Bromaghin, Stanley and McLane immediately formed a fraternity-style singing group which they dubbed "The Latrine Quartet," and committed to practicing and writing ski songs whenever breaks from skiing on Mount Rainier would allow. According to McLane, "We knew right away that, in the Army vernacular, we had pulled good duty." The barracks of the 87th Mountain Regiment, at least temporarily under McLane's influence, had become a sort of Dartmouth Campus West.

On Sunday, December 7, 1941, the burgeoning songwriting team of McLane and Bromaghin went with a group from Fort Lewis to Mount Rainier for a day of skiing in the sunshine, where they climbed up to Camp Muir (10,188 feet), the halfway station between the summit and famous Paradise Inn below. The weather was glorious, the snow deep, and the camaraderie reminiscent of the heady days at lunch rock below the headwall at Tuckerman's. Thoughts of war were very far away that morning. By late afternoon, sadly, that was no longer the case. Near dark, word finally arrived at Paradise of the attack on Pearl Harbor which had resulted in the deaths of thousands of American soldiers, sailors and airmen. The United States had joined the Second World War. The group headed back to Fort Lewis with a whole different mindset.

"We were really concerned about being shipped out to the Pacific theater immediately," recalled McLane, "but we ended up patrolling the area around Fort Lewis for several weeks until things on the West Coast settled down. When the Army figured out the Japanese invasion of California, Oregon and Washington wasn't coming, we finally got back to training."

With America now at war, a wave of new mountain troop volunteers poured into Fort Lewis. Led by Coach Prager (fresh from the Alta paratrooper experiment), former Dartmouth ski team captains Percy Rideout and **John Litchfield '39**, former Dartmouth student and 1934 US National Downhill Ski Champion **Joe Duncan '40**, and former Dartmouth Ski Team and Casque and Gauntlet member **John Montagne '42** the Hanover gang formed the nucleus of what would become one of the most "glamorous" specialized military units in history.

Due to incomplete information in the remaining files of the US Army and the college itself, it is not possible to say with certainty the exact number of former, current and future Dartmouth students and faculty that served with the 10th Mountain Division during the Second World War. Various reliable estimates, however, place the figure at approximately 120, representing a number equal to an astonishing five percent of the 1940 student body and certainly making Dartmouth the largest single contributor of manpower to the US ski troops.

Famed Dartmouth ski coach, Walter Prager, was used as the featured person in a
Life Magazine *promotional story to encourage enlistment in the mountain troops in late 1942;*
and recruitment numbers went up dramatically.

There has likely never been a military division with a higher mean level of education than the 10th Mountain Division during World War II. That is not to say, however, that despite its initial reputation as a glorified college ski club, joining the ski troops was for the faint of heart. According to another former Dartmouth ski team captain and mountain trooper **Bob Meservey '43**, many of the recruits looking for glamour by joining the ski troops "were shocked to find that it was indeed the infantry, but in the cold and with a heavier pack." Nevertheless, despite the rigorous training regimen that included skiing (but far more frequently climbing) in freezing winter conditions at high altitude carrying equipment so heavy that it frequently weighed more than fifty percent of the skier's body mass, the troopers still seemed to enjoy the idea that they were being paid to ski in an atmosphere that was decidedly not "regular Army."

That attitude was enhanced in no small part by the fact that the ski troops were originally quartered in luxury digs at the base of Mount Rainier in the Paradise Inn and Tatoosh Lodge. Snow piled up so high around the buildings that troopers coming in from maneuvers could ski into their rooms through the second floor windows. "So could the girls," one elated trooper later confided.

"The training experiences at Paradise led to the building of an unusually robust esprit de corps among the mountain troops that would become very important in combat," according to charter ski troop officer Major John Woodward of the University of Washington, a key participant in the 1935 Olympic Alpine skiing trials on Mt. Rainier that were led by Dartmouth skiers. "Officer or enlisted man," said Woodward, "we all had deep feelings in common, including a love for skiing and the outdoors in winter that bound us together very tightly. The training created a camaraderie that comes from shared outdoor experiences in the mountains that is very difficult to replicate in any other way. We were a fraternity of mountain men, regardless of background or anything else." " That," added his friend Percy Rideout, "and we had our songs."

More than any other of the thousands of aspiring ski troopers who arrived with their own music and mountain singing traditions, it was Charles Bradley and Ralph Bromaghin who led the way in regard to using songs as the glue that held the Regiment and later the Division together. The two penned dozens of musical parodies recounting the experiences of the ski troops that each new recruit had to learn and perform, but one in particular became and remains the theme song of America's mountain military. Sung to the tune of "Bell Bottom Trousers," the composition "Ninety Pounds of Rucksack" sums up the pride, fraternity, and humor that characterized the members of the elite US ski troops during the Second World War:

Ninety Pounds of Rucksack (to the tune of *Bell-Bottom Trousers*)

I was a barmaid in a mountain inn;
There I learned the wages and miseries of sin;
Along came a skier fresh from off the slopes;
He's the one that ruined me and shattered all my hopes.
Singing:

[Chorus:]

Ninety pounds of rucksack
A pound of grub or two
He'll schuss the mountain
Like his daddy used to do.

He asked me for a candle to light his way to bed;
He asked me for a kerchief to tie around his head;
And I a foolish maiden, thinking it no harm,
Jumped into the skier's bed to keep the skier warm..
Singing:

[Chorus]

Early in the morning before the break of day,
He handed me a five note and these words did say,
"Take this my darling for the damage I have done.
You may have a daughter, you may have a son.
Now if you have a daughter, bounce her on your knee;
But if you have a son, send the young man out to ski."
Singing:

[Chorus]

The moral of this story, as you can plainly see,
Is never trust a skier an inch above your knee.
For I trusted one and now look at me:
I've got a bastard in the Mountain Infantry.
Singing:

[Chorus]

By early 1943, the Army had completed work on a new training facility for its ski troops in Pando, Colorado, about halfway between Aspen and the Vail Valley, which it dubbed Camp Hale. At over nine thousand feet above sea level, it was the most complete, high-altitude military training facility in the world, quite literally a "ski city" made of redwood. Thousands more of the world's most famous skiers arrived to join the 87th Mountain Regiment, which was relocated there from Mount Rainier in its new and expanded form and renamed the 10th Mountain Division.

10th Mountain Division college hijinks in a snowbound car.

Combat training for the 10th Mountain Division at Camp Hale (1943).

Simply walking down Camp Hale's unpaved boulevards was a treat for a young skier or climber, who was likely to run into any number of winter sports heroes on the way to and from his barracks. Among the large contingent of world-class athletes from outside of the Dartmouth family that took up residence at Hale were European ski champion Friedl Pfeifer, Austrian Toni Matt (the Tuckerman headwall meister) and his Mt. Greylock ski buddy Rudy Konieczny, Swiss mountain guide Peter Gabriel, European Nordic skiing expert Arthur Tokola, North America's most famous mountain climbers Paul Petzoldt and David Brower, ski instructors extraordinaire Luggi Foeger, Andy Hennig, Flokie Haemmerle, and Pepi Tiechner, civilian four-discipline ski champion Alf Engen, Herbert Schneider (whose father Hannes had invented modern ski technique in St. Anton, Austria, before being forced by the Nazis to flee, eventually, to North Conway, New Hampshire), and the world's greatest ski jumper, the handsome and personable Torger Tokle of Norway. Even two members of the von Trapp family, whose story of escape from Austria would later be celebrated in the Broadway musical *The Sound of Music*, arrived from Stowe, Vermont.

By the time Bob Meservey and yet another former Dartmouth ski team captain, **Jacob Nunnemacher '42** arrived at Camp Hale and joined the Division, Hollywood had already dispatched a film crew to Pando to shoot a feature film depicting America's very photogenic, white uniform-clad "fighting mountaineers." New clothing and equipment were being invented and tested every day by the 10th Division, including the forerunners of modern ski bindings, arctic sleeping bags, hiking boots, fleece sweaters, quilted parkas, full-track snow cats known as "weasels," and snowmobiles. And whenever the training got too rugged during the week (such as when temperatures on the top of Homestake Peak and Cooper Ski Hill dipped to fifty degrees below zero), the troopers could always relax nearby on the weekends in a small mining town with a promising ski mountain called Aspen.

Everywhere the ski troopers trained, photographers and reporters tagged along for a story. The men rappelled off the balconies of the Brown Palace Hotel in Denver to impress the girls. They sang their songs on the radio. They pioneered near impossible ski routes through the Colorado Rockies that got them from Hale to Aspen quicker, and then celebrated their arrivals by downing wicked concoctions known as "Aspen Cruds" at the Jerome Hotel Bar. Charlie Bradley, promoted to being a Mountain Training Group ski instructor, became famous for shocking visiting dignitaries by tossing a straw filled, uniformed dummy off a cliff, while his fellow instructors feigned shock that he had lost patience with a recruit. The observers watching from a distance got excited every time. "All that was missing," said one former Ivy League ski instructor "was the football stadium."

But then came Kiska.

After more than a year of high-altitude training at Mt. Rainier and Camp Hale, the Army brass decided that it was time to test the ski troops under fire. In the summer of 1943, members of the 87th Mountain Regiment were sent to help clear Japanese invaders from the Alaskan island of Kiska in the far-western reaches of the Aleutian chain. It proved to be a brutal and humiliating introduction to combat for the untested infantry.

Forced to deal with horrendous weather conditions that included a swirling, blinding fog and lashing rain, the landing force hit the beach on Kiska and headed directly into the mountains to search for an enemy that had stealthily vacated the island a few days prior. With their troops in top condition and primed for a fight, the only thing that the untested 87th Regiment officers found in the mountain mist was each other—on what they mistakenly perceived to be opposite sides of the line. The resulting confusion led to the friendly fire deaths of nearly two dozen members of the ski troops, including a former Hanover area ski instructor named Roger Day Emerson. The 87th returned to Hale and to its sister 10th Mountain regiments (the 86th and 85th) heavy-hearted and minus several of its earliest members.

The Division's training intensified during the harsh winter of 1943-44 with a three-week set of maneuvers known as "D-Series," which took place in the Colorado Rockies in weather conditions that surpassed the misery of Kiska. Temperatures dipped to a steady thirty degrees below zero and blinding snowstorms kept troopers shivering in the field for twenty consecutive days without an indoor respite. During that time, many were trapped in the snow for days without food. As a whole, however, the Division came through the test remarkably well. Other than some serious cases of frostbite, their training had prepared them well for such difficult challenges of weather and terrain, and they impressed most Army analysts with their individual resourcefulness and tenacity. One Washington, D.C., military observer called D-Series the most difficult set of maneuvers the Army had ever conducted and he referred to the 10th as among the best-trained and most highly educated units in the American Armed Forces.

Still, the specialized nature of their training, and the stain of Kiska, seemed for better or worse to be keeping the 10th Mountain Division out of the war. When D-Day and the Allied invasion of Europe arrived on June 6, 1944, the Army used its Rangers, not the 10th Mountain Division, to scale the cliffs of Pont du Hoc above the Normandy landing beaches. A planned invasion to retake Norway from the Nazis was cancelled. Worse, when autumn came, the 10th was sent to Texas for flatland desert training. Many of its members feared the division was to be broken up into replacement units (an extremely dangerous combat role with an inordinately high rate of mortality) unless a need for its specialized talents could soon be identified. Though the situation appeared hopeless, there was, as it turned out, one American field general with his eyes on the ski troops.

General Mark Clark, who had presided over the terrible slog of American troops up the spine of Italy that served as a tactical Allied diversion in 1943 and 1944, was facing a difficult situation in the days after the D-Day invasion. His bogged-down Fifteenth Army Group and US Fifth Army troops and equipment were being siphoned off to be used on the more critical Western Front even as the German mountain troops continued to dig into the mountains of Northern Italy, potentially in preparation for a final stand in the Alpine Redoubt that stretched across the Italian, Austrian and German frontiers.

General Clark was neither a particularly well-liked nor gifted general, having already earned a reputation—through debacles at Anzio, Rapido River, and Monte Cassino—as a military leader prone to placing self-aggrandizement over the lives of his men. It was Mark Clark, however, who was the only military commander that requested the services of the 10th Mountain Division, and with the war in Europe clearly nearing its end phases, General Marshall granted his request. The members of the US Ski Troops promptly shipped out and landed in Northwest Italy at Christmastime, 1944, where they were attached to the US Fifth Army.

With the last gasp German offensive known as the Battle of the Bulge raging across Belgium and the Western Front, the 10th Division was rushed into position in the Apennine Mountains north of Florence and ordered to hold in place. Their main objective, as directed by Supreme Allied Command, was to ensure that the Nazis could not remove their entrenched Waffen SS units and mountain troops either to the Western Front, or more troubling, north into the Alpine Redoubt in preparation for a long, final siege. The 10th was to react only to an attack or an attempted withdrawal by the enemy.

General Clark, predictably, had other ideas. His Fifth Army had three times failed to secure Mount Belvedere, the towering heights above the main highway connecting the Northern Apennines to the Po Valley and the southern alpine entrance to the Redoubt beyond it. The units under his command had suffered horrendous losses in the process. Still harboring dreams of subduing the enemy on Belvedere and marching his Army north to seal off the Alps, however, Clark now believed he finally had at his disposal the specially trained troops necessary to carry out just such a mission.

The key problem in successfully attacking Belvedere, though, remained unchanged. German troops on the high shoulder adjacent to the massif (code named Riva Ridge) still had unobstructed views across the valley where attacks on the mountain had to originate. General George Hays, Commander of the 10th Mountain Division, studied the past failures to take Belvedere and determined that unless Riva Ridge could be captured first, a successful assault on Mount Belvedere was a near impossibility.

While the snow remained deep, General Hays sent out ski patrols to do reconnaissance and to map climbing routes up Riva, the only such ski patrols the 10th utilized in the war. "Skis make a lot of noise in anything but powder," concluded Johnny Litchfield, concerning the limited use of skier reconnaissance. "As military tools, they are worse than useless in icy, hard-pack conditions as one finds most of the time in the Apennines. Stealth becomes impossible."

Riva Ridge was a two-thousand-foot, near vertical climb that the Germans steadfastly believed could not be conquered. On the night of February 18, 1945, in one of the most audacious and difficult feats in the history of mountain warfare, it was scaled by a group of elite alpinists of the 10th Division that included former Dartmouth ski team captain and coach, Captain Percy Rideout. Arriving at the top of Riva at dawn after an all-night climb across freezing streams and under icy waterfalls, the Americans captured the high ground after intense fighting and then repelled a series of deadly German counterattacks. "It was very bad," remembered Rideout, "but we were very proud. We saved a lot of lives by knocking out those positions."

The following night, with former Nazi artillery observers lying dead in the snow on Riva, the remainder of the Division quietly crossed through the valley below Mt. Belvedere and started their climb. "When we got to the jump off point at the base of the mountain, we were told to fix bayonets," remembered **Phil Puchner '43**. "That order, believe me, got everyone's attention. My reactions fluctuated between 'you've got to be kidding' to 'brother, this is serious.'"

Puchner recalled that the troopers were ready to fight despite the wet, miserable cold, but lamented that the land mines which had been placed all over the mountain by the Nazis came as a complete surprise. "It's hard to prepare yourself for that, moving through the darkness, and suddenly realizing you are in an unmarked mine field, with friends all around you getting blown up. But you just keep going. You have no other choice."

The resulting explosions killed dozens of American ski troopers and tipped off the enemy that they were coming. Heavy fire poured down the mountain onto the advancing Americans and casualties mounted quickly. Toward the top, the fighting was hand-to-hand and foxhole-to-foxhole, with only the light of exploding mines and enemy fire to illuminate the battlefield. But by dawn, Americans controlled the mountain.

Once Mt. Belvedere had been secured, the division moved on to attack the adjacent peaks, Mount Gorgolesco and Mount della Torraccia, where the fighting intensified. The Germans, who were determined not leave their Apennine defenses without a fierce struggle, fought back with an intensity that shocked even hardened troops of the Fifth Army. Della Torraccia, especially, was a nightmare for those unfortunate enough to be ordered to capture it.

The 2nd Battalion of the 85th Regiment, led by Lt. Colonel John Stone, was the unlucky combat group assigned to that task. On February 21, Stone led his untested troops onto the slopes of della Torraccia. They were immediately hit with a barrage of Nazi shelling so sustained, violent, and effective that by the end of the day, those few of his officers, platoon and squad leaders that had not been killed could do little but try to comfort and rally the young infantrymen clinging to the rock-hard ground as their only hope of survival. With Company F that day was Staff Sergeant and squad leader **Roger William Herrick '40**.

Roger had grown up in Hollis, New Hampshire, near Nashua, and was a member of one of New England's oldest, non-Native families, with a long tradition of military service. The Herricks, in fact, traced their lineage back to the Vikings, with the first Herrick having arrived in America from Leicester, England, in the mid-17th century. A distant cousin, Ebenezer Herrick, died serving with the Continental American Army in the battle of Bunker Hill in 1775.

Young Roger, however, had a distinctly more artistic view of the world than many of his forebears. As a youngster, he was captivated by the scenic beauty of New Hampshire and Maine and wrote poetry celebrating his enchantment over the Maine seacoast near Boothbay Harbor where he summered each year with the extended Maine branch of the Herrick family near Herrick Bay.

Roger learned to ski at Phillips Academy in Andover, Massachusetts, and passionately embraced the sport. It was therefore only natural that he would chose to attend Dartmouth, not just because of his family's connection to the school (his father Ralph was in the class of 1907), but because of the skiing traditions and competitive dominance of the college's winter sports programs in the mid-1930s. Though the muscular and athletic Herrick did not make the college ski team, he continued to excel recreationally at the sport while studying Engineering and Physics and joined the Sigma Alpha Epsilon fraternity and the Dartmouth Outing Club. As a freshman, he toured Italy and was struck by the natural beauty of the mountains and valleys in Tuscany and to the north, places to which he hoped some day to return.

Following graduation in 1940, Herrick worked as an inspector for various New England airplane manufacturing firms while living in the home of family friend Mrs. William Cheney, who spoke glowingly of his good-natured friendliness , the joy he took in the outdoors, and the gentle nature of his soul. The war, however, weighed heavily on Roger. In 1943, at age twenty-seven and still a bachelor, he decided to answer the call of family friend Minnie Dole and joined the steady stream of former classmates into the 10th Mountain Division.

Herrick arrived at Camp Hale late in 1943, and because of his mountain experience and outdoor skills, was selected to teach skiing and rock climbing to new recruits on an informal basis. However, a stint in the hospital with pneumonia (developed from the coal smog that perpetually hung over the camp and an ailment so common that the coughing which accompanied it was referred to by troopers as "the Pando hack") caused him to miss the opportunity of being selected as a member of the elite Mountain Training Group.

Herrick recovered to participate in the D-Series field maneuvers, spending three full weeks in the snow convincing others that they, too, could survive the ordeal. As a result, he was elevated to the rank of staff sergeant, and made a squad leader. "He was a blueblood, we all knew that," remembered company-mate Don Montgomery, a tough kid from Western Pennsylvania. "But Hale was a place full of bluebloods and college boys. What set Roger apart was that despite being a quiet and refined person, a gentleman not prone to profanity or carousing –which kind of made him a fish out of water around the rest of us-- was that he was still a really good guy. As a sergeant, he didn't need to be friendly and encouraging to privates. But he was. And as I buck private, I really appreciated that."

Carl Cossin, another friend in Company F of the 85th, remembered Roger in exactly the same light. "Ordinarily, you didn't get men like that, as smart and formally educated as he was, who would talk to the regular guys about serious things with sincerity. But he was willing to do that. That's one of the reasons I admired him so much. I'm willing to say, quite frankly, that I looked up to him, which is something I don't admit about many people I've known."

Roger wrote home frequently to his mother, informing her openly of the joy he took in teaching outdoor skills to the new division volunteers, and the pride he took in leading the men under his command. "Among the things that were different about Roger was how close he was to his mother," remembered Cossin, and he didn't care who knew it or ribbed him about it. They were in constant contact. He made sergeant for her, basically. But not everything she did pleased him. She sent him a very expensive, crooked-stem pipe one time, and he didn't like it because his idol, Bing Crosby, smoked a straight stem. So I got a very generous gift, but I had to promise not to tell her if I ever met her."

The tenor of Roger's letters home changed upon his arrival in Italy. Shocked by the devastation that had been visited by war on the beautiful landscape he had so admired as a student, Herrick could take solace only in the fact that the people were still so warm and friendly despite the deprivations of war. Like so many members of the American Army in Europe, he wrote of sharing rations with the malnourished local children and was welcomed into local homes to enjoy a glass of *grappa* and the company of a family now and then. Those same children and families now stared up from the villages onto the carnage raking Belvedere and its sister peaks and silently wept for their new American friends.

By the morning of February 22, 1945, Roger Herrick had few men left in his squad to lead forward up della Torraccia. "Our company was all shot to hell...we had no food or ammunition," remembered Wilmer Trodahl, another of Herrick's company mates. "We had mine fields on both sides of us, and every time we'd try to move, in would come the [artillery]." Lt. Col. Stone radioed headquarters and informed General Hays that he could no longer press the attack under such conditions. He was told to move forward anyway, but Stone refused. Overnight, Hays sent supplies to the 2nd Battalion by mule, and issued an order that still sends a cold chill through the surviving members of Company F/85: "Continue the attack until your battalion is expended."

At dawn, the 2nd Battalion moved forward and once again gained ground, only to be stopped by waves of counterattacks that resulted in hand-to-hand combat and a sustained artillery barrage worse than the previous day's battering. At some point that morning—the exact details remain confused because of the level of savagery taking place on the hill—an artillery shell exploded in the trees above Roger Herrick's squad and the sergeant was hit in the head by shrapnel. Carl Cossin remembered the wound being to the top of his skull although the Army reported that the shrapnel tore out his upper jaw.

"He was unconscious from the moment he got hit, at least I hope he was," remembered Cossin. "We carried him down to the aid station through the remaining snow and ice as soon we could, but he was real bad, and he was gone before we got there. For some reason they listed him as having survived for two days, but he didn't. How do I know? Because I was the one who dug the shallow grave on the mountain, put him in it, and marked it with his helmet for the graves detail. That broke my heart. You don't ever forget something like that."

Herrick's mother accepted the Army's claim that her son died peacefully in the aid station after being treated for an extended period, a gift that no one was willing to take away from her. It brought her comfort to think that Roger might have been imagining Linekin Bay when he passed, remembering the poem that he had written during the summer of his 17th year:

Sergeant Roger Herrick '40 did not make it out of Italy. He was killed late in the War in a battle that may not have been necessary.

Linekin Bay

Oh, look to Linekin,
From Bayville on-the- hill.
To watch the wind make love to her,
As only wind will.
To behold her beauty,
Thru the warm summer air,
Would rest the eyes of anyone,
And calm the soul of care---
Broad and deep, with islands green,
Looking out to sea.
All complete within herself,
And satisfied to be.

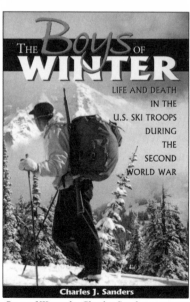

Boys of Winter by Charles Sanders captures the story of the 10th Mountain Division by describing the personal lives of several soldiers, some of whom did not return from the war. Many of his stories involved Dartmouth men who played significant leadership roles in the 10th.

With no wife and no children back home, the Herrick family elected to have Roger's body permanently interred at the American Cemetery in Florence, where he is buried with several of his men. His mother received his Purple Heart medal and a form bereavement letter from a chaplain after the war. Roger W. Herrick was 29.

Eventually, Lt. Col. Stone's battalion was reinforced by another unit and the attack on della Torraccia was brought to a bloody but successful conclusion after five days of fighting. Of the two hundred men in Roger Herrick's beloved Company F, reported Wilmer Trodahl, "there were only about ten or fifteen of us left [walking] when we were finally pulled out of the line." General Hays later relieved the shattered Stone of his command, the Nazis already having relieved him of most of his battalion. The fighting on the Belvedere chain took close to a week and claimed the lives of hundreds of other 10th Mountaineers. Through horrific shelling and counterattacks, however, the Americans held their ground until the Germans finally withdrew. Captain Ralph Bromaghin, Charles McLane's songwriting partner, had been with the relieving force on della Torraccia that finally fought its way to the top through vicious, hand-to-hand combat. In doing so, he earned a Bronze Star for saving the life of renown American mountaineer Duke Watson by braving heavy enemy fire to pull the wounded Watson to safety. Now, with the fighting having subsided, Bromaghin was visited by his old skiing buddy Captain Percy Rideout, whose company was to take over Bromaghin's positions so that his exhausted men could get a well-earned break.

Rideout remembered that there was coffee and laughter, congratulations, and back-slapping all around, everyone just thankful for having survived such an ordeal. "The mood was a bit somber, of course, but also celebratory," he remembered. "We were enjoying a few moments in the sun we thought we might never see again." And then came the flash and sound of a mortar round fired by the last of the retreating Germans.

Ralph R. Bromaghin died in the arms of a chaplain from an eviscerating abdominal wound caused by the shrapnel from that shell, which landed right next to him. He was the last American casualty in the Mount Belvedere action. "Some things in life are just too painful to talk about," remembered his buddy Charles McLane some sixty years later. "And for me, that is one of them."

After a short respite, General Clark, fearing a flanking counterattack by the Germans, sent the 10th back into action to straighten the Fifth Army line across the Apennines. In three more brutal days of fighting, dozens more American ski troopers lost their lives, including world-class Nordic skier Arthur Tokola and the world's best ski jumper, Torger Tokle. They were killed together while firing a bazooka on a German machine gun position that was threatening to wipe out their platoon. A split-second after firing a round that destroyed the German battery, the two were hit by a short artillery round fired by Allied troops in an adjacent sector.

"Friendly fire deaths were so common in that kind of combat," remembered Percy Rideout, "that you just took it for granted that these things happen." Many 10th Mountain Division veterans remember the deaths of Tokle and Tokola as the most emotionally devastating moment of the war. "If it could happen to them," said one grieving trooper, "it could sure as hell happen to you."

Combat, however, also had a way of hardening even the most green of the division's young skiers. The natural fears of an athlete frequently gave way to the grim resolve of an infantryman over the course of just a few days on the line. In fact, the prevailing attitude of these soldiers at the end of their nearly three-week baptism by fire was neatly summed up by trooper Harry Poschman, who noted with cynical pride that at least the division could no longer be derided as "just a damn ski club."

The mountaineers had suffered nearly two thousand casualties, including 350 dead, in taking Belvedere and its surrounding peaks. After less than two months at the front, one of every eight 10th Mountain Division members had already been killed or wounded. But the division had succeeded in keeping the German Army in Italy from either reinforcing the Western Front or withdrawing to the Redoubt, and in the long run, that saved lives. Even the enemy commander, Field Marshall Albert Kesselring, had been moved to refer to the 10th as a "remarkable division."

By early March 1945, the Italian Campaign had quieted down enough for the fifteen thousand members of the 10th Mountain Division to get some rest and recuperation. One especially deserving recipient of R&R in Florence was former Dartmouth ski team captain, Staff Sergeant Jacob Nunnemacher, who had fought his way up Mount Belvedere and participated in several of the other bloody combat operations that followed over the ensuing weeks.

In a better time, Jake Nunnemacher '42 on the slopes with Hampie Wentworth '42 in 1940.

Nunnemacher enjoying the climb up Tuckerman Ravine in 1941.

Nunnemacher, a happy person at the 1941 Dartmouth Winter Carnival.

Jake Nunnemacher had grown up in privilege as a member one of Milwaukee, Wisconsin's leading Swiss-German families, the descendant of wealthy businessmen and public benefactors on his father's side and of artisans and painters (including Carl von Marr) on the other. He and his brother, **Hermann Nunnemacher '35**, learned to ski as children on a two-year family sojourn to the Alps. When the family returned to Pine Lake and Milwaukee in the early 1930s, Jacob developed into one of the most talented and successful lake sailors in the Midwest. He and his brother also founded and led the famed Heiliger Huegel Ski Club so that they could have "fun in the wintertime, too," according to Hermann.

With all of his success in athletics, however, the immensely popular Jake had two passions that outshone all of the others: The first was the love of his life, Jean. The second was teaching children to ski and sail. "The kids at Pine Lake just idolized him," remembered a boyhood friend, Fritz Trubshaw. "They followed him around everywhere, imitating everything he did. And he and Jean were *the* couple wherever they went. It was a fairy tale existence that the two of them led as teenagers."

In 1938, at the urging of his father, Jake decided to follow his older brother to Dartmouth. Gradually, the good-natured but competitive Jacob became one of the most admired students on campus, helping mightily with the clean-up effort in Hanover following the great hurricane of 1938 and spurring the Yachting Club to stellar seasons in his sophomore and junior years (it won the collegiate championships a year later). In his junior year, Jake was selected to head Casque and Gauntlet, and as a senior, he was elected Captain of the Ski Team and President of the Dartmouth Outing Club, one of the few Dartmouth students ever to serve in that dual capacity.

"In every way Jake lived and acted the part of the ideal Dartmouth skier," wrote teammate **Jack Tobin '42**. The same integrity, intensity, and sportsmanship that were so appreciated by his young sailing students at Pine Lake had similarly moved his Dartmouth teammates enough to want to make him lead them, despite the fact that he was clearly not the fastest skier on the team.

According to Bob Meservey, there was one incident that perfectly encapsulated both the affection for Jake felt by his teammates and Jake's reputation as someone who could truly take a joke. The Dartmouth ski team was headed across the Canadian border to McGill for a race in 1941, he explained, at a time when the British Commonwealth was already at war with Germany. "Jake looked about as stereotypically German as anyone I've ever known," he recalled. "Blond hair, sharp, handsome features, and he spoke German fluently from the time he spent there as a kid." Meservey was in the first car carrying half the team, and Jacob in the follow car with the rest, as they reached the Canadian border.

"It was just one of those moments you have in college," Meservey continued. "We couldn't resist. We told the Canadian border guards that we were very suspicious of one of the guys we had seen in the car behind us at a rest stop. He was talking in German, and we feared he might be a spy, and that they had better check him out." It took hours for Jake to convince the Canadians that he was the captain of the Dartmouth ski team and not an agent of the Reich. "We arrived at McGill, had a few laughs, ate some dinner, and waited for Jake and the rest of the victims to straggle in," continued Meservey, "which of course they eventually did. Jake took some time to see the humor in that one. But eventually, he did think it was pretty funny. That was the kind of guy Jake Nunnemacher was."

After graduation in 1942, Jake defied his parents in order to join the ski troops as an enlisted man, rather than as an officer in a "safer" branch of the service than the infantry. He married his beautiful Jean, who accompanied him to Camp Hale and nursed him back to health from a serious lung infection that he, like Roger Herrick, had contracted from the coal smoke that frequently choked Pando. After his recuperation, Jake was selected to serve as an instructor in the elite Mountain Training Group, and during his time in Colorado with that unit he befriended and skied daily with Friedl Pfeifer, who was busy laying out plans to turn Aspen from a backwater into a ski mecca.

Nunnemacher, on the mountain above Camp Hale, became a leader of the 10th, but continued to ski recreationally whenever possible.

Eight months before his orders to ship out came through, Jean announced the happy news that she was pregnant. It made Jake nervous to leave her when his time came to go, but he knew that choice was not his to make. It was the Army's.

In January 1945, a few weeks after arriving in Italy, Jake received a letter from Jean with photos of his new daughter, Heidi. "He was head over heels," remembered his platoon-mate Lewis Hoelscher. "We saw those pictures a whole bunch of times. Jake was in love with that little baby." "Like the song says, he was accentuating the positive," remembered Percy Rideout. "Jake was like that."

Following the horrific action he endured on Belvedere, Jake wrote home to Jean not about combat, but rather about his excitement over being a father and his trip to the Cattedrale del Duomo in Florence. "I had a guide take me through, and then went on my own for a much longer time of the precious day than I had bargained," he wrote. "There were sculptures by Michelangelo and his famous followers—many of which I remembered from my art courses at Dartmouth (credit for liberal arts school!)"

Within a few days, however, Jake was back on the line, and his letters began to reveal the level of strain that he and his fellow soldiers were living under as they shivered in foxholes through the Northern Italian winter. "My writing is unusually scratchy," he wrote, "because my fingers are stiff and cold. They're also quite painful from cracks and sores which develop from the usual cuts and wear and tear. They are always filthy, and that doesn't help, either." Time dragged on as the troops sat in their wet foxholes for weeks more.

As the snows melted and spring flowers began sprouting in the Apennine hills, though, an optimistic feeling quickly spread throughout the Italian theater that the war would soon be coming to a close. In the meantime, the members of the 10th Mountain Division continued busying themselves by organizing feeding programs for the starving local children. And some started thinking about singing again, especially when news arrived that American Army units sweeping through Germany had crossed the Elbe River and were sixty miles west of Berlin, while the Soviet Red Army was already shelling the city from its eastern outskirts in anticipation of sacking the Nazi capital. The end was unmistakably near and both sides knew it.

Moreover, the Allies had already captured much of Bavaria and south Germany, making a retreat by Nazi forces into the Redoubt for one last stand now nothing more than a Wagnerian pipe dream. The Southern Front was quiet, and although there was concern among the western powers about the Red Army potentially moving south through Austria toward the Italian frontier, that was an argument among Allies, at least for the time being.

Nevertheless, General Mark Clark was itching to get back into the war. He still wanted to seal off the Redoubt, he asserted, and continue to tie up the German divisions remaining in Italy. As one historian from the US Army's Center of Military History put it, it was Clark's nature to want to "be in on the kill," and with the permission of Supreme Allied Command, he determined to launch a spring offensive using the 10th Mountain Division as the tip of the Fifth Army spear. As Division trainer and historian Hal Burton wrote in his popular treatment of the subject, *The Ski Troops*, "[t]he final battles in Italy epitomized the needless gallantry of war, the compulsiveness that drives generals to commit their troops, the irresistible urge to share in victory that could be earned more prudently by simply standing still."

Jake Nunnemacher's Company B of the 87th Regiment was ordered to lead the attack, which would eventually commence on the morning of April 14, 1945. The Germans had spent more than a month reinforcing their positions on the last high ground protecting the Po Valley and the routes to the Alps, and the fanatical SS troops that remained were determined to hold their ground or die trying. Everyone was expecting a bloodbath. They were correct for having thought so.

In one of his last letters to Jean before the offensive commenced, Jake described an overwhelming desire to leave the front even for a little while to ski on the highest peaks of the Apennines. Recalling Jean's winter visits to Dartmouth, he wrote "they seem to offer better slopes than the White Mountains, and day after day we look longingly at them." And then he closed: "During the last few days I think I've been more homesick than ever before. I think of you during these sunny days and even more at night when I lie in my dugout and gaze at the stars….If I could but hold you and look into your eyes. I love you, Jeanie, always."

That Saturday morning, the Spring Offensive began with furious Allied artillery barrages and air strikes against the last of the German positions in the Apennines. None, unfortunately, were aimed at the town of Torre Iussi, a name still recalled with bitterness and grief by surviving 10th Mountaineers. Company B started across a completely exposed valley toward the heavily defended town right after the Allied shelling ceased. The Germans answered immediately with artillery of their own, pinning down the company for hours and killing dozens of American soldiers. The bloody road into town, troopers recalled, was littered with broken bodies.

Sergeant Nunnemacher's squad was the first to reach Torre Iussi's outskirts. It was instantly targeted by snipers, who began picking off his men off one by one. Again pinned down and left with no good alternative, Jake jumped up, scrambled across open ground toward the source of the fire --a three-story house sitting far below an ancient monastery-- and tossed a grenade through a ground floor window. It was an incredible act of bravery and it saved the lives of many of his men. The firing ceased when the grenade detonated.

Calling out in German to those still inside, Sergeant Nunnemacher demanded their surrender. A few moments later, several enemy soldiers emerged from the house with their hands in the air. It was quiet. Jake called out in German again, asking if there were others inside. There was an exchange during which the surrendering German soldiers apparently said "no."

According to Lewis Hoelscher, who had been with Jake in Company B since the first days at Camp Hale, "I was five feet or so away from him when he went by those prisoners and into the house to check things out. I think he suspected they were lying to him because we'd seen this kind of thing before, but Jake was a very brave guy, and you never know how you're going to react in a situation like that until it happens. He went ahead."

John Montagne, Jake's close friend from Dartmouth, remained mystified over why such an otherwise meticulous person with so much to live for would place himself in such extreme danger, especially against his own instincts. "In heavy combat," he explained, "I think anger sometimes plays a part, and at times so does the disorientation of battle. Whatever it was, Jake took a calculated risk in doing his job that we all wish he hadn't taken."

Jake slipped into the building while the others waited for his word at the doorway. Jake was their ranking non-commissioned officer, he spoke German fluently, and he made it clear that he regarded this search as his responsibility.

According to those who witnessed it, Jake cautiously moved across the room and started up a stairway. The momentary calm was broken by a single rifle shot which rang in the ears of the soldiers standing frozen in the doorway. Profanities were blurted in anguish. Fired from behind by a Nazi sniper who had remained secreted on the first floor, the bullet hit Jacob just under the rim of his helmet, killing him instantly.

His men wept openly, even as they dispatched the sniper. For saving their lives and giving his own, Jacob R. Nunnemacher received a Silver Star, presented posthumously to Jean and Heidi. Jean later received a letter from an officer who had come upon the scene just after Jake's death. "I have never in my life heard any group of men," he wrote, "give such unanimous and sincere praise to a fellow soldier."

Jacob Nunnemacher was 26. There is an island in Pine Lake, Wisconsin, and a Dartmouth Outing Club cabin named in his honor.

Captain Percy Rideout's company, meanwhile, fought its way into Torre Iussi a short time later with orders to capture a target known as Hill 868 above the town. His men were similarly pinned down by sniper fire and taking heavy casualties. A cautious Rideout moved from position to position rallying his men, telling them to stay down until he gave the order to move forward. General Hays, however, impatiently demanded by field telephone that Rideout move up and denied his request for artillery to clear the ridge from which they were taking fire. The captain agreed, raised his head, turned to shout instructions to his lieutenant, and felt something slam into the side of his head.

Joe Duncan, the colorful 1934 National Downhill Champion. This was the second such race ever run and the first in the West.

A sniper's bullet ripped through soft tissue on one side of Rideout's face and exited through the opposite cheek. Miraculously, though he was evacuated in excruciating pain, Percy Rideout survived. "It's one of those strange things in war," he remembered. "If I hadn't turned at that precise instant, that bullet goes straight through my skull, just like my friend Jake Nunnemacher. Instead, I received pretty much a sew-up wound that I'm able to describe more than sixty years later." For leading his men up Riva Ridge and through Torre Iussi onto Hill 868, Percy Rideout was awarded a Silver Star.

April 14, 1945, was the worst single day of combat in the history of the 10th Mountain Division. The ski troops took well over 500 casualties in the twelve-hour battle below the mountain known as Rocca di Roffeno; the world's greatest skiers and climbers were well represented in that group. Sergeant Friedl Pfeifer lost a lung and nearly his life from shrapnel wounds. Lieutenant Bob Dole of Kansas (no relation to Minot) permanently lost the use of his right arm and was temporarily paralyzed when he was hit pulling a comrade to safety. A few days later, Rudy Konieczny, who had raced valiantly against the best that the Dartmouth had to offer on the Thunderbolt Ski Trail on Mount Greylock, lost his life in hand-to-hand combat taking Mount Serra. And still, the carnage was not over.

Joe Duncan '40, captain of his high school basketball team.

On April 17, an exhausted Captain Joe Duncan led his men toward a tiny hamlet known as Casa Costa and the very last ridges protecting the Po Valley. One of the most respected officers and combat leaders in the 10th Mountain Division, Captain Duncan had already earned three medals for valor in the Italian Campaign. Now, a German 88-mm artillery battery, the most feared field weapon of the Second World War, was harassing what remained of his company and he intended to put a stop to it.

Joe Duncan of Estes Park, Colorado, was perhaps the most unique character among all of the individualists that populated the 10th Mountain Division. He had grown up climbing and skiing in Rocky Mountain National Park, the son of a local lawman known as "The Judge," who ruled that portion of Colorado with an iron sidearm. The ruggedly handsome Joe, however, quickly moved out from the shadow of his larger-than-life father. Not only was Joe Duncan named captain of his high school's football and basketball teams, he was also its valedictorian. Those accomplishments, however, paled in comparison to the fact that under the tutelage of famed US Park Ranger Jack Moomaw, he helped cut the "Suicide Trail" at Hidden Valley in Rocky Mountain National Park on which he beat **Linc Washburn '35** to win the US National Downhill Ski Championship of 1934.

Joe Duncan with his young daughter, Doriane.

With his new-found glory as an academic ski hero who happened to bear more than a passing resemblance to film star Gary Cooper, Joe Duncan headed straight for New York, not to ski, but to begin working as a European tour guide for wealthy Americans. In 1935, he enrolled at Dartmouth with aspirations to become an hotelier, but after a short stay, the lure of the party circuit beckoned once again. It was on to Sun Valley, where he taught skiing with Rideout, Litchfield, Bromaghin and Pfeifer. Eventually, due to his Continental manners and experience, Duncan ended up serving as a mountain escort on behalf of the Union Pacific Railroad (owners of the resort) for some of America's best-known celebrities, including Clark Gable, Claudette Colbert, Ernest Hemmingway, and Gary Cooper himself.

Joe capped off his time in Sun Valley by marrying a young and beautiful French heiress and moving back to New York to accommodate her social wants. Together they had a daughter, Doriane, but life in Manhattan's upper social strata quickly became a bore for the man who remained a child of the mountains at heart. When he heard about the formation of the 87th Mountain Regiment, whatever his reasons, he was one of the first to join up.

Capt. Joe Duncan with his men in Italy, most of whom were killed shortly thereafter.

"Joe Duncan was the quintessential ski trooper," recalled Captain Hal Ekern. "From Paradise to Hale to Italy, this guy was a leader. Tough, fair, a good teacher and officer, and he did it without any bragging at all. Hell, we didn't know he was the national ski champion until after the war. He never even mentioned it." Duncan's leadership was equally evident on the battlefield. He won two Bronze Stars, one for protecting his men in horrendous fighting at a place so pockmarked by shells it was later nicknamed Punchboard Hill, and a Silver Star for personally leading a charge to knock out enemy positions at the top of another promontory known as Banzai Ridge. There, he personally charged directly into machine gun fire in order to save the remaining members of his company, three quarters of whom had already been killed or wounded in the action.

In the early afternoon of April 17, 1945, after three days of intense combat without rest during which his company had been absolutely decimated, Captain Joe Duncan located the 88- mm gun that had been killing his men and ordered it silenced. He sent a patrol out on a "seek and destroy" mission, and then crawled out onto an exposed position below a rock ledge to track their movements in case any of his boys ran into trouble. "He took his responsibility for his men's safety very personally," remembered his aide, Albert Soria, "and when he lost someone, he grieved." The captain was thoroughly exhausted, grief-stricken, angry beyond comprehension, and perhaps not thinking as clearly as he otherwise might have been had he been able to get just a few hours of sleep.

Spotting Duncan in the clear watching his men through field glasses, the wide-eyed German gun crew likely could not believe its luck over such an opportunity. They fired a single shell which hit the pre-sighted ledge above the Captain, showering rock and steel down onto him and two of his aides. All three died from shrapnel wounds. Only Al Soria, standing with them but miraculously unscathed, survived. As with Jake Nunnemacher, the surviving members of Duncan's battered company wept, regrouped, and swept forward, sparing no one in a German uniform. Joseph Duncan was 33. The Army Reserve Center at Fort Carson, Colorado, the Estes Park American Legion Post, and a mountain peak near Sun Valley, Idaho, are all named in his honor.

The 10th Mountain Division was the first Allied unit to cross the Po River. Just as General Clark had envisioned it, the men fought their way to the foot of the Alps at Lake Garda just before the end of the war in Europe on May 2, 1945, with the surrender of the genocidal Nazi regime. In all, close to one thousand members of the division were killed in action, most in Clark's Spring Offensive, some of whom died at Lake Garda *after* the news had been received that German Fuhrer Adolph Hitler had taken his own life in a Berlin bunker. In the days following the German surrender, General Clark congratulated the 10th Mountain Division, calling it one of the best fighting forces he had ever seen. (Clark eventually rose to the rank of four-star general and went on to serve in the Korean War and as President of the famed Citadel Military College in South Carolina, where he died at the age of 87 in 1984).

Meanwhile, the war in the Pacific raged on. After its successes in Italy, there was talk of using the 10th Mountain Division to spearhead the invasion of Honshu if that horrendous choice was made necessary by Japan's refusal to surrender. The atomic bombs dropped on Hiroshima and Nagasaki, as regrettable as the use of such weapons might have been, probably saved the lives of each and every member of the division who had survived combat in Europe. "I saw those beaches and the Japanese batteries above them," said 10th Mountain Division Artillery Officer, Colonel Bill Gall, "and I can assure you that none of us would have been coming home."

The surviving members of the division did come home, and their legacy in peacetime remains as impressive as their wartime sacrifices. Some, like **Newc Eldredge '50**, came back to study at Dartmouth under the G.I. Bill and joined the ski team. He also helped lead the controversial effort to establish the global peace organization known as the International Federation of Mountain Soldiers, a group which today is universally supported by the veterans of the 10th Mountain Division.

Others helped found great American ski areas, including Aspen (Friedl Pfeifer, Percy Rideout, Johnny Litchfield), Arapahoe Basin (Larry Jump), Vail (Pete Seibert. Sarge Brown and Bob Parker), Crystal Mountain (Duke Watson and Ed Link), White Pass (Nelson Bennett), Jackson Hole (George Fleming), Sugarbush (Jack Murphy), Mount Bachelor (Bill Healey), and Sandia Peak (Bob Nordhaus). Some two thousand members of the division, in fact, ended up working in the US ski industry— an industry they not only fostered and expanded, but essentially reinvented.

Walter Prager became the US Olympic Ski Team coach and led five former ski troopers to the 1948 Winter Games. Bill Bowerman coached the US Olympic Track Team and co-founded the Nike shoe company. David Brower became President of the Sierra Club, founded Friends of the Earth, and was three times nominated for a Nobel Peace Prize as one of the 20th Century's greatest environmental naturalists.

John Litchfield '39, a leader of the 10th Mountain Division, an early participant in Sun Valley and one of the developers of Aspen.

Monty Atwater became the world's leading expert on avalanche control. Paul Petzholdt founded the National Outdoor Leadership School in Jackson Hole, Wyoming, and his climbing partner Ernest Tapley began the American Outward Bound program. Bob Lewis pioneered skiing and hiking programs for the handicapped. John Jay made ski movies into an art form. Bob Dole went to the US Senate and ran for President of the United States.

Ed Ketchledge helped found the Association for the Protection of the Adirondacks. Albert Jackman extended the Appalachian Trail in Maine. John Montagne taught at the University of Montana with Charlie Bradley and founded the Montana Wilderness Association.

And Charles McLane came home to teach at Dartmouth.

Roger Herrick, Jake Nunnemacher, and Joe Duncan are the three known members of the Dartmouth family killed in action with 10th Mountain Division. There were many other Dartmouth students, instructors and friends who served and gave their lives with other units in this and other wars, and all are remembered with equal respect and appreciation for their patriotism, their bravery, and their sacrifices.

TUCKERMAN RAVINE

The history of skiing includes many adventures at Tuckerman Ravine involving Dartmouth skiers, and it is still one of the most iconic venues in all of skiing.

A near perfect picture of Tuckerman Ravine (photo by Dick Durrance I '39).

HoJo Lodge, the meeting point for skiers at Tuckerman.

CHAPTER VII

DARTMOUTH FIGURES AND THE SKI MOUNTAINS OF NEW ENGLAND

By Jeff Leich '71
Executive Director, New England Ski Museum

With Peter Q. Graves, Meredith M. Scott '96, Johannes von Trapp '63 and Sam von Trapp '94

BEFORE THE SKI TOW

From the very beginning of the Dartmouth Outing Club, skiers from the college fanned out on journeys of exploration into the foothills and ranges of the nearby White Mountains. A full generation before rudimentary ski tows were invented, DOC stalwarts pioneered ski ascents of several New Hampshire peaks that would come to be the focus of ski expeditions and early ski competition in the pre-tow era. In one of the earliest uses of skis in Hanover, the actual skis were brought in from Portland, Maine, by **Weld "Pa" Rollins, Class of 1897**, and by his friends, including diarist **Herman "Cap" Holt, Class of 1897**. Their expeditions to Mink Brook, Balch Hill, the Lebanon road, and across the frozen Connecticut River typified the back-pasture venues that sufficed for the limited skills of the day.[1] Once skiers outgrew the barnyard hills of upcountry farms and raised their sights to higher elevations, Outing Club skiers were confronted with mountains that were thickly forested with tangled vegetation. The few feasible routes of ascent on skis were the summer carriage roads built on significant mountains, most notably New Hampshire's Mounts Moosilauke and Washington, and the DOC founders were quick to claim those first ski ascents.

Fred Harris '11 and **Carl E. Shumway '13** were the most prominent of the early ski explorers from the college. Harris led the first DOC winter trip to Mount Washington in 1911; he was the only skier. The group trekked from the Ravine House in Randolph over today's Dolly Copp Road to the Glen House, and then up the first four miles of the carriage road to timberline. One year later in February 1912, Shumway and **Goodwin LeBaron "Eric" Foster '13** completed the first known ski ascent of Mount Moosilauke via its carriage road, traveling from Hanover to the mountain and back on skis as well. In 1913, Harris, Shumway, and **Joseph Y. Cheney '13**, were able to make the first ascent of Mt. Washington, again using the carriage road. On the 8-mile descent, they roped themselves together on the icy, windswept expanses above tree line. Back in the trees, they found a different challenge, as Shumway later wrote: "Planks on some bridges on the Carriage Road were taken up in the fall so water would drain off. This meant we would have to ski-jump over the openings. In those days, poles were not used, not steel edges or wax."[2]

Harris '11 and Shumway '13 in first ascent of Mt. Washington.

Almost as an afterthought, while waiting for favorable weather for their summit attempt, the Dartmouth skiers on the 1913 trip killed a day by skiing up the carriage road to the Raymond Path and into Tuckerman Ravine. Most of the larger party used snowshoes for the trek, but Shumway, Foster, and four others were on skis, the first of hundreds of thousands of skiers who would follow them to Tuckerman in the ensuing decades, as the ravine came to be an enduring emblem of the robust side of New England skiing. Climbing partway up the headwall in poor visibility, Shumway recorded his descent for the *Boston Evening Transcript* in the March, 15, 1913 edition: "It was one grand, wild coast down through the ravine. The blizzard added a spice of uncertainty to the performance, for the boiling of the snow flurries in the great cauldron made it impossible to see. The frozen snow waves kept me rocking back and forth."[3]

Other Dartmouth figures were among the few ski pioneers of New England's highest peaks, notably College Librarian **Nathaniel L. Goodrich**, who made the first ski ascent of Vermont's Mount Mansfield with Charles W. Blood.[4] But it would be Harris and Shumway who would have lengthy careers and long-lasting influence in the development of skiing in the region.

Very few skiers shared the desire of DOC mainstays like Shumway and Harris to ascend New England's highest mountains on skis, much less ski to them from home and then back as Shumway had done on his Moosilauke adventure. Consequently it wasn't until the 1930s, when mechanization in the form of scheduled railroad transportation to ski venues and ski tows and lifts on the ski slopes themselves appeared, that skiing reached anything close to popular acceptance. Carl Shumway and Park Carpenter, acting as members of the Appalachian Mountain Club (AMC), were both instrumental in convincing the Boston & Maine Railroad (the B&M) to begin operating "Snow Trains" from Boston's North Station to various ski hills in 1931.[5] This idea was closely tied to the publication of a small sheet titled *The Ski Bulletin*, edited by Carpenter in its early years, which grew into one of the most influential ski periodicals in the country between 1931 and 1942. It originated largely because the AMC, in general a rather staid group, declined to schedule club trips on Sundays; to get around this prohibition, AMC skiers circulated postcards with up-to-date snow reports and suggestions for informal outings. The postcard campaign evolved into *The Ski Bulletin*, which drew on a regional network of telegraphed snow reports and listed the snow train destinations for the upcoming weekend, as well as reporting on developments in the sport in general.

Snow train advertisement; one of the many contributions to skiing by Carl Shumway '13 who led the effort to organize snow trains for skiers.

From that year well into the 1950s, snow trains run by the B&M and other rail lines carried thousands of skiers north to ski country and made entry to the sport both easier and more enticing for neophytes: beginners could not only rent skis and boots on the trains, but ski clothing as well. What's more, they could mix with a ready-made social circle in the cars on the way to and from ski destinations. This option freed scores of weekend skiers from the tedium and associated perils of a long drive home in the dark, by physically fatigued drivers, over narrow roads whose surfaces varied according to the whims of nature and mood of snowplow operators. And perhaps as importantly, it also provided ski area access to those who did not own cars during the Depression era but who could still afford the modest train fare.

The Ski Bulletin would grow into a national publication at a time when interest in downhill skiing was expanding nationwide. It is fair to state that these two linked initiatives—the ski trains and *The Ski Bulletin*--did a great deal to build what had been a limited backyard amusement into a sport that was routinely covered in the sports pages of major newspapers and one that would become a booming industry within a few decades.

Carl Shumway was deeply involved in the promotion of the new sport as author, editor, and ad salesman. He convinced the *Boston Evening Transcript* to begin a ski section titled "Old Man Winter" which he edited beginning about 1930 for one year, and picked up again in 1936. In 1935, he became the promoter of the Winter Sports Exposition at the Boston Garden, one of the first indoor ski shows in the country.[6]

The early trips of Harris and Shumway up significant peaks of the White Mountains depended on the existence of carriage roads, but skiers quickly became aware there were many more appealing mountains than there were summer roads providing access to the heights. An opportunity to create dedicated downhill ski trails arose in 1933 when the incoming Roosevelt administration announced plans to create an outdoor and conservation-focused jobs program which came to be called informally the Civilian Conservation Corps (CCC). Several Dartmouth alumni were key figures in obtaining funding for creating ski trails on White Mountain National Forest land in the very earliest days of the CCC program. While the CCC ski trails of New England were a very minor part of the program as a whole, they were remarkably effective in enlarging skiing opportunities, and the ski areas that subsequently grew up around several of the major trails—Cannon, Mount Mansfield, and Wildcat—are still important resorts today.

Charley Proctor '28 (2nd from r) and friends at the Pinkham Notch Camp.

"It is hard to say just how it got started," wrote **Charles N. Proctor '28**, in December, 1933. "There took place a ski banquet or two, a few informal meetings on ways and means, and a conversation that should be historic between James E. Scott, supervisor of the White Mountain National Forest, and John P. Carleton of Manchester."[7] While at Hanover, **John Porter Carleton '22**, had dazzled Dartmouth audiences with his acrobatic ski somersaults and his ski jumping abilities. He was a Rhodes Scholar and US Olympic team member at the first Winter Olympic Games in 1924. He continued his lifelong pursuit of skiing while establishing himself as a prominent attorney in Manchester, New Hampshire. In 1931, along with Proctor, he had made the first documented descent of the Tuckerman Ravine Headwall, an inconceivable feat on the primitive skis of the day and still a New England test piece today.

"It strikes me that we have the opportunity of a lifetime," Carleton wrote to **William Plumer Fowler '21**, Chairman of the AMC Committee on Skiing. James E. Scott, Supervisor of the White Mountain National Forest, looked favorably on the concept of having ski trails cut in the forest. "I saw Scott yesterday afternoon and he is apparently flaming to go ahead on this thing in a big way." Given one or two experienced people to lay out the trails, Scott was prepared to put the CCC recruits to work on the project quickly. This would be "too big a job for anyone to do in spare time. I suggest we get someone like Charlie Proctor who can put all his time on laying out the trails under the direction of a committee," advised Carleton.[8]

May 1933, the New Hampshire State Development Commission and its Publicity Director, **Donald Dickey**

Bob Monahan '29 (right) ready to go to work.

Tuttle, Class of 1900, hosted a meeting in Concord to which hotel owners and skiers were invited to further plans for the trails. A New Hampshire Ski Trails Committee was appointed and charged with locating and surveying routes for the ski trails. Carleton was appointed chairman of the committee. The committee arranged for Proctor and the Marquis Nicolas degli Albizzi, a Russian-born son of a noble Italian family, to mark out the routes of the trails that the CCC crews would cut. The Marquis was the summer equestrian instructor at Peckett's Inn on Sugar Hill and had helped lay out the Taft Trail on Cannon. He had a colorful background, having served in the First World War with the Italian cavalry and later commanded a detachment of Italian ski troopers on the Austrian front.[9] The plan had been that Proctor would survey the eastern White Mountains while Albizzi marked ski trails in the Franconia Notch area, but the Marquis resigned in the summer of 1933 and was replaced by another of Peckett's instructors of noble birth, Duke Dimitri von Leuchtenburg.

The new conservation group was organized with astonishing speed under the direction of the US Army. On July 17, 1933, **Robert Scott Monahan '29**, a newly minted CCC foreman fresh from a winter spent on Mount Washington where he and **Joseph Brooks Dodge (Honorary '55)** had just established a weather observatory, directed his crew as they started cutting the Wildcat Trail following Charley Proctor's markings.[10] Working out of the 35-man Darby Field Sub-Camp of the Wild River CCC camp, this group finished the Wildcat, the first CCC ski trail in the northeast, and many miles of other ski trails in the Pinkham Notch region.[11]

The CCC ski trails in New Hampshire became a model for Vermont, where shortly the Nose Dive Trail was constructed down the face of Mount Mansfield by CCC crews; other New England states followed this example. The four foremost downhill race trails of the 1930s in New England, all built by the CCC, spawned three major ski mountains: Mount Mansfield grew up around the Nose Dive; the Taft Trail on Cannon Mountain spurred construction of an aerial tramway in 1938 (with help from Carleton); and the Wildcat Trail would see a lift-served area build around it by a group with strong Dartmouth connections in the 1950s. The larger legacy of the CCC ski trails was the vast expansion of ski terrain that became available just as the snow trains began to bring increasing numbers of skiers northward, attracted to the sport by widespread publicity.

All of the Dartmouth personalities who figured in convincing the CCC to begin building ski trails made further contributions to the growth of the sport. Foremost among them was Charley Proctor, who surveyed the majority of the CCC trails in New Hampshire. Described by historian Morten Lund as "the first

The AMC's Cardigan Ski Reservation.

150

consummate American-born skier,"[12] Proctor was a partner in a Boston ski shop, wrote books on skiing, and, as a consultant for the Union Pacific Railroad when they planned their Sun Valley resort, was instrumental in bringing plans for the world's first chairlift, which had languished in a pile of proposals, to the fore.[13] Bob Monahan, after several years with the CCC, moved to the Washington, D.C. headquarters of the US Forest Service, where he authored a nationwide survey of skiing operations on national forest lands just before World War II. Representing the Forest Service, Monahan was involved with selecting the site for Camp Hale, Colorado, the military base for the newly formed 10th Mountain Division where thousands of soldiers would be trained in skiing and winter warfare during World War II.[14] Don Tuttle, as editor of *The New Hampshire Troubadour*, a travel monthly published from 1936 until 1945 by the state of New Hampshire featuring elegant photography and short teaser articles on skiing in season, joined Carl Shumway as a significant popularizer of the growing pastime.[15] Alumnus Bill Fowler spearheaded the purchase and renovation of the AMC's Cardigan Ski Reservation in southwestern New Hampshire in 1934, one of two ski proto-resorts that the outdoors club developed in the years before the modern model of the ski resort as a constellation of lodging, lifts, ski instruction, ski patrol, and entertainment emerged.

There was considerable convergence of interests and missions of the DOC and the AMC, and it is indicative of that overlap that Bill Fowler, who in college was one of the most zealous DOC hikers of any generation, would head the Appalachian Mountain Club (AMC) committee that in the 1930s made many contributions of its own to the growth of skiing in New England. In the spring of 1920 Fowler and **Sherman Adams '20**, (who found that serving on the AMC summer trail crew "provided an incomparable means of physical flagellation") engaged in a distance-hiking duel that culminated in a successful one-day, 83-mile traverse of the DOC cabin chain.[16] A lifelong advocate of the view that Edward de Vere, 17th Earl of Oxford, wrote the works attributed to William Shakespeare, Fowler was also very much involved, albeit mostly behind the scenes, in the small network of passionate skiers

Harry Nichols and Joe Dodge H '55.

who worked to develop the infrastructure of skiing in the 1930s.[17] While his participation in the purchase and renovation of the former Shem Ackerman farm in Alexandria, NH, into the AMC Cardigan Ski Reservation, which provided lodging, meals, and ski trails for club members within a reasonable distance of Boston, denotes the more public side of his involvement in ski development, Fowler also seems to have been instrumental in bringing the skills of Otto Schniebs, then teaching skiing to the AMC in the Boston area, to the attention of **Dan Hatch '28**, Comptroller of the DOC when Dartmouth was seeking a ski coach in 1930.[18]

The AMC's second nascent ski center, Pinkham Notch Camp at the eastern foot of Mount Washington, was the hub of a thick network of CCC-cut ski trails, and was the jumping off place for treks to Tuckerman Ravine. DOC trips to the Presidential Range commonly passed through the place, and Joe Dodge, the genial, earthy, creatively profane hut master, came to know generations of Dartmouth students. Although not a Dartmouth graduate, Dodge did receive an honorary Master of Arts degree in 1955 when President Dickey presented him with the tribute "as from one New Hampshire institution to another."[19] In the winters he spent at Pinkham Notch from 1926 through 1958, Dodge became an important figure in organizational skiing. An early adopter of shortwave radio technology, he developed a system to time ski races via radio communications between the Mount Washington Observatory and the roadside camp. He was a long-time race official and hosted a branch office of the Hannes Schneider Ski School at Pinkham in the late 1930s and 1940s. By virtue of the camp's location near popular ski terrain, he and his crews became a *de facto* mountain rescue unit before the creation of a ski patrol. Joe's son, **Brooks Dodge '51**, was raised in that remote mountain

Brooks Dodge '51, Th '54 skiing Tuckerman.

The challenge of skiing Tuckerman.

location, where he grew to be a world-class skier as he would demonstrate on the US Ski Team in two Winter Olympic Games in the 1950s; but it was on the slopes and gullies of Tuckerman Ravine just above his home that Brooks would first showcase his skiing talents.

Each winter the bowl-shaped cirque of Tuckerman Ravine on the eastern side of Mount Washington fills in with almost unimaginable quantities of snow, blown there by the prevailing northwest winds from the acres of treeless plateau that rim the ravine, so that what summer hikers perceive as a cliff-like headwall is gentled somewhat into a smooth, steep, expansive snowfield that has attracted skiers since the 1920s. The 45-to-55 degree gradient of the skiable snowfields and gullies of the ravine approaches the limit at which wind-drifted snow will adhere and is at the upper edge of what humans on skis in excess of seven feet can reasonably expect to descend. Tuckerman Ravine is unique in the East in its alpine appearance, its notoriously steep skiing, the changeability of its often-arctic weather, and its potential for avalanches of sometimes catastrophic proportion. In the 1930s, as the ravine became known as a distinctive ski destination, the pioneers of its early ski descents were most likely Dartmouth ski team members and a few Harvard alumni like Alec Bright and Bob Livermore. Charley Proctor and John Carleton made the first recorded run over the 45-degree headwall in April 1931, a descent of the route today known as The Lip. Over the next decade, about five further ski routes were pioneered, though when each was skied for the first time is undocumented. That one major couloir is called Hillman's Highway, after **Harold Hillman '40** of the Dartmouth team, is suggestive that he was the first to ski the prominent gully.

In 1937 another Dartmouth ski team member, **Dick Durrance '39,** presided over the Tuckerman Ravine christening of a form of ski racing new to the U.S., today called the Giant Slalom. As downhill racing became popular and competitive, and the speed and enthusiasm of entrants outran their technical abilities on the narrow trails of the time and casualties mounted. Durrance wrote an article for *The Ski Bulletin* advocating a more controlled event which was essentially a stretched-out slalom, and his suggestion was put into action when a well-liked skier from the Amateur Ski Club of New York, Franklin Edson, died from injuries received in a 1936 downhill in the Berkshires.[20] Durrance and Dartmouth Ski Coach **Walter Prager** set the course, which ran from the top of Right Gully all the way to Pinkham Notch Camp, and a stellar field of eastern skiers competed. In contrast to the casualty lists that were becoming the norm for downhills, no injuries occurred in this race and the new format became a fixture of ski competition. Dartmouth can thus fairly claim to have imported and organized the earliest US competitions in slalom (1925 in Hanover), the modern-form downhill (1927 at Moosilauke), as well as the giant slalom. One other early outbreak of skiing modernity took place at this event: prior to setting the course, Walter Prager observed signs of recent avalanche activity and sent out some of his ski team to throw dynamite charges in avalanche zones to attempt to bring down potential snow slides before they could threaten spectators. It would be another decade before snow rangers in Utah discovered that dynamite is not the most effective explosive for initiating a preemptive avalanche, but Coach Prager's attempt is surely the earliest application of the concept on record in the East, if not the country.[21]

Hillman '40 crashing, maybe on Hillman's Highway, Tuckerman.

MECHANIZATION CHANGES THE SPORT

Accounts of first ascents on skis of narrow, switchbacked carriage roads on mountains like Mansfield, Moosilauke, and Washington provided interesting newspaper articles, but in the 1920s and 1930s most skiing took place on lower elevation terrain more suited to the open slope style of skiing that was emerging in the Alps. One such location was Woodstock, Vermont, about 20 miles southwest of Hanover. There, the numerous dairy farms provided pastures on hills with 400 to 600 feet of vertical drop, "possibly the best ski-ing country east of the Rockies," marred only by "that diabolical American invention, the barbed wire fence," as the 1932 *British Ski Yearbook* noted.[22] There, on Gilbert's Hill a few miles out of Woodstock, in January 1934, the first ski tow on American soil went into operation, and a Dartmouth winter sports team alumnus was close at hand. **Wallace "Bunny" Bertram '31** was a Rhode Islander who specialized in snowshoeing at college and picked up skiing in Hanover about 1930. Woodstock was a winter sports destination dating back to 1892 when the Woodstock Inn was opened for winter operation; in the 1930s, the center shifted across the town green to the White Cupboard Inn run by Robert and Betty Royce. Several of the Royce's guests had traveled to the Laurentians to ski on Alex Foster's rope tow in Shawbridge, Canada, built the previous year and the first rope tow on record in North America; they asked Royce if he couldn't provide something similar so they could maximize their ski vacation days by avoiding the inevitable uphill slogs. Royce obtained rough sketches from Foster and hired a mechanical engineer named David Dodd to build a similar tow. Bertram was in town as a part time ski instructor and gravitated to operating the tow, thereby witnessing the many mechanical problems that plagued the tow in its first year. Sometime after the 1934-35 season, he reported the annual costs of the tow operation to a committee in Hanover that was advocating building a tow there. The total expense came to $978.90 for the season, with Bertram's labor at $4.00 per day being by far the largest line item.[23]

The Oak Hill lift, the first overhead cable lift in the US (Hanover, NH).

The next season, 1935-36, he operated the rope tow on Gilbert's Hill after making some improvements but moved the entire apparatus the next year to a steeper hill outside Woodstock called "The Gully." As Woodstock became a rope tow center—eight had been built within a few years—Bertram finally settled on a steeper, longer pasture hill

The first rope tow in the US (Woodstock, VT).

153

that was designated only as "Hill 6" on a contemporary map. This became Bertram's legendary Suicide Six, where rope tows, and later Poma lifts, brought skiers to the top of the wide-open slopes terraced with wave-like rolls and dotted with sugar maple islands. The terrain was similar to European ski slopes that would challenge American racers, and this attracted Dartmouth ski team competitors who trained there even long after the Oak Hill J-Bar was built in Hanover. Bertram played host to an early citizens' race in which coveted pins, in the shape of the figure 6 in bronze, silver, and gold, were awarded in time trials down the moguled face of the slope. Dartmouth's **Tom Corcoran '54** set the record in 1951 that still stands today—and which will forever remain unbroken since the configuration of the slope was changed when Bertram sold the area in 1961.[24]

"The Hanover Community looked on this Woodstock development with some envy," according to a report drafted to study a tow in Hanover, accustomed as Dartmouth was to being the center of the ski universe in New England. After experimentation in the winter of 1935 with a portable rope tow modeled after Bertram's operation in Woodstock that ran for several weeks near the Outing Club house, the DOC and its General Manager, **Dan Hatch**, sought a more permanent solution.[25]

As we outlined earlier, it is pretty clear how an overhead cable ski tow with J-bars, very similar in form to the earliest such installation in the world—the 980-foot Bolgen-Davos J-Bar tow invented by Swiss engineer Ernst Constam and first operational in 1934—came to be built on Oak Hill in 1935 and put into service in January 1936. The evidence we have unearthed suggests that Dan Hatch saw photos of the Davos device in a news article and decided it was something useful to replicate at Dartmouth.[26] Hatch worked with Split Ballbearing, a local machine shop, plus a student and faculty group at Dartmouth's Thayer School of Engineering to design a workable facsimile for Oak Hill.

When the DOC, with Hatch at the helm, committed to building the J-bar tow in Hanover, they obtained a quote of $4,675 from an AS&W tramway engineer based in Worcester, Massachusetts.[27] Just after the tow went into operation, an unprecedented full-page ad in *The Ski Bulletin* was taken out by the builder, Split Ballbearing Corporation of Lebanon, NH, celebrating the construction.[28] The major components of wire rope, sheaves and bullwheels of the tow were supplied by AS&W, with Split Ballbearing acting as the local building contractor. AS&W, which built wire ropeway installations with impressive statistics like their 13,300-foot tramway with a 2,400-foot unsupported span crossing the American River Canyon in California, was the leading industrial supplier of circulating wire ropeways, but they had bigger projects to engineer than the DOC's 1,200-foot experimental rig for pulling decidedly non-industrial passengers a mere 350 vertical feet uphill. However, they were willing to sell materials needed for the ski lift project, and perhaps, they were already envisioning themselves as the future sole supplier of a new product to a growing market.

Eventually, Ernst Constam arrived in the U.S. to oversee the installation of his patented T-Bars at Pico Peak, VT, and Mont Tremblant, Quebec. While in the area, he visited the offices of the DOC and after hinting at legal action against the college for infringing his patent on the shape of the J-bar carrier, the college reached a settlement. Constam also had success enforcing his patent against Fred Pabst, a brewing heir (and brother of **Harold "Shorty" Pabst '38**) who assembled a collection of J-bar tows at Bromley, VT and other locations. Because of the dust-up with Constam, though, it is on record via a letter from **Hans Paschen '28** of the DOC to college trustee **John R. "Judge" McLane '07** that in its first five years of operation the Oak Hill tow made a net income of $3,500 on ticket sales of $10,000 for the period.[29] The pioneering tow would operate almost continuously for the next 50 years until the winter of 1985 with the exception of two years during the Second World War.[30] This durability is testimony to the excellence of the design created by the Dartmouth team from the relatively crude images on which their mechanism was based and to the industrial skills of the two companies that manufactured and assembled the component parts.

For several years it appeared that aerial tramways rather than tows would be the uphill conveyances of choice for emerging ski resorts. Ski enthusiast Alec Bright, Harvard class of 1919, wrote a 1934 study of New Hampshire mountains titled "Survey of Possible Aerial Tramway Locations" and worked with AS&W to conduct detailed surveys of three sites: Cannon Mountain, Belknap Mountain, and Mt. Blue, a subsidiary summit of Moosilauke.[31] For a brief time in the summer of 1934, Moosilauke and Cannon both seemed to be in the running for a passenger tram for skiing, with both Bright and DOC's Dan Hatch favoring the Mt. Blue location. There, the tram was planned to stretch roughly along the route of the Beaver Brook Trail to the east of Moosilauke. In the end, the DOC withdrew its support for the Mt. Blue location and efforts to install an aerial tramway shifted to Cannon.[32]

Dartmouth's skiing development at Moosilauke remained centered on the area where the Ravine Lodge would be built, and in 1933 the most ambitious of the major down-mountain ski trails in the White Mountains, Hell's Highway, was cut by DOC crews headed by Otto Schniebs. The construction of Hell's Highway was a conscious response to the opening of the Richard Taft Trail at Cannon which overshadowed the Moosilauke Carriage Road as a downhill race trail the moment it opened, threatening Dartmouth's position of predominance within the skiing cosmos. But Hell's Highway and its corollary trail, Hell's Byway, which

The Mt Washington Cog Railway Sign (photo by Jim Hamilton '65).

bypassed the awesome 38-degree pitch named the Rock Garden, had an all-too-brief moment of existence; the prodigious hurricane of 1938 rendered it impassable until the mass of blown down timber was finally removed in 1941. Hell's Highway was so steep and intimidating a run that several alternatives were built in about 1936, most notably the Snapper and Dipper trails which gained popularity as Hell's Highway fell into disuse. After the war, a rope tow was installed to the east of the Ravine Lodge, and trails were cut under the direction of Bob Monahan. But the rapid evolution of skiing developments had left the relatively inaccessible and comparatively primitive ski area that the DOC and alumni had funded at Moosilauke functionally obsolete, and after the winter of 1953 the Ravine Lodge did not open in the winter. [33]

THE PROFESSION OF SKI AREA PLANNING

Despite the DOC's veto of Mt. Blue as a tramway site, the effort to sponsor a ski tramway somewhere in New Hampshire eventually culminated in the approval by the State legislature of a plan to build one at Cannon Mountain. John Carleton was the chairman of the committee charged with bringing this about; but when federal funding could not be found in 1934 the project stalled until a new bill passed authorizing a state bond issue several years later. When the tramway opened in 1938, the nation's first professional ski patrol was hired, and among those patrollers was **Sel Hannah '35**, who had prior trail-building experience cutting Hell's Highway for the DOC and the Mt. Tecumseh ski trail for the CCC. One of Hannah's first tasks at Cannon was to assist the CCC with the construction of a new ski trail, the Cannon Mountain, which provided a more direct link between the tramway's mountain and valley stations than did the pre-existing Richard Taft Trail. Hannah's 1938 hiring at Cannon led him into a career in ski resort engineering, a profession that he did much to invent, and the company he and his partners created would have worldwide significance for ski resorts after the Second World War.

Sel Hannah '35, the founder of Sno-Engineering.

American participation in the war essentially brought a halt to ski area development from 1942 until about 1947. The recruitment, training, and short but intense combat participation of the first American military unit devoted to mountain and winter warfare, the 10th Mountain Division, set the stage for a postwar growth and geographic expansion that was unimaginable in the prewar years. The targeted recruitment of mountaineers and skiers for the Army's new mountain unit had the effect of assembling most of the leading skiers in the nation, along with those most passionate about skiing and mountaineering, and by concentrating them together at Camp Hale for years of specialized training, it melded them into a cohesive group that formed a ready-made network waiting to be accessed in later years. As might be surmised, Dartmouth skiers figured prominently in the 10th Mountain Division. (See Chapter VI.)

When the war was over, Sel Hannah foresaw that demand for ski area development would resume and grow, and in 1958 he assembled a team of engineers and ski lift and snowmaking specialists under the firm name of Sno-engineering. Having learned the trail-building trade with the CCC when axes, saws, and grub hoes typified the available tools, he came to appreciate the need to control erosion on exposed trail surfaces, so he developed methods like water bars, seeding, mulching, and pinning log barriers to exposed ledge to retain and build soil. As early as 1957, Hannah had written a paper titled "Environment, Ecology & Autumn Trail & Slope Maintenance," a decade or more before the terms entered the public consciousness.[34] Hannah was personally involved in the design of more than 200 ski area sites, often acting as a gatekeeper to those who would build a new resort. He pointed out the pros and cons of each venue, approving most of those that had the essential elements, advising against mountains without the basic factors necessary for a strong economic base, and on occasion opposing projects that offended his sense of what a later generation would term "wilderness ethics", as he did in New Hampshire's Pemigewasset Wilderness on the grounds that "I was convinced that to develop it would be a terrible thing, because there is so little land like that left".[35]

Ski area planning was a sideline for Hannah at the time; his main efforts were being devoted to his potato farm in Franconia, NH. About 1957, he hired **Joseph Cushing, Jr. '52** as summer help on the farm, and by 1961 Cushing was assisting Hannah on some of his ski survey jobs. "He and I both found out I could find my way in the woods," Cushing recalls.[36] Among the resorts that Cushing helped lay out in the early 1960s were two in New Hampshire that were each founded by Dartmouth graduates, Loon Mountain and Waterville Valley.

Cushing's Dartmouth roommate had been **James R. Branch '52, Tu '53**. Branch was general manager of the Aleyska resort in Alaska until 1967 when he decided he wanted to go back East. He turned up at Cushing's home and soon became involved with Sno-engineering. He and Cushing would purchase the company when Hannah retired; unfortunately, business slowed considerably in the early 1970s as the ski industry went through its first period of flat growth since its inception in the 1930s. A project at Keystone, CO, founded by **Chuck Lewis '58**, got the company back on track, and projects flowed from that time on. Branch remained deeply involved in the ski industry until his death in 1991. Over this time he moved Sno-engineering from a firm with a strong regional reputation to an international concern that offered complete resort mountain and land planning to new and existing ski areas all over the world. Some of the firm's early 21st century projects are in such exotic locales as the Ping Tian Mountain Resort in the Tianshan mountain range in northwestern China, and Palandöken and Konakli, the skiing venues for the 2011 University Games in Turkey.

For his part, Cushing remained with the company until his 1995 retirement. He worked on at least 450 ski resorts in the U.S., Canada, Australia and New Zealand, with some of the most memorable for him being Deer Valley, UT, Loon Mountain and Waterville Valley, NH, Mount Mansfield and Stratton, VT, Copper Mountain, CO, and Mont Sutton, Quebec.[37]

VERMONT

Killington, the pacesetter of the Vermont ski industry in the 1960s, felt the Dartmouth influence in the person of **Paul Bousquet '53**, a Dartmouth student until he transferred to the University of Vermont in search of a feminine element he found lacking in Hanover. Bousquet grew up in the ski business, as his father, Clarence Bousquet, was one of the first to refine the simple back-pasture with a rope tow into a ski area complex with most of the elements we today recognize as constituting a ski resort. Clare Bousquet adapted industrial machinery from idled western Massachusetts factories to his rope tows, adding features like counterweights and safety gates that the earliest tows lacked. Bousquet's ski area, at first named "Bousquet's Ski Grounds" and later simply "Bousquet's", is credited with being one of the earliest to introduce night skiing, which was unveiled in December 1936 using resources from the nearby General Electric plant in Pittsfield, Massachusetts. He was also the first in the US to use the now-ubiquitous ski area promotional brochures. Another of his inventions was a rope tow gripper that provided skiers with an individual handle with which to grasp the wet, twisting, glove-ripping rope, and the proceeds from that invention financed Paul's college education.

Walter Prager recruited Paul Bousquet for the Dartmouth ski team but the University of Vermont's ski coach, Bob Searles, enticed him to continue to ski for the Catamounts after his freshman year in Hanover. Bousquet later became the first general manager and vice president of Vermont's

Suicide Six Ski Area in Vermont, once Dartmouth's "other" home alpine mountain.

extensive Killington ski area from 1959 until 1967, a period of tremendous growth under its founder, Preston Smith. He then hired on with Polish-born engineer Jean Pomagalski, inventor of the Poma Lift, and served as CEO of the ski lift manufacturer Poma North America. In the late 1960s he was able to re-acquire Bousquet's ski area, which had been sold out of the family, and he operated it until the early 1980s when rising energy and insurance costs coupled with poor snow years forced many ski areas to close. He was soon hired as manager at Beech Mountain, NC, and in the early 1990s worked for alumnus Sherman Adams at Loon Mountain, NH. Paul Bousquet's remarkable career in skiing, beginning when rope tows were a new invention until an era when a major ski area could be built around artificial snowmaking in the Southern Appalachians, spans virtually the entire developmental period of skiing as a major industry in the US. It is somehow apt then that Bousquet should serve as the gatekeeper to the US National Ski and Snowboard Hall of Fame as Chair of its Selection Committee.[38]

Donald deJong Cutter, Sr. '45 was one of many Dartmouth recruits to 10th Mountain Division late in the Second World War. Cutter trained at Camp Hale where he served as a skiing and rock-climbing instructor. He was called up for a second stint in the Army during the Korean War, this time stationed in Garmisch-Partenkirchen, Germany, as director of the Army's recreational winter sports program there. Cutter and his wife Rosalie brushed up against one of the enduring mysteries of skiing history while residing in Germany, as they were neighbors and acquaintances of Dr. and Mrs. Karl Rösen. Just after the Anschluss in 1938, Dr. Rösen was instrumental in extracting Austrian skimeister Hannes Schneider, considered one of the founders of modern ski technique, from a Landek prison where he was being detained by Nazi party members from Innsbruck. [39]

Upon his discharge from the Army in 1956, Cutter was hired on as general manager of Okemo Mountain in Ludlow, VT, then in its second season. It was a shoestring operation at the time, and Cutter doubled as ski patroller while building ski trails, overseeing lift operations, and running the ski shop. In his time at Okemo, there was rapid expansion of lifts and trails; as a consequence, visits increased from 11,800 in 1957 to 39,900 in 1962. Cutter also became involved with a ski-in/ski-out "A-Frame Village" at Okemo in 1961 just as real estate developments coupled in with recreational skiing were beginning to become common. When the time came in 1962 that the ski shop was more profitable than the mountain itself, Cutter realized that equipping skiers might be more rewarding than transporting them up the mountain. So he resigned from Okemo and soon purchased the Art Bennett Ski Shop in Hanover, which he operated until about 1982. As a major Okemo stockholder—he was compensated with shares of stock in some of the early lean years—Cutter served on Okemo's board in the 1960s and later took a turn as general manager of Ascutney Mountain in the winter of 1968.[40]

Vermont is also home to two other illustrious ski venues that were started by members of the Dartmouth Family. The first, the Harris Hill Ski Jump in Brattleboro, was originally built in 1922 under the leadership of arguably the most important person in the entire Dartmouth ski story, **Fred Harris '11**, who founded the Dartmouth Outing Club in 1909. He was enamored with jumping all his life and Brattleboro was his home area. Meredith Scott '96 (Director of the Vermont Ski Museum) and Peter Graves (a member of the Vermont Ski Museum Board, ski coach, commentator at many major ski races, and a member of the greater Dartmouth family thru his connection to Dartmouth ski coach Cami Thompson) have detailed a brief history of this important New England facility, and it's rebirth in 2009 as one of the most important ski jumping venues in the United States.

Following this is another intriguing story by Johannes '63 and Sam '94 von Trapp about possibly the first, and arguably the US's leading, cross country resort venue, the Trapp Family Lodge. Only in the ski world and at Dartmouth, can one of the most romantic stories of our time, *The Sound of Music*, come together with a ski theme, many Dartmouth skier contributors, lots of innovation, and plenty of grit to result in another fantastic facility that is today used by many recreational skiers, and most serious cross country racers. Vermont is home to many skiing stories and facilities, but the presence of both Harris Hill and the Trapp Family Lodge Cross Country Center provides a very unique flavor to the Vermont ski operation.

***

HARRIS HILL REBORN

By Peter Q. Graves and Meredith M. Scott '96

In 2009, after a huge three-year rebuilding effort, the historic Harris Hill ski jump once again played host to the Harris Hill Ski Jumping Tournament. The story of the jump's extensive reconstruction combines elements of the sport, the community, and of public generosity. The legendary promoter of popular skiing Fred Harris (1887-1961) built the original 60-meter jump back in 1921 for $2000. Viewed by ski jumping fans as one of the nation's most venerable jumps, it fell into serious disrepair in 2005. About $575,000 was needed to bring the jump up to current standards. Grassroots appeals by the local community raised more than $257,000; most of the additional funds came in the form of gifts from the Manton Foundation and other non-profit groups. With much fanfare, the now-enlarged 90-meter jump reopened for the 2009 Pepsi Challenge and 85th Harris Hill Ski Jumping Tournament the weekend of February 14-15.

Harris, a Vermont native, became attracted to skiing during his early days in Brattleboro where he became afflicted with what he would later laughingly describe as "skeeing on the brain." While a junior at Dartmouth, he founded the College's famous Outing Club and, in 1910, organized the first of many winter carnivals, a series of athletic events with an interest in "stimulating attention in winter sports and the outdoors." Harris not only encouraged athletic pursuits, he also took part and was a high achiever, winning an extraordinary 26 Vermont State

Championships in tennis. He was also a crack naval aviator in World War I.

After Dartmouth, he returned to his hometown from where, not surprisingly, he played a major role in organizing ski competitions on a local, national, and international level. An Olympic official, FIS delegate, co-founder of the United States Eastern Amateur Ski Association, President of the Brattleboro Outing Club, he also financed, designed, and built Brattleboro's first ski jump, aptly named Harris Hill. He wrote the following about his passion for ski jumping:

"Any sport to be worthwhile must be one in which there is always something more to learn – one in which no matter how proficient you become, there is a chance to keep on improving. It must not be too easy and there must always be fascination in what lies ahead. It must improve and build up both physically and morally. It must require courage, co-ordination, speed and daring. It should be held outdoors and require the best in a man in every way. Finally it must lend itself pleasure and convenience to the "fans" who support it. Ski jumping answers all these requirements and more." [41]

The fans have supported the sport ever since Harris started to make Brattleboro a regional center for ski jumping. Three thousand paying spectators gathered to watch the first Vermont State Championship Ski Jump at Harris Hill on February

4, 1922. With so large a gate, Harris was able to reimburse himself for the full cost of building the jump after the first day's event, which was won by **John Carleton '22**.

In the past, the tournament has included a bevy of world-class jumpers including Norway's former world-champion, Birger Ruud, who leapt to victory in 1938. Olympic trials and national championships have been held here. Back in the halcyon days of the sport, as many as ten thousand people would gather for the events, which enjoyed an international reputation. Following a weekend of competition in 2009 over Valentine's Day with two-day crowd estimates of well over 8,000 spectators, one thing is certain: Harris Hill is back.

Fred Harris's dream of some 85 years ago exemplifies how a sport can transcend raw athletic pursuit to become a way of life. Welcome signs in Brattleboro present an image of a ski jumper greeting visitors; its residents have seen the likes of Torger and Art Tokle, Art Devlin, Roy Sherwood and many other famous jumpers soar off the huge Harris tower. The jump is a much-respected symbol in Brattleboro, much like Holmenkollen is in Norway. The vision of Fred Harris reverberates still; more than just the ski jump that bears his name, he gave the nation the gift of

an indomitable spirit to pursue and excel that endures today—one for which all of us are the richer.

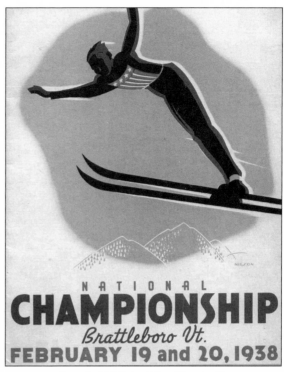

Poster for 1938 National Jump Championship on Harris Hill (Brattleboro, VT).

***

HISTORY OF THE VON TRAPP FAMILY LODGE IN VERMONT

By Johannes von Trapp '63 and Sam von Trapp '94

The family's early history has largely been defined by *The Sound of Music*, which is based on a book by Johannes's mother, Maria. Most people know that story about how Captain Georg von Trapp, his second wife, and their nine children escaped from Nazi-occupied Austria across the Alps and eventually came to America in 1938. The family's later history has evolved in large part from the creation of the first significant cross-country resort and lodge in the US over the last 30 years.

At the start of 1939, Johannes became the first American-born von Trapp. After some visa problems, the family applied for American citizenship. Two of the sons, Rupert and Werner, who had already had skiing experience in Austria, joined the US Army and served in Italy in the 10th Mountain Division. While in the 10th, the brothers frequently encountered Dartmouth graduates, many of whom were unit leaders.

By 1942, the family had bought a farm in Stowe, Vermont. Maria rented out rooms in the house while many of the von Trapps were on tour singing. The family farm became their home and the home eventually became the Trapp Family Lodge.

In 1960, Johannes entered Dartmouth College with the Class of 1963; the school was in his region, well regarded for its education, and known to the family through Rupert and Werner's 10th Mountain Division associations with alumni. A year earlier, the stage production of *The Sound of Music* had debuted on Broadway, and in 1965 the movie was released. Name recognition from the musicals gave the family an amazing level of fame, and Johannes's interactions at Dartmouth with some exceptional cross-country skiers set up the next stage of the family's development.

In 1968, with the help of his Dartmouth contacts, Johannes created a 15-kilometer cross-country course on a combination of summer hiking trails and existing logging roads. It was the first privately owned, publicly accessible x-c course in the US at the time. It has since been lengthened to some 65 kilometers of touring/racing trails, about 15 of which have snowmaking ability.

Important in these developments was the work of **Ned Gillette '67**, a legendary Dartmouth and Olympic cross-country racer, and **John Dostal '68**, a backcountry skier and writer. They, plus others, developed the trails and marketed the facility to a wide range of interested parties, including the Dartmouth ski team. In the next few years, the Trapp Cross-Country Center became the back-

Johannes '63 and Sam '94 von Trapp striding out on the Trapp Family Lodge X-C trail.

up to Dartmouth's home course for the all-important Winter Carnival races whenever the snow conditions in Hanover were poor. It also became the venue for many college x-c championship races. In 1976 the Dartmouth men won the NCAA championship on this course, and in 1977 the Dartmouth ladies won the AIAW Ski Championship here.

Although her husband had passed away 20 years earlier, Maria stayed active in the Trapp Lodge until her own death in 1987. As time passed, the development of the lodge into a successful resort enterprise fell increasingly to Johannes, the youngest of Maria's ten children. To eliminate family conflicts,

he engineered a buy-out in 1994 and resolved various other problems, finally assuming full responsibility. Johannes may have wanted to do other things with his life and says, "I honestly resented the fact that none of my older siblings took over the business.... so I could've run off and done whatever I wanted to do." But he has created a major success—and a New England landmark--out of the Trapp Family Lodge.

In 2007, Johannes's son **Sam von Trapp '94**, returned home from a career as a ski instructor in Aspen, Portillo, Chile and Stowe to begin the process of taking over the helm of Trapp Family Lodge, Inc. from his father. Sam's first project was to install and be the primary operator of the snowmaking system for a portion of the resort's cross-country ski network, allowing the center to maintain trail skiability without interruption even during winter thaws. Together, Johannes and Sam continue to build the lodge and its ancillary facilities into an even bigger business. Today, the Trapp Family Lodge stands as a premier resort and cross-country center, now further enhanced for summer use with ecologically designed mountain bike trails, and continues to be used regularly for x-c training and competitions by Dartmouth and other Eastern schools.

MAINE

With one exception, construction on skiable mountains in Maine lagged behind the development activity in Vermont and New Hampshire. For the most part this seems to have been the result of land ownership patterns in the state, where large forest tracts were held privately by timber companies, in contrast to the other northern New England states where the expansive acreages of state and federal land were more readily made available for recreational uses like skiing from the Depression years well into the 1960s.

That exception was Pleasant Mountain, ME, which opened in 1938 around a nucleus of two CCC ski trails, the creations of a Portland skier, Walter Soule, who spotted the mountain on his way to ski in North Conway.[42] The resort, renamed Shawnee Peak when it was purchased by a Pennsylvania group in the 1980s, has been owned by **Chet Homer '73** since the autumn of 1994.

In an age when snowmaking has become essential to ski resorts even in the snowy West, one of the elements that attracted Homer as he studied the mountain located on Moose Pond was its prodigious water supply. He increased the water pumping capacity of the area by 100%, while simultaneously lowering overall snowmaking costs by a third through his investment in energy-efficient snow guns. Homer's focus on snowmaking allowed him to recover quickly from the thaw-freeze cycles that are a fact of life in New England. That capability to rapidly resurface ski trails in the aftermath of a mid-winter rainstorm has become the gold standard for New England snowmaking systems.

Shawnee Peak's location within an hour's drive of Portland, as well as its status as the largest night-skiing area in New England, allowed Homer to concentrate on his local market and not compete with more remote destination resorts. A well-established mid-week night ski-racing league centered on the Portland vicinity draws a good crowd at a time when most ski areas are dark and vacant. Homer made continual improvements in the mountain in the years of his ownership and has rebuilt or replaced every lift on the mountain. Being the owner of a well-managed, mid-sized ski resort with many natural advantages, and having a history of making textbook decisions in terms of reinvestment, energy efficiency, and effective marketing, Homer shares his expertise with others in the industry as a board member of the National Ski Areas Association and Chairman of the New England Ski Areas Council.[43]

After World War II, a handful of Maine communities and groups looked to skiing as an avenue for new economic development, and often their first call was to Sel Hannah. Hannah had a hand in the selection and design of three Maine resorts that would in time be owned or managed by Dartmouth alumni: Sugarloaf, Saddleback, and Sunday River. Sugarloaf Mountain was the first to be built, with construction underway in 1955, and by the winter of 1957, two Constam T-bars provided access to the mountain's high snowfields.

The Sugarloaf Mountain Corporation's entry into bankruptcy in 1986 led to **Warren Cook '67** being named president of the company in the fall of that year. Cook was a lifelong skier, having started the sport at age four at Jiminy Peak and Bromley. He was a hockey player when he came to Dartmouth and he made the team, which kept him off skis in his college years since skiing was a forbidden activity for hockey players. Following service in the Marine Corps and several years of private school teaching, he went into his family's specialized materials business for a decade before entering the ski business at Sugarloaf.

Cook presided over the formation of a new company at Sugarloaf and by 1988 had added over 100 acres of new ski terrain, three new lifts, and snowmaking systems. In the next decade, Sugarloaf became notable as a venue for national championship events in Snowboard, Alpine, Freestyle, Master's Alpine and Junior Alpine competition. In 1994, S-K-I, Ltd., owner of Killington and other major resorts, purchased a 51% stake in Sugarloaf and within two years sold that to American Skiing Corporation (ASC), a massive ski industry conglomerate assembled by Leslie B. Otten of Sunday River. Cook spent several years as Senior Vice President of Operations at Sugarloaf under ASC before resigning in 1998. "He steadied a foundering ship," wrote Sugarloaf and ski industry veteran John Christie, "…devoted every ounce of his energy and considerable talent to refocusing the Mountain on what had accounted for its initial success—its skiing…"[44] After five years spent in the biotech business, Cook reconnected with the ski industry through Sugarloaf Global Partners, which was involved with resort development in Japan and China, and later became General Manager of Saddleback in Maine at a time of renewal for that resort.

At Sunday River in Bethel, ME, Dartmouth graduate **Murray "Mike" Thurston '43** was involved from the very beginning. A skier from his youth in Bethel, when he occasionally skied through family apple orchards lit at night with kerosene lanterns, Thurston also skied at Dartmouth at Oak Hill. After Army service and graduation, he was president of J. A. Thurston Company, the family wood products business. As a community leader in the Bethel area, he was a founding member of the Bethel Area Development Council, which explored the possibility of a local ski area.

Sel Hannah was hired to conduct a feasibility study in 1958 and found good terrain with the proper exposure and deep soil that he predicted would lower the costs of trail construction. By the time of its December 1959 opening, Sunday River Skiway had realized considerable savings in construction operations due to a good deal of community involvement in the building of the access road, parking lot, and ski trails. Financing was provided in part by a Small Business Administration package. After only three years of operation, the ski area showed a modest profit of $2,613 and had added a second T-Bar lift.

Thurston was president of Sunday River for a decade and was involved with the sale of the mountain to Killington in 1972 and 1973. That purchase brought an infusion of cash that was put into snowmaking and grooming, beginning the transformation of the small, locally owned ski hill into the behemoth ski resort that would be the hub of the ASC conglomerate that Les Otten would assemble in the 1990s. For his part, Mike Thurston kept involved in skiing as a volunteer instructor for the Maine Handicapped Ski program, teaching skiing in the program into his 80's at the mountain whose development he had initiated. [45]

NEW HAMPSHIRE

The Oak Hill lift and slope that opened in the winter of 1936 was a very significant step in the evolution of uphill transportation, but occurring as it did in the earliest phase of the progression of alpine skiing as a sport, it was quickly surpassed by newer technology and larger hills. By the early 1950s Dartmouth suffered by comparison to Middlebury, which had a substantial ski area near its campus. Dartmouth officials, most notably **John Meck '33**, felt that a new ski venue was necessary if the college was to retain its primacy in skiing. In 1953, Meck assembled a team to search for a ski area site within a reasonable range of Hanover and created a list of criteria a new site must meet. The prime attributes he sought were a northeast exposure and a vertical drop in excess of 600 feet. Meck, **John Rand '38**, Bob Monahan and Walter Prager made up the team, and after an extensive search they settled on Holt's Ledge in Lyme Center. Sepp Ruschp, Charley Lord and Henry Simoneau of Stowe, VT, visited the site in the spring of 1955 and hiked up the mountain to give a second opinion on the committee's selection. This was no random group: Charley Lord was the original architect of the Nose Dive Trail on Mt. Mansfield; Sepp Ruschp, an Austrian instructor hired to teach at Mansfield in 1937, built a career at Stowe and oversaw its ascent to the most respected ski area in the East; and Simoneau was an instructor and racer whose skiing style in the 1930s was remarkably similar to that of Dartmouth's Dick Durrance. [46]

Expert opinion being of one mind, the site was approved. Following an intense summer of construction financed by alumni contributions, the Dartmouth Skiway opened with one Pomalift and one rope tow in December 1956. The January 1957 grand opening ceremony included a feature unmatched by any other ski area in the country—a slalom demonstration by five Olympic skiers associated with the area's proprietors, in this case Brooks Dodge, **Bill Beck '53**, Tom Corcoran, **Ralph Miller '55**, and **Chick Igaya '57**. [47]

The Skiway, under the management of **Howard Chivers '39**, was such a success that skier numbers quickly overwhelmed the capacity of the area. So Meck cast his eyes to the east, to the western slope of Winslow Hill which faced the original Holt's Ledge slopes. In the summer and fall of 1967, four trails were cut there, surveyed by Don Cutter Sr., and a Savio double-chair was installed on this second face of the Skiway.

Owning a sizable ski area and eking out a net gain from operations in a weather-dependent, five-month season has always been an iffy proposition, and the college would come to learn this as the Skiway dealt with what seemed to be crisis after crisis; but this was in actuality just business as usual for ski area operators. The original Poma on Holt's Ledge became problematic, and the cost of a new installation was out of reach. The solution came in 1977 when a virtually new Hall double-chair from a closed ski area in Newburgh, NY, was moved to Holt's Ledge by the lift company at a considerable savings over that of a new chair. The Poma, in turn, was dismantled and given to Arrowhead in Claremont, NH; such migrations of lifts from one ski area to another were not unusual in the industry.

The need for snowmaking at the Skiway was the next hurdle, one that all Eastern resorts faced in the 1970s and 1980s. In the spring of 1985, challenged by an offer of a financial gift for Skiway snowmaking by Dartmouth parent and ski business veteran George Macomber, the college approved the project subject to achieving fundraising goals. Construction of the system got underway, overseen by **Don Cutter, Jr. '73**, who replaced Chivers in 1983 as manager of the Skiway, bolstered by a last-minute gift by **Lowell Thomas, Jr. '46** which put the fund campaign over the top. [48] This ability to draw on alumni gifts does distinguish college-owned areas from the rest of the ski business (Middlebury is the only other in the East), and in 2000 the Skiway benefited again from alumni generosity when the McLane Family Lodge was built as a replacement for the smaller and less accommodating Brundage Lodge base building. Alumni again came to the aid of the Skiway in 2008 when the four **Dupré sisters, Denise '80, Rosi '82, Anni '83** and **Michele '88**, donated the funding to greatly expand the area's snowmaking capability with high-efficiency snow guns and equipment from Snow Economics, Inc., the Natick, Massachusetts-based company their father Herman Dupré had founded in 1991 with his son-in-law, **Charles Santry Tu '89**.[49]

The Macomber and McLane families, prominent in the story of the Dartmouth Skiway, also figured in the creation of Wildcat. The Wildcat Ski Trail, laid out by Charley Proctor and cut by a crew overseen by Bob Monahan in the summer of 1933, became the core around which the Wildcat Mountain Corporation constructed a major ski area in 1957-58. Two Dartmouth graduates, **Malcolm McLane '46** and Brooks Dodge were among the group of four founders of the area. With their two partners, Mack Beal and **George Macomber** (father of three Dartmouth ski team captains: **John '77, Grace '81** and **George '85**), they built the first ski area on US Forest Service land in the East.

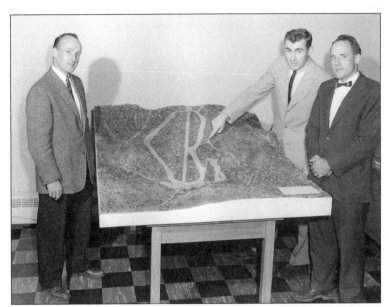

Wildcat Mtn founders: (l. to r.) M. McLane '46, B. Dodge '51, Th'54 and G. Macomber (D parent).

Malcolm, a son of "Judge" John R. McLane, grew up a skier with frequent family ski trips to places like Pinkham Notch and Tenney Hill. At Dartmouth he was on the ski team, though his tenure was interrupted by World War II when he served in the Army Air Corps and was shot down after flying 73 missions and spent the first part of 1945 in a German POW camp. He and his father were involved in an attempt to purchase the Glen House property and the Mount Washington Auto Road in the late 1940s to build a ski area. In the end, the owners of the property chose not to sell; but in November 1955, when the Forest Service announced it would consider proposals to develop Wildcat, just a few miles southwest of the Glen House, the group of four (Dodge, McLane, Macomber and Beal), all of whom had been competitive skiers at the international level, quickly determined to put in a bid. They were successful in this and construction commenced in June 1957.[50]

Financing was achieved through the sale of stock that came with lifetime lift privileges, and Malcolm, an attorney with a Harvard Law degree, drew up the prospectus. In years to come, he was bemused to note that as this form of ski area financing became more widespread, he could see verbatim portions of his legal language repeated by in other ski area prospectuses.

Brooks Dodge was by then retired from international skiing competition having been on the 1952 and 1956 US Olympic ski teams and placing fourth in the slalom in 1956, the best Olympic finish of an American male skier to that time. Trained as a civil engineer, he surveyed and supervised the cutting of new ski trails that would complement the existing Wildcat Trail.

While Dodge was in the Army stationed in Garmisch-Partenkirchen, Germany, he had seen enclosed gondola lifts that offered full protection to its passengers from the cold and wind, and he suggested a gondola lift be considered by the Wildcat Mountain Corporation. The company settled on a Carlevaro-Savio installation, a two-person gondola manufactured by an Italian firm; when this was christened in late January 1958, it became the first gondola ski lift in the U.S. and an instant way to promote Wildcat to the eastern skiing population.

In its first few years, Wildcat received a good deal of notice as the grandest and most glamorous new ski development in the East and also as host of the 1959 Eastern Championships and the 1961 National Championships. Soon however, the area was overshadowed as larger and more elaborate resorts, notably Sugarbush in Vermont, came on line. Wildcat's founding was also at just the point in time when it was becoming evident that lodging accommodations and sales of real estate at ski resort base areas would be a necessary component of financial success. Wildcat's location in the White Mountain National Forest, which had seemed a great advantage in 1955, came to be a hindrance to financial stability for the corporation since the Forest Service permitted no such activity within its preserves.

Wildcat was just one of the contributions to skiing that Dodge and McLane would make. Growing up as he had at the trailhead to Tuckerman Ravine, Brooks Dodge frequented its slopes as a teenager, and by the late 1940s he had added significantly to the roster of chutes and gullies on record as having been skied. Of the twenty routes considered skiable in the ravine, Brooks Dodge likely made the first descents of twelve or fourteen--partly because he could await ideal conditions for some routes that are not skiable every spring, and partly as the result of his use of a tighter, more efficient ski technique than the then prevailing Arlberg method. At Dartmouth, he was a key member of the second wave of ascendant Walter Prager ski teams that coalesced in the early 1950s, teams that echoed the dominance of the Dartmouth ski teams of the 1930s. Farther afield, Dodge was an early advocate of Canadian helicopter skiing when he prevailed on backcountry ski guide Hans Gmoser to switch from pedestrian ski touring to helicopters as the access mode to the vast powder fields of the Canadian Rockies in 1965.[51]

Malcolm McLane was another major force in organizational skiing, serving in numerous posts in the US Eastern Amateur Ski Association, National Ski Association, and the International Ski Federation. He was Chairman of the US Olympic Ski Committee from 1957 until 1972, presiding over that committee as it selected competitors for four consecutive Winter Olympics.[52]

One of Brooks Dodge's teammates on the Dartmouth ski team, Tom Corcoran, like Dodge the owner of a Winter Olympic fourth place finish (1960, Giant Slalom), became the founder of the Waterville Valley resort in NH. While Wildcat was limited by its lack of ability to provide commercial lodging and private homes, Waterville benefited mightily by the symbiotic development of a major ski mountain with a municipality at the base. Having grown up skiing at Mont Tremblant in Quebec, Corcoran was aware of the resort's pioneering ski village located at its base area, conceived by Philadelphia owner Joe Ryan, and the sense of homecoming that the settlement evoked became something he strived to incorporate at Waterville Valley.

After graduating from Dartmouth, Corcoran went to work in Aspen, CO, as assistant to Darcy Brown of the Aspen Ski Company. He was also friendly with Pete Seibert, a founder of Vail. One of the lessons he learned from Aspen and Vail was the need for a good relationship between the resort and the local municipality—the Vail resort had a constructive relationship with its town while Aspen's did not. The positive relation with the town of Waterville Valley that Corcoran would achieve in the future when he developed his own ski resort there was one of the legacies of his stint in the West. He resigned from Aspen in 1964 and moved east to develop Waterville Valley, site of a CCC ski trail that Sel Hannah had helped build in the 1930s on Mt. Tecumseh.

Corcoran was not the first Dartmouth man to influence Waterville Valley. **David S. Austin, II '04** leased and managed the Waterville Inn, a 19th century summer hotel, in the 1920s and 1930s and became a fixture in the small community. He was active on the committee that advised the CCC on locating ski trails in New Hampshire in the early 1930s, and in 1936 when the Forest Service hired Sel Hannah to scout out a ski trail location on Tecumseh, Austin hired Hannah for a supplementary job in the inn's kitchen.

As an Exeter student, Corcoran had run a race on the walk-up ski trail that Hannah surveyed in the 1936, and when he moved to the East to open a ski area he consulted with Hannah, who pointed out the Waterville area, and commented that Bob Monahan had identified it as one of the best potential ski area locations in the National Forests when he conducted a survey of possible locations. Corcoran moved quickly to lease private land in the valley and to obtain a use permit from the Forest Service.[53]

Waterville Valley opened for the winter of 1966-67 and rapidly became an important destination resort with more than a few touches of glamour, signified by ski vacations taken there by former US Attorney-General Robert F. Kennedy and his family, whom Corcoran had first met while guiding him around Aspen.

Corcoran's racing career and Western interlude influenced the design of his ski area. Ski competition was important and he located racing areas where they would not conflict with general skier traffic. Eleven World Cup races, including two finals, were held at Waterville in Corcoran's years even though the ski area was easily the smallest resort on the World Cup circuit. Waterville's trails, cut wider than was then customary in New England, were laid out like the fingers of a hand, radiating out from a central point. The ebullient Corcoran was also one of the first in the ski industry to film frequent on-slope television commercials for the resort, featuring himself as the spokesman.

Like the snow trains of the 1930s, the advent of a new transportation network in the form of the Interstate highway system in the 1960s eased skiers' approach to ski terrain, and this shift in access benefited some areas more than others. Waterville Valley was one beneficiary, and its competitor up Interstate 93, Loon Mountain, was another.

Loon Mountain was the brainchild of Sherman Adams whose career took many unique directions. Before leaving Hanover, he had been involved in starting the first official Dartmouth, and a first for any US college, ski team in 1921. He was then by turns a Chief of the Parker-Young Company in Lincoln, NH, and thereby the professional heir of the 19-century timber barons; Speaker of the New Hampshire House, and then Governor; the nation's first Presidential Chief of Staff (under President Eisenhower); and finally, ski area developer and owner.

On his retirement from politics, Adams was needled by his wife Rachael to find a viable ski area location on the Kancamaugus Highway, a newly opened scenic road running through the Pemigewassett forest from Lincoln to Conway. Adams himself scouted the mountains in the region and settled on Loon Mountain after a 1964 snowshoe climb which convinced him that the mountain had all the attributes he sought. As did so many other prospective developers, he brought in Sel Hannah, who confirmed Adams's evaluation and set to work designing a trail network. The land ownership pattern was similar to that of other successful mountains—flat lands at the base in private ownership, and therefore feasible for development, and mountain slopes on National Forest property. The Forest Service permit was complicated by the plans of the Army Corps of Engineers for a flood control dam at the base, and while that conflict was finally resolved in favor of the Forest Service and the dam plan was shelved, it was a harbinger of lengthy environmental battles that Loon Mountain Recreation Corporation would fight in seeking to expand their permit acreage in the 1980s and 1990s.[54]

Loon's distinctive base lodge was designed by architect and former Dartmouth skiing standout **Ted Hunter '38**, though his original plans had to be scaled back somewhat for budgetary reasons. A Pohlig gondola and two Hall chairlifts were installed, and Loon Mountain opened on the same fast-track timetable as Waterville Valley in the winter of 1966-67. A major expansion onto terrain called the East Basin in 1968-69 and installation of snowmaking in 1970-71 were all made possible by skier visits that increased steadily thanks to the easy access from Boston and environs.

Sherman Adams's Washington experience proved to be critically important to the ski industry in the fall of 1974 when Congressional worries over the gasoline shortage brought on by the Arab-Israeli War almost led to an embargo on travel for recreational purposes. Adams was able to brief Pete Seibert and Cal Conniff, President and Director respectively of the National Ski Areas Association, and Tom Corcoran, President of Eastern Ski Areas Association, on actions to take in Washington to delete the offending language from legislation already passed by the Senate. Following Adams' blueprint, the three traveled to Washington where they called on key legislators and mobilized a rapid industry-wide response that caused the language which would have restricted "non-essential" travel to be dropped.[55]

Another New Hampshire ski area built in this period of great ski industry growth of the mid-1960s was Attitash where **Norman E. "Sandy" McCulloch, Jr. '50** was a founding board member and eventually the chairman. Sandy, best known as a College Trustee from 1975 to 1988 and Chairman of the College Board of Trustees from 1986 to 1988, is another Dartmouth alumnus who grew up on skis. His father, **Norman E. McCulloch, Sr. '17**, took the family on ski trips to Moosilauke, Hanover, and Tuckerman Ravine. After college and marriage, McCulloch and his family bought a second home in North Conway; there he got to know Jack Middleton, a well respected New Hampshire attorney (and brother-in-law of Brooks Dodge), along with Phil Robertson, General Manager of Mt. Cranmore and a pioneer of the ski industry. Middleton drew McCulloch into a group that formed the Mt. Attitash Lift Corporation and proceeded to build Attitash, located just north and west of North Conway in the town of Bartlett.

Attitash opened in January 1965 calling itself "the red carpet ski area" for its customer service policy of limiting ticket sales to shorten lift lines. In an era of 30- or 45-minute lift lines, this was an appealing philosophy to many, but it was quietly dropped by the end of the decade as financially unsustainable. Phil Robertson, perhaps recalling the success Cranmore had in developing an entirely new form of ski lift with its Skimobile, became an advocate for a new form of ski lift at Attitash: a cog monorail. In early 1967, a full-size model was installed at the base and the line of the track was eventually cut to the summit; however, low skier capacity, uncertain prospects for financing, and doubt as to Forest Service approval for the expensive, unproven, and ultimately impractical experiment resulted in its abandonment.

McCulloch's association with Phil Robertson at Attitash brought him into contact with a North Country original who was one of the true pioneers of the ski industry. Robertson was one of three partners in the Moody Farm overhead cable ski tow that opened in Jackson, NH, in the same month in 1936 as the Oak Hill J-Bar, though it got so little notice that Oak Hill is generally conceded to be the first of its kind. While he was General Manager at Mt. Cranmore, the earliest mechanized ski slope grooming process on record was initiated in the winter of 1940.[56] In the later 1950s, when chairlifts were two decades past their invention and there were concerns among various states and insurance companies about the lack of standards of operation and maintenance, Robertson chaired a series of committees that led to the creation of the New Hampshire Passenger Tramway Safety Board, the model for other state tramway boards and for what is today the American National Standards Institute B-77 Committee that sets—and continues to devise—the governing standard that ski areas, insurers and state tramway boards must observe.

Jim Griffiths '65 is loading the chairlift in his Ski Patrol parka. In small ski areas like Whaleback, the owner does everything. (1975).

As Chairman of the Board of Attitash, McCulloch had to navigate through low-snow winters in the late 1970s and guide the corporation through the installation of snowmaking equipment. In the late 1980s, banks tightened credit substantially, and in the 1990s McCulloch presided over the sale of Attitash to Les Otten of Sunday River. The mountain was Otten's first acquisition on his way to creating the American Ski Company that would be such a force in the ski business for a short time.[57]

Following a great wave of ski area abandonment in the 1970s and 1980s brought on by high energy costs, competitive pressure to add snowmaking, and high insurance rates, there came in the late 1990s and early 2000s a modest rediscovery of the small area roots of skiing, accompanied by a realization that the grandiose atmospherics of large resorts are enhancements to the recreational pursuit of downhill skiing that not all ski areas need to offer. In addition, energy prices eased somewhat and the efficiency of snowmaking improved greatly, allowing faster coverage at lower cost and quieting concerns that climate warming might devastate the industry in the short term. Smaller areas realized an advantage in having smaller acreages to treat with snowmaking equipment and could open with 100% cover faster than could the larger areas.

Perhaps most significantly, the advent of snowboarding boosted the ranks of potential buyers of lift tickets at a time when the skier population was no longer growing, and the increasing appeal of terrain parks in ski areas, traceable to the influence of snowboarding, allowed skiers and boarders to find fulfilling new experiences without the necessity for vertical drops of major league proportions that had been a driving force in ski area expansions in the 1960s.

These trends are illustrated by the story of Whaleback in Enfield, NH, which was built in the mid-1950s as Snow Crest Ski Area by local resident **Ernest Dion**, an Olympic ski jumper who had informally coached Dartmouth skiers in jumping.[58] Dion sold the area in 1968 to a group of investors that included **Clark Griffiths '57** and his brother **Jim Griffiths '65**. The Griffiths brothers, having bought out their partners, expanded the area, and Jim Griffiths managed it until 1985, at which point the Griffiths group sold it to another Dartmouth group, including **Thomas W. Kent '72** and **Jeffrey B. Reed '76**. They optimistically invested in snowmaking devices and lights for night skiing, only to be forced to close after several poor winters.

The area sat vacant for several years until it was re-opened by Jim Griffiths' daughter Sally and son-in-law Tim, with participation by his other two daughters, Kate Griffith '90 and Jessie Griffith '93. In turn, these owners sold the mountain to Evan Dybvig and partners, who now operate the area as a snowboarding and freestyle park. [59]

SUMMARY

New England skiing has been led by the members of the Dartmouth family since the very beginning. Many of the large ski areas have been founded, designed or managed by people associated with this single institution that from its own founding has been located in the middle of the ski terrain for northern New England. Over the decades many smaller ski areas have come and gone. The positive sign for small and large ski areas is that the growth of snow making facilities and the resurrection of a small ski area, like Whaleback, represent hopeful expectations that skiing can remain a pastime within the reach of all who have a passion for the sport, and not become an exclusive prerogative of the elites. Broad demographic participation in the sport created the business of skiing that Dartmouth alumni did so much to influence in decades past and it remains a necessary precondition to its future success.

Notes

1. Herman Holt Diary excerpts, New England Ski Museum Collection, Franconia, NH, 1983L.031.001. 2. Shumway, Carl E., "Notes by Carl E. Shumway, Lynnfield, Mass. Concerning White Mts 1911-1913," photocopy of manuscript in New England Ski Museum collection, 2002.131.001. 3. Tucker, Richard E., "Skis in Tuckerman Ravine," *Journal of the New England Ski Museum*, 57, (Winter 2002-2003), 8. 4. Hagerman, Robert L., *Mansfield: The Story of Vermont's Loftiest Mountain*. Canaan, NH: Phoenix Publishing, 1965, 66. 5. Dudley, Charles M., *60 Centuries of Skiing*. Brattleboro, Vermont: Stephen Daye Press, 1935, 62. 6. "Shumway Back to Winter Page After Six Years," *Boston Evening Transcript* (November 27, 1936), 5. 7. Place, Edward, "Old Man Winter," *Boston Evening Transcript* (Friday April 7, 1933), New England Ski Museum collection 1998L.100.13. 8. Carleton, John P. to William Fowler, May 8, 1933, Appalachian Mountain Club Library, Fowler Papers; photocopy in New England Ski Museum collection, 2004.054.001. 9. Strom, Erling, *Pioneers on Skis*. Central Valley, NY: Smith Cove Books, 1977, 44-50. 10. Monahan, Robert S., "Original Wildcat Ski Trail Swamped Out by CCC in 1933," , *Eastern Ski Bulletin*, VI, 8 (March 7, 1958), 16, reprinted from "Off Main Street" in *Hanover Gazette*, n.d. 11. Proctor, Charles N., "New Ski Trails," Various Notes, *Appalachia*, December 1933, pages 599-603. 12. Lund, Morten and Eddy Ancinas, "An American Skier for All Seasons: Charley Proctor, Part I," *Skiing Heritage* (First Issue, 2000), 10. 13. Proctor, Charles N., Letter to Dick March, April 22, 1986, New England Ski Museum Collection, 1986L.103.001. 14. Putnam, William Lowell, *Green Cognac: The Education of a Mountain Fighter*. New York (AAC Press), 1991, 11. 15. "Rites Sunday for Donald Tuttle," *Manchester Union* (December 22, 1945), photocopy from Rauner Special Collections Library. 16. Adams, Sherman, "Mission Impossible," *Appalachia*, XXXVI, 15 (December 15, 1971), 53-64. 17. Sullivan, Robert, "No Holds Bard," *Dartmouth Alumni Magazine* (March 1994), 14-21. 18. Fowler, William P., "New Hampshire Becomes Ski Conscious," *Appalachia*, XLII, 8 (December 15, 1978), 123. 19. Putnam, William Lowell, *Joe Dodge: One New Hampshire Institution*. Canaan, NH: Phoenix Publishing, 1986, 131. 20. Durrance, Richard, "Controlled Downhill Skiing," *The Ski Bulletin*, VII, 3 (January 1, 1937), 3. 21. "Cream of Nation's Skiers Will Compete Sunday in Tuckerman's Ravine Races," *Manchester Union*, 75, 4 (April 3, 1937), 1. "US Eastern Slalom Championships and Franklin Edson Memorial Race", *Amateur Ski Club of New York News Letter*, IV, VII, (April 28, 1937), 2; Denver Public Library Dole Box 1, FF 4. 22. Brown, Daniel L., "New England Ski-ing," *British Ski Yearbook* VI, 13 (1932), 397. 23. "A Plan for Developing Ski Terrain With Ski-Tows at Hanover," ca. 1936, Rauner Special Collections, DO 1, II-25-9, page 7. 24. Adler, Allen, *New England & Thereabouts—A Ski Tracing*. Barton, VT: Netco Press, 1985, 50-52. McQueeney, Michael, "Bunny Bertram," 1980, transcript of oral history interview in New England Ski Museum Collection. 25. Dan P. Hatch, "Dartmouth Ski-Tow," *The Ski Bulletin* V, 15 (March 29, 1935), 6. 26. Bob Monahan wrote that Hatch viewed brochures: Monahan, Robert S., "20 Years of Uphill Work," *New Hampshire Profiles* (February, 1955), 29-31. Ed Newell, who grew up in Hanover and attended the Clark School and later was an aerial tramway proponent, stated that Hatch had seen the lift in person: Noble, Susan, "Interview with Ed Newell," November 29, 1980, transcript of oral history interview in New England Ski Museum Collection. Ernst Constam, in negotiations with Hans Paschen of the DOC in 1941, stated that Hatch saw photos of the Davos tow: Paschen, Hans, "To the Trustees of the D.O.C.", January 27, 1941, Rauner Special Collections, DO 1, Box 62, photocopy in New England Ski Museum Collection. 27. D.P. H., "Memo on Ski Tow," Rauner Special Collections, DO 1, 3:27, photocopy in New England Ski Museum Collection. 28. Split Ballbearing Corporation, "Modern Ski Tramways," *The Ski Bulletin* VI, 8 (February 7, 1936), 7. Extensive advertising and ski press coverage of the Oak Hill tow left the impression it was the first overhead wire rope ski tow in the US. In fact, a companion overhead cable lift opened in the same year in Jackson, New Hampshire at the Moody Farm; this tow featured short ropes hanging from the overhead cable for skiers to grasp and never became a target of Constam's patent infringement efforts. 29. Paschen, Hans, "To the Trustees of the D.O.C.", January 27, 1941, Rauner Special Collections, DO 1, Box 62, photocopy in New England Ski Museum Collection. 30. Kenyon, Jim, "Ford Sayre Plans to Cease Operations at Oak Hill," *Valley News*, (June 8, 1985). 31. Bright, Alexander, "Survey of Possible Aerial Tramway Locations," July 25, 1934, State of New Hampshire Archives, Concord, NH, Box 081111, photocopy in New England Ski Museum Collection, 2002.044.001. American Steel & Wire Company, "Engineering Report, Passenger Tramway Project for State of NH," January 18, 1935, State of New Hampshire Archives, Concord, NH, Box 081111. 32. Ripley, Damon, "The Tram's in the Air," *Yankee* (December 1936), 26. 33. Hooke, David, *Reaching That Peak: 75 Years of the Dartmouth Outing Club*. Canaan, New Hampshire: Phoenix Publishing, 1987, 158, 181, 196-97. 34. Hannah, Sel, "Environment, Ecology & Autumn Trail & Slope Maintenance," August 1957, typescript in New England Ski Museum Collection. 35. Spaulding, Ann, "An Interview with Mr. Seldon Hannah," November 14, 1979, typescript in New England Ski Museum Collection. 36. Cushing, Joseph Jr., Telephone interview with Jeff Leich, July 9, 2009. 37. Cushing, interview with Leich. 38. Bousquet, Paul, Telephone interview with Jeff Leich, June 19, 2009.

Dick Durrance '39, three-time winner of the Harriman Cup at Sun Valley.
(Handwritten inscription on photo: To Dick Durrance who helped put Sun Valley on the map & then stole
"the Cup". With my warm thanks and love to Miggs and all the best to all the Durrances. Averell Harriman
S.V. Jan 1940 Good luck in Nepal.)

Chapter VII Notes Continued...

39. Cutter, Rosalie, Letter to the Editor, *New England Ski Museum Journal*, 68 (Spring 2007), 27. It is anecdotally thought, though without hard documentation, that Dr. Rösen had performed some legal service for high-ranking German Nazis at the time of the 1923 Beer Hall Putsch, and while not a party member himself, could exert enough influence to have Schneider released to house arrest in Rösen's Garmisch-Partenkirchen residence. Schneider lived in that safe haven until a deal with Harvey Dow Gibson, an American banker, chairman of a committee of creditors holding German debt, and developer of Cranmore Mountain in North Conway, NH, was able to obtain papers for Schneider and his family to emigrate to America, whereupon Schneider took over the ski school at Cranmore. The details of Rösen's connection with the German Nazis, and Gibson's negotiations with the German government, remain obscure. 40. Lorentz, Karen D., *Okemo: All Come Home*. Shrewsbury, Vermont: Mountain Publishing, Inc., 1996, 46-55. Hagen, Dennis, Denver Public Library 10th Mountain Division Resource Center Curator, E-mail message to Jeff Leich re: database records for Donald Cutter, Sr., June 24, 2009. 41. The Dartmouth 2/11/24, Rauner files 42. Parkinson, Glenn, *First Tracks: Stories from Maine's Skiing Heritage*. Portland: Maine Skiing, Inc., 1995, 57. 43. Homer, Chet, E-mail message to Steve Waterhouse, March 13, 2009. 44. Christie, John, *The Story of Sugarloaf*. Camden, Maine: Down East Books, 2007, 102-112. 45. "Ski Area Developer Sees Prospects Good at Bethel," *Portland Press Herald* (April 22, 1958), 15. "Sunday River, Bethel Maine, Mike Thurston", Folder in Sno-Engineering Papers, New England Ski Museum Collection 2001.018.001a. *Bethel Citizen*, "Murray W. Thurston," http://www.bethelcitizen.com/story.php?storyid-5485. Meyer, Judith, *Bethel Citizen*, "Sunday River Trailblazer Mike Thurston Remembered," http://www.bethelcitizen.com/story.php?storyid-=5475. Lorentz, Karen, *Killington: A Story of Mountains and Men*. Shrewsbury Vermont: Mountain Publishing, Inc., 1990, 141-142. 46. Wood, Everett W., *Skiway: A Dartmouth Winter Tale*. Hanover: Dartmouth College, 1987, 2-10. Meck, John F., E-mail message to Steve Waterhouse, May 16, 2009. 47. Wood, *Skiway*, 23. 48. Wood, *Skiway*, 49-50. 49. Dartmouth College Office of Public Affairs, "Dupré gift funds major snowmaking upgrades to Dartmouth Skiway," press release, December 5, 2008,http://www.dartmouth.edu/~news/releases/2008/12/05.html. 50. McLane, Malcolm, Interview with Jeff Leich, October 15, 2004, transcript in New England Ski Museum Collection, 2004.146.002. 51. Dodge, J. Brooks, Jr., Interview with Jeff Leich, January 6, 2005, transcript in New England Ski Museum Collection, 2005.016.003. 52. Thomson, Robert, "Malcolm McLane", Nomination paper to US National Ski Hall of Fame, photocopy in New England Ski Museum Collection. 53. Bean, Grace Hughes, *The Town at the End of the Road: A History of Waterville Valley*. Canaan, New Hampshire: Phoenix Publishing, 1983, 57-58; 75-76; 99-100. 54. Adams, Sherman, "I Wanted a Mountain," *Yankee* (February 1971), 66-70. Merryman, Richard, "Sherman Adams: the Quintessential Doer", *Yankee* (April 1978), 68-76. 55. Rowan, David, "Ski Industry Mobilizes," Ski Area Management, 13, 1, (Winter 1974), 29-30. 56. Robertson, P.A., "Snow Maintenance of Open Slopes", *American Ski Annual* (1945-46), 209-210. 57. McCulloch, Norman E., Telephone discussion with Jeff Leich, July 7, 2009. 58. Dion, Doug, "Ernest D. Dion", Nomination paper to US National Ski Hall of Fame, photocopy in New England Ski Museum Collection. 59. Griffiths, Jim, E-mail message to Stuart Keiller, April 21, 2009.

CHAPTER VIII

WEST: DEVELOPMENT OF SKIING IN THE WESTERN U.S.

By Tom Washing '63
Founding Partner, Early Stage Technology Businesses Investment Fund

With Blair C. Wood '30, George W. Wood '67, and Kevin Whitcher '99

The business visionary who launched the expansion of skiing into the western United States was W. Averell Harriman, his point of departure being a resort he founded in Ketchum, Idaho: **Sun Valley**.[1] The skier protagonist of the narrative was a Dartmouth graduate whose entire adult life appeared destined to interlace with the critical ideas, places and events that initiated, and ultimately accelerated, the growth of skiing in the western United States: **Dick Durrance '39**.[2]

Harriman, who would become a prominent diplomat, cabinet member and Governor of New York, was a successful investment banker and railroad executive when he founded Sun Valley in 1936. An avid skier who had visited many of the elegant ski resorts in Europe (he was particularly fond of St. Moritz, Switzerland), Harriman was the Chairman of the Union Pacific Railroad and was enamored with the prospect of boosting the company's patronage by creating the first destination ski resort in the United States on one of his western rail lines. When a Union Pacific employee observed that the company spent more money for snow removal on the rail line to Ketchum, Idaho, than anywhere else in the country, the location for Harriman's new ski resort was no longer in question.[3]

Tom Washing '63 with Bugaboos in the background, location of the first modern ski traverse in 1959 by Briggs '54, Corbett '58, Neale '59 and French '56.

The prominent role Dartmouth would play in the advancement of skiing in the western United States was activated when Harriman hired **Charley Proctor '28** as a consultant to advise him in designing the new resort and to teach Ketchum locals to be ski guides. Proctor had been the captain of the 1927 Dartmouth ski team and had competed for the United States in the 1928 Winter Olympics, which had been held in St. Moritz.[4] He had already served as a technical advisor for several emerging ski resorts, including Yosemite's Badger Pass. Proctor helped design the first ski runs and assisted in devising and locating the early ski lifts at Sun Valley. The first of these lifts was installed in late 1936 on what became known as Proctor Mountain and is now listed in the National Register of Historic Places.

During the 1930s, the Dartmouth ski team was coached by Swiss skiing champion **Walter Prager** and was considered, as one writer observed, "the New York Yankees of collegiate skiing."[5] The Dartmouth team was generally acknowledged to be the preeminent college ski team in the United States and, possibly, the world.[6] By the winter of 1936-37, although he was only a sophomore at Dartmouth, Dick Durrance was widely recognized as the best Alpine skier in the nation and was the luminary of the Dartmouth ski team. Although the American-born Durrance had been raised in Germany and had skied throughout Europe for years, he had never skied in the western U.S. until 1935 when he, along with several other members of the Dartmouth ski team, attended the US Olympic tryouts on Mt. Rainier in Washington in the spring of that year. Even by European standards, he and his Dartmouth teammates were impressed with the mountain.[7]

Having thus experienced the exhilaration of western skiing for the first time, when Harriman invited him to participate in the first Sun Valley International Open (soon to be dubbed the Harriman Cup) to be held in

Dick Durrance I '39 on a winning run in the Harriman Cup at Sun Valley, the first American to beat the best European skiers.

March 1937, Durrance leapt at the opportunity, not only to participate but also to enjoy his first airplane ride which was paid for by the resort.[8] Durrance won the first of his three Harriman Cup victories that year, the first time an American had prevailed over the best European skiers in international competition.[9] Harriman's elation over an American winning the first international race at Sun Valley persuaded him to change the name of the mountain on which the race was held to Durrance Mountain. The country's first major destination ski resort now had two mountains named after Dartmouth skiers. With this historic victory, Dick Durrance's name and future became inextricably bound to Sun Valley.

John Litchfield '39 and Dartmouth ski coach Walter Prager.

The following winter of 1937-38, the Dartmouth ski team traveled to Sun Valley to meet the University of Washington. In route, the team was invited to stop and train at a ranch on the outskirts of Jackson, Wyoming, owned by Fred Brown, founder of the Jackson Hole Ski Association. According to the official Jackson Hole Resort History, the Dartmouth team "demonstrated the latest ski technique, use of two poles, and fixed heel binding to more than 200 spectators on Telemark Bowl near Teton Pass."[10] In addition to Durrance, the team featured several other Dartmouth skiers who would become instrumental in the development of skiing in the western US, including **Steve Bradley '39** and **John Litchfield '39**. Western skiing, and more specifically Sun Valley, was becoming a frequent topic of conversation among skiers on the Hanover campus.

In March of 1938, Durrance returned to Sun Valley to win his second Harriman Cup, and when school ended in the spring he accepted Harriman's offer to spend the summer working for the resort. He was hired as the resort photographer, and helped to promote Sun Valley as a western destination resort by photographing visitors and events and sending the pictures to newspapers around the country.[11] It was during this summer that Durrance's fascination with ski trail design and resort management was kindled. He spent a good deal of the summer surveying Bald Mountain, laying out runs, and cutting trails for future development, including the Warm Springs run which would become the site of the Harriman Cup in 1939.[12] Based in no small part on Durrance's work that summer, Mt. Baldy would emerge as the resort's signature mountain and premier ski racing venue.

Averell Harriman, who made no secret of his desire to glamorize the sport of skiing in the U.S. in general, and his fledgling Idaho ski resort in particular, was captivated by Dick Durrance's skiing prowess as well as his cinematic skills, both of which would enhance the reputation of the resort if Durrance settled in Sun Valley after graduation from Dartmouth.. Harriman tendered the offer and Durrance accepted following graduation in the spring of 1939.

Harriman's fascination with Dartmouth skiers was not confined to Durrance. **Percy Rideout '40** recalls that Harriman was said to have expressed a preference for those "virile, handsome Dartmouth men" as ski instructors because they would attract the Hollywood crowd and wealthy New Yorkers. Rideout modestly added that 'knowing this, we tried to fulfill his wishes as best we could."[13]

In December of 1938, Harriman dispatched his new ski school director, Austrian skier Friedl Pfeifer, to tour the East Coast promoting Sun Valley at ski shows in New York and Boston.[14] Pfeifer took a side trip north into New England, including a visit to Hanover to recruit Dartmouth skiers as future employees for Sun Valley.[15] Pfeifer's visit was predictably well received, and the following summer a band of Dartmouth men descended on Sun Valley including the aforementioned John Litchfield and Steve Bradley, plus newcomers, **Ned Jacoby '40, Bob Skinner '40, Joe Duncan '40, Harold (Hal) Hillman '40**, and, of course, the indispensable Dick Durrance.

Percy Rideout, the Dartmouth ski team captain in the winter of 1939-40, missed the Pfeifer visit to Hanover and was unable to join his teammates that summer as he was called home to work at his family's country inn in rural Massachusetts. But in September the following year, to his parents' dismay, Rideout moved to Sun Valley. Rideout recalled that when he told his mother, who had rarely ventured out of New England, that he was "moving west," it was clear "she did not know what that meant." Because he had not yet had the opportunity to meet ski school director Pfeifer, Rideout registered at The Lodge as a guest until his money ran out, ultimately securing a job on the trail crew, explaining that he was from Dartmouth and was desperate to work off his hotel room bill.[16]

In 1939, Sun Valley also welcomed guests for the summer months, a concept that was considered somewhat astounding for a ski resort at the time.[17] At least some of the Dartmouth boys were anticipating a rather cushy summer excursion in the Sawtooth Mountains of Idaho mingling with Sun Valley's glamorous guests. To their surprise, most were assigned to working under the sweltering sun on the trail crew, clearing sagebrush and timber for the planned Warm Springs run that had been surveyed by Dick Durrance on Bald Mountain the preceding summer. As the summer drew to a close, the Dartmouth boys finished their trail crew assignments and most were preparing to return to Hanover and their studies, undoubtedly aware that, sequestered in a room at the Sun Valley Lodge, Ernest Hemingway was composing the final chapters of *For Whom the Bell Tolls*.[18]

For the young skiers from Dartmouth, Sun Valley offered the ideal environment to become acquainted with the latest innovations in ski area management from the ground up. Sun Valley was not only the first destination ski resort in the United States, it also pioneered many of the

John Litchfield '39, Steve Bradley '39, Dick Durrance '39, Ned Jacoby '40, Bob Skinner '40, Joe Duncan '40, and Harold (Hal) Hillman '40 spent the summer of 1939 in Sun Valley cutting trails and climbing (Photos by Jacoby '40).

innovations that transformed skiing into a national pastime. For example, Harriman resolved that his guests should not suffer the inconvenience of grappling with a rope tow in order to be transported up the mountain. Charley Proctor, who was providing Harriman with technical advice on the project, had seen the first operating J-Bar ski lift in the country during a recent visit to Dartmouth. At Proctor's urging, Harriman's Union Pacific engineers created a "chair lift" by modifying banana-loading equipment used on fruit ships in the tropics, in effect substituting seats for the crook of the J-bar,[19] and the world's first chairlifts were installed in the fall of 1936.[20] Sun Valley also instituted the first ski school in the United States outside of New England,[21] thereby affording future employment opportunities to many Dartmouth men as well as teaching expertise for the resort's winter guests.

During the summer of 1939, three chairlifts were installed on Bald Mountain at the sites where Durrance had surveyed and the other Dartmouth boys had cleared the trails. In the fall, John Litchfield returned to Sun Valley where he would eventually become Head Ski Instructor and later Director of the Sun Valley

Phil Puchner '44 commenting to Tom Washing for this book.

Ski School.[22] He was eventually joined by Percy Rideout, Steve Bradley, Hal Hillman, Joe Duncan and **Charles McLane '41**.

It was during 1940 that Dick Durrance shot the footage for Sun Valley's first promotional film, *Sun Valley Holidays*. He also formulated the plot for his iconic award-winning *Sun Valley Ski Chase,* which was filmed by his former Dartmouth ski team pal Steve Bradley and starred Durrance being chased down the slopes of Sun Valley by various Dartmouth skiers including Steve's brother, **Dave Bradley '38**.[23] After returning from his tour in Italy with the 10th Mountain Division, **Phil Puchner '44** saw the Ski Chase movie for the first time in a bar in Leadville, Colorado, and judged it "the best ski movie I ever saw."[24] Puchner would shortly move to Sun Valley where he would join the ski school as an instructor.

The early1940s turned out to be a marvelous interlude in the lives of the Dartmouth team working at Sun Valley. John Litchfield recalled that many of the guests returned every year and asked for the same ski instructors they had the year before. "The guests all knew each other and knew the ski instructors. It was like one big family."[25] Occasionally, a small band of teen-age skiers from McCall, Idaho, would visit the resort wearing coonskin caps and dazzle the guests as they raced around the mountain. Litchfield only later realized that one of these hotshots was **Bill Brown**, a future sergeant in Litchfield's company in the 10th Mountain Division, a future member of the Dartmouth faculty, and a future honoree of the Skiing Hall of Fame.[26]

The Sun Valley instructors and employees had ample opportunity to mingle with the celebrities and that could be frustrating at times. Percy Rideout remembered Bing Crosby arriving with his "unruly bunch of kids" who preferred engaging in snowball fights with instructors at the bottom of the mountain to enduring ski lessons at the top. Crosby would end the day's outing by leading the guests and instructors in song on the bus ride back to The Lodge. These distractions were eclipsed by tranquil evenings during which Ernest Hemmingway, often accompanied by his hunting companion Gary Cooper, would invite the trail-crew members to join his table after dinner in the elegant Duchin Room, pouring wine all around and recounting tales of his assorted exploits.[27] Phil Puchner recalls being assigned as a Sun Valley Ski Patrol member to follow Daryl Zanuck, the prominent producer and executive at Twentieth Century Fox Studios, around the slopes carrying a box of Zanuck's favorite cigars to protect them from being crushed when Zanuck fell, which he apparently did with some regularity.[28]

As the Dartmouth skiers became increasingly smitten with the western mountains, they also experienced first-hand the initial consequences of the war looming in Europe. The 1940 US Olympic team, which featured an astonishing nine Dartmouth skiers, including Dick Durrance, John Litchfield, Hal Hillman, Dave Bradley, Steve Bradley and alternate Percy Rideout, was denied the opportunity to compete when the Olympics were cancelled following the German invasion of Poland in 1939 marking the beginning of World War II.

In the winter of 1941-42, the Dartmouth Ski coach, Walter Prager, was drafted into the Army and Dartmouth summoned its former ski team captain, Percy Rideout, to return to Hanover to succeed Prager as coach.[29] Within a year, the remaining Dartmouth boys at Sun Valley dispersed to serve their country. Rideout

Dick Durrance I skiing powder in Alta (1941).

recalled that if a Dartmouth boy was drafted it was understood that, by writing a letter to Minot Dole, the founder of the National Ski Patrol and driving force behind the formation of the 10th Mountain Division, and mentioning his Dartmouth skiing credentials, he would be accepted into the division.[30] Coach Prager, Sun Valley Ski School Director Friedl Pfeifer, Percy Rideout, John Litchfield, Charles McLane, and Joe Duncan would all volunteer to join the 10th Division, along with over 110 other Dartmouth students or graduates.

Dick Durrance visited Alta, Utah, with his future wife Miggs for a ski race in early 1940 and, in his words, "fell in love with the place."[31] Miggs remembered, "Alta was one of the most beautiful places we'd ever seen. There was only one lift and one lodge that was half built and not open for business. Well, this stuck in our minds."[32]

Alta, located at the upper end of Little Cottonwood Canyon in the Wasatch Mountains eighteen miles east of Salt Lake City, was a proto-typical boom-bust western mining town for most of its history. In the late 1930s, a group of Salt Lake City businessmen and skiers organized the Salt Lake City Winter Sports Association, negotiated a permit from the US Forest Service, and raised $10,000 to build a ski lift, which opened in 1939.[33] After Dick and Miggs were married in June 1940, Dick reached out to the Salt Lake City Winter Sports Association, asking if they might consider bring-

Durrance leading a ski class in Alta (1941).

ing him in to help launch Alta as a serious ski resort. Aware of Durrance's reputation as a world-class skier and early participant in the creation of Sun Valley, the Association responded enthusiastically in the affirmative and Durrance promptly immersed himself in his second major western ski area development project.[34]

Durrance raised money from a wealthy skiing friend from the East to complete the lodge. With initial funding in hand, he and Miggs agreed to "finish and run the lodge, establish and run the ski school, establish and run the ski shop, manage and run the mountain, and dig out from under the occasional avalanche."[35] Then, in late 1941, Durrance was asked by the Army to organize a ski school in Alta for paratroopers from Fort Benning, Georgia, who might face potential mountain combat in Europe. Durrance agreed, inviting several of his racing buddies to join him in Alta as instructors, including his brother **Jimmy Durrance '45**, Bob Skinner, **Sel Hannah '35**, and his Dartmouth ski coach, Walter Prager.[36] Durrance recalled the paratroopers "were mostly Southern boys who had never seen snow, never seen mountains or anything to do with skiing." Although the instructors successfully completed their training mission, Durrance concluded "it was easier to train skiers to jump than to teach jumpers to ski."[37]

Ned Jacoby, having joined the Air Force after graduation, delivered an aircraft to Salt Lake City in 1941 and drove up Cottonwood Canyon to visit the Durrances. As a veteran of the ice-encrusted slopes of New England, he was astounded by the depth of the powder, not to mention the challenge of maneuvering through it with narrow seven-foot long skis. As he piloted his plane out of Salt Lake at the end of his visit, Jacoby executed a low altitude farewell pass over Alta hoping he would not trigger an avalanche.[38] By the end of the winter of 1941-1942, Miggs was pregnant with their first son, **Dick Durrance '65**, and the family reluctantly abandoned the remote confines of Alta, moving first to Los Angeles and then to Seattle to work for Boeing in its flight test department during the war, and eventually settling in Denver to enter the ski manufacturing business.[39] Friedl Pfeifer, who was awaiting his orders to report to the 10th Mountain Division, was hired to replace Durrance as Alta's ski school director.

Aspen, a silver mining town in the Roaring Fork Valley of the Rocky Mountains in Colorado, had a population of about 700 people in the 1930s during the Great Depression. The initial effort to bring skiing to Aspen was the inspiration of a local rancher, Tom Flynn, who recruited two other investors to join him in forming the Highland Bavarian Corporation in 1936 to build a ski lodge at Ashcroft, an abandoned mining town south of Aspen. Flynn and his partners hired Andre Roch, a Swiss mountain guide, to teach European-style skiing to the locals.

The first ski run on Aspen Mountain, designed by Roch, was cleared in 1937 by the Aspen Ski Club. Morten Lund, one of our foremost ski historians, described Roch Run as "the longest, narrowest, meanest ski trail in the fledging sport of alpine skiing in America, at a time when alpine skiing was in its infancy and when long downhill race trails were scarce."[40] The Ski Club also built Aspen's first ski lift, a cumbersome affair called the "boat tow," consisting of two eight-passenger sleds, an automobile motor, and a mine hoist.[41]

Captivating tales about Roch Run quickly radiated through the ski world and in 1941 Aspen was chosen to host the National Alpine Championships. Austrian champion Toni Matt won the downhill calling it the "best downhill course I have ever skied."[42] Dick Durrance won the slalom and was the runner-up to Matt in the downhill. The Japanese attacked Pearl Harbor the following December. With World War II effectively suspending major ski competition for the next several years, this would be Dick Durrance's last major ski race.[43] It would not, however, conclude his affectionate association with Aspen.

The propitious selection of a valley near Leadville, Colorado, as the training venue for the fabled 10th Mountain Division would reunite many of the Dartmouth ski team members in the midst of the Rocky Mountains during the war. In no small part due to this wartime convergence of Dartmouth skiers, Camp Hale, as it would be named, would also emerge as the most prolific breeding ground of visionaries, founders, and developers of the future of skiing in North America.[44]

Reporting to Camp Hale in late 1942 and early 1943 were many of the Sun Valley Dartmouth contingent including Charlie McLane, Joe Duncan, Percy Rideout and John Litchfield. Litchfield commanded a company in which his First Sergeant was none other than Bill Brown from McCall, Idaho, whom Litchfield had observed skiing in a coonskin cap with his school buddies in Sun Valley a few years earlier.[45] When Litchfield was reassigned to headquarters, Charlie McLane replaced him as company commander, affording Brown a further introduction to Dartmouth.[46] In the spring of 1943, Friedl Pfeifer, the Sun Valley ski school director, joined his Dartmouth friends in the Tenth, as did the Dartmouth ski coach, Walter Prager.

Because Aspen resided within Camp Hale's "maneuver circuit," the town was inevitably discovered by some of the troops on exhausting cross-country treks over mountain passes in deep snow carrying ninety-pound packs.[47] In his autobiography, Friedl Pfeifer wrote that, upon seeing Aspen for the fist time on one such outing, the "mountain peaks looming over the town made me feel like I was returning to St. Anton."[48] He undoubtedly echoed the sentiments of many of his Dartmouth friends in the Tenth when he reflected, "I felt at that moment an overwhelming sense of my future before me."[49]

The weekdays at Camp Hale were extraordinarily grueling, especially for the boys who had never skied or climbed mountains as a recreational pastime. The Dartmouth skiers not only survived the rigors of the weekly routine with some degree of subtle gratification but also looked forward to the alternate weekends off as an opportunity to go skiing unencumbered by military gear and supervision.[50]

Percy Rideout '40 in his racing days.

Percy Rideout recounts the occasions when six men would pile into Charlie McLane's station wagon and drive eight to ten hours to Alta for a weekend of deep powder skiing.[51] Because gas was rationed during the war, the avid skiers made a practice of hoarding and bargaining for ration cards on a weekly basis in order to fund the gas for the round trip. Eventually, they established relationships with gas stations along the route where they would leave ration cards behind on one trip with the proviso that the station would open up at two o'clock in the morning as they passed through to fill the tank on the next trip. There was only one primitive ski lift in Alta at the time, but the lodge that had been completed by Dick and Miggs Durrance provided accommodations. The group would routinely climb the various bowls with skins strapped to their skis and then plunge down through the powder snow.[52] The only constraint on the weekend festivities was the stipulation that they fall in for Camp Hale's reveille at 6:00 am on Monday morning.[53]

Aspen was within a few hours of Camp Hale depending upon whether the troops took the train through Glenwood Springs or were able to hitch a ride in a car. For the eastern boys, the culture in the mountain mining communities occasionally proved to be somewhat startling. A youthful Phil Puchner, who had raced for Dartmouth in 1940-1941 under ski coach Percy Rideout and dropped out of school to join the Tenth in 1942, remembers checking into a hotel in Glenwood Springs on a weekend leave and reacting with some dismay when the miner checking in ahead of him dropped two six-shooters on the counter for safekeeping.[54] In stark contrast to the experience the Dartmouth ski instructors had enjoyed socializing with celebrities in Sun Valley, when the miners came into Aspen on the weekends it was a "rough town with brothels, fist fights, you name it" recalls John Litchfield.[55]

If they were lucky, the Dartmouth boys would secure a room at the Hotel Jerome where soldiers from the Tenth could stay for one dollar a night, including a steak dinner.[56] Sergeant Bill Brown found he could avoid even that minimal charge by washing dishes in the Jerome kitchen on weekends in exchange for meals and a lift ticket on the boat tow.[57] The Jerome also attracted the occasional miner who would bring the wife and children to the hotel for meals on the weekend. The Jerome bartender initiated the tradition of serving the whole family milkshakes, it being understood that the adult version always contained several shots of assorted hard liquors. The drink, denominated the "Aspen Crud," became a memorable highlight of every excursion to Aspen.[58]

Although the Aspen boat tow offered an uneventful 400 vertical feet of skiing at the bottom of the mountain, the primary goal of the trip was to ski Roch Run from top to bottom. To do so involved hitching a ride up the first two thousand feet on a mining truck that left in the dark of early morning for the Midnight Mine on the back side of the mountain, followed by an exhilarating hike up the remaining thousand feet to the summit with skins strapped on one's skis.[59] After descending the three thousand foot vertical drop though seemingly endless pristine powder to the valley floor on these weekend expeditions, Pfeifer, Rideout, Litchfield and others envisioned Aspen as a splendid setting for a new Sun Valley style destination resort in Colorado.[60]

During these weekend visits, Percy Rideout joined Pfeifer in talking to the local members of the Aspen Ski Club about the possibility of transforming Aspen into a world class ski resort after the war ended. In Rideout's words, it was in these meetings that "the seeds were planted" for the future of Aspen.[61] Pfeifer and Rideout at one point boldly appeared before the Aspen Town Council contending that skiing could be the catalyst that would revitalize the fading mining community. In Pfeifer's words, "the soldiers of the Tenth Mountain would help build the resort at Aspen, if we could just survive the war."[62]

Pfeifer, Rideout, Litchfield and the rest of the 10th Mountain Division shipped out for combat in the Italian Alps beginning in December 1944 Most of the Dartmouth boys were dispersed among different regiments and companies in Italy and, as a result, did not see much of each other. John Litchfield noted: "In Italy, we didn't really think much about the Dartmouth connection. It was you and your buddy and that was all you focused on." By the end of the campaign the following spring, nearly a thousand members of the Tenth had been killed, including Colorado native Joe Duncan, who had shared the Sun Valley experience with the other Dartmouth boys prior to the war.[63] Among those who returned home severely wounded were Pfeifer (who had a lung blown out by shrapnel), Rideout, and "Sarge" Brown. Also seriously wounded the same day as Percy Rideout was a young sergeant in Rideout's company named Pete Seibert who was told he would probably never walk again and that, certainly, he would never ski.[64]

Friedl Pfeifer skiing Aspen Mountain which he helped build into a major ski resort.

Percy Rideout returned to Camp Carson in Colorado in the early summer of 1945 and, having successfully recovered from his head wound, went to the nearby Army hospital where Friedl Pfeifer was convalescing from his chest wound. He was surprised and elated to learn that Pfeifer was not only thinking about Aspen but had hired a Denver lawyer to start identifying and acquiring decades old Aspen mining claims to facilitate the creation of new ski trails on Aspen Mountain.[65] John Litchfield had also contacted Pfeifer and the three agreed they would meet in Aspen as soon as Pfeifer was released from the hospital in October.

John Litchfield fondly recalls that when the three 10th Mountain comrades returned to Aspen after the war it "was like going home. We were welcomed with open arms. Everyone knew who we were and why we

During the research for this project, Steve Waterhouse sought the counsel of Friedl Pfeifer, the Aspen ski legend. (photo by Linda L. Waterhouse).

were there."[66] The locals not only helped them find homes but also hung wallpaper and painted their new residences. Litchfield reflected "it was a great time in our lives, doing something we loved."[67] By December 1945, Pfeifer, Rideout and Litchfield had formed the Aspen Ski School, relying for transport up the mountain on the old boat tow and a new rope tow they installed with the help of the Aspen Ski Club. **Charles Webb '43**, another former Dartmouth ski team member and 10th Mountain Division alum, joined them as an instructor.[68]

As the ski school founders labored to improve the mountain and expand the ski school, it became apparent that serious capital would be needed to create a quality destination resort. Chicago industrialist Walter Paepcke and his wife had developed a fascination for Aspen and, although Paepcke "didn't know anything about skiing,"[69] he began purchasing commercial real estate and many of the old Victorian homes in town with the objective of establishing Aspen as a western cultural and intellectual center.[70] In early 1946, Paepcke, Pfeifer, Litchfield, Rideout and others formed the Aspen Skiing Corporation and set about raising money to build a new ski lift.

Percy Rideout recalled leading the trail crews up the mountain to clear timber and open new ski runs, then rushing back to town on Friday afternoon to sign payroll checks. Once construction of the new lift started, Rideout worked on bolting together the steel towers, experiencing the "thrill of being one step closer to the top of the mountain with each tower." The team hired an amateur photographer to make a ski movie, entitled *Why Aspen?,* featuring Rideout, Pfeifer, and Litchfield (and his new wife), skiing and hiking on Aspen's scenic slopes. Rideout and his wife (whom he had met as a student in one of his ski classes) then visited the Midwest before the first snows in the fall to promote the embryonic ski resort, displaying the movie at upscale clubs, hotels and private homes, drawing on the team's acquaintances from their Sun Valley days.[71]

By December, the world's longest chair lift (actually two connecting lifts) was completed on Aspen Mountain and an official opening ceremony was held in January 1947. The three-mile, forty-five minute ride to the top cost $3.75 for a full-day pass. Just over one year from the day Pfeifer, Rideout and Litchfield met in Aspen after the war, the *New York Times* proclaimed Aspen "the winter sports center of America."[72] Shortly thereafter, John Litchfield purchased land in town to build the Red Onion Restaurant which in short order

At one time, Aspen had the world's longest chair lift.

became an Aspen landmark. One of his first employees at the Red Onion was Percy Rideout's First Sergeant from the 10th Mountain Division, the once seriously wounded Pete Seibert, who also became a member of the Aspen Ski Patrol and eventually an instructor in the Ski School.[73]

The next major phase of Aspen's expansion was set in motion with the hiring in late 1947 of a dynamic new manager, Dick Durrance. He had been working in Denver selling a new T-bar lift and had installed one on the Little Nell run at the base of the Aspen Mountain. The Aspen Ski Company, increasingly concerned about attaining profitability, invited Durrance to stay around and manage the resort. His international celebrity and personal connections empowered him to dramatically enhance Aspen's reputation as a world-class destination resort. In line with his mission to expand the mountain's terrain, he designed, cut and opened the Aspen's first broad intermediate slope, known to this day as Ruthie's Run.[74]

Durrance's most illustrious contribution to the growth of Aspen involved his decision to secure the 1950 FIS World Alpine

Championships for Aspen Mountain. With strategic assistance from his Dartmouth ski team buddy Steve Bradley, who was nearby pursuing a graduate degree at the University of Colorado in Boulder, a successful proposal was drafted for the 1950 championships.. Durrance later said, "If I've made a contribution to American skiing in general, I think that the 1950 FIS in Aspen would be it..."[75] The event was the first World Alpine Championship held in the United States and indelibly identified Aspen, and western North America, with the world's finest skiing.

Stein Eriksen skiing in the 1950 championships.

Prior to moving to Aspen, Durrance spent two years in Denver working for ski manufacturer Thor Groswold who had developed the "Dick Durrance" model ski while Durrance was running Alta.[76] Groswold and his business partner, former Dartmouth skier **Edwin "Ned" Grant '30**, had also supplied skis and snowshoes to the 10th Mountain Division during the war[77]. In 1946, Durrance began discussing the creation of yet another ski area in Colorado with an old friend, former Dartmouth ski racer and 10th Division veteran **Larry Jump '36**.

After graduation from Dartmouth, Jump had traveled in Europe where he joined the ambulance service of the French Army in 1939, was captured by the Germans during the invasion of France, and was eventually released to the US Consulate in Germany. Upon returning to the U.S., Jump volunteered for the ski troops in 1942, spent time training skiers at Camp Hale, fought with the Tenth, was severely wounded in Italy, and made his way back to Colorado. In 1946, Jump and a partner were employed by the Denver Chamber of Commerce to conduct a statewide survey of potential sites for a new ski area[78].

The site they selected was **Arapahoe Basin**, a spectacular natural ski bowl located west of Loveland Pass on the Continental Divide at an altitude of over 13,000 feet. When their research revealed that the US Forest Service was considering accepting bids for development of the area, Jump recruited Dartmouth teammate Dick Durrance to join the project, believing his impeccable ski industry credentials, expertise and experience would be invaluable in convincing the Forest Service to accept his bid.[79] Durrance persuaded his boss, Thor Groswold, to join the effort and, in May 1946, Jump, Durrance, Groswold and Jump's survey partner formed Arapahoe Basin, Inc., submitted a development plan to the Forest Service, and won the bid.[80] Financing for the new venture was provided in part by Dartmouth friends **Keith Anderson '39** and **Henry Buchtel '29**, both 10th Mountain veterans, and **Blair Wood '30**.

Arapahoe Basin opened for business in the winter of 1946-47 with a single rope- tow located halfway up the mountain to which skiers were driven by a war surplus four- wheel drive truck.[81] To this day it remains the highest ski resort in Colorado.

Larry Jump's leadership and innovation in the subsequent development of A-Basin, as it became known, is documented and memorialized in a massive historical collection which resides in the Denver Public Library. Under Jump's direction, A-Basin held the first National Senior Giant Slalom Championship in 1953, installed the first Pomalift in the United States in 1954, and with his wife Marnie initiated the first amputee ski program in Colorado, for which the Jumps received a National Citizens Award from the Department of Defense. Jump also founded Pomalift, Inc., in 1954 through which he sold Poma and other lifts to over 400 ski areas in the ensuing years.

Following his early investment in Arapahoe Basin, Blair Wood, an Iowa judge, became a regular winter visitor with his family and eventually built a family cabin down the valley on the Snake River. It was there in 1968 that Wood and some of his Iowa friends convinced Max Dercum, a long-time resident of the valley who also had helped get Arapahoe Basin off the ground, to fulfill his dream of building a new ski area on the mountain overlooking the Wood family cabin, to be called Keystone. Wood introduced Dercum to one his Iowa friends, Bill Bergman, who was in attendance at the meeting. Bergman rounded up most of the investors for the new area from his friends in Iowa and, when Keystone opened in November of 1970, became its first president. The location of the Wood cabin eventually became part of the Keystone Resort base area. *(See the articles at the end of this chapter on "Blair Wood '30 and the Wood Family" and "Larry Jump '36, Entrepreneur".)*

As is evident from the events described in this chapter, the name of Steve Bradley pervades any discourse on the history of skiing in the United States. A member of the legendary Bradley family of Wisconsin, Steve would easily merit the title "Skiing's Renaissance Man." He was not only a world-class skier, coach, inventor and executive but also "an excellent water-colorist, kayak designer, expert marksman, an accomplished dramatic actor and a gifted photographer."[82]

After serving in the Army Signal Corps in World War II, Bradley moved to Boulder where he earned a Master's Degree in Fine Arts at the University of Colorado. He also assumed an unpaid position as the first coach of the University of Colorado ski team. In order to facilitate team practices, Bradley helped create and manage the Mesa Ski Slope in the Boulder foothills near campus with a two hundred foot rope tow powered by a Dodge gasoline engine[83] and built a ski jump for the team by burying 50- gallon drums he recovered from a friend's dry cleaning plant in Boulder.[84] It was also during his tenure as coach that Bradley assisted Dick Durrance in securing the 1950 FIS World Alpine Championships for Aspen.

Pete Seibert worked for Dick Durrance in Aspen and sought his advice on starting Vail.

Among the very earliest skiing venues in Colorado, **Winter Park** is located in Grand County at the western end of the Moffat Tunnel which penetrates the Continental Divide west of Denver. Beginning in 1938, trains carried skiers from Denver to Winter Park and the area became increasingly popular with skiers from the Front Range of Colorado. In 1950, the City of Denver formed the Winter Park Recreational Association to operate and develop the ski area and hired Steve Bradley as its first director.[85] Under Bradley's inspired leadership over the next twenty years, the resort transitioned from a handful of rope tows and T-bars to a major national ski resort with 13 chairlifts. He introduced a range of ski area innovations including summer trail grooming, passive solar heating of resort buildings, the food scramble system for on-mountain restaurants,[86] and was instrumental in starting the Winter Park disabled skiing program.

In the world of skiing, Steve Bradley is best remembered as the "Father of Slope Maintenance" for his revolutionary designs of snow-grooming equipment. Until the early 1950s, most of the terrain in the larger ski areas was not maintained, or in today's parlance, "groomed," and was, therefore, suitable for only the more advanced skiers. In 1952, Bradley invented the first ski slope-grooming device, known as the Bradley Packer, consisting of a 400-pound roller which was maneuvered down the hill behind a single skier who himself risked being "groomed" if he lost control of the apparatus.[87] Eventually, the roller was modified to be drawn by a tractor and Bradley convinced large machine manufacturers to produce equipment specifically for grooming. Referring to his revolutionary invention in his 50th Dartmouth reunion yearbook, Bradley wrote "Like many inventors, I made no money from it." Needless to say, the advent of groomed slopes was instrumental in attracting a much broader audience of aspiring skiers to the sport.

Following his return from action with the 10th Mountain Division in Italy in 1945, Sergeant Bill Brown, unlike most of his fellow soldiers in the Tenth, elected to pursue a career in the Army. During combat in Italy, and later in Korea, Brown had earned five Purple Hearts, two Silver Stars and three Bronze Stars[88] and, by 1958, was one of the most highly decorated and highest ranking enlisted men in the United States Army. In 1958, Sergeant Brown was offered the opportunity to run the Mountain and Winter Warfare Training Center for the ROTC program at Dartmouth College, the only school in the country with such an operation. Familiar with Dartmouth by virtue of his many Dartmouth companions in the Tenth, Brown accepted. "Sarge" Brown later recalled that his eight year tenure at Dartmouth was "the best job I ever had in the Army", adding: "I could teach those kids in two hours what would take two days or two weeks to teach others."[89] In 1966, Brown volunteered to go to Vietnam and, when the Army declined his offer,[90] he chose to retire and called his old friend and fellow sergeant from the Tenth, Pete Seibert, who promptly invited him to join the founding team at Vail.

After working on the Aspen Ski Patrol and teaching in the Aspen Ski School with his 10th Mountain friends John Litchfield and Percy Rideout in the late 'forties, Pete Seibert traveled, worked at Aspen Highlands, and managed the Loveland Ski Area in Colorado. In 1957, he and his friend Earl Eaton made their celebrated hike to the top of what is now **Vail Mountain** and Seibert resolved to build a major new ski resort in Colorado. By the time of Sarge Brown's retirement from the Army in 1966, Vail was methodically gaining a reputation as America's premier ski resort. When Brown arrived in Vail, he was put in charge of the trail crew, but "within months he was running the entire slope maintenance department, and before long he was Mountain Manager and then Director of Mountain Operations."[91]

During his more than twenty years working at Vail, Brown set a new standard of excellence in ski area operations; his innovations and techniques were being emulated throughout the world. Burnishing his reputation for unwavering discipline, he told his employees if they did what he told them to do "we are going to have the best ski area in the world. If you can't do that, there's the door."[92] Brown's many Vail innovations included installation of Vail's first snowmaking equipment, creation of wider, more skier friendly trails, addition of overnight grooming, and improvement of snow cat grooming technology. In his final year with Vail he played a pivotal role in securing and managing the World Alpine Skiing Championships for Vail and Beaver Creek. Sarge Brown was inducted into the Colorado Ski and Snowboard Hall of Fame in 1982 and the United States National Ski Hall of Fame in 1990.

Bill Ashley '45 was a member of the Dartmouth ski team before he served in the Pacific Theater in World War II. Following the war, Ashley moved west to seek a Master's Degree in Geology at the University of Wyoming where he founded the University's ski team. After working as an oil prospector for a few years, he settled in Jackson, Wyoming, where he became a partner in a local retail sports enterprise and eventually acquired and taught at the **Jackson Hole** Ski School at Snow King, the town ski resort. When the developers of the new Jackson Hole Ski Resort were preparing to open for business in1965, they realized Bill Ashley owned the rights to the Jackson Hole Ski School name. In an auspicious transaction for both parties, Ashley swapped the name for the right to open the first ski shop in Teton Village at the base of the new resort. His shop, Teton Village Sports, remains a Jackson Hole landmark to this day.[93]

Just a month after Vail's grand opening in December 1962, another new ski resort opened, this one in **Crested Butte**, a remote silver mining town in south central Colorado. Three Kansas entrepreneurs bought a ranch near town and raced to precede Vail in christening the nation's newest gondola. Hampered by a number of setbacks, they lost the race by two months, opening in late January 1963.[94] Crested Butte ski area muddled through the next several years lacking adequate management and capital to achieve sustained viability. The first step on the road to gaining stature as a destination resort occurred in 1970 when Howard "Bo" Callaway, a wealthy Georgia businessman and politician, bought the area.

The Dartmouth connection emerged in the early 1980s when Bo's son, **Ed Callaway '77**, moved to Colorado and assumed an active role in the management of Crested Butte. The younger Callaway, who had earned graduate degrees in Accounting and Business from New York University and Stanford, had worked for the consulting firm McKinsey & Co., and served as President and CEO of Crested Butte from 1987 to 2003, then became its Chairman. Ed was one of the new breed of business savvy operators who recognized the ski industry's need for cutting-edge business and marketing expertise if it were to continue expanding. To that end, in 1985 he called upon his Dartmouth classmate **John Norton '77**.

After graduating from Dartmouth, John Norton became a highly regarded marketing executive in a succession of companies like Proctor & Gamble and Dunn & Bradstreet. John's wife, **Robin Clark '76**, was a member of Dartmouth's first class to accept women and was a competitive ski racer. When Callaway called Norton in 1985, Crested Butte was struggling to create a national and international clientele and was in desperate need of sophisticated marketing expertise. After John recommended an executive search firm to find the right person for the job, the firm proposed Norton himself. John and Robin moved their family to Crested Butte and he began a new career as ski area executive.[95]

Following John Norton's arrival, skier days on the mountain doubled and Crested Butte became the fastest growing ski area in the West from 1985 to 1991. John orchestrated an aggressive expansion of the mountain into more extreme terrain and negotiated the ski industry's first contract with a major airline to secure scheduled flights into a local airport. His relentless expansion plans, however, were frustrated in the late 1980s by opposition from some residents in the local community.[96] Norton's accomplishments at Crested Butte had drawn national recognition and, sensing his frustration with his current job, in 1991 Aspen Skiing Company hired him as Vice President of Marketing. Aspen had been struggling for several years with virtually no growth, a poor reputation for service, and disquieting labor issues. Norton became COO, managing a four-mountain ski complex, and playing a major role in recreating Aspen during the next eleven years, elevating the ski school to one of the world's best, expanding Aspen's international business, establishing a central reservations system, and bringing the now infamous X Games to the resort.[97]

In 2002, with Crested Butte again facing financial challenges, Ed Callaway asked Norton to return to stabilize the company and find a buyer. Norton did come back and was able to mobilize the community to support tax increases for marketing and airline subsidies; the locals even expressed support for "his edgy approach to differentiating their hill."[98] Norton fulfilled his mission in 2004 when Crested Butte was sold to Tim and Diane Mueller, owners of two major New England ski resorts.[99]

Chuck Lewis '58 was introduced to ski area management in the early 1950s when he landed a job in high school working summers for Steve Bradley at Winter Park cutting trails and running trail crews.[100] In 1954, Lewis enrolled at Dartmouth, which suggests that Bradley's enthusiasm for his alma mater made a favorable impression on the young man. Lewis continued to work for Bradley while in college but dropped out in 1955 to join the Army, serving as a Mountain Warfare Instructor in the Mountain and Cold Weather Command at Camp Hale.[101] Eventually earning a degree from the University of Denver, Lewis became a CPA and was hired by Pete Seibert, becoming Executive Vice President and Treasurer of Vail Skiing Corporation in 1965.

In 1967, a committee was formed in Denver for the purpose of securing the 1976 Olympic Winter Games for the State of Colorado. The US Forest Service suggested **Copper Mountain** as an ideal site for the competition.[102] Copper Mountain, known as Wheeler Junction at the time, was an abandoned copper mining camp at the junction of the Gore and Ten Mile mountain ranges about half way between Vail and Frisco. Chuck Lewis, then working as a consultant in Denver, initiated discussions with a group of Denver businessmen about developing the Copper site into a new ski resort. By 1971, Lewis had raised enough money to purchase 280 acres of land at the base of the mountain and secured Forest Service approval to develop the ski area.

Although Colorado's Olympic dream was quashed by the state's voters in 1972, Lewis was undeterred, announcing "I'm gonna build me a killer ski resort."[103] With Lewis planning and executing every detail "from the ground up," Copper Mountain opened for business in November 1973. One of his first employees was **Ned Gillette '67**, Captain of the 1967 NCAA runner-up Dartmouth Ski Team, NCAA Cross-country Ski Champion, and 1968 US Olympic Ski Team member. Gillette spent the winter of 1969-70 living in a trailer at Wheeler Junction exploring the mountain and laying out trails for the new ski area.[104] Ned Gillette subsequently taught cross-country skiing at Yosemite Park and at the Trapp Family Lodge in Vermont and went on to become a world-renowned adventurer, mountain climber, sailor, skier, photographer, journalist and author.[105]

The creation and development of Copper Mountain by Chuck Lewis was a watershed episode in the history of North American skiing, marking the transition of industry leadership from passionate early visionaries to seasoned business professionals. Shortly after Copper Mountain opened in 1973, *Time Magazine,* in a lengthy article exploring the current state of the ski industry, described the emergence of a "new class of ski entrepreneurs, who combine a love of the sport with hardheaded managerial techniques...backed by banks or syndicates of investors and aided by business-school-trained executives."[106] The article focused on Chuck Lewis as epitomizing this new breed of manager who hired a range of business, engineering, construction, and recreation specialists to execute his plan. Lewis confirmed, "Ski resorts are becoming refined, structured businesses...they can't be run by the seat of one's pants any more."

One of the experts hired by Chuck Lewis shortly after the opening of Copper Mountain was another Dartmouth skier, **Fred Jones '63**. Fred had skied for Dartmouth in the early 1960s and participated in its ROTC program under Sergeant Bill Brown and then joined the Army. While working for a small company in New England in the late 1960s, Fred spotted a help wanted ad in *The Wall Street Journal* for a position as General Manager of a New Hampshire ski area. The ad had been placed by **Tom Corcoran '54**, Dartmouth skiing great and the founder of Waterville Valley Resort. Jones was hired and served four years as General Manager of Waterville Valley under Corcoran until 1973 when Chuck Lewis offered him the opportunity to become Vice President of Operations at the new Copper Mountain Resort in Colorado.[107]

Fred Jones considered the experience of working with Lewis from the early days at Copper to be invaluable to his career as a ski area manager. He recalled Lewis as not only a visionary but also "a great manager and business person," a combination "unique in the ski industry at that time."[108] Skiing in Colorado was booming during the 1970s and, under the leadership of Lewis and Jones, Copper matured into a major destination resort and became the largest ski area in Summit County. Jones moved on to become Chief Executive Officer of three other ski areas: Kirkwood Ski Resort in the Lake Tahoe area of Northern California, Sugarbush in Vermont, and Whitefish Mountain in Montana.

WESTERN HOSPITALITY

As the western ski towns developed, the opportunity to provide a comfortable night's sleep and après-ski entertainment for visiting skiers became apparent to those like-minded entrepreneurs seeking to permanently settle adjacent to their favorite ski towns. Not surprisingly, Dartmouth grads were instrumental in establishing many of the landmark skier hospitality venues in the western US.

John Litchfield '39 was not only a founder of Aspen Ski Corporation but also started The Red Onion, one of Aspen's most popular restaurants. In 1946, Litchfield bought a red brick building on what is now the Cooper Avenue mall in the middle of Aspen. The "New Brick", as it was originally known, was built in 1892 and had been a gambling hall and saloon during the historic silver boom of the late 1800's. Litchfield refurbished the building and renamed it the Red Onion (which had been its local nickname up to that point). Litchfield's new establishment "became one of Aspen's first venues for après-ski and late-night entertainment that famously once included a performance by Billie Holiday." The Red Onion continued to attract and entertain skiers for over 50 years until it closed in 2007.[109]

Ralph Melville '49, who, like John Litchfield, had grown up in New England, graduated from Dartmouth with a degree in physics. Melville's passion was to someday own a ski lodge and, like Litchfield, the emerging ski scene in the western US became the focus of his vision. Melville visited Aspen in 1951 and "thought the place was overbuilt" with lodges erected for the 1950 FIS championships. Nevertheless, in 1953 he purchased two lots in the center of town for $2000 and opened the Mountain Chalet in December 1954 with three rooms.[110] After 55 years, the Mountain Chalet is one of Aspen's largest and best-known hotels. It is still managed by Ralph and his family today and is thought to be the oldest lodge in Aspen managed by the original owners.[111]

Not long after Ralph Melville started the Mountain Chalet, **Mead Metcalf '54** opened another Aspen landmark, the Crystal Palace restaurant and nightclub.

John Litchfield's historic Red Onion in Aspen.

Aspen's Mill and Main streets looking up at the mountain.

181

After serving in the Army in Germany following graduation, Metcalf, a former president of the Dartmouth Glee Club, had migrated to Aspen from his home town of St. Louis in 1957, skiing during the day and playing piano at the Jerome Hotel in the evenings. Shortly thereafter, he opened the Crystal Palace, naming it after a nightclub in St. Louis which was going out of business. Metcalf himself became the nightclub's biggest attraction, playing the piano and singing ribald ballads to loyal patrons and eventually joined by a versatile staff of singing waiters and waitresses. They would present over 10,000 shows over the next 51 years.[112]

Another St. Louis resident, **Ron Riley '65**, visited Aspen with his high school class in 1961, stayed at Melville's Mountain Chalet, and instantly fell in love with western skiing. In the fall of 1967, Riley traveled to Vail and Aspen with a partner in search of business opportunities. They bought a basement bar in Vail called The Slope whose only notable characteristic was a tiered floor which was covered in plush carpeting on which skiers, having dropped their ski boots at the door, would lounge around at the end of the day. In December, Rick Isaacson '64, T '65 came to Vail to visit Riley. Rick was working as a sales manager for Warren Miller at the time and brought with him a stack of Miller's legendary ski movies. When Riley showed the movies to his patrons, the enthusiastic reaction was immediate and The Slope served up the hottest ski movies in the West for the next 23 years.[113]

When Ron Riley arrived in Vail, the population of the town "was four or five hundred people, the main street was a dirt road, and there was no other development in the Vail Valley." For the first couple of months, Riley slept on the floor of The Slope in a sleeping bag, skied every day, and then went directly to work bartending in his ski pants late into the night. He eventually found a small apartment, although so many friends came to visit, Riley recalled "I didn't know if I was in the bar business or running a youth hostel." [114]

Since 1967, Ron has opened and operated many of the premier restaurants and bars in Colorado including Aspen Mine Company, Alice's Alley, the Char Room, Danny's, and a second Slope in Aspen and The Top of the Slope, Baxter's, the Bridge Street Shuffle, Nick's, Los Amigo's and Russell's in Vail. In addition to his hospitality ventures, Ron has become one of the leading real estate developers and a prominent philanthropic and community leader in the Vail Valley.[115]

SUMMARY

The emergence and growth of western skiing over the last two thirds of the twentieth century were unquestionably fueled by the west's unique combination of natural attributes: stunning mountain landscapes, spectacular vertical descents, deep dry powder snow, and abundant sunshine. Beginning with Sun Valley in 1936, and continuing through the end of the century, members of the Dartmouth Family were instrumental in founding and developing at least fifteen major destination ski resorts in the western United States. One might argue that much of this growth would have occurred even without the involvement of these Dartmouth visionaries. It seems only fair to observe, however, that without these players the growth in western skiing would not have occurred as rapidly, or in as many places, or with so many of the fundamental innovations which enhanced skier enjoyment and, thereby, attracted millions of new participants to the sport. And, most certainly, the story of how the West was won for skiers would not have been nearly as interesting.

***

THE WOOD FAMILY - SKIING FROM EIGHT TO EIGHTY

Excerpts from Blair C. Wood 1930's *Ski Life* by George W. Wood '67

Toward the end of his life, my father, Blair C. Wood '30, wrote a personal history of skiing spanning his early days of skiing in Iowa through his final skiing years in Colorado. Highlights of Blair's narrative include introducing skiing as an organized sport to the "Black Hawk County Alps" of Iowa in the 1950's, populating the sport by raising four Dartmouth skiers (Michael Wood '60, Blair Wood, Jr. '63,

George Wood '67 and John Wood '73)**,** and contributing to the development of the ski industry in Colorado.

Blair and his wife Eleanor made their first ski trip to Colorado from Waterloo, Iowa in 1947. "We made reservations at the Hotel Jerome for the opening of Aspen in January, 1947, There, at the afternoon tea dances or on the slopes we became intimates of all the skiing greats at that time, Friedl Pfeifer, Fred Iselin and the like. Our instructors were often Dartmouth men, often Tenth Mountain Division, Percy Rideout and John Litchfield, also Klaus Obermeyer, Ellie Iselin and Pete Seibert ... There were no easy trails, just the Roche Run and the Silver Queen. I can remember Eleanor, after one of them, looking back and remarking tearfully and with spirit ... 'that G** D***** mountain'."

On his second ski trip to Colorado, Blair took Eleanor and his young son, Mike, to Berthoud Pass. "Berthoud raised skiers to the summit of the Continental Divide by a single, fast, heavy rope tow. One learned not to tackle it alone because it was too heavy for one person. It also dug a dangerous trench in the snow and I remember that among the few of us present at our first weekend of skiing there were five broken legs or ankles."

Soon after, Blair found himself skiing the "Mine Dump" off the summit of Loveland Pass with his friend

The Wood family: Blair '30, four Dartmouth sons and a grandchild.

Henry Buchtel '29: "Once, we stood on the Continental Divide and Henry pointed to an area far below where he said they were building a ski resort, which came to be named Arapahoe Basin." The resort first opened for the 1946/47 season, but without any lifts. It began its 1947/48 season with "a single chair lift that served the Davis Cut-Off and Molly Hogan trails. The Molly Hogan trail was named for a woman of questionable virtue who frequented the lumber camps; the name is still applied to an iron ring used in lumbering operations. Other chair lifts were added along with a Poma." On the latter, the rider placed a wood or plastic disk attached to a rod attached to an overhead cable between the legs and began the ride by being catapulted 10 or 15 feet forward before the tension spring recovered and smoothed out the remaining ride. "It was at best unpredictable and at its worst would nearly saw off the legs of a lady skier. I have too much sensibility to dwell further on these contretemps which are unavoidable in any place where the law of averages has not been repealed." Blair Wood was one of the original investors in Arapahoe Basin.

By this time, I was old enough to accompany my family on their trips to Colorado. I have a fond recollection of the Poma lift, because to a youngster this was a great adventure. From my diminished perspective at the time, however, I recall the "lift-off" being more on the order of 30 feet. Coming of age in those days was to muster the courage to ski the famous Palivacinni avalanche chute and be rewarded at the bottom with a "Pali Pin" by the Ski Patrol.

It was at Arapahoe that the Wood family became close friends with skiing families from all over the country, most notably Max and Edna Dercum and the Merritt Paulson family from Barrington, IL. Max and Edna operated Ski Tip Lodge at the base of Loveland Pass and later founded the Keystone Ski Resort. The oldest Paulson son, Hank Paulson '68, went to Dartmouth where we continued to ski together on holidays and occasionally traded girlfriends. After Dartmouth, Henry (Hank) Paulson moved on to become CEO of Goldman Sachs and eventually Secretary of the Treasury under George Bush.

In 1957, the Wood family and several other Iowa skiing families, including the Bill Bergmans, jointly purchased the Alhambra Mine, a small log cabin near Arapahoe Basin. In the early 1960's the Wood family branched off and spent two summers building a family cabin on the banks of the Snake River just downstream from Max and Edna Dercum's Ski Tip Lodge.

And this is where Keystone got its start: "What began as a vision that Max Dercum had fostered for more than 20 years took shape one snowy evening in 1968 in a snug cabin near the Snake River. Max had skied every inch of the mountain and surrounding terrain until he had it memorized. With his dream of a ski area close to his heart, he worked diligently on his plans, creating a prospectus, hand-sketching maps and models he hoped would sell the concept. Until that night, he had been unable to get it off the ground. "Gathered around a fireplace on New Year's Eve of 1968 at the home of Blair Wood, a judge from Waterloo, Iowa...the group (Max Dercum, Bill Bergman and the Blair Wood family) began discussing Max's plans. 'This was when the enticement began,' Bill said. He admits that in the beginning, he really wasn't interested in getting involved, but Max and the others "ganged up" on him until he finally gave in. Bill shook his head remembering how fast it all happened and said 'We saw an entire ski area evolve in a matter of minutes'."[116]

With few exceptions, all the initial money for Keystone was raised in Iowa. Many of the skiing families from the Black Hawk County Alps in Waterloo were original investors (including the Wood family), and Bill Bergman an attorney from Cedar Rapids who knew my father from having skied often at Black Hawk, became the first president of Key-

stone when it opened in November, 1970.

In the 1980's, Keystone purchased the Wood property along the Snake River, demolished the cabin, and expanded its operations by adding the River Run Complex, a gondola and a high-speed quad chair lift.

Blair Wood began his skiing career in 1916, at eight years old, on the gentle slopes of Iowa. He took his last run on Keystone Mountain in 1988 at the age of eighty. He now lies beside Eleanor back in Iowa near his beloved Black Hawk County Alps. The four Wood brothers live in Colorado today, and all 18 members of their immediate families are active skiers, including my three-year-old granddaughter, Ava, who has already demonstrated her enthusiasm for the sport on the practice hill at Keystone.

The four Wood sons (Mike '60, Blair '63, George '67 and John '73) still maintain homes near the Keystone Ski Area.

***

LARRY JUMP - AN ENTREPRENEUR AND LEADER OF COLORADO SKI DEVELOPMENTS

By Kevin Whitcher '99

"Our venture into the ski-resort business is proving terribly interesting, exciting and in some instances, a bit trying. However, we are definitely pushing ahead into what may prove to be the most outstanding ski area in the entire Rocky Mountain region."[117] —Larry Jump, in a letter to a friend dated December 12, 1946.

Despite the glamour of founding one of America's iconic ski resorts with friends and investors from Dartmouth, the early years of Arapahoe Basin were as rocky and daunting as any entrepreneurial venture. Larry's correspondence from that time demonstrates the passion he had for his democratic vision of a ski resort designed "for the real skier"[118] at a site, that in his opinion, was "the choicest chance we have run across throughout [Colorado]."[119] But his letters also divulge the degree of hardship he endured as he struggled to make his vision into a reality.

Although Larry had recruited his famous teammate, Dick Durrance '39, (and Durrance's famous boss, Thor Groswold) to his roster for their draw with potential investors, he was struggling to sell enough stock to get the funds he needed to make the Basin operational. As Larry prepared to open the still largely undeveloped resort for its first winter ('46-'47), the stock market slid almost 25%[120] and investors closed their wallets. While Larry was getting his hands dirty on the operations side, his partners were out on the road trying to drum up investments which, Larry noted in a bleak update to another partner, "adds up to many hopes and few checks."[121]

The sport of skiing was still a very young one, and trying to divert the small base of skiers from developed areas like Berthoud Pass or Aspen (where Durrance had a significant conflict of interest and ultimately played a much more material role) was difficult. But by routinely paying his staff before himself and his partners, he managed to keep the fledgling resort going long enough to attract a few new investors, including his future wife, Marnie.

In a letter whose "aw shucks" opening sounds as much like a plea for a date as for investment cash, Larry wrote Marnie "I may be shooting completely in the dark, but I gather…you might be interested in a stake in what a lot of people believe is going to be one of the top three ski areas in the country."[122] With humility and bravado in equal measure, Larry's pitch illustrates the strength of his character and his vision, although both the relationship and Arapahoe Basin lasted much longer than he had probably anticipated in those days.

For several years, his cash flow difficulties didn't ease until both the resort and the sport were more established. The long off-season without revenue was particularly taxing and he nearly reached the end of his rope more than once. After a summer spent cutting roads and runs around 11,000 feet for virtually no pay, his exasperation was tangible as he told a colleague in September of 1948, "I never want to go through another summer like this one and won't…There is a limit to the amount of sacrificing I can do..."[123]

But Larry was not one to give up on something in which he believed. As he once warned a persistent adversary, "A principle… is at stake here. And for a principle, persons like myself will sacrifice much."[124] Both principles and sacrifice were evident throughout Larry's life and career. Having already been a prisoner of war *before* he volunteered for and was seriously wounded in combat, adversity was not an unfamiliar, or even an unwelcome, companion for Larry. And rarely was it an adequate obstacle to prevent him from achieving success, whether in his days at Dartmouth or in the military. So it is no surprise that under Larry's stewardship Arapahoe Basin not only survived, but that his vision of a mountain "for the real skier"[125] persists and thrives among real skiers today.

Larry's work was highly appreciated by others and he was inducted in to the Colorado Skiing Hall of Fame in 1982. The Colorado Hall of Fame statement reads….

Colorado is fortunate that Larry stopped here. Born in Ann Arbor, Michigan he started skiing at age 11 and roamed the world at an early age; he skied in the Alps, and became a member of the French Army. This experience prepared him for commissioned service with the 87th Regiment, part of the 10th Mountain Division at Camp Hale, Colorado. Larry later became a state-wide surveyor for potential ski areas and met Colorado Ski Hall of Famers, Max Dercum, Thor Groswold, Dick Durrance and Sandy Schauffer. They formed Arapahoe Ski Basin, Inc. While there he introduced the Wedeln technique, the famous Willy Schaeffler ski school, the first amputee program in the state, the Junior Courtesy Patrol, and many other innovative programs, such as Colorado Ski Country, USA, to improve skiing in Colorado and throughout the country.

Notes

1. See Pfeifer, Friedl, Nice Goin', and Lund, Morten, My Life on Skis, Missoula, Montana, Pictorial Histories Publishing Company, Inc. 1993, 61-70, for a first hand account of Harriman's creation of Sun Valley. 2. See Chapter XIV herein. Also see Durrance, Richard, The Man on the Medal; The Life and Times of America's First Great Ski Race, as told by John Jerome, Aspen, Colorado, 1995, Durrance Enterprises, Inc. 3. Wikipedia Sun Valley history, http://en.wikipedia.org/wiki/Sun_Valley,_Idaho. 4. Pfeifer, Nice Goin', 63; Proctor moved on to California in 1938 where he spent the next twenty years as Director of Ski Operations at Yosemite National Park. 5. Shelton, Peter, Climb to Conquer, 32, Scribner, New York, NY, 2003. 6. See Chapter IV herein. 7. Durrance, Man on the Medal, 24. 8. Durrance, ibid, 24. 9. Pfeifer, ibid, 65. 10. Jackson Hole Mountain Resort Official Website, http://www.jacksonhole.com/faq.history.dates.asp, Resort History. The visit was confirmed by Richard Bradley, brother of Steve Bradley. Email from Richard Bradley to Stephen Waterhouse, June 25, 2009. 11. Durrance, ibid, 54. 12. Durrance, ibid, 56. 13. Percy Rideout, Video in-person interview in San Francisco, California, March 26, 2009 ("Rideout Interview"). 14. Pfeifer, ibid, 66-67. 15. Jacoby interview, Litchfield interview, Rideout interview. 16. Rideout interview. 17. Ned Jacoby, telephone interview, March 14, 2009 ("Jacoby Interview"). 18. Pfeifer, ibid, 96. 19. Lund, Morton, "Ernst Constam and his Marvelous Uphill Device," Skiing Heritage,(December 2005). 20. Sun Valley histories.; Pfeifer, ibid, 63. 21.http://www.gonorthwest.com/Idaho/central/sun-valley/svhistory. Sun Valley, Idaho, USA, History. Sunvalley.govoffice.com, Sun Valley, Idaho Web Site, History. The Sun Valley Web site suggests that Sun Valley had the first ski school in "the world" but this claim is apparently erroneous. See, e.g., the following article from Time Magazine dated December 21, 1936 indicating St. Anton has a stronger claim to the title. 22. Litchfield interview. See also John Litchfield resume on file at the Tenth Mountain Division Collection, Denver Public Library. 23. Durrance, ibid, 65 and 70. 24. Puchner interview. 25. John Litchfield, Video in-person interview, June 24, 2008, Denver Colorado ("Litchfield interview"). 26. Litchfield interview. 27. Rideout interview. 28. Puchner interview. See also Pfeifer, Nice Goin', 70 in which Pfeifer remembered that Zanuck "liked to ski fast, puffing on his ever-present cigar, which was frequently bent out of shape after a bad fall in the snow." 29. Rideout interview. 30. Rideout interview. 31. Durrance, ibid, 70. 32. Durrance, ibid, 70. 33. See Duane Shrontz, Alta, Utah: A People's Story, Two Doors Press, 2nd Edition, 2002. 34. Durrance, ibid, 72. 35. Durrance, ibid, 74. 36.

Durrance, ibid, 81. 37. Durrance, ibid, 81-82. 38. Jacoby interview. 39. Durrance, ibid, 88. 40. Lund, Morten, "Aspen: The Birth and Metamorphosis of a Skiing Icon," Skiing Heritage Magazine, March 2008, 16, 17. 41. Fay, Abbott, A History of Skiing in Colorado, Lake City, CO, Western Reflections Publishing Company, 2000, 49-51. 42. Lund, Aspen, 17. 43. Durrance, ibid, 84. 44. The contribution of members of the 10th Mountain Division to skiing and the development of ski resorts in the United States has been widely reported. See, e.g., Whitlock, Flint and Bishop, Bob, Soldiers on Skis, A Pictorial Memoir of the 10th Mountain Division, Paladin Press, Boulder, Colorado, 1992, 190-192. 45. Litchfield Interview. 46. Sergeant Bill Brown, in-person video interview, Manor Vail Resort, Vail, CO, 3 March 2007 ("Brown Interview"). 47. Sanders, ibid, 74-75, Shelton, ibid, 102-103. Same documents; the experience of skiing soldiers at Camp Hale and weekends exploring ski country. 48. Pfeifer, ibid, 111. 49. Pfeifer, ibid, 111; Sanders, ibid, 75. 50. Litchfield and Rideout interviews. 51. Rideout interview. 52. Rideout interview. 53. Rideout interview, Shelton, ibid, 102. 54. Phil Puchner, In-person interview, Ketchum, ID, September 11, 2008. 55. Litchfield interview. 56. Pfeifer, ibid, 113. 57. Brown interview. 58. Litchfield and Rideout interviews; Boys of Winter, 75. 59. Litchfield and Rideout interviews, Climb to Conquer, 102. 60. Rideout and Litchfield interviews. See Boys of Winter for a discussion of others who shared the original   Aspen ski resort vision. 93-95. 61. Rideout interview. 62. Pfeifer, ibid, 111-115. 63.Sanders, ibid, 191-192. 64. Rideout interview; Seibert, Peter W., Vail, Triumph of a Dream, Mountain Sports Press, 2000, Boulder, Colorado 59-61. 65. Rideout interview. 66. Litchfield interview. 67. Litchfield interview. 68. Charles Webb obit. 69. Rideout interview. 70. Shelton, ibid , 228-229; Rideout Interview. 71. Rideout interview; See also Pfeifer, ibid, 134,136. 72. Shelton, ibid, 228-229. 73. Seibert, Vail, 65-71, 79. 74. Durrance, Man on the Medal, 98. 75. Durrance, Man on the Medal, 101. 76. Durrance, Man on the Medal, 80, 88-89. 77. http://www.coloradoskihalloffame.com/images_bio_htm_files/Edwin_Ned_Grant.htm. 78. Fay, A History of Skiing in Colorado 79; The Lawrence(Larry) Jump and Arapahoe Basin Records, H1220, Western History Collection, The Denver Public Library, Biographical Note. 79. See Arapahoe Basin Website, The Legend, http://www.arapahoebasin.com/ABasin/about/default.aspx. 80. Arapahoe Basin Website, the Legend; Jump Collection, Denver Public Library, Biographical Note. 81. Ski History of Colorado 79-80. 82. ISHA Newsline, November 14, 2002, Steve Bradley Obituary by Larry Groswold. 83. Cushman, Ruth Carol and Cushman, Glen, Boulder Hiking Trails: The Best of the Plains, Foothills and Mountains, Edition 4, Pruett Publishing, 2006, ISBN 0871089408, 9780871089403, 91. 84. On the Corner, Lower Chautauqua Newsletter, Volume 2, Issue 4; University of Colorado Yearbook, Class of 1948, 203. 85. ColoradoSkiHistory.com, Winter Park Resort, Resort History. 86. Steve Bradley Obituary, Jerry Groswold, ISHA Newsline, www.skiinghistory.org/newsbradleyobit.html. 87. Fry, John, The Story of Modern Skiing, ,Lebanon, NH, University Press of New England, 2006 52. 88. Vail Daily, September 14, 2008, A11. 89. Brown Interview. 90. Seibert, Vail, Triumph of a Dream, 122. 91. Seibert, ibid, 122. 92. Vail Daily, September 15,2008, A2. 93. The History of TVS, Teton Village Sports.com, http://www.tetonvillagesports.com/our-history.html. 94. Fay, A History of Skiing in Colorado, 93. 95. Interview with John Norton, April 6, 2009. 96. The Denver Post, August 6, 2004, "John Norton, President and DEO of Crested Butte Mountain Resort, Resigns." 97. The Aspen Times, May 31, 2002, "A Big Man Leaves a Big Void.", Interview with John Norton. 98. The Denver Post, November 24, 2002, "Character Comes to Forefront, New Ski Chief For Crested Butte Buffs Vintage Hamlet's rowdy Image." 99. The Denver Business Journal, March 2, 2004, "Triple Peaks Closes on Crested Butte Purchase.". 100. Rocky Mountain Skier Magazine, November 1972, Skier Interview with Chuck Lewis. 101. Colorado Ski and Snowboard Hall of Fame biography. 102. Fay, A History of Skiing in Colorado, 113. 103. Allsummitcountry.com, Copper Mountain History. 104. John Meck '67, e-mail to Tom Washing dated July 6, 2009. 105. Frank Litsky, "Ned Gillette, 53, Adventurer, Is Killed In Northern Kashmir", The New York times, August 14, 1998. 106. Time Magazine, December 25, 1972, "Skiing: The New Lure of a Supersport." 107. Fred Jones, telephone interview, March 24, 2009. 108. Fred Jones interview. 109. "The Last Call at the Red Onion", Aspen Times, November 28, 2006. 110. Mountain Chalet – the Melville Family History, http://www.mountainchaletaspen.com/history.htm. 111. Aspen Sojourner, Midwiter 2009, Staying Power, Mary Eshbaugh Hayes. 112. Rassenfoss, Joe, "Metcalf turned Crystal to gold in Aspen," The Rocky Mountain News, April 11, 2008. 113. Interview with Ron Riley, August 11, 2009. 114. Interview with Ron Riley, August 11, 2009. 115. See Chapter 11, Financial Entrepreneurs: Real Estate, Management, Finance. The Wood Family footnote: 116. Summit Pioneers by Alison Grabau (1999); chapter on Bill Bergman. Larry Jump footnotes.: 117. Box 1, FF4- 1951 - Inquiries regarding rates, accommodations, The Laurence (Larry) Jump and Arapahoe Basin Records, WH1220, Western History Collection, The Denver Public Library. 118. Box 4, FF22 - 1946-1970 - Plans, maps, news releases, The Laurence (Larry) Jump and Arapahoe Basin Records, WH1220, Western History Collection, The Denver Public Library. 119. Box 4, FF22 - 1946-1970 - Plans, maps, news releases, The Laurence (Larry) Jump and Arapahoe Basin Records, WH1220, Western History Collection, The Denver Public Library. 120. Box 4, FF23 - 1946-1948 – Prospectus, The Laurence (Larry) Jump and Arapahoe Basin Records, WH1220, Western History Collection, The Denver Public Library. 121. Box 4, FF23 - 1946-1948 – Prospectus, The Laurence (Larry) Jump and Arapahoe Basin Records, WH1220, Western History Collection, The Denver Public Library stockcharts.com, Thomson Financial. 122. Box 4, FF9 - 1946-1959 - Early development, friends: correspondence, The Laurence (Larry) Jump and Arapahoe Basin Records, WH1220, Western History Collection, The Denver Public Library. 123. Box 41, FF11 - 1941-1949 - Jump, Marjorie Brown: correspondence, The Laurence (Larry) Jump and Arapahoe Basin Records, WH1220, Western History Collection, The Denver Public Library. 124. Box 4, FF9 - 1946-1959 - Early development, friends: correspondence, The Laurence (Larry) Jump and Arapahoe Basin Records, WH1220, Western History Collection, The Denver Public Library. 125. Box 4, FF4 - 1946-1972 - Business correspondence, The Laurence (Larry) Jump and Arapahoe Basin Records, WH1220, Western History Collection, The Denver Public Library. Seibert, Vail, 65-71, 79. 74. Durrance, Man on the Medal, 98. 75. Durrance, Man on the Medal, 101. 76. Durrance, Man on the Medal, 80, 88-89. 77. http://www.coloradoskihalloffame.com/images_bio_htm_files/Edwin_Ned_Grant.htm. 78. Fay, A History of Skiing in Colorado 79; The Lawrence(Larry) Jump and Arapahoe Basin Records, H1220, Western History Collection, The Denver Public Library, Biographical Note. 79. See Arapahoe Basin Website, The Legend, http://www.arapahoebasin.com/ABasin/about/default.aspx. 80. Arapahoe Basin Website, the Legend; Jump Collection, Denver.

CHAPTER IX

OTHER US SKI AREAS AND IMPORTANT FIGURES

By Stephen Waterhouse

With Douglas Tengdin '82, Alan Kouns '78 and Valerie Jaffee '78

The major ski area developments have already been discussed except for two significant ones: Buck Hill, Minnesota, and Alyeska, Alaska; they are discussed in this chapter. The first skiing activities were Nordic—mostly cross-country and then jumping; these could take place anywhere there was snow. Alpine skiing areas in the US started on small ski hills in New England; these were mimicked by hundreds of small ski areas that sprung up on hills across the country wherever, and whenever, there was reasonably persistent snow. And there was no holding back the local Dartmouth alumnus or Dartmouth-influenced skier from seeking out the best of the skiing opportunities in his home community. They would often become very creative in the design of ski runs, and in the early years, the building of lifts. We will discuss a few of these innovative individuals as well as the ski areas or ski activities they became associated with.

We have arbitrarily divided this discussion in to 4 regions: Mid-Atlantic, South, Midwest and the Far North. The Mid-Atlantic area contains large urban populations and is close to the mountain ski resorts of New England. This combination provided for an active interest in having local skiing facilities to use in between the moderately long ski trips to New England in the early days of Alpine skiing and the considerably longer ones to the Rocky Mountain ski resorts today. The Midwest is home to some of the earliest skiers in the country, many of whom were of Scandinavian stock and particularly well versed in Nordic skiing activities. The South has a range of mountains running through part of it that is similar in height to New England. Most of this chapter will be allocated to the Far North as that is clearly a major location for serious skiers having many different ski related interests, not all involving Alpine skiing since most of Alaska's population is not particularly close to skiable mountains. This chapter will provide comments on both ski area developers and on people who have influenced skiing in various other ways.

MID-ATLANTIC

The states of New York, New Jersey, Pennsylvania and Maryland all have local ski areas, but the two most well-placed skiing states are New York and Pennsylvania. In the case of New York, Fred Pabst, brother of **Harold "Shorty" Pabst '38** who skied with many Dartmouth alumni, built 17 ski areas in 6 states and was the early conceptual leader in the creation of a chain of ski areas. Fred actually started the ski area that has the most name recognition in New York State, Lake Placid. Today, there are some 50 ski areas in the Mid-Atlantic region. Several other Dartmouth-connected people started other ski areas in this region, but we will focus most of our attention on the Seven Springs Resort, an area with a large Dartmouth family.

SEVEN SPRINGS MOUNTAIN RESORT

This story is multifaceted and involves not only the creation of a significant Mid-Atlantic ski area, but also many contributions to the ski scene in Hanover, NH. In the resort part of the story, the Dupré family entered the ski business in 1932 when **Herman K. Dupré's** parents bought a small Laurel Highlands, PA, farm plot and this grew into a 5,000-acre concern called Seven Springs Mountain Resort. Herman Dupré was born on the property in a farmhouse—now an upscale restaurant. He grew up, learned to ski right there on the property, and dreamed of skiing for the legendary ski college, Dartmouth. He applied, was accepted, and was elated When the time came to leave home, his bags were packed and he was ready to head for Hanover; but at the last minute, he was told he was needed there to run the family farm. He never was to make it to Hanover as a student, but that did not end his Dartmouth story.

He never forgot his dream and sent four of his children to take on the task he failed to complete, becoming the father of four Dartmouth ski team members, sisters **Denise Dupré '80**, **Rosi Dupré Littlefield '82**, **Anni Dupré Santry '83**, and **Michele Dupré '88**. The daughters say, "It was his and our mom's hard

Michele Dupré '88, the youngest of Herman Dupré's four Dartmouth daughters who all skied for the D team.

work and encouragement that enabled us to attend the College and ski competitively. They were both avid skiers and passionate about our educations, skiing, and the ski business." In later years, this dedication to skiing and to Dartmouth resulted in a gift by the Dupré family of a significant addition to the Dartmouth Skiway's snowmaking system which their father helped design. And the Herman Dupré name is now part of the Dartmouth lore because he even has a trail at the Dartmouth Skiway on the Winslow side named Herman's Highway and a tribute to him placed in the new McLane Family Lodge.

The snowmaking system was not a matter of making a financial contribution to the college; there is also a technical aspect to the Seven Spings and the Dupré story. Anni Dupré and **Charles Santry Tu '89** met, appropriately enough, on the Dartmouth campus in the mid-1980s when Charles was making a preliminary visit to Tuck School and Anni was visiting her sister Michele. Charles had an inventive mind and he worked with Herman at Seven Springs to develop some innovations in snowmaking to solve one of the major problems of the resort's location. And now Charles is one of the experts in the industry, which is what led to the helpful addition to the Dartmouth Skiway.

In explaining the art and science of snowmaking, Charles says: "Basically, snowmaking is trying to take water and atomize it into small droplets and freeze each one into a snow crystal from the time it leaves the nozzle to when it hits the ground. There are many ways to make it happen and create a crystal that's a snowflake. There needs to be an actual snow crystal that starts to form an actual white core that's really natural snow, but we're doing it in a short time frame. The crystal has to form in about 10 seconds—from when it leaves the nozzle to when it hits the ground—and that's the hard part. To get that to happen is what most of the companies in the snowmaking business are doing."[1]

The Dupré Family has supported recent Skiway snowmaking developments.

Although the family sold the Seven Springs Resort in 2006, Charles Santry continues to look forward to completing the technological innovations they are pursuing to improve snowmaking efficiency while conserving energy, reducing cost, increasing automation and increasing the flexibility to cope with changing weather conditions. Charles has a number of relevant patents that he has yet to fully incorporate into his work.

This one family has not only created a significant ski resort in the Mid-Atlantic States, sent several of its members to ski for Dartmouth, but is also available to provide on-going technical support for the Dartmouth Skiway in one of the long-term problems of ski resorts most everywhere. And it all started with the dream of a man named Herman.

MIDWEST

The Midwestern ski hills started appearing in the 1930s when locals, mainly of Scandinavian descent, switched from a love for cross-country and jumping to an enthusiasm for Alpine skiing. We have commented earlier on the work of Ski Clubs like the Heiliger Huegel Club in Wisconsin and the Waterloo Ski Club in Iowa to develop their own home hills. In 1935, Heiliger Huegel (HH) founders **Hermann '36** and **Jacob '42 Nunnemacher** searched throughout Wisconsin to find their spot at Holy Hill. This area has turned out a lot of skiers who have gone on to bigger mountains and other activities in skiing. But the enthusiasm still lives on at HH, and even today family members gather together to participate in friendly skiing on their hill.

In 1937, **Blair Wood '30** and his participants conducted a similar search in Iowa to find their hill in the Black Hawk County Alps. The resulting Waterloo Ski Club appears to have been Iowa's only significant skiing venue. They initiated many activities familiar to all skiers such as annual Ski Carnivals, and in the Carnivals of 1951 through 1953 they created the official "Iowa Combined Ski Championships" with skiers competing in slalom, cross-country and jumping events, drawing teams from various Iowa cities and thousands of spectators. They managed to even hold an "International" ski jumping event in 1953 with foreigners like Emil Thum of Germany who soared 70 feet off the trestle ski jump, probably a record long jump for Iowa.

Although club activities were the most frequent method of starting skiing in the Midwest (and some of these early organizations/ski hills still exist), ski industry entrepreneurs like **Freddie Pabst,** the first President of the Heiliger Huegel Club, were even more active. Freddie started Granite Peak in Wisconsin and Pine Knob in Michigan, but in time, Pabst moved out of these areas, so we will not dwell on their development.

Another active ski entrepreneur was Everett Kircher. Born in 1916, Kircher received his first set of skis at age nine, and he later took ski trips to Lake Placid, NY, and Sun Valley, ID, where he became an accomplished downhill skier at these areas, each of which had been developed to a greater or lesser degree by enthusiastic Dartmouth skiers and/or their associates. Kircher was frustrated by the lack of skiing options in Michigan, which back then had just one private and one public ski hill. In the 1947, he and two partners bought 40 acres of land in the northwest corner of Michigan's Lower Peninsula on which stood a 1,150-foot mountain; it was eventually to become a leading Midwest ski area named Boyne Mountain. The seller was so incredulous that Kircher wanted to use the remote, undeveloped site for skiing that he sold it to him for a dollar.

After buying the land, Kircher moved north and soon completed two ski trails which had been laid out by Victor Gottshalk, a German ski instructor he had taken lessons from at Sun Valley. Gottshalk alerted Kircher to the fact that Sun Valley was willing to sell one of its single-chair ski lifts, and so he bought it. The lift, which could transport 400 skiers per hour, had originally been built in 1936, and in fact was one of the very first chairlifts ever constructed. It was an improvement over existing lifts and its status as a first chair lift in the Midwest immediately put Kircher's operation on the map. As an indication of the long reach of the "Dartmouth factor," it is interesting to note that Kircher gained his interest in skiing at ski areas developed by men with Dartmouth connections and that his initial success was based on re-installing a ski lift created partly from the overhead cable concept first put in operation in the U.S. at Dartmouth's Oak Hill ski area and brought to Sun Valley by National Ski Hall of Famer **Charles Proctor '28.**

Today, there are over 100 ski areas spread from the Great Lakes to the Great Plains and the Black Hills of South Dakota. The rest of this Midwest section will concentrate on the developments at Buck Hill, an award winning ski area that has been developed in novel ways by a passionate skier, **Chuck Stone '53**, whose personal experience included working with the Dartmouth ski operation and the marvelous **Wallace "Bunny" Bertram '31** at Suicide Six in Woodstock, Vermont. The story below was researched and written with the help of many enthusiastic skiing supporters in Minnesota.

***

THE IMPACT OF CHARLES STONE '53 ON MINNESOTA SKIING

By **Douglas Tengdin '82**

One little-known aspect of Dartmouth's impact on skiing in the U.S. involves an unlikely location: Minnesota. In late 1953 **Arthur Ide '39** met with **Charles "Chuck" Stone '53** over dinner and the two discussed the prospects for a ski area in the Minneapolis area. These two were natural boosters for the sport in the Twin Cities. While Ide hadn't skied before coming to Dartmouth, he was a gifted athlete and he was introduced to the sport by fellow classmate and skiing legend **Dick Durrance '39**.

Stone had been a skier before coming to the Upper Valley, and his passion for the sport was unquenchable: in addition to his studies and athletics he worked part-time as a lift operator at Mad River Glen and Suicide Six. While at Suicide Six he had the opportunity to work with and learn from Bunny Bertram, who popularized the rope tow in the U.S. Shortly after he returned from Dartmouth, Stone began to search for suitable terrain on which he could install some ski lifts.

He was directed to a small rise south of the city that was owned by a woman from Northfield, MN. She was also interested in working with "young people" to see her land developed. In 1954, Stone formed a corporation and leased the hill. He and some friends cleared the land with chainsaws and dynamite and installed three rope-tow lifts on the 310-foot vertical rise. Before lifts were installed there had been a lot of freelance skiing: locals would hike up the *bucha*, (the Norwegian word for "hill") and ski down. This location therefore came to be known as "Buck Hill." In 1960 Stone led a consortium in a private equity offering which raised funds to build a base lodge, add a T-bar, and install snowmaking equipment.

In 1963, a couple of small junior racing clubs had formed around local ski shops. Ide had helped start the Tatra Ski Club, and in 1965 Stone sponsored a junior racing program based at Buck Hill. In contrast to the parent-run ski-shop sponsored clubs, the Buck Hill club was sponsored by the area and the coach was a ski-area employee. While some parents were put off by this, it anchored the ski team in one location and provided a stable income source for the head coach.

In its early days the racing team went through a succession of head coaches. At the time a number of Europeans were coaching U.S. junior racing programs. Tatra's head coach, Heli Schaller, also coached Olympian Cindy Nelson from Lutsen, MN. Ide suggested to Stone that he hire a European coach from out West, but Stone was convinced that he should sign up someone already in the Midwest who knew how to build a race program in a Midwestern city.

Accordingly, he recruited former Austrian National Ski Team member Erich Sailer to come to Buck Hill from Telemark, Wisconsin. Initially, Sailer was put off by the small size of the Buck Hill program. Stone had charged him with gathering over 100 racers, and at the time Sailer remarked to another local coach that he didn't think there were 100 racers in the entire State of Minnesota. Nevertheless, the program grew. Sailer has continued to coach at Buck Hill for 40 years, garnering multiple coaching awards and in 2006 being inducted into the US Skiing Hall of Fame.

Stone's concept of having a ski area sponsor an alpine ski-racing team provided a stable training platform and enabled the race team to cooperate effectively with the area. One innovation necessitated by

Minnesota's higher latitude was to install powerful lights to facilitate night skiing. This allowed the race program to offer midweek training in the evening and helped it become more rigorous while remaining family-oriented.

Over the years Buck Hill's race program has produced over 20 US Ski Team competitors, including 2009 US Men's Alpine Development Team member **Michael Ankeny '13** (brother of Dartmouth ski team member **Peter Ankeny '12)** and Sterling Grant (just named to the Women's Alpine B Team), as well as world-class racers Kristina Koznick and Lindsey Vonn, the all-time record holder for US women's World Cup victories. Erich Sailer brought Vonn's father to Minneapolis to work with him in the mid 1970s.

In the early 1970s Ide and **DeWalt "Pete" Ankeny '54** cooperated to form a successor club to Tatra as an alternative to Buck Hill, based out of another local ski shop. The Bonne Equipe team was formed and it produced several outstanding Alpine racers. While it never had the numbers of the Buck Hill program, it did engage some excellent coaches and sent many junior racers to national competitions. While this particular club was small, the friendly competition between the various clubs in the Minneapolis area kept the racing programs vital in the region.

Having multiple competitive junior ski clubs in the Minneapolis area facilitated local competition and pushed the skiers and their coaches to innovate. Many Minnesotans were thus encouraged to pursue Alpine ski racing when they otherwise might have ended up playing hockey. Eventually, dozens of racers who grew up skiing on the small Midwestern hills came back east to race for Dartmouth or other colleges, completing the cycle.

In 1973 Stone pioneered the idea of a "homecoming" race for Minnesota alumni to compete in when they returned home for the holidays. When Stone passed away in 1994 the race was dedicated to his memory. The Chuck Stone Memorial traditionally includes US Team members and elite collegiate athletes and has gained a reputation as the marquis national point competition in the region. Year after year, top-ranked skiers "come back to give back," in Vonn's words--a fitting tribute to a Dartmouth man who gave so much to so many.

The entire program was so conspicuously successful that the United States Ski Association awarded the Buck Hill Ski Team the highest achievement possible with the 2008 Club of The Year award. All this would not have been possible but for the early vision of a few Dartmouth skiers and the passionate, gritty determination of Chuck Stone.

SOUTH

The South is not blessed with great snow conditions. However, it does have snow, and the story of the first ski area south of the Mason-Dixon Line, which was built by the Ski Club of Washington, D.C. (SCWDC), serves perhaps as the best illustration of how the Dartmouth spirit could be introduced to a different region and thereby change the pace of ski area development there.

Southern U.S. skiing is clearly not as interesting as activities in the Northeast, the West, or Europe. However, most locals cannot afford the time or money to travel frequently, so having local ski areas would be the only way to take advantage of the sport with any regularity and to stay in shape for visits elsewhere. The one positive is that the southern Appalachian Mountains are quite similar in height to those of New England. Therefore, at higher elevations, snow survives for sufficient periods of time and skiing runs are acceptable, if short in length. There are roughly 20 ski areas in this region today.

Jim Collins '84 researched the background on the SCWDC story and how it helped create this active ski region. In his chapter, he tells how **Hal Leich '29** skied in the 1927 Moosilauke Down-mountain race organized by the Dartmouth Outing Club, moved to Washington, D.C., and took over as president of the SCWDC before the war. He led the Washington club to set up a ski area in a cleared glade in the Shenandoah National Park. A few years later after the war, seeking more reliable snow, Hal led a search that found a new ski area in West Virginia, often called "little Tuckerman's" This area became so popular that special ski trains were arranged to carry loads of skiers out from D.C. The club provided ski lessons, a ski patrol, and hosted an annual winter carnival, the social highlight of their ski year.

That's just one story, but it's an example of many early Dartmouth ski efforts. In this case, they introduced skiing to thousands of young people up through the early 1960s and spawned a sizeable ski industry in West Virginia. The SCWDC now has almost 2,000 members and is an active participant, a group of 22 ski clubs in the Blue Ridge Ski Council.

FAR NORTH

In this section, our focus is on Alaska and its main ski mountain, Alyeska. Few recognize that early skiing activities were organized near Anchorage as early as the 1930s, that the Alyeska Ski Resort has slowly risen to become one of the exciting ski areas of today, and that there has been a long involvement of Alaskans in the skiing of open terrain that is part cross-country, part mountaineering and very much a matter of endurance. Dartmouth's presence in Alaska is huge with over 500 graduates and in excess of 200 of them in the Anchorage Area. The vast number of these alumni participate in one way or another in this major Alaskan sport. Just in the Anchorage area there are reputed to be 40,000 Nordic skiers, so the local alumni are part of a great ski-oriented community. Research for our comments on Alaska was undertaken by **Valerie Jaffee '78.**

ALPENGLOW, ARCTIC VALLEY

Alpenglow in the Arctic Valley is the oldest downhill ski area in Alaska with four lifts and an altitude of 4000 feet. It has about a 1200 vertical drop—all above tree line—and is located just on the edge of Anchorage. It is a very family-friendly area and is known for its great powder skiing. And as in other regions, the local ski club is very important to the

Russell Dow '38 and wife Dusty at Anchorage ski area.

story; the Anchorage Ski Club (the oldest ski club in Alaska) and its board of directors manages the small non-profit and volunteer-run community ski area, Alpenglow.

The club dates to the beginning of 1937 when ski tournaments were first planned. A past president of the Club is former Dartmouth Alpine racer **Karen Loeffler '79** who was nominated in July 2009 by President Barack Obama to serve as the US Attorney for Alaska. Karen grew up ski racing in Minnesota. Dartmouth was her first choice for college for a number of reasons, but particularly because she wanted to be a member of the Dartmouth Ski Team. She skied on the team all four years. When she graduated, she put skiing on a back burner to complete law school at Harvard; she then moved to Alaska. She returned to skiing in 1985 and has done a lot of Nordic skiing, completing the 50-kilometer Tour of Anchorage every year since it began in the early 1990s. She is also enjoying more time on the alpine slopes as the teacher of her young niece and nephew. She got involved with Arctic Valley because of her love of the sport and her family's love for this area.

An important early figure at the Anchorage Ski Club was **Russell Dow '38.** He was a New Hampshire native, and a member of the Dartmouth Ski Team, who moved to Alaska upon graduation and never left. Russell was a typical rural New Englander who worked hard his entire life. In Alaska, he first labored at remote mines, did odd jobs all over, and cleared a wilderness area to make a homestead for himself and his wife. He also worked as a ski instructor for the Army and his final career was as a plant operator for the Eklutna Power Plant, which he helped construct. Russell was not a founding member of the Anchorage Ski Club, but he joined soon after it was established.

During World War II, Dow trained Army ski troops at Anchorage's City Ski Bowl. He was part of an illustrious team including Major "Muktuk" Marston and a member of the elite Alaska scouts known as "Castner's Cutthroats" that searched the mountains around Anchorage for an improved ski training area. With the Dow's help, the Army found and developed the Arctic Valley site in the Chugach Mountains, north of the city. In the late 1940s, with civilian skiers crowding the military warm-up building, the Anchorage Ski Club moved up the valley and built its own lodge and rope tows there.

Russell Dow was much liked by the Army troops. On one ski adventure, he was involved in pioneering trip across what is today likely to be the most popular backcountry ski touring route near Anchorage[3]. The Arctic Valley to Indian Alaskan Ski Traverse is a 21-mile route that goes over Indian Pass between these points. Back in the 1940s, Russell would lead army skiers along this route when there wasn't even a road back to Anchorage on this old Indian trail. Skiers had to catch a ride on the Alaska Railroad train back to Fort Richardson. The trip took three days and involved staying overnight in the remains of an old, abandoned turn of the century Iditarod trail roadhouse which is long gone.

ANCHORAGE CROSS-COUNTRY COURSE

Most of the Alaskan skiing activities up to the late 1930s were Nordic in nature. And Dartmouth folks have been and still are greatly involved here. Diane Moxness, Director of the Nordic Ski Association of Anchorage (NSAA), also known as Nordic Ski Club (NSC), has a Dartmouth son, **Anson Moxness '11**. **Jim Reeves '67**, long-time Anchorage Municipal Attorney, and Dartmouth parent **Parry Grover**, are past Presidents of the Anchorage Nordic Club.

Jim Collins has also outlined how **George Moerlein '52** and his wife Judy, with the Anchorage Nordic Ski Club, helped build a 5-km cross-country trail network for a new school in the Hillside area of the city. George headed up the club for years and became a leader in Alaskan cross-country skiing. His son, **Tim Moerlein '79,** learned on that course and helped Dartmouth win the 1976 Men's NCAA National Ski Championship. Tim later returned to Alaska, and became a dogsled racer, including placing well in the annual Iditarod race. His two daughters, **Janelle Moerlein '06** and **Katie Moerlein '08,** continued the Moerleins' Alaska-Dartmouth connection.

ALYESKA SKI RESORT

Alyeska is the only major ski resort in Alaska. Over fifty years ago, pilot Ernie Baumann found the "perfect" ski mountain forty miles from Anchorage. In 1954, eleven local men formed the Alyeska Ski Corporation with the dream of creating a first-class ski resort. In 1959, **Jim Branch '52, Tu '53,** took office as President of Alyeska to make the dream happen, and in 1960, the first chair lift and a day lodge were built. The

Dartmouth impact has been significant since early years. A few of the individuals who have been involved are noted below.

Jim Branch was a Dartmouth ski racer and jumper who initially worked with **Tom Corcoran '54** on the development of Waterville Valley Ski area in New Hampshire. When Jim took over Alyeska in 1959, the area had a small rope tow, a Pomalift, and a helicopter to haul advanced skiers to the top of the mountain on suitable weekends. He was the ski area's second manager and worked there during its early struggle to become viable. At one time, the resort could not afford to pay its employees; instead, the corporation gave them land in Girdwood, which was considered "worthless" in those days, but it's not worthless today! In 1967, Branch moved to Franconia, NH, and joined **Sel Hannah '35** to develop and expand Sel's Sno-engineering company and he remained as a co-owner for twenty-five years. In 1994, Branch was inducted to the Skiing Hall of Fame.

***

ALASKAN ENTREPRENEUR: JOHN BYRNE, III '81

By Alan Kouns '78 and Valerie Jaffee '78

John Byrne, III '81 is possibly the most significant current economic contributor to Alaskan skiing. Still skiing 100 days a year, including 32 helicopter days last season, John bought the Alyeska Ski Resort in late 2006. John has been passionate about skiing since his teenage years. He taught at Okemo Mountain Vermont where the family had a house. He taught weekends and was PSIA certified. John took winter terms off at college to teach at Okemo, Sugar Bush and King's Ridge. Son of insurance industry mogul John "Jack" Byrne II, the former head of GEICO, John has good business roots.

John Byrne '81 with Alyeska in the background.

The road to Alyeska for John Byrne, III has been of deep skiing tracks across the West. After a couple years making his own money at Salmon Brothers on Wall Street, Byrne bought The Inn in Teton Village in 1987. In 1991 he moved to the mouth of Alta canyon, investing in apartments, and calls Alta home. When he is not at Alyeska, he is a regular on Snowbird's early morning trams and with Wasatch Powder Bird Guides. Having done projects (bar / hotel /developments) in at least six areas and working closely with the various owners, he chose Alyeska as a place he could use this experience and to fulfill his dream for the love for skiing.

Alyeska Resort now includes ten lifts, a 60-person tram, several restaurants, a "hand tram" (a typical Alaskan air method of crossing a river), the 300-room Hotel Alyeska, and base area real estate with huge plans for development over time. An extensive mountain bike network is being built. At its peak, in a Girdwood population of about 2,000, the resort employs 700 workers with 450 on payroll year round. Potentially the most intense inbounds skiing in North America (631 inches of snow annually) rising from almost sea level to over 5,000 feet, Alyeska has hosted US Alpine Championships, World Freestyle Championships, World Freeride, and would like another chance to be an Olympic venue down the road. John's approach involves building great customer relations, taking a personal approach with all his staff, and making the resort more family friendly. He is a working owner and general manager with a top-notch ski resort management team, including **Dick Rosston'73** as real estate legal counsel.

His recent accomplishments have received much publicity, including being featured on the Travel Channel, and he had a three-part interview with the local ABC affiliate. When John bought Alyeska in 2006 from the Japanese corporation Seibu, it was losing several million dollars a year and failing as a destination resort. In a 2007 edition of *Skiing* magazine, as a sign of his immediate impact, Alyeska was ranked # 6 on its list of best ski resorts in the nation.

"A ski area is like an oil tanker. It takes three miles to turn around the ship", says John; his mission is to navigate the ski area through its growing pains to economic and environmental sustainability. John is looking into building a co-generation plant this summer. He envisions this plant heating the hotel, functioning for 50 years, paying for itself in 20 years, and reducing the resort's carbon footprint by 50 percent. He has a history of success and can demonstrate a model eco-sensitive, environment friendly 900-acre development in Telluride, CO, at Sunny Side Ranch. Having had success in such an anti-development community, John feels extraordinarily optimistic about his future at Alyeska.

High on his list of priorities was to make the resort more child friendly. He created a "magic-carpet" ski lift (that children can simply step onto); and he also created the "kid camp" for ski instruction. When he brought his now ten- and twelve-year old daughters to the ski area they hated the pizza because the resort had the wrong kind of oven. As an attentive single father, John listened; the resort now has better pizza. One day he hopes to completely have built out the ski area and hotel and leave it debt free for his girls. One daughter has already laid claim to the hotel and the other to the ski area as their future hegemonies. The question is, will his daughters also go to Dartmouth?

John Byrne's efforts for Alaska provided a great backdrop to the National Alpine Championship races run in March, 2009. **Annie McLane Kuster '78**, proud mother of 4th generation McLane family skiers **Travis Kuster '14** and **Zachary Kuster '11,** reported briefly via email on progress at Alyeska:

> *"So here is the report from our Alaska Adventure cheering for a gang of Dartmouth skiers, including alums **Paul McDonald '06**, and **Brian Freedman '02** plus current Dartmouth Team members **"Ace" Tarberry '11** (4th in Downhill) and **Trevor Leafe '12, Tommy Ford '12** and **Max Hammer '12**; and admittees Nolan Kasper (2nd in Combined; Admitted but not yet matriculated), **Keith Moffat '13** and **Michael Ankeny '13**, as well as **Annie Rendall '13, Abby Fucigna '13,** and **Maddie Packard '13**. What a great tradition! Highlights: 1) 100 inches of snow since our arrival this week, and skiing in fluffy powder up to my thighs with spectacular views of soaring white peaks in every direction! 2) Cheering for Travis who finished in the top 50 or better of the best ski racers in America and among the top dozen junior racers his age in the downhill, giant slalom and slalom, 3) Sharing this whole adventure with two great friends, both mother's of ski racing girls and Dartmouth alums (one my freshman year roommate whom I have hardly seen in 30 years), 4) Priceless: skiing after the last race from the summit of Mt Alyeska."* [2]

Dartmouth alumni have had many regular involvements at Alyeska over the years. **Phil Livingston '58**, a resident of Girdwood, is a former member of Sourdough Ski Patrol at Alyeska and currently a Master's ski racer. He is the former President of Girdwood Rotary as well as the District Governor of Rotary District 5010. He is also on the board of Davis Boyd Foundation, the charitable arm of the Skiing Rotarians and on the board of **Girdwood 2020,** whose mission is to establish Girdwood as a Four Seasons Destination Resort. One of the past accomplishments (of many) for this group was assisting in the effort that found John Byrne, III as the buyer of the Resort in lieu of a tour group who was going to it shut down in its entirety and use it for a time-share condominium in the summer only.

Now the 2020 group is looking forward to Byrne's vision of **Alyeska Resort 2020** and needs a new buzz. The board is establishing an endowment to assist Girdwood Four-Season athletes. Girdwood has had a number of US Ski Team members over the years including Tommy Moe, now the Director of the Alyeska Ski Club and winner of both a Gold Medal and Silver Medal at the Lillihammer Olympics (1994); Rosie Fletcher, a National Champion snowboarder and a Bronze Medalist at the Torino Olympics (2006); and a several A and B team Alpine skiers who could jump to the top. Phil Livingston himself is going back to Italy to get his Gold in the geriatric races for Masters in, as he calls it, the "halt and blind" over-70 group.

Phil is yet another example of a Dartmouth alumnus who learned to ski as a freshman in 1954, served as a ski instructor for former DOC President **Dick Perkins '56** at the Dartmouth Ski School, and 54years later is still skiing. He has been a National Ski Patroller, Alpine and Adaptive Instructor, and Masters Racer. Our major interest in Phil is for his work as the sponsor of Adaptive Ski Programs which ranges from Alaskan schoolchildren to disabled veterans.

The story of Phil's work via his Rotarian role with a severely disabled and potentially suicidal sixteen-year-old Russian boy, Igor, brought to Alaska for treatment is very special, and is one of the many contributions of Dartmouth-connected skiers in the area of Adaptive skiing. After local Rotarians and volunteer physicians provided this young man with prosthetics for his crushed left hand and amputated right hand (suffered in a climbing accident), Phil took him to Alyeska Resort and their Challenge Alaska Adaptive Ski School for therapy. Igor didn't speak English, but Phil correctly assumed that since Igor's father was an extreme skier, the son might be a skier, too. That was indeed the case, and this thoughtful therapeutic effort by Phil and the Alyeska team produced amazing results leading to the rebirth of Igor's confidence. He is now a practicing Russian lawyer with positive views of his American friends. In much the same way, Phil and the Alyeska Adaptive Skiing program have had a positive impact on veterans returning from battles in Iraq and Afghanistan with disabling injuries.

Richard Rosston '73, an Anchorage attorney, worked with the new owner of Alyeska, John Byrne, III '81, on the purchase of the mountain in 2006. He has served as the lawyer for Alyeska Resort since. He is also an extremely experienced member of the Alyeska volunteer Ski Patrol which relates to training received while a Dartmouth undergraduate. Richard first worked as a ski patroller at the college and then served as patrol leader his senior year. With this background, he was able to work on the patrol everywhere he has lived, including a year as the Assistant Director of the Bridger Bowl Ski Patrol in Bozeman, Montana, several years at Alpine Meadows in Lake Tahoe, California, and he has been on the Alyeska Ski Patrol since 1977. He was certified as a National Ski Patroller in 1974, and was the Far West Division Certification Advisor. He has also been a toboggan patrol advisor and helped write the NSPS national toboggan training manual and various other instructional manuals. He has continued to serve as the Alaska Division NSPS Certified Advisor since 1996. Dick's son, **Ryan Rosston '04**, may follow a similar path.

OTHER ALASKAN SKIING TERRAIN
The Unusual Alaskan Skiers and their many ways to impact the further development of all kinds of skiing.

Almost unique to the Alaskan environment are the adventurers who ski out in the wilderness in much the same way that a **Bill Briggs '54, Barry Corbett '58** and **Colin O'Farrell '03, MS '05** might climb an unskied mountain like the Grand Teton and ski down. There is no specific ski area, just a giant unexplored panorama with unlimited skiing opportunities open to the person willing to break a trail. The Dartmouth community has long been involved with this kind of challenge. Russell Dow '38 was one of the earlier alumni to step up and take advantage of such opportunities. And perhaps the greatest of them all, **Tim Kelley '79**, is still at it.

The Thomas Family: Lowell, Lowell, Jr. '46, Anne Thomas Donaghy '77, David Thomas '79

In Alaska, there are many legendary families. Lowell Thomas, Jr. is a patriarch of one of these. Tim Kelley tells a story of when he first moved to Alaska in 1981 and Lowell invited him to help:

> "Hey, I'm bringing supplies out to a trapper north of the Alaska Range and need some help. Want to come?" I said sure and the next thing I knew I was flown 250 miles out of Anchorage and dropped on a snowy river bar. Lowell sent me off to snowshoe up into the hills, find the trapper's cabin and his snowmobile – which I would use to haul his supplies in while Lowell went back to Anchorage for a second load. Before Lowell left he said: "I should be back in 6 hours, but you never know. This is Alaska … so it could be two weeks."

Lowell Thomas Jr. '46 is among many Dartmouth skiers who have called Alaska home.

Lowell junior started alpine skiing as a child in the Northeast, visiting Stowe, North Conway, and Lake Placid most New Year's. He learned the Arlberg technique from Austrians at Pecketts in Franconia, NH, and skied several times in Sun Valley and Aspen. He first skied the headwall at Tuckerman Ravine with his father at age twelve. And it was during one of these trips that Lowell senior connected with Chris Young, creator of the "Dr. Schlitz" movie, and agreed to do the narration for the film, one which. has probably been seen by more Dartmouth alumni than any other single short film. Lowell arrived at Dartmouth in the summer of '42, played JV football in the fall, and then left to join the Air Force's pilot training program before ski season. At one point, he roomed with Alpine racer **Malcolm McLane '46**, who remained a family friend for life and whose daughter **Annie McLane Kuster '78** is noted earlier in this chapter, was on the Dartmouth Ski Team and is now running for the US Congress.

Back in Hanover after the war in the fall of 1945, the junior Lowell became a member of the Dartmouth ski team under Walter Prager. He raced on the Alpine team, but also enjoyed jumping. **Steve Bradley '39** coached him to become a pretty good jumper. Lowell says that he loved leaping off Dartmouth's 40-meter hill on the golf course and that his best jump was during Carnival in '48 when he out-jumped the two Norwegians on the team. In Alaska, Lowell and his wife Tay have been extensive supporters of Nordic Skiing and provided funds to Alaska Pacific University a couple years ago to establish a summer Nordic training program on a nearby 5,000-foot glacier.

Lowell Thomas's two children, Anne Thomas Donaghy and Dave Thomas, were both cross-country skiers and ski team captains at Dartmouth. After his senior year, Dave Thomas guided climbers on Mount McKinley with the legendary Alaskan guide Ray Genet (who would later die on Mt. Everest). Dave introduced Tim Kelley, his former college roommate, to future wife Tammy Thiele, a pilot for Alaska Airlines. The ski coach at Diamond High School in Anchorage that Anne, Dave, and Tammy (and **Dan Billman '79**) all attended was **John Morton,** who would later become the Dartmouth and Olympic Ski Coach.

Anne Thomas Donaghy, who is grateful to be a "legacy child", writes:

Anne Thomas '77, Captain of the Dartmouth X-C Ski Team; and a leader in securing Dartmouth's first women's skiing championship, the 1977 AIAW Championship.

"I really couldn't imagine going anywhere else. Dartmouth had started a women's ski team the very first year the college went co-ed. Since Al Merrill was coaching the cross-country women, I went to Dartmouth mostly to become coached by him. He'd been a family friend of my granddad's and my father's, and some of my happiest memories of Dartmouth center around skiing with the 'Silver Fox', as everyone called him. I plan to stay involved in cross-country skiing my whole life. I'm in my 15th year as an editor and board member for the New England Nordic Ski Association (NENSA) and have just been tapped as the new President of the Board of Directors. All prior NENSA board presidents have been Dartmouth Alums."

The Nordic Skiing Family: George Moerlein '52, Andy Moerlein '77, Tim Moerlein '79, Janelle Moerlein '06, Katie Moerlein '08

Also notable in Alaska is the Moerlein family. The first Dartmouth forebear is George Moerlein, Dartmouth Class of 1952. He and his young wife Judy lived in Hanover in George's senior year. They arrived in Alaska in 1961, and in the early 1970s, George and his wife pioneered the start of the Anchorage Nordic Ski Club and created many cross-country ski trails in Anchorage area.[4]

The Moerleins had five sons, and most of them raced cross-country, as well as participating in jumping. George served as Race Director, Chief Timer, and Trail Groomer during his sons' many years of active competition. From 1967-73, mom Judy served as President of the Alaska Division of USSA (United States Ski Association) and USSA Foundation. In 2003, Alaska Pacific University and the Nordic Ski Club awarded George and Judy honors for their role in promoting cross-country skiing in Alaska.[5]

Professionally, George was a geologist in Alaska. He has traveled extensively in the state and apparently was quite a hunter, even killing a polar bear with a bow and arrow—and he has the rug to prove it. In one of Tim Kelley's visits to the Moerlein house, there were several rehabilitating owls perched on roosts in the kitchen (evidence that George's respect for wildlife) and he once awoke to George practicing the bagpipes.

Without question, George brought a special character to the forty-ninth state and the Moerleins have been a unique Alaskan family.

Sons Andy and Tim Moerlein both skied for Dartmouth. Andy coached cross-country skiing at Derryfield high school in New Hampshire for many years. Tim, freshman-year roommate of fellow Alaskans (and Dartmouth ski team members) Tim Kelley and Dave Thomas, was on Dartmouth's 1976 NCAA ski champions and went to the World Junior Skiing X-C Championships in 1977 in Switzerland. Two Moerlein grandchildren have now graduated from Dartmouth, Janelle '06 and Katie '08.

Uniquely for Alaska, Tim Moerlein got into professional sled dog racing after he graduated. In 1984, he was the "Rookie of the Year" in the Iditarod Sled Dog race, placing 11th in his first run up the trail from Anchorage to Nome across Alaska. Tim does not race sled dogs any more, but he is probably the only Dartmouth ski racer to change from gliding winter trails to "mushing" them.

Ned Gillette '67, a former Dartmouth skier, Olympic skier and an early developer of the von Trapp Family cross-country program, was a noted adventure skier all around the world. He made some memorable trips to Alaska to ski on cross-country and mountaineering trips. He is reputed to have made the first ever one-day ascent of Mt. McKinley (1978), the first circumnavigation of Mt. McKinley (1977), and a very difficult, long-distance ski trip to Alaska's Brooks Range in 1972.

Nina Kemppel '92, Tu '05, has been one of Alaska's most productive ski racers. She grew up in Anchorage and was a former Dartmouth Ski Team member. She has been elected to the Alaska Sports Hall of Fame as a four-time Olympian and a 20-time National Champion. See a full profile of Nina in Chapter XIV.

Tim Kelley '79 was a huge contributor to this Alaska Chapter as he is one of the most knowledgeable repositories of Alaskan ski history. From Vermont to Dartmouth to Alaska, he has shown exceptional skiing abilities. He was not only a member of the 1976 Dartmouth ski team that tied for first in the NCAA's with Denver University, and an All-American, but also a skier on the US Ski Cross-Country racing team. After graduation, he moved to Alaska, developed computer skills, and took up "peak bagging" (i.e., accomplishing first ascents), setting a record of 90 so far that continues to grow and may never be exceeded. He skied the Iditarod Trail, besting two bikers in the process, and has engaged in scores of similar adventures. A full profile on Tim is in Chapter XIV.

Nancy Pease '82 is famous in Alaska because she has held the Mount Marathon record since 1990. On the 4th of July every year in Seward, the tradition known as the Mount Marathon Race takes place. Testing their stamina on a layout that features an elevation gain of over 3,000 feet and which covers just over three miles in distance, competitors scramble through an exhausting racecourse that has been around since 1915. It is at this event that Nancy Pease has created a legacy for herself. As a six-time winner at the Mount Marathon race, she has truly established herself as the "Queen of the Mountain". Not only is Nancy a champion at this event, she still holds the 19-year record time of 50'30" set in 1990.

Dave Thomas '79, Captain of Dartmouth's Men's X-C Ski Team.

Kemppel '92, Tu '05 is one of U.S. and Alaska's most significant X-C racers.

Kelley '79 (r), holder of the Alaskan "peak bagging record" and, with his partner Baker, the winner of an unusual Iditarod Race.

Nancy raced for four years at Dartmouth in a period of rapid transition for the women's Nordic team. When she arrived from Alaska with a background of tough disciplined training, the Dartmouth team was still stuck in the "gentle-lady athlete" mentality under Coach Merrill. The women didn't even have a locker room...and no one questioned why not. But that changed as the women became more demanding of themselves and their success increased accordingly.

Jon Underwood '86 was an excellent competitor on the Dartmouth cross-country ski team and its team captain in 1986. Jon has followed the suggestions of his Dartmouth coach, John Morton, in cross-country trail design in Alaska. His technique of making narrow yet sustainable and maintainable multi-use trails is remarkable; and is changing the way folks view trails in Alaska. In 2008, he made an extensive trail system for the Hillside Park in Anchorage that is, in the opinion of some experts, the coolest and most amazing mountain biking trail in the entire state.

Cory Smith '96, Th '98 grew up in Littleton, NH, and always wanted to ski for Dartmouth. He was Captain of the Dartmouth Cross-Country Ski Team for two years (1995-96) and was a two-time NCAA All American. He raced in three World Cup races in 2001 and competed on the national circuit from 1997-2002. He was ranked in the top ten in the country several times.

Cory Smith '96, an All American X-C racer.

While still racing after college, Cory started a website (www.xcskiracer.com) to chronicle his travel and racing experiences. In those days, he was very probably the first skier in North America (and maybe the world) to have a blog site of this particular kind. The site was well-known throughout the ski world because he often posted race results and photos before anyone else. Many others skiers soon followed with websites of their own.

In 2002, he founded his Fasterskier web site (www.fasterskier.com), which grew to be the most popular Nordic skiing website in North America. It became the virtual cyber center of the cross-country community in the United States, but Cory sold the website in 2007. For the last six years, he has been the Executive Administrator of Cross-Country Alaska (similar to NENSA, but in Alaska and much smaller). This group runs the races, including the Junior Olympic qualifiers, and is the governing body for cross-country skiing for Alaska. One major accomplishment in that role has been his creation of an on-line Trail Reports forum that has grown into an Internet community for skiers throughout Alaska. It is checked by about 1000 people a day during the winter.

Cory has also completed Internet work for NENSA, XCSkiWorld.com, TeamToday.org, Nordic Equipment, and many other ski organizations. This is often the first such on-line experience for these groups. He has not done any ski racing for the past several years but instead focuses on fun Alaskan adventures on skis, on foot, and by raft (many of these have been with Tim Kelley) all of which are recorded on his blog, www.endurefun.com.

SUMMARY

The Far North is a hotbed of Dartmouth skiing today. The mixture of activities and interests there is probably greater than that seen in any other region, from pure Alpine to Nordic to snowboarding to rigorous adventure skiing in the expansive outback of the Alaskan wilderness. This is a region that deserves more attention than most have previously given to it. And certainly the transformation of Alyeska into a world-class ski resort under John Byrne, III's leadership will be particularly exciting to watch.

Notes

1. "Leopard Report.com", Feb. 3, 2007 2. Annie McLane, in an e-mail dated 4/1/2009, 7:04:20 P.M. EDT 3. Tim Kelley's Lost Ski Areas web site, www.alsap.com 4. http://www.anchoragenordicski.com/Trails/trailsHillside.htm 5. http://alumni.alaskapacific.edu/contact/archive/fall2003/page2.html

CHAPTER X

POPULARIZING SKIING

By Dick Durrance II '65
Professional Photographer and Author; Former Dartmouth Ski Team Captain

With Eric Lambert MALS '07, Rick Moulton, Richard Isaacson '64, Lisa Feinberg Densmore '83, Meredith Scott '96

Kneeling behind his rugged Cine Special movie camera filming the world's greatest ski racers bouncing through the twists and bumps of Schuss Gully at the 1950 World Championship downhill in Aspen, Colorado, my father, **Dick Durrance '39**, must have known that this moment was simultaneously the apex of his extraordinary life in the ski world, and the beginning of the next chapter of his life, his career as a filmmaker.

The 1950 World Ski Championships in Aspen brought together all aspects of his life in the ski world: world-class ski racer, designer of ski trails, developer of ski resorts, sports photographer, and pioneer filmmaker. His participation in the championships began in 1947. As the general manager of the fledgling Aspen Skiing Company, he conceived the idea of bringing the championships to Aspen as a way to put the resort on the world map of skiing. Together with classmate **Steve Bradley '39**, local activist Frank Willoughby, and renowned Bauhaus artist Herbert Bayer, he helped prepare the sophisticated proposal for hosting the event in Aspen. It was he who caught the train to Chicago in 1948 and sold the proposal to the United States Ski Association. Then, when US delegates persuaded the European dominated FIS to grant the US its first world skiing championships, he designed and directed the construction of racing trails for the event and organized the races. Now that the competition was underway and his official duties done, he was meticulously filming and photographing the races both to promote Aspen and to communicate the excitement of ski racing to future generations of skiers.[1]

Like many Dartmouth graduates who preceded him, and many more who followed him, my father was passionate about sharing his love for skiing. For some graduates, celebrating skiing was their job; for others, it indirectly advanced their careers or aided their business enterprises; and for a few, it satisfied needs totally separate from their professional endeavors.

Dick Durrance I '39 filming in the mountains.

For all of these Dartmouth men and women, extolling the joys of skiing—whether speaking on lecture tours, creating photographs and films, writing books and magazine articles, or blogging on the Internet—it was a vital aspect of their lives. In celebrating the sport, they contributed hugely to the growth of skiing from an activity with but a few thousands of participants in the early 1930s to millions of skiers today. It is a tribute to the quality of our Dartmouth education that so many graduates developed the rigorous communication skills necessary to share their insights and enthusiasm with national audiences. Some of the many distinguished alumni who did so much to promote the sport of skiing are discussed below.

***

Jack McCrillis '19

In addition to running an insurance business and serving as part-time judge in New Hampshire, Jack somehow found time to directly influence the development of skiing in the US in general and at Dartmouth in particular through his voluminous correspondence with early leaders of the skiing establishment, people like

Harold Grinden, an early president and historian of the National Ski Association, Coach Otto Schniebs, William Fowler of the Appalachian Mountain Club, and Carl Shumway, president of the Shumway Advertising agency in Boston. He authored an article for the *American Ski Annual* on technique, "The High Speed Turn," with Otto Schniebs in 1934 and filmed an early Dartmouth Outing Club race down Hell's Highway on Mt. Moosilauke, using the film to persuade the National Ski Association (now named the United States Ski and Snowboard Association) to sanction a National Championship Downhill in the winter of 1933. He participated in devising the rules that guided United States Eastern Amateur Ski Association (USEASA) competitions for years; he also created instructional films and co-authored a book in 1932 with Otto Schniebs, *Modern Ski Technique*, that helped inspire and instruct legions of skiers in the early 1930s. Through friendships with ski industry manufactures like B. F. Moore and Harold Hirsch, president of White Stag, he influenced the design for ski clothes and ski bindings.[2] In addition to playing an instrumental role in securing a place for my father at Dartmouth, he produced a playful film of Dad skiing on pine needles one fall that was widely distributed at the time and revived with a showing at the Telluride Film Festival in the early 1990s.[3]

Budd Schulberg '36

Far more famous for his novels (*What Makes Sammy Run, The Harder They Fall, The Disenchanted*, etc.) and for his Oscar-winning screen play for the 1954 film *On the Waterfront*, Budd nonetheless helped stoke popular interest in skiing for vast numbers of Americans who were just learning about the sport when he collaborated with F. Scott Fitzgerald on the screenplay for the Hollywood film *Winter Carnival*, a light comedy set at Dartmouth.[4]

Much less well known is the fact that it was Budd Schulberg who was sent to arrest legendary German filmmaker Leni Riefenstahl shortly after the end of World War II. In gripping detail, *The Washington Post* writer Philip Kennicott described the scene:

"He [Schulberg] was in Germany, assembling a film to be used at the Nuremberg trials as evidence against the Nazis. Riefenstahl knew where the skeletons were. He needed her to identify the seemingly endless gallery of faces on film that he had been collecting. So Schulberg, dressed in his military uniform, drove to her chalet on a lake in Bavaria, knocked on her door, and told the panicked artist that she was coming with him. 'I tried to calm her down,' said Schulberg, 'but she said, "You know, I'm really so misunderstood. I'm not political."' It is an argument that would define the rest of her life, and no one would ever believe."[5]

(Editor's Note: In the small world of skiing and Dartmouth, Leni Riefenstahl is the same woman mentioned in Chapter I as having had a relationship before WW II with Dartmouth coaching legend, Walter Prager, at the time she directed perhaps the most widely known of Nazi propaganda movies, *Triumph of the Will*, which featured all the leaders of Nazi Germany from Adolph Hitler on down and involved Prager being credited as an Assistant Director.)

Dr. David Bradley '38 and Steve Bradley '39

In a letter dated September 23rd, 1936, written to his mother, my father describes the early days in his life-long friendship with David and Steve Bradley:

"I have found a brilliant scholar and friend this year—a junior—who likes sketching as I do. His brother is crazy about photography and both of them are on the ski team—the Bradley brothers by name. David and Steve are our [Dad and his brother Jack's] best friends up here I guess."

The four of them remained friends through the rest of their long lives.

In 1937 the two Bradley brothers joined Dad on a trip to New Zealand and Australia organized by Jay Laughlin, an enthusiastic skier from Harvard, to promote skiing "down under." Jay and my father would later work together to develop Alta. David wrote about the trip in the February 1941 issue of *SKI Magazine* and later gave a lecture on the trip in Hanover. My father and Steve, as Dad describes it in his biography, *The Man on the Medal*, "both had Leicas and were camera nuts, as excited about shooting pictures as we were about anything else. Wherever we were we would go into the bathroom at night and develop the negatives we'd shot during the day." He continued: "One action shot that Steve would take of me, skiing near the Ball Hut on the South Island in New Zealand, turned out to be the model for the medals that were awarded for U.S. National Championships."[6]

At Dartmouth, David Bradley served as Captain of 1938 Ski Team, won the 1938 National Nordic Combined Championship, and was named to the 1940 Olympic Team. Because the 1940 games were cancelled due to the outbreak of World War II, he would never get to compete in the Olympics, but he did participate in the 1960 Olympics as Team Manager of the US Nordic Ski Team.

While he is widely known to the global anti-nuclear community as the author of the highly influential early study on the effects nuclear radiation at the Bikini atoll, *No Place To Hide*, published in 1948. David Bradley also brought his considerable intellect (*Summa Cum Laude* graduate) and writing skills (English major) to the world of skiing as the co-author (with **Dr. Ralph Miller '55**, former Olympic skier, and **Al Merrill**, Dartmouth and Olympic Nordic coach) to their best-selling book, *Expert Skiing*, published in 1960.[7]

David remained active in the ski world throughout his life, writing at least six articles for *SKI Magazine*, including a beautifully written two-part essay on the college's great 1930s ski team titled "Dartmouth in the Old Days". He also devoted considerable time to renovating 66 ski jumps in New England and to coaching jumping for Hanover's Ford Sayre junior ski program for 28 years. In 1985 David was inducted into the US National Ski and Snowboard Hall of Fame.

Sharing a passion skiing and photography, my father and Steve teamed up—one would ski and the other photograph, and then they would switch—to create some of the most iconic ski photographs of the 1930-40s during their trip to New Zealand in 1937, and then as collaborators on two films for Sun Valley in 1940. The first, *Sun Valley Ski Chase*, drew international attention to skiing, winning first prize at the Cortina Sports Film Festival in 1941 in Italy. The second, *Sun Valley Holidays*, helped the Union Pacific railroad generate excitement across the nation about skiing in general and at Sun Valley in particular.

John Caldwell '50

A member of the 1952 Olympic Nordic Combined team and coach of two US Olympic and World Championship Nordic teams, John Caldwell wrote what John Fry, longtime editor of *SKI Magazine*, describes as the best- selling specialized ski book ever published in the United States, *The Cross-Country Ski Book*. It has been published in more than eight editions and has sold more than half a million copies between 1964 and 1987. The book fueled the explosive growth of this Nordic sport in the 1970s.[8]

Brooks Dodge, Jr. '51

Renowned as a ski racer (4th in 1956 Olympic Slalom), Brooks Dodge was also an avid pioneering student of ski technique. Brooks grew up in Gilford Notch, NH, with Tuckerman Ravine as his backyard. His fascination with technique showed up as a teenager when he devised a two-pole turn for skiing the steep, tight gullies of Tuckerman's.[9] Between 1944 and 1952, using his new techniques for extreme skiing, Brooks notched multiple first ski descents in Tuckerman Ravine, including such classic "no-fall" lines as Dodge's Drop and Cathedral that feature dogleg turns, rock obstacles, and pitches exceeding 50 degrees.[10]

In 1956, upon his return from the Olympics at Cortina, Italy, Brooks and a photographer from *SKI Magazine* climbed up to the ravine where Brooks demonstrated the new Austrian technique of linked turns called "wedeln" for an article titled "Ski the New Way." Variations on wedeln went on to become the standard for a generation of skiers. While the turn that Brooks demonstrated involved less reverse shoulder than the pure Austrian version, it was, as John Fry wrote in his book, *The Story of Modern Skiing*, "breathtakingly modern...It wasn't a turn anyone was typically doing. It was something of the future..., something that might appear in a magazine published twenty, thirty, or even forty years later."[11] The article was published in the October 1956 issue of *SKI Magazine*.

In 1965, it was Brooks Dodge who brought the very first clients to Han Gmoser as he was launching Canadian Mountain Holidays in the Bugaboo Mountains of British Columbia, the first commercial heli-skiing operation in North America.[12] The flying techniques and skiing skills honed in the Bugaboos have fostered an increasing participation in big mountain extreme skiing ventures such as those described in Eric Lambert's article at the end of this chapter, and now taking place in remote ranges across the world.

Tom Corcoran '54

Tom's contributions to the development of skiing cover a remarkably broad spectrum of the sport: an Olympic skier at the 1960 Games, where he finished 4th in the GS; a columnist for *SKI Magazine* that John

Fry, his editor, describes as "a very influential voice in skiing in the 1960's, an opinion molder"; and a ski area developer who transformed Waterville Valley, NH, from a local family ski area into a world-class destination resort. As both an English major at Dartmouth and a graduate of the Harvard Business School, he had an exceptional understanding of the synergistic relationship between exposure in the media and the growth of businesses like ski areas.

The friendships he forged with sports writers as an undergraduate continued to flourish when he joined their ranks as a columnist for *SKI Magazine* and began his career as a ski area developer. At the Aspen Skiing Company, he was given responsibility for overseeing the feasibility studies for developing Snowmass. In that capacity he organized Snow-cat tours of the Big Burn for, among others, members of the press. He confided in me that he had a secret weapon for creating a positive impression on his visitors: bowls of wonderful homemade soups that were heavily laced with sherry. "Worked like a charm every time." He was also given the job of handling the huge media contingents covering the Kennedy family visits to Aspen. The Kennedy's love for skiing generated cover stories in popular magazines like *Life*, publicity that helped fuel the explosive growth of the sport in the 1960s.

At Waterville Valley, Tom followed the example set by my father at Aspen when he brought the World Championships there in 1950. Tom hosted eleven World Cup competitions at Waterville so that the global media and their audiences of prospective skiers would recognize that, as Tom put it, "if this place is good enough to put on World Cup events, then maybe it's good enough for me to go skiing there." [13]

In 1968, when John Fry came up with the idea of a National Standard Race, known as NASTAR, he asked Tom, who was at the time the magazine's racing editor, how he would structure it. Tom suggested they have local pacesetters work off of a percentage of a national standard set by a recognized racer.[14] Thanks to John and Tom, more than six million racers at 120 ski resorts have had the opportunity to test themselves against some of the world's top skiers since that first NASTAR race at Waterville Valley in 1967.[15]

Tom didn't just stop with traditional competitions. In 1971 Doug Pfeiffer, Editor of *Skiing* magazine, asked Tom who he thought the best skiers on the mountain were. Tom said: "The racers, of course." Doug replied, "What about all those guys on the other side of the mountain skiing the bumps and getting air?" They agreed they needed to hold a contest to see who was the best, and so the first freestyle contest was born at Waterville Valley in March of 1971.[16] The rest, as they say, is history. And Tom Corcoran had a hand in creating a lot of skiing history.

Dr. Ralph Miller, Jr. D'55, DMS '59

Born and raised in Hanover, Ralph was introduced to Dartmouth, skiing, and medicine at a very young age by his father, **Dr. Ralph Miller, Sr., Class of 1924**, who was an avid skier and a professor at the Dartmouth Medical School. Ralph said that by "the age of two I was walking around on a little pair of skis. But, my parents tell me, at the age of four my passion for skiing suffered a setback. I fell down on my tail early in the winter and gave up for the whole season." Such are the early disappointments of youth. "But, of course, I started up again the next winter, at age five, and by the age of twenty-five I had skied *a lot* of winters, skiing virtually every day of every winter plus the better part of the three summers spent training in Portillo, Chile."

For many of us who follow in our father's footsteps, their ways of thinking influence how we approach and describe our own challenges. Ralph agrees that he brought to skiing generally, and to ski racing in particular, the same analytical thought processes that he inherited from his father and that later guided his medical research in endocrinology. For instance, here is his description of his world record-setting speed run in Portillo, Chile, in 1955 when he was clocked at 109 mph, a record that stood for fifteen years, an experience shared with readers of the December 1955 issue of *SKI Magazine*.

"It just seemed like the logical extension of the run we had done the day before. Nobody had run it from the top, and it seemed like the logical

Ralph Miller '55 was one of many skiing legends who grew up in the unique ski mad world of Hanover, NH.

thing to do. It wasn't terrifying or intimidating. I just went as far up the hill as I could go. That's the only reason I went faster. It's the most logical reason."

The full story of Ralph's amazing speed record in Chile is more fully outlined by Stephen Waterhouse in an article at the end of Chapter XIII.

In 1957, before entering Dartmouth Medical School, Ralph wrote the Alpine Skiing section for a book titled *Expert Skiing*, with co-authors Dr. Dave Bradley (on jumping) and Al Merrill (on cross-country). Asked why he devoted the time to the book as he was preparing for medical school, he said:

"I felt that I was leaving skiing and I wanted to put down what I had learned and some of my ideas. I was interested in the evolution of technique. When I started skiing, people were skiing Arlberg technique. I was influenced by Emile Allais, the great French racer who was in Portillo all three summers I was there. He had his own technique. The [then] modern technique from Austria called Wedeln was showing us that if you stood on a little knoll and spun your shoulders one way, your skis would go the other way. That seemed to be a very efficient way to turn. I wanted to convey all that." [17]

Amazingly enough, between January 1958 and February 1960, while he was in medical school and in his residency, Ralph wrote at least eight articles for *SKI Magazine*, educating readers with his scientifically oriented insights into ski techniques with articles like "How to Pre-Jump", "You Can Ski on Ice", and "More Speed In Slalom". From 1960 on, Ralph focused his attention on medical research and teaching at the Walter Reed Army Medical Center in Washington, DC, Stanford University in California, and the University of Kentucky in Lexington.[18]

Roger Brown '57 and Barry Corbet '58

As a ski mountaineer, Barry Corbet, like his mentor Bill Briggs, could see the possible where others saw only the impossible. Standing at the top of Jackson Hole's Teton Village ski lift, looking into a steep, narrow couloir, he saw a ski run where the owners saw only a cliff. When he showed them it could be skied, they named it after him.

As a filmmaker, Barry, and his partner Roger Brown, likewise created films like no one had seen before. They opened their groundbreaking film, *Ski the Outer Limits*, with a spectacular slow motion sequence showing Tom LeRoy and Herman Gollner somersaulting, appropriately enough, into Corbet's Coulier. The two of them attracted a generation of skiers to the sport with their spectacular films that were shown again and again in skier's hangouts like The Slope in Aspen and Vail, both founded by **Ron Riley '65**. As John Fry said, "Roger and Barry took smaller things that were happening in skiing and made them more important by using them in their films." [19]

Richard Taylor '59

As Brooks Dodge, Tom Corcoran, and Ralph Miller look at skiing through the lenses of their Alpine racing experiences, so Dick Taylor views the ski experience from his vantage point as an international cross-country and biathlon competitor. Like them, he shares his views with fellow enthusiasts by writing. He serves as Contributing Editor to *The Master Skier*, a publication for cross-country racers, and he authored the book *No Pain, No Gain*, an intensive look at the culture of cross-country skiing in the United States. Having served as Captain of the 1959 Dartmouth Ski Team, member of the 1960 Olympic team, and Captain of the 1964 Olympic Cross-Country Ski Team, Dick draws on his experiences as a competitor to take a fresh look at the development of the athlete over the long term, focusing primarily on the physiological development.[20]

Johannes von Trapp '63

One of the catalytic events that sparked the phenomenal growth of cross-country skiing in the United States was Johannes von Trapp's idea in 1968 to offer cross-country skiing as an additional winter amenity at the fabled Trapp Family Lodge in Stowe VT. He was the first person to recognize that guests would be willing to pay for professionally prepared cross-country skiing trails in the same way they paid for skiing at alpine skiing resorts.[21] In the early days, he hired former cross country Olympian **Ned Gillette '67** to run the ski center for him. While working for Johannes, Ned wrote a number of articles on cross-country equipment and technique for *Cross-Country Ski Magazine*, augmented with his own photographs, that helped launch him as a writer/photographer.[22] Ned's articles in the magazine combined, with Johannes's advertising and personal promotional efforts for the resort, would help fan the wildfire of enthusiasm for the evolving sport, and by 1975 there were 23 professionally operated facilities with prepared tracks available in the United States.[23] Prior to the Trapp-Gillette partnership there had been none. There is a more complete article on the cross country course at the Trapp Family Lodge in Chapter VII.

H. Richard Isaacson '64

Public fascination with sports often begins with a hero. When Jean-Claude Killy won all three Alpine Gold medals at the 1968 Olympics, he became an instant global hero. Powering that explosion of public visibility was the unique marketing machine, International Marketing Group (IMG), that was created by Mark

Rick Issacson '64 and Jean-Claude Killy were frequently together.

McCormack to promote marketing endorsements for golfers Arnold Palmer, Jack Nicklaus, and Gary Player.

One of the operators wielding the marketing levers on McCormack's machine was former Dartmouth ski team member Rick Isaacson. Rick was the agent responsible for developing the licensing agreements for Killy. In promoting him, Rick was instrumental in increasing the global awareness of skiing among large numbers of people all over the world who had never before thought much about the sport. Working with McCormack, Rick helped to devise many of the sports marketing strategies that have lifted many top professional athletes in all sports into the financial stratosphere.[24] In an article at the end of this chapter, Rick outlines the "Killy effect" on televised skiing.

Charles Lobitz '65

Just as Dick Taylor analyzed the physiological aspects of skiing, so Dr. Charles Lobitz studied the psychological facets of the sport. Charles melded his skiing experiences, both as a member of the 1963-1965 Dartmouth Alpine ski team and as coach of the Stanford and the University of Oregon ski teams, with his experiences as a practicing clinical and sports psychologist to explore how mind and body interact within the dynamics of peak performance. He deals with this theme in two collaborative books: *Skiing with Your Head Down*, written in 1977 with Dr. Leonard A. Loudis, and *Skiing out of Your Mind*, co-authored with Dr. Loudis and Dr. Ken Singer in 1986.

Charles and his co-authors were among the pioneers in the field of sports psychology that swept through professional and amateur athletics in the 1970s and '80s. Inspired by the wisdom of Gaius Sallustius Crispus, who wrote in 40 B.C: "All of our power lies in both mind and body; we employ the mind to rule, the body to serve," [25] Charles and his co-authors "show us ... how to perform at peak performance levels by choice, not chance".[26] There are now millions of sports enthusiasts who have benefited from works published by sports psychologists like Charles, whether their passion is carving clean turns on the slopes or crushing a drive at their favorite golf course.

Heinz Kluetmeier '65

Heinz was one of four professional photographers to emerge from the Dartmouth Class of 1965 and graced with the ability and opportunity to reach millions of people with their images. Virtually all of them celebrated skiing in the mass-market publications for which they were working, helping spread the popularity of skiing in the 1960s and '70s. After serving as chief photographer for the Dartmouth yearbook, *Aegis*, and as a stringer for the news wire services as an undergraduate, Heinz landed a position at *Sports Illustrated* shortly after graduation. For more than forty years as a staff photographer, including periodic stints as Director of Photography, Heinz has gotten the magazine's legions of sports fans excited about skiing with his coverage of more than ten winter Olympics and countless World Cup events.

Heinz also applied his talents toward helping skiers learn the sport by creating the photographs for two books: *Sports Illustrated Skiing: Six Ways to Reach Your Skiing Potential* by Tim Petrick in 1978, and *Skiing* by Gary Paulsen, Roger Barrett, and Willis Wood in 1980.

Dewitt Jones '65

Shortly after graduation, along with classmates **Chris Knight '65** and **Dick Durrance '65**, Dewitt Jones was fortunate enough to find himself not only taking photographs but creating films for *National Geographic*'s 30 million readers. In stories, films, and lectures on Robert Frost and John Muir, Jones shared with international audiences the beauty of cross-country skiing in the Sierra Mountains of California and the White Mountains of New England.

In creating photographs for the book *Robert Frost: A Tribute to the Source*, Dewitt worked with and photographed David Bradley '38 who had agreed to write the text for the book. After a day spent touring the snow-covered fields of New England, Dewitt asked David what he wanted to write about Frost; David answered, "I want to tell people what they need to know." When he turned in his manuscript, the editor called back after reading the 35,000-word text to say, utterly astonished, that he had cut only three words. David's response: "I guess I told them too much." [27]

Chris Knight '65

Although Chris produced photographs for four *National Geographic* articles before devoting himself full time to documentary filmmaking, none of them included skiing. However, together with Dick Durrance '65, he photographed a story on skiing in the Tatra Mountains of Czechoslovakia for *SKI Magazine* in 1966. He also took the pictures for a number of children's books written by his wife, Kathryn Lasky Knight, which featured skiing and helped introduce several generations of kids to the sport.

Dick Durrance '65

As a boy raised in Aspen, Colorado, by a father who was a legend in the ski world and a mother who was an alternate on the 1940 Olympic ski team, it is easy to assume that I should have been a *really* good racer. I was talented enough to at least dream about following my parents to the Olympics—twice Skimeister at the Dartmouth Carnival, Captain of the 1965 ski team, two-time All-American. However, the next rung, international competition, proved to be beyond my reach. That disappointment proved to be a blessing. I learned, as we all must at some point in our lives, that when the limits of our abilities get defined, we often have to adjust our dreams. One afternoon, while working on an English paper in Baker Library, I came across a book by the great American photographer Ansel Adams, *Eloquent Light*. As I turned the pages, staring at those beautiful black and while landscapes, I realized that his world—the world of photography—could be my world too. I instinctively understood images, another gift from my parents who were both photographers. In that moment I knew that I wanted to spend my life creating photographs.

Upon graduation, thanks to an article on a canoe trip down the Danube River that Chris Knight and I had photographed for *National Geographic*, I was lucky enough to land an assignment from John Jerome, Editor of *Skiing* magazine, to create an impressionistic photo essay showing what ski racing felt like. The story was a rare chance to meld my love for ski racing with a passion for photography. Being a staff photographer for *National Geographic* in Aspen, on the Appalachian Trail, and amid the Rocky Mountains offered me the opportunity to share my passion for skiing with an enormous readership.

Dick Durrance II '65 speaking at Dartmouth-Tuck Winter CarniVAIL - 2009.

Ned Gillette '67

After competing in the 1968 Olympic cross-country championships, Ned combined his love for skiing and passion for photography to create a unique career as a professional adventurer. Alumni Bill Briggs and Barry Corbet skied epic routes down big mountains mainly because the possibilities were there and just waiting for someone to ski them. Making a living from their adventures was not foremost on their minds. Ned, on the other hand, fashioned himself into a professional adventurer who created remarkable journeys that were designed to intrigue book and magazine editors and their publications' audiences. And they did. His expeditions to traverse the immense Ellesmere Island in the Canadian Arctic, circumnavigate Mt. McKinley and Mt.

Everest on skis, and to ski from the summit of Argentina's Aconcagua (the highest mountain in the Western Hemisphere at 22,834 feet) and from that of Mustagh Ata in the Pamir Mountains of Tibet (at the time, the highest mountain [26,750 feet] that had ever been skied from the summit), expanded the perception of what skiing—and life itself—could be for untold millions of readers of magazines like *National Geographic* and *Outside* magazine.

"I don't undertake these things to please my fellow skiers or my fellow climbers or my fellow rowers. I do them to please myself and, I like to think, to give something back to the man in the street, the guy who sits at a desk and maybe isn't doing what he wants with his life. If anything, I'd just like to think I remind people that it's possible to do what you want. If adventuring is about anything, that's what it's about." — Ned Gillette, *Outside*, December 1986

In 1998, Ned was needlessly killed by bandits in the Haramosh Valley of Pakistan while trekking with his wife, Olympic skier Susie Patterson, in a remote area near Nanga Parbat, the world's 10th highest mountain. Susie was severely injured but survived the attack. After Ned's murder, Kevin Fedarko wrote in a piece for *Outside* magazine: "One of the most successful adventurers of his era, Ned Gillette spent a lifetime courting the edge of risk and disaster. The thing he never expected, however, was to die in his sleeping bag." [28]

John Russell '68

Of the many Dartmouth photographers who celebrated skiing in pictures, one towers above all the others in terms of his impact on the development of skiing: John Russell. As John Fry, longtime editor of SKI Magazine, said: "John, more than anyone, was the first to define ski racing photography. I got [from him] action pictures that just blew your mind, images that I had never seen before. It was a combination of intelligence and a mastery of equipment."

John, unlike most of those featured in this book, skied only once while at Dartmouth. As a member of the swim team, he was officially discouraged from risking his limbs on the ski slopes. However, one spring after the swim season was over, he hiked up to Tuckerman Ravine with some college buddies –wearing *lederhosen*—to try his hand at skiing. By the time he got back to the bottom, after throwing body checks all the way down Hillman's Highway to keep from flying into the trees, his legs looked like hamburger from their repeated close encounters with granular snow. Standing in the parking lot, wiping the blood off of his legs, he vowed to all within hearing range: "I will never do this sport again." And, as he said, "I was pretty good to my word."

Indeed, the fact that he didn't ski helped him land his first job after finishing up his service in the Air National Guard. Cal Morris, the West Coast sales representative for *SKI Magazine*, put him in touch with a guy introducing a new sport called "ski bobbing" in which you rode down the mountain on a rig that looked a lot like a bicycle except it was mounted on skis instead of wheels. The head of the company hired John specifically because he didn't like to ski, perhaps anticipating more productive hours; yet when it was a beautiful day, John would be out there riding his ski-bob obviously having great fun. What better way to promote the product!

Traveling around the ski world promoting the ski-bob, John found that "It seemed like everywhere I turned there were all of these Dartmouth guys." Through his brother, who was building the Head Tennis division, he met **Clay Freeman '58**, a rep for Head Skis. When John happened to meet Clay at Lake Tahoe doing a shoot with the great French ski champion Jean-Claude Killy, Clay let him grab a couple of shots of Killy. John also ran into Ned Gillette, who was helping to get Copper Mountain started, and Roger Brown, who saw a video of John jumping his ski-bob off a cornice and asked him to repeat the feat so he could shoot it for one of his films.

When the ski-bob company went bankrupt, John moved to Breckenridge, CO, where Roger let him tag along and shoot production stills while Roger filmed Killy for ski clothing manufacturer Mighty Mac.

John continued doing production stills for Roger, quickly building a portfolio of ski pictures that convinced John Fry to hire him for *SKI Magazine*. John Russell went on to shoot skiing photos for the magazine, as well as advertising images for major ski industry manufactures, for twenty years, establishing the style and the standards that guided the next generation of ski photographers and "the look" of skiing that helped attract a whole new generation of skiers to the sport.

Russell has philosophically reflected: "Looking back, we realize we're not self-made men and women. Tons of people, the majority of them Dartmouth graduates, helped me along my way. And I in turn have helped a few who followed." Many of us who worked on this book and those who are reading it probably have similar stories to tell. Perhaps we are paying forward; perhaps paying back. But we are all benefiting. It is a wonderful exchange.[29]

Jeff Leich '71

Listening to his father's stories about skiing in the first down-mountain race at Mt. Moosilauke in 1927 and spending years as a "career ski bum"—operating a ski shop and directing a ski patrol—probably did as much for Jeff Leich as did his Dartmouth education to prepare him for his current position as the Executive Director of the New *England Ski Museum* (NESM) in Franconia, NH.

Like his father, he loves to share historical stories with young people. One of the most interesting tales he shares is the one uncovered by the New England Lost Ski Areas Project of the more than 592 small and medium-sized New England ski areas that are now gone. Jeff featured the project as the museum's 2008 exhibit and wrote a three-part front-page story for the Journal of the New England Ski Museum. As he says: "I don't think anybody had any idea that there were that many areas that are now gone."

As custodian of one of the nation's most comprehensive collections of books, posters, photographs, manuscripts and films related to skiing, Jeff is now striving to locate and preserve the personal papers of ski pioneers that remain in family hands. "I would love to be able to preserve and share some of the surprising gems hidden away in those dusty boxes and trunks. The information would, I am sure, fill gaps in our knowledge of what went on in the early days of skiing." [30]

As the digitization of information opened broad new channels of communication, the media options available have changed extensively. But the message about their passion for skiing that Dartmouth people are communicating on their websites and blogs, LinkedIn pages, and tweets on Twitter remain pretty much the same. Not to be left out of the conversation, the NESM maintains a web site at www.skimuseum.org.

Tim Kelley '79

Tim Kelley contributed to the 1976 Dartmouth Ski Team NCAA victory with a 3rd in cross-country as a freshman and then raced for the US National Team. In a change of competitive venue, he went on to organize, compete in, and win the first human-powered race on the famous 1149-mile Iditarod Dogsled Course. His current passion is opening up new cross-country treks all across Alaska.

In 1998 he launched a website formally titled *Alaska Performance Backcountry Skiing* (www.crust.outlookalaska.com) which he describes as a skier's resource for exploring south-central Alaska on cross-country (x-c) skis. His website offers far more than ideas on gear, weather factors, and tips for trips; he also celebrates the beauty found in his distant corner of the nation and shares his passion for skiing it, inspiring others to follow in his tracks. As he says:

"I love Alaska. And I love adventuring in Alaska. I want to show people that winter x-c skiing adventures can be local, plentiful and cheap. You don't need expensive backcountry or x-c racing ski gear, you don't have to travel far, and you don't have to commit lots of time for skiing adventures. You just have to grab the x-c skis you have, drive out of Anchorage and ... open your eyes!" [31]

Tim Kelley '79 out on the trail in the Alaskan wilderness.

Bill Hunt '80

As is true for many of the people featured in this book—particularly Dick Durrance '39, who spent his teenage years in Garmisch, Germany in the early 1930s, and Brooks Dodge, who was raised at the trailhead for Tuckerman Ravine in the 1940s—Bill Hunt was at the right place at the right time. As a result, he emerged as one of the nation's earliest extreme snowboarders. At Dartmouth, his main passions were rock climbing and mountaineering. When he arrived in Alta, Utah, in the early 1980s as snowboarding was really catching fire, it was natural for him to take his board off-piste and high into the mountains he loved. He went on in the late 1980s and early 1990s to pioneer the first snowboard descents into some of the most dramatic chutes in Little Cottonwood Canyon: South Face of Mt. Superior, Pinball Alley and The Wave Arete on Mt. Superior, The Pfeifferhorn, The Hogum Sliver, The Ice Chute in the Hogum cliffs, the Shooting Gallery, and Hellgate Cliffs. As he did many of these descents solo and prior to the advent of the web, he made little effort to document them or share them with anyone. Now, like Tim Kelley, he posts blogs featuring pictures and stories from his adventures online so others can share in his love for extreme skiing.[32] (www.gravityfields.blogspot.com)

Lisa Feinberg Densmore '83

Lisa is a rarity: she is one of the few Dartmouth skiers to develop a career in television. While she excelled from the beginning as a producer of and host for shows celebrating skiing—earning three Emmys— Lisa would be the first to say her career in TV came about purely by accident. However it started, she shared her passion for skiing with television's vast audience before expanding her beat into traveling the world covering dozens of other sports and outdoor pursuits for NBC, CBS, PBS, TNT, OLN, A&E, the Travel Channel, and the Weather Channel. She would reach another audience when she described her passion for and insights about racing in her book, *Ski Faster: Lisa Feinberg Densmore's Guide to High Performance Skiing and Racing*, published in 1999. Hers is a wonderful story that says much about how Dartmouth graduates, with their well-rounded education, manage to acquire the skills they need to share their passion for skiing through a variety of media.[33] Lisa comments on television contributions to skiing in an article at the end of this chapter.

Diana Golden Brosnihan '84

After retiring from her remarkable ski racing career, Diana became a motivational speaker and brought to audiences the energy and commitment to excellence with which she had approached ski racing. She became internationally famous for her ability to inspire crowds and traveled the world sharing her passion for skiing and delivering her positive message of overcoming obstacles with steady persistence and solid commitment to goals. Unfortunately, the cancer that claimed her leg when she was twelve came back for her when she was only thirty-eight. But what she accomplished in her short life stands as her personal inspiration for all of us to make the most of the time we have left to us.[34]

Bill Hudson '88

Bill's stellar early racing career, one that included competing in the 1988 Olympics, never fully recovered from a crash so spectacular it is listed among Skiernet.com's *Most Memorable Runs*. Bill was racing in Kitzbühel's Hahnenkam downhill when he lost control on the fabled *Mausfalle* pitch (the Mousetrap) and flew completely over the safety fence into the trees, breaking his shoulder, arm, and rib, and injuring his lung.[35]

But Bill did recover enough to ski in segments of three Warren Miller's films: *Snowriders*, *Snowriders 2*, and *Freeriders*. Segments were filmed in Kazakhstan, Norway, Scotland, and on Mt. Hood, Oregon. As he said, "I had a very good time 'skiing professionally' without the pressures of competition, traveling and skiing in places I would have otherwise never experienced." And by skiing for Warren Miller's cameras, Bill excited the multitudes who view Warren's many films about the exotic places to which more and more skiers are now traveling.[36]

David Page '90

While "old media" like magazines and newspapers are under pressure from "new media" like blogs and Facebook, there are still Dartmouth men and women producing stories and pictures about skiing for the medium of print. David Page has written about skiing Death Valley's highest peak for *Men's Journal*, about skiing California's "14-ers" (mountains over 14,000 feet) with freeride mountaineer Chris Davenport for *Backcountry* and *Eastside* magazines, about spring skiing for *The New York Times*, and about historic CCC ski huts (and other things) in his award-winning book, *Yosemite & the Southern Sierra Nevada: A Complete Guide*.[37]

Jamie Meiselman '91

An English major, Jamie combined his knowledge of snowboarding with his writing skills to land an internship with a brand new publication founded in San Diego by fellow "boarders." He spent spring semester of his sophomore year at the newly-formed *TransWorld Snowboarding Magazine* that would quickly become the "bible" of the snowboarding industry; and while still an intern, he became the founding editor of *TransWorld Snowboarding Business*, the trade book variant of the consumer magazine.

Upon graduation, Jamie spent a year at Telluride, CO as a snowboard instructor and freelance writer before moving to New York City to write for *Skiing Magazine*. Within three months, he was back at *TransWorld* in San Diego as publisher of their trade magazines. He became Managing Editor of TransWorld Snowboarding during a period of tremendous growth for the sport and the magazine. He has since taken on another entrepreneurial role in snowboarding, but his writing will continue.

Charlotte Moats '03

Although a very successful junior racer (winner of the 1995 Junior Olympics slalom), Charlotte is among the first Dartmouth students to switch from conventional ski racing to compete in international freeskiing competitions while still an undergraduate at Dartmouth.

She is so successful at freeskiing—two World Heli Challenge Downhill wins and a victory at the 24 Hours of Aspen—she is now a professional big mountain freeskier, sponsored by Columbia Sportswear Company, and specializing in stunt work for film, television, and print media. As one of today's leading extreme skiers, seen in every conceivable media category, she is a role model attracting young girls to follow her to higher peaks, in the mountains and in their lives. As she says in her video on the Columbia website, "I'm living my dream." [38]

Erik Lambert, MALS '07

With a background in special-interest online journalism, and having edited a mountaineering website (www.alpinist.com), Erik knows better than most that the Internet has created a world beyond books, magazines and film: "Diverse online communities can spring up overnight. They devour special-interest sports news from media sites and blogs—most of which is unavailable in any other form—then banter incessantly. By shrinking the world, the Internet allows isolated pockets of interested users, like Dartmouth skiers, to connect regularly, share information and generate buzz, for free." [39]

FINAL THOUGHTS

The popularizing of skiing has been achieved thru the actions of ski interested media folks everywhere, particularly many members of the greater Dartmouth family. Sometimes it has been the publicity generated by their own exploits, and sometimes it has involved their own work in various types of media to highlight the exploits of others. In the five articles that follow, several involved contributors provide more details on some of the subjects already mentioned. Eric Lambert discusses the many noteworthy Dartmouth folks involved in aspects of extreme skiing over the past 100 years; Rick Moulton discusses the making of ski movies and the contributions of a select group; Rick Isaacson shines the spotlight on the important contribution of one leading ski industry celebrity (Jean-Claude Killy); and Lisa Densmore provides some further comments on the combination of television and skiing. Finally, Meredith Scott '96, Director of the Vermont Ski Museum, highlights some current important Dartmouth keepers of historical knowledge on skiing. Appendix 11 provides brief details on the major ski historical organizations across the US. All these historical centers will have relevant commentary on the greater Dartmouth family's contribution to their area of interest. I fervently hope that this book will further popularize this sport that has so intrigued us all and create more opportunities for us to connect regularly though the many channels now available to share memories and dreams from our years as skiers.

***

EVOLVING THE IMPOSSIBLE: THE IMPACT OF THE EXTREME

By Erik Lambert MALS '07

Bill Briggs '54 was alone, armed with an ice hammer. His skis poked high above his pack as he kicked crampons into steep alpine ice. From snow-capped gneiss he peered down to Wyoming's Teepe

Glacier, a thousand feet below. Though exhausted, he was only a few irreversible moves from the upper snowfields of the Grand Teton.

He summited, stepped into his skis, pointed the tips downhill, and made about 20 turns on the east face, then eased over the 60-degree lip of the Stettner Couloir. Skis still on, he slung a chockstone—a boulder wedged between two walls—and rappelled through spindrift. Below waited three friends who had seen him to the top of the couloir. As they continued to descend on foot, he schussed off, ecstatic, for the verdant valleys of Jackson Hole.

Most would argue that North American ski mountaineering was born on that day, June 16, 1971. Though widespread interest didn't catch until the late 1970s, Bill is quick to point out that his winter mountaineering exploits began two decades earlier at Dartmouth.

Bill learned to ski in his hometown of Augusta, Maine. At Dartmouth in the early 1950s, he met others gripped by mountains: his roommate **Mike Marx '54**, **Barry Corbet '58** and **Roberts "Bob" French '56**. In summer, they climbed rock; in winter, they explored the college's 4,802-foot Mt. Moosilauke and the iconic and always challenging Mt. Washington on skis. "Out there on our own, looking for adventure," as Bill remembers, these outings became their ski mountaineering foundation.

Bill Briggs '54 is a man of many legends, and singing ski songs is one of those.

Ski mountaineering has captured the interest of many Dartmouth undergraduates over the century past. DOC founder **Fred Harris '11**, **Carl Shumway '13** and **G.S. Foster '13** were early pioneers of both Moosilauke and Washington. Shumway was first to explore Tuckerman Ravine, soon to be the birthplace of high-risk skiing, and today the Northeast's most famous backcountry skiing spot. Two decades after Shumway's reconnaissance, **Charley Proctor '28** and **John Carleton '22** were first to rocket down Tuck's 50-degree headwall. Even before he was a student, **Brooks Dodge '51** pioneered many of Tuck's steep gullies.

In the 1950s, Bill Briggs considered the head-wall "the *piece de resistance* of skiing ability... something that all great skiers wanted to have done to prove their merit." [40] And earning that badge, for the likes of Bill Briggs and Barry Corbet, was just the beginning. Barry's motivated, prolific mountain-craft later took him up and down new routes from the Tetons to Mt. Everest. Most skiers today recognize his name from Jackson Hole's boldest in-bounds ski trail, Corbet's Couloir.

"We were doing more because of Barry," Bill said of his time at college. "His courage, stamina, insight and brilliance were inspirational for all of us, so we went to pushing." [41] Pushing meant matching the feats of mountain legend **Jack Durrance '39**—a prolific climber whose brother, **Dick Durrance '39**, revolutionized American ski racing with his "Tempo Turn."

Skiing, climbing and music have driven Bill for a long time. At Christmastime in 1952, he promised himself to focus all his energy on those three loves. Two months later he was expelled from Dartmouth, but his skiing education had just begun. With a Dartmouth crew in 1959 he made a 100-mile ski traverse in British Columbia's Bugaboos—the first of its kind in North America. He skied what is likely the first or second descent of Mt. Rainier in Washington, and pioneered classic descent lines in the Tetons, like the Skillet Glacier on Mt. Moran and Buck Mountain's east face. But on that June day of 1971, he knew he had skied his own *piece de resistance*, the classic of his era that might never be replicated in prominence and scope.

The morning after, when Bill spotted his tracks from the valley floor, he called in the press. Local skier and co-publisher of the *Jackson Hole News*, Virginia Huidekoper, immediately arranged for photos and a story. As Bill tells it, Virginia took him up in her airplane and gave him the controls; "Don't touch anything," she warned him. They made four passes of the Grand so Virginia could photograph his tracks for an upcoming story. Word spread, eventually reaching *The Denver Post* and *SKI Magazine*. Today, films like *Steep* continue to recognize the importance of his descent. In the film, Steve Casimiro of *Powder Magazine* describes it as this country's "singular, crystallizing moment for big mountain skiing."

Bill transformed Virginia's best photograph into a poster. He sells signed copies out of his Jackson home to this day. The popularity of the poster was one small sign that the skiing industry was entering adolescence in the 1970s. As exploits like Bill's splashed across magazines and television, the popularity of adventure skiing exploded, initiating an upward cycle of demand. Extreme skiing was born.

"At first it's mystique, then it's commonplace, taken as the common experience," Bill said. "The popularity takes the mystery out of it, [and it] becomes a commodity. Ski mountaineering as a sport—gosh, how many people do we have climbing up and skiing? … That's I think a direct result of having skied the Grand, the popularity. But it became known and popular by way of the poster and Virginia's beautiful photograph. It's the aesthetics of that poster which has sold it. Sold it big." [42]

Extreme skiing embraced the sport's flavor of danger. Wildly steep terrain and increasingly complex aerial maneuvers began to outpace ski mountaineering as media accounts fixated on speedy, exhilarating descents rather than slow, grueling ascents. Powder hounds began experimenting with snowboards, the new symbol of the off-piste counterculture. One of them was **Bill Hunt '80**, whose trailblazing accomplishments include numerous first and second descents in Utah's Wasatch backcountry.

No matter the method of descent, those charismatic and talented enough to capture media attention were becoming professionals. **Edward "Ned" Gillette '67**, whose expedition sponsors ran the gamut from Rottefella ski bindings to Camel Cigarettes, defined the word "pro." After winning the NCAA cross-country ski championship for Dartmouth in 1967 and attending the 1968 Olympics with the U.S. Nordic Ski Team, he began a life of adventuring. By the mid-70s, he shared company with the world's finest mountaineers while pitching colossal, outlandish expeditions to corporate sponsors. In 1979 Ned made a ski traverse of Ellesmere Island, Canada's northernmost point of land. The next year he skied Muztagh Ata (24,757') in China's Xinjiang Province, north of Tibet, then the highest summit ever ascended and descended on skis, and made a visionary 300-mile ski traverse of Pakistan's rugged and desolate Karakoram

Range. He concocted the Mt. Everest Grand Circle expedition, which took a 300-mile skiing, climbing and trekking orbit around the mountain in 1981-2. In 1988 he rowed 600 miles across the Drake Passage, some of the roughest seas on earth, from Tierra del Fuego to Antarctica. These unusual adventures landed him in the National Ski Hall of Fame and on the covers of numerous magazines, from *Dartmouth Alumni Magazine* to *Outside*.

Extreme Snowboarder Bill Hunt '80 is barely visible in a crevice in the right-hand corner.

While trekking in Kashmir with his wife in 1998, Ned was brutally and senselessly murdered in his tent. A new generation now carries his flame. Just a teenager in the late 1990s, **Charlotte Moats '03** would curl up by a fire with *Freeze Magazine* and the latest Teton Gravity Research movie. Soon, she was at Dartmouth and starring in those magazines and films.

Charlotte split her college time between classes in Hanover and international freeskiing competitions. In 2000, she won three international events, including the Canadian Freeskiing Championships World Tour and 24 Hours of Aspen (she was the youngest-ever winner of both events). She has two dozen first descents in Alaska and British Columbia and the media has taken notice: Charlotte was featured in four major skiing films and has appeared on 162 pages of 73 American skiing magazines between 2003 and 2007.

Like Ned Gillette, her profession brings her to the world's most magnificent ranges. The price is making it look flashy for the camera. "It's about getting images that are going to get published and make people want to ski," she said. [43] And that, too, has satisfying benefits. By catering to ski media, Charlotte entices others, especially women, to join the community and innovate within the industry.

Tim Kelley '79 is an extreme skier of another sort. He explores Alaska on cross-country racing skis, often for long stretches in remote corners of the state.

In 1990, Tim and a friend, Bob Baker of Fairbanks, skied all 1,149 miles of the famous Iditarod dog sled trail in 23 days in a race against two bikers—and won; this was the first recorded human-powered race of the full length of the Iditarod Trail. In 1993, he became first to cross-country ski the 1,000-mile Yukon Quest trail from Whitehorse to Fairbanks, a 20-day outing.

After having climbed Mount McKinley in 1984, he developed a passion for climbing more of Alaska's still unclimbed peaks, and in 2008 he was awarded the Mountaineering Club of Alaska's Vin Hoeman award for achieving a record 91 documented first ascents, the most by any climber to date. Tim maintains his Alaskan ski blog to share his expertise and passion for Alaskan ski exploration on lightweight cross-country skis.

Although even skiing in-bounds still has its risks, venturing on long treks or out of bounds—especially at Bill's or Charlotte's level—certainly has more. But with advancements in snow science, improvements in gear, and the electronic resources available today, the backcountry has become safer—and more crowded. Born from Bill's Grand Teton descent and the mounting wake of media that followed,

interest has grown and skiers have sub-divided into categories. Terminology has evolved, but today most of what's considered big and bold falls under the term "freeskiing": off-piste descents unencumbered by arbitrary boundaries. The irony is that, at the high end, even those guided by helicopter must gauge conditions, choose a line, and navigate speed and danger as a mountaineer would.

Some of us still climb in order to ski down. **Colin O'Farrell '03, MS '05** led a charge in the Tetons upon graduating. To cap dozens of descents reserved for only the most expert skiers, his descent with **Brian Feinstein '05** of the Otter Body Couloir—perhaps the Grand Teton's most harrowing line to date—marked only the couloir's fifth descent ever. Brian also has skied the Grand Teton's Ford Couloir solo. Successes such as these are the stuff of local blog posts that travel the ski world, forever recorded. The film *Steep* reminds us that four decades ago, before Bill's ski down the Grand Teton, only a handful of skiers even thought to frequent untracked hinterlands. Today, whether beneath Tuckerman Ravine or the Grand Teton, the Dartmouth tribe is lured upward by a hundred years of tales on the wind.

***

DARTMOUTH AND SKI FILMS

By Rick Moulton

Up to and in to the 1930s, skiing in the United States was primarily Nordic, that is, cross-country and jumping. The public view of skiing as portrayed in newspapers, and later by newsreels, was of daredevil ski jumpers, and largely because of these images it appeared that ski jumping was the real ski sport.

The first Alpine ski films to influence Dartmouth (and most Americans) were no doubt those of Dr. Arnold Fanck. Teaming up with the legendary Austrian skier Hannes Schneider, Fanck created the German mountain/ski film genre, producing nearly a dozen films from 1921 to 1933 in which he captured and communicated the excitement and daring of Alpine skiing.

In the 1920s, Dartmouth's **Charley Proctor '28** starred in the annual films taken by Winston Pote and shown in conjunction with his fall lecture circuit. In that same era Charley joined hands with **Johnny Carleton '22** to perform the first tandem jumps off Dartmouth's big Intervale ski jump for delighted cameramen. In early 1930s he made a two-part film

with Rockwell Stevens, a founding partner of Dartmouth Skis, demonstrating ski technique.

By the early 1930s, 16-mm film was available for the home moviemaker. **Jack McCrillis '19** filmed the annual Dartmouth Outing Club Invitational Race held on the old Mt. Moosilauke carriage road. He then joined a delegation headed by Roger Langley, who later served as President of National Ski Association for 17 years; they went to Chicago to get the Nordic-minded National Ski Association to officially recognize Alpine skiing. After seeing his film of the race, they agreed to sanction the first National Downhill Championship which was successfully run by the DOC at Moosilauke in 1933. Jack McCrillis went on to make some instructional films on downhill ski technique with Dartmouth coach Otto Schniebs. In autumn of 1933, Jack sponsored **Dick Durrance '39** for admission to Dartmouth when the young racer moved from Germany to the U.S., and put him up in Newport, New Hampshire, during a postgraduate year. Before the first snow fell, Jack made his most sensational film, a short entitled *Skiing on Pine Needles*, featuring Dick flashing through the trees behind the Newport high school.

The Dartmouth undergraduate experience is never complete without seeing the film of Dr. Schlitz in action at Tuckerman Ravine.

For many years, every incoming Dartmouth class gathered at the Moosilauke Ravine Lodge for several days of orientation. One of their activities was to view the classic film *Dr. Schlitz Climbs Mt. Washington*. This film was made in 1936 by Chris Young who had hired White Mountain filmmaker Winston Pote to help him. Young's script was a parody of a near-tragic account of an early ascent up Mt. Washington by a "Dr. Ball." Casting himself in the lead as the intrepid "Dr. Schlitz", Chris was on Mount Washington filming a scene in which a "Mad Monk" tries to push Schlitz off the headwall but misses and takes the plunge himself. Witnessing this filmmaking from the bowl was national newscaster Lowell Thomas, who was skiing there with his son **Lowell Thomas, Jr. '46**. Taken by this young filmmaker, the elder Thomas volunteered to do the film's narration free of charge.

That film has stood the test of time, and no wonder. Chris Young's surrealist films *Object Lesson*, and then *Subject Lesson*, won the "Best Short Subject Film" category back to back in 1948 and 1949 at the Cannes Film Festival. Chris filmed his wife, 1936 Olympian Mary Bird, during their honeymoon on Switzerland's Mt. Arosa in 1938, and called the film *Ski Girl*. He sold it to Warner Brothers and it opened in Radio City's Music Hall. Young later went to work as Lowell Thomas's cameraman, shooting all over the world and doing the animation for his feature, *Lost Horizon*.

In 1939, **Walter Wanger '15**, **Maurice Rapf '35**, and **Budd Schulberg '36** were involved in the creation of an unsuccessful film based on Dartmouth's Winter Carnival. In that same year, Dick Durrance began his own film career. Renowned as America's best Alpine skier of the 1930s, Dick had grown up in Germany where he was the Junior National Ski Champion in 1933 and had seen Dr. Fanck's films. After graduating from Dartmouth in 1939, he went to Sun Valley and, together with classmate and fellow ski team member **Steve Bradley '39**, produced *Sun Valley Ski Chase*, which closely followed Fanck's model. This scenic 35-mm film was commissioned by Sun Valley's owner, Governor Averill Harriman of New York, and his Union Pacific Railroad to promote the Sun Valley ski area and the soon to be opened ski lifts on Mt. Baldy. The film also starred **Dave Bradley '38** and **Ted Hunter '38** as well as Steve and Dick.

Rick Moulton's parents, Virginia & Dick '49 Moulton, were the models for the 1948 Winter Carnival poster.

Durrance later brought the 1950 FIS Championships to Aspen, Colorado, and co-produced a film of the race, just the first of many Aspen promotional films he was to create. Throughout his career, Durrance produced many mountaineering and ski-related productions. Riding up a chairlift over the Dipsey-Doodle run (named after Dick's unique low, crouching, modified tempo turn) on Aspen's Ajax Mountain with him this writer, Dick grimaced as pain shot through his lower back. "Justifiable," I thought, "I hope I'm still skiing as I approach 80." "How did you hurt it," I asked, expecting to hear of an injury from the years spent racing down narrow trails and catapulting off the biggest ski jumps in the world. "Carrying that damn film equipment!" was his immediate reply.

213

Dick Durrance I '39 and Steve Bradley '39 on location making the legendary Sun Valley Ski Chase movie.

Throughout the 1950s, Dartmouth skiers like **Brooks Dodge '51**, **Tom Corcoran '56**, and **Chick Igaya '57**, were more often out in front of the camera than behind it. Much of that footage would find a paying audience. There came to be a uniquely American travelogue genre, the Ski Lecture film, which thrived in this period. Following a distinct formula, these were shown every fall in person by traveling filmmakers visiting ski clubs, college campuses, and ski towns. John Jay, Warren Miller and, in the 1960s, Dick Barrymore, to name the form's grand old men, set the standard that others copied. Their itinerant presentations gave way to recorded narrations, VCR tape and the DVD.

In the early1960s, **Roger Brown '57** and **Barry Corbet '58** formed Summit Films and led the departure from the formulaic ski film being repeated by Jay and others. Corbet had moved to Jackson, Wyoming, to pursue mountaineering full time and became a member of the first American Everest Expedition. Brown was in on the start of the Vail ski area and began making sponsored ski mountain films. Barry became his partner, and they created a niche producing films that promoted skiing not only at Vail but at other new Western resorts. Summit Films also found patrons in the airline industry, where ski travel productions were an established format; Swissair and Air France had been promoting skiing in the Alps with short travel films since the late 1950s. Summit Films proceeded to Americanize the genre. In 1966 they bought a high-speed Michael camera that shot slow motion with exceptional clarity, and they combined this capability with extreme skiing sequences in making their landmark production *Ski the Outer Limits*.

One day, while Corbet was leaning out of a helicopter getting some dynamic powder shots near the Maroon Bells above Aspen, the craft caught a downdraft and slammed into a ridge. Corbet survived the crash but was permanently paralyzed from the waist down. As he recovered, he insisted upon finishing the editing he had started on his film. He and Roger followed *Ski the Outer Limits* with *The Great Ski Chase* (with Fred Iselin and Susie Chaffee), and then *The Moebius Flip*, with its strange psychedelic twist. One can argue that Dr. Fanck's films were filled with early versions of what we now call "extreme skiing," but I would say that the American fascination with extreme skiing can be traced back to the mid-1960s and to Brown's and Corbet's small film company in Gypsum, Colorado. It seems that almost every ski film that followed had to find bigger air and steeper pitches to capture.

In later years, Dartmouth ski racers like **Lisa Densmore '83**, **Gale "Tiger" Shaw '85** and others were seen in movies made for the television screen, often in the TV-magazine type format such as seen on "Wide World of Skiing." As extreme skiing increasingly dominated the fall ski film line-up, Dartmouth's **Charlotte Moats '03** emerged as a major star featured in the Warren Miller and Teton Gravity Research productions.

Although not a Dartmouth alum, movie-making legend Warren Miller provided many a Dartmouth alum the opportunity to ski in his over 100 ski movies and 400 commercial films.

The story of American ski films owes a lot to Dartmouth's sons and daughters. Over the years, the effect of the College's alumni upon the sport has been not only spread but magnified by these films. As long as ski films continue to include Dartmouth skiing stars, to be made by Dartmouth filmmakers, and to be produced by Dartmouth alumni, the College will continue to be associated with that sense of adventure and the outdoor spirit that called to **Fred Harris '11** at the start of the 20th Century.

***

THE "KILLY EFFECT" ON TELEVISED SKIING EVENTS

By Richard Isaacson '64

Prior to Killy's retirement from amateur racing and his signing with IMG in 1968, televised ski competitions were largely relegated to the network sports anthology programs (such as ABC's "*Wide World of Sports*" and CBS's "*Sports Spectacular*"). Skiing, as "stand-alone" TV programming, did not exist outside of the Olympics and the FIS World Championships. You want to watch skiing on television in the late 1960s – tune in to the network's sports anthologies.

Killy changed all that with the airing of "*The Killy Style*," an eight-part television series introduced on network television in the winter of 1969 under the sponsorship of Chevrolet, for whom Killy did extensive promotional work. Formatted as a "Ski-with-Killy" travelogue, the series showcased Killy "skiing the globe" – from the Tasman Glacier in New Zealand to the trails of Vail. It was a hugely popular and widely watched series featuring, for the first time, a ski personality in stand-alone, multi-part television programming.

Following the success of that series, Killy was again featured in a new eight-part stand-alone network series in the winter of 1970, this time a head-to-head competition called "*The Killy Challenge*" (also sponsored by Chevrolet). The series showcased recent Olympians and popular ski personalities in simultaneous "knockout competition" to see who

Killy visits Aspen on his promotional tour.

would challenge Killy in each segment's final race. Challengers ranging from Austrian Olympians Pepi Steigler and Anderl Molterer to US freestylers Tom Leroy and Herman Goellner competed in a four challengers per show format – a total of 32 challengers over the eight shows.

In each show, four skiers would be paired off in two-challenger side-by-side semi-finals on parallel courses, with the emerging winner going head-to-head against Killy. The kicker was that the challenger would be given a handicap: a head start out of the parallel gates – using red, yellow, and green lights as in drag racing – of up to two seconds (calculated from his performance in the preliminary races.)

This series represented two "firsts": it not only served as "stand-alone," multi-part television programming built around ski competition, but it also served to popularize head-to-head skiing competition (a format that would soon be further exploited on the rapidly developing pro ski circuit). I was instrumental in formatting "The Killy Challenge" competition and was also responsible for recruiting and indoctrinating the thirty-two challengers (eight shows, four challengers per show) into this innovative TV concept that initiated a new era (or format) of ski racing that had never before been shown on TV or as a regularly recurring event.

***

TELEVISION CONTRIBUTIONS TO SKIING

By Lisa Feinberg Densmore '83

I find it odd that so many influential people in the ski world are from Dartmouth with one exception, television. Granted, skiing on television is but a small pinpoint in the extremely broad world of broadcasting. If you had asked me when I was a student at

Dartmouth if I had ever imagined I would become a television producer and host, I would have laughed. As a student, the drama department (which was the closest thing to television studies) was as foreign to me as a language study abroad program in Arabic.

I was an Economics major with a job offer at Irving Trust, One Wall Street, after graduation. I abandoned my high performance race skis and obscenely painful ski boots in Hanover for a high performance job and obscenely painful high heels in New York the summer after I graduated.

Funny how life rarely works out as planned. One fair-weather weekend the following March, I made the fateful decision to join a friend at a Women's Pro ski event at Okemo, Vermont. She talked me into racing. I placed 8th, made $500.00, and resigned from the bank on Monday morning to return to my first love, ski racing. It was the 1980's, the heyday of pro ski racing in the United States, when stars like Austrian Bernard Knauss would earn $1 million and friends like **Peter Dodge'78**, Dartmouth drop-out, superb ski racer and now Dartmouth Men's Alpine Coach, were ripping it up in duel-format racing.

Six years later, in 1990, after a moderately successful pro racing career and a helluva lot more fun than I would have had working 80-hour weeks in the Big Apple, I was ready to retire from the pro tour. My last competitive season seemed a string of bad luck culminating with the loss of my ski bag en route to Sierra Summit, California. My skis accidentally got mixed up with the Japanese World Cup Team's gear while transferring planes in Denver. It took United Airlines a week to find them—at Narita Airport in Tokyo. So instead of being on the course and in contention, I spent the races as a guest commentator with the local Sports Channel affiliate, mainly to keep busy.

Sometimes careers happen simply by being in the right place at the right time. Mine did. The next year, ESPN signed a two-year agreement to cover pro ski racing and needed a commentator. I was the only one with any experience, limited though it was. At the same time, a small independent television station in Manchester, New Hampshire, needed a host for a new show called "Ski New England," which would air locally and then go to The Travel Channel, which was in its infancy. Suddenly, I had a full-time job in television. I loved it, and the rest, as they say, is history.

There have been highpoints – certainly winning my first Emmy, which I consider the Olympic medal that I never got. It required the same effort – 15 years of intense training and competition – and a little bit of luck.

I remember interviewing Bob Beattie for *RSN*

Outdoors, the national morning show that airs on the resort network at 100+/- ski resorts throughout the United States. Bob consented to the interview because it was with me. Imagine that! I didn't think he knew me from a snowflake on Aspen Mountain.

I interviewed Bode Miller for ESPN's World Cup coverage at the top of the Birds of Prey downhill at Beaver Creek. He talked candidly just before entering the starting gate, when normally he would never have consented to a mic in his face at such an intense moment. It helped to have had World Cup experience myself. I knew what to ask beyond the mundane, "How do you feel?" or "What's your strategy?"

A&E hired me as a commentator for the 2002 Paralympics in Salt Lake City, the only time the Winter Paralympics have received national television coverage. I cried on camera when I hosted the profile I had written in memory of my dear friend **Diana Golden '84**, the Olympic gold medalist who succumbed to cancer after a lifelong battle with the disease.

I was the color-commentator at the first-ever World Cup snowboarding event in the United States. It was at Mount Bachelor, Oregon. In an era when skiers were considered uncool to snowboarders and a completely separate culture, I agonized whether to wear my skis to the half-pipe, which was part way up the mountain. I was a beginner on a snowboard, yet I had a practical need to get around the slopes efficiently. What a relief to see every coach and course worker on skis!

Peter Graves was the play-by-play guy at that event and at many other events with me. A booming baritone, I usually lost my voice trying to keep up with him. I later learned that I could have whispered and the viewers would have thought we spoke at the same level if the sound mixer was worth his fee. Peter's roots are in Nordic skiing and his heart now belongs to **Cami Thompson**, Dartmouth's Director of Skiing and Women's Nordic coach.

I remember returning after a grueling day in the Adirondack backcountry working on a feature during the 2000 Winter Goodwill Games only to be told that four people had died in an avalanche on Mount Marcy and that I needed to cover the tragedy for CNN, the sister network of Turner Sports. My feature never aired.

I remember hosting a made-for-TV skiing event in Jackson Hole with Picabo Street. We had to dress up as cowgirls to open the show. She stormed off when a grip moved her skis, thinking he was trying to steal them. Chock it up to a redhead's temper? I had to talk her down and get her to return to the show, or there would be no show.

I sat next to Andy Mill in a studio in Portland, Maine, laughing hysterically at fellow Dartmouth skier, **Paul Hochman '84**, who had taped his first gear feature for a morning show that Andy and I hosted.

Paul had been on Dartmouth's Development Team when I was skiing on the varsity squad. He may not have set any college skiing marks, but he is perhaps the one other Dartmouth grad with a truly far-reaching impact on skiing television through his segments, first on RSN and later on NBC's Today Show. He's certainly the funniest and most creative Dartmouth skier on television!

***

DARTMOUTH AND SKI MUSEUMS

By Meredith Scott '96

Most Dartmouth alumni can attest to seemingly endless New Hampshire winters. At Dartmouth, as at other snow-blessed states across the country, skiing is a way of life. Its athletic, recreational, and social aspects not only make the long winters much more enjoyable but are also important economic drivers. The lift ticket sales, the lodges, the nightlife, and the equipment rentals and sundry purchases sustain many local economies. From a sport dotted with diverse adventuresome characters derive colorful tales, creative marketing, collectible art, memorable fashions, and ingenious inventions now preserved in nine major ski museums across the United States. Putting their liberal arts education to good use, Dartmouth alums have made many of these museums possible and sustainable.

Considering the broad impact of Dartmouth grads on the sport, it is not surprising that most museums hold in their collections periodicals, archival material, objects, and photographs documenting the achievements of numerous Dartmouth men and women, many of whom populate various Ski Halls of Fame. Understandably, our alumni have supported these museums as members, donors, volunteers, founders, and board members. Here are four examples who are working to preserve

Jeff Leich '71 and Meredith Scott '96 at the 2009 New England Winter Sports Summit at Bretton Woods.

the accomplishments of their fellow alumni and other notables in the sport.

Alex L. "Buzz" Bensinger '44 served as a Staff Sergeant with the Army Air Corps in WWII before graduating with a law degree from Temple University in 1949. He returned home to Stroudsburg, Pennsylvania, where he and his brother **Charles "Chud" Bensinger '40** built two rope tows, four trails, his-and-hers outhouses, and a hot dog stand on Camelback Mountain. This area closed, but, in 1959, they formed the Camelback Ski Corporation which opened in 1962 on the same mountain (in a different location) with one double chair, three ground lifts, and 100% snowmaking. Both brothers remained active in the area's development. Alex, along with his friend Albert Dowden, founded the Pennsylvania Ski and Winter Sports Museum in 1995; its primary exhibit is located in the base lodge of Camelback Ski Area.

Dean Ericson '67 spent his youth skiing in the Northeast, and as an undergrad he served on the Dartmouth Ski Patrol. After receiving his SM in Management from the Sloan School at MIT, he moved to Denver in 1978 where he opened a branch office of Abt Associates, Inc, followed by an executive level career in consulting and new business development. Life in Colorado led to a multiple-decade love affair with the Colorado Rockies and with skiing. In 2002, Ericson "discovered" the International Skiing History Association (ISHA) and soon joined the Board, becoming Vice Chairman in 2006 and President on January 1, 2008. His responsibilities include: overseeing the quarterly *Skiing Heritage Journal* (the only publication focused solely on chronicling the sport's history), approving annual awards for excellence given to skiing history authors and film makers, organizing ski history academic congresses, maintaining a content-rich web site, conducting an annual Skiing Heritage Week, and participating in historical preservation projects with other ski history museums. Ericson is heir to a legacy born at Dartmouth: in fall 1991, the first ISHA Board of Directors was chosen at a meeting at the Hanover Inn.

Jeff Leich '71 prepared for his current position as Executive Director of the New England Ski Museum by listening to his father's stories of the great 1927 downhill race at Mt. Moosilauke and by spending the 1970s -1990s in the ski industry. He managed retail, rental and repair for the Jack Frost Shop of Jackson, NH, at three areas - Black Mountain, Tyrol, and Wildcat - before working in Alta, Utah from 1983-1986. From 1987 to1997, when he took over the helm at the New England Ski Museum, he patrolled at Wildcat.

He is proud of helping to share the story uncovered by the New England Lost Ski Areas Project (NELSAP) of the approximately 600 small and medium sized ski areas that are now gone. Leich featured the project as the museum's 2008 exhibit and wrote a three-part front-page story for the *Journal of the New England Ski Museum*. Jeff is now striving to locate and preserve the personal papers of ski pioneers that still remain in family hands.

Meredith Scott '96, a History and Art History double major raised in a non-skiing Dartmouth family, found her way to the Vermont Ski Museum via the decorative arts. After working in museums in Washington, DC, and Colorado, she got a Masters degree from the University of Glasgow. Writing her dissertation on Scottish export pewter did not prepare her to research ski bindings. However, her interests in material culture and the stories objects can tell about the past and present have been applied to interpreting ski history. As the Museum's first professional staff member, Scott was instrumental in getting the museum opened in a new facility in Stowe in 2002.

A list of the main ski historical organizations is included as Appendix 11.

Notes

1. John Jerome, The Man on the Medal: The Life and Times of America's First Great Ski Racer, Durrance Enterprises, 1995, Chapter Two. 2. Douglas C. Leitch '65. from research Doug did with the McCrillis letters archived at the New England Ski Museum. 3. Ibid, Man on the Medal, p. 16. 4. Wikopedia. 5. Philip Kennicott, Art of Justice: The Fimmakers at Nuremberg, The Washington Post, Nov. 29th, 2005. 6. Ibid. Man On The Medal, p. 43. 7. Margalit Fox, The New York Times, Published: January 30, 2008. 8. John Fry, The Story of Modern Skiing, University Press of New England, Hanover 2006. 9. Jeffrey R. Leich, Recreational History of Tuckerman Ravine www.tuckerman.org/tuckerman/history.htm. 10. Louis W. Dawson, Wild Snow: 54 Classic Ski and Snow Descents of North America, American Alpine Book Series, 1998, p 228. 11. Ibid, The Story of Modern Skiing, p. 98-99. 12. Ibid, The Story of Modern Skiing, p. 214. 13. Tom Corcoran in a telephone interview with Dick Durrance II, June 2009. 14. Ibid, The Story of Modern Skiing. Chapter 9. 15. NASTAR website, www.nastar.com. 16. Craig McNeil, Rocky Mountain News, Apr. 14, 2008. 17. Dr. Ralph Miller, Jr., in a telephone interview with Dick Durrance II, June 2009. 18. Seth Massia, Skiing Heritage, June 2009. 19. John Fry interview. 20. Dennis Donahue, New England Nordic News, early fall issue, p. 8. 21. Ibid. The Story of Modern Skiing, p. 192. 22. Ibid. Durrance interview with John Fry. 23. Ibid. The Story of Modern Skiing, p. 192. 24. Durrance telephone interview with Isaacson June 2009. 25. Gaius Sallustius Crispus, The War Wtih Catiline (circa 40 B.C) quoted in the preface to Skiing Out of Your Mind, Leonard A. Loudis, W. Charles Lobitz, Kenneth M. Singer, Leisure Press, Champaign, IL, p. xv. 26. Horst Abraham, Skiing Our Of Your Mind, ibid, Foreward, p. xi. 27. Durrance telephone interview with Jones July 2009. 28. Kevin Fedarko (with Jon Bowermaster), Dispatch, Outside Online, November 1998, www.outside.away.com. 29. Durrance telephone interview with Russell, July 2009. 30. Durrance telephone interview with Leich, July 2009. 31. Alaska Performance Backcountry Skiing, www.crust.outlookalaska.com. 32. Email from Bill Hunt to Steve Waterhouse dated 13 April 2009. 33. Dartmouth Office of Alumni Relations, http://alumni.dartmouth.edu. 34. Biography, Golden Opportunities Fund, www.dsusa.org/DianaGolden/bio.html. 35. www.skiernet.com/legendary-runs.html. 36. Email from Bill Hudson to Pam Hommeyer dated 6 April 2009. 37. http://www.sierrasurvey.com/yosemitebook/ 38. www.columbia.com/who/athlete_detail. 39. Erik Lambert, email, 2009. 40. Erik Lambert interviews Bill Briggs. Virginian Restaurant, Jackson, WY. 9 April, 2009. 41. Erik Lambert interviews Bill Briggs. Virginian Restaurant, Jackson, WY. 9 April, 2009. 42. Erik Lambert interviews Bill Briggs. Virginian Restaurant, Jackson, WY. 9 April, 2009. 43. Erik Lambert interviews Charlotte Moats. Pearl Street Bagels, Wilson, WY. 7 May, 2009.

CHAPTER XI

SUPPORT INDUSTRY ENTREPRENEURS

By Stuart J. Keiller '65, Tu '66

Owner of Ski Clothing Company; former Chairman of Ski Industries America (SIA)

With H. Richard Isaacson '64 and Stearns A. Morse '52

Support industry entrepreneurs came in many shapes, and they evolved their careers from chance meetings as often as planned ones. The following summaries of some three dozen Dartmouth alumni will provide many examples of how the passion for skiing has led to lifelong involvements in areas of business that one may not necessarily think about when discussing skiing, but all have been critical to the exceptional growth of the greater ski industry over the past 100 years. As you will see, many of these Dartmouth entrepreneurs carved out new territory, created new or improved products, and built beneficial relationships to continue enjoying their passion for sliding on snow. In some cases, they were greatly aided by Dartmouth-connected people or they joined up with non-Dartmouth industry legends like Howard Head or Jake Burton (inventor of the snowboard); but more than any other contributing factor, they took charge of their own destiny. To provide a better way of understanding the growth of this side of the ski industry, we have subdivided the roster of names into six categories: Early Pioneers; Early Post-World War II Years; Ski Retail; Ski Equipment; Ski Clothing; and Ski Financial, Real Estate and Other. In some cases, there is overlap as they worked back and forth within these groups.

THE EARLY PIONEERS

John Piane, Sr. '14 is first up and rightly so as he forged an early leadership in the retailing of commercial ski equipment and apparel. He entered the business world in 1911, his sophomore year[1], with the purchase of the Dartmouth Student Union, then known as the College Book Store. Piane was the eldest of six children whose parents had emigrated from the Milan area of Italy. His active nature was on display even before matriculating at Dartmouth. Piane had been accepted to Princeton, but in the fall of 1910, "after riding to Norwich, VT, with a trainload of rowdy Dartmouth freshman, Piane boldly marched straight to the Dartmouth Admissions Office and asked to be enrolled."[2]

By the time Piane returned from the military at the end of WWI, Winter Carnival had generated so much interest in skiing that demand for skis far outpaced the supply being hand-made in enthusiasts' barns and garages. Piane's daughter said, "I don't ever remember seeing him on a pair of skis."[3] However, **John Piane, Jr. '50** added, "Dartmouth was the starting spot for skiing and dad immediately recognized a business opportunity."[4] In 1919 Piane changed the name of his retail store to The Dartmouth Co-op and began having skis made by the Gregg Ski Company in St. Paul, Minnesota.[5] A Hanover neighbor, Charlie Dudley, traveled Europe for pleasure and began sending samples of ski socks, sweaters, hats, wax, and assorted other goods to Piane. Piane began importing such ski-related merchandise for resale in the Co-op.[6] One of his suppliers was Marius Eriksen of Norway, father of Stein Eriksen.[7]

The 1930s were a time of innovation and growth for John Piane, Sr., and for the Dartmouth Ski Company and Dartmouth Co-op. "Dartmouth men would leave Hanover knowing how to ski but with nowhere to purchase ski equipment and apparel where they settled. Orders started coming to the Co-op from all over the country."[8] The cadre of aficionados like **Fred Harris '11** and his Outing Club band expanded to a growing group of passionate recreational skiers. Piane established his first warehouse in 1930 in what is now the Christian Science Building on Hanover's West Wheelock Street. By 1933 he had engaged sales agents across the country to sell his ski gear.

One of the major technical problems with early ski equipment was binding the boot to the ski. The system of leather straps in use from the earliest skis provided only rudimentary control and reliability was marginal. A Swiss music-box maker, Guido Reuge, tackled the problem in 1929 in an effort to diversify his company and survive the economic upheavals of the period. Reuge invented a heel plate and spring system to secure both the toe and heel of the boot to the ski and named his new invention the Kandahar Ski Binding, probably after the relatively new Kandahar Ski Club formed by Sir Arnold Lunn in Great Britain. Reuge's company still makes music boxes.

John Piane, Sr., learned of the revolutionary new binding and secured a license in 1930 to manufacture and sell them in the United States. He found a failing machine tool shop in Springfield, Massachusetts, Universal Tool, and bought the stock, retained the German master toolmaker, reorganized the shop floor, and began to manufacture the Kandahar binding. He did all of this in the depths of the Great Depression. The Kandahar–Dartmouth–Hanover Ski Binding quickly became a widely distributed product throughout the developing retail market for ski equipment. In Ithaca, NY, three local retailers, The Cornell Co-op, Treman, King & Co., and The Sport Shop all advertised this product heavily during the 1930s and '40s in *The Cornell Daily Sun*, the college's student newspaper. Treman, King & Co. actually advertised itself as "Ski Headquarters for this Section of New York State" and "We carry the famous Dartmouth-Co-Operative line–conceded by many experts to be the finest line in America."[9] Treman even offered yearly ski insurance for 60 cents to insure Dartmouth Hickory and Ash Skis against normal use breakage.

In the mid-1930s, Piane senior also began selling ski equipment to the premier national retailer of the time, Sears Roebuck & Co of Chicago. The Sears Catalog was the Home Shopping Network of the time and Dartmouth Skis became available to a wide swath of consumers across the nation. Sears had but a single buyer for the budding ski category, and on one of his early annual visits to Hanover this lone customer asked Piane where he could purchase ski apparel to compliment the equipment he'd received from Sears. Piane referred him to a young Dartmouth graduate who had just joined the family business down the road in Lebanon, **Lane Dwinell '28**, about whom more will be said later in this chapter.

Carl E. Shumway '13 combined a passion for skiing with the skills of a consummate promoter to almost single-handedly create the first commercially viable ski market in Boston. Skiing in the 1920s was more a test of nerve and skill for a small cadre of experts rather than a recreational activity readily accessible to anyone inclined to take up the sport. It was a period when skiing was being organized rather than becoming commercialized. Shumway was a man of many firsts. Right out of Dartmouth, Carl joined F.T. Shumway & Company, the first advertising agency in Boston, founded by his father in the 1880s. A writer for *Boston Evening Transcript* said of Shumway: "In 1913 upon graduation he brought his skis to Boston and for years lone-handed preached and taught skiing to thousands."[10] Carl's advertising career was interrupted by the outbreak of World War I; he decided to join the Navy and fly. At age twenty-seven, turned away for being too old, he went back to the recruiting office with press clipping documenting his "flying days" at Dartmouth as a ski jumper.[11] Recruiters were impressed, he was accepted, learned to fly both fixed-wing and lighter-than-air blimps, and soon found himself leading blimp patrols out over the North Atlantic hunting German submarines.[12] He was discharged in 1919 and started his advertising career again in earnest.

Carl Shumway focused his energies on the nascent ski industry to develop his client base. Many of his first clients were the inns and hotels in the White Mountains of New Hampshire. Eagle Mountain House and the Wentworth Lodge are two in Jackson that are still operating today. At his urging, the *Boston Evening Transcript*, in 1929, became the first American newspaper with a weekly page dedicated to skiing.[13] Entitled "Old Man Winter," it became the most successful page in the paper and spawned similar skiing pages in newspapers across the country. In that same year, Shumway began pushing the Boston and Maine Railroad to run ski trains to the White Mountains so people could get to the wonderful hotels he was promoting. An article in the November 27, 1936, *Boston Evening Transcript* recalled: "It was therefore but natural that this railroad went to him in 1931 and with his recommendation started the Snow Trains that winter. Destinations, fare, time, advertising, etc., he was consulting on each week–and each week that winter an operating profit was made."[14]

He approached the Boston Garden about holding an indoor ski show. After three years of persistence, management gave him the green light. "For four months he developed a plan, personally sold all the exhibition space, contacted the talent, etc., and only two and a half weeks before the (1935) Winter Sports Exhibition, single-handed convinced the Boston Garden, that instead of canceling it as they were considering, that it would be a real success. Over 40,000 persons attended the three days."[15] A headline promoting the 1936 show the following year read: "Mammoth Ski Hill Mounts to Boston Garden Rafters for Show. World Combed for Winter Sports Experts to Thrill Thousands – Austrians Arrive Today."[16] Shumway had sold skiing to Boston.

Another of Shumway's clients was **Jack McCrillis '19** who advertised and promoted his books on skiing. He did advertising work for the B.F. Moore Company of Newport, Vermont, promoting their Slalom Ski Wear. On December 31, 1933, McCrillis wrote B.F. Moore with a retail referral in Reno, Nevada, and then added: "I have noticed your advertising appearing in many places where the advertising for our book has appeared. I know Mr. Shumway handles your advertising as he does ours. I think he is doing a very good piece of work for both of us."[17]

Carl Shumway remained in the Naval Reserve after World War I and was recalled to active duty in 1941 to hunt the German submarines that were sinking ships in the North Atlantic. He ultimately became Executive Officer and Assistant Commander, Northern Air Patrol, Boston. [18] Later in the war, he was transferred to the Aleutian Islands. Carl's dad died during the war and the advertising agency closed. He came home to his wife and three children and began a new career in the booming post-war financial services industry. He never stopped skiing. A grandson, Bo Adams, recounts: "He influenced my life. He had me up on Mount Washington at age five. This year will be our family's forty-seventh consecutive spring trip to Dolly Copp [the largest campground in the National Forest systemnear Pinkham Notch, NH], skiing and hiking the mountains above."[19]

Harold Hirsch '29 arrived on Hanover Plain in the fall of 1925 from Portland, Oregon. The Hirsch family owned and operated the Hirsch-Weis Manufacturing Company, founded as the Willamette Tent and Awning Company in 1883.[20] Harold's father Max and uncle Leopold purchased the company in 1907 from founder Henry Wemme. Hirsch-Weis engaged in the manufacture of sails and canvas gear for blue water sailing ships. As demand for sails disappeared with the clipper ships, the company shifted to the manufacture of work clothes for loggers, mill hands, and stockmen.[21]

Harold recalled: "My going to Dartmouth in the first place has its roots in a ski trip I took as a fifteen-year-old kid at Moran School, up on Bainbridge Island in the state of Washington. One of my teachers there was a skier, my physics professor. His name was John McCrillis. He came from Newport, New Hampshire, and he was the class of 1919 at Dartmouth College. He took us on a ski trip, climbing Mt. Rainier and he was the one who was influential in my applying to Dartmouth College."[22]

Harold Hirsch '29 was an early leader in developing ski clothing and a mentor to many in the industry.

Harold recalls the trip: "Well, actually it was a very peculiar way to get into skiing: so many things start with a mishap, and if you like it well enough, even the mishap doesn't make any difference."[23] After climbing all day on skis, "I suddenly realized my toes inside both of these soft-toed moccasin-tipped boots were like a solid block of ice. I found that I had cut off the circulation, and I had frozen my toes, all ten of my toes. Well, I'll never forget. They sat me up all night on blankets. Both my feet were shoved in the snow, and different groups of boys, all night long, took turns rubbing my toes with snow to bring back the circulation. The boys carried me down off that mountain and to a hospital in Seattle, where I spent time having my toes treated. And all I can say is, I was very, very lucky that gangrene didn't set in. I didn't lose my toes…[but] I never got my circulation quite perfectly back in my toes." [24] It is a measure of the man that despite this vexing introduction to skiing, he had a life-long passion for the sport and for the design and manufacturing of ski apparel.

Hirsch and McCrillis became life-long friends. When McCrillis moved back to Newport, NH, a few years later to become a prolific writer and filmmaker of instructional ski books and films, the two men corresponded frequently, with Hirsch asking McCrillis for help selling ski clothes and finding sales representatives and McCrillis asking Hirsch for references to sell his books in the Northwest. In 1936, McCrillis recommend that Hirsch hire Dartmouth's varsity ski coach, Otto Schniebs, as his Northeast representative, and shortly Hirsch was writing McCrillis extolling Schniebs' salesmanship.

At Dartmouth, Hirsch won several inter-collegiate ski-jøring championships at an annual race during Dartmouth's Winter Carnival. Hirsch heeled for the Freshman Green Book and was slated to become the editor in his senior year, a big deal in terms of prestige and an opportunity to make a lot of money personally from the sales and advertising revenues. However, Hirsch was asked to withdraw from contention. In 1977, he could still recall the 1928 confrontation with the then editor who wanted him to drop out despite being the leading candidate as no Jew had ever been editor of a publication on the Dartmouth campus. Hirsch had teamed up with the prospective business manager in his bid to become Green Book Editor, and he said he would not serve without Harold. "He was not a Jew and he was furious when I told him that I had been asked to drop the competition. So…we made a campus political issue out of it, and it created quite a stink."[25] "The faculty took sides, the students took sides, and it really became a very embarrassing thing…Dartmouth being a liberal college, as well as a liberal arts college, was, I think, finally shamed."[26] Both men won office. The most important character trait for any entrepreneur is to never give-up, even the face of seemingly overwhelming odds. Harold Hirsch, to his personal and professional credit, demonstrated this time and time again in his long productive career.

Harold wanted to be a college professor, and on graduating he went to Oxford to do graduate work. The Crash of 1929 brought him home from England due to the financial challenges "…since the only other thing that I knew besides teaching,…was skiing."[27] The young Hirsch went to work learning the family garment business by spending time in virtually every department from sewing floor to warehouse and went to night school to learn pattern making. Harold recalled: "I felt the United States needed a good domestic mass-producer of ski clothing."[28] "Not an expert in textiles, Harold fell back on experience he gained as a former member of the Dartmouth ski team. In a corner of the Hirsch-Weis factory, he began work on a ski suit, which he marketed in 1931 as 'White Stag,' an English translation of the German words 'Hirsch' and 'Weiss'."[29] Some of these were sold to the Dartmouth ski team.

As he recalled, "Back at Dartmouth in the twenties they wore wool Melton jackets on the campus… They were called 'ski jackets.' I designed one from heavy green and black plaid virgin wool used in my family's Portland, Oregon, work clothing factory for loggers coats in Oregon and Washington. I called it a 'ski jacket' and paid a group of Dartmouth students to sell it room to room in Dartmouth dormitories. It became so popular that the Dartmouth Co-op, run by John Piane, Sr., and Campion's [clothing store] in Hanover, N.H., both agreed to handle them if I quit competing. I quit and they bought. White Stag's first ski jacket was inadvertently born."[30] In large measure this is when the ski apparel industry in the United States was also born as Hirsch developed both his ski jacket and ski suit designs.

Lane Dwinell '28, Tu '29, was born in Newport, Vermont in 1906. His family moved to Lebanon, N.H., in 1923 when his father, Dean, took an ownership position with Carter & Churchill, a garment manufacturer founded in 1877 and located in a building just off the town square that still stands. The company was established to supply work clothes to a growing manufacturing and rail center[31] by William Carter and Lyme, NH's general store manager, Frank Carroll, whose mother's family name was Churchill. Carter was the brother of Henry Carter, founder of Carter Overalls, so the product line was familiar.

Dwinell graduated from Lebanon High School in 1924, Dartmouth in 1928, and Tuck Business School in 1929. Lane was a member of the Dartmouth Winter Sports Team, specializing in the snowshoe events. After graduating from Tuck, he went to work as a financial analyst for General Motors in New York City, returning to Lebanon in 1935 to become a partner with his father in Carter & Churchill. The company had diversified into sporting goods as early as 1886,[32] and by the time Lane joined the firm it was described as a "major manufacturer of skiing apparel."[33] The Dwinells developed their ski trade under the Profile brand name, a reference to "the Old Man of the Mountain", or "the Profile", a great stone face on Cannon Mountain that was New Hampshire's state symbol for well over 100 years until it collapsed from natural causes in the spring of 2003. John Piane's goodwill gesture of sending a Sears customer to Dwinell for skiwear led to Sears becoming a client that gave the fledging ski apparel line a big boost during the 1930s.

By 1949, Lane Dwinell had become principle owner of Carter & Churchill. Starting in politics as a member of Lebanon's town budget committee, Dwinell became a member of the New Hampshire state legislature, was Speaker of the House (1951/52), President of the Senate (1953/54) and a two term Governor (1955/59) as well as Assistant Secretary of State in the Eisenhower administration (1959-61). Ms. Vincent had become Lane's personal secretary at C &C and went with him to Concord and Washington, D.C. The day-to-day management of Carter & Churchill was handled by Lauris Blake and Clayton Ramsdell who became minority stockholders in the company.[34]

THE EARLY POST-WORLD WAR II YEARS

World War II brought the rudimentary recreational ski equipment and apparel market to an almost complete stop as everyone turned to the war effort. At Dartmouth Ski, all production was turned to the manufacture of special ski poles designed by Piane and his team that could be adjusted for length;[35] these were made under contract for the US Army's 10th Mountain Division as well as the Russian and Turkish armies. Ruth Vincent, who joined Carter & Churchill in 1940, remembers the company devoting 80 to 90 percent of its production to manufacturing army uniforms during World War II. The company did, however, continue to produce small runs of Profile skiwear throughout the war years.[36]

The one-piece ski suits worn by the 10th Mountain Division were derived from the early one-piece ski-jumping suit that Harold Hirsch had developed for the Dartmouth Ski Team. A second and more ubiquitous "uniform" was developed from Harold's original design for use in war factories[63], and "Rosie the Riveter" made the jump suit famous in patriotic magazine ads and newsreels. Fashion writer Virginia Pope, writing in *The New York Times* in December of 1942, stated: "A maker of ski suits, White Stag, has adapted this one-piece for plant workers and it has been accepted by workers in the Kaiser shipyards...."[37] Ms. Pope went on to inform her readers of other practical uses for skiwear: "The classic ski suit with downhill pants is useful to the plane spotter."[38]

White Stag prospered on war contracts, but Hirsch was already looking ahead to the post-war boom in skiing he knew would come. On November 7, 1944, he announced in *The New York Times* that White Stag would open a skiwear production facility in Kingston, NY.[39] In addition, Hirsch was looking for counter-seasonal business. In doing so, he pioneered the women's sportswear business; Hirsch introduced sailcloth, a lightweight canvas that became the most widely used fabric in the industry. He designed a roll-up jean and coined the term 'clamdigger.' Harold recalled: "And they became a standard for women's sportswear. From then on I started branching out. And I did a shin-length (instead of rolled-up), a tapered shin-length pant. Remember, in those days women weren't wearing slacks, except for active sports. This tapered pant I called peddlepushers [sic]."[40] Clamdiggers and peddlepushers are still part of the lexicon in the women's apparel business today.

One of the people Hirsch mentored in the clothing industry was **Emilio Pucci** who had won a skiing scholarship to Reed College in Portland, Oregon, in 1935. Born into one of the oldest noble families of Florence, Italy, Pucci grew-up excelling in academics and sports. At age 17, he was a member of the 1932 Italian Olympic ski team at Lake Placid, NY, an area he knew from his undergraduate days at the University of Georgia when, in 1924, he was the first student from a Deep South institution—and perhaps also the last—to enter the Lake Placid Club's annual College Week ski competitions. He received a Masters Degree from Reed in 1937 and was awarded a doctorate in political science from the University of Florence that same year.[41] While at Reed, Pucci started a career in apparel design which would span nearly sixty years and which began with his creation of the Reed ski team uniform. Harold Hirsch had already begun a long relationship with Reed and became a trustee for life in 1956; but Hirsch and Pucci very likely met prior to World War II because of their common interest in ski apparel. Pucci left the United States in 1938 to enlist in the Italian Air Force, served as a bomber pilot, and was decorated for valor.

In 1947 Pucci burst onto the fashion scene when a ski outfit designed for a female friend was photographed in Zermatt, Switzerland, by Toni Frissell working for *Harper's Bazaar*.[42] Pucci set up a design studio on the Isle of Capri in 1948 and one of his first clients was Harold Hirsch and White Stag.[43] It was the beginning of a fifteen-year business relationship that would culminate in 1962 with Pucci designing an entire collection for White Stag. Operating out of the restored Pucci Palace in Florence, Pucci became a personal and fashion magnet to the rich, the famous, and the newly emerging 'jet-set,' including the likes of Princess Grace of Monaco, Jacqueline Kennedy, Audrey Hepburn, Elizabeth Taylor and Marilyn Monroe.[44] The Pucci designs featured bold colors and prints that were considered avant-garde, but the White-Stag-Pucci ski wear collection was too far ahead of its time and lasted just two seasons. The Hirsch-Pucci collaboration is illustrative of the creative and entrepreneurial spirit in Hirsch that marked his long and successful career. He was a visionary, an innovator, and a risk taker who parlayed a life-long passion for skiing into an enduring commercial success.

THE SKI CLOTHING MAKERS

Steve Crisafulli '61, Tu '62, grew up on Long Island. His interest in Dartmouth began when his older sister, who was attending Mount Holyoke College, came home with tales of Winter Carnival. Upon graduating from Tuck, Steve worked for the New York Telephone Company, but found himself making frequent weekend trips to Hanover to ski. By 1965 Steve decided he preferred the life style in the Upper Valley, quit his job, moved to Hanover, and worked as a handy man while looking for a company to purchase.

Crisafulli heard that Dwinell was considering a run for the U.S. Senate and surmised he might be open to selling Carter & Churchill. He teamed up with **Fred Bedford Tu '61** and proposed a leveraged buy-out. At the closing in late 1965, Dwinell turned to Crisafulli and said, "You know you're buying my company with my money." [45] The company was renamed Profile Sports Wear. Crisafulli and Bedford bought the B.F. Moore Company in Newport, Vermont, in 1968 in order to add the Slalom brand skiwear to the Profile business.

By 1971 the Crisafulli-Bedford partnership had soured and Crisafulli purchased B.F. Moore from Profile and moved to Newport. B. F. Moore had been founded in 1891 in a general store in Newport, Vermont to manufacture work wear for the railroad workers that were streaming in as Newport grew into a major rail center for freight moving into Canada. As Steve recalls, "Harold Hirsch and I would have arguments about who made the first ski wear. At B.F. Moore we found old catalogs from the 1920s with 'ski jackets' sprinkled in with the work wear."[46] B.F. Moore began branding the skiwear products as Slalom. In 1933 B.F. Moore's letterhead read, "B.F. Moore & Company makers of the Slalom Ski Wear" signaling that skiwear had replaced work clothing as the company's primary product offering.

Steve Crisafulli built Slalom into a mini-conglomerate in the North Country. He built a modern apparel factory for Bogner sportswear of Germany and became a fifty-percent partner in Bogner's United States venture. The 40,000-square foot facility manufactured Bogner's complete line of ski and sports wear for the North American market. Steve purchased the old hospital building in Newport and renovated it as replacement to the nineteenth century wood structure that housed the Slalom factory. He purchased the Alpine Designs brand of skiwear and expanded into technical sailing wear with the acquisition of Sea Gear and then into golf apparel with the purchase of DiFini. The most fortuitous acquisition proved to be a technical outdoor/ski apparel company based in Grand Junction, Colorado, called Marmot that had been in business for nineteen years and "lost money every year."[47]

A combination of poor snow conditions and a banking crisis brought on by the collapse of New England commercial real estate forced Crisafulli to close all the Vermont operations. Marmot had shifted all production to Hong Kong by this time, so Steve moved the company to Santa Rosa, California, in 1991 to be near a convenient port of entry (Oakland, CA) and take advantage of a depressed real estate and labor market. After a rocky start, Crisafulli and his team built the business to $100-million in sales and sold it to K2 Sports in 2004. His is a story of true entrepreneurial persistence that resulted in 'overnight success' after more than forty challenging years.

Stu Keiller '65, Tu '66 grew up in New Jersey where skiing was not something he or his contemporaries had any contact with. With a Navy ROTC scholarship paying tuition, books, and a living allowance, Stu attended Dartmouth. Once he was comfortable with the demanding academic program, he became more active on campus. With a Northland beginner ski package from the same legendary Co-op Ski Shop started by John Piane, Sr., he learned to ski and spent as many afternoons as possible at the Dartmouth Skiway. He obtained a Tuck MBA, and after serving his required four-year tour in the Navy sailing destroyers, he returned to Tuck to write case studies for Professor Ken Davis's graduate level textbook, *Marketing Management.* One of those cases was the acquisition of Profile Ski Wear by former Tuck graduates Steve Crisafulli and Fred Bedford. In 1971, when Crisafulli departed Profile to assume ownership of Slalom, Stu slid into his slot as Marketing Director, thereby continuing the Dartmouth line of Dwinell, Crisafulli-Bedford, and Keiller at Profile.

In 1975 Alex Schuster, Harold Hirsh's protégé at White Stag and then founder of Head Sports Wear (HSW), offered Stu a job as Merchandise Manager at HSW in Columbia, Maryland, just south of Baltimore. By 1979 had Shuster moved back to his native Germany to run Head Sports Wear Europe and Stu assumed the presidency of HSW-USA. He guided the company through its sale by AMF to Leslie Faye in 1981 and stayed with HSW for 3 more years. Immediately after leaving Head, Stu co-founded Kaelin Sports Wear with Stefan Kaelin, a former Swiss National Champion and Olympic skier who had competed against Jean-Claude Killy. Kaelin Skiwear quickly established itself as one of the leading premium-priced skiwear brands in the United States and the alpine countries of Europe. With over five hundred leading ski specialty retailers selling Kaelin, the skiwear was prominent on the slopes from California to New England. The company was sold in 2000, but Stu stayed on as CEO of the Kaelin division until retiring in 2008. Stu was a board member of trade association Ski Industries America (SIA) from 1982 through 1993 and Chairman from 1994 to 1996. In 1997 SIA changed its name to SnowSports Industries America in recognition of the growth in snowboarding.

Beginning in the late 1990s Stu developed a niche consultancy that mapped key ski industry data to measure the size of the ski market in state, county, and local markets. He has worked with over twenty ski areas mapping their clients and measuring market share and opportunities for growth. In 2003 he developed the inSight mapping program for SIA using Microsoft software to map and measure member firms' market penetration and unmask market areas that offer high potential for increased sales. The program was sold to over one hundred leading ski equipment and apparel manufactures and has already gone into its sixth edition.

Diane Boyer '78 has international roots. Her father "grew up in France and loved skiing. He would do anything to be out on the hill from dawn till dusk. Her mother grew up in Canada and always sported the most fashionable skiwear. She was the first to wear a one-piece suit at Stratton Mountain, VT in the late 1960's."[48] The family was an early investor in Stratton Mountain and would spend every winter weekend traveling from their home in Greenwich, Connecticut to ski. In 1972, her dad decided to make his passion his business. He pulled her mother's ski suit from the closet, looked at the label, and traveled to France to talk with the skiwear maker about importing their product to the US. Skea. (Ski-Sea) was thus formed, and by late winter the entire family was in Las Vegas at the SIA trade show exhibiting and selling the Skimaer collection.

Diane was a sophomore at the Miss Porter's School in Farmington, Connecticut, the year Skea was formed. Already an accomplished freestyle skier, she was competing with the likes of Wang Wong and other professionals while touring the preeminent ski venues of North America and Europe. She competed in all three freestyle disciplines— ballet, moguls, and aerials—and won the over-all Freestyle USAA New England Championship in 1974. When it came to college, Diane wanted to continue to "travel the world."[49] Her parents had other ideas, and a tour of colleges included a visit to Hanover. Diane "fell in love with Dartmouth,"[50] and told her parents she would go to college if she got into Dartmouth, which she did. However, Diane was not eligible under NCAA rules to compete on the ski team because she had already "turned pro" by collecting prize money on the freestyle circuit.

So Diane filled in her spare time as the New England Sales Representative for the family ski apparel business. Her family and their business moved to Vail, Colorado in 1978. After graduation, Diane joined Skea full time. The company had started manufacturing the French skiwear collection under license in Denver and but by 1980 had transitioned fully to their own Skea brand designs. Diane's mother, Jocelyn, became Skea's chief designer and the entire family worked in all phases of the business. Diane moved up as sales manager, then president in 1991, and CEO in 1995. Under Diane's leadership the company grew and firmly established Skea as "a luxury brand that actually works."[51] In 2005 Diane became the first woman to be elected Chairman of SIA. Diane says, "I made the fifty-year old 'boy's club' co-ed."[52] The mother of two teenage alpine ski racers, Diane's passion for skiing and the skiing life-style has been passed to the next generation.

SKI RETAIL DEVELOPMENTS

The Dartmouth Co-op continued to be the flagship store for Dartmouth Ski equipment as well as for a full-line of ski apparel and accessories. It was a one-stop shop for outfitting Dartmouth men for skiing. Because the Wagner Labor Act of 1939 mandated the separation of wholesale and retail businesses, Piane, Sr., had set-up separate companies and turned over the day-to-day operation of the Co-op to three department managers handling the textbook, men's clothing, and ski departments.[53]

The ski-happy children of Hanover were able to outfit themselves for ski school in the Dartmouth Co-Op basement.

John Piane Jr. '50, Tu '51, remembers his first job at age ten sorting imported slippers and stacking ski waxes in the Dartmouth Ski warehouse. He would take shifts working in the dipping room lacquering ski poles made of cane imported from the Tonkin province of China and come out drunk from inhaling the vapor.[54] After graduating Tuck in 1951, John Jr. had to quickly assume responsibility for running the Dartmouth Ski Company as John Sr.'s health was failing. For the next twenty years John Jr. transformed the business from a domestic manufacturing operation to an importer of European ski equipment with world-wide brands such as Fischer and Kneissl skis, Nordica boots, and Marker bindings. John Jr. was a pioneer, starting at the 1956 Olympics, in sponsoring world-class Alpine racers to use the equipment he was selling. He was one of the founding members of the Ski Industries Association (SIA) that continues to serve as the major tradeshow organizer and industry trade association.

In addition, John Jr. developed real estate and other businesses in the Upper Valley. He continues to own and operate the original Universal Tool machine shop purchased by John Sr. to manufacture the Kandahar ski binding. Today the company is known for the manufacture of Peerless® handcuffs and leg irons. The markets for ski bindings and handcuffs are about as far apart as one could imagine, but common requirements for precision, strength, and safety have provided a continuous link through two Piane generations spanning over seventy years.

John Piane, Sr.'s daughter, **Joan (Posey) Piane**, met **Richard (Dick) Fowler '54**, the son of **William P. Fowler '21**, not on a ski slope, but at the New Hampshire seacoast. Dick's father had been a member of the

Gene Kohn '60 bought the Dartmouth Co-Op in 1986, returning to a place familiar from his undergraduate days.

first Dartmouth Winter Sports Team, participating as a snowshoe runner in events held on the Dartmouth green and he later served as President of the Appalachian Mountain Club. Dick remembers the beautiful trophy cups his father brought home and stories of snowshoe sprints from the Hanover Inn to the library. Dick married Posey upon graduation, went into the Air Force, and returned to Hanover to take over management of the retail operations at the Dartmouth Co-op. Dick and Posey had a great 29-year run building the Dartmouth Co-op into a retail institution on Main Street. The expanded store sold fine books, had an extensive men's clothing department, and outfitted generations of Dartmouth men and women with ski equipment and apparel. Dick carried on the tradition of John Piane, Sr. offering affordable ski equipment packages to thousands of Dartmouth students, most of whom had never been on skis or even seen a ski lift prior to arriving in Hanover. John Piane, Jr. said: "Dick was a strong businessman and did a marvelous job."[55]

The Fowlers sold the Dartmouth Co-op in 1986 to **Gene Kohn '60** and a group of investors led by **Allen Stowe '60, Tu '61**. Gene had become acquainted with the Fowlers and the Dartmouth Co-op while an undergraduate. He founded an advertising agency and counted the Dartmouth Co-op and the Dartmouth Ski Company among his clients. Upon graduation he went to work for Grey Advertising, but moved on to retailing after six years on Madison Avenue. In 1970, Gene got into the ski business with the purchase of Dick Fischer's Sporting Goods in Buffalo and Rochester, New York. Gene quickly expanded the operation to eighteen stores. His format was a precursor for metro-area ski retail with a small offering of ski hard goods to authenticate the store and heavy emphasis on apparel and accessories to sell to the skier "want-a-bees."[56] The business was sold to rapidly expanding Herman's Sporting Goods in 1973. Gene owned and managed a variety of retail operations before returning to the ski business with the purchase of the Dartmouth Co-op. The Co-op phased-out of the ski business in the late 1990s to focus exclusively on Dartmouth logo apparel products and the iconic Dartmouth chairs and diploma frames. Gene and his investors remain Keepers of the Green as the Co-op enters the tenth decade of continuous operation under Dartmouth alumni ownership.

Art Bennett's Ski Shop was located across Main Street from the Co-op. Bennett had founded the shop prior to World War II in a "hole in-the-wall"[57] on Allen Street. **Tony Morse '52** worked at Art Bennett's as an undergraduate and remembers Art's merchandising plan: "In all his products he sought the best and most attractive for serious skiers and racers. As a result, almost all the racing fraternity patronized Art Bennett's and that was good for business.[58] Tony recalls: "Art was gregarious and all the ski business people, including manufacturers and designers, showed up in the shop. One of these was Howard Head, whose radical and resourceful mind was hard at work perfecting the metal-plastic ski that we now take for granted."[59] (See the article on Art Bennett at the end of this chapter)

Don Cutter, Sr. '45 was the descendant of a family that started sending sons to Dartmouth with **Benoni Cutter, Class of 1796**.[60] Don's father, **Victor M. Cutter '03**, was a Dartmouth Trustee for Life and President of United Fruit Company. Don Cutter was groomed for Dartmouth and skiing at Vermont Academy. In the fall of 1941, shortly after having matriculated at Dartmouth, Don enlisted in the Army's 10th Mountain Division on the day he turned eighteen. After training stops at Fort Lewis, Washington and Camp Hale, Colorado, Don participated in the retaking of Kiska in Aleutian Islands, Alaska. At the close of WW II, he was aboard ship headed for the Philippines as part of the force being assembled for the invasion of Japan.

Don returned to Dartmouth in early 1946 and started a trucking and excavating company while completing his undergraduate studies, graduating in 1948. He met Rosalie, a Hanover girl, and their marriage in 1948 lasted for fifty years. The Army recalled him to active duty in 1950 for the Korean conflict. But instead of heading West, Don and **Rosalie Cutter** were sent to Garmisch, Germany, where Don served as captain of the Army Ski Team, competing all over Europe, and utilizing his skills gained on the Dartmouth ski team. With over one-half million troops in Europe, ski meets were considered a great wintertime recreational opportunity for spectators and participants alike (as well as very desirable duty for those who could get it.)

Returning home in 1956, Don helped design the Dartmouth Skiway and then became operations manager of Okemo Mountain in Vermont which opened for business the same year. The Cutter's also operated a retail ski shop at Okemo to provide basic services for skiers and to supplement their income. Due to Don Cutter's efforts, along with those of others, Okemo has become a premier New England ski area.

Rosalie worked part-time for Art Bennett in 1963 "in order to pay for a pair of Rogg ski boots, my 4th pair of the season."[61] Art once told Rosalie, "If anyone else can run this place, it would be you."[62] Rosalie held Art to his word when she and Don bought the business in 1964. In the early years, Rosalie ran Art Bennett's while Don was building the Robert Trent Jones golf course at Sugarbush in Warren, VT. Don would get fully involved during the winter when work on the golf course was suspended due to weather. The Cutters continued to operate the ski shop in the tradition of Art Bennett and it remained the go-to place for ski racers and the experts.

With four young children, it was also natural that Rosalie would get involved with the Ford Sayre ski school program. She taught for seventeen years and served as Chairman for seven years as the program grew to over 800 youths.[63] Don taught and coached skiing on a different level. He was the long-tenured and highly successful coach of the Hanover High School Ski Team. Rosalie recalled: "…to my knowledge his team never was beaten in the New Hampshire Championships."[64] In respect for Don, scores of his former students traveled from all over the country to attend his memorial service in 1997.[65]

Rosalie also turned her attention to ski racing apparel. There was very little of it readily available in the Hanover area, and what there was did not perform up to the Cutter standard. Working with a New Hampshire fabric mill, Rosalie designed stretch fabric and crafted stretch racing suits for each of the four events—downhill, giant slalom, cross-country, and jumping—that her son, Don, Jr, skied. Others soon wanted the same slick suit that made one go faster or jump farther and Rosalie was inundated with orders every Monday after one of her protégés won a race or meet.[66] The ski coaching, special apparel, and technical knowledge of skis led to a growing retail business.

In the Hanover environment, the classic connector for retail, clothing and skis was Art Bennett who is profiled in more detail below by one of his acolytes from long ago. It is important to recognize that this store was in many ways an important center of the ski industry in its day as well as the center of attention for skiers in the Hanover area.

***

ART BENNETT'S SKI SHOP IN HANOVER

By Stearns A. "Tony" Morse '52

The original Bennett shop was a hole in the wall on Allen Street, barely remembered from ca. 1941. When Art was released from the Army after WWII, he moved the store to the west side of Main Street under the Dartmouth Printing Company (next to the fire station), and then to the east side of Main Street, next door to the Porter Florist Shop (later Roberts Florist.) It was a long, narrow area with a display window, counters and shelves for jewelry, accessories, shirts, and jackets, then it widened a bit where the skis were displayed. At the end was Eleanor Bennett's business office, from which she kept a sharp eye on any possible profit-diminishing philanthropic tendencies from Art, who liked to help create a loyal following where he could. Then the back stairs on the left, leading down to a big storage area for boots and other things, and finally the workshop, reaching back under the entire store, and where I worked from time to time.

Art was not a skier but rather a dedicated, alert, and fastidious businessman. Most ordinary students and townspeople tended to go to the Dartmouth Co-Op across the street, where Stan Starzyk held forth. His store sold both Northlands and its own brand of skis. Northland skis are described by Franz Gabl in his autobiography "Franzl II" as wonderful hickory gifts from Hannes Schneider to his young friends in St. Anton after the war, but to Art (and some others) they were clunky and heavy. Art sold Groswold skis, used by the US Team in the 1948 Olympics in St. Moritz. The later Groswolds included the ridge-top Dick Durrance model and the radical new flat-topped Barney McLean model.

Art also promoted Dovre bindings. He imported some of the first little-known brand skis into the U.S. before they were available anywhere else in the country—and before they became famous. He also led in waxes and skiwear, importing the first of the Bogner ski pants, which would finally replace the baggy look.

In all his products he sought the best and the most attractive for serious skiers and racers. As a result, almost all the racing fraternity patronized Art Bennett's and that was good for business. "You saw there any number of **Chivers** brothers, **Durrance** himself on rare visits, **Phil Puchner, Bradleys, McLanes, Neidlingers,** Millers (elder and younger, the latter the "fastest man in the world" for a while), George Macomber, Andrea Mead (two magnificent Golds at the Oslo Olympics), Dave Lawrence, Tor Arneberg, Per-Jan Ranhoff, Chris Bugge, coach **Walter Prager** (almost every day), **Brookie Dodge, Tom Corcoran, Pete Kirby, Bill Beck, John Caldwell,** Charley Furrer and in later days, Betsy Strong (Kent), Betsy Snite (Silver medal at Squaw Valley), **Chick Igaya** (Silver medal after Tony Sailer at Cortina), Rusty Sachs, and dozens of other fast skiers. Sometimes even Red Austin, despite the fact that he worked in the "other place."

To Art's mind, the workshop was the key to excellence in his product and services. He deplored the factory-installed steel edges, which were set too deep into the wood, leaving a proud surface that caused drag as well as lessening the effect of the steel. So he bought skis without edges and mounted them himself.

This was in the infancy of the offset edge. There was a special bench in the cellar that held the clamped ski. The meticulously set and guided router, ever sharp and only ever sharpened by Art himself, carved the channel for the gleaming Alpina edges. These were interlocked at the ends. The first ones at the shovel of the ski were skillfully tapped by hammer into a double curve; the first hole was drilled with a Handee drill furnished with an automatic spring-loaded stop to avoid over-drilling the hole, and then the first screw was set. Next, the piece of edge was teased into the curved channel and fastened again with the tiny standard screws (no Philips heads, please; too much drag.) And so on down the ski; then on to the other side, using the small Yankee ratchet screwdriver.

Apart from Art, who commanded the edging bench, the cellar was presided over by the kindly, skilled, and elegant Marsh Fitzgerald, brother of Marion Fitzgerald (Eastman) Blodgett. Marsh mounted all the bindings, fixed what needed fixing, and kept peace in the shop. We mended skis when the damage was within our skills; when tips broke off, the ski was sent to Wrisley in New York, where the vee-shaped cuts were mated together almost invisibly with the skill of the finest inlay.

Art and Eleanor were a great pair—sardonic, bristly with one another at times, but close. They were strong supporters of the town and of the ski community and of Ski Club Carcajou, for which they obtained and sold the black-and-white Carcajou pin with its tasteful brass letters and border. I met a gray-haired woman in North Conway in 2009 who proudly exclaimed that she still had her Carcajou pin from a half century ago. I have at least three.

In time, Art would travel to Europe during the summers, importing stuff straight from the source. This led to a corner on Henke boots and eventually to the arrival of a Henke associate, entrepreneur Eric Riess and his family from Germany, who set up shop as the Transcontinental Service Corporation in the old railroad station in Lewiston, VT. There they imported the boots and lovely close-knit turtleneck sweaters that became all the rage. I am told that today, 90% of the ski gear that comes into the United States comes through New Hampshire. Maybe that's the legacy of Art Bennett.

Art was gregarious, and all the ski business people, including manufacturers and designers, showed up in the shop at one time or another. One of these was Howard Head, whose radical and resourceful mind was hard at work perfecting the metal-plastic ski that we now take for granted. Remarkably, the brand still flourishes, and the team still fields the best,

as in Bode Miller who skis on Heads. Howard was energetic and very fun to listen to. We also saw Ernie McCullogh with his crazy hollow-ground skis—oh, didn't you know that at one time skis had only a single groove down the middle? I guess all downhill skis are hollow-ground now. Ernie was ahead of his time, and he knew it. Then the Stein Eriksen ski came along from Marius, with many small grooves.

There came a time when, in the dying days of shop-mounted steel edges, there appeared the Parsenn 4-star wedged edge. This came in pieces about 4 or 5 inches long and with a wide running surface, perhaps a centimeter. The steel was tempered and case hardened and the pieces thereby slightly warped, so they presented some challenges to the installer. The cross-section was wedge-shaped so that the ski must be routed on an outward-sloping angle. Walt Prager introduced this interesting design to us, and Art bought a few sets, but swore he'd never go through the fiddling job of mounting them. So I tried them on my downhill skis, and that was good enough for Tom Corcoran, who had me mount a set on his as well.

Soon after the Parsenn edges, Kästle appeared on the scene with the continuous hidden edges that we have today. Their skis were very fast, and the company supplied Buddy Werner, who was also very fast. But at the 1955 Nationals at Cannon Mountain, Buddy put his shiny new Kästle downhills too close to the furnace down in the cellar and they warped all to hell and gone.

And then there were the customers who discovered their skis were warped so that the running surface was not flat to the ground. Red Austin tells the following story, which to me is the essence of our life with Art Bennett. Red says that one day I had been in the shop and Art had a suspect ski sole-up in the vise down cellar. He had asked me first what I thought, and I took a straightedge, laid it on the tail of the ski, went to the front, laid another straight edge across the shovel, sighted down the length at the now-exaggerated extended surfaces, and pronounced the presence of a warp. Art stomped upstairs in disgust. Minutes after I had left, Red Austin drifted in, so Art took him down to check the ski in the vise, and *he* took two straight edges and laid them on the tail and the shovel, and pronounced the same result. "G*d-damn you, Austin, you're as bad as Tony Morse!"

Art was plagued from time to time by customers who came in complaining that their ski tip "broke; it just fell off in the middle of a turn" or "broke when

I stepped down on it" (on a rock). He did his best to give credit when he thought it was deserved—even if he doubted the integrity of some of the complaints. Most important of all, Art was an honest broker, dedicated to excellence in everything he did, critical of shoddy things or ideas, prickly at times and yet funny, sardonic, and wonderful company. Although hardly a soft touch, he was generous and supportive of the sport and the team members. He welcomed salesmen who knew what they were doing, but had little time for the fast-talkers. If he saw one coming far enough away, he might suddenly grab the nearest friend and hurry down the street for a cup of coffee at Lou's. For us and for him, life was never dull.

Some time after Art died from cancer, Don and Rosalie Cutter bought out the Art Bennett brand and re-established it in bigger quarters down the street where they, and it, flourished till they retired. They kept up the practice of getting the jump on new equipment and got Howard Head to build a metal ski for juniors. The first pair came to Don, Jr., and has been passed down through the generations.

THE SKI EQUIPMENT MAKERS

As the Art Bennett Ski Shop grew stronger under both Art Bennett's and the Cutters' stewardship, **Howard Head** became a frequent visitor to Hanover over the years. He came to talk skiing with many members of the community as he developed his ski products. In the early 1960s, his step-son **Richard Couch '64, Th '65,** was on campus and Rosalie Cutter remembers frequent telephone calls and occasional visits from Howard. Dick Couch recalls: "Howard was very ethical; the first pair of skis I owned he paid retail price for from Art Bennett's."[67] Dick spent summers in Baltimore and says: "I learned a lot about engineering and entrepreneurship from Howard."[68] Dick later invented and patented water injection plasma cutting equipment. He founded Hypertherm in 1968 and forty years later the Hanover-based company holds seventy-five patents, employs over 1,000 associates worldwide, and sells its products in over sixty counties.[69] Dick and Barbara Couch made a contribution to the new McClane Family Lodge at the Dartmouth Skiway to honor the memory of Howard Head[70] and his congenial Dartmouth connections.

The Cutters' son, **Don Cutter, Jr. '73**, was a star on skis from the time he could walk. At Rosalie's and Don senior's urging, Howard Head developed a junior ski and young Don was an early recipient. He recalls: "I didn't get the skis until March and I remember taking them to Tuckerman's in the spring. They were the famous Head black metal vs. the wood skis I had been using. [They] also had yellow "p-tex" bottoms vs. what I recall most skis having had black bottoms at the time. They were sharp looking, and I was proud to ski on them. They did perform better in that they had hidden edges and held the ice better than the other skis we had."[71] The ski was marketed nationally and was a big success.[72]

Howard Head's involvement with Dartmouth was multi-dimensional. First, he had many relationships in the ski world that were connected to Dartmouth in unusual ways. For example, Howard knew AIG founder **C. V. Starr** who sponsored many great skiers at his favorite ski college, Dartmouth, and often skied at Stowe using some of the ski instructors to test his new ski designs. Through Starr, he was introduced to **Kazuo Tajima** who was the original connection between Starr and **Chick Igaya '57**, the legendary skier for both Dartmouth and Japan. In the late 1950s, Starr had worked with Tajima to introduce Marker safety bindings in Japan. Mrs. Starr gave some nylon and quilted skiwear to Chick Igaya that he showed to Tajima. This led Tajima to introduce similar skiwear in Japan, creating a modest revolution in Japanese skiwear. In 1962, Howard Head asked Tajima if he would undertake the production of Head metal skis in Japan.[73]

As another example, Howard Head employed a number of Dartmouth alumni in his business, particularly as sales representatives. For example, **Roger Brown '57,** a former Dartmouth

Howard Head's team tested the first Head skis at Tuckerman Ravine.

Ski Team member, worked for Howard and the Head Ski Company as the West Sales Representative early in Roger's career selling ski equipment in the western ski areas he so loved. Roger's real passion was pursuing a career in outdoor cinematography and making ski movies as commented on in Chapter X, and he shifted fully into this area in 1963. Early that year, by mere coincidence, Roger met Dartmouth alum **Clay Freeman '58** who was passing through Aspen looking for employment on his way home after discharge from the Navy in San Diego. At Roger's suggestion, Clay drove to New York City to catch up with Howard Head at a trade show being held at the Statler-Hilton Hotel. A twenty-minute interview led to a job offer from Howard and a forty-three year career in the ski industry for Clay.

Clay Freeman's dad, **W. Brownell Freeman '27**, was an outdoorsman from his time as a member of the DOC and he brought up his two sons, Clay and his brother **Peter Freeman '61,** with frequent mention of stories about Dartmouth and the mountains of New Hampshire. Clay's early life involved recreational skiing at Dartmouth, playing on the hockey and lacrosse teams, attending Naval Officer Candidate School and training as an Underwater Demolition Team (UDT) covert interdiction expert, the precursor of today's Navy Seals, along with several other Dartmouth alums, including **Fred Bagnall '58**, **Clive Carney '61**, **Jon Stockholm '60** and **Mike Welch '58**. In one operation, Clay was standing by off the coast of Cuba as part of a planned 1962 invasion force during the Cuban Missile Crisis.

Clay said, "After my UDT experience, I could not see myself in the corporate world. None of the interviews clicked." [74] The suggestion from Roger Brown to contact Howard Head worked perfectly for him and his first assignment was making skis at the Head factory near Baltimore. But by the fall, Roger had left the Head Ski Company to work full-time as a cinematographer and Clay inherited his West sales territory plus the Alberta and Saskatchewan provinces in Canada. Clay's first sales trip took him to Bend, Oregon, where the US Ski Team was training for the 1964 Olympics. As Head's 'racer chaser', the former hockey player and frogman fit right in with Buddy Werner, Billy Kidd, Rip McManus, and Jimmy Huega along with Jimmy's young French skier friend and future star, Jean-Claude Killy, that he had befriended that summer training in Chile and who later promoted Head skis.

The late 1960s were a period of explosive growth in skiing and in particular for the Head Ski Company. Clay has said: "A big part of my job was telling retailers why they could not get more Head Skis." [75] Howard Head sold the Head Ski Company to AMF Incorporated in 1969. By 1972, with his heavy travel schedule wearing him down, Clay accepted a position as Western Sales Manager for Solomon bindings that enabled him to travel less and to maintain his home in Vail. Clay later held various executive positions in the ski equipment and apparel industry, including a ten-year assignment working with two-time Olympic skier and entrepreneur Chuck Ferries at Wintersports International that marketed US ski manufactures' products in the European and Japanese markets. Clay's last assignment prior to retirement in 2006 was with Production Finance International, a financial services company providing short-term production financing to ski industry manufacturers. He looks back his ski industry career with fond memories of "wonderful people doing what they loved to do." [76]

Another Howard Head employee was **Peter Hawks '60** who grew-up in Brattleboro, Vermont, in a single parent home, contracted polio at age seven and his doctors recommended skiing as exercise to help combat the debilitating effects of the disease. Peter said, "I headed for the hills, never stopped, and knew that's what I wanted to do." He was a junior ski patroller and four-event skier for Brattleboro High School when the skiing legend of Brattleboro, Fred Harris '11, got him to attend Dartmouth where he raced four events for four years. After graduation, Peter had an unhappy work assignment with Mobile Oil Company. A chance encounter with Howard Head, ever interested in recruiting Dartmouth men, after a Dartmouth-Harvard football game led to a job as the Head Ski Company's Northeast Sales Representative. Peter vividly recalls the halcyon days at Head: "The definition of a Head Ski rep was to be the eyes-and-ears for Howard and keep the dealers happy. We had a company car, generous expense account, and freedom. It was like a seven-year vacation." [77] As with Clay Freeman, the 1969 AMF sale led Peter to look for new challenges. Another chance encounter led to a job offer from the Animal Trap Company, a manufacture of steel animal traps and duck decoys, [78] that wanted help to diversify into the ski equipment business. This venture failed as the market was challenged by the oil embargo, high interest rates, and slowing growth. Peter ended up working for Dean

Witter in the financial services industry, but remains a "powder hound," an out-back guide at Sugarbush, and a frequent heli-skier with his son.

Churchill Ettinger, father of **Tom Ettinger '60,** moved the family to Vermont in the early 1950s to pursue his career as a preeminent outdoor painter and illustrator. Tom learned to ski early. He skied for teams at Burr and Burton Academy (Manchester, VT), Northwood Academy (Lake Placid, NY), and was on the Dartmouth B-team for two seasons. After graduating and spending two years with the 2nd Armored Division in Germany to fulfill his ROTC commitment, he followed a familiar path, contacting the Head Ski Company. An interview led to a job as Head's Middle Atlantic Sales Representative in the fall of 1962. After two years on the road, Tom moved inside to become the advertising and sales director. A clash with consultants Howard Head had brought into the company led to a new career at *Sports Illustrated* in 1966. In 1991, Tom finally left SI to form his own book publishing business.

Not everyone got in to the ski equipment business via Howard Head. For example, the father of **Sabin Abell '54** had run a sporting goods retail business, L.P. Wood, in Burlington, Vermont since 1941, and Sabin grew-up helping-out. A star student and skier at Burlington High School in the late 1940s, Sabin attracted the attention of a mutual friend teaching at Phillips Exeter and consequently transferred there for his junior and senior years. **Tom Corcoran '54** was a classmate and captain of the ski team. Sabin commented, "Dartmouth was a natural choice for me,"[79] and, after graduation, "it made sense to go home and work with Dad."[80] It was also natural that ski goods would take a more prominent place in the family business. Woods Sporting Goods became the first retailer in Burlington to sell Head Skis, Lang Boots, and Bogner ski apparel. The Abells sold their retail store in 1968, but Sabin had established himself as a full-time sales representative with Kastle skis. He was one of the founding members of the New England Ski Reps Association. In the 1980s and '90s, Sabin became deeply involved with the development and sale of the first molded lens ski goggles. Made of a new polycarbonate by Leader of Canada, the goggles represented a significant technological improvement in goggle safety and performance. In the early 1990s Sabin transitioned to selling custom tradeshow exhibit booths manufactured by a company in Maine. The Abells moved to Vero Beach, Florida, in 2000 and today Sabin splits his time performing his duties as Mayor of Vero Beach, and continuing his lifetime involvement in the ski business.

Rand Garbacz Tu '63, taught Winter Mountain Warfare to Dartmouth ROTC students while attending Tuck Business School and got to know the legendary "Sarge" Brown. Rand had participated in the Mountain Warfare program at Norwich University as an undergraduate and received a two-year deferment from the Army to attend Tuck. Rand's close working and personal relationship continued when Sarge moved to Vail in 1967. At Tuck, Rand also studied the feasibility of installing snowmaking for the owner of Bromley Mountain and determined it would work there to maintain Bromley as a viable ski area during periods of low natural snow. After his active duty tour in Army Intelligence at the Office of the President, Rand joined Cummins Engine in 1966. He was put in charge of mergers, acquisitions, and diversification. A 1969 ski slope meeting with Bill Kirschner, inventor of the fiberglass ski and founder of K2, resulted in Rand taking a leave of absence from Cummins to work with Kirschner [in Vail or where?] to commercialize K2. Cummins subsequently purchased K2 in 1970 and Rand became its president, after which K2 experienced explosive growth, overtaking Head in market share. While the Head ski was built for durability, K2's was made for performance. The Maher twins, Phil and Steve, exploded onto the world ski scene with K2's and propelled the brand to prominence. Rand left K2 in 1971 to pursue new challenges as a business consultant turning around under-producing companies. He continues his life-long passion for skiing and business from his home near Vail, Colorado.

John Stahler, Tu '69, a Long Island native, was a natural at basketball (captaining his University of Vermont team) and a skier. After the Army, John encountered an opportunity to attend Tuck while working on Dartmouth's early computer network for New England Telephone. These were the early days in the development of Dartmouth's revolutionary Time Sharing System and Basic language software by the inventors, Professors John Kemeny and Thomas Kurtz. Tuck's Director of Admissions, **Bob Kimball '46, Tu '48**, urged John to attend Tuck for his MBA. After Tuck, John began a thirty-eight year career in the ski industry at AMF Corporation. One of his first assignments was to monitor the apparel division of the newly acquired Head Ski Company, initially run by Alex Schuster and then by **Stu Keiller '65, Tu '66.**

In 1973, Stahler met John Piane, Jr. and moved back to Hanover to work for Dartmouth Skis. After losing important lines like Nordica boots and Dolomite skis, Stahler and Piane restructured the business model, setting up partnership deals with Tecnica ski boots and other products. In 1978, through a complicated deal, Piane sold his shares to Stahler. For the next thirty years, John Stahler built the West Lebanon-based company into one of the major hard goods suppliers to the U.S. ski market with product line expansion to brands like Völkl skis, Marker bindings, and Rollerblade, the firm became the model for product innovation, customer service, and continuity of success. John, an industry leader, served two terms as chairman of SIA and on the Executive Committee for over twenty years. John sold his company in 2007, and has served Tuck School as a project leader for its Global Consultancy program leading groups of students on European consulting missions.

John Schweizer '70, Tu '75, was preceded at Dartmouth by brothers **Stu '66, Th '67** and **Paul '68, Th '69**. His family founded Schweizer Aircraft in 1930 and it endures to this day. John remarked: "I did not want to go to Dartmouth precisely because my brothers went there. I ended up at Dartmouth because it offered the best combination of engineering and skiing."[81] Not up to the ski team racing standard, John taught skiing, raced independently, and averaged one hundred days a year skiing. On a summer cross-country hitch-hiking trip, he arrived in Portland, Oregon, contacted his college skiing buddies **Chuck '65** and **John '67 Lobitz** who introduced him to **Harold Hirsch '29**. Several years later, after time in the Army (spent fortuitously at the Army's Cold Regions Laboratory in Hanover), and then graduating from Tuck, John wrote to Hirsch to inquire whether he would hire him at White Stag. John recalls Harold's reply was an embarrassing life lesson admonishing him to correct his many errors of grammar before sending out his next job application. More than forty years later, John still values Hal Hirsch's helpful rejection.

John's first job landed him with the Rossignol Ski Company in Burlington, Vermont. After time in sales and running a tennis equipment factory in Boston, John had met **Jennifer Lucus, Tu '78,** who got him interested in cross-country skiing. The mountains and skiing were the magnets that drew John and Jennifer back to Vermont in 1981 to found the Merrell Boot Company in Burlington. Combining his knowledge of skiing and mountaineering, John focused Merrell on the burgeoning market in Telemark skiing. John and his partner sold Merrell to cross-country skimaker Karu in 1987, running it for them until 1993 when the parent company was sold. Today Merrell is a part of Wolverine World Wide, Inc. with sales of about $500 million. John was then approached by a hundred-year-old Italian boot manufacturer to help resurrect the Garmont brand ski boot that been abandoned in 1987. John put the Garmont ski boot start-up with an existing company distributing Excel cross-country boots and Roces in-line skates. After turning around the existing business and re-launching Garmont, John and his Italian partner broke away in 1996 to form an independent company to develop the Garmont Ski Boot business. John built up Garmont to become number one in both Telemark and ski mountaineering boots before selling out in 2008.

David Lampert '75 was raised on a dairy farm in Topsfield, Massachusetts. David junior followed in the footsteps of his father, **David Lampert '46**, taking advantage of the DOC ski instruction program and all-year academic operations. He became a PSIA certified instructor in his sophomore year, and took the winter term off his junior year to teach skiing full-time at Sugarloaf Mountain in Maine, working part-time at the leading specialty retail shop. Through a contact at the Rossignol Ski Company, David accepted an offer to teach skiing for two years after graduation at the French ski resort of Les Deux Alpes. He fondly recalls his time in France: "Wearing the French ski instructor sweater made you a skiing hero. We were wined and dined everywhere we went and could not pay for a beer even if we wanted to."[82]

Returning to the United States in 1977, David held a series of ski industry jobs in New England with the Molmar Ski Company, the Head Ski Company, and then the rapidly growing K2 Ski Company. In 1985, he met and married Norwegian Olympic Bronze Medalist Toril Forland. One of Toril's sponsors was a Norwegian cross-country ski wax company, Swix. David joined Swix as Vice President of Marketing and Sales for Swix's U.S. distribution company. Promoted to President of Swix Sport USA, Inc. in 1990, David guided the company to a five-fold increase in revenue over the next nineteen years via diversification into Alpine waxes, graphite ski poles, and ski bags; an acquisition of a Rhode Island-based bicycle chain lubrication company; and a distribution agreement with Montana Sport of Switzerland, the world's leading manufacturer of ski tuning machines. He served on the Board of SIA from 1995 to his retirement in 2008 when he was Vice Chairman.

Len Johnson '56 got into the ski business in 1989 with the founding of Jenex, Inc., in Milfred, New Hampshire to make roller skis. Len was fifty-six years old and recently retired from managing the electronics company he had founded in 1968. While Len was late coming to the ski industry, he was early coming to skiing. His parents sent him to Sweden to live with his grandparents as a toddler because it was thought the clean air of north-central Sweden would help his asthmatic condition. Len was on skis at age two and half and skied to school every day. Trapped by World War II in Sweden, Len returned to the United States in 1946 and "bounced around"[83] in locales without access to skiing. While living in Stamford, Connecticut, Len excelled at the prestigious Staples High School in Westport, and was able to attend the college of his choice, Dartmouth, "because of the skiing."[84]

Having not skied for six years Len arrived in Hanover determined to ski for Dartmouth. He was in peak physical condition and won every cross-country race he entered while skiing for the Freshman Dartmouth team. Determined to make the US National Team, Len spent too much time skiing and not enough studying—until his parents ended his competitive skiing activities. After taking a year off, Len came back and graduated with a major in geology and then enrolled at UCLA to study engineering. After working for ITT-Cannon for several years Len invented and patented an improved computer motherboard and founded Genex in 1968. After building a successful business and selling his company to Teradyne, Inc, Len retired from the electronics business in 1989.

Dartmouth skiers on roller skis, a familiar sight around the streets of Hanover, NH in warm weather.

In 1972, Erik Jebsen '73 (front left), Captain of the 1972-73 X-C Team, brought an early roller ski to Hanover from his native Norway, perhaps the first use in the U.S.

Len reverted back to his lifetime passion for skiing in his founding of Jenex which evolved from his engineering background and patenting breakthrough technology for roller skis used for dry-land cross-country training. Today Jenex has over seventy-percent market share for the North American roller ski market. Jenex roller skis are used by the world's elite skiers with sixty-eight Olympic medalists having trained on Len Johnson's skis. Kazakhstani Vladimir Smirnov won thirty World Cup and Olympic medals while training on Johnson's roller skies. Patented speed reducers provide friction resistance so athletes can generate the same metabolic rates in dry-land training as they do when snow skiing. A patented braking system permits training on courses that would be hazardous without the added safety of a brake. Len Johnson's skiing odyssey that started in Sweden in 1935 continues full-tilt in 2009 as the seventy-five year old entrepreneur pursues his lifetime passion with a constant stream of new products engineered to improve the performance and pleasure of dry-land skiing and to hone the abilities of champions and their challengers.

Jamie Meiselman '91 remembers going to see John Stahler at his West Lebanon office in 1988 as a freshman undergraduate to ask permission to use the rivet gun in Tecnica's boot repair shop.[85] Jamie was designing and building prototype snowboard boots on a consulting assignment for **Jake Burton Carpenter**, founder of Burton Snowboards in Manchester, Vermont. Growing-up in Westfield, New Jersey, in the late 1970s and early 1980s, Jamie typified a new wave of "skiers" that were appearing on hills and mountains on the East Coast, Utah, and California. Eastern skate-boarders and western surfers were taking to the snow, sliding down hills on wide single boards that resembled their summertime implements. Just as it was for Carl Shumway and his band of Dartmouth ski pioneers sixty years earlier, there were no dedicated areas for these young sliders. Most ski lift operators allowed only people with two "boards" on their feet to buy a ticket or use their slopes.

The snowboard phenomenon had its roots on Christmas Day 1965 when a Michigan father "seeking to entertain his children after the plum pudding, nailed crosspieces onto two skis to make a single piece, which he called a "Snurfer."[86] Sherman Poppen licensed his invention to hometown sporting goods company, Brunswick Corporation. They marketed it as a wintertime backyard toy.[87] The first picture of a snowboarder appeared in *Ski Magazine* in 1974. "It was not of a Snurfer, but of someone with one foot in front of the other, riding a device called a Winterstick, deep in Utah's powder-rich Wasatch Mountains. In all likelihood, the unidentified rider was Wayne Stoveken, who made boards that could be used for both water and snow surfing."[88] In 1977 at age twenty-three, Jake Burton Carpenter started making snowboards at his home in Vermont. He had played on a Snurfer growing up on Long Island in the 1960s. Jake would later say: "I didn't invent snowboarding the way Poppen did. No, I believe what Howard Head said about dogged persistence. If there's anything I give myself credit for, it's perseverance."[89]

By 1979 annual sales had reached 300 boards.[90] Jamie Meisselman bought one of them from Burton in person after he cajoled his parents to drive him to Vermont. "We showed up at Jake's house, knocked on the door, and Jake took us out to the garage that served as his factory. We bought a Burton on the spot."[91] At Dartmouth, Jamie, ever the entrepreneur, felt snowboard boots were rudimentary and did not provide the control elite snowboarders needed to compete. He set out to build a better boot using the metal shop in the college's Hopkins Center to fabricate prototypes from parts scrounged from old ski, hiking, and miscellaneous footwear. He also traded Burton boards for his own prototypes and ultimately patented and licensed his designs to K2 Ski Corporation. After graduation, Jamie spent the next six or seven years starting and editing *TransWorld Snowboarding Magazine* that was to become the "bible" of the snowboarding industry (See Chapter X). By 1998 Jamie was back working for Jake Burton managing the Burton boot business. Burton had become a large company and Jamie's entrepreneurial spirit still burned, so he left to improve his business knowledge by enrolling in the MBA program at Columbia University. While in business school, he conceived/founded yet another concept, Surfparks for boarders, with seed money from an Entrepreneurial Fund. Since receiving his MBA in 2002, Jamie has been working to design and build the world's first truly realistic artificial surfing facility in Orlando, Florida. The Ron Jon Surfpark will have a football-field- sized pool generating surfing waves for the next generation of riders[92] who, like Jamie, will take their boards to both the hills and the beach as they live their passion year-round.

CREATING CELEBRITY BRANDS

Today, it is pretty common to see a celebrity "name" or brand tied to the products associated with a particular sport and used by marketers to promote their equipment, clothing etc. The first significant skiing celebrity brand was Jean-Claude Killy. He was merchandised by the folks at IMG, including a former Dartmouth ski team member. See the article below.

***

THE "KILLY EFFECT" ON MERCHANDISING PRODUCTS

By Richard Isaacson '64

I graduated Dartmouth in 1964 and received my MBA from The Tuck School in 1965. In April 1968, I moved from New York City to Cleveland, Ohio, to become one of the first employees at The International Management Group (IMG), the evolving athlete representation and sports marketing company founded by Mark H. McCormack. In May 1968, I was part of the three-man team (headed by McCormack) that signed French superstar Jean-Claude Killy to a client representation agreement. The subsequent commercial activities centering around the charismatic Killy–on the heels of his three Gold medals in the 1968 Grenoble Olympics and his repeat 1968 World Cup victory–changed the landscape as to how ski products were marketed and ski television programming was presented.

The marketing of Killy centered on bringing new companies–not yet associated with skiing–into the sport.

The established ski-products companies were reluctant to climb aboard the Killy bandwagon, as they felt that Killy had not "paid his dues" to the sport (as had Stein Eriksen and Toni Sailer). They also balked at paying a ski personality huge dollar sums to promote their products. And, finally, there was strong resistance in the ski industry to subordinating traditional brand names to the Killy label and name.

So IMG went outside of the established ski industry and licensed Killy's name to a number of quality companies that introduced a broad spectrum of products under the "Killy" label. Among those were Mighty-Mac (outerwear), Wolverine Worldwide (after-ski footwear and gloves), Eagle Shirtmakers (tops), Champ Hats (headwear), and Clairol (skin-care products), among others.

The Killy "branding" also extended to hard goods through endorsement deals lined up with Lange Boots and Tomic poles, and a licensing arrangement with Head Skis, which introduced their new fiberglass skis under the Killy name.

Killy was the first personality in skiing to market his name across an untapped spectrum of product categories, bringing new companies into the industry, all for what were—at the time—huge monies paid to an athlete, and particularly a skier. Certainly, Jean-Claude Killy's broad portfolio of ski-related licenses and product and service endorsements transformed the landscape as to how those products and services were advertised, marketed, and sold.

Isaacson '64 and Killy were a hugely successful marketing combination.

Skier product endorsements and licensed goods, not prevalent before Killy, are now the mainstay of the snow sport retail landscape. I am proud to have been an integral, albeit behind-the-scenes, part of that transformation.

FINANCIAL ENTREPRENEURS: REAL ESTATE, MANAGEMENT, FINANCE

In order to build ski communities, there is a need for significant real estate development and financial management. Similarly to develop celebrity ski racers, there is a need for business managers. The folks who manage to be successful in any of these areas have great financial skills and, when breaking new ground, uncanny entrepreneurial instincts. Dartmouth has graduated many individuals who have gone into this sort of work, some in skiing and some in other areas of life. To provide a sense of this arena, we have outlined the lives of a few such skiing financial entrepreneurs.

Art Kelton, Jr. '61 "grew up skiing" [93] at Bromley Mountain as a pre-schooler. He went on to ski at Vermont Academy where **Warren Chivers '38** was his coach. In addition to being a member of the Dartmouth Ski Team, Art ran the student ski instructional program under George Ostler, was on the ski patrol and active in the DOC. After graduation, Art moved to Colorado. First he coached the ski team at the Lowell Whiteman School in Steamboat Springs and then, after a chance encounter with a "guy in a bar," Art started selling real estate in Vail. Within a year he bought the agency, and in 1972 he launched the first large-scale residential project in the area at nearby Eagle Vail. This successful 800-unit project led to several more on the same scale with more complicated financial arrangements, SEC filings, and limited partners. President Ford acquired a home in the area, and his presence on the golf course that Art developed provided national exposure to his projects in the mid-1970s. Kelton has made a significant

Warren Miller and Art Kelton '61(right) at Warren's 1995 Mad Mountain Marathon charitable event in Vail.

impact on the real estate market in Vail as well as redeveloping properties in Boulder and the new Denver International Airport. Living in Vail, where he skis regularly, Art is still active in ski-related projects with land holdings in southeastern Idaho and central Vermont where he also enjoys spending time.

Ron Riley '65's connection to skiing and Dartmouth began with annual class trips from his St. Louis, Missouri, high school to Aspen, Colorado, for spring-break skiing. He chose Dartmouth because he read somewhere that "an athlete with brains will love it."[94] Ron was recruited for football, but failed his physical due to suffering a shoulder rotator cup tear in an accident on Aspen Mountain. The injury also upset a potentially successful wrestling career, so he spent his Dartmouth years providing ski instruction to students almost every afternoon at the Skiway. After graduation "[His] overriding compulsion… was that somewhere or somehow [he] would end-up skiing. The hook was too deep."[95]

First, he returned to Aspen looking for skiing or ski bar opportunities, and finding none, he shifted to Vail. He purchased The Slope, a well know bar/night club, in the fall of 1967. Vail Mountain had opened just five years earlier and the town had been incorporated the prior year. As Ron says, "In those early years you could count on a 20-25% increase in business every year."[96] After two years, it was back to Aspen and a much bigger bite of the apple with the signing of a twenty-year master lease for the 18,000 square foot Woodlander building that had a mix of commercial and residential units. Ron and his partner operated three of the four bars in the complex and leased the remainder of the building. Aspen real estate exploded in value in the early 1970s and the venture proved extremely lucrative.

Next, he turned to real estate acquisitions in Vail. First, the Oar House building next to the Covered Bridge in the heart of Vail in 1971; and then 25 acres in East Vail for a 26-year project named Timber Falls starting in 1972 that involved single-family and multi-family housing. Timber Falls was the first development in Vail to incorporate on-site avalanche control. It was so popular that the Vail Chief of Police, Director of Planning, two city-council members, and the vice-president of the bank all were property owners there.[97]

To have reasons to develop real estate projects, it is also necessary to have reasons for people to come to the community. Ron was a long-time member of the board of directors for the Jerry Ford Invitational Golf Tournament that was a major contributor to the positive reputation of Vail. He founded the town series of ski races featuring teams from the local business community competing for pride and bragging rights. He started the Town Championships, a full-blown downhill race that is the culmination of the local racing season. He has played a quiet role in many of Vail's community improvements. Ron still skis but at normal recreational speeds as he has been slowed by multiple injuries over the years, including repair of the rotator cup torn forty-five years ago in Aspen.

Rick Isaacson '64, Tu '65, grew up skiing in Winter Park, Colorado, where his family owned and operated a ski lodge. After surveying the collegiate ski powers of the day, Rick decided on Dartmouth because it was "far enough away from home and sounded better than Middlebury." [98] Financial reversals in the family business almost terminated Rick's Dartmouth career in his sophomore year. **John Meck '33**, Dartmouth's Treasurer and long-time ski team supporter, was able to find scholarship money for Rick and he went on to obtain degrees from both Dartmouth and Tuck. After leaving Tuck, Rick first spent two years in advertising in New York, but decided he wanted to work in a more entrepreneurial setting. A friend introduced Rick to Mark McCormack, who had started a sports management company in Cleveland, Ohio, in the early 1960s, representing Arnold Palmer. That company, International Management Group (IMG), was still in the start-up phase when Rick joined in 1968 and moved to Cleveland.

Early that year, Jean-Claude Killy burst on the world scene by winning the triple crown of Alpine skiing with Olympic Gold medals in downhill, giant slalom, and slalom at the 1968 Winter Olympics in Grenoble, France. The combination of worldwide TV coverage and Killy's good looks and charm made him an overnight media sensation and one of the most recognized sports personalities in the world. Rick combined his competitive ski background with a very persuasive and engaging personality to convince the French star that he and IMG should represent Killy's business interests.

Killy had dropped out of school at age fifteen to concentrate on skiing. He put his trust in Rick and the collaboration resulted in many firsts in sports marketing. Rick and IMG were the first to do a licensing deal with a skier, and it was the first time a sports personality was named on a major product launch with the "Killy

800" by the Head Ski Company in 1969.[99] Rick was the first to bring companies from outside the ski industry like Mighty Mac® and Wolverine Worldwide® to launch ski apparel and accessories collections under the Killy brand. It was the first time that a ski personality was used to endorse products not related to skiing, popular items like Rolex® watches, Bic® pens and Bristol Myers fragrances. Rick and Killy made skiing a stand-alone sport for TV with a pioneering series on CBS. Up until then, ski coverage had been treated as part of sports anthologies such as *ABC's Wide World of Sports©*.

Rick Isaacson went on to open IMG's New York City office in 1974, to found IMG Consulting in 1975, and then found IMG Licensing in the early 1980s. He built IMG Licensing into the largest independent celebrity, trademark, and event licensing company in the world. In 2008, Rick celebrated 40 years of continuous employment at IMG, making him the longest tenured active employee in the firm's history.

Harry Lewis '55 starting skiing in Colorado in 1938 at age five. He thought he had racing talent, but that didn't work out. However, his interest in skiing never wavered. He was President of Dartmouth's Carcajou Club from 1954-1955, initially joining as a freshman. He returned to Colorado after graduation and organized financial backing via setting up extensive municipal bond underwritings required for many of the ski communities to build out their facilities. His brother **Chuck Lewis '58** (see Chapter VII) was CFO of Vail Mountain in the 1960s and then founded Copper Mountain.

Marshall Wallach '65 saw the *Dartmouth Bulletin* had a front cover picture of the Ledyard Canoe Club and decided this was the college he had to check out. When he first stepped on campus, he "knew immediately Dartmouth was the place for him."[100] A varsity tennis and hockey player, and an accomplished rock climber, Dartmouth was a perfect fit. The son of a career Army officer, Marshall assumed a leadership role in Dartmouth's Army ROTC unit. He learned to ski at Dartmouth and "skiing often took priority over Economics classes on winter afternoons."[101] After three years of active Army duty and earning a Harvard MBA, Marshall moved to Denver to begin a long and successful career in the financial service industry. As he said: "My Dartmouth experience is the reason I ended up in Denver. At Dartmouth I grew to love the mountains and outdoors."[102]

Like so many before him, Marshall pioneered many firsts in the financing of ski areas and ski industry related business. As a senior member of management at Boettcher & Co., he engineered the first federally guaranteed loans to the ski areas at Copper Mountain and Vail to finance lift and restaurant construction. Marshall found a provision buried in the Agricultural Department's Farm Bureau regulations that made federal financing available for capital investment in rural areas; and he was the first to qualify ski areas' large capital investments as fitting this rule. In 1984 Marshall formed Wallach Company and engineered the sale of Vail Mountain by its founders to entrepreneur George Gillette. The transaction was the first auction sale in the ski industry (and only the second in the U.S.) Rather than the seller placing a price on the property, Marshall asked potential buyers to make their own valuation and make an offer. Within five years, eighty percent of all business sales followed this practice. Wallach Company also provided financial services to a wide range of ski companies including apparel maker Obermeyer of Aspen and the ski areas of Steamboat Springs and Purgatory. Wallach Company prospered and was sold to Key Bank Corporation in 2001.

Marshall fondly recalled his years working with the people in the ski industry: "It is a tough business to make money in. The people work in the industry because of their passion for the sport and the life-style it provides. They have their priorities squared away. It was fun and exciting."[103] Marshall's thoughts serve as a succinct and fitting summary of the experience Dartmouth men and women have had pursuing their passion for skiing not only on the snowy slopes but in the competitive arenas of the sport's essential and ever-evolving support industries.

SUMMARY

Little could have been achieved in modern skiing as we know it without the entrepreneurial and spirited work of the people highlighted in this article and many more who are not mentioned. The Support Industries for skiing employ thousands of people and has provided a substantial economic benefit for the U.S. every year. There is no doubt that many more support functions could be added to this list. Our main objective was, and still is, to provide the reader with insights on the involvement of members of the Dartmouth family in this area as well as the many others we have mentioned.

Notes

1. Oral history, John (Squeak) Piane, Jan 10, 2009. 2. Dartmouth Co-op.com, dartmouthcoop.com/history.html. 3. Oral history, Joan (Posey) Flower, Jan 6, 2009. 4. Oral history, John Piane, Jr., Jan 10 and Apr 12, 2009. 5. Piane, Jr., ibid. 6. Piane, Jr., ibid. 7. Piane, Jr., ibid. 8. (Squeak) Piane, ibid. 9. "The Cornell Daily Sun" ad by Treman, King & Co., Jan 18, 1938. 10. Boston Evening Transcript, Nov 27, 1936, page 5, from the archives of the New England Ski Museum. 11. Oral History, Peter Shumway, son of Carl Shumway, Mar 16, 2009. 12. Carl Shumway hand-written notes on Naval Service, from daughter Nancy Shumway Adams collection. 13. Boston Even, ibid. 14. Boston Even, ibid. 15. Boston Even, ibid. 16. Boston Even, ibid. 17. Jack McCrillis letter to B.F. Moor Co., dated Dec 31, 1933 from archives of the New England Ski Museum. 18. Shumway, ibid. 19. Bo Adams, oral history taken Mar 12, 2009. 20. Oregon History Project, created by the Oregon Historical Society. www.ohs.org. 21. Oregon History, ibid. 22. Harold S. Hirsch Interviews conducted by Helene Hirsch Oppenheimer, from The Oregon Historical Society Research Library, Portland, OR. 23. Harold S. Hirsch, ibid. 24. Harold S. Hirsch, ibid. 25. Oral interview, Harold Hirsch with Shirley Tanzer, July 26, 1977, Oregon Historical Society. 26. Hirsch with Tanzer, ibid. 27. Hirsch with Tanzer, ibid. 28. Harold with Tanzer, ibid. 29. Oregon History, ibid. 30. "If I Had to Do It All Over Again" a talk given by Harold Hirsch at Ski Magazine Business Week, Vail, CO, Dec 1, 1979. 31. http://en.wikipedia.org/wiki/Lebanon,_New_Hampshire. 32. Carter & Churchill, Manufactures of Sporting Garments, etc., trade catalog dated 1886. 33. Theta Delta Chi, spring 1998 newsletter, obituary of Lane Dwinell. 34. Piane, Jr., ibid. 35. Ruth Vincent, oral history, February 9, 2009. 36. New York Times, Dec 13, 1942. 37. New York Times, ibid. 38. New York Times, Nov 7, 1944. 39. Harold S. Hirsch Interviews conducted by Helene Hirsch Oppenheimer, from The Oregon Historical Society Research Library, Portland, OR. 40. hhtp://en.wikipedia.org/wiki/Emilio_Pucci. 41. hhtp://_Pucci, ibid.. 42. http://dlxs.lib.wayne.edu/d/dhhcc/pucci.html. 43. http://www.holiday-apartment-tuscany.net/tuscany_travel_guide/florence_palazzo.htm. 44. Stu Keiller worked with Blake and Ramsdell, 1971-75. 45. Oral history, Steve Crisafulli, Jan 21, 2009. 46. Crisafulli, ibid. 47. Crisafulli, ibid. 48. http://www.skealimited.com/about.html. 49. Oral History, Diane Boyer, May 5, 2009. 50. Boyer, ibid. 51. http://www.skealimited.com/about.html. 52. Boyer, ibid. 53. Piane, Jr., ibid. 54. Piane, Jr., ibid. 55. Piane, Jr., ibid. 56. Oral history, Gene Kohn, Jan 5, and Apr 16, 2009. 57. Art Bennett's Ski Shop in Hanover, Reminiscences by Tony Morse, Apr 13, 2009. 58. Bennett's, ibid. 59. Bennett's, ibid. 60. E-mail from Barbara L. Krieger, Archives Supervisor, Rauner Special Collections Library, Dartmouth College, dated Apr15, 2009 and e-mail from Rosalie Cutter, dated Apr 22, 2009. 61. E-mail from Rosalie Cutter, Apr 20, 2009. 62. Oral History, Rosalie Cutter, Apr 14, 2009. 63 Oral History, Cutter, ibid. 64. E-mail, Cutter, ibid. 65. E-mail, Cutter, ibid. 66. Oral History, Cutter, ibid. 67. E-mail from Richard Crouch dated Apr 15, 2009. 68. E-mail, Crouch, ibid. 69. http://www.hypertherm.com. 70. E-mail, Crouch, ibid. 71. E-mail from Don Cutter, Jr. dated Apr 15, 2009. 72. E-mail, Don Cutter, Jr., ibid. 73. K. Tajima autobiography, Chapter on CV Starr. 74. Oral History, Clay Freeman, Apr 21, 2009. 75. Freeman, ibid. 76. Freeman, ibid. 77. Oral History, Peter Hawks, Apr 29, 2009. 78. http://www.asomagazine.com/magazinepdf/04/09/015.pdf. 79. Oral History, Sabin Abell, Apr 21, 2009. 80. Abell, ibid. 81. Oral History, John Schweizer, May 14, 2009. 82. Oral History, David Lampert, May 7, 2009. 83. Oral History, Len Johnson, May 20, 2009. 84. Johnson, ibid. 85. Oral History, Jamie Meisselman Apr 14, 2009. 86. John Fry, The Story of Modern Skiing, (Lebanon, NH: University Press of New England, 2006), p.236. 87. Fry, ibid. 88. Fry, ibid. 89. Fry, p.237, from author's taped transcript of interview with Jake Burton Carpenter, Stowe, VT, Sept 4, 2001. 90. Fry, ibid. 91. Meisselman, ibid. 92. http://www.surfline.com/surfnews/article.cfm?id=1520. 93. Oral History, Art Kelton Jr., Feb17, 2009. 94. Oral History, Ron Riley, Apr 20, 2009. 95. Riley, ibid. 96. Riley, ibid. 97. Riley, ibid. 98. Oral History, H. Richard Isaacson, Mar 27, 2009. 99. http://en.wikipedia.org/wiki/Jean-Claude_Killy. 100. Oral History, Marshall Wallach, Apr 2, 2009. 101. Wallach, ibid. 102. Wallach, ibid. 103. Wallach, ibid.

TECHNICAL ACHIEVEMENTS TAKE MANY FORMS

*The Oak Hill Overhead Cable lift in Hanover was the first in North America;
here an adjustment is being made to a J-Bar Tower (late 1930s).*

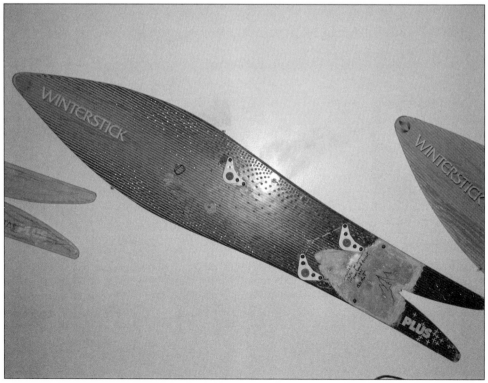

This is the exotic snowboard that Bill Hunt '80 used for his first descent of an invisible chute at Mt. Superior (1991).

CHAPTER XII

MEDICAL AND MOUNTAIN TECHNOLOGY

By H. Roger Hansen, M.D. '65
Retired Orthopedic Surgeon and Partner, Orthopedic Group

With Phil Livingston '58, Fred Hart '58, and David Durrance

In the evolution of the ski industry, there have been many technical advances. Some of these have been medical-related to help skiers recover from injuries and get back out on the slopes. Some have been safety-minded improvements such as better ways of laying out ski trails, providing groomed slopes, developing more effective ski lifts, etc. And for all of these technical situations, there has been a need for people trained in mechanical or medical activities to handle the implementation of these advances. Dartmouth- connected individuals have been at the forefront of all these issues, and continue to be.

PHYSICIANS IN SKIING

Dartmouth College graduates many students who become involved in some aspect of sports medicine, whether as doctors, nurses, technicians, researchers or administrators. It boasts one of the oldest medical

schools in the country — and is the only one with its own slopes and ski lifts. — one might expect that involvement to have begun to snowball around the same time the DOC was founded and the incidence of skiing-related injuries became a matter of increasing frequency. And so it did. Two of the winners of the first DOC Winter Sports Day in 1910 were local Hanover school students John P. "Jack" and Richard "Dick" Bowler, sons of **Dr. John W. "Doc" Bowler DMS 1906**. They also both skied with the Dartmouth team, along with John Carleton, in the first ski meet with McGill University of Montreal in 1914. Jack described that event in 1949 in a letter to Elmer Stevens, Jr. of the Dartmouth News Service.

Roger Hansen '65 with friends Campbell '65, Danson '60 and Waterhouse '65 at the DSW Weekend-2009 in Keystone.

"At the time, the Montreal Ski Club invited the Outing Club to compete against McGill in connection with the Canadian Open championships. Four members of the Outing Club were sent up; and because we lacked entrees for a jumping team, we took along a couple of "ringers" – John P. Carleton and my younger brother, Dick Bowler, who were then high school boys. Even at that time, they were the best jumpers in town, and later both were members of the Dartmouth Class of 1922 and relatively famous as ski jumpers who put on somersault shows, both singly and in doubles."[1]

Both Bowler boys graduated from Dartmouth, Jack in 1915 and Dick in 1922 (having captained the first official Dartmouth Winter Sports Team). "Doc" Bowler was the Athletic Director and trainer at Dartmouth for 36 years and a significant force in the development of many activities at Dartmouth, including raising funds from alumni in 1909 to build a new gymnasium. His role as the trainer, coupled with his medical degree and his sons' enthusiastic participation in skiing and ski jumping, drew him into sports medicine before the term was even coined.

Like his father, **Jack Bowler '15** also became a doctor. He was the leader of a group of five physicians who started the Hitchcock Clinic in Hanover in 1927. This was one of the first group medical practices in the U.S. at a time when doctors typically practiced alone, and it grew to become the highly respected **Dartmouth-Hitchcock Clinic** (DHC), a not-for-profit organization with historical roots in the Mayo Clinic, where Jack had once practiced. The DHC now has a network of over 900 primary and specialty care physicians located throughout New Hampshire and Vermont, some of whom provide services to skiers in the local ski areas. Jack also served as the Dean of the Dartmouth Medical School, and Chairman of the Board for the Mary Hitchcock Hospital. Few other individuals have contributed as much to the leadership and development of the substantial Hanover medical complex as Jack Bowler did from 1927 – 1960 when he often served in multiple leadership roles. Throughout his life, he continued to enjoy skiing, and encourage others to enjoy it as well.

Jack Bowler '15, leading the race on the Hanover Golf Course at which his father, Doc Bowler DMS '06, is serving as an official (man with chart to right). Jack and his father played leading roles in Hanover medical activities.

Dick Bowler '22 about to show his jumping skills on the old Hanover ski jump

Another early medical and skiing connected family in Hanover was that of **Dr. Elmer Carleton DMS 1897**, father of the very same **John Carleton '22** mentioned above. Elmer, who played on the 1893 football team, joined Jack Bowler and the Hitchcock Clinic staff in its early days and also served on the faculty of the Dartmouth Medical School. He was one of the physicians at the Glencliff tuberculosis sanatorium, founded in 1909, at Mt. Moosilauke before skiers started regularly traveling out to enjoy its ski slopes and pure mountain air, the latter deemed particularly healthful for the patients. Elmer's son John was a key link to the international skiers in Europe and the first American-born Winter Olympian (Chamonix, France, in 1924.) Yet another early Hanover medical/skiing connection involved Colin Stewart III who also served the Hitchcock Clinic as its president; he was the father of Dartmouth skier **Colin Stewart IV, Class of 1948**, who represented the U.S. at the 1948 Winter Olympics in St. Moritz, Switzerland.

When combined with their love for skiing, it is little wonder that Dartmouth-connected medical professionals can be found at virtually every sizable ski area in the United States. A few examples follow.

Alta, Utah: Dr. Kenneth Libre '86, DMS '94

Here is one of the various comments that have come in to us on the Dartmouth connection in the medical world. **Larry Goodman '47** sent us a note with the following:

"I'm almost 82 and have been skiing since I was seven. My father was an early ski enthusiast. I read *Skiing Heritage* [magazine] with great interest, and their archives should be a priceless source of information. I still ski about forty days a year–mostly at Alta where I hear stories about Dick Durrance's influence in the early years. Alta never had a medical clinic until one was established by Dr. Ken Libre '86 a Dartmouth graduate. Good luck! Larry Goodman '47."

Aspen, Colorado: Dr. John Freeman, MD '66, DMS '67

John has been in Aspen for 32 years. He is an orthopedic surgeon and partner in the Snowmass Clinic. He learned to ski as an undergraduate and at Dartmouth Medical School where he completed his first 2 years of medical school. His exposure to skiing and ski injuries was enhanced by participation in Dr. Ellison's Ski Clinic at Haystack Ski Area in Vermont when he was a in his residency training program after receiving his MD at Harvard. Following his residency at Columbia Presbyterian Medical Center, he completed the Sports Medicine Fellowship at the Cleveland Clinic in 1977. In addition to treating ski-related injuries, he has participated in the training of orthopedic fellows who come from Cleveland for a two-month rotation in Aspen through the Aspen Foundation for Sports Medicine, Education and Research. John has also served as an orthopedist for the US World Cup Ski Team.

From an analysis of basic medical problems, he reports that the majority of ski injuries relate to fractures as well as soft tissue injuries of the knee and upper extremities, especially the thumb. In recent years the increased population of older skiers has presented the added challenge of concomitant disorders such as osteoporosis, neurological conditions, and other health problems which complicate the treatment and rehabilitation of ski injuries in the more senior skiers.

Jackson Hole, Wyoming: Dr. Amos R. "Bud" Little '37

The Bud and Mary Little Award of the United States Ski Association recognizes individuals who have contributed significantly to US skiing interests through long-term involvement in the International Ski Federation or the Olympics. Quite fittingly, it has also been awarded to Bud Little himself.

Bud was a slalom specialist at Dartmouth, racing on teams in the late 1930s. In graduate medical school at Johns Hopkins University in Baltimore, MD, Bud won the first ski race south of the Mason Dixon line. During his military service in the US Air Force Rescue Service doing parachute duty during World War II, he earned the Legion of Merit, the Air Medal, and the Army Commendation Medal. After medical school, Bud settled in Helena, Montana, where he had previously gone on a number of parachute rescue missions.

For more than 30 years he served as a ski administrator on an international level. This has taken him on many trips outside North America, including six Winter Olympics and seven World Skiing Championships. He has played a key role with the International Ski Federation (FIS) for 29 years, the last 22 as vice president and board member. He was a member of the US Olympic Ski Games Committee for seven different Winter Olympics and managed the Alpine team at the 1960 Olympics and at the 1950 and 1962 World Championships. He served on the FIS Alpine Technical Committee for seven years and was Chairman of its Medical Committee from 1971 to 1988. He was elected to the USSA Ski Hall of Fame in 1965. Bud says, "I will ski until my joints don't let me anymore. That is what is great about the sport. It goes on all your life."[2]

Bud's brother, **Edward F. Little '41**, was also in the Dartmouth Outing Club and a ski team member. Edward returned to Hanover to coach the Dartmouth ski team after World War II. In 1948, he and John Clark wrote *Fundamentals of Skiing*, an instructional book on how to ski.[3]

Dr. Bud Little '39 has participated in all levels of skiing.

Vail, Colorado: Dr. Peter J. Millett, DMS '95

The Dartmouth effect at the Vail Medical Center, the Steadman Hawkins Clinic, and the Howard Head Physical Therapy Center includes board leadership from locals such as **Art Kelton '61** and experts in orthopedic surgery like Peter Millett as well as other doctors, nurses, administrators or associates like **Michelanne Shields '08**, a former Captain of the Dartmouth Ski Team and a participant in Dartmouth's 2007 NCAA National Championship team.

Peter Millett is a partner at the renowned Steadman Hawkins Clinic in Vail and the director of the shoulder program. Steadman Hawkins is recognized worldwide as a leading center for orthopedic rehabilitation treatment of professional athletes in many different sports as well as dealing with private individuals. Peter specializes in disorders of the shoulder, knee, and elbow plus other sports-related injuries. His special focus is complex shoulder surgery and the treatment of athletic injuries to the shoulder.

Prior to moving to Vail, Millett had served in a number of senior orthopedic roles. He held a faculty appointment at Harvard Medical School in Boston where he was Co-Director of the Harvard Shoulder Service and the Harvard Shoulder Fellowship, directing the Musculoskeletal Proteomics Research Group. His clinical practice in Boston was based at both the Brigham & Women's and Massachusetts General hospitals. He has worked at other leading orthopedic centers in New York and England, authored over 60 peer-reviewed scientific articles, and numerous book chapters on orthopedics. He has received awards from several international societies and serves as a shoulder and sports medicine consultant to Bermuda.

From a sports medicine standpoint, Peter advises the United States Ski and Snowboard Association and provides specific services as a team physician for the US Ski Team. He also serves as an associate physician for the Denver Broncos professional football team and the Colorado Rockies major league baseball team.

Monterey, California: Dr. Wylie Scott '58

During the early 1980s, Wylie traveled with the US Ski Team as an orthopedist for both the US Women's Team and the Men's "B" team. In those days, physicians paid their own travel and living expenses during a two-week period overseeing the medical needs at three different race areas.

Wylie stayed with the team members and coaches, working with exceptional skiers like Silver medalist Cindy Nelson and the Mahre twins among others. This was a difficult role because the teams were frequently in remote areas with minimal or no facilities for acute medical care. His travels took him to famous ski areas like Val d'Isere (France) as well as to some much less well known to Americans, such as Isola Deux Mille, Ein Klein Kirchen and other areas in Austria, France, and Southern Germany.

He eventually stopped making these trips as the malpractice issues increased worldwide and there was no insurance coverage available for them. Wylie says it was "a shame because it was such fun and adventure. I learned much from these extraordinary people. I'm not referring to their athleticism, but to that special something they all possessed to strive and focus on being the best. I don't think that I ever saw that elsewhere in life. I'm sure it was there, but it never so impressed me as during those special years."[4]

Portland, Oregon: Dr. Augusta ("Gusty") B. Swift '01

Born and raised in Jackson, Wyoming, where she developed a love for the outdoors, she blossomed early as an Alpine ski racer. At the age of fifteen, she moved east to attend Burke Mountain Academy (BMA) in Vermont to further her skiing skills. For Gusty, the next logical step in this progression was Dartmouth. Throughout her high school and college years, she competed at both the national and international levels and spent time training with the US Ski Team. While enrolled in Dartmouth's pre-med program, and also studying Art History and Studio Art, she was on the Women's Alpine Ski Team and attained Academic and Athletic All-American honors.

Following graduation, she returned to BMA to teach science and ski racing for a year and spent another year teaching art, soccer, and ski racing in Vail, Colorado. She then moved to Portland, Oregon, to attend the National College of Natural Medicine to pursue her longstanding passion for naturopathic medicine. Since Dr. Swift has been a competitive

Dr. Gusty Swift '01, a woman with a passion for skiing and naturopathic medicine.

athlete for much of her life, her practice concentrates on sports medicine, performance enhancement, and injury prevention. In combining her natural aptitudes and intense interests in skiing and medicine with a Liberal Arts education, Dr. Swift has earned the status of "Renaissance Woman" among her peers—of which there are few—and among her admirers, of which there are many.

Denver, Colorado: W. Chuck Lobitz '65

In order to achieve peak performance in skiing, as with other human endeavors, there must be a meeting of body and mind. Chuck Lobitz, a practicing psychologist and former Dartmouth ski team member, joined two other writers in creating a book on the sport psychology of skiing. The forward to their book, *Skiing Out of Your Mind*, states: "Skiing bombards a person almost simultaneously with tension and relaxation, with terror and exhilaration, with clarity and illusion, with exhaustion and recuperation".[5] The book lays out strategies and methods for striking the proper balance between these often conflicting emotions and reactions so as to attain optimal pleasure and performance in one's skiing.

Hanover, New Hampshire: Dr. Edward J. Merrens '88, DMS '94

Ed has been Chief of the Hospital Medicine Section at Dartmouth-Hitchcock Medical Center. He was an Alpine ski racer in his earlier years starting at his local area, Beartown ski area, north of Plattsburgh, NY, and moving on to Whiteface. He organized his own Nordic skiing activities because there were none in his area. He chose Dartmouth because it had the right combination of outdoor activities and academics along with a certain esprit and confidence not seen elsewhere. He came from a high school where no one in recent memory had gone to an Ivy League school except for his family doctor.

He skied on the development Nordic team under Dartmouth coach John Morton from 1984-1988. Then he went to medical school. Since 1998, he has continued his racing involvement by becoming team physician for the US Biathlon Team. He has gone to numerous World Cup and international ski events including the Olympics in Salt Lake City (2002) and Torino, Italy (2006). And like many Dartmouth doctors, he has worked with alumni members of various US Biathlon ski teams including **Laura Spector '10**, **Sara Studebaker '07**, **Zach Hall '06**, **Carolyn Treacy '06** and **Sarah Konrad '89**.

In addition to these specific examples, other Dartmouth alumni pop up in a quick survey of a few ski communities in the mountains across the US. For example: Stowe, Vermont: **Richard Bennum '76**, **Matthew Collins DMS '95**, **Richard James '88**, **Simone Margalit Rueschmeyer DMS '97**, **Theresa Sullivan DMS '05**; Park City Utah: **William Compton DMS '69**, **Lisa Hazard '95**, **Deborah Seaver '87**, **Cynthia Vitko '79 DMS '94**; Aspen, Breckenridge, Steamboat, Vail, Colorado: **John Freeman'66 DMS'67**, **Neill Hirst '68**, **Julie Colliton DMS '90**, **Granville Lloyd DMS '93**, **Phillip Freedman '68**, **Peter Millett DMS '95**, **Edward Crane '45**, **James Gruber '78**, **Paul Veralli '71**, **Graftom Seiber '53**, **Brian Harrington DMS '91**, **Lori Harrington DMS '91**, and **William Philip '68 DMS '70**. Many more are based in ski resort communities everywhere and they will fit the profiles we have outlined.

ADAPTIVE SKIING AND RACING

Adaptive skiing in the United States reached a critical mass in the late 1960s. Although limited numbers of disabled veterans with amputations or other problems from earlier wars had learned three-track skiing, it was the Vietnam Era veterans who were first aggressively encouraged by the military and veterans hospitals to get into skiing.[6] And the vets returning home from Iraq and Afghanistan have found a welcoming ski community where many programs have grown up over the last few years aimed specifically at helping this group. The benefits to the veterans is much greater than just the opportunity to learn—or relearn—to ski. It has often made an amazing life-changing impact on the individual vets as they begin to understand that they can still handle vigorous athletic activities, often better than many others who lack their injuries or disabilities. Many Dartmouth graduates have played a major role in the development of adaptive skiing, both in the continental United States and Alaska.

And in an interesting offshoot of the Dartmouth involvement in the history of Adaptive skiing, many alumni have participated in Olympic-level disabled skiing both as racers and administrators. Coaches and administrators on the US Disabled Team with Dartmouth roots have included **Joe Walsh '87**, the US Olympic Committee's Managing Director for the Paralympic program; **Sarah Billmeier '99** who has won 13 medals in four different Paralympic games and is now an athlete services coordinator for the team; and **Trygve Myhren '58** who was the US Chief of Mission to the Paralympic Games in Torino and Sestriere, Italy, in March of 2006, and was recently named to serve on a selection committee to choose the next CEO of the US Olympic Committee, as was **Nina Kemppel '92, Tu '05**.[7]

THE DEVELOPMENT OF ADAPTIVE SKIING

The individuals highlighted below are only a few of the Dartmouth alumni who have been instrumental in the development of adaptive ski training programs. Many of our alumni in ski areas all around the world participate in adaptive ski instruction and a large number have experienced the rewarding opportunity to assist disabled skiers to improve their performance on snow. And some Dartmouth alumni are successful adaptive skiers themselves.

Larry Jump '36

Larry was the developer of the Arapahoe Basin Ski Area in Colorado. His wife, Marnie, received a National Citizens Award from the Department of Defense for their Adaptive program. The adaptive program at Arapahoe Basin (A-Basin) was backed by the then Fitzsimmons Army Hospital in Aurora and the Denver Children's Hospital. Much of the work completed to actually develop the program was undertaken by Willy Schaeffler, head of the Arapahoe Ski School. He gained considerable information by contacting the International Ski Congress, Interski, about an amputee ski program which had been developed for German amputee WWII veterans.[8]

Steve Bradley '39

In 1970, the Children's Program moved to Winter Park, CO, and became the National Sports Center for the Disabled (NSCD). Jerry Groswold, a director of Winter Park and son of Thor Groswold, a Ski Hall of Famer who worked with many Dartmouth skiers and was a founding supporter of A-Basin, was the key person who proposed bringing the Children's Hospital adaptive program to the ski school at Winter Park. Steve Bradley, Executive Director of Winter Park, was very supportive of the program and recruited a senior instructor, Hal O'Leary, from Arapahoe Basin to run the program. NSCD has grown to a dozen full time employees and 1000 volunteers. They teach skiing to individuals with a wide variety of disabilities including blindness, deafness, multiple sclerosis, paraplegia and other neurologic disorders, amputations, and emotional disorders as well as autism.

Steve Bradley's interest in adaptive skiing possibly arose from the fact that his brother Bill Bradley had polio at age 25 in 1950 and lost his chance to continue a very athletic life style. Like the rest of the seven Bradley brothers, he had been a good athlete and had been encouraged as a skier by their father, Dr. Hal Bradley, who started a ski club at the University of Wisconsin partly through contact with the Dartmouth Outing Club. In 1973 Bill started the adaptive program at Snowmass. Bill wrote this note to his niece, Steve's daughter, Kat, about two major contributions that Steve made to Winter Park and skiing generally:

> "Dear Kat, It's worth emphasizing your dad's other great contribution to handicap skiing in addition to his large slope grooming program at Winter Park. He had the concept and he built the first models. Slope grooming was well established by 1973 when I took lessons. The whole learning process was accelerated by smooth slopes. One could become an independent skier in only a week. Excellent instructors and groomed slopes made handicap skiing thrive, and your dad was a major player in both. Love, Bill"[9]

Murray "Mike" Thurston '43

Meanwhile on the East Coast, Mike Thurston was among several businessmen in Bethel, Maine, who were examining ways to reinvigorate the economy of their region. Logging and textile mills were on the wane. They determined that a ski area could be developed on nearby Barker Mountain, and in 1959 they cut two trails and set up a rope tow powered by a Model A Ford engine. According to Murray's wife, fellow Dartmouth graduate **Sel Hannah '35** often came to Bethel on weekends to help plan and cut trails. Over time, the area flourished and became the Sunday River Mountain Ski Resort.

When Chip Cruthers, a physician from Portland, suggested starting an adaptive ski program, Murray was an early supporter and learned some of the required techniques through training in Winter Park. His son, **Dave Thurston '73**, said that it was his service as an instructor in the handicapped skiing program of which Murray was most proud. He continued teaching adaptive skiing well into his seventies. In his eighties, Murray began having trouble with his balance and became a pupil of the adaptive skiing program himself. Murray died November 25, 2008, at the age of 87. His origination of Sunday River and his early adaptive skiing program were the main reasons for his election to the Maine Ski Hall of Fame.

Phil Livingston '58

Ex-Marine fighter pilot Phil Livingston has been a ski instructor at the Alyeska ski area in Alaska for many years. As president of the local Rotary Club region, he became involved in ski instruction with a young Russian who had become injured while mountain climbing in Siberia (an area within Phil's immense Rotary region); and this has led to a successful adaptive skiing program being established at Alyeska for returning injured combat veteran from Iraq, Afghanistan and elsewhere. Phil has provided more detail on this experience in his article at the end of this chapter.

Chet Homer '73

Chet Homer is the owner of Shawnee Peak, another ski area in Maine. He has an adaptive ski program in which 150 children who are emotionally disturbed have weekly ski instruction for seven weeks each year. He also provides free season ski passes for children with cancer and their families in cooperation with Maine Children's Hospital. Chet also supports an annual Moonlight Charity Challenge fundraiser for Camp Sunshine that has been very successful.

Dr. Michael Mayor, MD

Michael Mayor is an influential orthopedic surgeon at the Dartmouth-Hitchcock Medical Center (DHMC) and the Dartmouth Medical School. He lost one leg above the knee as a result of bone cancer as a teenager. Nonetheless, he started three-track skiing with equipment he got from Stein Eriksen at Mad River Glen and says he promptly tore the handle off the right outrigger. After repairing his equipment, he worked with local Peg Kenney, who was running a lodge nearby. He took some pointers on technique, joined the NH Handicapped Skiers Association, and made triple-tracks thereafter all over New England, the Rockies, and Europe. As for so many other adaptive skiers, this new skill opened a huge and breathtaking world of snow and vistas that were previously all but inaccessible. Mike's example was noticed by others.

Mayor is not the normal adaptive skier...if there is such a thing. He is a longtime Professor of Orthopaedic Surgery at the Dartmouth Medical School and has also been Co-director of the Thayer School of Engineering's Biomedical Engineering Center for Orthopaedics at Dartmouth College. He has been heavily involved in surgical implant retrieval and analysis of joint replacement components and is a world-renowned expert at improving as well as implanting replacement joints. When he himself received a new polymer knee replacement on his good knee, and knowing his schedule required him to cover vast distances within the DHMC, he was concerned about wearing out the new joint. One day, Mayor was stopped by a patient whose husband works for Dean Kamen, a New Hampshire engineer who invented a "human transporter" called the Segway®. Mayor was smitten. It not only worked like a charm indoors, it could even negotiate ice and snow outdoors in the winter. No word yet on its skiing capabilities!

DISABLED SKIER RACERS AT DARTMOUTH COLLEGE

The development of adaptive skiing has opened new vistas on mountains for many people. Some are just interested in personal fun and some are actively using these new skills to develop as international ski racers. Although the racing side will be covered in more detail in Chapter IV, we provide a sampling here of how the adaptive techniques have impacted skiers who have elected to ski while attending Dartmouth. This in turn has reinforced the further involvement of Dartmouth-connected people in developing adaptive skiing programs elsewhere. Here are a few examples....

Diana Golden '84

Diana Golden was one of the greatest, most successful, disabled athletes of all time. She was a woman of incredible spirit who overcame tremendous physical and emotional challenges to triumph in her quest to live fully and completely right up until the end of her short life. Diana lost her right leg to cancer at age 12. She accepted that loss with optimism when she learned that she would still be able to ski after amputation and chemotherapy. She then re-learned to ski as an amputee with the help of the New England Handicapped Skiing Association at Mount Sunapee. There, in the company of Vietnam veterans and other physically disabled athletes, she caught the desire to pursue championship success as a ski racer. She entered Dartmouth College in 1980 and became part of the ski team there, participating fully in the team training regimens.

Diana Golden Brosnihan '84, the first great woman medalist and inspiration to all.

While earning a B.A. in English at Dartmouth, Diana was part of the US Disabled Ski Team, which she continued to ski with after graduation until 1990. Her achievements in disabled skiing competition are legendary. In eight years of racing she amassed an extraordinary total of medals, including 10 Gold medals, while racing in the World Disabled Ski Championships. Diana made the skiing world recognize the amount of competitive ability that a disabled ski racer could possess. With Diana's powerful influence, US skiing instituted the "Golden Rule," which now permits disabled ski competitors in able-bodied events to race as early seeds in all USSA-sanctioned events. Diana's career achievements led to her induction into the US National Ski Hall of Fame and the International Women's Sports Hall of Fame in 1997 as well as other awards and honors. As perhaps the ultimate tribute to Diana's place in the skiing world, she was named the "U.S. Skier of the Year" by *Skiing Magazine*, the US Olympic Committee, and the North American Snow Journalists Association in 1988.

After retiring from ski racing, Diana became a motivational speaker and took to this profession with all of the energy and commitment to excellence with which she approached ski racing. At age 29, Diana was diagnosed with breast cancer and underwent bilateral mastectomies. Diana applied herself to writing in her later years and was published in several magazines. Personal essays on her life experiences appeared in *Chicken Soup for the Woman's Soul* and the *Dartmouth Alumni Magazine*. Before her death at age 38 in August 2001, Diana completed a book about her experiences as a child losing her leg to cancer and finding acceptance and self-esteem by becoming a ski racer. Diana established the Golden Opportunities Fund shortly before her passing. Its goal is to provide financial assistance for young, disabled athletes striving for excellence. The fund is administered by Disabled Sports USA. (Golden Opportunities Fund Website. www.dsusa.org/DianaGolden/scholarship2.html)

Sarah Billmeier '99

Sarah Billmeier lost her left leg above the knee to bone cancer when she was five years old. Growing up in Maine, her family, which included three brothers, was active in skiing. With their support, Sarah started down the slopes when she was eight and began racing at ten; "I was addicted to the speed and freedom of being on the snow," she recalls.

At one time or another, Sarah has been involved in soccer, softball, swimming, bicycling, and whitewater kayaking. "She has always been competitive, always looking for new challenges," said her mother, Nancy.

Sarah Billmeier '99, leading all-time medal winner who now works with new Paralympians.

"She is very driven, somewhat stubborn, and very focused." At age 14, Sarah made the US Ski Team that competes at the Paralympics, the disabled athlete's equivalent of the Olympic Games. She won Paralympic medals in France in 1992, Norway in 1994, Japan in 1998, and Salt Lake City in 2002. The year after Lillehammer, she enrolled in Dartmouth College. For the next six years, she went to classes in the spring and summer and skied in the fall and winter.

By the time she was 25, she was a six-time World Champion and had won 13 Paralympic medals. Sarah has numerous awards and honors, including inductions into the New England Women's Sports Hall of Fame in 2005, US Olympic Committee skier of the year in 2000, and the Arete Award for Courage in Sports in 1992. In 2002, she put aside her skis to enter Harvard Medical School. In June 2006, she graduated with her M.D. degree and has gone on to train as a general surgeon so she can use her knowledge to help others.

Carl Burnett '03

Carl Burnett is another Dartmouth alumnus who has distinguished himself as a racer in the world of disabled ski racing. Injuries in an auto accident at age five resulted in Carl's paraplegia. He took up disabled ski racing at age 12. By age 15 he had swept all four junior national titles. And where does he ski? The very places where Dartmouth alumni have been instrumental in developing adaptive skiing: Sunday River and Winter Park. He has finished well in each World Cup he entered and now edits an online dictionary of skiing terminology.

Carl Burnett '03, leading Paralympic racer.

MOBILITY EQUIPMENT DESIGN

Henry Hof, 3rd '58

Henry Hof transcended a crippling mid-life neurological condition by combining his personal talents with a concern for others. Since 1993 he has served as an adviser to and steady supporter of Whirlwind Wheelchair International, a San Francisco-based group that has helped thousands of needy individuals in developing countries to build, use, and own inexpensive wheelchairs. The models range from the basic to the newest RoughRider™, which has the potential to facilitate mobility in snowy areas and promote active recreational participation there by those who are physically disabled. (A more detailed account is presented in Chapter XV.)

Athletic in his younger years, Henry captained the 1954/1955 freshmen basketball team during Al McGuire's first year as coach, a tenure which would bring the Ivy League title to Hanover twice by the time Henry graduated in1958. He also played on the varsity tennis team, earning his "D" sweater. But at age 42, he began to notice increasing difficulties in running, walking, and even standing. By 1989, he was using a wheelchair and still does so today. Taking to heart Helen Keller's words, "When some doors close, others open," Henry found the chance to collaborate with fellow members of the disabled community. Taking advantage of his collegial contacts at the United Nations, he collaborated with Whirlwind to help individuals around the world with similar disabilities. He hopes the newly designed RoughRider, a wheelchair that is maneuverable over a variety of terrains, will someday find wide acceptance in snowy environments as a means of mobility for the non-ambulatory.[10]

ON-MOUNTAIN TECHNICAL DEVELOPMENTS

This next section deals with a wide variety of roles, including designing and equipping ski mountains to provide an outstanding ski experience. We will discuss Dartmouth alumni who have been active as ski area consultants and designers and others who have developed significant equipment advancements.

SKI AREA CONSULTANTS AND DESIGNERS

Selden J. Hannah '35, Dartmouth graduate and Olympic skier, describes getting his first consulting job in notes he was compiling for an autobiography. He and his wife, Paulie, were newlyweds in 1938:

> "We headed north looking for a farm and work. We located one on Milan Hill [NH] that caught our fancy and then drove down to Franconia. The Tramway had just opened on Cannon Mountain and we went in to look around. Roland Peabody happened to see me in the lobby and asked if I was working. He hired me on the spot to supervise the construction of the ski trails." The CCC did the construction. Sel became co-head of the maintenance crew and the ski patrol. There is a trail on Cannon Mountain called 'Paulie's Folly'. Lower Cannon had been laid out by **Charley Proctor '28**. He went up until he got stuck. Ken Boothroyd had started the layout from the top. I had the impossible job of connecting the two trails. I got $80.00 per month—rather good pay for those days."

Sel and Paulie went on to run a small potato and vegetable farm, as well as milking cows and driving a

Two legends: Sel Hannah '35 (left) has planned more ski runs than any other person in history; Sherman Adams '20 was a former NH Governor and Chief of Staff for President Eisenhower in addition to starting the Loon Mountain ski area.

milk route. Their home also served as a small ski lodge, which earned them added income.[11] Sel's daughter Joan, a former Olympic skier, lives in the house currently.

Sel stayed in touch with other Dartmouth skiers. "Dear Potato King," began Steve Bradley in his March 1946 letter to the Franconia potato farmer and ski trail designer. It continued:

"We were talking of trails, particularly at Cannon…May I suggest an experimental idea? It really hasn't been given a try anywhere, though lots of people have discussed it. Why not try an experimental Slalom Glade, with trees forty to fifty feet apart and everything else thinned out?… The more you think on the subject the more reasonable it seems as one answer to the limitations that surround Eastern skiing."

This letter, now in the New England Ski Museum collection, is the first written reference to formal construction of glades in a ski area. Skiers in the Alps and in the western U.S. did not need to think about cutting trees to create skiable glades, mainly due to the widely spaced nature of the forests there[12] and the extensive skiable snowfields above timberline.

Over time, Sel became known for his talents as a consultant who could assist ski areas with lift and trail layouts as well as market analysis and planning for lodges and related matters. In 1958 he formalized this business by forming Sno-engineering. Initially it was based at his home and Paulie was part of the business, along with Sel's brother, Paul.

His son, **Selden Hannah '65**, also worked with Sel on several projects in the late sixties. Thereafter, young Sel went on to design and engineer ski lifts, working for Bob Kinney in New Jersey and later New Hampshire. Since 1985, he has done loss control and prevention inspections of ski areas. He is now semi-retired and living in New Hampshire.[13]

One of Sel's early consultations at Sno-engineering was at Barker Mountain in Maine, now the Sunday River Mountain Resort. Fellow Dartmouth alumnus, Murray Thurston, was president of Sunday River's board and one of its founders. Sel's analysis included items like snowfall, exposure and contour of the mountain for holding snow, and proximity of the ski area to population centers. Sel returned in 1963 and recommended further development, including new trails for novice skiers, increasing lift capacity, and increasing the size of the base lodge. Similar consultations were furnished in 1969 and 1981.[14] This was typical of his relationship with many ski areas across the country. In its 1968 Holiday Edition, *SKI Magazine* comments about Sel Hannah as president and founder of Sno-engineering: "It is safe to say that more than half of all America's skiers at one time or another have skied on Hannah-designed trails".

In 1956, Sel consulted with the US Forest Service regarding development of Wildcat Ski Area, including the design of the first gondola. He stated that: "Wildcat is located in one of the most dependable snow areas of the East with a season from early December to mid-April or later". He expected snowfalls of 150 to 170 inches per year. The consultation covered the need for proper grading, with water bars to minimize erosion and facilitate grooming, first aid facilities and ski patrol coverage. A further consultation in 1973 addressed increasing the daily skier capacity substantially and adding four chairlifts and a new bowl.

Sel took on a variety of assignments over the years. One of the more unusual jobs was to advise the State of West Virginia on potential sites for ski areas. This involved flying over various parts of the state as well as on–the-ground assessments to determine possible locations. In 1966 he worked with Professor Dean of the Thayer School of Engineering on "A Study of Evacuation Procedures for Chair Lifts", concluding that the then current methods were economic and effective[15] Sno-engineering compiled data and drafted reports for various organizations including the US Department of Commerce, for whom they wrote "The Skier Market in Northeast North America, 1965 Edition." A similar report was done annually beginning in 1967 for the National Ski Areas Association and called "Economic and Financial Statistics." In 1967, Sno-engineering donated the services of a team of employees to assist in the preparation for the North American Alpine Championships being held at Cannon Mountain that year.[16]

All together it is estimated that Sel consulted at approximately 200 ski areas. Over the years many other Dartmouth-connected folks have been part of Sno-engineering (S-E). Succeeding Sel as president of S-E was **Jim Branch '52, Tu '53**. Jim's son, **Ted Branch '83**, **Sel Hannah '65**, and **Jim Westfall '65** each worked there for varying times. Tim Beck, who had coached the Dartmouth Alpine Ski Team, worked for S-E from the mid-eighties to the early nineties. **Joe Cushing '52** was the lead ski area designer for most of his career at Sno-engineering, which extended from 1961 to 1995. The company continues to thrive under its current name of SE Group. This reflects the increased breadth of services to resorts of all types on an international basis.

Former Dartmouth racer, Jim Branch '52, Tu '53, ran the Alyeska Ski Mountain in Alaska before coming back to NH to spearhead the activities of S-E Engineering.

Scott Barthold '78 Th'81 – Sno.matic Controls and Engineering, Inc.

When the water system for Dartmouth Skiway in Lyme, NH, needed to be redone, the college had no need to go out of town for the design work. Scott owns Sno.matic Controls and Engineering, also located in Lyme. Scott skied for Dartmouth and then was an assistant coach there while going to the Thayer School of Engineering. He graduated from Thayer in 1981 and has been working on snowmaking systems since then, originally with Sno-engineering, from which he spun off Sno.matic. The company operates primarily as a consulting engineering firm. They analyze what snowmaking capacity is required and recommend the best type of equipment, and then design the system infrastructure (water supply, pumps, compressors, piping network, controls, etc). An overarching theme is energy conservation. Scott says, "I figure if 'Skiing is a way of Life', somebody needs to make sure there is enough snow around to enjoy that life."

Fred Jones '63 – Manager of Ski Areas

One of the experts hired by **Chuck Lewis '58** shortly after the opening of Copper Mountain in 1973 was alumnus Fred Jones. Fred had skied for Dartmouth in the early 1960s and participated in the ROTC program under Sarge Brown before joining the Army. While working for a small company in New England in the late 1960s, Fred spotted a help-wanted ad in *The Wall Street Journal* for a position as general manager of a New Hampshire ski area. The ad had been placed by **Tom Corcoran '54**, Dartmouth skiing great and the founder of Waterville Valley Resort. Jones was hired and served four years as General Manager of Waterville Valley under Corcoran until 1973 when Chuck Lewis offered him the opportunity to become Vice President of Operations at the new Copper Mountain Resort in Colorado.[17]

Fred Jones considered the experience of working with Lewis from the early days at Copper to be invaluable to his career as a ski area manager. He recalled Lewis as not only a visionary but also "a great manager and business person," a combination "unique in the ski industry at that time."[18] Skiing in Colorado was booming during the 1970s and, under the leadership of Lewis and Jones, Copper matured into a major destination resort and became the largest ski area in Summit County. Jones moved on to become Chief Executive Officer of three other ski areas: Kirkwood Ski Resort in the Lake Tahoe area of Northern California, Sugarbush in Vermont, and Whitefish Mountain in Montana. Then he started using his expertise to consult with other areas on the development and growth of their operations.

Valarie Jaffee '78 – West Coast Ski Area Consultant

Valerie came by her involvement in skiing about as naturally as one could. Her mother was a competitive skier before World War II in her native Japan and she got Valerie involved in the ski world at the age of two. After immigrating to the U.S., she began ski racing at age seven and continued until the fall of her fresh-

Valerie Jaffee '78 skiing on cotton seed.

man year at Dartmouth, though she did not race in college. She has had the unusual experience of training on straw and cottonseed when snowfall was sparse, which is not too dissimilar from Dick Durrance's experience of skiing on pine needles just for the fun of it behind his school in Newport, NH, in 1934. Valerie has competed at the National Alpine and international collegiate level, earning the FIS "Elite" ranking, participating in US national and international race camps, placing 1st in the British Alpine Championships, 2nd in the European Collegiate Championships, and winning various corporate events. She raced for the London School of Economics while studying there and later while working for Charles Schwab & Co.

Valerie has also been a professional ski instructor and has been trained for the National Ski Patrol, not surprising since both her parents were patrol members at their local ski areas in the 1950s. With a background in telecommunications, finance, and planning, she began consulting in the ski industry in 1985. Her firm, Jaffee Associates, focuses primarily on marketing issues for ski areas in or near California.[19] Valerie is dedicated to promoting the sport of skiing both on the West Coast and around the world because, as she says, "it is in my blood."

Dick Durrance '39 – Ski Mountain Designer

Back in 1937, Dick Durrance had set the first American Giant Slalom race course in Tuckerman Ravine in an attempt to control the speed of racers after a downhill race had claimed the life of Franklin Edson in 1936 on the Ghost Trail in Pittsfield, MA.[20] Later, he fell in love with the big mountains of the West where he worked directly on designs in Sun Valley, Alta, and Aspen, but indirectly influenced the ski area layouts of most of the major Western ski mountains.

The following comments about his father's mountain design work were written by **David Durrance**, who is one of Dick Durrance's sons and a former Dartmouth Alpine ski coach and professional ski racer.

David Durrance, former Dartmouth ski coach, speaking at CarniVAIL - 2009.

Having grown up in the sponge-diving community of Tarpon Springs, Florida, Dick Durrance hardly had the credentials to be a ski area designer. But as a teenager, he learned to ski in Europe where there were great wide open spaces above the timberline and narrow tree-lined trails below. Then in New England, while at Dartmouth, he skied narrow corkscrew trails like Moosilauke, Nose Dive, the Taft Trail, and Hillmans Highway. As he traveled West for ski races he saw bigger mountains with great possibilities for skiing.

When Averell Harriman invited him to Sun Valley, ostensibly to shoot publicity photographs, he talked Mr. Harriman into letting him design and cut a few trails on Baldy Mountain. With no restrictions on how many trees he could cut, Dick cleared wide swaths through the forests that opened up a whole new way of skiing for the West. He had created the open feel of the alpine skiing in Europe, but with the trees as protection from the wind.

He went on to start Alta with Jay McLaughlin. Jay took care of the financial matters and Dick did the lifts and trails. He cleared out gullies so they could be skied and opened up the natural bowls and rolls to let skiers enjoy the great powder snow that Alta had to offer.

After the war, when he became the first General Manager of the Aspen Skiing Company, he had a great new mountain to play with.

He designed trails like Ruthie's Run, Dipsy Doodle, and Silver Queen. He cleared the deadfall and blowdown from Bell Mountain and opened up Spar Gulch. When he was able to bring the FIS World Championships to Aspen in 1950, he adjusted and added to what he had already done to make racecourses that the European skiers said set the new standard for international racing.

His mission was to use the natural terrain of the mountain and open it up so that skiers could use all of their creativity to enjoy all of the possibilities. Most who have skied his runs would agree he did just that.

Charles Proctor '28 – Ski Area Designer and Consultant

In addition to Charlie Proctor's other accomplishments, he consulted on the development of ski areas. In 1931 he laid ski trails and established a weekend ski school at Newfound Lake near Bristol, NH. In 1933 he worked as a ski consultant, laying out the trails to be worked on by the Civilian Conservation Corps, which had just been founded that same year. He also laid out trails on Pico Peak in Vermont for the Mead family, whose daughter, Andrea, was a future Olympic champion.

Three years later he was hired by Averell Harriman, Chairman of the Union Pacific Railroad, to consult on the resort to be built at Sun Valley, ID. Charlie went to Ketchum to teach a class of eight local boys to ski in order to raise interest in skiing among the townspeople. The class climbed what was later to be called Dollar Mountain to make runs and ventured onto the slopes of Mt. Baldy. In a report to Harriman, Charlie advised against building a ski area at Mt. Baldy because the terrain was too advanced for most skiers of the day. He also advised against the terrain picked by Harriman's advisor, Count Schaffgotsch, above Elkhorn Creek as too inaccessible. Charlie fixed on Dollar and Proctor Mountains (the latter named in his honor) near the site of the Sun Valley Lodge and suggested that a lift be built to both of these as well as a funicular to some higher terrain. Those choices proved astute and are still being skied 60 years later.

Charles Santry, Tu '89, and the Dupré Family – Snowmaking and Snow Economics

During the winter of 2008-2009 the Dartmouth Skiway in Lyme, N.H., improved its snowmaking production and energy efficiency through the work, expertise, and equipment provided by Snow Economics, Inc., a company that Herman Dupré founded in 1991 with his son-in-law Charles Santry. The college's newly updated snowmaking system is designed to allow more ski terrain to be covered in a shorter period of time, earlier in the season, and at lower cost—giving Dartmouth's ski teams a consistently usable training ground and the Upper Valley community more reliable snow conditions for this recreational facility.

Four former Dartmouth skiers, sisters **Denise Dupré '80**, **Rosi Dupré Littlefield '82**, **Anni Dupré Santry '83**, and **Michele Dupré '88**, and their families, supported this project with a gift to recognize the achievements of the family patriarch, Herman K. Dupré, an internationally known inventor and entrepreneur in the snowmaking industry. "Growing up in Pennsylvania in the 1940s, our dad dreamed of skiing for Dartmouth. His bags were packed, but at the last minute he was needed at home to run the family farm," said the Duprés. They acknowledge their parents' help and enthusiasm:

> "It was his and our mom's hard work and encouragement that enabled us to attend the College and ski competitively. They were both avid skiers and passionate about our educations, skiing, and the ski business. With our gift we wanted to show our appreciation and give Dartmouth first-rate snowmaking capabilities, which our father helped design."

A trail at the Skiway on the Winslow side will be named Herman's Highway for Herman Dupré and a tribute to him will be placed in the McLane Family Lodge." (Dartmouth News-December 2008)

Snow Economics, Inc., is based in Natick, Massachusetts. Since inception, the company has installed snowmaking products at more than 420 ski areas around the world, including in the United States, Canada, Korea, Japan, China, Austria, Switzerland, France, Italy, Germany, Spain, Sweden, Norway and New Zealand. Its basic air/water technology was conceived some 20 years earlier by Herman K. Dupré, founder of Seven Springs Resort in Western Pennsylvania and inventor of the HKD Tower Snowgun System. He spent numerous years developing and refining his technology in its practical application on the mountain. With the HKD system in place, Seven Springs has the unprecedented ability to make snow at a rate capable of blanketing 400 skiable acres of terrain with 12 inches of snow in approximately 48 hours.

Chet Homer '73 – Promoter of Green Skiing

Chet Homer purchased Shawnee Peak Ski Area in Maine in September 1994. In the winter of 2009 he was featured on National Public Radio in an interview about his efforts in energy conservation and promoting "Green Skiing". For the last several years efficiency and energy conservation have been a key driver in his business strategy. He reports:

> "Our water pumping capacity has doubled, we only use high energy efficient snow guns and as a result we can recover very quickly and have reduced on energy costs related to snow-making by approximately 30% — all our snowmaking pumps have variable speed drives and working with State of Maine agencies we got rebates for approx 35% of our investment — we pump 4000 gal/min. After this summer's improvements all the lifts will have been replaced or upgraded during my stewardship. In the summer of '08 we put an addition on the base lodge with R-50 value in the roof, R-35 in walls, 15-watt bulbs for lighting. We only use fluorescent lightening. We have special parking for hybrid cars."

Chet has worked with SE Group to lay out early stages of a master plan. To offset the area's carbon footprint he is working with a conservation group in Maine that plants trees in areas at risk. Additionally, he says:

> "We have cut our use of diesel by one third. We have been an early user of energy efficient snow guns and last year we purchased another $100,000 of equipment from Snow Economics, which is owned by the Dupré family who made the huge donation of equipment to the Dartmouth Skiway. We have testimonials from skiers that they come to ski with us because of our green policies. Shawnee Peak is a recognized leader in green practices within the ski business. For a mid-size ski area this has been a huge capital commitment."

Professor Charles Crane Bradley – Avalanche Control Research

In 1950, Charles Bradley, a member of the Wisconsin Bradley family and a brother of three Dartmouth alumni, drove to Montana in an old convertible roadster with his seven-year-old son Charles, Jr. and a rumble seat full of camping gear to scout for a house because Montana State College (MSU) had started a Department of Geography and Geology in 1947. The first staff member was Nicholas Helburn, a geographer, and he hired Charlie as the college's first Professor of Geology. Most colleges in the U.S. were understaffed and thousands of ex-GIs were enrolling after the end of World War II.

In 1957 Charlie was promoted to full professor and became Dean of the Division of Science at Montana State. After having accepted the administrative role at the college, Charlie realized he missed doing fieldwork. He made sure he was on ten-month teaching contracts so he could spend several months each summer doing research and field work.

After friends of his barely missed being caught in an avalanche while skiing in the Bridger Range near Bozeman, Charlie began to study snow dynamics and conditions related to avalanche initiation. During the period 1965-78, he published a dozen articles on snow and avalanches, many together with **John Montagne '42**, a former 10th Mountain Division trooper who had served in Italy. Under Charlie's leadership, MSU engineers and scientists gained an international reputation and became world leaders in snow mechanics. The accomplishments of the group (which included Montagne and his early associates Bob Brown, Ted Lang and, more recently, Ed Adams) are legendary.

John Merrill Montagne '42

John began an enduring acquaintance with the out-of-doors through experiences as a camper and counselor at Camp Morgan in Washington, NH. At Dartmouth, he continued that acquaintanceship through the Dartmouth Outing Club, became a speed skating athlete, and developed leadership skills and a lifelong commitment to service befitting his election as senior class president. Responding to the call for military service at the outbreak of World War II, John graduated early and, with his interest in the out-of-doors and mountain environments, he joined the newly created US Army Mountain Troops of the 10th Division. John married his wife, Phoebe, on a weekend pass signed by **Walker Weed '40**, the future father-in-law of Montagne's future son, Cliff.

After the war ended, John taught army mountaineering skills on the slopes of the Grossglockner, Austria's highest mountain. Then he and Phoebe settled in Jackson, WY. John served in Jackson as a school principal, teacher, and coach, and then became a Ranger Naturalist in Grand Teton National Park. He and others noticed the need for a trained mountain rescue group. Using his own background, and calling on friends from the 10th Mountain Division, he instigated and organized the first training for Search and Rescue teams in Grand Teton National Park.

John returned to Hanover with Phoebe and briefly worked in the Dartmouth College Admissions Office, but then followed his passion and completed graduate work in Geology at the University of Wyoming. Armed with his PhD, he joined the faculty at Colorado School of Mines; but when his 10th Mountain Division friend and fellow Dartmouth alumnus Prof. Charles Bradley began to build the Earth Sciences Department at Montana State University (MSU), John jumped at the chance to live and work within the Greater Yellowstone ecosystem.

As the skiing at the Big Sky ski resort in Montana developed, John and his students contributed useful information about the Big Sky rock glaciers and hazards. Montagne and Bradley created the first university course on snow avalanches in the United States and laid the foundation for the snow science program at MSU. This led to establishment of the biannual "International Snow Science Workshops" which blend theory with the realities of practice. John was also a founding member of the American Avalanche Association and served as its president from 1990-1994.

When John joined the faculty of the Earth Sciences Department, he also joined the Bozeman area community. A longtime member of the National Ski Patrol, he led the volunteer Bridger Bowl Ski Patrol and served as President of the Bridger Bowl Board of Directors. John and Phoebe embraced skiing as a way of life. Skiing Bridger Bowl or a backcountry tour with friends were weekly family wintertime events. They organized the cross-country events for the 1968 Junior National Ski Championships at Bridger Bowl and helped establish Nordic skiing in Bozeman. Always supportive of ski and outdoor activities, John participated with his family in co-ownership of Crosscut Ranch Ski Touring Center at the base of Bridger Bowl[21]. John Montagne died in 2008 from complications of melanoma which, according to his wife Joan, started with a severe sunburn he got at Camp Hale when he fell asleep on a snow bank during maneuvers!

SUMMARY

Whether working in the medical area, in ski mountain development, or in managing terrain and skier activities to enhance the skiing experience for all, there are usually Dartmouth folks involved. Some are managing and doing, and some are simply taking advantage of the experience and helping to grow the enthusiasm for the sport. In addition to Dave Durrance's article earlier on his father's mountain design work, the two articles below highlight ancillary technical contributions through an Adaptive Skiing program in Alaska and the involvement of faculty and students of Dartmouth's Thayer School of Engineering in ski activities over many decades.

***

ADAPTIVE SKIING PROJECT IN SIBERIA

By Philip K. Livingston '58
Senior Ski Instructor at Alyeska and a Community Leader

From 2000 to 2001, I was Governor of District 5010, Rotary International. Geographically, it is the largest Rotary District in the world. It includes the Yukon Territory, Alaska, Far East Russia, and Siberia. That position gave me a personal link with vast areas both east and west of Alaska. In my second life, after retirement, I became a certified Alpine and Adaptive Ski Instructor, having first taught skiing for **Dick Perkins '56** at the Dartmouth Ski School as an undergraduate. To make a long story short, I started an adaptive ski program in Russia in 2003.

The opportunity arose when I was invited to teach an adaptive ski clinic to members of the Russian Professional Ski Association (ARASIA). "Adaptive skiing" is a collection of special techniques and equipment to help disabled persons participate in the sport of skiing. The invitation came from a former President of our Komsomolsk Na Amur Rotary Club.

255

To my surprise, he also turned out to be the Director of the ARASIA in Far East Russia. Among his other credits, Alexander Shelopugin had guided a film crew for Warren Miller at some point. The International Fellowship of Skiing Rotarians and their Davis Boyd Memorial Foundation, Rotary District 5010, The Rotary Foundation, and our local Rotary Clubs underwrote a 'Rotary Foundation Discovery Grant' to help fund the trip.

This overture was a 'thank you' for an earlier Rotary project. In 2002 we brought a disabled Russian boy to Alaska for medical attention. The young man was Alexander's son Igor. His left hand was crushed and his right arm was severed above the wrist as the result of a climbing accident led by his father. He was clinically depressed and suicidal at age fifteen. The medical care available in Far East Russia is basic, and although the disabled are well taken care of, they are effectively ostracized from normal society. After our club meeting in Komsomolsk Na Amur, the Vice President of the club took me aside and told me he was certain that if Igor committed suicide, Alexander would surely follow. When I got home I could not get this out of my mind. I was not only sympathetic to the bleak future faced by Igor but aware that, but for the grace of God, Alexander's anguish could have been mine. I have four children and have taken risks with them more than once.

This is a long story filled with coincidence and serendipity, but the bottom line is that after many false starts trying to find a surgical solution, one of our local Rotarians fitted Igor with two prosthetics: a hook for his missing right hand and a custom fitting for his crushed left hand. Then, both for therapy and to accustom Igor to his new prosthetics, we took him skiing. Igor's father was an extreme skier and we assumed that Igor was a skier, too, although we couldn't ask because of the language barrier. The moment he stepped into his skis we knew we were right.

I have a picture of Igor, his father, and my wife Diana on top of Mount Alyeska during that first day, arms raised high in exultation. That night, he came to our Rotary Club and shook hands with every member of the club...with his hook. He went back to Russia and is now in law school.

With the ARASIA invitation in hand, we formed a training team from the adaptive ski school at the Alyeska Resort, Challenge Alaska, Inc., and went to Komsomolsk Na Amur. The results of that clinic were two-fold: first, new teaching techniques were learned by professional Russian ski instructors, and second, the experience of having used disabled boys from a nearby orphanage as our students opened the eyes of these instructors to the concept that disabled skiers could and would benefit from their sport. This epiphany resulted in the ARASIA adding a new division for adaptive skiing to their association in Russia. Subsequently, in 2005, we brought a Russian ski instructor to Alyeska Resort and Challenge Alaska, Inc., and certified him as the first Professional Adaptive Ski Instructor in Russia. And, lest we forget, Challenge Alaska, Inc., ski instructors Tom Beatty and I were also certified by ARASIA. I can't read the badge they gave me; it's in Russian. But I wear it.

We recently received a second invitation to teach an adaptive ski clinic in Russia: this time in Magadan, Far East Russia. This clinic will teach parents in a "village specifically for the disabled" how to teach their children to ski. Coincidentally, this approach is very similar to the one Dick Perkins used at the Dartmouth Ski School to teach the children of Hanover "Dartmouth skiing." We brokered this second invitation to the Rotary Club of Whistler, BC. They are working to send a team to Russia to teach adaptive techniques from their adaptive ski school (W.A.S.P.) As tenuous as the string may be, Dartmouth skiing was the catalyst for three countries spanning half the world – the US, Russia, and Canada – to work together effectively in a unique humanitarian endeavor: that of enabling the disabled to participate in our sport.

Actually, that was not the end of the story: the same suspects – International Skiing Fellowship of Rotarians and the Davis Boyd Memorial Foundation with The Rotary Foundation – have also initiated other projects at Challenge Alaska, Inc., including a Bush Alpine Ski program, which gives rural Alaska children the opportunity to learn to ski, and also a Disabled Veterans Ski program which includes a Para-Olympic ski program. The latter has recently received additional support from two private foundations.

I believe in the "stone and puddle" analogy: when a stone drops in the water, the circles continuously expand. That is Rotary's concept of active involvement and it closely mirrors the concept Dartmouth's influence on skiing. Where there is passion and it is shared, there is progress.

***

THAYER SCHOOL CONNECTIONS

By Fred Hart, '58, Th '60
DOC Director of Competitions 1957, DOC President 1958

In the very beginning, when **Fred Harris '11** wisely realized that support from the faculty and administration would be essential to the Outing Club's success, he could hardly have imagined that not only would the College, but the entire Hanover community, unhesitatingly become involved in providing that support. Dartmouth's Thayer School of Engineering, founded by **Sylvanus Thayer '07** in 1867, has certainly rendered its share. Possibly the earliest example was **Allen P. Richmond '14** [22] who was part of the group of students and faculty that made the first down-mountain excursion on Moosilauke's Carriage Road as a senior in 1914.[23] He returned to teach Civil Engineering on the faculty at Thayer during the 1920s, and served as an advisor and member of the DOC Council from 1925-1929. He even used his engineering expertise to design and supervise the building of a new living room fireplace for the Moosilauke Summit House during this period, site of the original telling of the celebrated Doc Benton Ghost Story.[24] Other Thayer personnel would serve in similar advisory and support capacities in later years: for example, **William P. Kimball '28** (later Thayer School's Dean) was a DOC Trustee in 1948-1951 and on its Board in 1951-1953, and **Richard W. Olmstead '32, Th '33** (Dartmouth's Manager of Buildings and Grounds) served on the DOC Board from 1953-1956.[25]

During the 1950s, the Thayer faculty formed the backbone of the officials list for ski meets sponsored and run by the DOC. The Winter Sports Division relied heavily on the experience and expertise of these volunteers, lined up and organized by Civil Engineering **Prof. Edward S. Brown Jr. '34, Th '35**, led by Dean Kimball himself, and including Thayer faculty members Edwin A. Sherrard, **Jim Browning '44, Th '45**, Carl Long (also later to become a Dean of Thayer School), Millett G. Morgan, Huntington W. Curtis, **S. Russell (Russ) Stearns '37, Th '38**, and Kenneth A. (Ken) LeClair. These men turned out on their own time for event after event as timers, judges and scorers, with their warmest overcoats (and sometimes their own stopwatches), working closely and smoothly with other officials from all over New England, to make Dartmouth races among the safest and most professionally conducted ones of the era.

One of these Thayer faculty members, Electrical Engineering **Prof. Millett G. Morgan**, had grown up in Hanover and studied radio engineering at Cornell and later at Stanford (since Thayer School still had only a Civil Engineering curriculum). Eventually, he returned to Hanover as a member of the Thayer faculty briefly in 1941, and permanently about 1947 after serving in radio research for the Navy during World War II. While an undergraduate at Cornell, Morgan had put his Hanover background and organizational skills to good use, serving as President of the Cornell Ski Club in 1937 and starting a ski team. He participated with the team in the Dartmouth Winter Carnival, the Lake Placid Club's College Week, and other intercollegiate competitions, including a series of Dartmouth - Cornell match races on a home-and-home basis.[26]

Professor Millett Morgan continued to ski in Hanover, and promote skiing to his Thayer School students.

For a time in the 1950s, four out of six DOC presidents in a row were also Thayer or Tuck-Thayer graduates: **Roland B. Leavens '53, Tu-Th '54, Harlan R. Jessup, Jr., '55, Tu-Th '56, Clark A. Griffiths '57, Th '58** and **Frederick C. Hart, Jr., '58, Th '60**.

Perhaps the most interesting aspect of Thayer School's connection with skiing is technical, rather than organizational. Although it was only possible to readily search for skiing-related topics for Thayer School undergraduate and graduate degree projects for the years from 1963 to the present, several were found on a variety of subjects – most of them related to mechanical engineering and thermodynamics.[27] These projects are probably typical of the kind that Thayer students (with skiing obviously on their minds) might have selected during the pre-1963 years:

- "Cross-country ski no-wax base design", Mark Beauregard, Yu-Hwei Chou, Bachelor of Engineering Project Report, Winter 2008.

- "Designing an algorithm for use of the pulse electro-thermal brake in cross-country skiing", Gabriel P. Martine, Thesis (M.S.), 2005.

- "Audible speedometer project: an application for snow skiing", Samantha Abeyratne, Sean Sherrod, Tao Zhou, Bachelor of Engineering Project Report, Winter 1999.

- "The thermal characteristics of downhill skis", Guy Charles Warren, Thesis (M.S.), 1989.

- "Evaluation of artificial snow-making alternatives for the Killington ski area", John Alexander Meleney, Bachelor of Engineering Project Report, Spring 1971.

- "Design of an apparatus for snow and ice removal, and transportation, on a ski slope", George Edgar, Bachelor of Engineering Project Report, Spring 1964.

A number of Thayer graduates have gone on to prominent careers in the ski industry: **Selden L. Hannah '65, Th '66**, who was for a time part of the Sno-engineering firm started by his father, Dartmouth's former skier, coach and Ski Hall of Fame member **Selden J. Hannah '35**; and **W. Scott Barthold '78, Th '81**, another former team member and an assistant ski coach for Dartmouth while a student at Thayer, who also worked with Sno-engineering and later began his own consulting firm, Sno.matic Controls and Engineering, Inc.

We should also note that Olympian **J. Brooks ("Brookie") Dodge, Jr. '51, Th '54**, son of **Joe Dodge '55 (Hon)**,[28] the amiable Adirondack Mountain Club Hutmaster at Pinkham Notch, NH, and long-time friend and supporter of New England skiing, was also a Thayer graduate and an inductee into the National Ski Hall of Fame.

Closing the loop that encompasses Thayer School, skiing, and an engineering career in a remarkable way is Clark Griffiths (mentioned above), whose brother **Jim Griffiths '65** managed nearby Whaleback ski area for many years. Upon graduation from Thayer, Clark joined what was then the small Split Ballbearing Company in Lebanon, NH. He spent his entire 35-year career there and retired as their Head of Engineering after having helped the firm grow to a total workforce of about 900 employees. But in Clark's own words: "What I never knew was that Split Ballbearing received the contract and obtained or fabricated the components and built the Oak Hill lift for the Outing Club in 1935 according to agreed upon specifications." Clark's story is yet another example of the often unpredictable effect that a Dartmouth ski experience has had on countless lives, and in many careers.

Notes

1. Letter from J. P. Carleton to Stevens, Dec. 19, 1949; J P Carleton File in Rauner 2. Commented on Dick Jackson in the 1939 Dartmouth Alumni Magazine, DAM Class Column. 3. Published by the LCG Publishing Co., Hanover, New Hampshire. 4. Oral interview with Wylie Scott. 5. (Looudis, Lobitz, and Singer, "Skiing Out of Your Mind" Human Kinetics Publishers, Inc, Champaign, Illinois, 1986). 6. NESN Newsletter, Autumn 1999, Issue #49. 7. VOX of Dartmouth, February 2006). 8. E-mail from Jerry Groswold, Winter Park, CO. 9. E-mail from Bill Bradley, 11/26/08. 10. Based on e-mail comments from Henry Hof , May 29, 2009 and subsequent. 11. (Box 2001.1644.001B NESM). 12. Jeff Leich, NESM, 2/21/06. 13. Personal communication Sel Hannah. 14. Box 2001.048.001A NESM. 15. Box 2001.048.001C NESM. 16. Box 2001.164001B NESM. 17. Oral interview with Fred Jones. 18. Fred Jones, ibid. 19. Personal communication with Valerie Jaffee. 20. NESM Newsletter, ibid. 21. NY Times Jan 20, 2009. 22. Class numerals are only included herein for Dartmouth undergraduate and Thayer School classes. To avoid confusion, graduation dates from other institutions have not been included. 23. Doug Leitch, supra, chapter 2. 24. David O. Hooke, Reaching That Peak (Canaan, NH: Phoenix Publishing, 1987), 151. 25. Reaching That Peak, 449. 26. Millett G. Morgan, "Skiing in New York State Colleges and Universities," High Spots, Adirondack Mountain Club, January 1937, 20-1; copy provided by his daughter, Deborah Morgan Olsen. 27. We appreciate the assistance of Sarah J. Buckingham, Reference Librarian at Thayer's Feldberg Library for her assistance in generating this list. 28. Joe Sr. never attended Dartmouth but was awarded an honorary Master of Arts Degree by the College at Commencement of 12 June 1955 (William Lowell Putnam, Joe Dodge 'One New Hampshire Institution' (Canaan, NH: Phoenix Publishing, 1986), 132.

Chapter XIII

INTERACTIONS IN THE INTERNATIONAL SKI WORLD

By Stephen Waterhouse '65, Tu '67

With Ned Jacoby '40, Chik Onodera '58 and Valerie Chiyo Jaffee '78

It is fair to say that skiing has been a regular activity in many parts of the world long before it started in the U.S. As noted in the Introduction, the oldest ski artifacts recognized by the International Ski Federation (FIS) Historical Timeline of Skiing, specially researched by Elisabeth Hussey and her team of historians, are skis found in Russia dating from 6,000 BC. The FIS Timeline also refers to a number of early artifacts associated with the Scandinavian countries. The United States as a country did not exist in this era, but the American continent did. One must anticipate that there were artifacts in the northern areas of America as well but these have eluded researchers for now.

British Ski Club and FIS historian Elisabeth Hussey on the slopes.

What we might call modern skiing started developing actively in the 1800s with Telemarking races in Scandinavia, British travel companies taking skiers to Switzerland for skiing holidays, and a first ski club formed by Norwegian immigrants in Berlin, New Hampshire, near the location of the contemporary New England Ski Museum. As the 20th century began, travel to go skiing somewhere foreign and then return home was still limited. There were no major racing venues, or even established racing rules, to attract people to go see exceptional downhill or slalom skiers. There were no ski lifts to carry skiers quickly up a mountain to expand the potential of skiing events. However, as the 20th century unfolded, all this changed. And Dartmouth College's early involvement with these activities led to its playing a unique role in International or multi-country developments in skiing as well as impacting many aspects of US skiing. Its alumni, students, faculty and families became regular travelers to distant parts to participate in skiing adventures. Likewise, foreign skiers began to recognize Hanover, NH, as a special place on the world skiing map to both ski and obtain a high quality education. This has led to a number of different individual stories of Dartmouth connections with International skiing. This chapter will provide some details on a number of those stories.

According to the FIS skiing timeline study, ski racing and recreational skiing began in the 19th century with equipment innovations like the development of a heel strap in 1850 by Sondre Norheim of Morgedal, Telemark. He entwined shoots of birch tree roots with enough stiffness to provide adequate control, but enough elasticity to keep the heel in a snug position during both downhill skiing and ski racing. The study references a competition event in 1866 conducted by the Central Ski Association in the Norwegian capital, Christiania, where Sondre Norheim and his Telemarking team demonstrated what would later be called a Telemark turn and a Christiania skidded stop turn. In 1870, Norheim introduced the first modern sidecut ski. This narrow-waisted ski flexed easily on the snow, which facilitated smooth carving and turning. The Norwegians were active in the US as well. In 1882, Norwegian immigrants organized the Norske Ski Club in Berlin, NH, as the first ski club in America.[1] That ski club became known as the "Berlin Mills Ski Club", and in years to come would be the source of many Dartmouth skiers, including **Sel Hannah '35**.

The earliest international adventure for Dartmouth students appears to have been in 1914 when a group of Dartmouth winter sports athletes journeyed to Montreal to complete against McGill University and its newly formed ski club in the first intercollegiate ski race event ever held on the American Continent. As noted in the FIS Timeline, "The McGill Ski Club was formed as an affiliate of the Montreal Ski Club. A cross country and ski-jumping meet was held between McGill College and Dartmouth College of Hanover, NH USA in January 1914 – the first intercollegiate meet in America."

The start of the first Downhill ever run under the rules set up by Sir Arnold Lunn whose ideas were reflected in the first US Downhill (1927) on Dartmouth's Mt. Moosilauke.

The connections with international ski activities did not just involve skiers. In 1919, early ski retail merchant **John Piane '14** was reselling ski socks, sweaters, hats, wax, and assorted other goods shipped to him from Europe. One of his suppliers was Marius Eriksen of Norway, father of Olympic skier Stein Eriksen.[2] Piane was looking for all the opportunities he could find to source equipment that would be welcomed by the very active ski community around Hanover.

In the early 1920s, one of Dartmouth's star skiers, **John Carleton '22**, headed to Oxford University in the United Kingdom as a Rhodes Scholar. Carleton was regarded as the best US skier of his day and had a particular interest in ski jumping. John's ability to successfully complete somersaults off jumps was a forerunner of some of the more exotic freestyle skiing of current times. At Oxford, John got involved with the University's skiing crowd and joined them on trips to Switzerland to compete in races. There he met British ski pioneer Arnold Lunn, and as this book has detailed, the early connection of Lunn to Carleton, and later to **Charley Proctor '28**, sparked a regular exchange of new information on the development of skiing from the Old World to the New. The Dartmouth ski crowd took advantage of Lunn's innovations to start the first Slalom and Downhill races in North America.

Among Charley Proctor's activities in Europe was his participation in the first race of what was the greatest downhill and slalom ski racing event in the world for many years. That first race took place in 1928 at St. Anton, Austria (March 31, 1928)[3], and was known as the Arlberg-Kandahar Cup. The A-K race was started by the two most important European ski innovators, Britain's Sir Arnold Lunn and Austria's Hannes Schneider. As Warren Miller has mentioned in his foreword, Charley Proctor was one of the true great Dartmouth and US skiing innovators as well as a member of the US National Ski Hall of Fame, and a participant in the second Winter Olympics (1928, St. Moritz). Through his exposure to the skiing legends of Europe and his role as an early legend of skiing in the U.S., Charley Proctor became one of the most influential thought leaders in early US skiing

The Arlberg-Kandahar race, named for the "Kandahar Club sponsoring a race in the Arlberg"[4], was very important in developing relationships amongst the international ski fraternity as most of the world's leading racers prior to World War II met there, competed against each other, shared the spirit of the event and developed great camaraderie. Lunn wrote in the 1938 edition of his *British Ski Year Book*, the bible of European skiing history, that "it is the personality of Hannes [Schneider] which is more responsible than any other single factor for the A-K atmosphere....The ten years that have passed [since the first A-K race] have only served to deepen my respect and affection for this paladin of ski-ing… He dominates St. Anton,…his outstanding success as a teacher,… his great record as an active skier… and his engaging personality. There is a granite-like integrity about the man"[5] This is the same Hannes Schneider who would escape from a Nazi prison cell, and get transported to—of all places—New Hampshire, where he would establish one of the great ski instruction schools, one that still operates today. He was not a Dartmouth man, but his spirit, as reported by Lunn, of "granite-like integrity", is reminiscent of the Dartmouth song defining her

> On February 26th, 1928 Arnold Lunn as the representative of the Ski Club of Great Britain secured the official recognition by the Federation Internationale de Ski at the Oslo Congress for the British Rules of Downhill and Slalom racing which had gradually evolved from the Rules reproduced above.

The statement plaque in the British Ski Club Library to commemorate the acceptance of Sir Arnold Lunn's rules for Downhill and Slalom by the FIS in 1928.

alumni as having "the granite of New Hampshire in their muscles and their brains…"

The reason for commenting on Lunn and Schneider is to point out the tight connection of people who were Dartmouth alums and those who were to become connected with Dartmouth in the early years of the development of modern skiing via the active mixing of experiences in the international ski world. Schneider, as well as his son Herbert and his family, came to New Hampshire largely through the efforts of Harvey Gibson, who owned Mt. Cranmore and wanted to develop it into a major ski area. But it is not hard to appreciate that Schneider's mind rested easy on this move because he had to be aware of so many serious skiers whom he knew from past A-K races and other ski activities in Europe, had moved to the US. Many started out by skiing in New Hampshire, as part of growing migration of leading European ski legends from Europe to the U.S., particularly in the late 1930s.

Hannes Schneider skis Oak Hill, Hanover, NH with Dartmouth Olympian Brooks Dodge '51, Th '54 (Schneider is far right and Dodge is to his left).

One of those connections for Schneider would have been the leading racing star of the world in the early 1930s. This was none other than future Dartmouth ski coach **Walter Prager** who won the 1930 and 1933 A-K races and placed in the top three in at least one of the three featured races (Straight Race, Slalom, Combined) in two other A-K race years. Lunn comments on Prager's racing style during the 1931 Straight Race (the fourth A-K in Murren, Switzerland), illustrating his respect for Prager's skill: "Prager is recognizable even at a distance by his easy, unconcerned style. He ran beautifully"[6] That particular year, Walter fell and only placed 22nd in the Straight Race, which was won by Bracken of Great Britain. Walter recovered in the Slalom to place 2nd to the legendary Otto Furrer of Switzerland and 9th in the Combined.

And Hannes would have probably known of John Carleton because of John's racing in Swiss races in 1923-24 while he was at Oxford, being one of the American participants in the 1924 Olympics, and being a contact of Lunn's. He would undoubtedly have known Charley Proctor who was involved in the first A-K Race in 1928. And he would have known **Dick Durrance '39**, who had created a name for himself in Germany, and in the tight European ski world, as winner of the 1932 German Junior Championships, and by having placed well in the 1933 A-K (16th in the Straight Race, 35th in Slalom, 32nd Combined) where Prager was going 1st, 2nd and 1st. In the 1936 A-K, Durrance placed well (15th in the Straight Race, 8th in the Slalom and 11th in the Combined). In this same year of 1936, Prager almost became the first person to win the coveted A-K Diamond Award for placing 3rd or better in the races of 5 separate years. But as Lunn reported, "Prager ran the *Furrerhang* [straight race] superbly and missed his Diamond by three seconds, a narrow enough margin for a skier who returns to racing after breaking a leg." Prager finished 5th, 10th and 6th overall.[7] As reported earlier, he was eventually to be the fifth man awarded the A-K Diamond by Lunn in 1956.

Prager Wins Alpine Skiing Highest Prize

Walter Prager, College ski coach and former United States Olympic team ski coach, received alpine skiing's highest award Saturday night at the annual banquet of the United States Amateur Ski Association in Albany, N.Y.

The Diamond Alberg-Kandahar pin was presented to Prager by Edwin Eaton, President of the USEASA, on behalf of Sir Arnold Lunn of the Kandahar ski club. Lunn, one of the founders of alpine skiing as it is known today and author of books on skiing and mountaineering, asked that the award be presented in full recognition of Prager's greatness as a skier.

The Alberg-Kandahar ski race, first run in 1928 through the joint efforts of the Alberg and Kandahar ski clubs in one of the most famous of all ski competitions and fittingly it has the most famous of skiing's awards, the Diamond "A-K" pin, attached to its running.

In order to win the Diamond award a skier must have won either separately or in aggregate the slalom, downhill and combined five times. Only three other racers besides Prager have been able to accomplish this feat. These three are Otto Furrer, Swiss guide and father of the College's ex-assistant ski coach Charley Purrer; James Coutet; and Andre Molterner.

Named Assista[t] Dartmouth Coa[ch]

HANOVER, N. H.—Allison coach of the U. S. Olympi[c] Country ski team last winter, named assistant ski coach of [Dart]mouth Outing Club. Merril[l] former coach of the Leba[non] School ski team, will assist Walter Prager and will also [assist]ant supervisor of Dartmo[uth] Holt's Ledge Ski Area in L[ ].

In 1954 Merrill was coach [U.] S. FIS ski team in the Nordi[c] bined events. The followin[g] coached both the alpine [ ] squads of the U. S. Eastern [asso]ciation Junior ski team in [ ] Utah and held the same p[ ] at Whitefish, Mont.

Merrill is a graduate of [Univer]sity of New Hampshire.

WALTER PRAGER

Newspaper story on Prager's recognition as one of the greatest racers in the 1930s.

Jeff Leich '71, President of the New England Ski Museum in Franconia, NH, and a fellow writer in this book, once wrote: "In St. Anton, Hannes Schneider had collected what was essentially a bunch of peasants, friends of his, and helped give them professions. Those men, in turn, went around the world and created ski areas of their own." Many of these same people came together in North Conway, NH. While Hannes helped to develop Cranmore into a world-class destination, his son Herbert went on to serve his new homeland in WWII, traveling to Colorado to help train the US Army's elite 10th Mountain Division, and later fighting as a soldier on skis in the European theater. As summarized earlier, if Hannes had not been fully aware of the Dartmouth connection to skiing before, he most certainly would have been after his son's tour of duty with the heavily Dartmouth led 10th Mountain Division. Hannes also spent some time in Japan and would probably have gained some knowledge of the Igaya skiing contributions by both the father, Kunio, and his son, **Chick Igaya '57**. Hannes Schneider passed away in 1955, but his son ran the family ski business for decades after that.

In the 1930s, "Dartmouth men would leave Hanover knowing how to ski, but with nowhere to purchase ski equipment and apparel where they settled. Orders came to the Dartmouth Co-op from all over the country."[8] John Piane continued to look for the best products to satisfy this demand and kept a close eye on developments in markets around the world. One of the major technical problems with early ski equipment was in mating the boot to the ski. Swiss music-box maker, Guido Reuge, invented a heel plate and spring system to secure both the toe and heel of the boot to the ski, the Kandahar Ski Binding. Piane obtained a license in 1930 to manufacture and sell them in the United States. The Kandahar–Dartmouth–Hanover Ski Binding quickly became a widely distributed product throughout the developing US retail market for ski equipment.

Another important international factor involving Dartmouth was the series of European ski coaches hired from 1923 to1957 by the College to develop and lead its growing ski racing program. This sequence (outlined in Chapter II of this book) was started with wise input from the DOC's founder, **Fred Harris '11**, and others who had some exposure to the international racing scene. They brought the best racing techniques of the time to Hanover. The first such coach was Colonel **Anton Diettrich**, a solid skier and fencer. Diettrich served as ski coach first for the 1923-24 season. He was also the fencing coach His knowledge of ski techniques like Slalom and Downhill from his connection to skiing in Europe was important to the birth of these techniques in the U.S. and nurtured at Dartmouth in 1925 (slalom) and 1927 (downhill).

For the 1927-28 season, **Sig L. Steinwall** joined the Dartmouth staff as the new ski coach. Steinwall was a Norwegian ski jumper and a member of the prestigious Norge Ski Club of Chicago. He had won many Swedish jumping contests and enjoyed an international reputation as a jumper. However, his focus on jumping was not what the Dartmouth ski team needed as it developed its skills in the new ski alpine racing activity. **German "Gerry" Raab**, another well-known European skier and a graduate of the University of Munich, was engaged as the ski team coach for the 1928-30 seasons.

Jack McCrillis '19 and **William P. Fowler '21** encouraged a shift to professional ski instructor **Otto Schniebs** from the Black Forest in Germany for the 1930-31 season. Otto brought not only great ski coaching skills but also an outstanding personality to the job. He was well connected in all aspects of skiing, and he greatly influenced the development of skiing at not only Dartmouth but at many other colleges and universities, including some of the important women's colleges. Finally, in 1936, the last of the leading European ski coaches arrived, World Champion racer Walter Prager, who was to continue in this role until 1957 with time away only for US military service in World War II and at the Olympics. Each of the European coaches brought important skiing connections, knowledge of European ski history and activities, and a special focus on what was still an underdeveloped sport at most other schools. In the context of this book, these men all contributed significantly to the strong connection of Dartmouth to the International ski world.

The Dartmouth connection continued to evolve with individual skiers taking advantage of skiing facilities in Australia, New Zealand, Chile, Japan and other countries in addition to Europe. One was the early trip of **Dave Bradley '38, Steve Bradley '39** and **Dick Durrance '39** to New Zealand in 1937 that produced the now famous image of Durrance skiing fast across a slope discussed earlier. The Dartmouth ski team has been making regular trips to Chile for decades. Current Dartmouth ski coach, **Peter Dodge '78**, has been running an annual ski clinic there for several years.

Another factor was the importance of Winter Carnival to Dartmouth's skiing reputation. Carnival became known as the Mardis Gras of Skiing and also as a serious venue for talented ski racers. And because it was repeatedly featured in movies, magazine stories and other promotional vehicles, this event became a big enough draw to bring foreign ski teams to Hanover for the 2nd weekend of February. Over the years, teams from Norway, Switzerland, Germany, Austria, and Chile amongst others came to Hanover to race against the Dartmouth skiers. Other outstanding US ski racers and jumpers entered the Winter Carnival

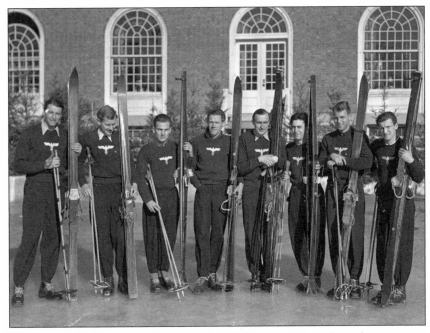

This entire German ski team skied in the 1938 Dartmouth Winter Carnival.

competitions. Each time a foreign team or individual skier came to visit Dartmouth, it added to the knowledge, prestige and reputation of Dartmouth in the ski world.

As this international reputation grew, Carnival also became a draw for individual racers from other countries. Starting after World War II, and heating up in the 1950s, some of the most talented younger racers on the world stage made the trek to Hanover to attend Dartmouth and obtain instruction from the legendary ski coach Walter Prager. This transition was aided by fans of Dartmouth skiing like international businessman and ski enthusiast, C.V. Starr. It was he who personally recruited and often financially supported some of the most outstanding skiers like Chick Igaya '57 of Japan to make the transition from other countries to Hanover, NH. These men would race on the college team and add much to the ski environment at Dartmouth and then race in the Olympics for their home country. Starr also sponsored trips to Hanover for some of the parents of these skiers. One such parent was an older legend of Japanese skiing, Kunio Igaya, father of Chick Igaya. C.V. hosted the elder Igaya on his trip to Hanover and on visits to many of the better US ski resorts. This in turn stimulated some ideas for Kunio Igaya to use in the development of his own ski area in Japan, Shiga Heights, which was, and still is, one of Japan's leading ski areas.

Another special category of international skier/student at Dartmouth encompasses those who may be a citizen of a foreign country and those of American nationality but also holding a passport of another country. They come to Dartmouth and yet still ski for the National and/or Olympic teams of the foreign country. When Dartmouth became coeducational in 1972, it concurrently initiated a new way of dividing up the school year. Unlike every other significant college in the U.S., Dartmouth splits the school year up in to four terms; this provides the opportunity for undergraduates to choose the terms they attend each year. To make it work smoothly, all sophomores are expected to attend the summer term after their normal sophomore year. But a skier can improvise and take every winter term off, attending classes every summer; or, as some do, just extend the normal four year college program to six, eight or as much as ten years. Other notable skiing colleges may permit students to take time off and extend the total number of years to graduate, but only the Dartmouth Plan is set up to handle this scheduling option as a regular activity for any student.

And for skiers, the Dartmouth coaching staff emphasizes to all new ski prospects that the Dartmouth program is set up to help every skier achieve his or her maximum potential. Thus any international skiers looking for a first-rate American education can matriculate at Dartmouth, attend classes for the terms that suit their specific needs, and eventually obtain a highly desirable degree while skiing to the limits of their skills in whatever country or ski region is required. This is a unique combination of attributes that, when recognized by leading international skiers with a desire for a degree from one of the top ten academic institutions in the US, is hard to pass up.

DARTMOUTH'S INTERNATIONAL SKIERS

As a result of many of these earlier connections, Dartmouth has had a frequent flow of skiers to Europe, Scandinavia, Japan and Australia/New Zealand where skiing has been established for a long time. In other places like Korea, China, India and many more, skiing has not been very active until recent years. The involvement of Dartmouth-connected individuals in these less active markets has often developed through an individual wanting to continue to ski so they seek out whatever facilities exist and ski or participate in activities they are familiar with like working on the ski patrol.

Steve Bradley skiing an Australian mountain in 1937.

In assessing the Dartmouth impact on many of these foreign environments, one could draw some parallels to the spread of products like MacDonald's hamburgers. There is a special excitement that American enthusiasm and entrepreneurial, can-do spirit has brought to many activities or products that have become common around the world. Skiing is no different. The enthusiasm shared by Dartmouth skiers for over 100 years has contributed significantly to the development of ski lifts, ski resorts, and ski related technologies of all kinds. Dartmouth skiers have visited and helped generate skiing enthusiasm in even the more distant places like Australia, New Zealand and Chile. They have intermingled with and been similarly stimulated by the older ski markets in Europe and the Scandinavian countries.

One other unusual contributing factor in the development of skiing around the world has been the presence of the US military in many countries, most often the Army, and the number of Dartmouth skiers that have been involved while in the service. Even before the formation of the 10th Mountain Division, Dartmouth alumni like **Russell Dow '38** were helping develop skiing via Army assignments in distant places. In his case, it meant building the rope tow for a small ski area in Anchorage, Alaska, and helping to build up the Anchorage Ski Club. This process was particularly enhanced with the activities of the 10th Mountain Division in World War II and the unusually large number of skiers that passed through that experience; but it continued after the war as elements of the military stayed in foreign countries. and people like **Bill "Sarge" Brown** racing successfully throughout Europe during post-World War II assignments; or **Ralph Miller '55** enjoying great racing success in Europe as a soldier in the mid 1950s; or **Doug Leitch '65** simply hustling up a mountain in Japan during time off from active duty in the 1960s to enjoy a limited skiing opportunity; and **Dave Mulliken, Jr. '00** or **Louie Cheng Tu '03** serving in the modern 10th Mountain Division in Iraq and Afghanistan. These last two would find little opportunity to ski in these regions today, but if the chance comes they will no doubt take it.

AUSTRALIA AND NEW ZEALAND

Skiing has been going on in Australia and New Zealand for a long time. Dartmouth skiers have been visiting there for over 70 years, and they still make regular trips to enjoy skiing during US summers. The two countries enjoy a healthy rivalry in skiing resorts. The average holiday ski or snowboard terrain is intermediate blue-groomed runs like most blue runs around the world. Australia has the largest ski resort, Perisher in Australasia, followed by Mount Ruapehu's Whakapapa resort on New Zealand's North Island. Skiing in New Zealand is above the tree line, while in Australia, the snow gum trees provide some definition to ski trails in stormy, low-visibility weather. Queenstown, a truly stunning lakeside resort town, is the New Zealand social hot spot with skiing all around.

Herman Muckenschnabl (Dartmouth Ski Coach)

Dartmouth's Alpine Ski Coach, Herman Muckenschnabl, started and ran a busy instructional program in Australia for many summers in the early 1970s. He encouraged members of his Dartmouth ski team to join him in Australia to participate in the clinics.

George Peter Perry '72

George grew up racing in Maine under the watchful eyes of Al Merrill. He first skied at age 3; won the USA Junior National Championships at age 18; and became an outstanding Nordic and Alpine skier at Dartmouth under coaches Al Merrill and Herman Muckenschnabl. He was a four- event skier; participated in the NCAA Championships (1969-1972); became an All American in Nordic and a US Ski Team Member (1972); and was selected as Captain of the Dartmouth ski team (1972). After graduation, he worked at White Mountain School (NH), Rumford High School (ME), and the Holderness School (NH). He first traveled to Australia in 1974 intending to join Muckenschnabl briefly at his ski school but ended up staying "down under" for 25 years. He was the first Fully Qualified Instructor to graduate from an Australian Ski Instructor Course. In 1999, during the Australian summer, he began teaching skiing in Aspen-Snowmass as well and now serves there full time as the qualifier of Professional Ski Instructors. He twice served as the Australian Representative at Interski (Banff, Canada in 1987 and Beitosterlin, Norway in 1999) and coached

George Perry '72 and his daughter Tahnee relocated from Australia to Aspen.

the Aspen Divas to second place in the World Championships (1999-2000). George's daughter Tahnee is the Director of Marketing at *www.stayaspen.com* in Aspen and her sister Toyah is a designer for Rip Curl, a skiing and surfing clothing and accessories company in Torquay, Australia.

Charles M. "Chip" Richards '92

A competitive Freestyle skier in high school from Colorado with a Dartmouth father (**Thomas Richards '63**), Chip went east for college. He continued his freestyle ways on the Hanover plain, often training with the Nordic and Alpine skiers, and was twice ranked the #1 Freestyle skier in the United States during his years at Dartmouth. His life of sudden crash landings, or just plain wear and tear, led to two consecutive knee injuries and reconstructions in the spring of 1990 and 1991 with his subsequent withdrawal as a competitive skier. Chip then discovered a second passion: coaching. After serving as a very successful Assistant Coach with the US Development team, he found his way to Australia to coach the Australian National and Junior National teams. The Australian ski job progressed to his becoming the Head Moguls Coach of the Australian National Ski Team in the middle of an Olympic campaign heading to Nagano (1998). In so doing, Chip fulfilled his own Olympic aspirations not as an athlete, but as a coach. And though his team did not win the

Chip Richards '92 was twice ranked the #1 Freestyle skier in the United States.

265

gold that year, it did claim Australia's first-ever top three finish at the World Cup level for moguls, paving the way for a string of Australian World Cup and Olympic victories that have come since.

Bradley Wall '02

Brad went to school in Australia, but ended up enrolling in Burke Mountain Academy in Vermont for his last three years of high school. He raced at World Juniors throughout his whole Dartmouth career as a member of the Australian National Team. He managed to get to the 2002 and 2006 Olympics and had some great experiences but did not place well. After graduating from Dartmouth, he traveled with the Australian Team until his retirement when he took a coaching position at his old high school, Burke Mountain Academy. In the summer of 2009, Brad and his wife returned to Australia. He is hoping to stay involved in ski racing, and the ski industry. A full profile is included in Chapter XIV.

CANADA

While the eastern Canadian resorts tend to get rather cold, they have a special appeal that is unmatched by their western sisters. Eastern Canada offers much variety in its resorts, and in general, the lift lines are shorter than those in New England. The people of British Columbia take great pride in their dynamic yet affordable western ski areas, of which Whistler Blackcomb is the "grand dame". The three ski areas of Banff are characterized by their overwhelming beauty. Lake Louise is famous for the ultra elegant Fairmont Chateau Lake Louise. Many Canadians attend Dartmouth and some return home, others don't.

Tom Corcoran '54

Corcoran grew up skiing at Mont Tremblant in Quebec. He enjoyed an outstanding skiing career as a competitor, ski area owner, developer and executive. During the 1950s and 1960s he was a member of two successive US Olympic Teams (1956, 1960) and one World Championship team (1958). His 4th place finish in the Giant Slalom in 1960 at Squaw Valley was the best by an American male skier in that event until 2002. Over seven years of racing internationally, he won three US national titles, the Roch Cup twice, the Harriman Cup, the Parsenn Gold Cup, the Kandahar of the Andes, and the Quebec Kandahar. He won national championship races in Canada, Chile and Argentina. He later became Director and Chairman of the National Ski Areas Association. In 1978, Corcoran was inducted into the US Ski Hall of Fame. A full profile is included in Chapter XIV.

John W. Peirce '68

John is a passionate cross-country skier. He is the timing "guru" for many of the cross-country Nor-Am and World Cup races held in Canmore, Alberta, and was selected to help at the Vancouver Winter Olympic Games. John is a successful geophysicist who has applied some of his technical expertise to cross-country skiing.

Marie-Hélène Thibeault '02

Marie-Hélène was a member of the Dartmouth Ski Team After graduating, she moved to Calgary in 2004 to work as Media Manager for Alpine Canada, the governing body for alpine ski racing in Canada, and

Marie-Hélène Thibeault '02 focused on the course.

the Canadian Alpine Ski Team which was led by Canada's ski legend Ken Read. At the 2006 Olympic Games in Torino, Italy, she served as the Media Attaché for the Canadian Ski Team. After the Olympics, she joined a geophysical software company owned by **John W. Peirce '68** as a marketing manager. She expects to be involved as manager of the media center in the 2009 Biathlon event and at the 2010 Winter Olympics in Vancouver.

In parallel to her work in geophysics, Marie-Helene has also taken on a new project as Executive Director for a foundation called Fast and Female (F&F). The foundation was started by Chandra Crawford, Olympic Gold Medalist in the 2006 Cross-Country Skate Sprint. The mission of the organization is to empower young women through sports. In the short term, they have been focusing on cross-country ski events. Fast and Female supports equal accessibility for women at all levels and the Olympics. F&F is intended to help female Aboriginals via a dry land camp underway in Ontario to encourage them in cross-country skiing. Given Dartmouth's early and continuing emphasis on the educating of Native Americans, this is certainly a very appropriate adventure for an alumna like Marie-Hélène to participate in.

Andrew G. Biggs '04

Andrew came to Dartmouth from Ottawa, Ontario, Canada. He raced on the Alpine Team and secured five top-ten finishes in Carnival races; he was Team Captain in 2003 and 2004. He represented Canada in the 2003 World University Games in Tarvisio, Italy. He is now working in finance in Boston.

Patrick R. Biggs '06

Patrick, Andrew's younger brother, came to Dartmouth to continue racing. As a freshman, he finished 4th in the Slalom and Giant Slalom in the Eastern College Championships and at the NCAA Slalom Championships. After his freshman year, he qualified to race with the Canadian Ski Team. More details on Patrick are included in the next chapter. His comment below from his first World Cup race is one of the reasons we are doing this book as the history of skiing should reflect what Dartmouth College has contributed to the sport, and a skier like Patrick should be recognized in that context as well as for his skiing ability.

"At my first world cup race, in Chamonix, France, 2005, I had one of my best finishes ever. I had start bib 59 and was the last competitor to qualify for the second run (top 30). Starting first in the second run, I laid down my best run ever. I sat at the bottom in the winner's circle as athlete after athlete came down and no one could top my run and take me overall until the 16th skier finally beat my overall time (I had clocked the fastest second run of the day). After the race I was interviewed by Austrian television. Their first question was 'Who are you, and where did you come from?' They had never heard my name before and never seen me in any other world cup competitions. I told them 'My name is Patrick Biggs and I raced in the NCAA university circuit for Dartmouth College.' They gave me a look like I was crazy. 'University circuit' and 'Dartmouth College' were two names they obviously didn't expect a top skier to come from."[9]

Dartmouth skiers enroute for Chile to race in the first international ski meet south of the equator: (l to r) Capt. Stephenson of the ship Santa Maria, H. Chivers '39, W. Chivers '38, Wells '39, Litchfield '39, Hunter '38 and team Mgr. du Bois. (1937)

CHILE

For 70 years or more, Portillo, Chile, and other relatively remote ski areas in Chile have seen the migratory arrival of Dartmouth skiers to take advantage of summer skiing at high altitudes with great snow. Many of the early skiers to take this trip were the established skiing stars like Dick Durrance, Ralph Miller, and Chick Igaya. As noted earlier, the Dartmouth ski team (shown in the photo on the prior page) skied in the first international race south of the equator in 1937. All of these skiers helped build an enthusiasm for this summer skiing activity, and this has led to frequent visits by the Dartmouth ski team and others. Today, in 2009, Dartmouth Ski Coach Peter Dodge is involved with running his annual ski clinic there. We are not aware of specific ski areas developed in Chile by Dartmouth connected folks, but we are confident that the enthusiastic use of the early ski areas has propelled the Chilean ski business forward. Certainly the extensive notoriety of Ralph Miller's World Speed Record, set in Portillo in 1955, was the kind of event that brought lots of positive publicity to the country's ski operations. At least one native Chilean skied for Dartmouth and a small number of Dartmouth alumni live, work, and ski in Chile.

CHINA

Around 2000, China started expanding its ski industry substantially. Today, there are 60 or so recognized ski areas.[10] There is an extreme gap in quality and amenities among the resorts: basic ski areas have primitive lifts powered by oxen towing sleds uphill while extreme luxury developments, such as the one under way at Yabuli, may include private gondolas. Beidahu and Wanlong are two other leading areas. Skiers from Europe and North America report a very poor quality experience, even at the most developed resorts. Although China is now the world's leading producer of ski clothing and, increasingly, of ski equipment, many of China's several million skiers (virtually all beginners) have to rent "ancient" skis and do not even own their own skiwear.[11]

Mark P. Inkster '85

Mark was involved in one of the earlier explorations of ski resort development in mainland China. He had a unique background for this adventure, having been on the Dartmouth ski team and having studied the unusual combination of Engineering and Chinese. Just before graduation, his mother (who had raced for the U.S. in the 1950s) and his coach, Mark Ford, noticed an article in *Ski Racing Magazine* about a group going to China in early 1986 to look into developing a ski resort there. It was led by Bob Parker, a 10th Mountain Division veteran, a friend of many Dartmouth alumni from that era, and one of the leaders in the development of the Vail Ski Area. Mark ended up joining this study team. Despite deciding at the end of the trip that it was still much too early to invest there because things were so primitive, they had some intriguing experiences. As it turned out, China developed much more quickly than they expected, building a ski area in a decade. Two of the three hills they had checked out in 1986, Yabuli and Beidahu, were developed around 1996 and are now booming resorts in 2009. Highlights from his trip included: 1) climbing up a forested mountainside in ski boots, accompanied by machine gun-toting Red Army guards, ostensibly to fend off Siberian tigers; 2) riding a Poma-lift that only had four metal bolts sticking up from a metal plate and which were remarkably uncomfortable; 3) seeing a beginner skier with two left boots; and 4) getting on an incorrectly-adjusted chairlift that ended up taking them two-thirds of the way up the mountain and then, when the cable started slipping backwards, took them all the way back down again.

FRANCE

As a country, France has some of the great ski areas of the world and has produced outstanding world class ski champions. The most famous is Jean-Claude Killy who is featured in this book as the first world-famous celebrity skier under the ground-breaking marketing innovations and management organized by former Dartmouth ski team member **Rick Isaacson '64, Tu '65**.

Edwina ("Nina") Cook Silitch '94

Nina grew up in southern Vermont, learned to ski at Bromley Mountain, raced locally, relocated to Sugarloaf, Maine, ski area where **Warren Cook '67** had become the General Manager. She attended Holderness School under Coach **Phil Peck '77** and became Captain of the Nordic team in 1989/90.

The Dartmouth ski team philosophy of welcoming all levels of skiers was what attracted Nina to enroll in 1990. The Development Team allowed student athletes to learn, train and compete alongside the Winter Carnival team. After graduating, Nina coached the Dartmouth Development team in 1995-1996.

The Ski Team and the Dartmouth Mountaineering Club provided a strong community of support and friendships. The ski team trained once or sometimes twice a day, ate together, and went to training camps and races together. When not skiing, Nina was often scaling a building on campus, climbing a peak in the White Mountains, or off to a Dartmouth Mountaineering Club climbing road trip for spring break. After taking a wilderness EMT course, Nina became Safety Coordinator for the Outing Club and developed her passion for mountaineering.

Silitch '94 ski mountaineering in France.

Nina worked for the National Outdoor Leadership School teaching mountaineering and then returned to classroom teaching in Boulder, Colorado, where she met her husband, Michael Silitch, one of the High-Alpine Mountain Guides. They moved to Chamonix, France, in 2001 where Michael obtained a job as an Alpine Guide. While in Europe, she and her husband traveled, competing in cross-country skiing all over Europe. It was not until Nina moved to Chamonix that she learned what ski mountaineering was all about. She completed her first Chamonix-Zermatt *haute route* in 2003 and was hooked. Ski mountaineering combined all the things Nina loved about the mountains: the endurance while skinning uphill, the technical climbing (often in crampons) up couloirs, and the fast downhill in off-piste terrain. The early Harvard/ Dartmouth races on Mount Washington were in the same spirit. In 1926, competitive Ski

Silitch '94 with the victory symbols of a successful race.

Mountaineering was declared a demonstration sport by the International Olympic Committee, but only military teams competed. The current International Ski Mountaineering Federation hopes the sport will make its Olympic re-debut in 2018.

For several years, Nina worked as head of the girls' outing program at Aiglon College in Villars, Switzerland, pursuing ski mountaineering by competing in local uphill races. These had a fun ambience of cowbells with raclette or fondue meals to follow. In 2006, her family returned to Chamonix, so Michael could focus on his guiding career and Nina could do more ski mountaineering races.

Nina was selected for the USA Ski Mountaineering Team in 2007. That year she was one of the first Americans to compete in the *Patrouille des Glaciers* (PDG), the famous ski mountaineering race conducted by the Swiss Army. This is considered one of the hardest ski races in the world. The course is over 54 kilometers long and climbs 3900 meters vertically. The race starts at midnight and teams begin by working their way up a glacier carrying certain mandatory equipment like rope, ice axe, shovel, headlamps, phone, a GPS and other necessities. In the 2008/2009 season, Nina competed in five World Cup Ski Mountaineering races and finished 13th overall. In 2010 she hopes to represent the U.S. at the World Championships in Andorra.[12]

JAPAN

The history of Japanese skiing is long, starting at the end of the 19th century when a Japanese general brought back a pair of skis from Europe. The first ski championship took place in Takada in 1913. The Winter Olympics of 1928, the second ever held, was the first to see a Japanese team compete. Among other visitors over the years, Hannes Schneider came to Japan in 1930 to teach downhill skiing. The first ski lift was built at Maruike, Shiga Heights, in 1946 by the US Army, which induced the Igaya family to move nearby. The "land of the rising sun" is now 4th in the world in the number of ski lifts and first in the number of chair lifts. There are over 500 ski areas in Japan and 15 regions with skiable terrain, but are mostly only 4-5,000 feet. And Japan's 23,000 hot springs offer salvation for weary muscles at many resorts.[13]

Yokichi Fujiyama '38

Mr. Fujiyama attended the college during one of the peak times in Dartmouth's long ski racing history. He was said to have enjoyed "graceful skiing" while in Hanover rather than racing. He was from an important and successful Japanese family. His father, Raita Fujiyama, not only built up a very large conglomerate, Fijiyama Concern (with subsidiaries in sugar refining, chemicals and other products), but was also a leading politician before WW II. Yokichi's elder brother, Yoichiro Fujiyama, graduated from Princeton, was appointed Japanese Foreign Minister after WW II after, and became the founder and first President of Japan Airlines (JAL).

As his family was involved in Japanese politics, it is possible that Yokichi went to Dartmouth to follow in the footsteps of Kan-Ichi Asakawa, Class of 1899, who became a key adviser to President Theodore Roosevelt in brokering the peace between Russia and Japan in 1905 at Portsmouth, NH. He was a Professor of Japanese Civilization at Yale University and also made an effort to encourage peace before Japan and the US became adversaries in WW II. The Dartmouth connection for Asakawa still creates a fascination in his small home town of Nihonmatsu where he remains its most famous person. Several years ago, the Tokyo Dartmouth Club arranged with town officials in Hanover and Nihonmatsu for them to become "sister cities". They have been exchanging high school students for reciprocal home stays ever since.

In the small world of skiing, Yokichi Fujiyama's future wife used to take ski lessons from Kunio Igaya, the father of Chick Igaya '57, in Shiga Heights and she participated in ski racing together with Fujiyama. Yokichi once owned a ski resort called "Bandai Lodge" in Fukushima Prefecture. He hired a celebrated ski instructor, Miura Yuichiro, to head up his ski school.[14] Yokichi is representative of many Japanese students at Dartmouth who often came from communities in Japan with some form of nearby ski activity, or they returned to Japan after their Hanover years with a passion for skiing based on their Dartmouth experience.

Chiharu "Chick" Igaya '57, and his father, Kunio Igaya.

In 1947, when Kunio Igaya saw the first ski lift built at Maruike, Shiga Heights, in 1946 by the US Army, he moved his family there from Amori. He arranged for his son Chick to get a job on the Ski Patrol on the Maruike ski slopes. He himself obtained a job as the Master of the Ski school at Shiga Heights. In 1952, the US Army turned the Maruike area over to Shiga Heights. Kunio Igaya gained a reputation as the most important figure of Japanese skiing in those days. He was the senior person running Shiga Heights, which continues to be regarded as one of the best Japanese ski areas. Through C.V. Starr, Kunio visited many US ski areas in the 1950s and saw new ways to improve Shiga Heights.

In 1952, Chick Igaya won the ski championship of Nagano Prefecture, and was selected to the Japanese Olympics team to go to the Oslo Winter Olympics. By his chance meeting with C.V. Starr he ended up going to college at Dartmouth and be hired later by Starr at AIU (American International Underwriters). Kunio Igaya was to refer to the relationship with C.V. Starr as a fairytale, and it took him a long time to accept that this fortuitous relationship had really happened for his son. Chick placed 9th in the Oslo Olympic Slalom and then 2nd at the Cortina Olympic Slalom to receive Japan's highest Winter Olympic medal, and he raced again in the 1960 Olympics at Squaw Valley. He won multiple races for Dartmouth, many races in Japan, and was a national champion in both countries. In 1961 he started his business involvement with AIU. He went on to an outstanding business career and has been a senior executive in the Olympic movement for decades. Further details on Igaya are included in Chapter XIV.

Valerie Chiyo Jaffee '78, her mother (Mary Weed Jaffee), and her family

No question this is a family of skiers with exotic backgrounds and a passion for skiing from Japan to the U.S., Switzerland, and Iran. A copy of a hand-written letter[15] from Valerie Jaffee's uncle (George Tilson Weed) in the Keio University archives tells the personal history of Valerie's grandfather (David Tilson Weed) and her uncle who both taught for decades in Japan from the start of the 20th century. Both

Mary Weed (on left) with 2 friends at Hutte Tsugui, Japan (1940)

were important figures in the history of Japan's highly regarded Keio University. Uncle George was also a ski racer in his early years.

Valerie's mother Mary was a young ski racer in Japan in the 1930s before World War II. She moved to the U.S. after the war. She and Valerie's father became early ski patrol members at their local ski areas in the 1950s. Mary was elevated to the National Ski Patrol as one of the first 170 women to be selected as members of the NSP. For the 1960 Olympics at Squaw Valley, Mary served on the Olympic Ski Patrol as well as being the translator for the Japanese team. Chick Igaya commented to **Chik Onodera '58** that "he is still thankful to [Mary Jaffee for her] help rendered to the Japanese team who were then almost deaf and mute in English at the Squaw Valley Olympics."[16] Valerie's father remarried after his wife Mary passed away, and Valerie's stepmother Susan entered the family with the same ski interests she had developed while at private school in Switzerland and maintained in her native Iran.

Arthur and Mary Jaffee on Chairlift 1 at Mt Baldy, CA with 2 year old Valerie (1958).

Mary Jaffee holding the Japan banner at the 1960 Olympics.

Valerie Jaffee herself has been involved in the ski world since age two and has had the unusual training experience of skiing on straw and cottonseed which is not too dissimilar from Dick Durrance's experience of skiing on pine needles behind his school in Newport, NH, in 1934. Valerie competed on the national Alpine and international collegiate level, earning FIS "Elite" ranking, participating in US national and international race camps, placing 1st in the British Alpine Championships, 2nd in the European Collegiate Championships, and winning various corporate events. She graduated from Dartmouth in 1978, has served as a Professional Ski Instructor, and has been trained for the National Ski Patrol. Valerie is dedicated to promoting the sport of skiing around the world because, as she says, "it is in my blood", pursuing skiing all her life and becoming involved in the ski industry as a consultant.

Clifford J. Bernstein '89

Moving from southern Japan to Hokkaido in 2008, Cliff Bernstein, with his company Eastern Mountain Planning, Inc., invested in the Freedom Inn, a Georgian-style building with essences of New England and a few tatami rooms next to the ski slopes in Niseko. The village is at the latitude of Rome, but the skiing altitude is lower than at Nagano, site of the 1998 Winter Games. The top of Niseko Annupuri Mountain is the height of New England ski mountains at about 4300 feet. Niseko has been called the "Aspen of the East" by the *Financial Times* and the mountain is Japan's largest ski area, with an annual snowfall of 600 inches. Close by, there is a beautiful nearly perfect volcanic cone, Mt. Yotei, which is often called "Fuji's Sister", and can be seen

A view of Cliff Bernstein '89's Freedom Inn, backed by Mt. Yotei in Niseko, Japan.

from Niseko. At the end of 2008, the Japanese government approved funding to connect the Niseko ski resorts with Tokyo by bullet train by around 2020.

As to why he invested there, Cliff remarks, "It is like being in Vail in 1972, where I first skied as a 5-year-old, and knowing what it will look like in 30 years". Cliff developed a love for the sport that has found outlets on the ski patrol at Dartmouth and as a ski instructor in Aspen prior to what has been a multi-decade odyssey in Japan as a student, businessman, attorney, banker and real estate investor.[17]

Kenta Takamori '92

Kenta's parents met in Japan through a mountaineering club and raised two sons to love the mountains. Kenta was born in Pennsylvania, moved to Hudson on Croton in 1972, started skiing at age five, racing soon after. In high school, he raced for the school team and the Tri State team in USSA races and competed at Eastern Junior Olympics While spending a term at the Killington Mountain School, he noticed how dominant the Dartmouth racers were at every event. As a teenager, he watched the DOC ski team unload cheerfully from their green vans at races and win most of the races. He set his heart on going to Dartmouth.

He was recruited to the ski team by John Morton, Nordic head coach, but he managed only to be a backup skier on the Dartmouth squad throughout his four years as he was hindered by major injuries in three out of four seasons. The ski team dominated his Dartmouth experience, and although he did not fulfill his goal of being on the Varsity team and race at Winter Carnival, he considered his time at Dartmouth to be a cherished life experience. Several years ago, he tried to get back to ski racing by joining a Masters ski race but blew out his knee and quit racing. He has in recent years become an avid backcountry skier in Jackson Hole, Chamonix, Greenland, and throughout Japan; and in May, he climbed Mt. Fuji using crampons and skied down.

After leaving Dartmouth, Kenta worked for Goldman Sachs in New York and Tokyo. He left Goldman Sachs in 2007 to get involved in ski resort revitalization in Japan, providing consulting services for private equity firms with Japanese ski resorts. Warburg Pincus, a small investment bank with an equity investment focus, asked him to participate in a deal to acquire Hakuba 47 (pronounced "four-seven", to indicate it is open four seasons a year, seven days a week), an extensive resort area of which Kenta recently became the CEO. Hakuba is in the northern Japan Alps, about a three-hour drive from Tokyo and is one of the most picturesque mountain valleys on Honshu. It has a long skiing history and hosted a number of Alpine and Nordic events during the 1998 Nagano Olympics. Hakuba 47 is one of the newest ski resorts in the Hakuba valley and an interesting challenge for Dartmouth's latest mountain manager.

KOREA

The Dragon Valley resort is considered Korea's premier ski area. It has been FIS certified for international races and it even has the potential to host a future Olympics (possibly in 2018).

Larry Hall '68, David Warner '69, Norwell Coquillard '74 and Jeff Bolton '76

Norwell Coquillard was transferred to Korea by his company, Cargill, in 1984 when there were still only four ski areas in Korea. On weekends at Dragon Valley, Norwell initially skied with his friends Larry Hall, David Warner, and later Jeff Bolton, with few Koreans in sight on a Saturday. More Koreans would show up on Sunday but there were never any lift lines. As the economy took off, it became a very busy place by 1987 because Koreans used lift lines as fashion runways. At the same time a number of new ski resorts were being built in and around Seoul. The US Military, with its sizeable presence, set up a foreign ski patrol that worked at the various hills. Norwell joined it. He worked at Dragon Valley on weekends, spending time picking up people who skidded down the resort's steepest slope–a slope they should have never attempted– usually on their backs, and Norwell's work involved more broken boot buckles or bindings than broken legs. Norwell has moved on to Shanghai, China, with more skiing adventures yet to come.

SCANDINAVIA

Hans Preben Mehren '68

Before coming to Dartmouth, Hans competed mainly in Norway, winning the Norwegian junior championship in slalom and combined slalom (1963); was a member of the Norwegian military team for the World Championships (1964, 1965; Bronze medal in 1965 for the combined giant slalom–cross-country). The Silver medal was won by **John Bauer** who later became a Dartmouth coach.

While Denver University was very popular with many Norwegian skiers, he knew that Dartmouth was a much better place to study and was lucky in getting a nice scholarship. During his Dartmouth years, he also represented Norway in World Cup races (1966–67; Slalom, GS and Downhill). Earlier, in 1964, he represented Norway in the Summer Olympics in Tokyo, sailing the "Flying Dutchman", an Olympic-class boat dinghy. His personal athletic goal was to be a member of the Norwegian Olympic team, in both summer and winter. He managed half the goal with a Sailing 9th place in Tokyo and also represented Norway in the Alpine World Cup series. To have equipment for his skiing dream, he became an importer of Kästle and Head skis, Tyrolia bindings, and Raichle boots to Norway. He also ran his own production company to make Landsem cross-country skis; this enterprise went broke, but he kept the famous name alive until around 1995. Hans proudly outlines the origin of the cross-country skiing in the village of Morgedal, around the 1880s in Telemark county, a place where the Winter Olympic torch has often being lit. Each year he still downhill skis about four weeks and cross-country skis some 500 miles, perhaps inspired by living directly next to the Hollmenkollen ski jump, the second-oldest jump in the world, which opened in 1892.

Per E. ("Couch") Coucheron '68, Tu '69

Per was recruited to Dartmouth through Norwegian alumni and by Al Merrill, the Dartmouth head coach. Prior to coming to Hanover, he had been on the Norwegian National Team in ski jumping, the best in the world at the time, and was the Norwegian Champion (1964) and 8th in the German-Austrian four-hill jumping tournament (1965), the equivalent of a world championship.

Working his way across the Atlantic on a freighter, he was linked up with the David Bradley '38 family, spending the summer with them in Maine. This was a result of David's long association with Norway and his long involvement in supporting the development of jumping. Couch worked on his English while being tutored by one of their children in math. He spent three years on the varsity Nordic team while an undergraduate and a fourth year during his first year at the Tuck Business School, which was also his fourth year in college. He won most of the jumping events at the various collegiate Carnivals and competed on the broader jumping circuit in New England; he also jumped at the major US/Canada venues and in Steamboat Springs for the NCAA title.

Arne Henrik Nielsen '76, Tu '78 [18]

In the 1960s and 1970s, many Norwegian ski jumpers went to US universities to get an education and ski the same time. Arne's sister used to date Per Coucheron, and when Arne told him he wanted to go the U.S., Per said, "There is only one place for you to go, Dartmouth!" So he applied and was accepted, not even considering any other school. After he left Hanover in 1978, Arne only jumped a few more years before working full time; he was concerned about his family life, and the revolution in training regimens and equipment was making competing ever more time-consuming and expensive. For the last ten years, he has joined a Friends of Jumping group in Norway, an organization that gives money to Norwegian ski jumpers.

SWITZERLAND

Peter J. Harvey '90

Former Dartmouth Nordic team member, Peter Harvey, is the Director of Hohliebi Programs in the Swiss Alps, an organization that operates "The Winter Term" skiing program each year (January-March) for approximately thirty-five 7th and 8th grade students from the U.K., the U.S., and countries around the world. The school is situated in a spectacular location in Switzerland--a mountainside chalet in the Bernese Oberland town of Lenk. Peter is from a Dartmouth family as his father, **Arthur Mosby (Mo) Harvey, Jr '65** and older brother **Lawrence H. (Lars) Harvey '87,** preceded him. Peter began this adventure on a leave term from Dartmouth in 1989, helping the Hohliebi School founder John Curtis, former head of the lower school at Buckingham, Brown & Nichols in Cambridge, MA, and of The International Schools of Lausanne and Bern, Switzerland, to establish the program in its first year.

Peter moved with his wife, **Anna (Cathcart) Harvey '90,** and their four boys to Switzerland in 2006 to assume leadership of Hohliebi and "The Winter Term". Over the years and among the 800-plus alumni of the program, a number of Dartmouth alums have sent their children to participate in "The Winter Term" to take advantage of the opportunity to simultaneously combine a unique and challenging coeducational experience with an outstanding Swiss ski experience. Families looking to expand their children's international exposure in a well-supervised environment can contact Peter to discuss details of "The Winter Term." Hohliebi also runs a summer program, "The Alpine Summer Term", an alpine leadership adventure, cultural immersion, and summer camp all in one place. More information is available on the Internet at www.hohliebi.ch and Peter can be contacted at hohliebi@forevermail.com.

Mark W. (Max) Saenger '88

In the spring of 1937, Max's father, **Werner Saenger '41**, was scheduled to attend Princeton University after having spent two years at the Ecole de Commerce in Neuchatel, Switzerland. On a weekend ski trip in the Bernese Oberland, his father met Walter Prager who convinced him to abandon Princeton and apply instead to Dartmouth. In the fall of 1937, Werner Saenger arrived in Hanover and thus began the family's connection to Dartmouth College.

Dartmouth and Swiss racer Max Saenger '88.

Beginning in middle school in Switzerland, Max already dreamt about attending preparatory school in New England and then Dartmouth College. In the summer of 1979 his family toured various prep schools armed with two critical questions: "How good is the ski program here?" and "How many students from here go to Dartmouth each year?" They chose Holderness School in Plymouth, NH, and Max hung a green Dartmouth banner in his dorm room for four years, regularly meeting Dartmouth alumni, skiers, coaches, and even attending the ski team scavenger hunt.

In the fall of 1984, he arrived at Dartmouth as an inexperienced yet enthusiastic Nordie; with training and much guidance, Max managed to qualify for the Junior Olympics his freshman year and two years later was captain of the Nordic team (1987, 1988) Although he went on to compete on the World Cup Circuit and at the World Championships, the camaraderie Max felt with the Dartmouth Ski Team was only equalled when he guided **Rob Walsh '88** (who is legally blind) in the '92, '94 and '98 Paralympics.

In 1992, Max began competing in Biathlon. Coach John Morton taught Max shooting basics and lent him a biathlon rifle. In 1993, Max represented the U.S. along with **Tim Derrick '89** and **Stacy Wooley '91** at the World University Games in Zakopane, Poland. His goal is to make the World Cup Biathlon Team, but Max Cobb '87, the Team Coach, decided to emphasize youth and Saenger, by then, was considered too old.

As an alternative, Saenger represented Switzerland in the World Cup from 1996 through 1998. In 1999, he returned to the U.S. as the Executive Director of the Maine Winter Sports Center, an economic stimulus project in Aroostook County, Maine. He worked to establish high level competitions in biathlon and cross-country culminating in a 2004 Biathlon World Cup at Fort Kent's 10th Mtn. Ski Center, Me. and a 2006 Biathlon World Junior Championships at Presque Isle's Nordic Heritage Center, Me. He has established two world-class ski venues, developed local ski trails, and regularly put thousands of kids on skis throughout the winters in this northern Maine location. Several of his athletes have the chance to represent the U.S. and the Maine Winter Sports Center at the Vancouver 2010 Olympic Winter Games. Max has now taken on the role of Biathlon Sport Manager for the Vancouver 2010 Olympic and Paralympic Winter Games.

TURKEY

Paul Kuhn '78

Paul taught skiing at Dartmouth for three years under George Ostler, a colorful figure in the history of the Dartmouth Ski School. He also spent a lot of time with the DOC's Winter Sports Division, helping and officiating at the ski races. **Paul** and **Steve Maynard '78** were the only Dartmouth skiers that Paul was aware of in Turkey in the early 1990's. Steve and a non-Dartmouth fellow geologist were probably the first to ever ski Kazdagi Mountain, which is an important place from Homeric legend and the Trojan Wars. They may also have been the first people in Turkey to ever ski in the morning and swim in the Mediterranean in the afternoon, despite the very cold water.

UNITED KINGDOM

Skiing in England itself is non-existent, but Scotland does have several small mountains with annual skiing activities. However, the history of British skiing is much more important than having local in-country mountains to ski on. The British have been at the forefront of creating many games. America might claim a first in basketball, baseball and football, but the Brits had been there first in lots of games and sports, even some of these. What has come through to the author in 35 years of living half of the time in England is that the inhabitants of the United Kingdom know how to play.

It would be hard to place skiing in the category of an English "first" as the first ski artifacts have been found in Russia and Scandinavia, but it's quite easy to define modern skiing as having a strong UK component. Sir Arnold Lunn and his father (who started the Lunn Travel Company) were involved with the early efforts of UK citizens taking ski holidays in Switzerland. Sir Arnold has been clearly identified as the person who started various racing techniques like the slalom. He wrote in his ski journal: "However difficult it may prove to hold our own in such competitions, we can at least console ourselves with the reflection that Englishmen were responsible for initiating the oldest of all downhill ski races (the Roberts of Kandahar), the longest of all downhill races (the Inferno), and the most popular of all international downhill racing meetings, to wit, the Arlberg-Kandahar and the Parsenn-Derby."[19] And they organized the first official downhill race under FIS rules, run on February 20, 1931 in Murren, Switzerland, and that very first race was won by Dartmouth ski coach to be, Walter Prager.

It is Lunn who started the British Ski club and the *British Ski Year Book* that became the annual bible of ski activity not only in Europe but other parts of the world as well. It is Lunn's long-time assistant, Elisabeth Hussey, who led the FIS History of Skiing team; and her sister was Lunn's early administrator of the Arlberg-Kandahar race event. So even though this country has almost no ski areas, and none of any prominence, it has been a major player in the history of Alpine skiing.

R. Geoffrey W. Pitchford '64, Tu '65

In Geoff's own words, "I never dreamed of being in the Olympic Games when I started skiing at my school in Switzerland in 1948. I loved skiing and spent every minute of every day in the mountains. Racing was never in my mind until my older brother told me he thought I could beat the ski racers we had seen at the Seilers Shield race. I entered that race the next year and, to my own amazement, I won it. The rest is history.

"I did several local races for the next couple of years, a major international (FIS) race in Zermatt and, after eight years of living and skiing in the Swiss Alps, was an alternate on the British Ski Team for the 1956 Winter Olympics in Cortina d'Ampezzo, but I did not get to race. My plan to make the 1960 Winter Olympic Games in Squaw Valley was endangered by the Suez Canal crisis in which Great Britain invaded Egypt, and I was called up. While in the military I skied on the British Army Team and raced with Buddy Werner who was on the US Army ski team. At the 1960 Winter Olympic Games in Squaw Valley, I finished in the middle of the pack in Downhill and Giant Slalom, but sadly was disqualified in the second run of the slalom. The downhill was the first ski race to ever be televised. I was one of the lucky ones to be shown from top to bottom. Within hours of finishing, I was swamped by telegrams and phone calls from past American friends and students I had coached in Switzerland. ...

"During all the racing from 1956 to 1960 I got to know the US national and Army ski team, and most were from Dartmouth. They told me about "the 3/2 program" at Tuck School, and after the Olympics I visited the Dartmouth campus and loved what I saw -- an excellent education in a rural outdoor-oriented community so unlike anything in Europe. I applied, took my SATs at the American Embassy in London, and was accepted. I arrived at Dartmouth having spent a total of twelve winters skiing and racing all over Europe from northern Norway to Sicily and even behind the Iron Curtain in Poland. While I did ski on the Dartmouth freshman team, I needed to do well enough academically to get into the Tuck School, something had to give — and that was further ski racing.

"While I was at Dartmouth and Tuck, I coached in several capacities. In 1961 I ran the largest USEASA racing camp; in 1962, I ran several private racing camps; I was head instructor of the Ford/Sayre program; head student instructor under George Ostler of the DOC Ski School with 800 students, and then became student manager. I had long written for various ski magazines and ski clubs, including the *British Ski-ing Monthly*, *The Skier*, The Ski Club of Great Britain and The Kandahar Ski Club; and continued writing about emerging ski techniques.

"In 1965 I started with McKinsey [one of the world's most significant consulting firms] in New York. Soon, I was dealing with recreational development, much of which was ski related. A couple of years later a Tuck classmate, Dick Chase '60, Tu '65, and I formed our own consulting firm and bought "Glebe Mountain" in Windham Vermont, a small (one T-bar) ski area where I spent 12 years and turned the operation into a private club called The Timber Ridge Club. The gasoline crisis and warmer no-snow winters took the toll on the small New England ski areas but we had our share of high profile visitors. Paul Newman skied at Timber Ridge when visiting his kids attending Vermont private schools. After a day of skiing, Paul would often bring out a six pack of beer which he shared with our lift crew in the chairlift engine building. His affinity for the common working man has since that time been well documented.

"I am particularly proud of instituting a branch of the Buddy Werner League at Timber Ridge in memory of my good friend Buddy Werner who was tragically killed by an avalanche and never made it to the 1960 Olympics. We had raced everywhere and he was the best US racer in the late 1950s. In the early 1980s, we sold Timber Ridge and are now retired. I have returned to New Hampshire as all Dartmouth Alumni should." [20]

Luke O'Reilly '71

Luke is a native of the United Kingdom, but he learned to ski in one of the early hotbeds of skiing, Murren, Switzerland, in 1953. As mentioned earlier, the first FIS Downhill Race was run in Murren in 1931. Yearly, Luke skied in the Alps or in Scotland, completing Juniors Training Camps, and competing in the British and Scottish Junior Championships. He water-skied in the summer, following in the footsteps of a family friend who competitively skied on snow and water. This is very common for British skiers. Peter Lunn, an early British racer and son of Sir Arnold Lunn, was still water skiing and snow skiing as he approached the age of 90 and was an early contact on researching this book.

After graduating from his school in 1966, Luke skied for Great Britain in the World Cup events in 1967 and 1968, meeting members of the US Team, and striking up an especially close friendship with 'Spider' Sabich. When Luke inquired about US colleges, Spider said that if he wanted to ski he should go to the University of Denver, but if he wanted an education he should go to Dartmouth. That is one of the key incentives for any skier to attend Dartmouth. The next day Luke wrote off for an application to Dartmouth, and was accepted.

Luke says Dartmouth gave him self-confidence. He remembers Dartmouth President Kemeny's opening speech at matriculation: "You are here because you are either bright or brilliant." He says he does not recall all the courses he took, nor what exactly he learned, but he knew he was "learning how to learn."

He skied for Great Britain in the 1968 Olympics (Downhill, Slalom and Giant Slalom) and 1970 FIS Alpine World Championships (Downhill [with a top 30 finish] and Slalom). He also skied infrequently for the DOC Alpine Ski Team, coming in second at the 1970 Middlebury Winter Carnival Downhill. This was his only race completed that year in North America because he was mostly in Europe for the FIS World Championships, racing with former mates from his 1969 Scottish Junior team.

His time and resources post-college were taken up by a non-skiing career. In late 1973, he was elected to the board of directors of the British Water Ski Federation, having been National Champion in 1968 and a member of the British Water Ski Team at the 1968 European Championships.

William B. Gaylord '90

Bill grew up in Flagstaff, Arizona, and started skiing at the local ski area, the Arizona Snowbowl. In his high school sophomore year (1982) and for a post-graduate year (1986), he lived in Vail, Colorado, and skied with Ski Club Vail. After he met Mark Ford, the Dartmouth coach, and talked to Tiger Shaw '85 he was on his way to Hanover. He skied on the varsity team all four years and participated in the NCAA Championships twice (1987 and 1990), earning All America (1990), the Cooke Award (1987), and the Norwegian Trophy (1990) for the best performing freshman and best throughout the season. His senior year at Dartmouth was a breakthrough year in his skiing, and he was very eager to continue racing to achieve his potential.

Being born in England, he held dual nationality with Great Britain. Peter Dodge suggested reaching out to the British Ski Federation to see if there was an opportunity there. He had not originally envisioned skiing for the British Team, but it provided a means to pursue ski racing. Peter asked, "If your dream in life is to become a doctor and you are only accepted at a state university, but not at Harvard, would you still go?" One of his professors, Professor Arseneau, was also very influential in helping him. He told Bill, "Young people need adventures. There will be plenty of time for work."

The British Federation agreed to grant him an FIS license to compete as a British skier, but with no affiliation with the national team. His first results qualified him for the world championships later that winter, and he was invited to train with the British team; he was later formally named to team for the following season. There were challenges in trying to compete with a British Team which carried a significant stigma from the notoriety of "Eddy the Eagle" (the inexperienced British ski jumper who tried to compete with the best in the world) in the Calgary Games. Funding was limited, and travel and training budgets paled in comparison to other national teams.

At the 1992 Winter Games in Albertville, France, despite a month of intensive rehab from an accident shortly before, he finished 36th in the Olympic Giant Slalom. He continued with the British Team for the next two seasons, winning several races and improving his world ranking. He qualified for Lillehammer (1994) where he competed in the slalom, giant slalom and combined downhill, but crashed in all three. Still, it was a highly gratifying experience.

William B. Gaylord '90

Dartmouth and British Olympic racer Bill Gaylord '90.

On the advice of various people (including the author of this book), he enrolled at Columbia Business School at the end of the racing season in 1994. During his first year, he skied at the 24-Hours of Aspen Race, where teams ski for 24 hours straight to see how many runs they can complete on Aspen Mountain. Bill next moved to San Francisco and participated in several corporate ski races, coached, and is now raising three young racers.

Both Bill's father and sister are still involved in skiing. His dad became a race official when he was young and officiated at the World Championships in Vail, the North American World Cup races, and the Olympics in Salt Lake City. His sister also grew up racing, but stopped competing while at college. After graduation she went to work for *Powder Magazine*, the US Ski Team, and currently works for the US Olympic Committee.[21]

INTERNATIONAL SUMMARY

The Dartmouth connection to the international world of skiing has been a two-way street almost from its earliest days. Certainly from the formation of the DOC onward, there have been Dartmouth connected skiers traveling to distant points to share their enthusiasm for sliding over snow. And from the first trips of McGill University skiers to Hanover for the earliest races in the second decade of the 20th Century, foreign skiers have come to Hanover just to race or to both race and get an education. This intermingling of foreign and domestic skiers has greatly influenced the development of skiing ever since the Alps became a favorite tourist destination for the British in the mid-to-late 1800s. The reality of this process (of foreign skiers coming to Hanover to be where the action was) taking hold in the Green and White Mountains of Vermont and New Hampshire is just one more unexpected consequence of the initial thrust of Fred Harris '11 to rally the local Dartmouth students to spend more time out of doors in the winter. Another result has been many unique stories, involving activities in different countries, that are important to the history of skiing and have involved members of the greater Dartmouth family. Three examples involving incidents in Chile, Japan and New Zealand follow to illustrate this special Dartmouth involvement with the international ski world.

***

CHILE — RALPH MILLER '55: THE LAST MAN STANDING SETS A WORLD SPEED RECORD OF 109 MILES PER HOUR IN PORTILLO IN 1955

By Stephen L. Waterhouse

Dr. Ralph Miller, Jr. was born and raised in Hanover, NH, growing up with exposure to Dartmouth skiing from the time he could walk. His doctor father was a skier and took both Ralph and his two sisters skiing as often as he could. Ralph was a 4-event racer in high school and elected to attend college at the best ski racing school of the time, joining the many other great racers on the 1950s Dartmouth Ski teams. After many moments of ski racing success, but too little time in the classroom, Ralph Miller left Dartmouth in 1954 after the World Championships in Are, Sweden to join the US Army.

In August of 1955, although Ralph was serving on active duty, he was given time off to travel to Portillo to train for the 1956 Olympics. He was not alone in going to Chile as several fellow Olympic prospects, including Buddy Werner, Ron Funk, Marvin Melville, and **Chick Igaya '57** were also at Portillo for the same

Newspaper photo of Miller '55 and Emile Allais in Chile during the record speed run.

purpose. While getting in some early runs, this group began speculating on what speeds they could attain over Portillo's Roca Jack slope. A former world-class French racer, Emile Allais, offered to be the timer on a 50-meter speed trap specially set up for this little challenge. The first two days, they packed out the course and did some test runs. On the third day, Melville, Funk, Miller and Werner all were timed at around 75 mph. By the 4th day, they were hooked on the process and wondered how much faster they could go. Werner ran the 50 meters in 1.30 seconds to lead the day. On the next day, Miller lowered it to 1.25 seconds (92 mph); Werner hit 1.30 seconds again and Igaya joined the effort, but with a slower

time of 1.40. Encouraged by their results, the group decided to try to achieve even greater speed, knowing it would be necessary to climb further up the mountain before starting down. They were not too far behind the world record of 99 mph set in 1947 but that was not yet on their minds.

The next day, Melville dropped out as he felt his skis were not up to the higher speed level. The other four continued. Igaya slipped to balance on one ski twice in his run and was close to losing control, so he quit. The remaining three climbed higher to get still more speed. Miller ran the course at the best speed yet, and then Werner flashed through, beating Ralph's time, and achieving an outstanding 98 mph. Finally Funk came shooting down the course, but he sped out of sight in an explosion with skis and snow flying. Funk had crashed badly at 90 mph, breaking an ankle. On the following day, only Miller chose to continue the chase for the speed record; Funk's crash had a negative effect on everyone else. Miller and Allais tested the track and found it too hard. Finally, in the afternoon, it softened up a bit and Miller ran the course at a now pedestrian 75 mph. After climbing a bit higher, he managed a faster 85 mph on what was a much faster track as the sun set.

On August 25th, Miller was first up the lift and climbed higher than ever before to a new starting point. He launched, skiing hard and going through the trap very fast 98 mph, but not new record. He believed his skis could go faster, but knew that the next day the track would take forever to soften, and speed on a hard track is extremely difficult to control. The next run needed to be the one. He headed up, climbing above any prior starting point and right to the uppermost possible limit, forcing him to launch his run at a 45 degree angle. Now everyone is out to see his run, some with cameras, and all are prepared to see a spectacle — one way or another. Down he goes, crouched, pressure all around, face out of shape, tips of his skis in the air and starting to wobble, but somehow he holds on, roaring through the trap and only just managing to stop way beyond the normal safe area. And as he collected his breath, Allais skied up to deliver the message: A new world record of 109 mph! C.V. Starr, the visionary developer of the Stowe, VT, ski area, was in Portillo at the time, and Ralph believes Starr called the *New York Times* shortly after the record; in any event, the paper published a short article on the achievement.

Ralph Miller's precise speed was challenged for not being electronically timed, but no one seriously contested that he had exceeded 100 mph or that he was the first to do so. Dick Dorworth did a speed test in Chile in 1963 that timed by the Chilean Ski Federation; he hit 106.5 miles per hour to set the official western hemisphere speed record. However, Ralph's unofficial speed was not surpassed until 1974. His skis were one part of his success. They had cellulose bases and special inset edges prepared for him by Nelson Griggs in Vermont. Today, those skis are on display at the New England Ski Museum. Ralph commented to us on these skis and his successful speed run:

> "Nelson Griggs was a fine man. When I met him he was already suffering from multiple sclerosis and showed courage in carrying on. He installed my special edges that gave me the control I needed to operate at the high speed, and he should get full credit for inventing this particular one piece edge. It was inserted at an angle into the edge of the ski. The ski had a type of plastic bottom. …. There was no planning for a record at all. We started schussing in powder down the last 1/2 of the slope at Portillo, Chile and slowly went higher and smoothed the slope more. On the last day I was the only one interested in continuing. Thus, I was the only one who started at the top of the slope. Even then I was not thinking about a record, just going faster since I started higher."

Prior to Ralph's amazing run down the slopes at Portillo, several skiing speed records had been set by racers building up maximum speed before flying thru similar speed traps. F. Huber (83.58 mph, 1933) and Leo Gasperl (84.39 mph, 1934) had set records at a special 20-meter trap set up in St. Moritz. Former World Champion Downhiller Zeno Colo (99 mph, 1947) had skied through a 100-meter trap at Little Mont Cervin, Italy. At Ste. Marguerite, Quebec in North America, lower speeds of 53 mph (Bill Trower, Dick Ball, 1936) and 70 mph (Louis Cochand, 1937) were obtained with a shorter run in to a 150-foot trap. Sir Arnold Lunn pointed out that none of these speeds compare to that of a car, but there are no springs to provide a shock absorber between the snow and skier, sensitive skis respond to every variation of the gradient, and all the skier has are just muscles, balance, and reflexes to protect his body. Equipment and snow conditioning improvements have led to ever-increasing speeds, as have shorter trap lengths. But Ralph's run in Chile was special because there was no organization behind it; it was the product of his own special determination.

Ralph went to the 1956 Olympics in Cortina with a US Alpine Team of **Bill Beck '54**, **Brooks Dodge '51**, Melville, Mitchell, Streeter, and Werner. Ralph faced big challenges, finishing 13th in the Giant Slalom, 22nd in the Slalom and he crashed in the Downhill. Dodge finished 4th in the GS, the best ever for an American male. Igaya, his fellow skier on the speed adventure in Portillo, finished 2nd in the Slalom as a member of the Japanese team, the best ever finish for a Japanese or any Dartmouth male racer.

After the Olympics, Ralph completed his military obligation, returned to Dartmouth College, and then went on to Harvard Medical School, taking time out in 1957 to win the US National Downhill Championship. His medical research led him to Walter Reed Army Hospital in Washington, DC, to Stanford University, CA, and in the early 1980s, to the University of Kentucky where he remains as a Clinical Professor of Medicine with a sub-specialty in Endocrinology.

Ralph earned his pilot's license at age 16, took up hang-gliding at age 44, and won his age group in the Columbus Marathon by three quarters of an hour shortly after turning 70. But in his mid-seventies, during a vacation in Mexico with his wife Pam (who learned to ski in Hanover's Ford Sayre Program), an ill wind swept his hang-glider into trees at the end of an otherwise idyllic flight. With Ralph's recent crash (2009), Brooks Dodge's sailplane crash (1979), Buddy Werner's death in an off-piste avalanche in the

Swiss Alps (1964) and similar mishaps by other excellent skiers, one might conclude that there is some inner wildness that pulls them and their kind beyond the near edge of disaster. The author is a member of the aggressive Streeter Ski Group in Vail, CO, named after Ralph's 1956 Olympic teammate, Les Streeter, who did not walk away from a plane crash in the early 1980s. Ralph's hang-gliding accident was perhaps just another result of that strong desire to do more—to test the limits of his own abilities—or maybe it

was just an unlucky break after many years of great results. Whatever the case, we trust he will find a way to harness his speed demons and live a much longer life…. and truly become the last man standing!

This Article incorporates information provided by Ralph Miller himself and noted ski historian John Fry based on personal letters from Miller at the time of the event and the writings of Fry (Modern Skiing, 2008), Sir Arnold Lunn (British Ski Journal), and others.

***

JAPAN — SERENDIPITY: THE FATEFUL FIRST MEETING OF CHICK IGAYA AND C.V. STARR
…AND A PAIR OF PLASTIC SKIS!

By Chik Onodera '58 and Stephen Waterhouse

In the setting of a Tokyo sporting goods store, a fateful meeting took place between Chiharu (Chick) Igaya '57, Japan's greatest ski racer and long time leader of the Olympic movement, with the man who was to become his most important mentor, Cornelius Vander Starr. The meeting was a unique and important step in Chick's transition from "genius child skier," as he was referred to in Japan, through his important education experience at Dartmouth, and on to his success as a superb and stylish racer, influential businessman, and senior leader in sports. The source of this story is the autobiography of Mr. Kazuo Tajima, who was the facilitator of that meeting and his son, Kazuhiko Tajima, who was like a brother to Chick growing up together.

A young Chick Igaya '57, one of Japan's and Dartmouth's all-time greatest racers

On the fateful day November 31, 1951, at Mizuno's Sports Goods Shop in the Ginza, a downtown district of Tokyo, Mr. Tajima, the store manager, was busily engaged in his office with the month-end closing when two foreigners entered the shop downstairs. A sales boy came to him to say that a pair of plastic skies, recently created by Mr. Tajima, had broken in the foreigners hands and they wished to see the manager to compensate him for the damage they had done. Mr. Tajima, not speaking English and feeling too busy, sent the boy back with the message that no payment was required since any damage was his fault for creating a faulty

product. In many situations, the issue might have ended right there.

This was not to be the usual situation. The foreigners asked again to see the manager. They wanted to know more about the unusual plastic skis. Finally, Mr. Tajima relented and went downstairs to find a short, younger man of mixed blood and fluent in Japanese accompanied by a tall older man in shabby pants with a button undone and no belt. The old man asked simply: "Who created the plastic skis, and why?" Tajima answered: "I did; maybe I am just ski crazy!" The old man signaled he was the same.

The younger man asked Tajima if he knew of the Stowe, Aspen or Sun Valley ski areas in the United States and said that the older gentlemen was the owner of Stowe. Tajima had not heard of Stowe and, looking at the older man's dirty shoes and poor appearance, did not trust what he was being told.

A rapid then conversation ensued. The older man asked if Japan was participating in the 1952 Olympics. Tajima answered: Yes, two Alpine skiers and eight Nordic skiers. Older man: Which one is more hopeful for a medal? Tajima: Alpine is best, and especially one young racer. Old man: Do you know of Toni Spiess? Tajima: Yes, an Austrian skier. Old man: Yes, and he won the European Championship this year. (Tajima thought but did not say: This guy seems to know a little about skiing.) The old man continued: I sent Tony to Dartmouth College under my sponsorship, and he is the strongest contender in the Alpine races at the Olympics. Tajima, feeling a bit agitated, said: My Japanese racer, Chiharu Igaya, who stays at my home for schooling, is also a very good racer, and I trust he will win a medal. Old man: When is he leaving for Europe? Tajima: Middle of January to be in time for the games. Old man: Oh, that is too late. All the contenders spend 1-2 months in Europe to gain points in order to secure a good starting position at the Olympics. Kazuo Tajima: I know, but it's not possible under the current Japanese situation….for this is Japan's first Winter Olympics since the war.

Then this tall old man became quiet for a while. A few minutes later, he proclaimed, "I shall bear the cost for the two Alpine racers from Japan." For a moment, Kazuo could not understand what had just been said. It was well translated into Japanese by the young foreigner, but Kazuo simply could not believe what he had just heard.[22]

The old man then said: "It is November 30 today. The American team is departing for St. Anton and my wife is escorting them. The Japanese team should also leave immediately and join the American team in training for the next six weeks. I am already committed to inviting all Alpine medalists at Oslo to participate in the American Championships at my Stowe in March. I will invite the two Japanese Alpine skiers to Stowe also." He then offered his card: *C.V. Starr, 102 Madison Lane, 5th Avenue, New York, NY.* At this point, the younger foreigner said: This gentleman is the boss of American International Underwriters (AIU) and the majority owner. A skeptical Tajima was finally convinced, but still astonished. Starr then directed him to contact the Japanese Ski Association to apply for passports and visas…immediately!

Just then, by sheer coincidence, Chiharu came into the shop on his way back from school (he usually went straight home, seldom dropping by the shop.) So I introduced him to Mr. Starr, saying: "This is the boy staying at my home and going to Oslo, Norway, representing Japan."[23] Tajima could not believe the fairy tale unfolding before him, but he quickly sent a telegram to Chick's father, Kunio Igaya, in Shiga Heights, seeking his consent, and asked the Chairman of the Japanese Ski Association to meet with Starr to organize the details. All was completed within 24 hours.

One week later, C.V. Starr returned to the shop to report that his research indicated that Chick's father had contributed much to skiing in Japan. C.V. invited Chick's father to Oslo as well, but the offer had to be declined because of post-war restrictions on Japanese travel.

And so it was that twenty days after an incidental enquiry about plastic skies, Chick Igaya and his racing mate, Hisashi Mizukami, left for St. Anton, Austria, then onward to the Oslo Olympics where Chick came in 11th in the Slalom, a tremendous achievement for the Japanese team.

The story did not end here. Starr arranged for Chick to attend Dartmouth, starting what Chick still acknowledges as the most important period of his life. Starr later invited Chick's father and mother to Hanover to observe Commencement Day and see their son graduate. He also organized visits for them to many US ski resorts. Chick continued to prove his ski racing greatness at Dartmouth, at the Olympics, and with multiple victories in other venues. He went on to hold senior positions at AIU or its subsidiary, American Insurance Group (AIG), in Japan for over two decades and to serve on several Olympic committees.

***

NEW ZEALAND — THE STORY OF THE "MAN ON THE MEDAL" PHOTO

By Ned Jacoby '40

The 1936-1937 competition ski racing winter had been a busy and successful one for **Dick Durrance'39** – skiing in the 1936 Winter Olympics at Garmisch, the infamous FIS downhill in Innsbruck, the King's Cup at Italy's new Sestrieres and the Arlberg-Kandahar held in Austria's St. Anton. Then, as the school year was ending in March, came a surprise

phone call from James ("Jay") Laughlin who was finishing his own school year at Harvard.

"How about coming with me to New Zealand and Australia this summer?" he asked. "It's their winter down there and the skiing is supposed to be great." Coming from an affluent steel industry family in Pennsylvania, Jay knew Dick only through his reputation but had spent several winters skiing in Europe's big resorts and was a solid recreational skier. (They would both be later involved in the development of Alta.)

Who could resist *that* offer? Dick accepted immediately and the Bradley brothers, Steve and Dave, who could afford to make the trip, signed on for the expedition also. Both Dick and Steve were devotees of the 35mm camera revolution just unleashed by the legendary German Leicas and photography "down under" was going to be a big part of their expedition. In preparation for it they took everything needed to develop their film after a day's shooting. Printing the pictures

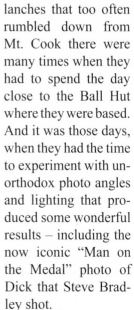

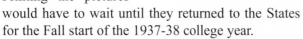
Possibly the most famous ski photo ever taken; used on some ski medals and as the logo for the New England Ski Museum.

would have to wait until they returned to the States for the Fall start of the 1937-38 college year.

Both Dick and I (and, possibly, my roommate of that year, **Dave Boyle '40**) were signed up for Prof. Charles Proctor's course in camera optics. Having a well equipped photo darkroom of our own was an impossibility for us as students but that optics course gave us full access to the well equipped one in the Wilder Physics Building!

Struggling along at the tail end of the ski team, I didn't really know Dick who was in the class ahead of me so, when we were sharing the Wilder darkroom together and he asked me to help him go through (and help print) the mountain of developed 35mm negative rolls they brought back from their trip "Down Under," I jumped at the chance.

I think Dick knew that the shots he and Steve Bradley had made in the European-like Alps of New Zealand's South Island might be the best of the whole trip and those film rolls were some of the first he chose for us to begin looking through. Because of the extreme danger of glacial crevasses and the avalanches that too often rumbled down from Mt. Cook there were many times when they had to spend the day close to the Ball Hut where they were based. And it was those days, when they had the time to experiment with unorthodox photo angles and lighting that produced some wonderful results – including the now iconic "Man on the Medal" photo of Dick that Steve Bradley shot.

It was that head-on photo of Dick that turned up the first day we started going through their trip negatives. Crouched low, almost on his side, back lit and with snow flying in a long curved stream behind him, it would go on to catch every skiers' imagination and, in that one shot, ended the old, formal, "big press camera" ski photography forever. There were a lot of other wonderful shots on those negative rolls but that, somehow, was "the" photo.

Many years later Dick said that many of the shots from their trip had never yet been printed or even looked at! So it might have been just luck that we started on those New Zealand rolls first. Still, I've always thought that from the beginning Dick knew it was hiding in there, waiting to be discovered!

Notes

1. http://ski.lovetoknow.com/Timeline_of_Skiing. 2. Oral history, Piane, Jr. '50, Tu'52, January 10 and April 12, 2009. 3. The 1928 British Ski Yearbook, p. 516-517. 4. The 1938 British Ski Year Book, 5. The 1938 British Ski Year Book. 6. The 1931 British Ski Yearbook, p. 276. 7. The 1936 British Ski Year Book, p. 360-371. 8. Oral history, Piane, Jr. '50, Tu'52, January 10, 2009. 9. Interview exchange with Jaffee '78. 10. http://industryreport.mountainnews.com/2009/04/chinas_ski_industry_slows_to_t.shtml. 11. http://www.chinaskitours.com/skiingchina. 12. Interview with Jaffee '78, July 19, 2009. 13. Email from Onodera '58 July 7, 2009. 14. Based on telephone conversation of Onodera '58 with Mrs. Muzue Yamaguchi, daughter of Mr. Yokichi Fujiyama, June 30, 2009 15. Dated January 20, 1963 under the letterhead of DuPont Far East Inc. to Keio University. 16. Interview of Igaya '57 by Onodera '58, July 9, 2009. 17. Interview with Bernstein '89 by Jaffee '78. 18. Interview with Nielson '76 Tu '79 by Jaffee August 6, 2009 19. P. 235, British Ski Year Book for 1932. 20. From Interviews with Jaffee '78 in August 2009. 21. Interview with by Jaffee '78 on August 4, 2009. 22. Page 267: Kazuo Tajima's autobiography. 23. Page 272: ibid.

CHAPTER XIV

LOOKING BACK AT SOME EXCEPTIONAL CONTRIBUTORS OF THE PAST 100+ YEARS

By Stephen L. Waterhouse '65, Tu'67

With David Hooke '84, Stuart Keiller '65, Tu '66, Doug Leitch '65, Newc Eldredge '50, Fred Hart '58, Warren Miller, James W. Page '63, Nate Dougall, Jan Stearns, William W. Cantlin '70, Joe Stephenson '57, Tu '58, Roger C. Brown '57, Gerry Huttrer '60, Edward Williams '68, Joseph Walsh '84, Chelsea Little '09, Pam Crisafulli Hommeyer '88, Max Saenger '88, Jamie Meiselman '91, Phil Livingston '58, Valerie Jaffee '78, David Durrance, Richard Durrance II '65, Tom Washing '63, Mary Kendall Brown '78, and Roger Urban '65

In this chapter, we present profiles on a mix of skiers who have contributed greatly to the substantial legacy of Dartmouth's impact on the development of skiing, including some who are still doing so. Our purpose is to illustrate the wide range of their contributions along with the interaction of some of the key players across the different areas of involvement presented earlier in this book. These profiles are divided into two groups: individuals and families. All of the people profiled here are important but by no means comprise all, or even necessarily the most important, of those to grace the Dartmouth skiing stage for well over a century. They simply represent a spectrum of the types of contributions made by Dartmouth alumni, staff and their families over these many decades.

The thirty-five individuals are listed in order of their Dartmouth class year or, in the case of staff, of when they were active at the college. Many of these individuals will be recognizable from early chapters; the same is true for certain members of the five families we have profiled. Each profile briefly highlights specific activities or thoughts about the Dartmouth connection that we feel illustrate an important element of the larger story. We start with some of the true legends of the Dartmouth story and then we roll on to some of Dartmouth's most recent contributors. They represent the substance of what Dartmouth Skiing has been all about—innovators and achievers across many aspects of what makes up the modern skiing industry. No other educational institution in the world can lay claim to a comparable cast of such influential contributors to the sport and business of skiing. And these we have space to include only scratch the surface of the long list of individuals who could be profiled in this way.

Each of the five families profiled here has influenced skiing from almost the very beginning of the historical scope of this book. And one finds many instances of interactions among them, both personal through marriage and via incidental overlaps throughout the progression of their intertwined careers. These overlaps often stimulated synergies that led to subsequent contributions by family members to the development of skiing. Although there is a common thread of ski racing success in the early years for each of these families, it is the range of contributions to the broader ski industry that is important to reflect upon.

For example, the McLane family has been involved in the development of Dartmouth's own history as well as in the creation of the 10th Mountain Division and the founding of major ski areas. And the latest generation of this family is setting a fast pace on the ski racing slopes today. The Durrance family provided much of the early impetus that led to Dartmouth's reputation as an outstanding ski racing school, but this is only one of its many contributions to the organization of the ski industry and the promotion of skiing. The Bradley family is an example of the broad influence of the Dartmouth Outing Club which roused the passion of Dr. Hal Bradley to get involved in skiing and led to multiple contributions by the next generation of the Bradley family in just about every aspect of this book. The Kendall family, too, has played a strong role in the evolving US racing scene for over 60 years by providing racers, coaches, race officials and other contributions of this sort. They are the State of Maine's greatest ski racing family and certainly one of Dartmouth's great racing-oriented families. And the Hannah family has contributed significantly to the technical development of the ski business and is still making an enduring contribution via the company started by perhaps the first person to bring multiple concepts to the evolving technologies in play at the ski resorts of today, Sel Hannah '35.

INDIVIDUAL PROFILES

Professor Charles Albert Proctor '00
By David Hooke '84

Charles Proctor, Professor of Physics at Dartmouth for over 40 years, was the "quiet leader" who brought slalom skiing to Dartmouth, provided key supervision of Dartmouth's enormous winter sports enterprises in the 1920s and '30s, and persuaded the College to fund the Moosilauke Ravine Lodge as a ski resort in 1938.

After completing his graduate work in Chicago, Proctor returned to his alma mater in 1909 as a Physics professor, and in 1910 he built a house for his family near the golf course. Finding some leftover pine boards from its construction, he fashioned some skis for his young son Charley who was immediately smitten; soon he was trudging all over the golf course as it became the focal point of the new sport of skiing.

Charley grew up in step with skiing's explosion of popularity in Hanover, taking part in every formal

Professor Proctor '00 dressed in his official outfit for the 1932 Olympics at Lake Placid.

and improvised contest, first in the shadow of the great **Johnny Carleton '22**, then in his own right. His father was drawn into this whirl in part to encourage his son's participation in sports, but Professor Proctor was equally fascinated by the new opportunities being presented as Dartmouth led the move away from the then typical snowshoe and cross-country ski events toward the Alpine events and became the center for ski innovation in the U.S.

In 1922 Prof. Proctor became part of a three-member faculty committee in charge of overseeing Winter Carnival. In 1923 he persuaded the College to hire the Czech Army officer **Anton Dietrich** as Dartmouth's first ski coach. Proctor was closely involved in the formation of the Intercollegiate Winter Sports Union (IWSU) in 1924, establishing three regional divisions and a Union Championship. That same year, John Carleton introduced Proctor to Arnold Lunn, head of the Ski Club of Great Britain; Lunn sent Proctor details of a type of ski race judged on time only that would replace the rule-intensive "alpine proficiency" contests then prevailing. On this basis, Proctor organized the first "slalom" ski race ever held in the US; it was on Balch Hill near Hanover in 1924 and was an immediate hit--a "compact alpine ski event confined to a compact space where a crowd could follow most of the action."[1] Proctor tried the timed event at the 1925 Carnival and it was again a great success; young Charley, now a Dartmouth freshman, was the winner. So for the first-ever IWSU Championship in 1926, Proctor had designed the first ski contest recognizable as a modern ski meet. Both a slalom and a "mile downhill" race were set on the face of Balch Hill.

With this success established, Proctor and Dietrich began looking further afield for bigger challenges and they settled on the Mt. Moosilauke Carriage Road as a new race venue. Charley Proctor won this first-ever Moosilauke Downhill Race, held in 1927 over a 4.5-mile course, in 21 minutes.

In 1928 Proctor had the idea of creating a physical focal point for Dartmouth Winter Sports activity and led the drive for the Class of 1900 to fund the Dartmouth Outing Club (DOC) House, to be located between Occom Pond and the golf course, as a locker room, meeting place, clubhouse and general hub of winter activity.

Dietrich departed at the end of that year and a series of less effective coaches resulted in some rough years for the Dartmouth winter sports teams. Prof. Proctor was eager to reverse this slide. By 1931 he was both Chairman of the Physics Department and a member of the DOC Council. He learned of the Austrian ski expert **Otto Schniebs** and had the idea to hire him as part-time lab assistant and part-time ski coach. Schniebs brought about a dramatic turnaround in Dartmouth's skiing fortunes; Proctor made this possible by gracefully and patiently dealing with the twin challenges of Schniebs' meager salary and sore neglect of his "lab assistant" duties. Schniebs, DOC General Manager **Dan Hatch '28**, and others pushed for the creation of a completely new ski trail on Moosilauke and for the improvement of a ski base lodge in an old lumber camp at the foot of that trail; Proctor tirelessly carried the administrative burdens so that the undergraduate DOC leaders would not feel overwhelmed by the Moosilauke project. Schniebs laid out the spectacular but almost un-skiable Hells Highway on Moosilauke cut in 1933 on land purchased by Dartmouth alumni; to attract a broader skill range of skiers, Prof. Proctor laid out the Hells Byway in 1936 that detoured the steepest section.

Professor Proctor maintained his connection with the larger world of skiing and winter sports; he was in the leadership of the 1932 Lake Placid Winter Olympics committee (and son Charley was Chief of the Jump.) He helped organize the first National Downhill race on Moosilauke in 1933 on the Carriage Road and the first National Slalom Championship in 1935.[2]

When the ski camp at the foot of Hells Highway burned in 1935, the DOC had to take stock of its priorities in planning for its replacement. For a while, the alumni pushed for a luxurious base lodge, but only a fraction of needed funds were raised. Then in the fall of 1937, Proctor led the effort to hire **C. Ross McKenney**, legendary Maine Guide, to be Woodcraft Advisor for the DOC and run summer programs at Moosilauke. Once hired, Ross soon presented the idea that the lodge could be built as a huge log building using old growth spruce on the site and that he could lead the effort. Available funds would only permit a very rustic building, but with momentum building for the project, Proctor went to Dartmouth President **Martin Hopkins '01**, with whom Proctor was close, and persuaded him to ask the College to grant $15,000 to put in full basements, a heating system and plumbing. The result was the Ravine Lodge, Dartmouth's base for skiing from the late 1930s through the early 1950s and one of the largest log buildings in New Hampshire. The Lodge continues to be used today as a mountain retreat.

With one other professor, Proctor essentially led the DOC during the war years while staff was away serving the nation; it afterward became clear that the massive ski-based enterprise of the club could no longer effectively be managed on a part-time basis. Ever the man of grace, Proctor led the committee that rewrote the DOC's charter with the College, devolving many of the enterprises he had helped found (the Outing Club House, Moosilauke, Oak Hill Ski Tow) onto the College's business managers.

All this he did while managing a distinguished academic career focused on Optics, including the design of lenses used by the German Leica camera company. He was also an avid ornithologist; my father, **Richard Hooke '53**, recalls many great trips in the early 1950s with Prof. Proctor, then retired, to the cliffs in Fairlee, Vermont, and elsewhere, studying peregrine falcons.[3] Professor Charles Proctor was elected to the US Ski Hall of Fame in 1966.

Fred Harris '11 — Innovator and Motivator
By David Hooke '84

Fred Harris of Brattleboro, Vermont, was founder and prime mover of the Dartmouth Outing Club in the winter of 1909-1910. He took up skiing in the winter of 1904 when he was about fourteen. Within a day he was completely hooked. That winter he started a diary of skiing, which he kept through the winter of 1911. As long-time ski historian Professor John Allen writes:

"…with seldom a day's activity unrecorded, and they show what it was like for one who had 'skeeing on the brain evidently' at a time when there were few to enjoy what he found so marvelous. He made his own skis, remarking when he had good bends…He…told of cross-country trips and of the successes and failures on his 'slides,' as he termed going down hill. He built jumps, broke skis, hurt his back, and once even confided to his diary that he had been 'overdoing lately and decided to lay off for one day.' Although he had occasional companions, his was a lonely pleasure in these early days."[4]

His greatest interest was ski jumping off homemade jumps, and by the winter of 1907 he was able to clear fifty feet. Arriving at Dartmouth, he soon found that winter was seen as an annual liability; the ritual of "stuffy rooms, hot stoves, card games and general sluggishness from lack of exercise" was firmly entrenched. Har-

Winter Field Day: Fred Harris '11 with trophies won in the first Winter Field Day races.

ris generally went out on his own, often far afield from Hanover, occasionally meeting other students "on the snowpath," and dreamed of forming a club of like-minded fellows. Late in the winter of 1908 and then again in 1909, Harris went with his father to see the Montreal winter carnival, with its thousands of spectators watching the big ski jump; it made a great impression on him. The other strong influence was James "Pop" Taylor, later founder of Vermont's Green Mountain Club and the Long Trail, and at the time headmaster of Vermont Academy. His "scheme to get the boys going" in winter came to fruition on Lincoln's Birthday 1909 with a field day involving ski and snowshoe races, obstacle courses, and jumps. Harris saw this and was inspired.[5]

So on December 7, 1909, the Dartmouth newspaper published the following letter from Harris:

The question "what is there to do at Dartmouth in the winter?" gives rise to the thought that we might take better advantage of the opportunities which the admirable situation of our college offers... The writer suggests that a ski and snow-shoe club be formed, the purposes of which would be:

1. To stimulate interest in out-of-door winter sports.
2. To have short cross-country runs weekly and one long excursion each season (say to Mooselac [sic]).
3. To build a big ski jump and hold ski jumping contests.
4. To hold a meet or field day during February at which a program of events similar to the following may be contested: 100 yard dash on snowshoes, cross-country run on snowshoes, 100 yard dash on skis, cross-country run on skis, ski jumping contest and other events that may be suggested.

...By taking the initiative in this matter, Dartmouth might well become the originator of a branch of college-organized sports hitherto undeveloped by American Colleges...[6]

Harris found a number of professors who were eager to serve as advisors. The editor of The Dartmouth wrote a key editorial in support, and Harris persuaded the captain of the football team to serve on the executive committee. At a meeting on January 10, 1910, some 60 men joined the new Dartmouth Outing Club (DOC), numerous faculty endorsed the scheme, and Harris was elected founding president. Harris then led the charge that winter, leading trip after trip, and "kept the papers supplied with DOC news, shouldered financial burdens and radiated enthusiasm."[7]

Fred Harris '11 was still involved with the DOC in later life.

Campus opposition from the old order crumbled with the success of the first "Winter Field Day" held February 26, 1910, with 300 spectators. Despite a sprained knee suffered in escaping a fire that severely damaged Harris's dorm the previous night, he nonetheless won the Ski Jump contest. The following year the DOC staged its first "Winter Carnival" enlarging the Field Day to include its first "Carnival Dance," bringing in women to all-male Dartmouth for the first time in winter. With this, the DOC was off and running, boasting nearly 800 members by the end of the decade.[8]

In 1920, Harris wrote an article for *National Geographic* magazine about the DOC entitled "Skiing in the New Hampshire Hills." It was read in more than two million homes across the country--many of them the homes of boys thinking about college. That spring, applications for admission jumped from 825 the previous year to 2625.

"The Secretary of the College observed that this... increase could only be accounted for by the *National Geographic* article. The increased volume of applications forced the College to adopt the selective process of admission with its accumulating benefits [to Dartmouth's stature] through the years."[9]

A believer that sport was important to one's everyday life, he was a year-round athlete; a three-time intercollegiate tennis champion, he was once ranked 14th in the United States. A devotee of junior skiing, Harris instigated the building of the 40-meter and 65-meter jumps in Brattleboro, VT. Known as Harris Hill, the site continues to host the annual Fred Harris Memorial Tournament.

Harris is also credited with a number of first descents including Mount Washington and Whiteface Mountain. In 1922 Harris became the founding president of the US Eastern Amateur Ski Association. Six years later was elected Vice-President of the National Ski Association; he also served as Treasurer from 1929 to 1931. Fred Harris was inducted into the Ski Hall of Fame in 1957.[10]

John Piane, Sr. '14 — Life of a Salesman
By Stuart J. Keiller '65, Tu '66

John Piane, Sr. '14, entrepreneur, pioneer ski retailer, and ski equipment manufacturer demonstrated he was a man of action and boldness even before being admitted to Dartmouth. The eldest of six children whose parents had emigrated from the Milan area of Italy to settle on Manhattan's Lower East Side, Piane had been accepted to Princeton when a chance encounter in the fall of 1910 "riding to Norwich, Vermont, with a trainload of rowdy Dartmouth freshman"[11] changed the course of his life. Piane "marched straight to the Dartmouth Admissions Office and asked to be enrolled."[12] Thus began an association with Dartmouth, the Upper Valley, and the ski industry that would span two family generations and which continues to this day with the Dartmouth Co-op on Main Street in Hanover and with Tecnica, USA in West Lebanon, the successor to Piane's Dartmouth Ski Company.

In 1911, his sophomore year, Piane purchased the student union, known as the College Book Store. After graduation, a brief period of working for the predecessor to Citibank in New York, and service in the United States Army during World War I, Piane returned to Hanover and resumed day-to-day management of his business in 1919. He changed the name to the Dartmouth Co-op and moved into a single storefront on Main Street. By this time the Dartmouth Winter Carnival had generated so much interest in skiing that the demand for skis far outpaced the supply being hand-made in enthusiasts' barns and garages. As **John Piane, Jr. '50, T '51** says, "Dartmouth was the starting spot for skiing and Dad immediately recognized a business opportunity."[13] Piane Sr. began having skis made by the Gregg Ski Company in St. Paul, Minnesota, and selling them under the Dartmouth Co-Operative brand name.[14] Charley Dudley, a Hanover neighbor who traveled in Europe for pleasure began sending samples of ski sweaters, socks, hats, wax and assorted other goods to Piane who then began importing such goods in lots for resale in the Co-op. One of Piane's suppliers was Marius Eriksen of Norway, father of famed skier Stein Eriksen.[15] The Dartmouth Co-op was likely the first ski specialty shop in the United States, and Piane certainly was the first entrepreneur to vertically integrate branded ski and retail operations.

The decade of the 1920s marked modest but steady growth for both Piane's ski manufacturing and his retail business. The 1930s became a time of innovation and expansion for his enterprise "Dartmouth men would leave Hanover knowing how to ski but with nowhere to purchase ski equipment and apparel where they settled. Orders started coming to the Co-op from all over the country."[16] The cadre of aficionados like **Fred Harris '11** and his band expanded to a growing group of passionate recreational skiers. By 1930, Piane had established his first warehouse in what is now the Christian Science Building on Hanover's West Wheelock Street.

One of the major technical problems with early ski equipment was in binding the boot to the ski. The system of leather straps in use from the earliest skis provided only rudimentary control and their reliability was marginal. A Swiss music-box maker, Guido Reuge, tackled the problem in 1929 in an effort to diversify his company and survive the economic upheavals of the day. Reuge invented a heel plate and spring system to secure both the toe and heel of the boot to the ski and named his new invention the Kandahar Ski Binding, after the Kandahar Ski Club formed in 1924 by Englishman Sir Arnold Lunn in Mürren, Switzerland.

John Piane, Sr. learned of the revolutionary new binding and secured a license in 1930 to manufacture and sell them in the United States. He found a failing machine tool shop in Springfield, Massachusetts, Universal Tool, and bought the stock, retained the German master toolmaker, reorganized the shop floor, and began to manufacture the Kandahar binding. He did all of this in the depths of the Great Depression. The Kandahar – Dartmouth – Hanover Ski Binding quickly became a widely distributed product throughout the developing retail market for ski equipment. In Ithaca, NY, three local retailers, The Cornell Co-op, Treman, King & Co. and The Sport Shop advertised heavily during the 1930s and 1940s in *The Cornell Daily Sun*, the student newspaper, that they sold this product. Treman, King & Co. actually advertised itself as "Ski

Headquarters for this Section of New York State [and] We carry the famous Dartmouth-Co-Operative line –conceded by many experts to be the finest line in America."[17] Treman even offered yearly ski insurance for 60 cents to insure Dartmouth Hickory and Ash Skis. The policy covered: "breakage from any cause, fire, theft, burglary, pilferage, including theft of permanent bindings."[18]

By 1933 Piane had engaged sales agents across the country to sell his ski gear. In the mid-1930s he also began selling ski equipment to the premier national retailer of the time, Sears Roebuck & Co. of Chicago. The Sears' Catalog was the Amazon.com of the time and the Dartmouth Ski product line became available to an increasingly wide swath of consumers across the country.

World War II brought the growing recreation ski equipment and apparel market to a virtual stop as everyone turned to the war effort. At Dartmouth Ski, Piane developed a special adjustable-length ski pole for the Army and all production was devoted to supplying the famous 10th Mountain Division--as well as the Russian and Turkish armies, both regarded as allies at the time. A new building was erected at 3 Lebanon Street behind the post office to handle this specialized production. As a defense contractor, Dartmouth Ski Company had to build its new facility to wartime government specifications for bomb protection. Though later converted to an office building and expanded over the years, the original core of the building with its three-foot thick walls still stands.

John Piane, Sr. married in 1921 and moved in to a house at 13 Rope Ferry Road in Hanover. John, Jr. was born in 1928 and Joan ("Posey") in 1930. John Jr. graduated from Dartmouth in 1950 and Tuck in 1951 and quickly assumed responsibility for running the Dartmouth Ski Company as John Sr.'s health was failing. John Jr. ran the company until selling it to **John Stahler Tu '69** in 1978. Joan married **Richard (Dick) Fowler '54** upon his graduation, and after his Air Force tour of duty Dick and Joan ran the Dartmouth Co-op for twenty-nine years before selling the business to **Gene Kohn '60** in 1986.

John Piane, Sr. was first in the United States to recognize skiing as a retail business opportunity, first to develop a ski equipment and accessory specialty store, first to integrate branded ski manufacturing and retail, first to bring the state-of-the-art ski binding to the US market, and first to recognize the power of catalog merchandising (Sears) to market ski equipment to a nation-wide client base of skiing enthusiasts. His entrepreneurial spirit, business sense, and bold but judicious risk-taking were character traits on display time and again in succeeding generations of Pianes and they are evident in those Dartmouth men and woman who made--and are making—their own special mark in the thriving ski industry.

John W. McCrillis '19 — Organizer and Promoter
By Douglas C. Leitch '65 with Newc Eldredge '50

Many of Dartmouth College's finest skiers had their first skiing thrill in their own backyards. Skiing in North America was in its infancy in 1897 when John W. McCrillis was born in Newport, New Hampshire. In a community which included a recent influx of Finnish immigrants, skiing was beginning to catch on in Newport just when McCrillis was a boy. Some of those Finnish immigrants had formed the Newport Ski Club in the 1890s. "Every boy had a pair of skis then…my grandmother gave me my first pair," McCrillis recalled about his early skiing efforts in his backyard by the age of 13. When he enrolled at Dartmouth College a few years later, he began to ski in earnest. In the winter of 1916, Newport planned its first winter carnival. Naturally, McCrillis wanted to return for the hometown festivities, so he "stepped into his bindings and skied the 35 mile route with a friend. 'It probably took us from about 2 p.m. to 8 or 9 p.m. We stopped for supper in Grantham.' "[19]

After graduating from Dartmouth, Jack headed west in 1919 to work in an Oregon logging camp. The following year he secured a teaching position at the Moran School for Boys at Bainbridge Island, near Seattle, Washington, where he remained for five years. During his tenure there, McCrillis took advantage of opportunities to pioneer new locations for skiing in the Pacific Northwest, including several skiing firsts in Paradise Valley and Camp Muir on Mount Rainier, and at locations on the Olympic Peninsula. Each winter, he took groups of students from the Moran School on skiing trips in the area. One student he introduced to the sport was **Harold Hirsch '29** who was so taken by that experience that he decided to attend Dartmouth. Hirsch later became the founder of White Stag skiwear and remained a lifelong friend of McCrillis. His other contacts in the Northwest helped to broaden McCrillis's network of skiing acquaintances from coast to coast over the years.

Returning to New Hampshire in the mid-1920s, McCrillis continued to pursue his interest in skiing and his association with other Dartmouth alumni like **William Fowler '21**, an active member of the Appalachian Mountain Club in Boston who served on its Committee on Skiing. Together they helped develop new opportunities for skiing in New Hampshire and were both involved in the search for Dartmouth's new ski coach Otto Schniebs in 1930. It was McCrillis's own close association with Schniebs that would become one of the key links in landmark developments for skiing's future.

McCrillis applied his filmmaking talents to meticulously record Schniebs demonstrating new Alpine techniques of turning and controlling skis. In coordination with the Dartmouth Outing Club (DOC), they filmed Dartmouth's early down-mountain races on Mount Moosilauke and used those images to collaborate in publishing the first ski instruction book in the United States, *Modern Ski Technique*. It initially appeared serially in the Dartmouth Alumni Magazine before being printed by the Stephen Daye Press of Brattleboro, Vermont, in 1932. McCrillis used the good offices of fellow

John McCrillis '19 was a real force in D skiing.

Dartmouth alumnus **Carl Shumway '13** and his advertising business in Boston to help market the book. Shumway, a fellow US Navy aviator and friend of Antarctic explorer Admiral Richard Byrd, succeeded in getting the admiral to endorse the book.[20]

The 1932 premier of McCrillis's films of downhill races on Mount Moosilauke at the annual meeting of the National Ski Association (NSA) in Chicago resulted in the NSA's agreement to officially sanction the first national downhill race at Moosilauke for 1933. In addition, requests from schools, colleges, and ski clubs across the country for film rentals helped to increase sales for their book and recognition for both the authors and their ties with Dartmouth. Before long, McCrillis would be the key agent for another connection between Dartmouth and the rapidly expanding world of skiing: just as he had been instrumental in inspiring a future leader in the skiwear industry to attend Dartmouth when he pointed Harold Hirsch toward Hanover, McCrillis was about to repeat that service to his alma mater.

William Davies, one of Jack's acquaintances, lived in Cleveland, Ohio, but also spent time in Newport, NH. He traveled to Garmisch-Partenkirchen, Germany, to ski where he met a young fellow named **Dick Durrance '39** on the ski slopes. Durrance was from Florida but attending school in Germany where he was becoming a very accomplished skier. His skiing skills attracted Davies' attention, something Davies later mentioned to McCrillis. Davies asked McCrillis to see if there were a way to get Durrance enrolled at Dartmouth where he could put his great skiing ability to good purpose while gaining a superb education. When Durrance returned to the States, McCrillis provided him with lodging while the young man spent a year to prepare for admission to Dartmouth. During that time, Durrance attended Towle High School in Newport where he competed very successfully on the school ski team. In the fall of 1934, Durrance matriculated at Dartmouth and immediately caught the appreciative eye of McCrillis's friend, Coach Otto Schniebs. McCrillis continued to serve *in loco parentis* for his protégé, Durrance, and advised him through the academic side of college life while also serving as a link for the young skier into McCrillis's growing network of influential contacts in skiing.

While Durrance went on to set records and show the national ski scene the tails of his skis, McCrillis continued to make his own impressive impact on the ski world both locally and nationally. Jack continued to offer his advice and experience to many who sought it regarding skiing. He advised new entrepreneurs about entering the ski industry and offered them contacts with his friends, evaluated early versions of skiwear sent to him for use and for comment by his friend Hirsch, tested new skis, bindings, and waxes and suggested improvements. He was well-connected and active among the national skiing organizations of the time, promoted Schniebs's efforts to establish ski schools, maintained his own close network of media sources like Frank Elkins of *The New York Times*, and found time to ski with old Dartmouth friends like **Sherman Adams '22**.

In late 1934, McCrillis, as president of the Newport Ski Club, began negotiations with property owners and the Society for the Protection of New Hampshire Forests (SPNHF) for permission to cut ski trails on Mount Sunapee for use by the Newport Ski Club. In the process of starting what would later become one of New Hampshire's state-owned ski areas, McCrillis again turned to his Dartmouth network and engaged his old friend Bill Fowler of the Appalachian Mountain Club to help forge a favorable relationship with the SPNHF. By the winter of 1934, the Newport Ski Club had one trail cut and more planned.

Jack continued to send out reels of his films and copies of his book to friends and strangers, all of whom eagerly sought these great new tools for learning how to enjoy skiing. He and Coach Schniebs once again collaborated with the DOC, this time to establish a new Schniebs-McCrillis Trophy for the best four-event man on the Dartmouth ski team. When specialization meant that there were no longer any four-event skiers, in 1974 McCrillis authorized changing the criterion for awarding the trophy to the skier who best embodies Schniebs's motto that "skiing is a way of life," a motto that could be said of McCrillis as well. He was a key agent in the overall development of skiing in North America and in the introduction, and then the growth, of Alpine skiing from the local and regional level to the national level and beyond.

John P. Carleton '22 — The First American Olympic Skier
By Stephen Waterhouse

John Carleton was an outstanding skier, a Rhodes Scholar, and an Olympian. He was a true skiing pioneer in the northeastern United States.

His famous somersault jumps off a ski jump were legendary, not only at Dartmouth, but throughout the East where he frequently demonstrated them. In 1922, at the first Winter Carnival to have use of the then new Vale of Tempe ski jump, he and his good friend **Dick Bowler '22** (Captain of the first Dartmouth Ski Team and also someone who had grown up in Hanover like Carleton) wowed the crowd with a display of their jumping skills. This comment from a 1922 classmate was included in Dick Bowler's obituary in the Dartmouth Alumni Magazine (April 17, 1981):

> "Dick was an expert on skis, and by class acclamation, he and Johnny Carleton were the first Dartmouth students to somersault off the new ski jump. The two of them skiing hand-in-hand at breakneck speed down the jump and flying off into a graceful somersault is an indelible memory of our college years."

Both boys had such good jumping skills that, long before they entered Dartmouth, they were invited in 1914 to participate in the first collegiate ski meet against McGill as the jumpers for the Dartmouth team. In a letter in 1949 to the head of the Dartmouth College News Service, **Jack Bowler '15**, Dick's older brother and another participant in the McGill races, said "Because we lacked entrees for a jumping team, we took along a couple of "ringers" – John Carleton and my younger brother, Dick Bowler, who were then high school boys. Even at that time, they were the best jumpers in town." (December 19, 1949; John Bower '22 file, Rauner)

Through his racing days in Europe after college, he became a friend of Sir Arnold Lunn, and helped initiate a connection between Sir Arnold and **Charles Procter, Class of 1900**, plus others at Dartmouth. Carleton was a leader of the Oxford University Ski Team, where he attended as a Rhodes Scholar from 1922 to 1924. He made the connection with Sir Arnold Lunn during early ski races in Switzerland that led to Lunn's frequent exchange of ideas with the ski oriented folks in Hanover, and the initiation of some of the early ski racing techniques by Dartmouth skiers like the first Slalom (1925), Downhill (1927) and contributed to starting the Giant Slalom.

John Carleton '22 grew up in Hanover and developed a crowd-pleasing somersault off the ski jump; this may have been John doing his favorite trick in 1916.

Carleton was on the first US Winter Olympic Team, competing in Chamonix in 1924 in Nordic events. He has the distinction of being the first American-born skier to compete in the Winter Olympics, as his teammates in France were of Norwegian descent. A total of three Ivy Leaguers made the trek to Chamonix: Carleton, Nathaniel W. Niles (Harvard) and Willard W. Rice (Harvard). Niles competed as a figure skater and Rice as a hockey player as they had also done in the 1920 Summer Olympics in Antwerp. Chamonix played host to 16 events for over 250 athletes from 16 nations, and the Games took over a month to complete.[21]

Despite Carleton's efforts, the US team did not star in the skiing events. He only entered the jumping events, and did not medal. These Games were dominated by the powerful Norwegian team. This was evident in the final medal tally, with Norway leading the pack at 17 and the US having modest results with a Gold only in the 500m Speed Skating event (Charles Jewtraw). Carleton did not return for the 1928 St. Moritz Games, but **Charles Proctor '28** represented Dartmouth in those Olympics. Other Dartmouth winter sports athletes have followed Carleton and Proctor as representatives of the college in every subsequent Winter Games as competitors, and its alumni have served as competition officials or Olympic team staff for most, if not all, of them.

As the years rolled on, Carleton continued an involvement in ski racing, ski explorations of various kinds, and as an advisor to the DOC and Dartmouth skiing. With Charles Proctor he was, in 1931, the first to climb and ski the Tuckerman Ravine headwall on Mount Washington. In 1932 he competed in the Eastern Amateur Ski Association's first downhill race on Mount Moosilauke. He was helpful in Eastern ski area expansion as he successfully promoted using Civilian Conservation Corps funds and personnel for the development of 15 ski trails in New Hampshire.

Carleton built a career as a lawyer in Manchester, NH. He was also a veteran of both World Wars. His law firm included Dartmouth Trustee and leader of the McLane family, **Judge John R. McLane '07**. It was Carleton who converted Judge McLane from skiing cross-country to skiing Alpine. McLane became an advocate for Dartmouth's increase of its Alpine ski facilities, particularly the construction of the Dartmouth Skiway in 1957.

Even sixty years later, classmates remembered vividly the image of Johnny Carleton '22 and Dick Bowler '22 skiing hand-in-hand at breakneck speed down the Vale of Tempe jump, and flying off into a graceful double somersault.

John Carleton is a member of the National Ski and Snowboard Hall of Fame, having been inducted in 1968 as one of the earlier honorees elected.

Charles N. Proctor '28 — East meets West
By David Hooke '84

Charles Proctor was dubbed the "Babe Ruth of skiing" in the late 1930s for his superlative skiing ability, his pioneering development of major ski resorts and ski equipment, and his authorship of key books on ski technique. Long and lanky, he was one of the strongest forces behind the emergence of skiing as a national sport in the late 1930s despite being described by fellow skier Dave Bradley '39 as "laconic, shy, and [extremely] taciturn..."[22]

Born in Missouri in 1906, Charley came to Hanover in 1909 when his father, Charles A. Proctor, Dartmouth Class of 1900, returned to his alma mater as Professor of Physics. In 1910 the Proctors built a house on

Occom Ridge near the golf course where, that same year, the college's first Winter Field Day was conducted to inaugurate the famous Dartmouth Outing Club (DOC). Also that year, Prof. Proctor made Charley a pair of skis out of leftover lumber from the new house. Charley instantly took to skiing and was soon tramping all over the golf course. Thus, Charley Proctor and the DOC began their intertwined skiing lives together.[23]

Charley was right in the thick of the action as the DOC expanded its winter sports events over the ensuing years. In 1917, at the age of 11, he won his calls at the Boys Jump at the Dartmouth Winter Carnival[24] and repeated this in 1921. In 1922, he competed at the inauguration of the new Fred Harris jump in Brattleboro[25] with 3000 spectators on hand[26]. There, competing with his longtime friend and Hanover ski companion Johnny Carleton '22, Proctor set the schoolboy record with a jump of 114 feet, while Carleton set the New England record of 150 feet.[27]

Son and father fed each other's enthusiasm and interest. Prof. Proctor helped found the US Eastern Amateur Ski Association in 1923 and organized its first contests.[28] These meets brought Charley into contact with the top Norwegian skiers and he learned from them. Charley entered Dartmouth in the fall of 1924, and in 1925, in an event designed by his father, won the first slalom race at a Winter Carnival.[29] He was individual high point scorer at the 1926 Collegiate Championship and that same year made an exhibition jump of 130 feet on the Dartmouth hill, a record that stood for six years.[30] Named Captain of the team in 1927, he won the Canadian Nordic Combined Championship[31] and the first-ever Moosilauke Downmountain race, also designed by his father, on a 4.5 mile course down the Carriage Road, in 21 minutes.[32] Chosen to compete for the U.S. in the 1928 Olympics in St. Moritz, he placed 14th in the jump and 26th in the Nordic Combined.[33] Meanwhile, his father attended the meeting where the FIS decided to adopt the first "time-only" slalom on an experimental basis; Charley thereafter skied in the first Arlberg-Kandahar race in 1928, the first European race ever held under the new slalom rules.[34]

Charley continued to be involved in the Harvard, Appalachian Mountain Club and Dartmouth ski world. In 1931 he founded a weekend ski school at Newfound Lake near Mt. Cardigan, NH[35], and on April 11 he and Carleton became the first to ski the famous Tuckerman Ravine headwall on New Hampshire's Mount Washington.[36] That same year he met Rockwell Stephens; the two founded "Ski Sport, Inc." in 1932 to make and sell ski equipment. Relying on the Harvard/Hochgebirge Ski Club old-boy skiing network for financing, they pioneered a number of innovations, including the first steel ski poles.[37] Charley traveled as far as California to sell ski gear and learn what was out there, and in the process he met Don Tressider, President of Yosemite National Park and the Curry Company (the primary concessionaire in the park), who would later hire him to run the Yosemite ski program.[38]

Charley married Mary Miller in 1932 and they moved to Brighton, Massachusetts, in 1933 when he was named coach of the Harvard ski team. In 1933, he and Stephens collaborated on *The Art of Ski-ing*, a popular early handbook on equipment, technique, and even on-hill ski etiquette.[39] He also began laying out ski trails in earnest, starting on Pico Peak, Vermont, for the Meade family, and then some 40 miles of ski trails in New Hampshire for the newly founded Civilian Conservation Corps. In 1934 he laid out the Sherburne Trail on Mt. Washington and, in 1935, its Gulf of Slides Trail; also that year, he designed the Alexandria Trail and the Fire Trail on Mt. Cardigan.[40] He skied with no falls in the second Inferno Race from the summit of Washington to Pinkham Notch in 1934[41] and that same spring, he set the course for the first Harvard-Dartmouth (H-D) Slalom at Tuckerman's; he and then high school student Dick Durrance '39 both foreran the course. The Inferno and the H-D Slalom inaugurated Durrance's famous skiing career.[42]

Perhaps Charley's most influential contribution to the business of skiing was his pivotal role in the design of the Sun Valley resort in Idaho. Envisioned by Averell Harriman, Chairman of the Union Pacific Railroad, as the first true luxury ski resort, it was to be the destination to which the rich and famous would flock. In 1936, Proctor trained a number of local men to ski and was hired by Harriman as design consultant; he explored the difficult Mt. Baldy terrain and wife Mary, who accompanied him, became the first female skier to make the descent. Nonetheless, recognizing the nature of the clientele, he recommended against the more difficult terrain in favor of the easier and more accessible. He proposed ski trails on Dollar Mountain and what became known as Proctor Mountain, and he approved the design of the world's first chair lift, designed by U.P. engineers, but with crucial details inspired by the Dartmouth lift at Oak Hill. With outstanding ski terrain, the country's first chair lift, and the million-dollar base lodge, Sun Valley instantly became the place to be seen on skis.[43]

Proctor built his reputation as the ambassador of the sport in ways large and small.[44] He was Chief of Jump for the 1932 Olympics in Lake Placid.[45] In 1933, for the first National Downhill Race, held on the Carriage Road on Moosilauke, Charley was the forerunner and had the best time at 7'22", a full 38 seconds faster than the first official contestant. In 1935, he wrote *Guide For Your First Ski Trip* published by Yankee; then *Skiing Fundamentals: Equipment & Advanced Technique* with Rockwell Stephens in 1936; and *Do's and Don'ts for Safe Skiing* with Charles C. Lund, Boston and Maine Railroad, in 1937. He was judge and exhibition skier at the first several years of the Boston National Ski Shows, starting 1935. In 1937 he traveled throughout the West, including Sun Valley and Utah; he lauded the skiing there, and a reporter in Salt Lake dubbed him "the number one man in skiing" and "the Babe Ruth of skiing."[46] He lectured in Chicago on "ski fever." That spring and summer he designed the Fire Trail on Mt. Washington and the Proctor Downhill Course in Hanover, site of Winter Carnival races until the early 1950s.[47] That fall, he opened a ski school at New Foundland, near Bristol, NH, becoming the first American to run a ski school in the East. At the second New York Winter Show, he and Frank Elkins Norwood Cox were listed as the two best all-around skiers in America.[48] All of this by the tender age of 32!

Finally in 1938, with Mary expecting their first child, he accepted the post of head of the winter sports program at Yosemite National Park, a position he held for the next twenty years. He settled into family life with a second daughter and son but was still highly sought after, becoming the first secretary of the Far West Ski Association in 1943.[49] He retired from Yosemite in 1958, was inducted into the Ski Hall of Fame in 1959, set race courses at the 1960 Olympics in Squaw Valley. Remaining active in skiing, he received numerous honors, including Life Membership in the Kandahar Ski Association. In 1981, the Western Division of the North American Ski Journalists Association established The Charley Proctor Award for individuals in the West contributing significantly to the sport of skiing. He died in California in 1996, aged 90, his life fully lived and dedicated to the sport he so loved.

Dan Hatch '28 — The "Beaming Baron" of the Dartmouth Outing Club
By Douglas C. Leitch '65

It was so unlikely that one of the most influential agents of Dartmouth's leadership in the sport of skiing would have been born in Los Angeles, California, in 1906, a year before Fred Harris matriculated. Daniel P. Hatch, Jr. was a member of the Dartmouth Class of 1928, and, as he noted later, "majored in DOC." Certainly his influence as an undergraduate officer in the Dartmouth Outing Club would be magnified for another decade to the benefit of skiing's rapid development.

As the Outing Club grew in complexity, stimulated by its centerpiece activity of skiing, so did the need for a full-time manager beyond the capabilities of its enthusiastic and energetic undergraduate officers. In 1929, the DOC nominated recent graduate Hatch to fill that role and made him Comptroller of the Dartmouth Outing Club, but soon he was functioning more as the first General Manager of the DOC.

Hatch began his job only one year after the Dartmouth College Athletic Council had formally approved skiing as a varsity sport even though the team had existed since 1921. Dan jumped directly into his new role in typical Hatch fashion. At the fourth annual Moosilauke Down-Mountain race, he was on the slope beside **William Fowler '21**, a DOC alumnus and active skier, discussing the need for a qualified ski coach when Fowler recommended Hatch look into hiring Otto Schniebs, a noted ski instructor near Boston. Hatch engaged the assistance of Professor Charles Proctor, a DOC faculty advisor, who met with and recruited Schniebs. Six years later, when Schniebs resigned after moving the Dartmouth ski team to the top of the intercollegiate skiing world, it was Dan Hatch who would lead the search for a successor. And it was Hatch who would direct the process to recruit, hire, and relocate champion skier Walter Prager from Davos, Switzerland to Hanover. Once Prager arrived, Dan arranged for housing and did his best to find him summer employment, doing everything possible to keep the popular new coach at Dartmouth.

Hatch worked tirelessly with local businesses to develop skiing in the region by promoting ski school programs, ski merchandisers, and the development of nearby facilities. As skiing expanded on Mt. Moosilauke, Hatch helped to open the summit camp for skiing in 1932. He served on a college committee to develop new ski slopes in Hanover, resulting in the use of Oak Hill as a ski area, and in the design and construction of an entirely new overhead cable lift for these slopes which had never been seen in North America before. In the meantime, he scheduled travel for the ski team to compete around the country and the world – Minnesota, Mt. Rainier, Sun Valley, summer training in Australia and New Zealand, sending another contingent to Chile at the same time he negotiated bringing the Swiss National team to race in Hanover.

He lobbied hard for a change in national eligibility rules to allow ski instructors to compete with amateurs and successfully pitched the idea of sanctioning new subdivision ski clubs within the DOC to expand skier eligibility in sanctioned meets, and he managed to engage prominent British ski promoter Arnold Lunn to lecture on campus in 1936, the first of several visits by Lunn. David Bradley '38, a future National Ski Hall of Fame member, called Hatch the "beaming baron of the DOC" for the influence he had on New England skiing. "His thoughtful direction of the Outing Club's Winter Sports program has been a thing inspired by a profound appreciation and enthusiasm for the spiritual as well as the physical side of the sport," Bradley wrote.[50]

Hatch was the first true General Manager of the DOC. He eventually elected to move out of a direct involvement in the DOC and skiing to assume a career in the insurance industry, but his time in this position was to have a lasting impact on the direction of Dartmouth skiing. He established a role for adult leadership of the DOC that carries thru to this very day. And even though removed from the DOC and skiing scene in future years, he maintained a lifelong interest in the on-going evolvement of Dartmouth as the center of US skiing developments.

Walter Prager — Ski Coach Emeritus
By Frederick C. Hart, Jr. '58, Th '60

Walter Prager was born in Bonn, Germany on April 2, 1910; grew up on skis near Davos, Switzerland; winner of the first Arlberg–Kandahar Alpine Combined title in 1930; Nordic Combined Swiss National Champion in 1931; first F.I.S. World Champion Downhill skier at Mürren, Switzerland in 1931, repeating in 1933; DOC ski coach from 1936-1941; author of the instructional book, *Skiing*, for the Barnes Sports Library

Coach Walter Prager: World Champion Skier, superb Coach, 10th Mtn Div Leader, and member NSSHF.

in 1939, later a US Army Training Manual; sergeant, US Army 10th Mountain Division from 1941-1945, and awarded the Bronze Star; DOC ski coach again in 1946-1947; US Olympic Ski Team coach in 1948; DOC ski coach again from 1949-1957; ski shop operator at Mt. Snow, Vermont from 1957-1960, and at Wilmington (Whiteface), New York from 1960-1980s; awarded the A-K Diamond Pin (belatedly) in 1956; elected to the National Ski Hall of Fame in 1977; named Head Ski Coach Emeritus by the trustees of Dartmouth College on 23 April 1982; died at Mountain View, California, 28 May 1984.

Walt arrived in New York on October 15, 1936 on board the *Europa* from Bremen, a "teacher" on the passenger list, destination "Dartmouth College, Hanover, New Hampshire."[51] He became popular immediately with the DOC ski team members, many of whom were already competing at an international level. This popularity wasn't only because of his skill and European experience in all four events, but also because of his coaching style – teaching by example, training and racing alongside his men. He was more like a slightly older brother to them. His first team's great leader, **Dick Durrance '39**, later said, "Walter was a technical coach [by comparison with his predecessor, Otto Schniebs], more quiet, more our age, really . . . He was still racing while he was coaching. So we were racing buddies as well as members of his team."[52] Coach Prager was indeed a quiet, modest and gentle man, with a ready smile, a musical Swiss accent, and a great love of skiing.

His popularity spread throughout the ranks of college skiers everywhere. It was on a trip to Tuckerman's as a high-schooler from Connecticut in 1953 – still unaware that I would ever attend Dartmouth – that I first realized the icon he had become. I heard a happy group of college guys singing songs about Walter: "Oh, Walter Lee, Oh Walter Lee, Oh Won't you teach us how to ski?" (as in, "Oh, Tannenbaum"). To my amazement, the singers were competitors from the UVM Ski Team – not Dartmouth at all!

I was fortunate to know him in his final years of coaching, when he was still beautiful to watch on skis – effortless, efficient, always faster than anybody else, and, in a word, graceful. He even *walked* fast, with "Vorlage" (German for forward lean or position), as if to illustrate a key feature of his skiing style.[53] I saw him make some of the first tracks ever down the Worden's Schuss at the new Dartmouth Skiway — on cross-country skis, no less. I saw how he was respected by and got along with the great Dartmouth skiers of that later generation: Dodge, Beck, Corcoran, Stigum, Igaya, and perhaps most significantly with Ralph Miller Jr., whose father had been instrumental in Walter's coming to Dartmouth in the first place.[54] He set slalom courses just as smoothly as he skied them. He was a waxing genius[55], and a respected mountain-climbing instructor. He consulted on ski area and trail design in several states, and especially for Dartmouth at both the Moosilauke Ravine Lodge and the Dartmouth Skiway.

When DOC Executive Director John Rand received Walt's telegram from Europe on September 9, 1957 that it was "impossible to continue coaching," my first reaction was disbelief. How could this be, at the start of the school year, at the peak of his career, at his relatively young age, with a super team and the DOC hosting the NCAA Championships later that season? But his hip was more of a problem than any of us knew, and it was increasingly difficult for him to continue with his style of physically leading and coaching by example. It was for real, and Walter's coaching career was over. We salute him now for his many accomplishments, and for his distinguished and amiable impact on Dartmouth Skiing.

In the 1957-1958 winter, a Wallace Silver bowl was commissioned as a new NCAA Ski Championship team trophy and engraved, "The Walter Prager Trophy / National Collegiate Champions / 1958."[56] The bowl also proudly displayed a small replica of the DOC team's snowflake emblem, originally designed by Otto Schniebs.[57] It was presented at the victory banquet on March 23, 1958 to Coach Al Merrill, representing his (and Walter's) team, with senior co-captains **Dave Harwood '58** and **Bill Smith '58**, that had just become the first Dartmouth ski team ever to win the NCAA championship.

Dick Durrance '39 — Man on the Medal
By Warren Miller

Today when a skier wins an Olympic medal in a downhill race by thirteen thousandths of a second, or half a ski length, he or she becomes an instant millionaire. Think how much a person could earn today if that person had been born in Florida and left home to become the junior alpine ski champion of Germany, United States Collegiate Champion in downhill, slalom, cross country and jumping all four years of his college career, U.S. Olympic ski team member twice, won the Harriman Cup three times, was a consultant to Sun Valley, Idaho and laid out trails on Mt. Baldy, co-developed Alta, Utah and was General Manager of Aspen Skiing Corporation for five years, organized and brought the 1950 FIS championships to Aspen, Chief-of-Race at the Squaw Valley Winter Olympics, and produced dozens of award winning movies as well as several hundred commercial movies? Certainly not the millions a top racer earns today. Well, don't even think about it.

This ski champion, Dick Durrance, is small in size and big in heart and accomplishments. He's a man who has devoted his life to the semi absurd sport of traveling all over the world to turn a pair of skis right and left, day in and day out, until the snow melts and then travels to the other side of the equator and does exactly the same thing there.

In the winter of 1927, his mother, together with his two brothers, and two sisters walked the streets of Garmisch-Partenkirchen looking for a place to live. None of them could speak a single word

Dick Durrance '39 winning his first Harriman Cup.

of German and they wound up staying for five years. Or until they could ignore Hitler no longer. Dick did everything the hard way because there was no book written at the time on how to do any of what he was doing. No interactive videos, no CD-Rom, no person to copy. There weren't even metal edges on his skis or lifts to ride. Dick was the one that everyone copied.

Dick was, and always will be, the influential trend setter wherever he travels. I can remember when I was a skinny fourteen year old kid living in Hollywood, California. I was just growing out of my career as a Boy Scout in favor of young girls when I saw pictures of Dick Durrance in a book in a sporting goods store. I think it was in 1937 or 1938. This was three years after someone invented the rope tow and one year after someone else invented the chair lift in a place called Sun Valley, Idaho.

By that time Dick Durrance had carved his skiing style into the minds of skiers from the slopes of Germany during the 1936 Olympics to the glaciers of New Zealand. He is the only skier I have ever known who has had a mountain named after him. As far removed from skiing as I was in 1937 living in Hollywood, I must have instinctively realized early in my life, that there was a man who had the unique capability of making molehills out of mountains.

Together with his wife Miggs, Dick has skied here, raced there, filmed everywhere and has the trophies to prove it. He's done it all. Several generations of skiers have come and gone since his third Harriman Cup victory. But there is no other person then, now or will there be in the future, who so completely dominated ski racing as Dick did. Nor has any ski racer ever designed the ski runs on a mountain like Baldy at Sun Valley and on Aspen Mountain or developed a ski resort like Alta, Utah. Dick did.

Yes, Dick spent his whole life making molehills out of mountains. I'm honored to have been asked to summarize a lifetime of achievements in a page or two. It's an impossible task.

You will have to read the book. It still doesn't tell all that Dick has done and done successfully. Not only has he done it all, he invented most of it, and he is way too modest to tell you about most of it. No other person has ever dominated skiing in America as much, or as long, as this short man with long skis who made molehills out of mountains.

[This profile was originally written by Warren Miller as the Preface for the book, *Man on the Medal – The Life and Times of America's First Great Ski Racer*, with text by John Jerome (1995; reprinted here courtesy of Durrance Enterprises and Warren Miller).]

Amos "Bud" Little '39 — The Doctor who made House Calls — by Parachute
By Stephen L. Waterhouse

Dr. Amos "Bud" Little was a member of the Dartmouth ski team during his undergrad days, racing with the many legendary skiers of the time. While at Johns Hopkins Medical School in Baltimore, MD, he is reputed to have won the first ski race south of the Mason Dixon line. As the story below by Curt Synness reveals, there lurked in Bud's body a fearless soul willing to put all on the line to achieve his objectives and to help his fellow man.

Bud Little '39 shows off his somersault style.

More than 60 years ago, before helicopters were used for mountain and wilderness rescues, Helena's Dr. Amos "Bud" Little was making rescues from the sky. In 1944, Little, then 27 and serving as an Air Force "paradoctor," gained national recognition for one of the most daring parachute rescues in U.S. history in a remote region of the Colorado Rockies known as Hell's Half Acre.

"Shortly after midnight on June 14, 1944, a B-17 Flying Fortress out of Rapid City, S.D., bound for Greeley, Colo., had crashed on the north side of Crown Peak in the Roosevelt National Forest, just below the snow and timberline at 10,800 feet," according to a July 1999 *Wildland Firefighter* magazine article titled "The Savior Who Fell From The Sky" by Mark Matthews.

Three of the bomber's 10 crewmembers were killed instantly. Another died the next morning. Two survivors were able to walk down from the mountain. The other four were injured too badly to leave the site, including one with a broken back. Little's heroics were reported in three national magazines — *Time*, *Coronet* and *Reader's Digest*.

"Soon, a bomber, with an Army doctor aboard, was on its way to the rocky ledge where the four injured men lay," stated the *Time* article of July 10, 1944. "The doctor first dropped a parachute load of supplies from the circling (UC-54), then jumped himself. When the main rescue party arrived by land, nearly four hours later, the patients had been fed, bandaged and drugged to ease their pain.

"The doctor is small, husky Lt. Amos Little, of Marlboro, Mass. He is one of six paradoctors attached to the Search and Rescue section of the Second Air Force." Little had been contacted in Casper, Wyoming, at 2 a.m. on June 15. "As soon as we spied the crashed bomber, I dropped the 85-pound kit containing equipment for treatment of shock, burns, fractures, lacerations and other injuries," Little told the *Great Falls Tribune* in 1945.

"It landed within 25 yards of the mangled B-17, but my landing was not quite as good. I bailed out at 12,500 feet, a thousand feet above the craggy mountain top where the wreckage was. The wind carried me (about 600 feet) from the crash, and I thought I was a goner for a minute. As I approached the ground, my chute snagged (the top of) an old dead tree, and I fell about 20 feet with that tree right after me. It landed with a hell of a thud a few inches from my head."

At the time, Little's rescue was unofficially the highest altitude for a parachute landing. He was recognized as the only physician to make a rescue jump in the U.S. during World War II. In 1994, one of the survivors of the bomber crash of 50 years earlier penned a tribute to his rescuer.

"How do you say 'thank you' to someone who risked his life to save you and your comrades by jumping from that altitude?" wrote David Phillips from his home in Chandler, Arizona. "It was an incredible effort, for which I and the others are forever grateful."

After graduating from Dartmouth in 1939 and Johns Hopkins University in 1942, Little enlisted in the U.S. Army. It was while stationed at Great Falls, MT, that he volunteered for jump school. "They gave us a choice to work on a tractor motor or learn how to jump out of airplanes, and I chose the latter," said the 91-year-old Little, who currently resides at The Waterford in Helena.

He attended jump school in 1943 with the smokejumpers at the U.S. Forest Service Parachute School at Seeley Lake and then finished his training at Fort Benning, Ga. Little made 52 parachute jumps between 1943 and 1946—45 practice and 7 rescue jumps. In the summer of 1944, he bailed out over a raging fire in Montana's Lolo National Forest to rescue a smokejumper who had broken his back. In October of 1945 in western Montana, Creek Morgan of Kellogg, Idaho, was accidentally shot in the arm by a high-powered hunting rifle by a hunting companion who was aiming for a bear.

"Capt. Amos Little parachuted to the spot where Morgan lay in the rugged timberlands of the Bitterroot National Forest to perform the operation," reported "The Missoulian." "Little said Morgan was 'darned near dead when we landed.' " Little and nine smokejumpers made the dangerous 2,000-foot leap to aid the wounded hunter. They administered three quarts of blood plasma during the all-day trek from the thickly wooded area to an awaiting plane, which flew him to a hospital in Missoula. "Dr. H. M. Blegen said Morgan's condition was serious, but 'the emergency work done by Capt. Little undoubtedly saved his life,' " according to "The Missoulian."

Bud Little relocated to Helena in 1947, where he operated a private medical practice for many years. He and his family — wife Mary and children Jim, Sue and Rogers — became key members of the Belmont Ski Club. The day after the Mann Gulch Fire in 1949, Little helped identify the bodies of the 11 smokejumpers who perished in the fire.

In 1958, he made the 24th documented ascent of Granite Peak (in the Beartooth Range and the highest point in Montana at about 12,800 feet,), an acknowledged validation of mountaineering skill. He was appointed Director of the 1960 U.S. Alpine Ski Team, and served as the vice president of the International Ski Federation from 1970-88. In 1955, Little received the A. Leo Stevens Medal for his para-rescue work, and in 1965 he was enshrined into the U.S. National Ski Hall of Fame.

An appropriate quote from an article on Little's profession six-and-a-half decades ago from the newsletter "The Slip Stream" reads: "There are times when they parachute rather blindly, floating down the hillside into the unknown. 'I am a doctor,' he utters. Words that have never sounded more sweeter in all your life."

Over the decades, Bud participated in major US skiing activities of many types. He served as president of the Northern Division of the U.S. Ski Association (1949-50), as well as co-chairman of the National Alpine Championships (1949). Little was Chairman of the Alpine Committee and manager of the U.S. Alpine team for the world championship meet in Aspen, Colo. (1950). He served on the U.S. Olympic Ski Games committee in 1952, 1960, 1964, 1968, 1972, 1976 and 1980. Little was the manager of the U.S. Alpine team for the 1960 Olympics in Squaw Valley, Calif., and at the World Championships in Chamonix, France (1962). He was a referee at two other Olympics (1964, 1968) and World Championships (1962, 1966). For 29 years, from 1960-88, Bud Little was part of the International Ski Federation (FIS), serving as the vice president the last 19 years, from 1967-88. He was on the FIS Alpine Technical Committee from 1960-67, and was chairman of its Medical Committee from 1971-88.

During his career, Bud Little attended six Olympics and seven World Skiing Championships and visited with kings, queens, prime ministers and the Pope. Little's lifetime commitment to skiing earned him the American Ski Trophy (1961), the Blegen Award (1962), induction into the USSA Ski Hall of Fame (1965), the John Clair Award (1987) and the USSF Bud and Mary Little Award (1989, named in his own honor by the USSF). He was a skier and a doctor who made many visits to ski activities of one sort or another around the world; and sometimes, he made house calls in a way that marks him as one very, very special person!

[The central theme of this profile was provided by Curt Synness, as published in the *Independent Record*, Helena, MT on March 31, 2008, and is included here with their agreement.]

William R. "Sarge" Brown — A Man of Many Legends
By Stephen L. Waterhouse

Calm, thoughtful, and demanding of himself and others, Bill Brown displayed many talents: world-class skier, a military leader and hero in the strongest definition of the term, a successful coach of National Championship ski teams, an important member of Dartmouth College's very special ski history, and, particularly thru his work at Vail Mountain, a leader in the creation of today's modern ski industry.

Affectionately known as "Sarge," he came to Vail in 1966 from Dartmouth, where he had created a special Army R.O.T.C. Program, to join his 10th Mountain Division buddies. Bill managed the resort until 1990, bringing new thinking to ski area management. Using military techniques, he created a highly professional organization, bringing in "big iron" bulldozers to widen ski trails as he had seen in Europe, devising new signage and safety barrier systems, developing better snow cat technology, standardizing slope maintenance and ski patrol scheduling, and creating world class race courses using a finishing device of his own design, "Brown's Brush." Bill's remarkable contributions are the primary reason for Vail's recurring selection as the best ski area in North America and one of the leading ski areas in the world.

Sarge Brown's smiling image as the Man of Many Legends.

Bill's impact was widespread. He proved to the Forest Service that trails could be created and maintained to be both fun to ski and environmentally sound by using vegetation in new ways to stabilize open slopes. Even after he retired, and right up to his death in 2008, he was in regular touch with the management who followed his advice on how to care for "his" mountain. The Vail ski experience owes its existence largely to the wisdom of Bill Brown, and he is immortalized in various ways around the mountain; for instance in the dining area, Sarge's Shelter, with its case of his early ski racing trophies in Mid-Vail; and on a plaque at the top of the Riva Ridge ski run, named after the 10th Division's greatest battle.

Bill Brown's legendary status is based on more than his years in Vail. Born in 1922 in Cascade, Idaho, his father was a US Forest Service Ranger who introduced Bill to his lifelong passion for the outdoors. In his early years, Bill was a star athlete in several sports, gaining All-America status in six-man football. When he entered ski racing and jumping, he became an instant success, winning the Idaho State Cross Country-Championship in 1937 at age 15. Over the next 20 years, Bill was a frequent winner in cross-country, downhill, slalom and jumping. In 1941, he led his U. of Idaho team to the National Intercollegiate Championship. In 1948, he was the Pacific Northwest Ski Association Alpine Combined Champion.

He was selected for the US Olympic teams in 1948 (St. Moritz) and 1952 (Oslo), but injuries prevented his participation. In 1954, he was the European Military Ski Champion in Slalom, Giant Slalom and Downhill. With his experience as a winning competitor and having great management skills, he became an outstanding coach, race official, and leader of race events. He was repeatedly selected as Chief of Race and a member of race juries. In 1948, he organized the first National Junior Championship and coached three National Champion youth teams. In 1989, he organized and directed Vail's highly successful World Alpine Championships.

Bill's first career was the military. From 1942 to 1966, Bill carved out a special niche as the Army's most successful and heroic mountain soldier. He was the youngest First Sergeant in the 10th Mountain Division — and the Army — at age 19. He joined with many Dartmouth alumni, his lifelong friends, as key leaders of the 10th. He was wounded twice in WWII and twice in Korea, earning many medals for valor, including two Silver Stars, two Bronze Stars, and two Purple Hearts. He became the Army's Senior NCO in mountain warfare in Austria, Korea, Alaska and Colorado.

In 1958, he was assigned to run a special Mountain Warfare Program for Dartmouth's Reserve Officers Training Corps (ROTC) Program. He designed a program, and inspired or browbeat his "officers-to-be" into becoming exceptional skiers, mountain climbers, and soldiers. Dartmouth's ROTC Program became one of the best in the nation, and Bill was recognized as the Soldier of the Year. And just as important to Bill, he became a beloved member of the ski world's greatest fraternity, the alumni, staff and extended family of Dartmouth College. When the Army refused to allow him to go to Vietnam at age 44, Bill retired as one of the five highest-ranking NCO's in the US Army with the title of Senior Sergeant-Major.

In 1990, Bill "Sarge" Brown was elected to the National Ski Hall of Fame in Michigan, adding one more name to a long list of Dartmouth alumni and associates, far and away the institution with the most members enshrined there.

John Caldwell '50 — Father of American Cross-Country Ski Racing
By Jim Page '63

John Caldwell competed in the Nordic Combined event in the 1952 Olympics in Oslo, Norway. It wasn't a great experience. No American had ever competed well in this event at the international level. Nonetheless, as John explains it, "...competing in the Olympics was a defining moment for me. I don't think I have ever, before or after, been so totally unprepared for any athletic event as the Games in Oslo. I came home telling myself that if I had anything to do with it, no Nordic skiers would ever go abroad and be so embarrassed."[58] He has spent his life fulfilling that vow and generations of American skiers were better as a result.

John was a very good four-event skier (downhill, slalom, cross-country and ski jumping) and became a member of the 1949 and 1950 Dartmouth teams, perhaps the most dominant ski teams the college ever assembled. They "cleaned up" competing against all the ski powers in both the East and the West.[59] The NCAA hadn't come along yet to sponsor intercollegiate championships, so Dartmouth doesn't even count these wins as official national championships, but these guys were that good!

Caldwell started teaching and coaching at The Putney School in Vermont in 1953, where he headed

John Caldwell '50 and his brother Pete Caldwell '54.

a program that developed many of the best skiers ever produced in the U.S. The 1982 five-man team that rose in rank to 4th in the world was composed of three Caldwell products his son **Tim Caldwell '76**, Bill Koch (still the only US Olympic Cross-Country Ski Medalist), and Jim Galanes.

Not satisfied to be "just" a coach, John started doing volunteer work for the Eastern Ski Association by running the committees that organized the sport, managing the cross-country (x-c) training camps for top athletes, and conducting first-rate ski competitions. Ultimately (somewhere in the 1980s), he got involved with organizational politics at the national level as well. He served with **Tom Corcoran '54** on the US Ski Association Board and later was one of the groups that split off and formed the US Ski Team. It now controls the entire US Ski and Snowboard program.[60] His "Hey, we gotta do this better" attitude shook up the complacent x-c ski world and led to many important changes. He is still doing that today.

John started coaching international teams in 1966, returning with the US Nordic Team to Oslo where he had been so unsatisfied fourteen years earlier. He coached at three World Championships and three Olympic Games for the U.S. and at Lake Placid in 1980 for the Australian Cross-Country Ski Team. His teams were noted for their prodigious training feats, like hiking the entire Long Trail down the spine of Vermont in ten days and for their strong belief, instilled by their coach, that they could compete with the best in the world.

In 1964 he wrote the first book in English on cross-country skiing. It went into "eight editions [between 1964 and 1987] eventually selling a half-million copies, greater than any specialized ski book ever written".[61] The book "made Caldwell a significant mentor–in print at least–to tens of thousands of people who took up the sport. He combined his skill in teaching and his Nordic knowledge to quickly gain a reputation as America's most talented, native-born cross country coach."[62]

He feels his most significant contribution to the sport was the formation of NENSA (New England Nordic Ski Association). "As the U.S. Ski Association started to centralize and spend less time and effort promoting the cross-country sport in New England, it became clear that competition would die here if something wasn't done. And so a group of us started the NENSA, something totally outside of organized skiing at the time. It has served as a model for the development of skiing in other regions"[63]

It is characteristic of a lot of Dartmouth alumni that they do things well, and that if they don't do so initially, they will somehow figure out how to excel. John Caldwell has been figuring out how to improve the sport of cross-country skiing in the U.S. ever since his personal setback in 1952. His less than stellar racing there has benefited athletes, coaches, and cross-country ski sport organizers for more than 50 years.

Bill Briggs '54 — The Compleat Ski Mountaineer
By Nate Dougall

William Morse Briggs was born appropriately on the first day of winter in Augusta, Maine in 1931. Fate had decided to spice things up and Bill was born without a right hip socket. A short two years later, doctors hammered out a hollow in the young boy's pelvis. Undaunted, he began to ski at the age of seven, being heavily influenced by his sister and later her husband, **Dick Kendall '44**.

When Bill arrived at Philips Exeter Academy in 1949, he had the good fortune to have Bob Bates as one of his teachers. Bob was a gregarious and accomplished mountaineer who later became President of the American Alpine Club. This was during what many have called the Golden Age of Mountaineering (1946-1956) when some of the great mountains were conquered — if only for a moment. Bates encouraged Briggs to join the Exeter Mountaineering Club, which he did; Bill particularly enjoyed the group sing-alongs after the climbing. Bates had climbed with noted experts Glen Exum and Paul Petzoldt out in the Tetons in the 1940s and his influence on a young Briggs was significant; he decided there was adventure to be had out West.

At Dartmouth, Bill quickly gravitated to the DOC and Dartmouth Mountaineering Club, a natural extension of his interests and a more satisfying environ for Briggs than on-

Steve Waterhouse '65 with the master of ski songs, Bill Briggs '54, who performed for D skiers gathered for the CarniVAIL Lunch in Sarge's Shelter at Vail.

campus fraternal organizations. Freshman could select a trip and Bill chose Ravine Lodge near Mount Moosilauke, a place known for the Brown-McLane parties where there was lots of music making. This moved Briggs enough to purchase a banjo and teach himself. That took care of the music side, but the events at the Etna, NH, farmhouse of Beanie Nutt (Dartmouth Associate Professor and oceanographer) and his wife Babs inspired him even more; here Briggs was able to rub shoulders with and listen to impromptu stories by arctic explorers on adventure and survival. This was an education in itself.

In 1952 Briggs, his brother John, **Peter Robinson '54**, and **Bob Collins '54** climbed in the Purcells in British Columbia. Briggs was inspired by two Dartmouth legends, brothers **John (Jack) R. Durrance '39, DMS '42** and **Richard (Dick) H. Dick Durrance '39**—one a great climber, the other a great skier; and Briggs

aimed to be both. In 1957, Bill had a chance meeting in Wales with Sir Arnold Lunn, an Englishman and one of the first ski mountaineers; he enlisted Bill to take responsibility for the sport of skiing by keeping the history and traditions of the sport. Lunn "invented modern downhill and slalom racing" with the hope that they "would help to develop the kind of technique suitable for ski mountaineering."[64] Bill knew that the life of a ski mountaineer was for him--a culmination of all of his talents (climbing, skiing and music). Briggs taught **Barry Corbet '58** how to ski parallel during a tip pull lesson (pulling the skis around a pole plant). Corbet asked if anyone else knew about tip pull parallel. He exclaimed, "Briggs, we're in on the ground floor!" In 1958, Briggs led a group of Dartmouth students — Corbet, **Sterling Neale '59** and **Bob French '56** — on the first successful Grand Traverse in British Columbia from the Bugaboos to Rogers Pass; this 100-mile crossing through previously unmapped territory stunned the many Canadians who had unsuccessfully attempted a similar journey.

Music is important to Briggs, an outlet first developed at Exeter and on the train returning from skiing at North Conway. His appreciation of music was enhanced at Dartmouth during the parties at Moosilauke Lodge around New Year's Eve. When Briggs first moved to Jackson, Wyoming, he started the infamous "Teton Tea Parties" underneath the bridge leading into Grand Teton National Park. Later, Briggs was a co-founder of the Hootenanny, a musical gathering held at Dornan's bar, very close to the Teton Tea Party bridge. In 1969, Bill was a co-founder of the Stagecoach Band in Wilson, WY which has now played over 2000 consecutive Sunday shows, affectionately called "Church." An accomplished yodeler, Briggs developed an interest in the history of alpine yodeling songs and is working to immortalize them in the Smithsonian Institution.

In 1959, Bill signed on with the renowned Exum Mountain Guides, taking clients up the Tetons for pay

The image of the tracks from Briggs legendary
first descent of the Grand Teton (1971).
(Tracks highlighted for reference; photo courtesy of Nate Dougall.)

much like Jack Durrance did so many summers before. In the winters, Bill was a ski instructor with Junior Bounous (who Warren Miller called the greatest off-piste skier in American history). Bill was surrounded by great men--great climbers and great skiers; Briggs became both. In 1966, Bill skied Buck Mountain in the Teton Range, first skied by Barry Corbet. In short order Bill then skied the Middle and South Tetons in 1967, and in 1968 the Skillet Glacier on Mount Moran on the northern end of the Teton Range, a feat about which Yvon Choinard (famed mountaineer and founder of Patagonia, Inc.) had quipped that anyone would need to rappel to get down.

On June 16, 1971, Briggs stunned the ski world with his seemingly impossible first descent of the Grand Teton, the central mountain in Wyoming's Teton Range. Near the bottom Briggs came across a couple on a hike that noted the skis on his back and asked what he had skied. Briggs calmly replied that he had skied the Grand Teton. The gentleman then asked, "How many times?" obviously unaware of the significance Briggs was too taken aback to reply. It wasn't very surprising that few believed Brigg's claim when he returned to town that evening, so he arranged for Virginia Huidekoper, who was not only a pilot and a prestigious skier but co-owner of the *Jackson Hole News*, to fly him up the following day to photograph his tracks. The visibility was perfect and the tracks were still there; Virginia documented the proof with her camera. The resulting photo created an indelible image that has inspired many to pursue their own mountains.

Later that year, Bill founded the Great American Ski School which focused on the mechanics of skiing for teaching to all abilities. It became a rite of passage for the youth of Jackson to get ski lessons from Briggs at Snow King Mountain Resort. Bill's contribution to skiing is still evolving; his multi-media compendium of ski instruction, *The Certainty Training Method*, will be released soon, as will his biography, *The Snow King*. So if you hear a distant yodel in the mountains out west, it just might be Bill Briggs making fresh tracks where none have skied before.

Tom Corcoran '54 — Champion Entrepreneur
By Bill Cantlin '70 and Jan Stearns

Tom Corcoran was one of Dartmouth's most successful ski racers while at the college as well as during a subsequent international ski racing career that spanned six years and included participation in two winter Olympics and a world championship. His passion for skiing, whetted initially by racing, grew to become a career that involved almost every aspect of skiing:

- Forty-five years of mountain resort development and operations (Waterville Valley, NH);
- Significant ownership stake in a leading ski equipment company (Scott ski poles);
- Start-up of a specialty ski retail shop near Los Angeles;
- Racing editor of *Ski Magazine* for seven years with a column in every issue;
- Eighteen-year elected board member of the sport's governing body, the U.S. Ski Association;
- Twenty-year board member and 2-year chairman of the National Ski Areas Association;
- Former chairman of the American Ski Federation;
- Fully certified ski instructor.

It all began when Tom was six; his American mother remarried and they moved to Canada. Tom's stepfather was the chief engineer for a bush airline based at the Gray Rocks Inn in the Laurentian Mountains of Quebec, north of Montreal. Tom and another boy the same age, **Pete Kirby '54**, went to a small English-speaking school and every afternoon skied on the little rope tow hill behind the inn. No instruction, no coaching; just miles and miles of skiing every day, learning by instinct, imitation, and lots of trial and error. It was an idyllic life for a kid.

When the boys were twelve, their parents decided their formal education was deficient and sent them off to boarding schools, Pete to a school in Quebec and Tom to a pre-prep in NH, then to Exeter Academy. Both boys later applied to Dartmouth, were accepted, and roomed together in their freshman year. Walt Prager, then the ski coach, had recruited a number of skiers that year who had illustrious racing records, but he had never met or heard of Tom and Pete before they arrived, which was not surprising because they had done very little schoolboy ski racing. But they could ski well, and they came to Dartmouth to be with great ski racers, to get coached by a great trainer, and to realize their dream of making the Dartmouth Ski Team.

By the end of their first season, Tom, Pete and fellow freshman **Bill Tibbits '54**, from North River, NY, had developed, with Walt's coaching, into three of the best ski racers in the country. They were mainstays of the Dartmouth team for the next three years, when Dartmouth won far more winter carnival competitions than any other college or university. Pete Kirby went on to make the Canadian World Championship Ski Team in

1954, and, in a twist of fate, received an Olympic gold medal not in skiing, but as the brakeman, a key position, on the Canadian 4-man bobsled that won the event in the 1964 Olympics. In Tom's senior year he won every winter carnival slalom, the Harriman Cup at Sun Valley, and both the Canadian Championships and Quebec Kandahar at Mont Tremblant, very close to the hill where he learned to ski. The next six years for Tom were a blur:

- He was NROTC in college, graduating with a naval commission and a two-year active duty obligation, most of which was served as a line officer on a destroyer escort in the Atlantic Fleet;
- He made and participated on the 1956 & 1960 Olympic Teams and competed on the 1958 World Championship Team;
- He earned an MBA at the Harvard Business School, graduating in 1959.

During that six-year period he won many ski races, including four National Championships, the Roch Cup at Aspen twice, the Parsenn Gold Cup in Switzerland, the Kandahar of the Andes, and the Chilean & Argentine Championships. His best Olympic performance was at Squaw Valley in 1960, at the end of his active career, when he placed 4th in the Olympic Giant Slalom after starting 24th, the best finish for a North American man in that event until Bode Miller got a silver medal 42 years later.

After Squaw Valley, Tom got jobs in finance in San Francisco and Los Angeles until it dawned on him that he wasn't a city guy. He got a job as Assistant to the President of the Aspen Skiing Corporation. A superb ski area operator, Darcy Brown was Tom's boss and mentor and gave him four principal responsibilities: do acquisition feasibility studies on the nearby Buttermilk Mountain Ski Area and run it if acquired; conduct skiing feasibility studies of the potential Snowmass Ski Area; plan and implement the first comprehensive marketing program for Aspen; and reorganize the ski school and make it a major profit center.

Three years later, in 1965, Tom decided to return east and search for a suitable mountain on available real estate to build a medium-sized, high quality mountain resort community with year-round facilities that would appeal to upscale families. **Sel Hannah, '35**, head of Sno-Engineering, Inc. and an old friend, told Tom that 425 acres of private land in Waterville Valley, NH, were up for sale, including Mt. Tecumseh, in the adjacent White Mountain National Forest, an area eminently suitable for skiing development.

Corcoran '54 winning his 2nd straight National Slalom Championship in 1957, and the first of 2 Roch Cups.

Tom flew over the site, recognized its potential, met the owner, negotiated a purchase option, and formed the Waterville Company, Inc., a small private concern with mostly family members. He then hired Sno-Engineering to help design the skiing, did the feasibility studies, got the ski area permits from the U.S. Forest Service, arranged the financing, and built the ski area on Mt. Tecumseh, opening in time for Christmas 1966 with four chairlifts and a J-bar, serving 18 runs and over 2,000 vertical feet. It was an instant success.

During the next 28 years the company served as master developer of the award-winning resort community which is self-contained and complete, having all facilities within walking distance or just a short shuttle bus ride away. At present there are over 6500 beds in the community in a mix of inns, lodges, resort condominiums and single-family homes. There is a specialty shopping center next to a six-acre pond, with shops, restaurants, services and offices. Mt. Tecumseh now has 12 lifts, including two high-speed quads, and 53 runs with 100% snowmaking cover. The resort has hosted ten Alpine World

Cup ski races, including two World Cup Finals. Other facilities include a cross-country skiing center with 105 km of trails; an indoor hockey-sized ice arena with refrigeration; a tennis center with 18 outdoor clay courts and two indoor courts, just part of a complete indoor athletic complex; a 9-hole golf course; and many miles of hiking trails to the summits of the surrounding 4,000-foot peaks. In addition, the Waterville Valley

Black and Blue Trail Smashers Ski Club is the largest ski & snowboard competition club in the country, annually providing new talent to the US Ski & Snowboard Teams.

In 1994 the company divested most of its operating assets, including the ski facilities, but retained the remaining developable land, the golf course, and its real estate sales company, Waterville Valley Realty. The company continues to serve as the master developer of the resort community.

Tom retired in 1999 and recruited **Bill Cantlin '70**, formerly a Dartmouth ski jumper, to be his successor as President and CEO. Tom and Bill had worked together for many years back when Tom had brought Bill into the company to start Waterville Valley Realty, and later to build condos and a lodge in the valley. Tom remained involved with Waterville Valley as the largest shareholder of the Waterville Company Inc. and served as the Board Chairman. He and a partner also owned the cable TV system serving the community.

In 1978 Tom was inducted into the U.S. National Ski Hall of Fame as both a skiing athlete and ski sport builder. In 1991 he received the Blegen Award, the highest award of the U.S. Ski Association. And in 2006 he was selected to be the first recipient of the "Spirit of Skiing" award given by the New England Ski Museum.

Tom's impact on the ski industry careers of other Dartmouth alumni was remarkable. At various times Tom had 9 Dartmouth grads working for him: **Sel Hannah '35**, founded Sno-Engineering, Inc., preeminent ski area consulting firm, oversaw ski area design & skiing feasibility studies for Waterville Company, Inc.; **Joe Cushing '52**, worked for Sno-Engineering and designed ski trails at Waterville Valley; **Roger Brown '57**, made early promotional films about Waterville Valley; **Fred Jones '63, Tu '64**, served as V.P. & G.M. for Waterville Company, Inc.; **Pete Aydellot, Tu '64**, served as V.P. & Dir. of Mktg. for Waterville Company, Inc; **Sel L. Hannah '65, Th '66**, a son of the elder Sel Hannah (not a jr.), worked as a lift designer for the engineer who drew up the specs for WV's first lifts, and later became an insurance inspector for WV lifts; **Bill Cantlin '70**, brought in to start up Waterville Valley Realty, became an independent developer in WV, brought back by Tom in 1999 to be his successor as Pres.& CEO of the Waterville Company, Inc. (WCI) when Tom retired; **Bob Ashton '73, Tu '76**, started at WCI as V.P. & Treasurer, then became V.P. & G.M.; and **Kathleen Corcoran '87**, one of Tom's daughters, worked in the Marketing Dept. for WCI.

Chiharu ("Chick") Igaya '57 — The Eternal Olympian
By Joe Stevenson '57

Dartmouth skiing great **Tom Corcoran '54** called Chick Igaya "the most successful male alpine ski racer ever to ski for Dartmouth." But whether or not Chick was "the most successful," without a doubt he is among a handful of the very best Dartmouth skiers of all time.

The Igaya Ski Legend. Chick dominated American skiing in the late 1950s, winning just about every existing intercollegiate skiing title. He was a five-time US alpine champion. In 1955, he led Dartmouth to victory in its own Winter Carnival and to a first-place finish in the 1957 Eastern Intercollegiate Ski Championships. In international competition, he won the Silver Medal in the slalom at the 1956 Winter Olympics in Cortina d'Ampezzo, Italy, Japan's first-ever Winter Olympics medal. And at the 1958 World Championship, he won the Bronze in the slalom, finished 6th in the giant slalom and 4th overall. In 1972, Chick was inducted into the US Ski Hall of Fame, and in 1988, he received the Imperial Purple Ribbon Medal in Japan, and in 2002 the National Order of the "Star of Romania."

If you ever saw Chick plunging down a slalom course, you will never forget his unique, fluid, aggressive style. A spectacle of athletic beauty and skill!

Development of a Champion. The story began in Hokkaido, Japan's northern island, where his father, Kunio Igaya, began teaching Chick how to ski. Igaya senior was Japan's most famous ski instructor and Chick was just three years old. The lessons took hold and young Igaya became Japan's Alpine-events

Chick Igaya '57 was awarded an Honorary degree (Doctor of Humane Letters) by Dartmouth College in 2006.

champion. Then, by sheer chance, he met C.V. Starr at a sporting goods store in Tokyo. Starr was a wealthy insurance executive, founder of American International Underwriters (AIU) in 1910, a ski enthusiast, a Japanophile, and the developer of the Stowe, Vermont, ski area. It all fit beautifully and it led to a whole new life for Chick. Mr. Starr arranged for him to go to the Winter Olympics in Oslo, Norway, in 1952 and, a year later, sponsored his enrollment at Dartmouth College.

The Dartmouth Years. Besides his athletic prowess, Chick was an excellent student and well liked by his classmates in the Class of 1957. He became a member of Theta Delta Chi Fraternity and Casque & Gauntlet Senior Society. The Dartmouth experience began on a humorous note at his matriculation in the fall of 1953. The then President **John Sloan Dickey**, a towering, revered figure in College history, signed each new freshman's matriculation document and chatted with him informally. Mr. Dickey misunderstood Chick's connection with skiing and underestimated Chick's command of English, asking him if he knew about the sport of skiing, describing it in the simplest language and using his hands to demonstrate the sweeping decent on a ski slope. Once beyond this bit of embarrassment, Dickey and Chick ultimately became great friends. Chick's undergraduate years concluded in triumph as he won the Dartmouth Cup, given to the "senior athlete who on and off the field reflects the greatest credit to the College."

Return to Japan and AIU. Life after Dartmouth for Chick Igaya was focused primarily on a career at AIU. C.V. Starr provided the important link with AIU and later with its parent company, AIG. Chick worked in New York for a few years before returning to Tokyo for a long progression of managerial jobs for AIU and AIG. He was made a Managing Director of AIU's Japanese insurance operations, holding that position for years. From 1994 to 2002, Chick was Chairman of AIG K.K and until recently served as Honorary Chairman of the Board of AIU Insurance Company, Japan.

During his early years in Japan, Chick served as private ski instructor for Crown Prince Akahito and his famous commoner bride, Michiko Shoda. The future Emperor and Empress and Chick were often seen together on the courts of Tokyo's Lawn Tennis Club.

Japanese and International Athletics. Besides skiing and his insurance profession, Chick's major interest has been the promotion of Japanese and international athletic competition. He has been a member of the FIS Alpine Committee and the FIS World Cup Committee, Chairman of the Japan Olympic Academy and President of the Japan Triathlon Union. He has been advisor to the Japan Amateur Sports Association, the Japanese Ministry of Education and the Japan Ministry of Foreign Affairs for Sports Issues. A member of the Ethics and Education Committee of the World Anti-Doping Agency, Chick was also the Vice President of the Asia Triathlon Confederation.

Chick has been connected to the International Olympic Committee (IOC) for five decades. In 1988, he served as Chairman of the Study and Evaluation Commission for the Preparation of the 1994 and 2006 Olympic Winter Games. The IOC has consumed much time and attention for Chick: he has served on various commissions and preparatory committees for Albertville in 1992, Lillehammer in 1994 and Salt Lake in 2002, and has held the important position of Vice President of the IOC since 2005. He was seen by millions of television viewers around the world in the grand opening parade at the outset of the Winter Games of 2002 in Salt Lake City.

Dartmouth Honors Chick Again. Dartmouth's love affair with their famous Japanese son has continued for more than five decades. Chick was given the Asakawa Award by the Dartmouth Club of Japan in 1998. This award, named for the first Japanese graduate of Dartmouth, Kan'Ichi Asakawa, Class of 1899, recognizes "those who have contributed to the betterment of US/Japan relations." In addition, he was awarded an honorary degree at the Dartmouth's 2006 Commencement ceremonies. President **James Wright** addressed the citation to Chick which concluded, "...you have always reflected 'the greatest credit to the College.' And you have, through the competitive bonding of sports at the highest level, followed Mr. Dickey's charge to make the world the better. We now salute you with the degree of Doctor of Humane Letters."

Barry Corbet '58 — A Higher Vision
By Roger Brown '57

Like most of us, Barry Corbet was exposed to a much larger world at Dartmouth than he ever experienced in his pre-college years. His gifts for writing and editing were honed there and he formed many lifelong friendships. But he could not resist the pull of the Grand Tetons, and so left Dartmouth early, perhaps because he recognized that rock, ice, and snow in all of their manifestations were his true mentors.

Writing about Barry Corbet is not a simple matter unless I just say the obvious. He was a superb climber, excellent skier, brilliant cinematographer, editor, and writer. But this says little about his incredible charm and grace, his poetic soul, his iconoclasm, and his uncompromising principles. He was a prince among his peers, respected and loved by all who knew him.

Skiing for Barry was both a means to an end—i.e., mountaineering—and a joy unto itself. Although not a serious racer, his study and mastery of skiing technique greatly expanded his ability to venture onto unskied terrain and return without injury. The skills of balance and recovery, reading snow conditions, and picking the proper lines of descent that he developed through skiing contributed to his mountain exploits as well.

And what exploits they were! In 1959, Barry went to Alaska with **Jake Breitenbach '57**, classmate **Pete Sinclair '58,** and Bill Buckingham, to make the first ascent of Mt. McKinley (20,320 feet) via its hitherto unscaled South Face. Widely recognized as the premier mountaineering accomplishment of the year in North America, *Time* magazine carried an article on the achievement. But how do you top being first to climb North America's highest peak by a new route? Corbet's answer: be the first US citizen to climb the highest mountain in the world. So in 1963 he joined what would be the first American expedition to conquer Mount Everest (29,035 feet); on that team were Mt. McKinley co-climber Breitenbach and **Dr. David Dingman '58**.

As the expedition unfolded, its members divided into two camps: one group focused on reaching the summit by the previously ascended South Col route; the second, led by Willi Unsoeld and Tom Hornbein, opted for the unclimbed West Ridge. Never one to seek the known when the unknown beckoned, Barry joined the West Ridgers. On the final day's push before reaching the summit, already at 26,250 feet, he hacked out over 300 vertical meters of steps up what has become known as Hornbein's Couloir, making it possible for the West Ridge team to camp at 27,200 feet and summit the following day.

Barry could have been a member of the final summit team. He was as capable as Hornbein and Unsoeld, but demurred when offered this opportunity. "You two have been climbing together, you know each other, you'll make the strongest team," he said. "What's more," he added, lightening the momentousness of his decision, "you're both just about over the hump. This is my first expedition. I'll be coming back someday."[65] Hornbein and Unsoeld's ascent of Everest's West Ridge was the finest mountaineering accomplishment of 1963. In retrospect, it is evident that Barry's skill, strength, and generosity were critical to their success.

The 1963 American Mount Everest Expedition was widely heralded. Four members had summited via the South Col route while Hornbein and Unsoeld had pioneered the more challenging West Ridge route and traversed the summit of Everest from west to east in doing so. For these accomplishments the expedition's members were honored by then President John F. Kennedy and presented with the National Geographic Society's prestigious Hubbard Medal. For Barry Corbet, the ceremony must have been a bittersweet occasion; his close friend and Teton climbing companion, Jake Breitenbach, was missing, having been killed by collapsing seracs in Everest's Khumbu icefall. A full account of the adventure is chronicled in the book *Americans on Everest: The Official Account of the Ascent*, written in 1964 by noted mountaineering author James Ramsey Ullman, who was engaged as the expedition's historian.

Having climbed in "the roof of the world," Barry headed toward its basement, so to speak. In 1966, he joined a ten-man expedition to Antarctica that included former DOC officer, ski patroller, and mountaineer **Dr. Sam Silverstein '58** who, in 1962 with **Chris Wren '57** and a few others, had blazed a first ascent of his own up Mt. McKinley's previously untracked Southeast Spur. The two-month expedition to the edge of the Antarctic Circle succeeded in conquering four of the continent's highest mountains, all never before climbed, including the two highest: snow-clad Mt. Vinson (16,067 feet) and the only slightly less towering—but technically more difficult—Mt. Tyree (15,896 feet). In 2006, the US Geological Survey named eight of Mt. Vinson's subsidiary summits in honor of members of this expedition, including Mt. Corbet and Mt. Silverstein (both about 15,700 feet). The June 1967 National Geographic reported the expedition's story in full and illustrated it with many of Sam's professional-grade still shots. Barry was the expedition's cinematographer, a task to which he brought his characteristic passion, precision, and proficiency.

Back in Colorado in the winter of 1968, Barry and I worked on several different film projects. But on a fateful day in May, while shooting skiers high in the mountains behind Aspen, the helicopter from which he was filming crashed. Within five short months of his near-death condition, he learned to cope with paralysis, edited and wrote our most recognized film, *Ski the Outer Limits*, and started a new independent life in a wheelchair. The Craig Rehabilitation Center doctors who worked with him had never seen anyone so seriously injured return to full activity in so short a time.

Barry then took up white-water kayaking and soon learned to run the larger rapids with some of the most talented river rats in the West. Unfortunately, he found that even he could not compensate for paralyzed lower limbs with sheer upper body strength. His determination and guts failed to stop his shoulder joints from wearing out. Barry's passion for the outdoor life, for climbing, skiing, and kayaking, made being a paraplegic very difficult, but he contained any open remorse about his misfortune, giving himself over to helping others by teaching them to learn to cope with their disabilities. Eventually Barry stopped talking about climbing and gave up writing and editing adventure films because the sports action sequences reminded him too painfully of what he was missing. Nonetheless, it is telling that he never gave up his founding membership in the American Mountain Guides Association. Corbet's greatest gift to society came after the accident, when he made films and wrote articles about and for people with disabilities. He asked for engagement, not isolation, for challenges, not sympathy, and for the elimination of physical barriers, not handouts. "Can you believe this? They still haven't made Timberline Lodge wheelchair-accessible!" he said, after attending his son Mike's wedding there in 2001. Mike tells me that omission has been corrected now.

His books, *Options: Spinal Cord Injury and the Future and Spinal Network: The Total Wheelchair Resource Book*, set a new tone and a positive, forward-looking, up-beat agenda for coping with spinal cord injuries. "We are humans too, and please respect that fact; and if you can't, get out of our way because we will not be suppressed." In this sphere as in every other, Barry was a larger than life presence. Throughout his difficult but productive years as a paraplegic, his children—Jonathan, Mike, and Jennifer—comforted him, as did his four attentive grandchildren. To many, Barry was a hero. On a mountain or in a wheel chair, it didn't matter: he had his own perfect vision about what was important and significant in life. As his friend and climbing partner Sam Silverstein says, "When you were with Barry it was never about Barry. It was always about you." He shines brightly in my memory. It was a wonderful privilege to know him.

Gerry Huttrer '60 — A Family With a Skiing Way of Life
By Gerry Huttrer '60

My parents, Fred and Elizabeth "Lilly" Huttrer, were brought up and lived in Vienna, Austria, from 1910 to 1939. They dated and "played" in the mountains of Austria, Switzerland, and Italy all year round, so they were very familiar with all the best climbs and downhill runs. Typically, they would take a train out of Vienna to some beautiful location, climb on skins to a hut (or "Hutte"), spend the evening eating, drinking, and horsing around, ski down the next day, and take a train back home, often in "high" spirits (with my uncle Willy safely tucked into the overhead luggage rack so that he could sleep off the tougher effects of the trip). To my knowledge, none of my grandparents skied, so my parents were "mavericks" and I just inherited their love for the sport.

Before WW II, my folks left Austria in much the same manner as depicted in "The Sound of Music," escaping across the Alps to France and thence to New York by boat. I arrived about two weeks later, being born in a New York City hospital.

I began skiing on bright red, paint-losing skis when I was about 4-5 years old. The "mountain" was my front yard in New Rochelle, NY. Soon the family graduated to the local golf course (vertical drop about 100 feet) and then we began skiing about every other weekend at Bromley Mountain in Manchester, Vermont, as well as in Stowe. I could ski about everything, but I do remember running my skis under a root, being stopped cold, and flying out of my leather boots to land head first

Gerry Huttrer '60 (left), Vail D Club Secretary-Treasurer, being recognized at CarniVAIL-2009 by Club President Waterhouse. (Holmes, 2009)

in a deep snow bank. I could not get out and had to be rescued by some kind passer by, as my parents were far ahead, completely unaware of my predicament.

When I went to Dartmouth in 1956, I soon hooked up with **Jay Emery '60** (deceased) and we skied constantly. The Skiway had just opened and we were on the first ski patrol together. When I learned that a small resort called "The Keenes" was looking for a ski instructor, I applied and was accepted. I was allowed to charge $10/person/hour and I could teach up to ten persons in a 2-hour class. The $200 I earned was unbelievable for those days and helped me pay my $2,000/year tuition.

While at in college, I joined the Dartmouth Outing Club and rose through the ranks to become first, the Director of Competitions, and then President. In these roles I rubbed shoulders with many of the Dartmouth skiing legends of yore since I regularly called on them to act as course setters and/or judges during Carnival and other competitions. It should be noted that Dartmouth was not co-ed when I attended, and there was no women's racing or any serious discussion thereof.

The top racers during my time at Dartmouth were **Chick Igaya '57, Ralph Miller '55**, and **Dick Taylor '59**. The coaches were **Walter Prager** and **Al Merrill**, with both of whom I had the pleasure of working closely. I knew Chick and Ralph and Dick casually, as they were several years ahead of me, but I remember all of them as being friendly, hard working, dedicated skiers and Dartmouth supporters. When Ralph's father crashed his plane in the Pemigawasset Wilderness, I helped organize and participated in the searches that went on for weeks until the wreckage was found.

By 1958, I had been certified in the USEASA so when I went to grad school in Oregon, I began teaching on Mt. Hood. I then met my wife-to-be (a Minnesota-born ski instructor) and the two of us left school and went to Sun Valley where I patrolled, taught, and played "Broom-Ball on ice skates (with Pepi Gramshammer, Conrad Staudinger, Jonny Iceland, *et al.*) I did not know about the Dartmouth-Sun Valley connections at the time.

I then returned to grad school at the University of Washington where one of the conditions of my acceptance was that I had to teach the children of my Geology Professor (Peter Misch of Himalayan climbing fame) how to ski. I also taught at Snoqualmie, Hyak, Stevens Pass, and Crystal Mt. At the latter venue, I was in the first ski school assembled by Jack Nagle, father of Olympians Cathy and Judy Nagle.

After graduate school, I began my career as a geologist. I started as an engineering geologist, first specializing in soils and foundations, then took on several jobs in the U.S. and in New Zealand related to dam construction, and later moved to Colorado where I worked as a mineral exploration geologist with assignments in Guatemala, Jamaica, Canada, and Spain.

Next, I became a geothermal geologist, first working for small and medium sized private firms, and then starting my own consultancy in 1985. In the past 38 years of geothermal work, I have operated in 42 nations, primarily exploring volcanic areas in third world countries for sites suitable for development of electric power generation projects. Of skiing-related interest may be the fact that I managed to wangle helicopter rides to peaks in Papua New Guinea, Alaska, and Chile so as to ski back down on previously unskied, unmapped snowfields. Recently, I sought geothermal resources for use in heating the Steamboat Springs Ski Resort base area. Unfortunately, no adequate resource was found near the end-use site and the project was discontinued.

I then moved to northeastern Washington and started a tiny ski area in Ione (population ~200). I got re-certified at Mt. Spokane (Level II) and continued teaching. We moved to Colorado in 1965 and there I signed on with the Loveland Ski School, staying 15 years until 1980. During those years, I had several occasions to be in Europe (for geologic reasons) and took the time to ski again in Spain, France, and Austria with Jay Emery who was stationed in several European Air Force bases.

We moved to California and remained there until 1984, so for four years my skiing was limited to a few weeks at Christmas when we returned to Colorado and I resumed teaching at Loveland. Finally, in 1988, I joined the Vail Village Ski School where I am still actively teaching together with my second wife Cat (my first wife died in 1988 after a 10-year battle with cancer). As chance would have it Cat was my student at Loveland in 1978, but since then she has become a better technical skier and instructor than I.

Some of my greatest pleasure comes from being able to slide around today with **Joe McHugh '60**, my Dartmouth roommate, **Mike Wood '60**, my geology classmate, **Art Kelton '61**, my Dartmouth Ski Patrol buddy, **Alan Danson '60**, my fellow Stowe Ski Patrol member, as well as a few more Dartmouth friends that regularly come out to Vail. In the summers, we ride road and mountain bikes and hike up all sorts of mountains in Colorado and Utah with Big D's Mike and Blair Wood, and Alan Danson.

When my mother died in 1996, my daughter Anne (now living in Vail), obtained a 300-picture collection of photographs that my father took while he and my mother were courting in the Alps. Anne had these photos transferred to dishware that is now being sold all over the western U.S. and in some European countries.

In my 64 years of skiing and 51 years of teaching I have been exposed to many "legends" of the sport. Some were Dartmouth alumni or staff like **Dick Durrance '39, Tom Corcoran '56**, and Walter Prager; others were just celebrities (US Presidents and Veeps Ford and Quayle come to mind), Princess Diana, with whom I skied and rode the lift while her Instructor Pentti Tofferi escorted others in her entourage, Saudi Sheiks (no names remembered), etc. It's been a great ride so far and I'm looking forward to continuing for at least 30 more years.

Edward F. "Ned" Gillette '67 — The Great Adventurer
By Stephen L. Waterhouse

Throughout this book, the reader will find references to Ned Gillette. He was a skier and a ski industry contributor with many dimensions to his efforts, and no short comment like this will truly do him justice. At Dartmouth, he was a success as a cross-country racer of considerable achievement. He was the NCAA Champion in cross-country skiing in 1967 and also the Captain of the Dartmouth ski team in that year which finished a close runner-up in the NCAA championships. He continued his racing after college and was selected as a

Ned Gillette '67 in his student days.

member of the 1968 Olympic team (Grenoble, France) competing in his Nordic specialty. But it is perhaps after his Dartmouth and racing years that his legend grew to unusual proportions. He created an interesting life based on his own philosophy of venturing out to ski and climb in unusual environments around the world. He is reputed to have said many times that he was a professional adventurer, and his post-Dartmouth years included a series of novel achievements.

Not far from Dartmouth's location, Ned played an important role in laying out the original cross-country course at the Trapp Family Lodge in Stowe, Vermont, the first privately-owned public course of its kind in the U.S.. He helped **Johannes von Trapp '63** promote cross-country as a resort sport just like all the downhill resort mountains did for alpine skiing. He created an initial 15-kilometer course by making use of summer hiking trails, existing logging roads, and open fields. This unique venture has grown into 65 kilometers of trails to become the leading such facility for both cross-country recreation and racing purposes. The Dartmouth cross-country team uses it as their back-up course, and Winter Carnival races are run there when snow conditions are poor in Hanover. In 1976, the Dartmouth men won the NCAA championship on this course, and in 1977 the Dartmouth ladies won the AIAW Ski Championship here. This facility is being further developed at the Trapp Family Lodge today under the leadership of a new generation led by **Sam von Trapp '94** who is expanding the snowmaking capability along the trails to extend their seasonal use.

In another ski business situation, Ned was hired by **Chuck Lewis '58** to help develop the Copper Mountain ski resort in Colorado. The mountain, initially known as Wheeler Junction, was once considered a site for the 1976 Olympics, but when that did not work out, Lewis took the opportunity to initiate the building of a substantial new ski resort out of an abandoned copper mining camp and the surrounding land near Frisco, Colorado. One of his first employees was Ned Gillette, and Ned spent time living in a trailer at Wheeler Junction to explore the mountain and lay out trails for the new ski area. Chuck later hired **Fred Jones '63** as the Vice President of Operations. Fred was another Dartmouth skier from the early 1960s, a participant in the

Dartmouth ROTC program under Sergeant Bill Brown (a major contributor to Vail's development), and an early general manager of the Waterville Valley Resort founded by **Tom Corcoran '54**.[66] *Time Magazine* suggested in an article on Chuck Lewis that he represented a new breed of manager who hired a range of business, engineering, construction, and recreation specialists like Ned and Fred to execute his plans.[67] Today, Copper Mountain is one of the major ski areas in the Rockies.

The most important stage of Ned's life involved his skills in developing unusual ski and climbing treks to exotic locations around the world. He was a highly regarded mountain climber as well as an extraordinary skier. For the last 25 years of his life, he spent his time climbing mountains like Mt. McKinley (over 20,000 ft), and skiing down or around their base. He made it around McKinley and Everest twice. He made the first snowboard descent of Mt. Aconcagua (almost 23,000 ft.) in Argentina, skied down the wonderfully named Mountains of the Moon on the border of Uganda, traversed the Karakoram Range in Russia, skied down China's Mt. Muztagata (nearly 25,000 ft high), made many treks across Alaska and much more. There has probably never been another person who has undertaken this mix of challenging activities in distant, typically hard to reach locales quite like Ned Gillette did.

In all his travels and experiences, Ned promoted skiing through his writings. He wrote instructional books on skiing, became a world class photographer and respected journalist, authored stories on his many adventurous escapades, and found as many ways as he could to highlight the more amazing aspects of this sport. And he was constantly on the move with some very widely traveled skis! Tragically, in mid-1996, he was killed by robbers while traveling in Northern Kashmir. It would be rare to encounter another Ned Gillette in one lifetime.

Dartmouth Coach Al Merrill – Cultivating Potential, Honing Excellence
By Edward "Gus" Williams '64

I was dejected and in despair after a terrible performance in the first Alpine time trials in my freshman year. What was I going to do? This was a different league; and I had no hope to be on the Dartmouth Ski Team. But then came this pivotal moment which would dramatically change my life for the next four years, and even in many ways, my life. Al Merrill came up to me on the way back from the Skiway, and said these words that I remember to this day: "Did you ever think of doing cross-country? We are short a runner for the freshman team; and I can teach you to ski cross-country…." I jumped at the opportunity. Al Merrill did in fact teach me to ski cross-country; and, under his tutelage, got quite good at it. By sophomore year, I was skiing on the varsity team.

Coach Al Merrill, or as he was known "The Silver Fox".

Just who was this upbeat, immediately likable and confidence-inspiring person? Who was this surrogate parent figure with whom I would have more contact than any other adult at Dartmouth, and who would have such a strong influence on my life? We knew, of course, that Coach Merrill was technically proficient, particularly in the Nordic events of cross-country and jumping. His ability to craft an effective training program was self-evident: those who followed his training regimen saw immediate improvement in their fitness and endurance. We also heard about, and later experienced, his unequaled abilities in waxing cross-country skies. The depth of his knowledge of all aspects of cross-country is evidenced by the fact that he was the Chief of Course for the cross-country events at the 1960 Olympics in Squaw Valley, California. But what else was on his "resume"?

Much of the following I learned about Al Merrill only much later. Al was born in Andover, Maine in 1921 (which meant that he was 39 years old when we first met him in Robinson Hall our freshman year). He graduated from Hebron Academy in Hebron, Maine and enrolled in the University of New Hampshire where the ski team he captained for three years won three successive Dartmouth Winter Carnival titles (1941-1943).

Al's college career was interrupted by WWII, where he served with the 83rd Infantry Division in Europe and was awarded the Purple Heart, Distinguished Service Medal and Bronze Star. After returning to UNH and graduating in 1947, Al taught physics and chemistry at Lebanon High School, where he also coached skiing. He took time off to also coach the US Nordic Team at the 1954 World Ski Championships and the 1956 Winter Olympics.

Al came to Dartmouth as assistant coach under **Walter Prager** and, when Prager retired in 1957, Coach Merrill became the first American-born coach of the Dartmouth Ski Team. The Team, under Al's coaching, won the NCAA Ski Championships in 1958 and in the twelve years that followed, his teams won seven Dartmouth Winter Carnival titles and never placed lower than fourth in the NCAAs. During his tenure as Dartmouth Ski Coach, Al was also head Nordic coach for the US Teams at the 1964 and 1968 Winter Olympics, served as the US Ski Association's Nordic program director from 1968-70, and was co-chief of the Nordic courses for the 1980 Winter Olympics in Lake Placid, NY. He also served for many years in various capacities with the US Eastern Amateur Ski Association (President in 1964); the National Ski Association; the US Olympic Ski Games Committee; and as a member of the International Cross Country Ski Committee of the FIS, the world governing body for skiing.

In 1970, Dartmouth created the Office of Outdoor Affairs and Al was appointed its first director. In 1972, Al retired as coach of the ski team, succeeded by **Jim Page '63**. Al continued working full-time for the College as Director of Outdoor Affairs and, in that capacity, oversaw the operations of the Dartmouth Outing Club, the recreational ski programs at the Skiway and Oak Hill, the operations at the College Grant, and perhaps most significantly, he initiated and saw to completion (in 1976) the rehabilitation of the Moosilauke Ravine Lodge.

Al Merrill retired from Dartmouth College in 1983, but continued his ski activities as a member of the FIS Cross-Country Committee and as a trustee of the US Ski Educational Foundation. His many contributions to skiing were recognized by the numerous awards he received: the Julius P. Blegen award for outstanding contributions to US Skiing in 1972; the Paul Bacon Award for his work in Nordic Skiing in 1989; and his election to the US Ski Hall of Fame in 1974.

These honors, while interesting and impressive, do not explain what Al, the person, was all about or how he influenced me and many of my Dartmouth teammates. Al Merrill was the person willing to spend untold hours teaching "a nobody" freshman from Rosendale, NY how to ski cross-country simply because the kid was determined and willing. He was a man who never mentioned his many accomplishments or the honors he had received. He saw no need to do that. His world was here and now. He had a quick and hearty laugh, and demanded much – but never more than it was possible to give; a man keenly interested in the personal welfare and development of "his boys." He was a coach who respected the fact that athletics, while important, were subsidiary to the demanding academic environment at Dartmouth. Kind, considerate, modest, and utterly self-effacing, Al was a role model for us, a true teacher, and a gentleman; someone for us to strive to emulate.

C. Allison Merrill, the "Silver Fox," died in July 1990 at the age of 69, two years after suffering a stroke while hiking near his home in Etna, New Hampshire. A cross-country race is held each year in his honor and memory called the "Silver Fox Trot" on a trail named after him on Oak Hill.

Tim Caldwell '76 — Four-Time Olympian
By Jim Page '63

Tim Caldwell is a fearsome trainer. His feats are legendary around his home in Putney, VT, among his Dartmouth and National Cross-Country Ski Team mates. and even today around Lyme, NH where some refer to him as the "iron lung."

His dad, **John Caldwell '50**, says Tim ("TC") started exercising early (note he didn't say "training") before he was in the 6th grade. He bought a bike and an odometer, and when asked by his dad how far he went, it was usually 35 or 40 miles. At one point, in high school, he and a training buddy rode the entire length of Vermont – 220 miles – in one day. In Hanover, in the spring or summer, when most collegiate athletes are training lightly, TC would grab a group of team skiers and ride 200 miles from the Canadian to Massachusetts border, or run from Woodstock to Hanover on the Appalachian Trail. Even today, at the end of the winter, he and friends will do a "fun" 55-km ski around Smarts Mountain north of Hanover. He enjoys training so much that he once told a TV interviewer that he raced so he could train.

Tim believes that Dartmouth played a big role in his ski career and in his life. "Coming back to Dartmouth after each season was great. It was a wonderful way to transition from the racing circuit to something different, engaging and constructive. Being able to combine a top-notch education with World Cup, World Championships and Olympic competition was perfect for me. I do not think I would have enjoyed my ski career as much as I did, nor would it have lasted as long, without the experience and education that Dartmouth provided me." He claims that "the ability to train with classmates during the off season was invaluable. I always felt welcome by the team and coaches. Although it [cross-country skiing] is an individual sport, the camaraderie of training and racing with friends and competitors is something I will always value."

It was great for Dartmouth Skiing as well. **Phil Peck '77**, a top racer at that time says, "Tim provided a model of training that was a joy, never a chore. For all of us on the Dartmouth team, he was the unelected captain during the off-season. He was the instigator behind training. The joy that Tim had was contagious. He had a great intuition about training properly. He didn't go out and 'hammer' every time. He was incredibly balanced. He cross-trained before people knew what that was. Imagine what it was like for the skiers after a long winter of racing and training to have Tim show up and want to do a weight workouts, or bike 200 miles, or run from Woodstock to Hanover. There was no off-season and no downtime. In Tim's world view skiing wasn't something you would take a break from: it was a way of life and living: every term, year around, every year!"

He skied in ten events in four Olympics from 1972-1984, the first, in 1972, as a senior in high school. During that same period, he skied in 30 World Cup events a year and in four World Ski Championships. His best individual result was a second place in the final World Cup of the winter in 1983 in Anchorage, Alaska. In 1982 the men's cross-country team, with Tim as its recognized spirit and leader, finished fourth overall on the season-long World Cup circuit, still the highest finish ever for any group of US skiers.

Tim never skied for a Dartmouth team and didn't win a varsity letter, but he made the team better and was at least in part responsible for the strong performance of the 1976 Dartmouth cross-country skiers that helped bring the NCAA Men's Championship to Dartmouth for, at that point, only the second time in its history. Every member of that team and others who traversed vast areas of Vermont and New Hampshire with him would want to award him an honorary "D."

Diane Boyer '78 — A Free-Styler in Every Way!
By Stu Keiler '65, Tu '66

Diane Boyer grew up in a skiing oriented family. By the time she was a sophomore at Miss Porter's School in Farmington, Connecticut, her dad had given up his career in the oil business to pursue his passion for skiing and the ski business. Diane's family was an original investor in the Stratton Mountain development and would make the trek to Vermont every winter weekend. Not content to ski the groomed trails, Diane "wanted to ski all over the mountain."[68] Moreover, she skied with the boys, including Wayne Wong and other young skiers who were inventing a whole new discipline of skiing first called "hot-dogging" and subsequently termed "freestyle".

Creativity, risk taking, and boldness were the prerequisites for anyone wanting to slam down a mogul field at breakneck speed, go airborne in gravity-defying aerials, and glide down the hill performing a ballet on skies. As a teenager, Diane had all of that plus an incredible athleticism and fearlessness that had her winning championships as a high school teenager. She competed in all three disciplines, was Junior National Freestyle Mogul Champion in 1973 as a junior in high school, and 1974 captured the Eastern Freestyle Championship.

Summers were spent training in Kaprun, Austria with her coach from Stratton Mountain and included travel to skiing Mecca's like Val D'Isere, Les Trois Vallees, Verbier, Lech, St. Christophe, and St. Moritz. "Free spirits" best describes the freestyle cadre as they created a whole new sport in front of enthusiastic galleries that idealized these young rebels who defied a century of ski traditions to do their own thing.

Diane wanted to continue the lifestyle that is every teenager's dream, and college was the last thing on her mind—until her father drove her over from Stratton to see Dartmouth. She "fell in love with Dartmouth,"[69] applied for early decision, was admitted and stormed the Hanover Plain in the fall of 1974. Already a "pro" on the freestyle circuit earning prize money, and with the NCAA still bound by the traditional ski disciplines, Diane could not compete with the Dartmouth Ski Team. The world-class skier played varsity lacrosse and field hockey for Dartmouth while continuing to compete in freestyle.

In 1972 Diane's dad and mom started a ski apparel company importing French fashion skiwear and selling to ski specialty shops across the country. Diane added New England Sales Representative to her plate and, as a 19-year-old Dartmouth freshman, she traveled the territory attending regional and national trade shows, including SnowSports Industries America (SIA) in Las Vegas.

Her family and its business moved to Vail, Colorado in 1978. After graduation, Diane joined Skea full time. The company started manufacturing the French skiwear collection under license in Denver and by 1980 had transitioned fully to their own brand. Diane's mother, Jocelyn, became Skea's chief designer and the entire family worked in all phases of the business. Diane moved up to Sales Manager, then President in 1991, and CEO in 1995. Under Diane's leadership the company grew and firmly established Skea as "a luxury brand that actually works."[70] In 2005 Diane became the first woman to be elected Chairman of SIA. Diane says, "I made the fifty-year old 'boy's club' co-ed."[71] She remains a member of the SIA Board of Directors and also serves on the Board of the Colorado Ski Museum. The mother of two teenage alpine ski racers, Diane's passion for skiing and the skiing life-style has been uncompromisingly passed to the next generation.

Tim Kelley '79 – A Collector of Lofty "Firsts"
By Stephen L. Waterhouse

After Dartmouth, Tim Kelley took a "road less traveled by." He has pursued his two main interests, cross-country ski racing and Alaskan exploration. He combines these interests in a 30-year (so far) foray to explore Alaska on lightweight cross country racing skis, setting new records for adventurous skiing in the process.

Tim grew up on a dairy farm in Cornwall, Vermont. As a high school student, he experienced some light-hearted foolishness, worthy of "Animal House," that led him to attend Dartmouth. At a cross-country race event, he was an unintended observer to the Dartmouth Women's Ski Team having a post-race celebration in a recreation center pool, less clad than normally expected! A flustered manager demanded that the wild Dartmouth ladies immediately depart the premises, and harangued their coach for not keeping the girls under control. What impressionable, red-blooded young male would not recognize the omen in this experience?

Tim graduated in the Class of 1979 at Dartmouth where his roommate was the Dartmouth Ski Team Captain, **David Thomas '79**, a member of a famous Alaskan family as the son of **Lowell Thomas, Jr. '46** and grandson of Lowell Thomas, famous national radio newscaster and remembered in Dartmouth lore as the voice of the Dr. Schlitz Ski Movie. Tim's other roommate was fellow ski team member **Tim Moerlein '79**, of the pioneer cross-country ski racing Moerlein family of Anchorage, Alaska, of which the patriarch, **George Moerlein '52**, helped found the Anchorage Nordic Ski Club.

Tim Kelley '79 at the end of the Idatarod Trail.

As a star skier in only his freshman year at Dartmouth, Tim Kelley was a member of the 1976 Dartmouth Ski Team that tied for first in the NCAA's with Denver University. He was an All-American that year, and placed 3rd in the NCAA cross-country championships. For the next several years, he did not ski for Dartmouth because he was a member of the US Ski Team racing regularly in the US and in Europe. Like many Dartmouth skiers, he took full advantage of Dartmouth's very flexible, year-round academic plan.

Tim moved to Alaska after graduation and worked as a commercial fisherman. Returning to graduate school at the University of Vermont for 1982, he obtained an MS degree in computer science and began a career of computer automation consulting in the Alaskan oil industry.

In 1984, Tim climbed Mount McKinley and developed a passion for challenging the "unclimbed" peaks of Alaska. A quarter of a century later, in 2008, he was awarded the Mountaineering Club of Alaska's prestigious Vin Hoeman award for climbing and documenting the ascents of 91 previously unclimbed Alaskan peaks, the most ever "bagged" by any climber on record. News writer Mike Campbell captured the essence of Tim's passion for peak bagging in his article[i] on this event:

"Last month,[Tim] Kelley, 51, became the fourth climber to earn the Mountaineering Club of Alaska's Hoeman Award for making 91 first ascents of remote peaks in the Western Chugach, Talkeetna and Kenai mountains -- and for sharing his discoveries with others. "(That's) more than any other known person, and he continues to add more every year," said Bill Romberg, head of the club's award committee. "It's probably safe to say that no other person since Vin Hoeman has climbed and named as many peaks in Alaska. ... Hoeman, who died in an avalanche in Asia in 1966, was a renowned local climber who became the first person to reach the highest point in all 50 states ... But while his [Tim's] determination to reach summits may be high, his focus isn't particularly narrow. "I don't tie a sense of accomplishment to individual peaks," he said. "My goal is to live a long life filled with adventures of my own making. So I get a sense of accomplishment if I can look back on a year and feel that I lived it to the Alaskan max."

Not limited to just bagging peak adventures, Tim and his ski partner, Bob Baker, skied the Iditarod Trail in 1990, skiing its 1149 miles across Alaska from Anchorage to Nome in 23 days. They completed this as a race against two bikers, and won! This was the first human- powered race the full length of the Iditarod Trail and set the stage for other races that traversed all or part of the Iditarod Trail like the Iditasport and the Iditarod Invitational.

In 1993, Kelley and Baker were the first to ski the sister sled dog race trail of the Iditarod Trial–the 1000-mile Yukon Quest Trail from Whitehorse in the Yukon Territories of Canada to Fairbanks, Alaska. It took them 20 days. For both of these long treks, they used racing cross- country skis, pulled sleds, and camped out or stayed in remote cabins. As far as is known, Kelley and Baker still hold the skiing record for both of these trails and no one has repeated their trek on the Yukon Quest Trail.

Since the early 1990s, Tim has continued to pursue Alaskan expedition skiing on lightweight cross-country skiing gear. He has skied from Kaktovik on the Arctic Ocean across the Arctic National Wildlife Refuge and the Brooks Range to Arctic Village, skied across the Wrangell Mountains, skied the 440-mile Kobuk dog sled trail above the Arctic Circle to the east of Kotzebue, and skied the Kuskokwim River in western Alaska from Chuathbaluk to Bethel. He also has skied numerous ambitious shorter Alaskan trips, many of which no one else has skied. Using his computer communication skills, he shares his expertise, his passion for skiing, and his effort to promote Alaskan ski exploration via his web site: www.crust.outlookalaska.com.

John Byrne III '81 - Living the Dream
By Stephen L. Waterhouse

In an interview with KTUU-TV in Anchorage, John Byrne III stated that he is now "living the dream"[72] as he operates a very personal acquisition, the Alyeska ski resort, which is the largest ski area in Alaska. John's life has involved a series of skiing adventures. Blessed to be born into a successful family—very much a Dartmouth family, with two Dartmouth brothers (**Mark Byrne '85, Tu'86, and Patrick '85**), some Tuck-graduate cousins, and parents who generously support the college—John's personal ski life started with an early family foray to the Okemo ski area in Vermont. He later became a weekend ski instructor at Okemo while in high school, and courtesy of the flexible Dartmouth Plan, took the opportunity to continue this work in the winter during his college years. After graduation, John became a very successful real estate investment banker at the reputable New York firm, Solomon Brothers. He spent his time acquiring real estate, particularly during the troubled times of an earlier banking system crisis. However, he did not lose the ski bug or the passion for a dream of one day spending his time working on a ski hill. A family outing at Alta, Utah, led to his acquiring a place there that he has kept for over 20 years—along with a love for the unique elements of Alta's operations. Some aspects of Alta, such as a world-leading avalanche control system, have been beneficial to his Alyeska development.John enjoys being on the go, taking regular winter ski trips that have included visits to over 100 ski resorts in the United States, summer hikes in the Alps, and a bike trip across the country in 1986. Six years ago, he started taking helicopter skiing trips to Alaska and fell in love with the wilderness and the great snow. In 2007, he came across the opportunity to buy Alyeska from its former Japanese owners and did so with the help of his purchase advisor, Anchorage attorney **Dick Rosston '73**. Now he is finally back working on the hill! And he expects to continue doing so for a long time, joined by Dartmouth friends, his extended family, and two young daughters, Kaelee and Noelle. And work it is as he has changed the face of Alyeska considerably to create a year-round resort operation with a revitalized hotel, heli-skiing tours, "magic carpet" ski lifts to encourage children, new ski trails and major lifts, fabulous night skiing, new Nordic trails, a longer ski season, summer mountain hiking trails and biking facilities, summer festivals and more. Alyeska is avalanche prone, so based on his experiences at Alta, he has four 105-mm howitzer canons (shades of the legendary 10th Mountain Division troops), including a new mount and covered shelter, to roll into action when needed to knock down the enemy snow masses.[73] He is spending a lot of money to create a resort that will become cash-flow positive and able to sustain itself.[74] However, not all is work as John takes advantage of the mountain's lighting system (necessary to permit skiing not only at night but also

John Byrne '81 skiing the wilds of Alyeska in Alaska.

during the darker hours of an Alaskan winter day) for some early morning cruising with no one else on the slopes. Due to Alyeska's position overlooking the coast, he may even one day spot a passing whale from the slopes of his mountain, an omen he believes will validate his Alaskan endeavors.

John is following a well-trodden Dartmouth path from Okemo to Alta and to Alyeska. The early work of **Don Cutter '46** led to the wonderful Okemo skiing experience; **Dick Durrance '39** started developments at Alta; and **Jim Branch '52** contributed greatly to Alyeska as a prior mountain manager there and has been recognized by having his name on a famous Alyeska ski trail. These are not the only Dartmouth connections. The Alyeska staff includes Dartmouth alums like **Phil Livingston '58,** and many other Big Green skiers have schussed down the slopes. To work out changes on his mountain, Byrne employs SE Group (formerly known as Sno-Engineering), the leading firm in ski mountain developments started by the legendary **Sel Hannah '35** and peppered full of Dartmouth connections. John spent a gleeful three hours skiing with **David Chodounsky '08** after David won the 2009 National Slalom Championship race at Alyeska. This early morning adventure focused John's mind on some trail expansions that are now taking place. Yes, the green thread of past, present and future Dartmouth skiers is still being spun...and still winding a path thru snow-covered hills and plains, far from those of Hanover.

Diana Golden Brosnihan '84 – A Champion of her Cause
By Joseph Walsh '84

Skipping across campus with her crutches and ever-present smile, Diana Golden was among the most recognizable students at Dartmouth in the early 1980s. She was the champion one-legged skier who had been featured on the sports page of *The Dartmouth* hopping up (and down) the bleachers of Memorial Field among her Dartmouth skiing contemporaries – NCAA All-Americans, Carnival skiers, former and future members of the US Ski Team – all of whom had two legs.

Several years later, one of the first IMAX productions began with a long-view of a lone skier racing down a giant slalom course. The skier dips behind a knoll in the foreground then reappears, cresting the knoll straight at the audience crouched over one leg, with hands jutting forward, tightly gripping her poles in perfect form. Of course, it was Diana.

Diana is the epitome of the Paralympic champion, pursuing performance and perfection under what most people would consider to be less than perfect circumstances. Having lost her leg to cancer at age 12, she continued skiing with New England Handicapped Skiing at Mount Sunapee, NH. Among injured Vietnam War veterans and others, she began her ski racing pursuits shortly thereafter and came to Dartmouth in 1980 already a gold medalist from the World Skiing Championships for the Disabled.

It was following graduation, though, when the ski champion that was Diana Golden really blossomed. She won all three events (SL, GS, DH) at the 1986 World Skiing Championships for the Disabled, added to

*Diana Golden Brosnihan '85,
an inspired skier of great skill.*

that two Gold medals at the 1988 Paralympic Winter Games, and led a USA 1-2-3 sweep in the disabled giant slalom demonstration at the 1988 Olympic Winter Games in Calgary (which included fellow Dartmouth alumna **Martha Hill Gaskill '82** who won Bronze).

Determined to get even better, she gave up her outriggers and went to skiing on one ski with just regular ski poles – a demonstration of her incredible athleticism as well as her commitment to excellence. While ultimately that technique proved to not be faster, she still won all three gold medals at the 1990 World Alpine Skiing Championships for the Disabled. With 19 national skiing titles to her credit as well, Diana Golden was indisputably the dominant Paralympic ski racer of her time.

Diana and her legacy as a champion are recognized and respected far beyond Hanover. Her celebrated accomplishments and persuasive advocacy led to adoption of "The Golden Rule" that seeds Paralympic skiers so that they can race before deep ruts develop in all US Ski Association sanctioned competitions. The Diana Golden Race Series provides entry-level competition at mountains all across the country for skiers who have disabilities. Diana has been inducted into the US National Ski Hall of Fame, the US Olympic Committee Hall of Fame, and the Women's Sports Hall of Fame. She received the Flo Hyman Award from the Women's Sports Foundation, the Buddy Werner and the Beck International Awards from the US Ski Association, and she was named the US Olympic Committee Athlete of the Year for Skiing in 1988.

Diana was diagnosed with breast cancer in 1991. Her competitive career behind her, she applied her extraordinary optimism and the lessons of a champion to inspire millions of people from all walks of life over the years that followed. Diana met **Steve Brosnihan '83** in 1996; they were married and lived a loving life together until Diana's death in 2001. Diana spent a great deal of her time writing in her later years including personal essays that were published in *Chicken Soup for the Woman's Soul* and the *Dartmouth Alumni Magazine*. She appeared on "The Today Show" and was profiled by *Sports Illustrated, LIFE, Reader's Digest,* and *TIME* in articles written by **Robert Sullivan '75**. In addition to her many other awards, Diana was honored with the Presidential Medal for Outstanding Leadership and Achievement from Dartmouth.

My two most vivid memories of Diana are watching that effervescent girl skipping across the Hanover Green and dancing with her in the snow covered streets of "Little Chicago," Team USA's housing block at the 1986 World Skiing Championships for the Disabled held in Salen, Sweden. We also navigated Logan and JFK together as we headed off to Europe on several trips, and although our paths crossed only occasionally, I knew I could always count on Diana for moral and practical support – as well as for a big laugh and smile. Diana was a giant in the world of Paralympic sport – truly a pioneer. As with many who gain such notoriety, her accomplishments pale in comparison with the positive effect she had on those of us who she touched personally. A champion, a legend and a great friend was Diana Golden.

Liz McIntyre '87 – Smoothing out a Bumpy Career
By Chelsea Little '09

In 2006, Liz McIntyre retired from coaching US Ski Team moguls skiers and returned to her home in Granby, Colorado. While it may seem that she disappeared from the skiing world, McIntyre hasn't been forgotten: in 2009, she was inducted into the Ski Hall of Fame, with a nod both to her twelve seasons as a US Ski Team athlete and her eight years as a national team coach.

McIntyre had already been competing in moguls at an advanced level in high school before coming to Dartmouth. While most universities would not grant students time off to ski internationally, and some of her competitors were forced to choose between competition and education, Dartmouth provided the flexibility to pursue both. Because she missed several semesters to train and compete – McIntyre skied her first World Championships in 1986 – she took a few extra years to earn her degree, a double major in Government and Environmental Studies.

After graduating, McIntyre competed in numerous World Cups and World Championships as well as three Olympics. She was part of a trio of innovative and incredibly successful American women, including Donna Weinbrecht and Anne Batelle. McIntyre rose above the fray to win a Silver medal at the 1994 Olympics in Lillehammer. Her last competition before retiring, the 1998 National Championships at her home resort of Winter Park, Colorado, ended fittingly: in victory.

Liz McIntyre '87 showing her mogul skills.

Soon thereafter, McIntyre was asked to join the coaching staff of the US Ski Team as a technical coach, and although she hadn't planned to stay on the circuit – and had thought that maybe she was finally done living out of suitcases and in laundromats – she accepted. In the early days of inverted airs, one of the coaches' jobs was to figure out what the heck their athletes were doing when they flipped upside down, and McIntyre was one of the first coaches to put together composite photos of athletes' jumps. McIntyre also diligently compiled an index of judges' scores so that athletes could change strategies based on who was in the judging box. She even cooked breakfast for her skiers when she thought it was important.

One of the last athletes McIntyre talked to before she retired was a young, red-haired skier on the Continental Cup team. This skier was applying to college, trying to decide whether she could balance skiing and school. McIntyre probably didn't pressure **Kayla Snyderman '10** to go to Dartmouth, because that's not how she operates. But whatever it was she said, Snyderman chose Dartmouth. After the first day of racing at the 2008 Saint Lawrence Carnival, four other Nordic skiers and I took the lift up Whiteface and watched Snyderman get on the podium of the World Cup for the first time, snagging a Bronze medal.

When interviewed, McIntyre's athletes from the US Ski Team always say that Liz was all about the skiers, not about the coach. When she was inducted into the Ski Hall of Fame, this was cited as one of the reasons why. Sure, she won that medal. Sure, she was a superb technical coach. But, even in this fast-paced, modern day where results often appear to be all that matters, character counts for something, too. One of McIntyre's greatest gifts to her athletes, according to the freestyle community, was her amazing selflessness. This doesn't surprise me at all: Liz McIntyre is my aunt, and she has always been the most generous, thoughtful mentor and friend I could have asked for. After her Silver medal, she signed a poster for me that says, "Be kind, eat your Brussels sprouts, and ski." Part of her message has always been that you gain the most by being a kind, decent person. She has given much to the ski world by the personal example she set, not simply the success of those she so caringly coached.

These days, you can find McIntyre skating on skinny skis or honing her telemark turns; ever the experimenter, she's still exploring what skiing has to offer.

Bill Hudson '88 — Winning at the Sugar Bowl
By Pamela (Crisafulli) Hommeyer '88

As he strides to the front of the room and reaches for the microphone, a sea of smiling, wind-kissed, goggle-tanned faces looks up eagerly and he delivers his well-known opening, "My name is Bill Hudson, Executive Director of the Sugar Bowl Ski Team Foundation, an organization dedicated to the development of the whole child: mind, body and spirit."

A member of the Dartmouth Class of 1988, Bill Hudson is a quintessential example of Dartmouth's impact on the world of skiing. This influence has taken two distinct forms: first as an accomplished ski racer himself, and subsequently as the leader of a first-class ski team and academy.

Born and raised in Squaw Valley, CA, Bill is a former US National Champion (1989 Combined), a member of the US Ski Team (1985-1993) and a US Olympic Team member (Calgary, 1988). Skiing is in Bill's blood—his mother, Sally, was also an Olympian (Oslo, 1952). Bill may be best remembered for his love of speed, which once resulted in a spectacular, bone-breaking crash when he sailed completely over a course barrier fence at the famed Hannenkam Downhill in Kitzbuehel, Austria in 1991. Bill was fortunate to survive this horrendously debilitating crash. Despite the serious injuries, Hudson returned to the World Cup circuit and was selected to the World Championship team in 1993. But according to Hudson himself, he never skied quite as fast after the accident. At the conclusion of the 1993 season, Bill decided it was time to move on.

Bill Hudson '88 shows his aggressive style.

After a short stint as an event marketer in San Francisco, Bill headed back to the mountains near Lake Tahoe and was hired by the Sugar Bowl Resort in Norden, CA, as Marketing Manger. Six years later, during a fierce snowstorm, Bill found himself chatting with Tricia Hellman Gibbs, Board Chair of the Sugar Bowl ski team and its college-prep high school, the Sugar Bowl Academy. Bill suggested several key improvement ideas for the team and the academy, including how a single leader might better integrate operations. Soon after this fateful conversation, Bill found himself as Executive Director of the combined ski racing entity, the Sugar Bowl Ski Team Foundation (SBSTF), a position for which he was uniquely qualified.

In this new role, Hudson's impact was both immediate and far-reaching. He now oversees the re-energized ski academy and a ski team that has grown to over 400 members, ranging in age from five to nineteen. The program aims to develop in kids a love of the sport through recreational and competitive skiing. The team adheres to the principles of the Positive Coaching Alliance, which stresses the importance of good sportsmanship and respect for one's teammates and coaches.

The Sugar Bowl Academy, a college preparatory ski academy for students in grades 7-12, was founded on the premise that the pursuit of academic excellence is a vital element in the development of outstanding individuals and athletes. And while the SBSTF's program certainly strives to nurture athletes who will achieve greatness in the world of ski racing, at its heart is the desire to develop great people who love and respect the sport and the outdoors. Bill's leadership and dedication to help produce student-athletes strong in spirit and ready to face life's challenges is a true tribute to the Dartmouth experience. As Dartmouth's alma mater refrains, *"Though 'round the girdled earth they roam, her spell on them remains!"*

Bill's family connections at Dartmouth run deep. His grandfather, **Lloyd Neidlinger '23**, was Dean of the College for 20 years; his uncle, **Malcolm McLane '46**, was Captain of the Dartmouth Ski Team; a cousin, **Ann McLane Kuster '78**, was a member of Dartmouth's first women's ski team, and her son, **Zack Kuster '11**, made the men's team. Bill and his family still reside in Squaw Valley. Each day he continues to make a difference in the lives of young people through his own love of skiing and the outdoors.

Max Saenger '88 – A Swiss Biathlete Trained at Dartmouth
By Max Saenger '88

In the spring of 1937 my Swiss father, **Werner Saenger '41**, was scheduled to attend Princeton University after having spent two years at the Ecole de Commerce in Neuchâtel, Switzerland. On a weekend ski trip in the Bernese Oberland, my father met a countryman named **Walter Prager** who convinced him to abandon Princeton and apply instead to Dartmouth. In the fall of that year, Werner Saenger arrived in Hanover and thus began my connection to Dartmouth College.

Beginning already in middle school in Switzerland, I dreamt about attending preparatory school in New England and then Dartmouth College. In the summer of 1979 our family toured likely prep schools armed with two critical questions: "How good is the ski program here?" and "How many students from here go to Dartmouth each year?"

We chose Holderness School in Plymouth, NH, and I promptly hung a green Dartmouth banner in my dorm room. Just one hour east Hanover, I spent the next four years meeting Dartmouth alumni, skiers, and coaches, and even participating in a ski team scavenger hunt

Admitted in the fall of 1984, I immediately reported to the ski team office. After years of Alpine racing in Switzerland and the U.S., I arrived at Dartmouth as a very inexperienced yet enthusiastic "Nordie" with only one season on the skinny skis behind me. Nevertheless, Coach **John Morton** allowed all freshmen to attend fall training figuring we would "self select" before winter arrived. I was always the last skier to roller ski into the feed station van parked on Route 10. Morty would drive me ahead to the next feed station, leap-frogging me to the front of the pack so that I could arrive back in Hanover before dark.

With a solid training program and much guidance from Morty, I managed to qualify for the Junior Olympics my freshman year and went on to captain the Nordic team in my Junior and Senior years. Working with John Morton and the rest of the team to try to achieve top results for Dartmouth at the weekend Carnivals and at the NCAA's was at different times challenging, thrilling and just plain fun. The highlight of my final season was at the last Carnival where I shared two 3rd places—one in the cross-country Individual and the other in the Relay. Although I went on to compete on the World Cup Circuit and at the World Championships, the camaraderie I felt with Morty and other ski team members during those Dartmouth years was only equalled when I guided **Rob Walsh '88** in the '92, '94 and '98 Paralympics.

In 1992 I began competing in biathlon. In exchange for helped John Morton chip tree branches and clean up his forest, he taught me some shooting basics and lent me his biathlon rifle. In 1993 I represented the U.S. with **Tim Derrick '89** and **Stacy Wooley '91** at the World University Games in Zakopane, Poland. My goal was to make it onto the World Cup Team and travel through Europe competing in a different resort each weekend.

In 1995, my former roommate and US Biathlon Team Program Coordinator, **Max Cobb '87**, made a bold strategic move and reduced the funding for the senior men's World Cup Team to invest more heavily in the future with a very promising junior program. While Max had made a great move for the future of US Biathlon, it left me with no chance to make it to the World Cup as I could never afford to self-fund the European World Cup trip. I teased him that I thought it was retribution for an incident from our college days when, during my year as its president, the Bait and Bullet Club burned down Stoddard Cabin while Max Cobb was President of the Outing Club.

As a Swiss I had competed on the Swiss Cup Circuit in Biathlon, and after hitting 19 of 20 targets in my first Europa Cup race I qualified for the World Championships and the remaining World Cup races that season. I represented Switzerland on the World Cup Circuit and at World Championships from 1996 through 1998. The Swiss Olympic Committee had a goal of maximizing the athlete to medal ratio for Nagano, Japan, and only one Swiss biathlete was allowed to go to those Games although we had earned the right to compete with a relay of four athletes and start two in each individual competition.

In 1999, after one year of teaching alpine skiing in Switzerland, John Morton and Max Cobb asked me to think about a career in the Nordic sports, beginning as the Executive Director of the Maine Winter Sports Center, an economic stimulus project in Aroostook County, Maine. I worked with community members to establish a culture of hosting high level competitions in biathlon and cross-country culminating in a 2004 Biathlon World Cup at the 10th Mountain Ski Center in Fort Kent, ME, and a 2006 Biathlon World Junior Championships at the Nordic Heritage Center in Presque Isle, ME.

By re-establishing skiing as a community lifestyle, building two world-class ski venues, and developing dozens of local ski trails and matching programs, I was able to put thousands of kids on skis regularly throughout the winters in Aroostook County. It is very satisfying to watch these young athletes progress and win medals at National and World Championship events. Several athletes have the chance to represent the US and the Maine Winter Sports Center at the Vancouver 2010 Olympic Winter Games. After a great experience with Max Cobb and John Morton in the Salt Lake 2002 Winter Olympic Games I jumped at the chance to move to Vancouver to take on the role of VANOC Biathlon Sport Manager for the 2010 Olympic and Paralympic Winter Games. My responsibilities center on the preparation of venue, the training and recruitment of the Competition Committee, and the management of the competitions and training sessions. During the Olympics I will work with the competition committee and International Biathlon Union to ensure a smooth operation of all aspects of the biathlon competition venue.

Rob Walsh '88 – Staying True to his Vision
By Joe Walsh '84

In March 2002, at the age of 36, Rob Walsh attended his last Dartmouth Ski Team practice. Well, OK, he still went out for a soccer game every now and again, and he certainly still crossed paths with the team up on Oak Hill during the winter; but no more over-distance roller-ski workouts, no more Oak Hill ski bounding intervals, no more technique drills at the old 9th hole of the Hanover Country Club. He essentially retired.

Rob Walsh '88 on his way to another victory.

Now make no mistake: Rob is no Cal Ripken. He missed a few practices in his 18 seasons of training with the Dartmouth boys, but that's only because he had to keep his job at the US Army Cold Regions Research and Engineering Laboratory out on Lyme Road. It was part of the critical combination of living, working, training, skiing and shopping for groceries all within walking—or at least biking—distance. Only part of the eligibility for being on the US Paralympic Ski Team is skiing fast; the other part is having a qualifying disability. Being legally blind (his best corrected vision is about 20/200) he qualifies; but that means no driving.

Rob had been on cross-country skis once or twice before arriving at Dartmouth in 1984, but his real introduction to the sport came on a borrowed pair of skis at a Christmas break training camp in the Second College Grant his freshman year. A regular scorer on the Braintree (MA) High School cross-country running squad, he had some endurance training under his belt, and he put that to good use in his new sport. The always supportive Dartmouth ski team development program welcomed him "as long as you're willing to make the commitment," Coach **John Morton** likely said to lay out the prerequisites. Few Dartmouth skiers have ever made such a commitment to the sport and to the team. Under the tutelage of Morty and his development coaches, **Sam Smith** and **Joe Holland**, Rob developed his skill and strength as a skier. He advanced to earn a varsity letter his senior winter–not for Carnival performances, but for representing Dartmouth and the USA at the 1988 Paralympic Winter Games in Innsbruck – and for winning a Gold medal in the 15-km. "I had a little extra motivation that day, having lost a bronze medal to Joe [i.e., me] by less than 3 seconds in the 30-K two days earlier. I had followed in Joe's footsteps since I started skiing and that was the first time I beat him." It was a proud occasion for both of us to have him win. And that was just the beginning.

Rob went on to win a Bronze medal at the 1992 Paralympic Winter Games and to win Silver and Bronze Paralympic World Championship medals. He represented the USA in the 1994, 1998 and 2002 Paralympic Winter Games as well and in three Paralympic Nordic Skiing World Championships. He was named to the US Disabled Ski Team 17 consecutive seasons. So, maybe he did miss a practice or two, but thanks to the support of John Morton and his successor as Men's Cross-Country Ski Coach **Ruff Patterson**, Rob likely holds the record for most Dartmouth Ski Team training sessions attended, although I don't think anyone was counting.

Said Morty, "During his undergraduate years, Rob unassumingly showed up for workouts with the Varsity and Development team skiers. He fit in the program so smoothly I suspect many of his teammates were unaware of his visual impairment. While his buddies were headed off to intercollegiate Winter Carnival competitions at Middlebury and UVM, Rob, without any hoopla or fanfare, joined the US Disabled Ski Team in Austria and returned to Hanover with a Gold medal from the Paralympic Games."

Rob is the first to admit that he gained enormously from his long-standing tie to the Dartmouth Team. "I couldn't imagine a better situation. I had the benefit of a team to help me in my training; I had a great coach to give me advice, and I had a connection to generations of Dartmouth students long after I graduated. As an undergraduate, I looked up to the Dartmouth skiers and biathletes competing on the national teams. As an alumnus, I fed off the energy and enthusiasm of the undergraduates. As a working professional, I found few things more relaxing than going to a ten-day training camp with the team at Mt. St. Anne where the toughest decision each day was which James Bond movie to watch that night!"

Rob's longevity with the team provided opportunity for other Dartmouth skiers as well. The partnership of a visually impaired Paralympic skier and his guide needs to be well cultivated before they can expect success at a national or international level. In addition to the technical elements of race speed, timing at transitions, and communications on the course, the pair needs to undertake the travel, race strategy, and race preparation together. That requires significant compatibility. Being a cross-country skiing race guide for a top skier requires significant capacity as well. Yes, the Carnival skiers could all keep ahead of Rob, but they were busy skiing Carnivals and NCAA's. Over the years, six Dartmouth skiers raced as Rob's guide at national or international competition: **Paul Blackburn '88, Herve Garant '90, Max Saenger '88, Pat Cote '98, Cory Smith '96** and **Levi Hensel '03**. While we all carry with us our experiences and add them to who we are and what we do, two of that group have gone on to prominent roles in the skiing world. Max Saenger became the first Executive Director of the Maine Winter Sports Center and was later chosen to serve as Biathlon Competition Manager for the 2010 Olympic and Paralympic Games in Vancouver, BC. As of this writing, Pat Cote serves as Executive Director of the New England Nordic Ski Association.

As for Rob, he took up the mantle of leadership as Chair of the International Paralympic Committee Nordic Skiing Committee which oversees competition globally. He also coaches the J5 (8-9 years old) group for the Ford Sayre Memorial Ski Council in Hanover, where he lives with his wife, **Tracy Walsh '91**, and their two children Shannon and Matt. Just as Morty described him unassumingly showing up for training, he quietly provides leadership to the international community. The consummate cross-country skier, he knows that from perseverance will come success. He also knows that his dedication and commitment is fueled by a love for skiing and the out-of-doors—a love he continues to share with past, present, and future generations of Dartmouth skiers.

Jamie Meiselman '91   Enter The Snowboarder
By Jamie Meiselman '91

In the late 1980s - early 1990s, snowboarding underwent the experimental, exciting, and sometimes awkward transition from childhood to adolescence. For fortunate early-adopters like Jamie Meiselman, opportunities to participate in the growth and direction of snowboarding were ubiquitous, especially in Jake Burton's New England backyard where the industry, the competition scene, and many of the world's elite riders were born and bred. With Hanover as a literal bull's-eye of the rapidly developing snowboard scene, Meiselman took full advantage of this rare and fortuitous opportunity to contribute to the progression of the sport in its most formative years.

A New Jersey native, Meiselman arrived on campus in the fall of 1987 with a skateboard, a snowboard, and a surfboard in tow. While these "action sports" are now fixtures in the mainstream sporting consciousness, Meiselman got plenty of sideways glances as he skated across campus from class to class. At the time, the Dartmouth Skiway didn't permit snowboarding, so Meiselman got his fix at nearby Whaleback Mountain just 15 minutes southeast of campus, a ski area formerly owned and developed by **Jim Griffiths '65**. Whaleback had recently decided to allow snowboarders, but no formal instruction was available at the time. Meiselman approached

Jamie Meiselman '91 on his board in 1991.

Whaleback management in late fall 1987 and proposed the formation of a snowboard instructional program. With nothing to lose, mountain management gave Meiselman the green light (and more importantly, a free season pass), and the Whaleback Snowboard School was born. While there, Meiselman made first contact with the select few Dartmouth snowboarders such as **Luke Smith '88**. In years prior, Smith had been hiking and riding his snowboard at the defunct Oak Hill ski area just north of campus, where he often encountered an older Dartmouth student (name unknown, but likely Dartmouth's first snowboarder) who rode self-made boards built in the Hopkins Center woodshop.

Snowboard competitions were still in their infancy in the mid-to-late '80s, but some of the world's best riders were competing in the New England Cup, the first organized snowboard competition series in the country. Those events were highly anticipated, competitive gatherings of the small but passionate East Coast snowboard community. At each event, competitors not only looked forward to testing their skills against peers, but to checking out all of the advancements in equipment that were occurring rapidly during the period. Each successive event saw riders showing up with a new wave of experimental designs and materials for boards, boots, and bindings. Meiselman was particularly obsessed with his boots. He considered the then standard soft boots with strap bindings too unresponsive and the alternative ski-influenced plastic hard boots too restrictive. So in his spare time between events, Meiselman cobbled together his own "special blend" snowboard boot to combine the flexibility of soft boots with the responsiveness of hard boots. While he usually finished middle-of-the-pack in the New England Cup events, he gained an enviable reputation in snowboard circles for his Rube Goldberg-like boot experiments.

In 1988, Jake Burton signed Meiselman (then a Dartmouth sophomore) to a consulting contract for developing boot designs. Burton gave him all of the boots and bindings he wanted to cut up and modify, and Meiselman took payment primarily in the form of free Burton boards. He developed his boot creations in the Hopkins Center metal shop and also gained access to the boot-repair shop at nearby Technica headquarters in Lebanon, NH, a firm run by **John Stahler Tu '69**. Meiselman ultimately received three US patents on his boot creations and licensed the patents exclusively to K2, which commercialized them in the form of the first "step-in" boot/binding.

The media side of snowboarding was also just emerging in the late '80s. *TransWorld Snowboarding* magazine (now the world's most widely circulated snowboard publication) ran its first issue in the fall of 1987. That winter, Meiselman met TransWorld publisher Kevin Kinnear at the US Open Snowboarding Championships at Stratton, VT. As both a competitor and an English major, Meiselman was a prime candidate to contribute informed and reasonably literate content to the fledgling magazine; Kinnear invited Meiselman to solicit article ideas for publication and he had several articles published in the final issue of *TransWorld Snowboarding's* first year of publication.

He then took advantage of the Dartmouth trimester plan by taking off his sophomore spring, driving to San Diego, and taking a position as the first intern at *TransWorld Snowboarding*. During his internship, Meiselman was given the task of creating the industry's first trade publications: *TransWorld Snowboarding Business* and *TransWorld Skateboarding Business*. These publications still exist today, both online and in print, in a combined format called *TransWorld Business*. Following graduation, Meiselman worked full time at TransWorld from 1992-1995, serving as Managing Editor of TransWorld Snowboarding. He also recruited Dartmouth surf/snowboard buddy **John Stouffer '90** to TransWorld. Stouffer became Managing Editor of *TransWorld Business* and held the post for nearly a decade. Stouffer currently serves as a marketing executive at *Fuel TV*, the first 24-hour Action Sports cable TV network.

Dartmouth and snowboarding had an informal, underground relationship until fall 1989 when **Tom Paganucci '92** posted flyers proposing to form the first "Dartmouth Snowboarding Club." Meiselman and a handful of other students, including now-famous actress/comedienne **Aisha Tyler '92** (*Friends, Talk Soup, Nip/Tuck, CSI, 24*, etc.), attended the inaugural meeting. The Dartmouth Snowboarding club caught on quickly, receiving recognition and funding from the DOC. The primary agenda item of the Snowboarding Club was to convince the Dartmouth Skiway management to open up to snowboarders. Seeing a critical mass of interested Dartmouth students, Skiway manager **Donnie Cutter '73** was receptive to the pleas of the club. Cutter organized a "safety demonstration" in late winter 1990 during which members of the Snowboarding Club rode with Donnie and the ski patrol to exhibit snowboarders' ability to ride the lifts, run the slopes, stop under control, and to generally co-exist peaceably with skiers. The demo went off without incident and Cutter not only welcomed snowboarders beginning in the 1990-91 season, but dove in head first, delegating the Snowboard Club authority to set up and run the Skiway Snowboard School.

Winter season 1990-91 was the first time Dartmouth students could snowboard at the Skiway and take snowboarding lessons for school PE credit. Meiselman developed the teaching methods and trained members of the Snowboarding Club to be instructors. The program caught on immediately, with nearly as many students signing up for snowboarding lessons as ski lessons in the inaugural season. The Skiway continues to offer student-taught snowboard instruction for the public and for student PE credit; as of the 2008-09 winter season, student participation in snowboard lessons outnumbered that of downhill skiing at the Skiway. Ironically, when snowboarding was first introduced to the Skiway, there was a bizarre "no jumping" policy in place, the management citing insurance restrictions. This forced snowboarders and skiers to "look before they leaped" in fear of being cited by ski patrolmen. The Skiway now touts a full-time snowboard park; and yes, the jumping ban has been lifted.

Meiselman moved from the media side of snowboarding back to his roots in product in 1996 when he set up and ran the US distribution of European snowboard brands Generics and Blax (now Head Snowboards). He moved on to run the boot division at Burton in 1999-2000 before returning to get his MBA in Finance and Entrepreneurship at Columbia in 2002. His quest to improve the lot of the board-sports community continues to this day; with seed financing from Columbia's Venture Capital fund and other private investors, he founded Surfparks LLC in 2003 to develop the world's first surfing wave-pool facilities. He is currently continuing on this quest to bring high quality, consistent waves to the overcrowded, underserved surfing community.

Nina M. Kemppel '92, Tu '05 – An Enduring Woman
By Phil K. Livingston '58

In 2001 Nina Kemppel was a speaker at a Rotary conference in Anchorage, Alaska, that featured a focus on "Youth". The other keynote speakers were notable but Nina's talk was extraordinary. The audience, young and old, was spellbound. Nina's talk was about determination and goal setting. This is a person who knows about these two subjects first-hand. When she was looking at potential colleges and universities she "focused on programs where I could excel both academically and athletically." Dartmouth College was the lucky winner of that competition.

When Nina was ten years old, she told her parents that she wanted to become an Olympic cross-country skier. I guess her parents had already learned to listen to their little girl. Although neither parent was a skier, they both put on the boards and joined her in the cold at 5:00 a.m. the next morning. To quote Nina: "My mother was afraid that I would be trampled by a moose while training during the dark morning hours on Alaskan trails." Initially motivated by her ten-year old, Nina's mother became a National Masters Champion and her younger sister, **Denali Kemppel '96**, became a Junior National Champion, an All American at Dartmouth, and competed in the 1995 World University Games and 1998 Olympic Trials. After Nina retired from skiing, one of her goals was to develop support for young athletes. In addition to those attending the Anchorage conference, it is hard to estimate the number of young people around the country who found the key to their future success from Nina's talks.

Kemppel '92, Tu '05 racing at the UNH Carnival.

The focus "upon programs where (she) could excel both academically and athletically" led Nina to Dartmouth College. A strong student at Dartmouth, Nina maintained her dual focus of academic excellence and cross-country skiing. In her freshman year there, she placed fifth in NCAA competition and was awarded All-American Honors. "The Dartmouth Women's Nordic team trained together and helped each other navigate the delicate balance between excelling academically and athletically." She was a two-time NCAA Cross-Country Skiing All American, a member of the US Ski team for thirteen years, and qualified for her first of four Olympic Games in 2002. She competed on five world championship teams. She had eleven seasons on the World Cup circuit and eighteen US National Championships. Her fifteenth place in the 30-km Classic event was the best Olympic performance of any American woman at that time. Her ties with Dartmouth resonate when she says, "my two best friends and roommates actually skipped one of their major final exams to travel to Albertville, France, and watch me compete in my first Olympic games."

Nina also received The Finlandia Award for the outstanding cross-country ski racer in the United States in 1994, 1996, and 2001; The Erik Judeen Award for the woman who scores the highest at the US Cross-Country Championships in 1994, 1997, 1999, and 2002; and The Martha Rockwell Award for the fastest woman in 5-km event at the US Cross-Country Championships 1994, 1997, 1999, and 2001.

In Alaska we have a few challenging events of our own. The premier event is The Mount Marathon Race. This demanding race features a running climb up a 3,022-foot mountain coupled with a dangerous descent to the bottom on a shale avalanche chute. Nina has won this race nine times with eight straight wins in a row. Another Dartmouth Alaskan, **Nancy Pease '82**, won this race six times. Nina has also won other mountain challenges: The Crow Creek marathon twice (1,950-foot vertical gain), the Lost Lake Run twice (1,800-foot vertical gain), and The Alyeska Resort Vertical Challenge uncounted times (2,410-foot vertical gain). She says she has lost track of the numbers here but can check with her mother, who is her scorekeeper. On the way to all of the above, she participated with a competitive team on an episode of TV's "Survival of the Fittest" and the Mount Hood Gorge Race filmed for PBS.

What can you do for an encore to that resume? For Nina, Tuck Business School was the first goal on the agenda. Assisting future athletes in the sport of skiing remained as a close second: "Upon retirement from competitive ski racing, I realized that the most effective support I could provide for my teammates and for future athletes was to be involved in programs for the development of elite athletics." On that platform, Nina has been the Ski and Snowboard representative to the US Olympic Committee Athletes' Advisory Council and on the Board of Directors of the US Ski and Snowboard Team. Her focus is on anti- doping issues and improved athlete support programs. Currently, she is the Vice-Chair of the USOC Athletes Advisory Council. She also helped establish the Alaska Winter Olympians Foundation (AWOF) which provides financial support for talented winter sports athletes in Alaska. Even while at Tuck Business School, she traveled extensively about the country giving her motivational speeches to young people. The subject was goal setting. She also volunteered to help with youth programs, including the Hanover, N.H., Ford Sayre Ski Program, youth ski camps in Minnesota, and several youth oriented organizations in Alaska. I remember one sequence from her talk back in 2001: 'In the summer, I trained on Eagle Glacier 6,000 feet above the Girdwood valley. I would wake up cold, stiff, and still tired from the day before. Who wouldn't want to stay in their sleeping bag? But I had a goal--*Gold*!'"

Nina has recently been inducted into the Alaska Sports Hall of Fame. She is now married and working as a management consultant on business strategies in Portland, Oregon. I think I can guess at the core concepts of those strategies: identify your goal, head down, pick up your pack and go!

Charles M. "Chip" Richards '92 – The Freestyle Anomaly
By Chip Richards '92

With hands braced on my knees, staring at the bottom step of the stadium, I remember thinking to myself, "This can't be just a warm up." Desperately trying to catch my breath, I prepared for another sprint to the top row of the Big Green coliseum – this time along with another guy about my size... on my back! I'd been invited by my dorm mate **Carl Swenson '92** (a Nordic team gun) to join the Alpine team for some pre-season workouts. As a competitive Freestyle skier from Colorado, I had always trained harder than most, so I figured I'd enjoy mixing with some stick-chasers for a few sessions. But here I was, ten minutes into my first session, and I was about to lose my Collis lunch.

Growing up in the Rockies, there had always been a palpable wall between the worlds of Freestyle and Alpine. The racers seemed to think themselves slightly superior, because of their intense work ethic and ability to hold an edge on icy ruts, while in their eyes Freestylers just seemed to be out catching big air and getting face-shots in powdered bumps all day. Freestyle skiers on the other hand saw themselves as slightly superior, for pretty much the same reason. We used to notice that whenever racers had time off, they would come and ski moguls. But strangely, we never felt tempted to pad up and run gates during our lunch break. We worked hard, but imbedded in all of our work was the thrill of adrenaline, fun, and hard play. So seeing as I was now at Dartmouth, the global epicenter of "work hard, play hard," I figured the playing field was level and I'd be able to hang with these guys. But as I hobbled back to my dorm with shredded lungs and jackhammered body, I began to understand why there had always been that wall between the two worlds in the first place. These racers were not normal human beings. In fact, I'm pretty sure they weren't human at all.

Needless to say, my time training with the Alpine team was brief and lactic-acidly bittersweet. It was complimented with mountain bike rides, plyometric sessions with members of gymnastic team, and a great diver buddy of mine, **Doug Jamison '92**, and I even took a 'Ballet for Sports' dance class with a bunch of football players. While my years at Dartmouth marked the climax of my competitive career (twice reaching the ranking of #1 in the U.S. as a combined Freestyle skier), the winter quarter worked out as the perfect window for me to be gone from the campus and back in Colorado training and competing. The Big Green became my arena for pre-season autumns and spring recovery.

Funny thing about Freestyle skiing: any way you slice it, no matter how hard you train, it's pretty darn hard on the body. Following two consecutive knee injuries and subsequent reconstructions in the spring of 1990 and 1991, I gave myself the gift of a season off in 1992 and enjoyed my senior winter in the Hanover ice instead. This pause in my Olympic aspirations allowed two great things to occur. Firstly, I was able to graduate with my class in the spring of 1992, and secondly it opened the doorway for me to discover an even bigger passion than competitive skiing – that of coaching.

In the winter of 1992-93, I joined my former coach in Colorado as assistant coach of a US Development Team… and loved it. Two seasons and many team podiums later, I found myself in the ski fields of Australia, coaching the Australian national and junior national team. My plan was to be there for three months and then to ride my bike across the country – and beyond. But those three months unfolded in ways I never could have imagined…. First, I met an amazing Australian woman named Peta. She had never even seen snow before the winter that we met. I fell in love almost instantly, and she must have too, because we were married three months later (we're still joyfully together fifteen years later, with a beautiful nine-year-old son, Joshua). Secondly, the Australian ski job just kept growing, and before I knew it I was the Head Mogul Coach of the Australian National Ski Team, deep in the middle of an Olympic campaign heading to Nagano 1998.

So my Olympic aspirations we fulfilled not as an athlete, but perhaps even more fittingly, as a coach. And though we did not get the gold in moguls that year, we did claim Australia's first ever podium finish at the World Cup level for moguls, humbly paving the way perhaps for the string of Australian World Cup and Olympic victories that have come since.

In the spring of 1998, I hung up my skis in my Australian garage, took a deep breath, and picked up my surfboard. After following the path of winter between the hemispheres for many years, I have now enjoyed a decade of summer, surf and subtropics. I have channeled my energy for coaching into various business and creative industries and have discovered that much of what I learned about human potential in the sporting realm crosses over quite powerfully into all areas of life. I do miss the mountains sometimes, but fortunately I have discovered that on the sliding scale of fun and fulfillment, an early dawn of glassy 4-foot waves in Northern New South Wales is just about equal to a crisp morning of fresh powder in the backcountry of Colorado. And while I never experienced either of those activities directly at Dartmouth, I do know that my time at Dartmouth, and all of my experiences there, somehow played a vital role in bringing me here.

Sarah Billmeier '99 — Paralympic Champion wears Gold, Green, and White
By Joe Walsh '84

I turned around and saw Sarah in the back of the van, her head bent over an open textbook. Studying in the van is a skill many Dartmouth skiers need to develop in order to capitalize on the daily drives to training and on longer trips to competition. But we weren't returning from a Carnival or the Skiway; we were transferring from JFK to LaGuardia airport on our way home from the 1992 Paralympic Winter Games in Tignes, France, just outside Albertville. Sarah was fourteen.

That may or may not have been the only studying she did on the trip–"cramming" for her return to class the next day after three weeks away; but I'm guessing she passed 9th grade algebra without difficulty. Having a sister about Sarah's age, my brother **Rob Walsh '88** and I had been keeping an eye on her during the trip, recognizing that a 14- year-old wasn't necessarily going to fit in or keep up during an international competition trip of that magnitude. But of course Sarah held her own, and she did much more than that when on the hill, winning two Gold medals and one Silver in the Women's Standing Alpine competition.

I next saw Sarah in Hanover the following summer, studying German in the Rassias Foundation's 10-day intensive program on a scholarship provided by the US Ski Team. She was introduced to canoeing at Ledyard, mountain biking at Oak Hill, and square dancing at Moosilauke in addition to learning a little German. I guess that all worked for her because two years later, after completing an introduction to first-year students on pre-medical programs at the C. Everett Koop Institute at Dartmouth, I was working through the queue of inquisitive freshmen when the last student surprised me with, "Hi, Joe. It's Sarah Billmeier."

A happy Sarah Billmeier '99.

I think that was the last time I was surprised by Sarah. Always poised, professional, friendly and enthusiastic, she continues to be impressive and thus no longer surprising. When I would by chance encounter her on campus as a student, she always stopped to catch me up on her studies, how things were going with the US Team, or her latest results. She continued to excel in her studies, and she continued to dominate national and international Paralympic skiing, including winning medals in all four events she entered (including two Gold) at the 1998 Paralympics in Nagano, Japan.

Sarah brought more to the table than just her athletic prowess. While still an undergraduate at Dartmouth she became the first athlete elected to the United States Olympic Committee (USOC) Athletes' Advisory Council (AAC) specifically to represent Paralympic athletes. The AAC was formed by a group of Olympians (including **Ed Williams '64**) in 1974 to provide a voice for athletes in the US Olympic movement. In 1998, Congress formalized the USOC's oversight of Paralympic sport in the United States – a responsibility that initially gave the USOC and the AAC significant pause. Sarah's reasoned, positive and cooperative approach to that issue, and to her role on the AAC more generally, balanced the more aggressive tactics of some other Paralympic advocates, which ultimately facilitated the true inclusion of Paralympic sport in the USOC. Subsequently, when Sarah went on to win the Gold medal in the Standing Women's Super G at the 2002 Paralympic Games in Salt Lake City, as well as Silver medals in the Downhill and the Slalom, she had many fans celebrating her accomplishments with her – including the AAC and the rest of the USOC leadership.

Sarah continued her off-snow leadership even after retiring from competition by volunteering as an Athlete Services Coordinator for the 2004 and 2006 US Paralympic Teams. Selection for these roles is generally very competitive, but Sarah easily rose to the top of the candidate pool. Filling the "big sister" role for athletes in these US delegations, she was actually still younger–though much more experienced–than most of them. Her outgoing, positive demeanor and her approachability, patience, and rational problem solving kept the team focused and upbeat. From basketball players to shot putters, they all quickly realized that Sarah was there to support them and that she had the skills and experience to do it.

Of course the real story on Sarah Billmeier's contributions to Dartmouth skiing, US skiing and skiing more broadly cannot yet be written, as the full consequence of her accomplishments to date are still without the context of time. Having graduated from Harvard Medical School and now a surgery resident in Boston, the influence that Dr. Billmeier will have on her patients, their families, and their friends is also still unknown; but through the strength of her example, the skill of her hands, and the wisdom of her counsel, Sarah will touch many lives. Her enthusiasm, optimism and competence consistently inspire her friends and colleagues to seek the positive, work harder, and stay focused on our goals. It seems likely, if not inevitable, that she will similarly inspire a new generation of skiers to live out their dreams–skiing and otherwise–on the Hanover Plain and in the wide world beyond.

Bradley Wall '02 — From Down Under to the Top: An Australian's Story
By Bradley Wall '02

I grew up in a small town called Jindabyne in NSW. It is about 5-hours drive south of Sydney, in the mountains and the snowfields. The population is about 1800, but it triples in winter with the seasonal work-force; the town is entirely dependent on winter tourism.

My first experience with skiing was in a backpack on my dad's shoulders. I first skied myself when I was three; I had a pair of wooden skis with little red leather boots screwed into them. I don't really remember my early days on skis, but my parents have memories of me terrorizing the bunny slope, unable to turn or stop.

I joined the Guthega Race Club when I was 8 or 9. I would ski on weekends and school holidays; that was when I grew to love skiing fast and competing. When I was 11, I started winning scholarships to travel overseas to the US and to Europe for ski racing. From that point on, because of the opposing seasons in the southern and northern hemispheres, I didn't see a full summer until after I retired in 2006, so I went 16 years without a summer and 17 without spending Christmas with my family.

I went to high school in Australia until the end of 10th grade. It was very difficult to ski competitively and go to school; the local schools in my area were not very good, so I went to an all-boys boarding school in Canberra, about two and a half hours away. They made it very difficult to race as much as I needed to, so I ended up enrolling in Burke Mountain Academy in Vermont for my last three

Bradley Wall '02 has been involved at many levels of skiing.

years of high school. Burke was an excellent program which involved skiing half the day and schooling half the day. Unlike my previous experiences at Canberra Grammar Boys School, when I needed to leave school for a week or so for a particular race series, the teachers at Burke were very accommodating, It was there that I first heard of Dartmouth.

There is a great history of Burke athletes attending Dartmouth, including the men's current ski coach, **Peter Dodge '78**. So I learned of Dartmouth through the skiing side of things, and quickly realized the academic reputation, too. At the time, and I still believe it today, Dartmouth had the best collegiate ski program in the country. It seemed a natural progression for me to apply. At the end of my senior year at Burke, I was on the Australian National Team, but funding was very difficult. I knew I wanted to continue my education and a degree from Dartmouth is a handy thing to have when your ski-racing career fizzles. So I applied and was accepted.

I skied for Dartmouth for three years with quite good success. My freshman year I qualified for the team and was selected to race at the NCAA championships on a 3-man team with two seniors. However, I was on the Australian Ski Team as well, and the NCAA's were being held at the same time as the World Junior Championships in France. That presented a conflict. But the philosophy of the Dartmouth Ski Team is that they want you to become the best ski racer that you can be, and Pete Dodge and I decided that it was in the best interest for my skiing that I miss the NCAA's and race at the World Juniors. It was a hard decision, but I went to France and had a great experience and achieved a good result: 5th in the Super-G event, the best result for Australia.

I have always appreciated that conversation with Pete Dodge and the philosophy of the program; he certainly could have told me that he worked hard to get me in to Dartmouth and that I owed it to the team, or any number of things; but the idea that Dartmouth should be a stepping stone to a bigger career in skiing was a really liberal approach.

My other two years competing for Dartmouth had their ups and downs. Both years I went to NCAA's; but in 2001 at Middlebury, after not crashing all season, I managed to do so in both the slalom and giant slalom events. In 2003, my senior year, Dartmouth hosted the NCAA's at the Skiway. It was heartening to compete on our home hill, and I had great personal success, finishing second in the GS and winning the Slalom title. Unfortunately, the team as a whole did not have similar results; but for me it is one of my favorite ski racing memories, right up there with competing in two Winter Olympics, and the perfect way to finish out my Dartmouth career.

Throughout my years at Dartmouth I remained a member of the Australian National Team. I would miss weeks at a time to go and compete at World Championship events, and I took a whole year off leading up to the Salt Lake Olympics. Again the philosophy of the team made this easy, and for the most part the professors were also accommodating.

Ever since I started ski racing, competing in the Olympics for Australia was my goal. I was fortunate enough to realize that goal in Salt Lake City in 2002 and Torino in 2006. The challenges in competing for Australia were mostly financial; skiing is a huge industry in Australia, but ski racing is a small, almost unknown sport in the country; financial support was hard to come by until you had qualified for the Olympics. Once you got over that hurdle, extra money came in from the Australian Olympic Committee. So the Olympic years were better, but all the years leading up to them, when all the criteria and qualifications had to be met, were very difficult.

Another thing that made competing for Australia difficult--not just in Olympic years, but every year I competed--was our geographical location. The majority of the World Cup circuit is in Europe; to follow the circuit and be competitive you constantly have to relocate. We would spend 5-6 months of the year living out of our bags, traveling from hotel to hotel in Europe. It was tiresome and far less than ideal, but it was the way it had to be then.

My Olympic experiences were incredible, and I will never forget them even though I did not have much success. In Salt Lake, I competed in the GS and finished 33rd, the only highlight being that I was one of the 15 fastest for one of the sections of the course. In Torino, the heelpiece of my binding shattered into three pieces in the middle of my first run and my ski came off. The binding company took a look at it and decided that it must have been a stress fracture that just gave way at the most unfortunate time possible. That was tough to take; to crash because of a mistake you made, you can live with; but when your equipment breaks at the worst possible time, that's really tough to swallow.

After graduating from Dartmouth, I began traveling with the Australian Team again. I competed for three years and retired after the 2006 Olympics. I then took a coaching position at my old high school, Burke Mountain Academy. I felt that ski racing had given me so much that I owed it something in return, and there was no better place for me to do so than at Burke, where I had learned so much and had really become passionate about ski racing. I coached boys for three years, and in the summer of 2009 decided that my wife and I would move back to Sydney, Australia, five hours away from the nearest skiing. My parents still live in Jindabyne, so I will still get down there and make some turns now and then. I will still have some involvement in skiing as the Ski and Snowboard Australia Federation have assigned me to the position of Athlete Liason on the National Alpine Committee which is responsible for alpine ski racing in Australia. I am glad that I will continue to be involved in ski racing, despite the fact that I am no longer working directly in the industry.

One quote that has stuck with me and that I have tried to pass on to athletes that I have coached over the last three years came from Peter Dodge, the Dartmouth coach. On bad weather days, or when the snow conditions were particularly difficult, days when it was tough to motivate for a race, Pete would say to the team, "Hey, some ass*** has got to win this thing; it might as well be one of us". Very simple, but very true. You can't concern yourself with things that are out of your control like weather or snow conditions; all you can worry about is being prepared and doing your best under the circumstances. On those tough days, you can see the morale and attitude drop in some athletes, but if you can stick to Pete's motto, then you will actually gain confidence in watching the other athletes lose it. I have tried to pass this on to the athletes I coached over the last three years, and hopefully they have found it as helpful as I did.

Patrick Biggs '06 – A Canadian Olympian
By Stephen L. Waterhouse

Patrick Biggs came to Dartmouth as a result of not having qualified for the Canadian National Team by his late teens; to ski for his country had been a cherished goal growing up. But he wanted to continue racing—and improving. The program structure, the availability of the near-by Dartmouth Skiway, and the competitive skiers he knew who went to Dartmouth made it an appropriate fit for him. In considering Dartmouth, "the D Plan" was a particularly attractive option when he was evaluating colleges. Talking with some of the team members at the time, they mentioned that it was possible to take a fall term off some years to get in extra training, or cut down to two courses in the winter semester during the competition season. It was also not unusual for ski racers to take six to ten years to complete their course work to obtain a college degree. In a sport where the time spent in training and racing conflicts with the schedule one normally allots to completing college work, this was very important. The D Plan has been helpful to many Dartmouth skiers and it would be for Patrick as well.

Dartmouth's Patrick Biggs '06 in full fly down the course.

In addition, Dartmouth seemed to stand out from other colleges by having a program where athletes significantly improved their performance through their years on the ski team. When you look at the world rankings of Dartmouth skiers as freshmen vs. their ranking two or three years later, the improvement is often vast. This is almost unheard of in the college racing world, and it says a lot about the college's coaching program and the drive these athletes have. There was also the lure of Hanover itself and of obtaining a coveted Dartmouth degree, which all Green alumni know is something special. It sounded to Biggs that Dartmouth College was fully organized to work constructively with outstanding skiers.

As a freshman, Patrick finished 4th in the Slalom and Giant Slalom at the Eastern College Championships (Middlebury), and 4th at the NCAA Slalom Championships (Dartmouth Skiway). After just his freshman year, he qualified to race with the Canadian Ski Team and had to stop racing for Dartmouth. When he learned he had been selected, Patrick was thrilled that Coach Peter Dodge was also genuinely excited, confirming Patrick's impression that the Dartmouth coaches truly believed their college system should be a stepping-stone to put athletes on national ski teams whenever possible—even at the expense of their talent to the Dartmouth team.

Patrick qualified for the World Cup in 2005, finishing in the top ten at several races, and he qualified for the 2006 Olympics in Torino, Italy. Since then, his best performance has been placing 9th at the Slalom World Championships in Are, Sweden, in 2007. He is now training for the Vancouver Olympics, his second Winter Games, and back in his home country.

David Chodounsky '08 — The 2009 National Slalom Champion
By Stephen L. Waterhouse

As an example of the continuing drive of Dartmouth skiers once they depart from the supportive skiing environment in Hanover, David Chodounsky is battling for a spot on the 2010 Olympic team after concluding a successful 2008-09 ski season with his first victory in the National Slalom Championships at the Alyeska Mountain Resort in Alaska owned by John Byrne III '81. This is David's second National Championship of any kind, having finished first in the NCAA Slalom competition in 2005. David was also a key member of Dartmouth's 2007 NCAA Championship team that won its first team championship since the late 1970s, greatly contributing with a 2nd place finish in the slalom. As reported by Tom Kelly of the United States Ski Team:

> Former NCAA slalom title-holder David Chodounsky (Crested Butte, CO) notched his first national championship, winning the men's race as snow continued to fall throughout the day. In the men's contest, Chodounsky laid down a crushing second run to move up from fourth and take the title by .38 seconds over first run leader Jimmy Cochran (Keene, NY), the 2007 and '08 slalom title winner. Cody Marshall (Pittsfield, VT) held forth in third, maintaining his spot from the first run. "I've been looking for this one all year," said Chodounsky, who was captain of the Dartmouth ski team before graduating last June. "I've been skiing well, but today felt really smooth. The course

David Chodounsky '08 in 2005, the year of his NCAA Slalom Championship.

held up really well considering all the snow we've had, but when the ruts started to form, you just had to stay inside the groove and it was fast." "David just outperformed everyone in the second run," said U.S. Ski Team men's Head Coach Sasha Rearick. "He traveled with the Europa Cup Team a bit this season and got some international experience. It's good to see him put together such a great race in some really challenging conditions."[75]

In the 2007 season, David was a key participant on what was in fact an unprecedented campaign for the Big Green Dartmouth team with victories in all six collegiate Winter Carnival meets around the East and a victory in the Eastern Regional Championship at Middlebury. The NCAA victory was also unusual for an Eastern college as none of them had won the NCAA championship since Vermont pulled it off in 1994. Even the Dartmouth team had not won an NCAA Men's and Women's Championship since the start of combined races in 1983, having last won a national team championship of any kind in 1977. But David was a regular on the podium for his specialty throughout the season and considered a sure point-getter for the team. In 2008, Chodounsky served as Co-Captain of the Dartmouth Men's Ski Team with classmates **Alexander Felix '08** and **Ben True '08.**

He was a happy skier after his Nationals win in Alyeska, commenting, " I've been working so hard and finally got the race I was looking for this year".[76] He was cheered on by a large group of Dartmouth alumni who traveled to Alyeska to race or watch others race, and he spent early the next day skiing Alyeska's trails with owner **John Byrne '81**. His victory adds to the record of Dartmouth's close to 200 individual national champion skiers since the first days of such competitions in the early 1930s. **Ted Hunter '38** was the first National Slalom Champion in 1935, preceded by several Dartmouth-bred National Champions in the Downhill. **Dick Durrance '39** then followed with three consecutive National Slalom Championship victories in 1937, 1938 and 1939. Many more have followed since and are mentioned throughout this book, champions like **Charles McLane '41, Bob Meservey '43, Tom Corcoran '54** and **Chick Igaya '57** amongst others. (See Appendix 3)

At the time of writing this book, the final team that will be chosen to ski for the United States at the Vancouver 2010 Olympics has not been determined. David is in with a chance as his 2009 National Championship victory would suggest, but the competition for spots on the US team is very stiff. If not this time around, perhaps we will see David in a future Olympics in 2014.

FAMILY PROFILES

Dr. Hal Bradley and the Bradley Boys
By Tom Washing '63

Dr. Harold Bradley was born in California in 1878, received his undergraduate degree from the University of California at Berkley and his doctorate in Physiological Chemistry from Yale. He joined the faculty of the University of Wisconsin in 1906. Within a couple of years he fell in love with and married Josephine Crane who was an undergraduate in her junior year. Although Josephine had been completely deaf since the age of two, the couple raised seven remarkable sons, several of whom, along with their father, left an indelible imprint on the history of skiing in the United States.

When he was 28, Dr. Hal witnessed a ski jumping contest in Wisconsin and "began a life long love and involvement with ski sport."[77] He encouraged all of his sons to take up skiing and drove them to jumping competitions all over the state throughout their childhoods. In 1931, Hal founded "Hoofers", the university's outdoor recreation club, which he modeled after the then flourishing Dartmouth Outing Club (DOC). There being no skis available commercially in Wisconsin at the time, he discovered that the DOC was acquiring its skis from Switzerland. With help from the Dartmouth club, Hoofers was able "to come by some twenty sets of hickory skis with leather thong bindings—it was the only thing available at that time—and boots to fit and poles, and so on."[78]

Hal went on to become an early member of the Sierra Club, eventually serving as its president. That club's Bradley Hut, located in Pole Creek, California (near Squaw Valley) is named after Hal's wife Josephine. In fact, he particularly loved and indulged in backcountry skiing all his adult life. He did two traverses of the Sierra Nevada, once alone in 1921 from Placerville to Truckee, using a pair of jumping skis and a garden rake handle for a ski pole, and once in 1935 from Lee Vining to Yosemite Valley with his son Charles. Both times he camped in the snow. After WWII, at age 69, he spent two months in the backcountry of Yosemite National Park with several of his sons, living in cabins he had stocked with food and wood the summer before.[79] Dr. Hal Bradley was inducted into the US National Ski and Snowboard Hall of Fame in 1969.

David Bradley in his college image.

His sons were all familiar with Dartmouth because of Hal's work with the DOC as well as through family friends and relatives who had attended Dartmouth. Son Ric recalled, "I think skiing was a big reason for all of us to attend Dartmouth. Alpine skiing was just coming to this country at that time and all of us were pretty hooked on that in addition to our background in Nordic skiing."[80]

Dave Bradley '38, Hal's third-oldest son, was the first of three Bradley boys to attend Dartmouth. While there, Dave was captain of the 1938 ski team, won the 1938 National Nordic Combined Championship, and was named to the 1940 Olympic Team which never competed due to the outbreak of war in Europe. After graduation, Dave attended Cambridge and served as a war correspondent for several Midwestern newspapers covering the Russo-Finnish War of 1939-1940. He earned his M.D. from Harvard in 1944 and later served as an Army medical officer on the Bikini atoll studying radiation levels following the nuclear tests there. He later chronicled his experience in the book, *No Place to Hide*, published in 1948.

Upon his return home, Dave never strayed far from skiing, designing or renovating more than 60 ski jumping hills in the Northeast and serving as manager of the US Nordic ski team at the 1960 Olympic Games in Squaw Valley. He also co-authored (with Ralph Miller and Al Merrill) the book *Expert Skiing* in 1960. Dave Bradley was inducted into the US National Ski and Snowboard Hall of Fame in 1985.[81]

Steve Bradley '39 and Elizabeth Durrance in their college years.

Steve Bradley '39 also competed as a member of the great Dartmouth ski teams of the late 1930's as a four-way specialist in slalom, downhill, jumping and cross-country. In his senior year he won the first of Sun Valley's Intercollegiate Four Event Ski Championships by such a decisive margin that the championship trophy was thereafter officially called the Bradley Cup.[82] Following military service during the war, Steve became one of the great pioneers in the development of skiing in the western U.S. (See Chapters 7 and 10). Among his most memorable accomplishments were his role as Manager of Winter Park Ski Area

THE DURRANCE FAMILY

Dick Durrance '65, showing his winning form (1963).

Dick Durrance '39 skiing the Logo run at Alta.

Dave Durrance in an early slalom race in Garmisch (1953).

Future D ski star, Dick Durrance II '65, and future D ski coach, Dave Durrance (left), on the T-Bar in the early days at Aspen.

Jack Durrance '39, a legend in mountaineering, rappelling down a mountainside in Sun Valley.

Dave Durrance, a star professional racer.

in Colorado for 30 years and his invention of the first slope-grooming device, which led to his nickname as the "Father of Slope Maintenance." Steve was inducted into the Colorado Ski and Snowboard Hall of fame in 1979 and the US National Ski and Snowboard Hall of Fame in 1980.

Charles Bradley graduated from the University of Wisconsin with a degree in Geology and served in the 10th Mountain Division during World War II where he met **John Montagne '42**. Charles later wrote about his experiences with 10th in Alaska in the book *Aleutian Echoes*, illustrated with his own drawings and paintings. Following the war, Charles completed his PhD at Wisconsin and joined Montagne on the faculty of the Montana State University where they created the first university course in the country on snow avalanches. This partnership led to the creation of one of the leading snow science programs in the world, one which led to better avalanche detection methods and procedures for triggering them without the loss of human life. Many an off-piste skier owes a debt of silent gratitude to Bradley and Montagne.

Ric Bradley '44 also skied for Dartmouth, then became a physicist and taught at Colorado College in Colorado Springs where he is now retired. **Bill Bradley** also served in the Tenth Mountain Division during the war, became a geologist and taught at the University of Colorado. **Joe Bradley** became an art historian and taught at the University of Wisconsin.[83]

The Durrance Ski Family
By David Durrance with Richard Durrance II '65

Dick Durrance '39 was certainly the epicenter of the family's involvement with skiing, and from him rings radiated out for several generations. If there is a theme for the Durrances it is one of breaking new ground. Dick was so far ahead of other American skiers when he returned to the states from Germany, where he had learned to ski, that he became the template for others to emulate. He was already an international caliber ski racer and he still had to finish high school. When he couldn't find adequate skiing on the golf course in Sunapee, NH, he just cut a racing trail on Mt. Sunapee without knowing who owned the land. He, of course, won many of his first races in New England. As a freshman at Dartmouth he won the National Collegiate Championships in all events. That was the beginning of what was to become a total of seventeen national championships including collegiate, amateur, and open championships. Of those, nine were considered to be the US National Championships, a record he shares with Bode Miller. He raced the whole winter of 1936 in Europe, including the Olympics, and won several races, most notably the Kings Cup Downhill week in Sestriere, Italy. The Olympics had been disappointing, so he wanted to prove that he was among the best skiers in the world.

The Harriman Cup, which was first run in Sun Valley, Idaho, in 1937, instantly became the biggest ski race in North America because Averell Harriman was willing to pay the way for the top European racers to come. The Europeans wanted to come to America because the possibility of working here after racing was terrific. Dick won the downhill and the slalom and the combined, beating all the top European racers, amateur and pro. Averell Harriman was so pleased that an American had won the race that he had the mountain where the downhill was held renamed Durrance Mountain. The two started a friendship that lasted the rest of their lives. It also gave Dick his first chance to be a professional photographer and his first chance to be a ski area designer.

In the summer of 1937, Dick was invited to New Zealand with the Bradley brothers, Steve and Dave, along with several other friends. During this trip, they made a number of interesting photographs. One ended up becoming an iconic image of a racer slicing across the hill and is on the cover of Dick's biography, *Man on the Medal*, as well as being used on the face of racing medals and as the logo of the New England Ski Museum in New Hampshire. An article in this book by **Ned Jacoby '40** outlines the history of this photo and how it came to be developed by Ned back in Hanover, NH, in Professor Charles Proctor's photo lab.

In the summer of 1938, Dick went to Sun Valley to work in the publicity department, photographing guests and sending the pictures back to their hometown newspapers. But Dick was interested in Sun Valley in general and in the development of skiing. That summer, he also sited and designed the Warm Springs part of Mt. Baldy, the mountain that would make Sun Valley a great international resort. He won the Harriman Cup in 1938 and again in 1940, thereby retiring the permanent trophy (if you could win it three times in five years you could keep it). This trophy was big enough to bathe his boys in when they were infants. After graduation from Dartmouth in 1939, Dick moved to Sun Valley as a full time member of the publicity department. He continued to expand on the design of Mt. Baldy and raced for Sun Valley, winning another spot on the Olympic Team for the 1940 games in Finland. In the spring of that year, he made his first film with **Steve Bradley '39**, the *Sun Valley Ski Chase.* It was during this winter of this same year that he met the love of his life, Miggs.

In the late spring of 1940, many of the skiers from Sun Valley went to Salt Lake City, Utah, for Friedl Pfeifer's wedding. After the wedding, they had a race at Alta, which was a ski club operation. Dick and Miggs were fascinated by the terrain and snow.

Later that summer, Dick would contact the Salt Lake Winter Sports Association to ask them if they had an interest in turning Alta into a going concern. They did, and with the financial help of J. Laughlin, a friend who had also been on the New Zealand trip, they built Alta, ran the Lodge, ski school, ski shop, and the lifts. Dick got to create a resort from the ground up. As WWII broke out, the Army wanted to establish a group of winter warriors who could jump out of airplanes into snow and then operate deep into a mountainous environment. They sent 200 paratroopers from the 82nd Airborne at Fort Bragg, NC, to Alta to learn to ski. Dick assembled a group of ski racing buddies to teach the predominately Southern boys how to ski. After a couple of months, about a third showed some promise and the rest were either injured, incompetent, or thoroughly disenchanted with winter and snow. In the end, the Army decided that it would be better to teach skiers to jump out of airplanes than to teach paratroopers to ski, and so concept of the Tenth Mountain Division was born.

After the winter of 1941, with Miggs pregnant, the Durrances decided it was not prudent to stay at the end of such an isolated canyon. Hugh Bauer, who had been one of the ski instructors for the paratroopers, was working in the engineering department at Boeing and told Dick that there were openings in the test flight department for a cinematographer. He went to Seattle to look into it and was fascinated by the challenge. Dick's job was to rig cameras around the airplane so that Boeing could have an accurate record of every instrument and control throughout the flight. The technical challenge was very rigorous and required a lot of experimentation. He worked with engineers to redesign many of the instruments in the cockpit so that the pilots and the camera could get a quicker, clearer read of the instrument. In the end, he advanced the testing cycle so that fewer people could do more analyses quicker. Eventually he moved on to making training films that dealt with emergency procedures in flight and then to making instructional films for use by the Air Force to teach crews how to fly the airplanes. This required more than just technical photography so he learned to work with scripts, soundtracks, and all the trappings of professional filmmaking.

After the war, Dick and Miggs were ready to leave the perennial moisture of Seattle and head to the Rockies. Dick had an offer to sell skis for the Groswold Ski Company in Denver, Colorado. For a while, he sold skis for Groswold and lifts for Constam, but couldn't keep himself out of product development. Solid hickory skis were formed with steam heat and therefore had a propensity to warp. Dick figured out a way to use a dry heat to form the skis, which meant they were much more stable and allowed him to make a more flexible ski. In order to gain even more control of the ski in the manufacturing process, he experimented with using strips of wood laminated vertically instead of solid wood and found that they make the skis lighter and much more consistent. This opened up new possibilities to build in more performance characteristics like making the skis hold an edge better and to float in powder better. At Groswold, they were interested in making more than skis; they also made bindings and wax. Dick was in charge of marketing and making the catalog. When he went to Climax, CO, to sell the mining company a ski lift, he learned about molybdenum and realized that its properties could be helpful in waxes, so he developed a line of waxes for Groswold with molybdenum that were very fast in cold snow. Over the years Dick had a lot of ideas for innovations in skiing, most too far ahead of their time to catch on. They included a breakaway slalom pole, fog-free goggles, a rear entry ski boot, and a safety binding.

In the fall of 1947 the Aspen Skiing Corporation asked Dick to come to Aspen to run the ski area. This was the first time a former ski racing great would manage a major ski area. But first he had to make it a major resort. Two chairlifts were already in place, and the T-Bar he had sold them the year before was installed but not working. The few trails that had been cut were narrow and very difficult. Dick started by cutting more trails--wide ones that would allow even intermediate skiers to get down the hill-- and he opened new terrain near the top of the mountain, which had a gentler slope. Ruthie's Run was a prime example: it was unusually wide for that time and today is still one of the best runs anywhere in the world. With a good product in hand, he had to get people to come. He knew the FIS would hold a World Championship in 1950 and he felt that the Europeans would see the merit in this mountain. He built an elaborate proposal for the FIS and in 1948 they accepted it. Then Dick went to Adolph Coors, the beer magnate, to head up the finance committee who raised the budgeted $72,000 to hold the races. All work done on the mountain for the races had to benefit the skiing public as well, because this was Aspen's chance to come out to the world. Race week arrived and with it came the sports press from around the world. Mother Nature helped with perfect conditions; the races were a great success, and most importantly, America and the world learned that Aspen was a great place to ski.

Somehow, in the midst of hosting the World Championships and running the Aspen Ski Corporation, Dick found the time to shoot a film about the event. *Ski Champs,* as the film was called, would be described much later as "a compelling feature-length documentary that stands today a priceless record of the personalities and racing world of the 1950's." It was the first feature-length film on skiing made in the United States and the first feature-length film made on ski racing. Dick produced a similar film of the 1952 Olympics in Norway two years later.

The success of *Ski Champs* convinced Dick that he should focus his attention entirely on filmmaking, which he did for most of the rest of his life. From here out it was more about quality than innovation. He went on to photograph, direct, and produce more than fifty films. Some were about skiing and others were travelogues, promotional films, documentaries, instructional films, and theatricals. His films won many awards along the way.

Miggs was a strong ski racer in her own right, making the team for the 1940 Olympic Games with top three finishes at the Nationals. In 1941 she would win the Silver Belt races at Sugar Bowl in California with son Dick cheering her on--from inside of her. She went on to become a noteworthy photojournalist shooting assignments for *Life, Look, Time, Sports Illustrated*, and *National Geographic*. Because of her stature as a photojournalist, she was invited to be part of a group of leading women in various fields who went to China and the Soviet Union before there was any official travel to those countries.

Brother **Jack Durrance '39** was also a member of the Dartmouth ski team and he founded the Dartmouth Mountaineering Club. He is more widely known for being the first American climber of international stature, much as Dick is credited with being the first American skier of international stature. Jack is known for many first ascents in the Tetons, including the North Face of the Grand, an attempt at K2 in 1939, and the rescue of a foolhardy stunt man from the Devil's Tower in Wyoming. Speaking of foolhardy, Jack was actually the first person to attempt to schuss the Headwall at Tuckerman Ravine. He did it on purpose the year

before Dick and Toni Matt did it inadvertently during the Inferno. Jack had cleared everybody out of the way and schussed the Headwall well until he hit some sticky snow on the knoll just before "Howard Johnson's" cabin, and went ass over teakettle spraining both ankles badly.

As a doctor he became a specialist in cardio-pulmonary diseases, perhaps as a result of his experiences at high altitudes while climbing. He also was the doctor who organized the first lung transplant. He became a beloved teacher at the University of Colorado School of Medicine and an expert reader of X-rays, which he continued to do well into his eighties. On the side, he became a preeminent breeder of irises with seventy new varieties to his name and he co-founded the Denver Botanical Gardens.

Dick and Dave (right) receiving an award to the Durrance family at CarniVAIL - 2009. (Holmes, 2009).

Sister Elizabeth was a ski racer in the late thirties and early forties who most often finished among the top ten women in national races. She was also the winner of the second slalom race ever held for women at the Dartmouth Winter Carnival in 1937. Her second husband was **Steve Bradley '39**, her brother's classmate at Dartmouth, a man of many skiing legends himself, and her former Dartmouth date in her younger years.

Dick Durrance, II '65 followed in his father's footsteps at Dartmouth as captain of the ski team and National 4-way runner-up before picking up a camera and becoming a lifelong, globe trotting photographer. Between his junior and senior years at Dartmouth, Dick II and several classmates created an opportunity to do a story about canoeing down the Danube River. So his first published photographs were the cover of *National Geographic* followed by sixteen more pictures inside. Right after college, he did articles for *Ski* and *Skiing Magazine* on skiing the High Tatra Mountains in Czechoslovakia and an abstract piece on the feel of ski racing. After a tour in Viet Nam as a combat photographer for the Army, *National Geographic* asked him to join their photographic staff. In his seven years there, he created the images for nine articles and three books and was honored as the 1971 White House News Photographers Association Photographer of the Year. His portfolio now includes corporate and advertising photography (for which he was named the 1989 American Society of Media Photographers Advertising Photographer of the Year), panorama images of the National Parks, golf course photographs, and two books, *Golfers* and *The PGA Tour: A Look Behind the Scenes*. **Dewitt Jones '65**, a classmate at Dartmouth, inspired Dick II to take up motivational speaking and he now travels from coast to coast speaking to association and corporate groups.

Son Dave stayed closer to the skiing. He raced for twenty years and coached for another fifteen. He competed at the junior, collegiate, national, World Cup, and professional levels, participating in two Alpine and one Nordic Junior Nationals. He had top ten finishes in both Alpine and Nordic. He skied for the University of Denver as their last 4-way skier and was captain his junior and senior years. He had top-ten finishes in Slalom and Cross-Country and was second and third in the Skimeister at the NCAA's. He had two more top tens at the US Nationals in Slalom and finally won a National Championship in Slalom at the Masters Nationals in 1974.

Dave coached at ski racing camps while he was racing professionally and then at Alyeska Resort in Alaska for three years. After that, he joined **Jim Page '63** at the Dartmouth Ski Team (1975-1978) as the Men's Alpine Coach and helped win the NCAA Championship in 1976. At the US Ski Team, he worked with the men's team at the World Cup, Europa Cup, and Development levels. In the early days of the Development effort, the ski team wanted to bring kids from around the country together in order to generate some sense of camaraderie and friendly competition. This could create considerable nervousness among the kids' home coaches who didn't want national coaches telling the kids something that was in conflict with what they were saying. Dave and some of the other coaches developed a minimally verbal curriculum of tasks that would let the national coaches evaluate the kids skiing without creating a conflict with the home coaches.

That curriculum would prove to be useful as Dave moved from the US Ski Team to Special Olympics in Washington, D.C., as the first full-time Director of Winter Sports. There he was tasked with developing a curriculum that non-ski teaching professionals could use to teach mentally retarded athletes to ski. Again he went to a non-verbal set of maneuvers that could be learned in a gym and then reapplied once on snow. With the curriculum in hand he could go to the rest of the ski industry (PSIA, NSAA, and SIA) to establish institutional relationships that would outlive any particular Director. **Walter Malmquist '76** would later hold the same position.

Finally it was time for him to return to Aspen and to ski retailing, which he had been introduced to when he was twelve. In 2001 he started his own store, Durrance Sports, and began to put in place innovations in merchandising and consumer ski testing that had long been on his mind. In the shop's third year, *Ski Magazine* recognized it as one of the top shops in North America with the Gold Medal designation.

Grandson Jesse took from both Dick I and brother Jack. He was a top-three finisher in his age class at Junior Olympics and went on to climb and to ski rarely-attempted mountains, including Denali in Alaska, 20,00-ft peaks in South America, and Pyramid Peak and the Maroon Bells near Aspen. Grandson Peter, who inherited Dick's gifts for skiing, now skis faster backwards than his dad can ski forwards.

The Durrance family, led by Dick Durrance, has had a substantial impact on the development of skiing.

And through Jack Durrance, the family has also had a substantial impact on mountaineering. Now the early work by these two Dartmouth pioneers has evolved over three generations, and long may it continue into the future.

The Hannahs — One of Dartmouth's First Skiing Families
By Roger Urban '65

Selden ("Sel") James Hannah '35 skied in all four events (downhill, slalom, cross-country and jumping) all four years at Dartmouth and was captain of the ski team during his senior year. He and his wife, Pauline, were lifetime skiers who started one of Dartmouth's great skiing families.

Growing up in Berlin, New Hampshire, amid Scandinavians who had come to work in the Brown Paper Company mill, Sel was surrounded by skiers. In Berlin, where jumping was an integral part of skiing, much of the sport included the actual construction of jumps. Berlin was also home to the Norske Ski Club, considered the nation's first, having been organized in the 1870s. As he grew up, Sel embraced this hometown sport and became a great jumper.

The Hannah's were Canadians by nationality and Scandinavians by birth. During his childhood, Sel remembers that "skiing was a completely different sport. The equipment we had was primitive." His only skis were a pair of jumpers that doubled for everything because "no one knew anything different." When he arrived at Dartmouth, he won his first cross-country race on those heavy jumping skis.

Sel was virtually unbeatable in the Alpine events, both in college and afterwards. Selected to represent the U.S. in the 1940 Olympics along with eight other Dartmouth skiers, his chance to compete was cancelled by World War II. Some of Sel's post-Dartmouth skiing achievements include:

1940 – US Nordic FIS Team

1941 – Eastern Downhill Champion

1942 – Ski instructor of paratroopers at Alta, Utah

1953 – First US Senior National Champion in Slalom and Alpine Combined

1968 – Inducted into the US National Ski and Snowboard Hall of Fame

A founder of Sno-Engineering Company in 1958, Sel Hannah served as its President and Chief Trail Designer until 1970. Out of 500 alpine ski areas in the United States, he had a hand in the design of about 250. Sno-Engineering not only designed ski areas but provided ski area operators with complete marketing support. Sel recalled that "We'd tell them not only how many tickets they'd be able to sell in an area, but what kind of tickets they were going to sell and what they'd have to offer."

Joan Hannah, the eldest of Sel's four children, was a US Olympic Team skier in 1960 and 1964. In 1962 at the world FIS championships in Chamonix, France, Joan won two Bronze medals. In total, she won six US National Giant Slalom titles. Joan Hannah was inducted into the US National Ski and Snowboard Hall of Fame in 1978, ten years after her father.

Frank Lee Hannah '64 and earned an advanced degree in Mathematics from Dartmouth in 1968. Frank skied all four events his freshman year at Dartmouth, but he concentrated on cross-country and jumping during his three years on the varsity ski team. For 36 years, he taught Mathematics at Philips Andover Academy. For more than a decade he coached the Andover

Selden Lee ("Sel") Hannah '65, Th '66 was a four-year member of the ski team. He also specialized in jumping and cross-country. For more than 20 years Sel was a ski lift

Sel Hannah '35 set the pace in ski area design.

engineer and inspector for Sno-Engineering. Today, Sel is still a sought-after consultant to the New England ski industry.

Lucy Hannah, the second daughter of Sel '35, was an avid recreational skier when she met a Swiss ski instructor working in Franconia, NH. She married that instructor, Paul Pfosi, and they lived in Malix, Switzerland, for their first two years together. Their daughter, Eva was born there. Lucy and Paul moved to Waterville Valley, Maine, in 1965, where Paul became the area's first ski school Director.

Eva Pfosi '88 was a three-year varsity skier for Dartmouth and team Captain in 1987. She remembers that "Dartmouth was an amazing experience for me. Being there actually reignited my love of the sport. I think a big part of it was skiing at a place that supported an NCAA team plus a development team – you don't find that anywhere else. We trained with them, shared the wax room, shared their energy and the things they were so enthusiastic about. I loved the camaraderie. It made me feel like I was part of a real team, part of something special."

In 1987, Eva completed one of the few undefeated slalom seasons ever in collegiate racing. Her smallest margin of victory was a remarkable 1.2 seconds. That year she won the NCAA Slalom Championship by the staggering margin of 2.02 seconds. **Eve Wood '34**, author of *The History of Dartmouth Skiway* and long-time veteran of the international ski racing scene said, "Nobody can win an international slalom championship by that much. This is phenomenal."

In 1988 Eva started four years of skiing on the US Pro Tour. In 1992 she married David Merriam, the current Director of the Ski and Snowsports School in Stowe, VT. Today their 15-year-old daughter Lucy is now a ski racer at the Mount Mansfield Ski Club, where Eva helps with the coaching. "That energy I felt at Dartmouth is still with me," Eva says. "Enthusiasm is something I feel that I bring to the club my daughter is in." Eva still regularly competes in local slalom races at Stowe. Records from the *Stowe Reporter* show that she consistently beats most of the women and many of the men in these races. This is another way that **Eva Pfosi Merriam '88**, granddaughter of Sel Hannah '35, keeps the Dartmouth skiing tradition alive in the North Country.

The Kendalls — "The First Family of Maine Skiing"
By Stephen L. Waterhouse with Mary Kendall Brown ' 78

The First Generation
Dick Kendall '45 and his wife Mary contributed eight children to Maine skiing with four of them becoming national champions. Despite the Kendall family having been in Maine for many generations, skiing is a recent family trait. Dick Kendall learned to ski at Dartmouth, like so many others, and credits his friend **William Eppley '44** with inspiring him. The family has long ties to shipbuilding in Maine and is of English heritage, having an early member who may have originally come over to cut timber for the ship masts of England's King George III…even before Dartmouth was chartered in 1769. Certainly there are "DAR" women on both sides of the family so they have been involved in the U.S. for a long time.

Dick served as President of the Auburn Ski Association, President of the Maine Alpine Racing Association, and as a founding investor/member of the first Board of Directors that helped get Saddleback Mountain started. The family was granted lifetime ski passes there as a result. As a ski instructor, Dick was the first director of the Lost Valley Ski School, established the Junior Racing Program, and coached winning teams. He served as a frequent race official, including the Nordic events at the 1980 and 2002 Winter Olympics. He was a timing official at numerous Junior, Senior and Collegiate National Championships.

Dick's wife Mary was just as active, working as a ski instructor at Lost Valley, creating the children's ski instruction program for the Auburn Recreation Department, and as a delegate to the Conference on Promotion of the Development Team for the US Olympic Ski Team. Like her husband, she was a race official at Junior, Senior, and Collegiate National Championships and an official for Nordic events at the 1980 and 2002 Olympics. The long involvement of Dick and Mary in Maine skiing earned them both membership in the Maine Ski Hall of Fame, a very unusual double act.

But this is only the beginning of the family's skiing leadership. Mary Kendall's brother is **Bill Briggs '54**. Dick credits himself with taking Bill and his sister on their first ski trip. If accurate, Dick can take partial credit for Bill's initiating modern extreme skiing, starting the American School Ski Instruction techniques, developing into a legendary ski song singer and becoming one of Dartmouth's most recent additions to the National Ski Hall of Fame.

And there is much more to the story as the Kendalls also taught their own children to ski, and ski well as noted below. All of the children stayed involved in skiing well beyond their competitive days. Each of the ten family members held at least two or more positions as ski racing coach, ski instructor, ski school director, Olympic timing official, president of a local ski association, president of a state ski organization, officer of a national ski association, certified jumping judge, certified cross-country instructor or similar activities. Every child was selected to Maine teams that competed in New England competition and seven skied in both individual national championships and team national championships. As a group, they won 32 team championships and 33 state, New England and US National individual ski awards. The Kendalls are the only Maine family to have had four of its members coach teams in the National Championships, two of which actually won those championships. They have been selected as Skimeisters at events from high school to college; and two (Kim and John) were NCAA Skimeisters while two were individual national champions (Mary and Bob)

For the Olympics, four members tried for the 1972 team. Bob Kendall competed with the 1972 Nordic Combined Team at Sapporo. Four members of the family (including the parents) were officials at the 1980 Winter Olympic Games, and five more acted in an official capacity at the 2002 Olympics.

The Second Generation

All six boys competed on teams that won both Maine and New England ski championships. During their competitive years, Edward Little High School won seven successive state championships and five New England championships. All six boys competed in Junior Olympic ski nationals.

William K. Kendall '68 — Received the Donald J. Cook Award (Excellence in 4- event skiing at Dartmouth; 1968) 3rd in the Junior National Nordic combined championships (1964); Captain, Freshman Ski Team (1964-65); Nordic Combined Champion at Dartmouth's Winter Carnival (1968); Runner-Up US National Biathlon Championship (1970); 1969-71, US Biathlon Team member (1969-71); Participant, World Games in Sweden (1970).

Bob Kendall — Sr. National Nordic Combined champion (1971); 2nd in Junior National Nordic Combined championship (1965); last man classified as US Senior "A" racer in all ski disciplines (1968); Skied Nordic Combined, 1972 Sapporo Olympics; Coached at University of Colorado, Boulder and had National Champions (1973); (attended the University of Colorado, Boulder, 1965-69).

John Kendall — First in 7 of 8 slalom meets including state championships and 2nd in NE Championships (1967); Maine and New England Skimeister Champion (1966, 1967); Member of both the Eastern Alpine and Nordic ski teams (1966, 1967); Participant, US National Ski Jumping Championships (1968); Set hill record at Eastern U.S. jumping meet at Rumford, ME (1968); Art Bennett Trophy Award, Dartmouth College Winter Carnival (1970, 1971); Eastern Collegiate and National NCAA Skimeister award (1970, 1971); (Attended the University of New Hampshire, 1967-1971)

Thomas M. Kendall '72 — Owns, developed, and operates BART Race timing service which is based on computer software in BASIC (developed at Dartmouth College) to time and score all ski events computer; BART times many ski competitions for multiple High School, College, NCAA and National Ski championships; Parents serve frequently as his co-workers when they are available and needed New England High School Skimeister (1968); Eastern Jr. National Alpine Ski Team (1968); Donald Cooke Award (Excellence in 4 event skiing at Dartmouth; 1969); Dartmouth Ski team (1969-72); Eastern Nordic Program Director (1972-75); Former president of the Auburn Ski Association; Developed computer software to manage annual Auburn Ski Swap fund raiser; Cross-Country Assistant Chief of Protocol (1980 Olympics, under Al Merrill); Chief of Timing (2001 Biathlon World Cup), Cross Country-Nordic Combined-Biathlon (2002 Winter Olympics), and the North American Biathlon Championships (2005).

Kim Kendall — Won Freshman Giant Slalom (First college race, Dartmouth, 1970); Won the Genesee Cup at Bristol Mountain, NY (1970); 3rd in the NCAA Skimeister (1971); Finished each college GS in top 10 for 3 years; Art Bennett Trophy as Skimeister (1973); NCAA Skimeister as he won all but one Skimeister title (1972, 1973); Coached University of Colorado Nordic team to 4 consecutive NCAA championships (1974-1977). (Attended University of New Hampshire, 1969-1973).

Steve Kendall — Won 10 individual ski events at 4 state championships (more than his 5 brothers combined; 1966-71); 2nd in U.S. National Junior Biathlon Championship (1969); Won cross-country and selected best 4 event skier at New England Championships (1971); Best 4-event skier at Collegiate National Championships (1975); Nordic ski coach at U. of Maine - Orono (1976); Coach of University of Utah Nordic teams who competed for National championships (Men and Women; 1976-77); Coached Women's Nordic team to NCAA Championship (University of Utah, 1977). (Attended University of New Hampshire, 1971-1975).

The next two ladies (as was their mom before them) were voted "Best Female Athlete" at their high schools. Both daughters competed on their high school ski teams that won six successive state championships.

Anne Kendall — Highest scorer overall for Maine High School Championship ski teams (1971-72); Coach of Auburn, ME, middle school girls and boys ski team (1993-96); President of Auburn Ski Association (1996-98); (Attended Nursing School in Lewiston, ME, 1972-1974).

Mary Kendall Brown '78 — Eastern Ski Association slalom champion (1967); Jaycee State champion for slalom and giant slalom combined (1969); Jaycee Junior National Slalom Champion and 3rd in Giant Slalom at Iron Mountain, MI (1969); Named to the All-East first team for intercollegiate skiing (1976); Eastern AIAW intercollegiate slalom champion (1977); Awarded Dartmouth Women's Most Consistent Skier Award (1977); Captain of Dartmouth Women's Alpine team (1977-78); Co-Captain of the first team to win the women's AIAW Skiing National Championships (1977); Coach of Div. I Alpine ski team at Bates College (1980-84).

The Third Generation

Jessica M. Kendall — Daughter of John Kendall; Macomber Award as the Best Female Junior Alpine Racer in New Hampshire (1999); Waterville Valley Academy Headmasters Award (2000); five-time Junior Olympic Alpine competitor, (5th in the 1999 Jr. Olympic Downhill Lake Placid, NY); Junior Olympic Downhill Champion (2000) Sugarloaf, Maine; Rand Stowell Downhill Champion, Sugarloaf, Maine (2000); participant in National Alpine Championship (speed events only; 2000), Jackson Hole, WY, World Cup Pre-Olympic Downhill Championships Snow Basin, Utah (30th; 2001); attended Waterville Valley Academy, (along with her brother Jason, from 1996-2000.

Lara Kendall '98 — Tom Kendall's daughter, she skied for the Dartmouth Nordic team under coach Cami Thompson. Lara continues to ski in Park City, Utah, and also does guiding, instructing, and bike racing.

The Kendall family is a large family that has shown exceptional skills in ski racing. The family has achieved greater race results than any other we are aware of and continues to send members to Dartmouth College. We expect to hear more of the passionate skiers in the Kendall family in the future.

The McLane Family — Leaders in Many Venues
By Stephen L. Waterhouse

From Scotland to New Hampshire to the business, legal and political worlds to the 10th Mountain Division to skiing around the world, the extended McLane family has produced many leaders and has had at

Legendary Fred Harris '11 and Malcom McLane '46 discuss skiing.

least a 100-plus-year relationship with Dartmouth College. And it continues to do so. The McLane-Dartmouth connection started with John McLane of Lennoxtown, Scotland, who moved to the U.S. in the mid 19th Century and developed a furniture business. He entered politics, became President of the New Hampshire Senate, and then Governor of the state (1905-07). In this role he was automatically an ex-officio Trustee of Dartmouth as all New Hampshire governors have been since Governor Wentworth assisted Eleazar Wheelock in securing the College's charter in 1769. Governor McLane was awarded an honorary degree in 1905.

His son, **John R. McLane '07**, was the family's first

Dartmouth graduate. He attended Oxford University as a Rhodes Scholar and then went to Harvard Law School, becoming a prominent lawyer, and in 1926 a Dartmouth Trustee. Eventually, he became Chairman of the Dartmouth Board of Trustees and was prominent in the development of the Dartmouth Skiway. His wife Elisabeth had two Dartmouth grandfathers in the **Class of 1841, Jesse Bancroft and Bartholemew Wood**. His sister Hazel married **John Clark '08**. Judge McLane's connection to skiing began in 1925 when he switched from snowshoes to skis through the efforts of his young law associate, and one of Dartmouth's first great skiing stars, **John Carleton '22**.

The list of family members who have impacted Dartmouth or skiing is a long one. Over 25 members of the greater family have played a role in a long Dartmouth family history that is still evolving. It is fascinating to also see the frequency of interconnections with other individuals who are important to the history of skiing at Dartmouth and elsewhere.

John R. McLane, Jr. '38, Judge McLane's son, was a Chairman of the Winter Carnival Committee.

Charles McLane '41, Judge McLane's other son, was Captain of the Dartmouth Ski Team and a downhill skier known for his straight line and power. Charles was the first recruit of the 10th Mountain Division, and later became one of its officers. He returned to Dartmouth to teach Government, and remained an active skier all his life.

John McLane Clark '32, Judge McLane's brother-in-law **John Clark '08**'s son, was a senior fellow, journalist and developer of President Dickey's Great Issues course.

Peter McLane '37, Judge McLane's nephew, was a founder of the Carcajou Ski Club, named for the fastest, most cunning, and wildest animal in the Northern Woods, to allow more students to enter ski racing competitions. Peter's son, **P. Andrews ("Andy") McLane '69 Tu '73**, was a Dartmouth ski patroller and serves on the boards of the US Ski and Snowboard Team Foundation and the Appalachian Mountain Club.

Patty McLane, Peter McLane's sister, was the first winner of the first ladies race at a Dartmouth Winter Carnival in 1936. Patty married Peter's classmate **William Rotch '37** who was a ski team member and leader in the DOC. This ladies race was to become a "must do" event each ski season for the leading women skiers of the East, and included several participants from the greater interconnected family of the Mclanes, Bradleys and Durrances, including Blanche McLane (wife of John McLane '38), Lilla McLane Bradley (Judge McLane's daughter and wife of David Bradley '38), and Elizabeth Durrance Bradley (2nd wife of **Steve Bradley '39**). Elizabeth Durrance Bradley won the 3rd Dartmouth Women's Ski Race in 1938. Patty and Bill Rotch's son, Peter, was a D'63.

David Bradley '38 was involved as a consultant in the formation of the 10th Mountain Division, an authority on ski jump-

Malcolm and Susan McLane at the 1955 Suicide Six Races.

Annie McLane Kuster '77 in her racing days.

The McLane Lodge at the base of the Dartmouth Skiway.

ing, a designer of many of the ski jumps in Northern New England, a member of war-cancelled 1940 Olympic team and a Professor at the Tuck School (who once tried to teach this author how to write!). **Darby McLane Bradley '67**, son of Lilla and David, was an active skier and DOC member.

Malcolm McLane '46, Judge McLane's son, brother to Lilla, Charles and John, served in the Air Force as a bomber pilot and was shot down in the Battle of the Bulge. He was a prisoner of war and eventually returned to Dartmouth to become a four-event skier and Captain of the Dartmouth Ski team. According to legend, he was particularly inept at waxing skis and was used by Coach Prager to demonstrate effective wax techniques. Like his father, Judge McLane, he also became a Rhodes Scholar and New Hampshire lawyer. Malcolm married another exceptional skier, Susan Neidlinger, who was a daughter of Dartmouth's Dean of students and sports legend, **Lloyd Neidlinger '23**. Lloyd was a Walter Camp Football All American choice and exceptional ice hockey player. Malcolm was a founder of Wildcat Mountain Ski Area in Pinkham Notch, NH, and with **Amos "Bud" Little '39** served as the Ski Representative to the US Olympic Committee. Bud's son, **Jim Little '65** came to Hanover from Helena, Montana and skied on the Dartmouth Ski Team. Malcolm founded Wildcat with **Brooks Dodge '51**, Mac Beal and George Macomber. The McLanes and Macombers shared a ski house in Jackson for 43 years, hosting generations of Dartmouth skiers at "Club Max." All three Macombers skied for the Dartmouth, including **John Macomber '78**, Captain in 1978, All American 1974 and '78, Dartmouth Carnival combined and GS winner in 1974 and '78, US Ski Team 1974-76, Jr. National GS champion 1974; **Gay Macomber Bird '81**, Captain in 1981; and **Jory Macomber '85**, Captain 1985, All American 1983, '84 and '85, Dartmouth Carnival Combined winner 1984 and '85. John's son, **Ian Macomber 2013** is the newest member of the family to join the Dartmouth team. The "Macomber Family Ski Team Room" accommodates the team in the McLane Family Ski Lodge at the Dartmouth Skiway.

President Dickey '29 (left) and Judge McLane '07 (a Trustee for some 30 years) at the dedication of the Dartmouth Skiway (1957).

Susan and her sister **Sally Neidlinger** were the most successful junior ski racers in NH winning every race 1-2. They were the first Eastern and then National Women's Champions, trying out for the 1948 US Ski Team at age 16 in Sun Valley. Sally skied for the US Ski Team and was a member of the 1952 Oslo Olympics team. Sally's youngest son, **William Hudson '88**, skied on the US team and in the 1988 Calgary Olympics. Mother and son were the first such combination to ski for the US Olympic Team. Bill Hudson is the head of the Sugar Bowl Ski Academy. Susan and Sally's sister, **Mary Neidlinger**, married **Robert Kilmarx '50**, another man destined to become a Dartmouth Trustee. Their son **Peter Kilmarx '83** was an active DOC skier in his college days.

Susan and **Malcolm McLane** have 5 children and 11 grandchildren. They are all skiers. **Ann McLane Kuster '78** raced for the Dartmouth Ski team, and also competed in Master's ski races after college. She is a lawyer in Concord with the firm headed up by **Thomas Rath '68**, and is currently running for a US Congressional seat. She and her husband Brad have two sons, **Travis Kuster '14** and **Zachary Kuster '11,** who race for Dartmouth today. Travis skied in the 2009 US Nationals at the Alyeska Ski area in Alaska. He plans to join Zach and Ian on the Dartmouth team next year.

Debbie McLane Carter, Ann Kuster's sister, skied for Harvard and married her coach Peter. They have three daughters, Ashley, **Maile Carter '06,** and Laurel who was on the US Ski team in 2006-08. Ann's brother Alan and his wife Alice have a daughter **Laura Kuster** who is a National Junior Olympic Champion in ski jumping and Nordic combined. She is one of the few highly successful female jumpers, sometimes competing in meets with her third cousin **Micah McLane**.

The recently completed McLane Family Lodge at the Dartmouth Skiway is a fitting memorialization of a lineage that has been so involved in Dartmouth's administrative, academic, and skiing history. Andy McLane led the charge to make this facility a reality, recognizing an amazing continuity with the participation of his great-uncle, Judge John McLane, at the dedication of the Dartmouth Skiway in 1957 and the entire skiing McLane clan at the dedication of the McLane Family Lodge in 1991.

Notes

1. Lund, Morten, unpublished monograph. 2. National Ski Hall of Fame citation. 3. Summarized from David Hooke, Reaching That Peak, 75 years of the Dartmouth Outing Club, Dartmouth College, 1987, see index. 4. Allen, E. John N., From Skisport to Skiing, University of Massachusetts (Amherst) Press, 1993, p. 45. 5. Hooke, David, Reaching That Peak, 75 years of the Dartmouth Outing Club, Dartmouth College, 1987 p. 3-4. 6. The Dartmouth, Hanover, New Hampshire, December 7, 1909. 7. Hooke, p. 5-7 . 8. Hooke, p. 13, 18. 9. R. S. Monahan, Dartmouth Alumni Magazine, quoted in Hooke, p. 19-20. 10. Harris's Ski Hall of Fame citation . 11. Dartmouth Co-op.com, dartmouthcoop.com/history.html. 12. Ibid. 13. Oral history, Piane, John, Jr. '50, Tu'52, January 10, 2009 and April 12, 2009. 14. Ibid. 15. Ibid. 16. Ibid. 17. "The Cornell Daily Sun" ad by Treman, King & Co., January 18, 1938. 18. Ibid. 19. "Downhill Pioneer," Georgia Croft, Valley News, 8 Dec, 1987. 20. Letter, Carl E. Shumway to McCrillis, 7 Aug 1933, NESM L1999.14.3a. "John W. McCrillis, 1919", Dartmouth College Alumni File, Rauner Special Collections John W. McCrillis Collection, papers and correspondence 1931-1937, New England Ski Museum (NESM). 21. http://www.iviesinathens.com/olympic/games.aspx?ID=201. 22. Bradley, David, interviewed by Dave Rowan, 4/18/2000. 23. Lund, Morten, unpublished monograph, [details?]. 24. Lund, "41A". 25. Lund, "B88 w 1922". 26. Allen, E. John B., From Skisport to Skiing, University of Massachusetts Press, Amherst, Mass, 1993, p. 79. 27. Lund, "53 A". 28. Lund, "54 A". 29. Lund. 30. Hooke, David, Reaching That Peak, 75 years of the Dartmouth Outing Club, Dartmouth College, 1987 p. 228. 31. Lund. 32. Hooke, p 230. 33. Ski Hall of Fame, Proctor citation 34. Hooke, p. 231. 35. Lund, 36. Ski Hall of Fame citation. 37. Allen, P. 155. 38. Lund,. 39. Lund, quoting. 40. Lund, quoting 33A Classic Backcountry Skiing by David Goodman. 41. Lund quoting 36A from the 1934 (first issue) of the U.S. Eastern Ski Annual. 42. Hooke, p 243. 43. Lund, "16A" and "29A" Shawn Gray thesis, Ski Hall of Fame citation. 44. Lund,. 45. Lund,. 46. Lund, "b19, B36A, B45, B57". 47. Lund, "B78" Ski Bulletin B11", Hooke p 254. 48.0 Lund, "B61, B61a". 49. Ski Hall of Fame citation, Lund "9a". 50. Bradley, David, "Dan Hatch," American Ski Annual, 1937-38. 51. "List or Manifest of Alien Passengers For the United States Immigration Officer at Port of Arrival, New York," NARA microfilm T715: 5886, list no. 38, ship Europa, line 8, image online at www.Ancestry.com, "New York Passenger Lists, 1820-1957." 52. Dick Durrance and John Jerome, The Man on the Medal (Durrance Enterprises: Aspen, CO, 1995), 34-5. 53. Vorlage was emphasized often in his own book, Walter Prager, Skiing (New York: A. S. Barnes and Company, 1939), 4, 24, etc. 54. David O. Hooke, Reaching That Peak – 75 Years of the Dartmouth Outing Club (Canaan, NH: Phoenix Publishing, 1987), 250. 55. See, for example, his intricate X-C waxing chart in Skiing (note 3), 56-7. 56. From the writer's personal contemporary notes. 57. Reaching That Peak (note 4), 249. 58. John Caldwell interview 3/26/2009. 59. Caldwell interview 3/26/2009. 60. Caldwell interview 3/26/2009. 61. John Fry, "The Story of Modern Skiing" (Lebanon, New Hampshire: University Press of New England, 2006) p 198. 62. Ibid. p 198. 63. Caldwell interview 3/26/2009. 64. Hornbein, Everest: The West Ridge, Mountaineers Books, 1998. 65. Fred Jones, telephone interview with T. Washing, March 24, 2009. 66. Time Magazine, December 25, 1972, "Skiing: The New Lure of a Supersport.". 67. Oral History, Diane Boyer '78, May 5, 2009. 68. Oral History, Diane Boyer '78, May 5, 2009. 69. http://www.skealimited.com/about.html. 70. Oral History, Diane Boyer '78, May 5, 2009. 71. Peak bagger: Climber tackles Alaska's unnamed peaks by Mike Campbell, Anchorage Daily News, December 13, 2008. 72. Television interview, August 2007, KTUU-TV, Channel 2, Anchorage, Alaska. 73. Telephone interview with Byrne by Waterhouse , August 5, 2009. 74. Girdwood Community Presentation, February 14, 2009. 75. From a USST e-mail summary by Tom Kelly, tkelly@ussa.org, March 29, 2009. 76. Ibid. 77. U.S. National Ski Hall of Fame and Museum. www.skihall.com/Honored Member. 78. Butts, Porter, "The Wisconsin Hoofers, An Early History", an oral history included in the publication The Wisconsin Union—The First 75 Years.79. Email from Ric Bradley, September 19, 2009. 80. Email from Ric Bradley, October 21, 2008. 81. Margalit Fox, New York Times Obituary, January 30, 2008. 82. Email from Ric Bradley, June 6, 2009. 83. "The Bradley Bunch . . . How Skiing Kids Grow Up Good.", Skiing Heritage Magazine, Fall 1995.

DARTMOUTH STUDENT WINTER ACTIVITIES

The Dartmouth Skiway is the center of local skiing activities and highly competitive racing as it has been for over 50 years. The new McLane Lodge (see P. 341), snow making systems and better lifts have added to the quality of the operation.

There may be fewer Ice Sculptures around the Dartmouth campus for Winter Carnival, but they are still created.

Hockey Fever

Once winter meant pickup games on frozen ponds.
Now parents and children chase dreams and ice time
while driving hundreds of miles to tourneys.

BY JIM COLLINS | PHOTOGRAPHS BY JULIE BIDWELL

I like almost everything about pond hockey: the potluck quality of the players (young and old, male and female), the 12-on-12 games that last all afternoon, the universally acknowledged rules (goals marked by winter boots a hockey-stick length apart) and rituals (teams sorted by sticks gathered and tossed into two random piles, to be collected by their owners, now teammates). I like the serendipity of finding a game in prog-

Hockey games still take place on Occom Pond as they have for a 100 years.

The Ski Team Office in Robinson Hall is still a room full of trophies from the continuing success of the Dartmouth ski team.
(Hart, 2009)

CHAPTER XV

DARTMOUTH SKIING TODAY

By Stephen Waterhouse

With Chelsea Little '09, Cami Thompson, Pam Crisafulli Hommeyer '88, Katie Fahey '06 and Henry Hof 3rd '58

It would be easy to make the judgment that the Dartmouth impact on the development of skiing has been waning in recent years. So much has already been done it may seem there is little room for anything except more of the same However, few are aware of the large numbers of Dartmouth alumni now involved, and fewer still recognize the reverse is true as the legends of Dartmouth skiing continue to develop. In this chapter, we will highlight both a few of the contemporary contributions mentioned in earlier chapters and provide details on several subjects not previously discussed.

As a starting point, the Dartmouth Outing Club is still an important component of the education process of Dartmouth College. It may not still be so totally focused on skiing as it was when Fred Harris started it, but the DOC is still very much involved as the administrative home of the Dartmouth ski team (perhaps the only major college ski program to be managed outside its athletic department, just as it has been since its start in 1921). The DOC also manages the Dartmouth Skiway; Mount Moosilauke, and the other huge tracts of wilderness property owned by Dartmouth, as well as ski instruction, the ski patrol, Winter Carnival and other winter-related activities. Today the DOC also plays a major role in many other outdoor activities on the Dartmouth campus or in the various wilderness areas of New Hampshire and elsewhere, among them trail and cabin maintenance, rock climbing instruction, and overnight hiking trips.

Perhaps the DOC's biggest single non-skiing function is to manage the annual four-day Freshman Trip experience by first-year students before they begin classes at Dartmouth. This unique adventure is unmatched by orientation programs for new students of any other institution and provides a wonderful initial exposure to Dartmouth's outdoor opportunities and serves as a bonding experience that promotes class unity. The new Director of Outdoor Programs, **Dan Nelson '75**, carries on the tradition of leadership by someone with a personal fondness for enjoying the outdoor experience and skiing. Dan is one who might just as likely be skiing down the side of Mt. Moosilauke in the winter, like Fred Harris and his early DOC mates loved to do, as spending time in an administrative role at his Hanover office.

The Dartmouth Winter Carnival still takes place in Hanover each year as the leading such event in the eastern college ski season. New Winter Carnival posters are still created and sold, the theme statue is still constructed out of snow each year in the center of the campus, and parties are still held at many venues around campus. That is not to say there are not changes from earlier decades. The arrival of women students in 1972 has had its impact on aspects of this weekend just as it has had with many other activities on the Dartmouth campus. Many of the features that might have been important in 1939 when F. Scott Fitzgerald was asked to create a script for the infamous *Winter Carnival* movie are no longer present. Great groups of young men do not gather at the train station to meet their dates and the frequent lack of sufficient snow has curtailed the enthusiasm for building the more elaborate fraternity and dormitory snow sculptures of the past.

Another thing that remains consistent is that the Dartmouth ski team is still the one to beat, just as it has been at eastern winter carnivals since the beginning in 1911. And Dartmouth skiers are regularly placing well in all the other annual college ski racing events. In fact, the recent record has been excellent as the ski team has won its Winter Carnival races in 2007, 2008 and 2009; the EISA Championships in 2007 and 2009; and in an exciting finish, the NCAA Men's and Women's Ski Championships in 2007. In the recent 2006 Torino Olympics, the greater Dartmouth family contributed more participating athletes, coaches and staff than any other institution.

The competitive drive of Dartmouth skiers continues long after college as seen by the record in the Olympics, National Championships, Masters races, and all the specialty racing techniques from telemarking to ski mountaineering to Pro-Am and local club races of all types. In the recent decade, these racing programs have involved Dartmouth alumni of all ages from **Sandy Treat '46** to **Phil Livingston '58** to **Steve Waterhouse '65, Tu '67** to **Alan Moats '70** to **Lisa Densmore '83** to **Liz McIntyre '87** to **Scott Macartney '01** to **Nina Kemppel '92, Tu '05**. All seek the joy of one more competition as much as the thrill of one more victory.

Alumni are still active in multiple ski clubs around the U.S. Some of these clubs have been around for decades, as we have covered in an earlier chapter. Some are relatively new, as in locations like Vail with its famous Game Creek Club, set up some ten years ago as the model of the new mountain clubs, and the recently formed Vail Valley Ski Club. Most of these new clubs are oriented toward year-round social activities and not just skiing. But occasionally you will find the really serious ski club formed by really serious skiers; a prime example is The Streeter Ski Group of Vail, named after Middlebury Olympian Les Streeter. Most of these clubs are heavily populated by Dartmouth-connected folks—just like the ones that were started decades ago.

As we have outlined in many prior chapters, the ski bug is not lost on Dartmouth alumni as a reason to get together for some skiing and camaraderie once they leave the encouraging slopes around Hanover. For many decades, a number of alumni groups have gathered for ski weekends in some form since the skiers of Dartmouth first got together around the turn of the 19th century. Members of many graduated classes still organize skiing odysseys to different ski areas in the U.S. and even to other parts of the world over the course of several years.

In recent years, Dartmouth alumni have also gathered in larger, multi-class groups to enjoy ski events and other activities reminiscent of winter carnivals on the Dartmouth campus; some of these are considerably more varied in scope than simple ski weekends. Several hundred alumni from the undergraduate college and each of the three graduate schools now join together for fun, skiing, and intellectual discussion at the annual Dartmouth/Tuck Winter CarniVAIL in Vail, Colorado. Reflecting a continuing enthusiasm for skiing, this event is now the college's largest annual alumni gathering outside Hanover. It is organized by the local Vail Dartmouth Club and the Tuck Business School under the leadership of Steve Waterhouse**.** A companion event is organized in nearby Keystone, Colorado, under the leadership of **Bob Downey '58** and the Class of 1958. The groups at these two events actually gather to ski together in Vail and Keystone for part of the weekend. Alumni clubs in Japan and Korea initiated a similar Carnival Ski Weekend under the leadership of **Cliff Bernstein '89**, reflecting the continuing presence of Dartmouth skiers far beyond our shores. Even some of the notorious Dartmouth alumni made famous in the novel *Animal House* by **Chris Miller '63**—and made even more so in the movie, a comedy classic so enduring that the History Channel did a two-hour retrospective celebrating the film's 1978 release—take part in these skiing weekends.

The 10th Mountain Division has been deactivated and reactivated several times since World War II. In the past few years, its troops have been engaged in counter-insurgency and mountain warfare operations in Iraq, Afghanistan, and elsewhere. Although skiing is no longer the main focus of the Division's contemporary training, Dartmouth alumni who can ski, like recent 10th veteran **David Mulliken '00** and current member **Major Louie Cheng, Tu '03**, still form a part of the force, but the alumni presence only exists today in very limited numbers.

The number of Dartmouth family members engaged in ski area development and management as well as other ski business occupations continues to be significant. Most major ski areas have Dartmouth alumni participating in roles from ski instruction to ski patrol to general management as has often been mentioned before. Alumni still own mountain resorts, including Alyeska in Alaska and Shawnee Peak in Maine. Many alumni now function as ski area consultants, principals in engineering firms supporting ski resort technical developments, owner-operators of medical facilities in ski resorts, entrepreneurs in the support industries from clothing to ski equipment, and in many other key positions throughout the ski industry. The extent of the greater Dartmouth family thus involved is probably greater now than at any previous time in the college's history.

Some of the important ski contributions of earlier decades such as the venerable Harris Hill Ski Jump in Brattleboro, Vermont, first developed by Fred Harris in 1922, are still up and running. The Harris Hill Ski Jumping Competition is a celebrated Brattleboro tradition, and the two-day tournament has always brought world-class jumpers from the U.S. and Europe to jump in one of the region's most popular winter sporting events. It has served as the site of 18 national and regional championships with the most recent in 1992 when Brattleboro hosted the US National Championships. Harris Hill was the personal vision of Fred Harris of Brattleboro, founder of both the Brattleboro Outing Club and the Dartmouth Outing club. Only an occasional snow drought and World War II have interrupted this annual tradition until recently when the jump had to be shut down in order to be rebuilt.

During this past year, extensive renovation and upgrading of the jump was completed and major jumping events were held. Situated on the edge of a Brattleboro cornfield, the brand new jump was rebuilt to FIS (International Federation of Skiing) specifications and is the only 90-meter jump in New England. The website for the Harris Jump makes the historical involvement of Fred Harris and the pride of the community in this operation very clear:

"Welcome to Harris Hill Ski Jump of Brattleboro, Vermont which is the only 90 meter ski jump in New England and one of only six in the USA of our size and caliber. We have completed an extensive renovation of the jump in order to continue its reputation of a first-class venue in the sport of ski jumping. Harris Hill is a symbol of pride for the Brattleboro community and throughout the Northeast. We look forward to continuing the tradition with the 85th annual Harris Hill Ski Jumping Competition presented by Pepsi February 14 & 15, 2009, a United States Ski Association (USSA) sanctioned event, where we will host the world's best ski jumpers on our brand new jump. Founded in 1922 by Fred Harris of Brattleboro, the Fred Harris Memorial Ski Jumping Tournament is one of the region's most popular winter sporting events, attracting thousands of fans from the Northeast for this two-day ski jumping competition."[1]

The Dartmouth Skiway still operates as one of only two college-owned ski areas of any size or significance in the U.S. Recent improvements in lift capabilities, a new mountain base lodge, and updated snowmaking equipment should enable the Skiway to remain a creditable center of skiing for Dartmouth ski racers, students, staff, and local residents for years to come.

Dartmouth College has new traditions that impact skiing in other ways. For example, over the past 20 years the US Ski and Snowboarding Team has taken advantage of the special language-training courses available during the Dartmouth Summer Term through The Rassias Summer Language Program, originally started by long time Dartmouth **Professor John Rassias** to pioneer language instruction for Peace Corps Volunteers. The Hoyt Foundation and Judy Hoyt currently underwrite this program in memory of her late husband Pete, a long-time Foundation Trustee. Mrs. Hoyt's generous contribution allows the US Ski and Snowboard Team to send a number of its athletes, coaches, and staff to the Hoyt/Dartmouth Language Program annually.[2] The purpose of the program is to enhance the students' practical language skills and cultural awareness in a country where they will train and compete.

***

There are many ways that Dartmouth people are involved in the contemporary world of skiing. Some alumni continue to race long after their last run as a collegiate skier. The Dartmouth ski team is particularly adept at teaching ski team members how to organize their schedules, their careers, and their own training in ways that will allow them to continue beyond college in this competitive sport that they have loved. The story below provides some insights into the activities of Nordic skiers after they leave the Hanover Plain.

DON'T FORGET THE NORDICS

By Chelsea Little '09 (Based on her article in *The Valley News*, February, 2009)

When Dartmouth Winter Carnival approaches every year, students hurry to finish their work so that they can drink and dance at the fraternities. But many Dartmouth students forget or do not realize that Winter Carnival was initially founded as a weekend to celebrate outdoor activities, particularly that fledgling college sport: skiing. The first carnival ski races were swept by **A. T. Cobb '12**. Since then, Dartmouth skiing has never looked back.

It is no secret that Dartmouth has been very successful in NCAA competition. But what happens to these skiers after they graduate? For many Nordic skiers, like their Alpine counterparts, it turns out that they keep racing. Now a graduate myself, I will be joining many of my former teammates in pursuing skiing at the national level and maybe, like some of them, even internationally.

These include **Mikey Sinnott '07** and **Kristina Trygstad-Saari '07**, both chosen to represent the U.S. in World Cup competition last season; **Sam Naney '06** and older graduates **Brayton Osgood '03** and **Kate Arduser '02**, who have raced all over the world; 2007 and 2008 captains **Sara Studebaker '07** and **Susan Dunklee '08** and **Zach Hall '06**, who are members of the U.S. National Biathlon Team; and **Carolyn Bramante '06** who has already represented the U.S. in one Olympics and is aiming for a second.

There are more Dartmouth grads on the international circuit than alumni from almost any other college. Why? I asked some of these athletes for their opinions.

First there are the details. Day-to-day life on the Dartmouth Ski Team forces athletes to take responsibility for their own training. While there is a weekly plan, we have to adjust each workout based on what our bodies are telling us. Dunklee said, "I came out of Dartmouth with a firm grasp of the theory behind the training plan and a good feeling for when and when not to push myself hard." This doesn't change on race day. We test our own skis and wax, and contribute to selecting the team's race wax. We are responsible for finding our own best warm-up routines, making intelligent breakfast choices, and nearly everything else that goes into race preparation.

Katie Bono '10 believes that these small things are what will help her most in her post-collegiate career. "The way the team is set up gives athletes skills to keep skiing after college. The coaches don't coddle you. You have to be on top of your stuff and strong in your sense of self."

While Mikey Sinnott agrees that the team has always had a culture of "never giving in, and being tougher than the rest," it's not all stoicism and responsibility. The coaches, **Cami Thompson** and **Ruff Patterson**, simultaneously teach two seemingly opposing approaches to athletics: the need to train hard and the importance of having fun.

Dartmouth emphasizes love of the sport and even has an annual award for the skier who most embodies "skiing as a way of life." Dunklee says, "The team has the right attitude: training hard balanced with playing hard. It keeps people enjoying the sport,

and as a result, they don't burn out as easily."

We are encouraged to run longer than we've ever run, to start a race without being afraid of failure, and to experiment. We go ski just for the pure joy of it. Racing is important, but if you don't love the skiing in its own right, you can't excel at it. We make sure we have fun. Says Bramante, "This fosters a love for the sport and others in the sport, which is absolutely important!"

Cami Thompson, the women's coach, agrees. The focus is never on just a single race result, or just the six-week college season, or even a collegiate career. "Our mission is to develop skiers; we want them to get better while they're here. It's just a step along the way in the process. Ruff and I feel strongly that it's a process. We want people to look at the bigger picture."

And so, while the program may force athletes to take responsibility for their own training and racing, and while it may promote grueling but fun adventures we would never have had the guts to try before we got here, it is perhaps a philosophical difference that separates Dartmouth skiers from the rest. It's certainly not just a matter of resources. Sinnott says, "The most interesting comparison is to the western schools, which have recruiting money, scholarships, less demanding academic standards, and

Mike Sinnott '07 represented the U.S. in 2009 World Cup competition.

Kristina Trystad-Saari '07 represented the U.S. in 2009 World Cup competition.

Brayton Osgood '03 has been competing around the world for years.

Susan Dunklee '08, Capt in 2008, and a 2009 National Biathalon Champion.

Chelsea Little '09 has raced and written about racing.

consistent snow. Yet they rarely produce American skiers who continue their career." Thompson points out that these western state schools are more interested in recruiting athletes – often from Europe – who are already going fast. They are most concerned with how their program will fare that year, or how that athlete will perform as a college skier. That's how they spend their money.

Dartmouth is different. Cami and Ruff are willing to work with skiers like me: kids who didn't come in with a lot of credentials. They take these skiers and develop them alongside their recruited talent, to the benefit of everyone. The team focuses not only on NCAA's, but also races at SuperTours, U.S. Nationals, Spring Series, and, occasionally, Canadian Nationals. Brayton Osgood says that "Ruff always made sure we were aware of skiing beyond the EISA circuit. College racing was important, but so were US Nationals and international competition."

One of the first times I was really aware of international racing was in high school. At the 2003 Cross-Country World Championships, Dartmouth graduate **Carl Swenson '92**, in a 50-kilometer skate race, was skiing well with a shot at the podium when

he broke a pole. He skied with the broken pole for a while, got a new one, and eventually ended up 5th. Swenson is now a public defender in New Hampshire and won't ski any more World Cups, but, Sinnott points out, "There has always been a Dartmouth skier at the Winter Olympic Games." Osgood, Sinnott, Bramante, Studebaker, Hall and Dunklee all state that they hope and plan to ski in Vancouver in 2010, and even beyond.

This winter, a whole new crop of Dartmouth alumni are joining the national circuit. The Class of 2009 is one of the most prolific in years for producing post-collegiate racers with six of the Nordic skiers who entered in the fall of 2005 now skiing professionally. While **Dakota Blackhorse-von Jess '09** from Bend, Oregon, and **Glenn Randall '09** from Collbran, Colorado, probably have the best shot of joining their former teammates in Vancouver—and perhaps a few undergrads, like **Rosie Brennan '10**, who has already started a World Cup race—the rest of us aren't giving up yet. If you watch a SuperTour this winter, you'll see **Audrey Weber '09** in the Central Cross-Country race suit, **Pavel Sotskov '09** representing the Maine Winter Sports Center, and **Hannah Dreissigacker '09** and me sporting the colors of the Craftsbury Green Racing Project. Maybe by 2014 we'll all be teammates again.

It is truly remarkable how many members of our class are pursuing skiing full-time; this isn't just a hobby, it's our life. Thompson says, "After years at Dartmouth, the thing we're the most proud of is the number of people who are still involved in skiing."

And so while Winter Carnival is our one chance to show the rest of campus—who probably aren't even awake when we start the races—how we excel in collegiate competition, our Nordic skiers can say with confidence that when they run out of carnival starts, there will be plenty more races waiting for them.

***

Many former Dartmouth skiers have participated in the coaching ranks at all levels since the early years of skiing. The article below highlights many aspects of this long-term commitment to coaching, but emphasizes how the number of alumni coaching has, if anything, increased in recent years.

DARTMOUTH COACHING ACTIVITIES

By Cami Thompson, Dartmouth Women's Nordic Coach since 1989

It should come as little surprise that while Dartmouth has developed a host of Olympic athletes—in

fact, at least one has competed in every modern Winter Olympiad—the College has also fostered much growth and development on the national coaching scene, as well.

As we celebrate the 100th Anniversary of the DOC we get a clearer picture of the role Dartmouth has had on so many different levels of the sport. We find that the same traditions that have developed outstanding skiers have also generated growth in the ski coaching ranks. The role they play in developing generations of athletes who share their love and passion for the sport is abundantly evident.

From the mentoring days of the legendary **Fred Harris '11** to the era of Dartmouth's current Men's Alpine Coach, **Peter Dodge '78**, who has been at the helm for more than 20 seasons, Dartmouth's legacy burns brightly. Consider the list of our Big Green skiers-turned-coaches; it includes the likes of **John Caldwell '50**, who coached four Winter Olympic Games, while his son, **Sverre Caldwell '77**, has served as a long-time coach not only with the US Ski Team but also as the Nordic Director of the acclaimed Stratton Mountain School.

The four current Dartmouth coaches, mentors of coaches to come, gathered at the White House in 2007 - (l. to r.) Christine Booker, Ruff Patterson, Cami Thompson, Peter Dodge '78.

They provide a sure sign that Dartmouth skiers who have gone on to coaching have set the standard.

US Winter Olympian, **Dick Taylor '59**, made his mark in coaching following his own successful racing career. Taylor has been one of the true intellectuals of the sport, and to this day, is always seeking ways to be faster and more efficient on skis. His stints with the US Ski Team and as the long-time coach at Gould Academy, and the athletes he has developed in those capacities, are a testament to Dick's skills, work ethic and love of sport. Dick remembers, "At Dartmouth the possibility and opportunity for anybody to excel through choice, diligence, reckless tenacity and plain hard work was simply a given, at every corner of campus life".

Alpine skier **Lindsay Mann '07**, who was on Dartmouth's 2007 NCAA Championship team, has used her experience to motivate younger skiers to race. Mann says that despite sensing the end of her own racing career, the adjustment to coaching did wonders to soothe her soul. She recently recalled, "I was becoming more and more upset about graduating and leaving college behind, but also ski racing. Ski racing has been the one consistent throughout my life and it has provided me many opportunities that have allowed me to mature a great deal by learning the struggles and successes of such an intense sport." She brings to her coaching skills a unique perspective of what winning takes: "After being part of the NCAA Championship Team in 2007, I realized that although I did not want to continue to pursue my individual career, I still wanted ski racing to remain a big part of my life. For those reasons I decided to give coaching a try. I've enjoyed seeing a different perspective and different challenges of the same sport."

Current US Ski Team coach, **Chris Grover '93**, a veteran of elite international racing circles, recalls what helped shape his coaching philosophy: "If there is one thing that I have probably taken from those years [at Dartmouth] and applied to coaching, it is perhaps the sense of being an underdog. Just as Dartmouth skiers often come against top foreign athletes attending larger universities on ski scholarships, so the United States must contend with traditional cross-country ski nations like Norway, Sweden and Finland. At Dartmouth we trained really hard and were confident in our success, which eventually did come. We take the same approach as coaches and athletes of the US Ski Team, and we are beginning to see the dividends."

As we span the circles of ski-sport in North American, we see the Big Green influence well represented by former athletes turned ski coaches. Here is a look at a small segment of the talent.

The contributions of John Caldwell to the

sport as x-c coach at the Putney School and for the US FIS and Olympic teams have placed him among the greats. During the eight years from late 1978 to early1987, **Jim Page '63** was successively the US Ski Team Head Nordic Combined Coach and then Nordic Program Director; he would later serve as the High Performance Director of the USOC. **Phil Peck '77**, now the Headmaster at Holderness School in Plymouth, NH, served as a National Team coach from 1982-84. The list goes on and on. **Max Cobb '87**, a former Development Team skier, is now leading the US Biathlon program, and teammate **Joe Walsh '84** has gone on to big things working with the USOC's adaptive program.

Many other athletes have landed top academy and junior program positions. More recently, on the Alpine side, they include **Brad Wall '02, JP Daigneault '97, Christin Lathrop '03, Lindsey Mann '07, Peter Anderson '06**, and **Eric Cates '07**. On the Nordic side, we find **Abi Holt '99, Eileen Cary '04, Scottie Eliassen '90, Poppet Boswell '90 and Will Sweetser '92**. And in the collegiate ranks are **Paul Stone '98** at the University of Vermont and **Evan Weiss '06** who coached first at Western State and then at the University of Nevada, Reno.

Around the nation, many former skiing alums have contributed time and talent in coaching young, local athletes. From three-time Olympians **Tim Caldwell '76** on the East coast to **Leslie Thompson Hall '86** in the Pacific Northwest and long-time International Disabled skier, **Rob Walsh '88**. This list only begins to tell the story, but you get the idea.

***

Some alumni involved in coaching and skier development are active in schools referred to as Ski Academies and which offer a special focus on the development of outstanding skiers, as is discussed below.

SKI ACADEMIES: A CIRCULAR PIPELINE

By Pamela Crisafulli Hommeyer '88

Until about forty years ago, Dartmouth ski team members came from either the New England preparatory schools or from public schools near ski areas scattered throughout the upper Midwest, Northeast and West. Many of today's stars are drawn from a growing group of ski academies that train these athletes for both the academic and athletic rigor required of a Dartmouth skier. Consider these facts: Over 40% of current US Ski Team members hail from a specialized ski academy and over 50% of today's Dartmouth ski teams, both Alpine and Nordic, is comprised of ski academy graduates. A large portion of these skiers hail from Burke Mountain Academy (BMA), Green Mountain Valley School (GMVS) and Stratton Mountain School in the East, but there are others just as prominent elsewhere. "Since the late 1970's when the earliest ski academies were coming into their own, they've had a strong influence on Dartmouth's Ski Teams," asserts **Peter Dodge '78**, Dartmouth Men's Ski Team Head Coach. "This impact continues today."

Ski academies give student-athletes a college preparatory education within a flexible schedule, allowing college ski racing hopefuls to receive the rigorous training and countless hours on the snow required to compete at the elite NCAA Division I level. In essence, these specialized schools are producing the quintessential Dartmouth student: passionate, hard-working, hard-charging, intellectually focused and committed. Dartmouth graduates have played and are playing a key role in this student-athlete evolution—as coaches, faculty and heads of school at these academies.

The first and maybe best known of these is **Burke Mountain Academy**. Founded in 1970 by Warren Witherall in East Burke, Vermont, Burke has become the model for other ski- and sports-specific academies around the country. In fact, BMA was the first sports academy of any kind in the United States. Not only has BMA sent over 50 students to Dartmouth since its inception, its team of coaches and educators has included scores of Dartmouth alumni over the years, currently including **Christin Lathrop '03** (Admissions Director and J3 Coach), **Bradley Wall '02** and **Sam Damon '04** (Men's FIS Coaches), and **Thomas De Carlo '78** (Academic Director and English teacher). Lathrop, herself a graduate of the Green Mountain Valley School in Vermont, says, "We're doing things here at Burke that cannot be replicated in a traditional school environment. These kids have to be focused and performing at a top level both in the classroom and on the mountain." Long-time Burke Head of School and now US Ski Team staffer, Finn Gundersen, looks beyond the over one hundred Burke graduates who have made the US Ski Team when he points out, "BMA graduates are great citizens of the world. Getting through the rigors of a ski academy program prepares them for just about anything in life. The students who end up at places like Dartmouth are not only ready to excel in their field of study but have a maturity not typical of incoming freshman." Two BMA skiers, Cody Marshall and Nolan Kasper, are presently on the US Ski Team and possible choices to compete in the 2010 Winter Olympics in Vancouver, British Columbia.

A bit farther south, in Waitsfield, VT, is an equally productive competitor, the **Green Mountain Valley School** (GMVS). With an average enrollment of about one hundred students (slightly larger than Burke's), it also turns out its fair share of top skiers, thanks in part to **Jean-Pierre L. ("J.P.") Daigneault '97**, the school's Alpine Coach, and **Jere W. Brophy '88**, its Dean of Faculty, Race Director and Athletic Coach. Their most recent national skiing success was the acceptance of two of its students, Jeremy Transue and Chelsea Marshall, to the 2009 US Alpine B Teams while another, Devin Delany, was named to the US Women's Alpine Development Team. And at the collegiate level, former GMVS student **Francis Fortin-Houle '05** was named by the US Collegiate Ski Coaches' Association as a member of the 2009 All Academic Intercollegiate Ski Team, thus helping to carry on the tradition of the student-athlete.

Today, we continue to see the expansion of this highly academic ski academy concept being advanced in Norden, California, by two former Dartmouth ski racers. Nestled in the Sierra Nevada Mountains near beautiful Lake Tahoe, **Sugar Bowl Academy** (SBA) was created to offer Western-based student-athletes the same college prep education and Olympic-caliber ski training offered by Eastern ski academies. Sugar Bowl Academy's Head of School is **Tracy Wilson '02**, a former Dartmouth Ski Team captain. "SBA was founded on the premise that the pursuit of both academic and athletic excellence is an important factor in the development of outstanding individuals," says Wilson. "Our mission indicates a commitment to the whole child—mind, body and spirit and embodies our belief that accommodating the training and travel schedules of competitive skiers should not compromise rigorous, college preparatory academic

standards." The students may be Olympic hopefuls, but the school's faculty and coaching staff maintain a no-nonsense approach to their expectations in the classroom.

Wilson collaborates with another Dartmouth skier, **Bill Hudson '88**, Executive Director of the Sugar Bowl Ski Team Foundation, who overseas the Sugar Bowl Academy as well as a 400-member team of young skiers. A former Olympian himself, Hudson has lived the punishing and demanding life of a competitive ski racer. He matriculated in the fall of 1988 and after a highly successful freshman year on the Dartmouth ski team, he made the US Ski Team. He competed at the World Cup level for over ten years, most recently at the 1988 Calgary Winter Olympics. "Schools like Dartmouth need skiers who can compete at an elite level, but who can also thrive in a highly competitive academic environment," asserts Hudson. "Student-athletes at ski academies learn how to balance these sometimes competing goals, preparing them for the intensity of being both a full-time Dartmouth student and ski racer." Like many "locals," Hudson grew up in Truckee, CA, minutes from the Squaw Valley Ski Area, and was able to coordinate his ski training needs with his nearby neighborhood school. Many other ski racers are not so lucky and must find other workable options. Some manage by splitting the year between their local school and an academy, attending the ski academy for the winter-only session. However, this solution can present logistical problems in transitioning back and forth, resulting in a more disjointed academic experience. Others make the move to a ski academy full-time, where they can have it all.

Ski academy students are exceptionally motivated, disciplined, and dedicated. Succeeding in this highly charged environment requires significant sacrifices. Routinely, days begin before sunrise and stretch far into the night. Generally, ski training happens in the morning, when the snow is at its firmest. Early afternoon sees the start of classes, ending at dinnertime. Evenings are spent doing homework and ski tuning. According to Wilson, "Ski academies are not for the faint of heart or the casual skier, given our 15-hour days packed full of ski racing, dry-land training, classes, studying, ski tuning and even community service." Certainly the required travel demands a flexible schedule, but administrators and coaches alike are committed to not allowing it to compromise a student-athlete's classroom endeavors. Recently when early season snow was inadequate on their

A LIFETIME OF RACING OPPORTUNITIES

The Dartmouth Ski Team visited with President George W. Bush in the White House after the 2007 NCAA championship.

Nina Kemppel '92, Tu'05 has won 18 National X-C titles.

The Dartmouth ski team gathered together with the Dartmouth Club of the Vail Region during their preseason practice in Vail (2005).

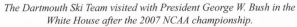

Tryg Myhren '58 (left) and Art Kelton '61 raced for Dartmouth; Myhren headed the U.S. team at the 2006 Paralympics and Kelton helped develop Vail; seen here at the Dartmouth Ski Weekend in Keystone, CO, (2009).

Steve Waterhouse '65 shown winning a race for the Game Creek Club of Vail over the Aspen Club. An example of many club racers.

Lisa Densmore '83, winner at the 2008 Masters Super G World Championships, Reiteal, Austria; one of her 57 Masters titles.

Sandy Treat '46 raced for over 60 years for Deerfield, the Army, Dartmouth, and on the seniors circuit.

home mountain, the Academy picked up its entire program—faculty and students—and temporarily relocated to another ski resort with more snow. This kind of flexibility is a hallmark of ski academies.

Wilson cautions us not to miss the bigger picture: "Let's not forget the value of a child's pursuit of a passion at this age." Jaqui Lebel, a junior at Sugar Bowl Academy, asserts: "My dream is to ski at Dart-mouth. I know I have to do really well in both school and ski racing to even have a chance of being accepted. Going to a ski academy increases my chances of making my dream come true." Time and time again, ski academy students graduated from Dartmouth have gone out to instruct and encourage new generations in the skills and joys of skiing — and are likely to continue doing so — thus bringing the process full circle.

***

Skiers are showing their enthusiasm for the sport in ways that are personally challenging to them, but not necessarily to anyone else--ways that are the result of this lifelong enthusiasm that permeates so many Dartmouth-connected skiers. The following story outlines a record-setting ski effort by an alumnus father and his undergraduate daughter to experience the extraordinary variety of skiing resorts that exist in North America. John Walters '62 commented, "I remember Peter [Fahey] talking about his odyssey back in 2005 at Bob Downey's Keystone weekend….Never saw a guy with a bigger smile on his face."[3]

2005: A Ski Odyssey – Seventy-two Areas Skied during Winter Term

By Stephen L. Waterhouse

Based on "Downhill All the Way," an article by Katie Fahey '06 published in the *Dartmouth Alumni Magazine*, Winter 2006

During the winter of 2005, **Katie Fahey '06** and her dad **Peter Fahey '68** finally realized Peter's long-discussed dream to make at least one top-to-bottom run at every major ski area in North America in a single season. This was carried out over the winter term of 2005 during which the pair racked up visits to 72 different ski areas in eleven weeks and which included periodic rendezvous with other Dartmouth groups around the country.

The story is a contemporary example of the passion for skiing that Dartmouth-connected individuals are still exhibiting each in their own way. Although this was a trip where the challenge of moving almost daily from one location to another—checking in an out of hotels, purchasing tickets, packing and unpacking, traveling to the next area, etc.—was almost as taxing as overcoming the physical demands of terrain and weather conditions, it nonetheless took staying power and serious commitment of time, funds, and endurance to complete. And in doing so, they demonstrated a never-ending enthusiasm for the joy of being out skiing or boarding on whatever mountains they encountered.

For years, Katie had heard her father express his desire to visit and conquer all the major ski areas in North America, a fantasy repeated at most family gatherings, and this special skiing "odyssey" had become hers as well. When she decided in 2004 to take Winter Term 2005 off, she suggested giving it a go… and go they did!

They started with 20 ski areas in New England and followed up with 52 areas in the West as their pace ever quickened. Along the way, they saw a lot of people, and in particular, Dartmouth alumni they knew. Many were enjoying informal ski reunions at various mountains. During a five-day stay in Breckenridge, Colorado,

Katie Fahey '06 (far right) on the mountain with members of the Class of 1968 at Big Sky, MT.

the Class of 1958, plus others, welcomed them at its annual gathering in Keystone. They joined the group for dinner, participated in a group sing-along of old John Denver songs, and heard many stories on a broad range of topics. Katie says she realized then that they were all part of something very unique, unforgettable, and undoubtedly "green"… and of something that would be one of her best Dartmouth memories.

A week later, they were in Montana to spend time with her dad's 1968 Class at their annual ski reunion which was an occasion of constant entertainment and fascination and a chance to be amazed again by the diversity of interests and pursuits of Dartmouth alumni. Katie began to realize something else about her college's alumni:

Peter Fahey '68 with a long string of lift tickets; from his 72 mountain; ski odyssey.

those who participated in the Dartmouth experience are independent-minded, usually outgoing, and very unique individuals no matter what their age. They have many interests in common but are also very different people, just like her own friends at Dartmouth—a thought that many of these alumni discover as the years pass by and a variety of interactions takes place.

By the time they returned home from their tiring 72-ski area journey, Katie felt closer to Dartmouth than she ever had before. Not a bad thing when you have a father and three older siblings who have also attended Dartmouth. And after years of crossing the college green, walking down Main Street, and stopping by fraternity basements, her off-term odyssey was the first time she truly understood and appreciated what Dartmouth is all about. Her trip illuminated many of the qualities that are represented in the special breed of individuals that Dartmouth attracts, encourages, develops, and graduates.

Peter and Katie would probably not have achieved their goal of visiting all these ski areas in eleven short weeks if they did not share the same passion that **Fred Harris '11** had when he started the DOC, or as did **Carl Shumway '13** who trekked out to Moosilauke in 1912, or Nathaniel Goodrich (Dartmouth's longest-serving Librarian) who made the first ski runs down Mt Mansfield, or **Tim Kelley '79** who regularly ventures across the wilderness areas of Alaska today.... or many others like them.

In total, the Fahey father-and-daughter team managed to ski at 72 ski areas across a very large territory far beyond the normal holiday skiing adventure. It ended up as something Peter calls his "2005 Ski Odyssey" and that both he and Katie will share and relive for years to come.

***

Other alumni contribute in special ways that are both unique and often helpful to different parts of our society. We have spent a significant amount of time in this book outlining the multi-decade contribution of the greater Dartmouth family to adaptive skiing. The story below reflects the involvement of one alumnus in a related aspect of this area of concern. **Henry Hof '58** has dealt with the problem of being unable to walk by associating himself with Whirlwind Wheelchair International, a group that has helped thousands of needy individuals around the world to build and use their own wheelchairs, including the Whirlwind RoughRider model which enjoys the potential to facilitate mobility even in ski areas if certain modifications can be funded.

WHIRLWIND WHEELCHAIRS

By Henry Hof, 3rd '58

As an undergraduate in the mid-1950s, I preferred the hoops and hardwood of our Alumni Gym to the snowy slopes of the Green and White Mountains. Having a high center of gravity, I was much better suited to the toboggan than a pair of skis. But I loved sports, even as I aged. Athletic activities halted rather abruptly for me, however, when my legs progressively stopped moving. In 1981, I was diagnosed with primary lateral sclerosis, a debilitating disorder that rendered me unable to walk—much less run, jump or glide—without artificial support. By 1989, I resorted to a wheelchair for mobility and have used one ever since.

HANOVER CAMPUS SCENES

Top: Dartmouth Hall and pathways thru the snow have been a prominent image for all students and skiers passing thru Hanover, NH, on snow-filled days since modern skiing began.

Middle: The dress-up X-C race has been a comic feature of Winter Carnival in recent years, and often ends with a ski-less belly slide down the old Golf Course Ski Hill. (Mehling, 2009)

Bottom: Crowds still gather daily on Occom Pond to enjoy skating and hockey, but the ski hill beyond no longer has a rope tow or skiers. (Waterhouse, Jan. 23, 2010)

ALUMNI SKIER GATHERINGS

Dartmouth alumni and friends get together in many places around the ski world every year, but these three locations have seen particularly large gatherings as alumni Winter Carnivals.

The Friday morning gathering of the first few Dartmouth skiers at the base of Vail Mountain to start CarniVAIL-2009.

Chris Jarnot, Operations Head of Vail Mtn, is inducted into the Dartmouth Vail Club by Vail Club President Steve Waterhouse at the group lunch in Sarge's Shelter.

Bill Briggs '54 (with banjo), is backed up by the "Carcajou Singers" (l to r: Huttrer '60, Brew '52, Danson '60 and Silverstein '58) at the CarniVAIL- Ball. (Holmes, 2009)

Japan D Club President Cliff Bernstein '89 and Korea Club President Euysung Kim '91 with their daughters (Cliff was once Euysung's Freshman Trip leader).

The "hard Core" skiers at the Dartmouth Ski Weekend (DSW) in Keystone CO, take time for a photo op (2009).

357

Consistent with my duties as an economic and social program officer at the United Nations Secretariat, I teamed up with Whirlwind Wheelchair International. This dedicated group, based at San Francisco State University, designs, constructs, and trains others to build wheelchairs in developing countries.

I relished the job. By helping individuals around the world with their particular disabilities, I could fight back against the frustrations of my own paralyzing condition, which was, as I came to learn, a minor-league form of Lou Gehrig's disease. Our clients were the poorest of the poor, socially isolated and economically disadvantaged, without even the most basic wheelchair to move around in. By working with Whirlwind it would be an overstatement to say that I found a way "to unite my avocation and vocation", but something did occur in me akin to that notion, expressed by Robert Frost's "Two Tramps at Mud Time." My so-called disability thus became a calling card for similarly concerned non-governmental organizations and a credential for interested United Nations member states ranging from tiny Malta to vast China.

Now retired, I am still associated with Whirlwind. Their MacArthur Award-winning chief engineer, Ralf Hotchkiss, designed their newest wheelchair, named the RoughRider™. Presently being produced in Colombia, South Africa and Vietnam, the RoughRider is an ultra-stable long wheelbase wheelchair for use, as its name suggests, where surface conditions are difficult. The chair is maneuverable over a wide variety of terrains including rocky surfaces and soft ground such as mud, sand, and even some kinds of snow. It uses wide mountain-bike rear tires and a unique 4-inch wide caster wheel to promote improved flotation. A five-position rear-axle mount allows the rear wheels to be situated so that the rider's upper-body strength is optimized as weight is reduced on the front wheels. This makes the chair easier to push without getting bogged down on soft surfaces. While not specifically designed as a snow chair, the RoughRider would allow disabled skiers to function independently in moderately sloped areas. This model is also notably safer for the rider, with or without a companion's help, staying stable where others would tip and thereby minimizing falls.

I wholeheartedly endorse Whirlwind's belief that the RoughRider is appropriate as an aid around skiing areas. Whirlwind is open to exploring with the Dartmouth ski community other practical ways to facilitate mobility for enthusiasts who have become injured in their sport as well as for those who are otherwise disabled. One example is our design project to equip the RoughRider chair with some form of ski- or saucer-type attachment that would allow the physically compromised to negotiate the less demanding ski slopes and so experience, in a somewhat different way, the exhilaration of sliding down a Stowe snow trail or Pico Peak's pike or the Dartmouth Skiway. Whirlwind is seeking entrepreneurs to finance the design of a lightweight RoughRider model for the North American market. This wheelchair would sell for a half to two-thirds the cost of competing models and be the only stable long-wheelbase everyday chair that is not a dedicated outdoor vehicle.

I should add that the Green Mountain State has the Vermont Adaptive Program conducted at various venues by a non-profit organization offering recreational sports opportunities to people who have physical and developmental disabilities. Some of Vermont Adaptive's training lessons, for which a range of fees applies, are stand-up, sit-down, 3- and 4-track cross-country, mono- and bi-skiing, as well as Alpine racing, snowboarding and snowshoeing. During the program's two decades of existence, Dartmouth College personnel have actively supported it. The upbeat motto of Vermont Adaptive is "Sports For Every Body." How apt!

[Supplementary Note: As noted above, Henry's efforts to further the use of the Whirlwind Wheelchair in skiing environments have yet to be realized. However, like the work of Dr. Michael Mayor to develop materials for better knee replacements or his use of the Segway transporter to help him move around the Dartmouth-Hitchcock Medical Center, any promising initiative to develop improved mobility options for the physically challenged is an opportunity worth supporting. The Whirlwind group requires financial support to cover design and development costs to create an add-on ski or saucer device to their latest wheelchair. Either Henry or the Director of Operations for Whirlwind, Marc Krizack, would be pleased to discuss project proposals with any interested parties. Some background information on the company, photos of the existing RoughRider model, and other wheelchair activities and topics can be found on their web site: www.whirlwindwheelchair.org. In addition, a two-minute online video is available at: http:// RoughRider.notlong.com. – Stephen Waterhouse]

SUMMARY

In completing this book with a discussion of things taking place in recent times, we cannot be certain whether any of the elements of the Dartmouth story happening now will evolve into important developments for the history of skiing. Impacts on history are rarely ever known until the years roll by and one has the wisdom of age to look back. For example, few could have predicted that the massive growth of major western ski areas would result from Minnie Dole's efforts to establish a unit of mountain troops at the beginning of WW II. However, the experience of skiing in the Western mountains by so many young men from the eastern states, and the strong and lasting friendships gained during the war, were of such impact that they motivated these men to become the leaders of a very substantial skiing movement for that part of the country. Had Dartmouth not had so many competent skiers and mountaineers of its own willing to help fill the ranks of the 10th Mountain Division, much of the history of Western skiing would surely have been different.

As it has over the past one hundred years, Dartmouth is still making skiers out of non-skiers and developing more than its share of champions out of the better ones. While some will continue to race long after having graduated, others will gravitate to the teaching or coaching side of the sport while yet others will engage in occupations to develop, maintain, or improve the quality of ski areas or to look for new ways to make the sport more accessible to a greater number of people, on better equipment, at lower cost, over a longer span of years. They will research, design, innovate, test, and refine their ideas to eventually produce something that is safer, more durable, more versatile, more stylish, or more practical. They will use their experience, knowledge, creativity and the collegial network of "ski people" to raise the quality of the skiing experience yet another notch higher in the passionate pursuit of making "the perfect run" a more consistently repeatable event. Many who have never been associated with the Hanover crowd will be doing the same. But in the world of skiing excellence, whether on the slopes, at the drawing board, in the workshops, or at the computer, there will scarcely be a place, a product, or a publication of note that does not have its own bright tint of Dartmouth Green.

Notes

1. Harris Hill Ski Jump: http://harrishillskijump.org/index/php/history. 2. Hoyt/Dartmouth Language Program website: http://ww.ussa.org/magnoliaPublic/ussa/en/formembers/nationalteam/education/hoytdartmouthlanguage.html. 3. John Walters '62, email November 18, 2008. 4. Artist/Maker: Paul Starrett Sample, American, 1896-1974; Title: Nearing Home (Near the River) Object Date: not dated; Materials: Oil on canvas; Dimensions: 39 1/2 x 50 1/2 in.; Inscriptions: Signed, lower right: PAUL SAMPLE; Credit: Hood Museum of Art, Dartmouth College. Gift of Sigurnd Larmon, Class of 1914; P.974.518.

Paul Sample '20, Dartmouth Artist in Residence (1938-1962), titled this painting "Nearing Home"
when he created it in the 1950s, and this is an appropriate way to enter the final chapter.

(This image used courtesy of the Hood Museum, Dartmouth College; Artist/Maker: Paul Starrett Sample, American, 1896-1974; Title: Nearing Home (Near the River)
Object Date: not dated; Materials: Oil on canvas; Dimensions: 39 1/2 x 50 1/2 in.; Inscriptions: Signed, lower right: PAUL SAMPLE;
Credit: Hood Museum of Art, Dartmouth College. Gift of Sigurnd Larmon, Class of 1914; P.974.518)

CHAPTER XVI

CONCLUSIONS FROM *PASSION FOR SKIING*

By Stephen L. Waterhouse

When this book began, we highlighted a broad range of contributions to skiing of the many members of the greater Dartmouth family. In the 14 main chapters that followed, we outlined the massive involvement that people associated with this one institution, Dartmouth College, have undertaken in every aspect of skiing in the United States and to a more limited degree—but still a significant one—in many corners of the globe. In this final chapter, we will recap a few of these involvements and achievements, but our main objective is to identify the factors behind why Dartmouth College has played this unique role in the development of skiing and related winter sports. As Paul Sample has so aptly named his painting *Nearing Home*[1], we are close to the end of this story.

We will also discuss the elements of campus life that have been at the heart of creating the passion for skiing that defines our story. These pragmatic considerations are an important contributing source of the legions of enthusiastic skiers coming out of Hanover. We will show how the life stories of these enthusiasts for this sport have played through the areas discussed in earlier chapters. As part of this, we will share a sampling of comments that have reached us during the past two years when we actively sought input and were overwhelmed with unexpected and unknown details. These volunteered thoughts represent a unique aspect of the Dartmouth experience and, as far as we know, have never before been collected or commented on as such an important component of why skiing has developed generally. For our research, they helped us piece together the diversity of the Dartmouth involvement in skiing and shaped the direction of some of our later research.

Finally, we will discuss some of the heroes of our skiing story, particularly those individuals we feel history has so far overlooked or whose contributions have not yet received due recognition. And we will finish with brief comments on things happening right now that will undoubtedly add to the richness of Dartmouth ski history of the future.

THE BACK-STORY: SOME DARTMOUTH HISTORY

To start, we need to answer a simple basic question: What is it that has enabled Dartmouth to play this major role in the development of skiing? To answer this question, it is necessary to understand and appreciate some background factors in the Dartmouth College history that are not skiing related but which have been crucial to enabling the college, its staff, and students to evolve Dartmouth's skiing contributions. There are several factors that fortuitously came together as a back-story in the first half of the 20th century, and provided a rationale for why the emphasis on skiing has taken hold at this one particular academic institution in the woods of New Hampshire.

Certainly, skiing was not a part of the rationale for forming the college when it was founded in 1769 under a Royal Charter as the ninth and final college established prior to the Revolutionary War in 1776. King George III of England, Lord Dartmouth (Secretary of State for the Colonies), and Governor Wentworth (the Royal Governor of New Hampshire) were the three people most critical to the process of granting the charter to Eleazar Wheelock, who had founded and run Moor's Indian Charity School in Connecticut to educate and train Indians for missionary work in Native American communities. Clearly, none of these people were skiers nor was skiing a topic of general discussion in those days. For some

Professor Charles Proctor 1900 has been referred to by some as a Father of American Skiing; here judging a ski jump at Dartmouth's Vale of Tempe Jump.

125 years, there was little in the activities of Dartmouth students that indicated the next 100+ years would involve such a marvelous effort to help develop so many aspects of this single sport. The spark provided by the original genius of one man, **Fred Harris '11**, who started the Dartmouth Outing Club and focused the early activity on winter sports, was no doubt critical. Fred's passion for skiing, jumping, and competition began the organized process of skiing, and his efforts were greatly aided by the interest and contributions of many others in the area like **Professor Charles Procter 1900 and Carl Shumway '13**.

But what is it in the water of Hanover, New Hampshire, the genes of Dartmouth College, or in other facets of this small New England community that has led to this amazing tale of dedicated commitment to this one sport? Here are the factors—some obvious, some less so—that we feel are the most important, not to the pragmatic skiing activities part of our story, but to enabling it to happen at all.

THE UNIQUE ENABLING FACTORS AT DARTMOUTH

The Environment

The environment is a first consideration. Dartmouth is one of few major colleges (and the only one with a history going back before the Revolution of 1776) that was founded in the wilderness with snow and mountains nearby. The area around Hanover, NH, has cold conditions in winter and, in times past, an abundance of natural snow. The terrain nearby is endowed with reasonable-sized mountains which provide opportunities to create interesting ski slopes. As we briefly noted in earlier pages, the location of Dartmouth College is by coincidence rather than plan. If Eleazar Wheelock had achieved his initial objective, his new college would have been based in Connecticut where Wheelock had been operating a school to educate Native Americans for many years. However, he was unable to obtain a royal charter there from the British king as Connecticut already was home to an existing royal college by the name of Yale University, the very school from which Wheelock himself had graduated. And in a side note, the first four graduates of Dartmouth College were all transfer students from Yale.

The only place that Wheelock could find to use as the base for his new college was the sparsely-settled wilderness of New Hampshire, and that was only achieved when Governor Wentworth granted him a huge land grant as the basis for a college operation. And some 140 years after the founding charter was granted in 1769, this environment combined with an all-male undergraduate body ready to consider something novel to do to ease the tedium of academic life in the winter months provided the backdrop for skiing to get started. Fred Harris '11 formed the Dartmouth Outing Club to take advantage of the outdoor opportunities presented by that very same cold, snowy, mountainous wilderness, and to provide something new and invigorating for his fellow students to do.

At the 1953 Commencement, President Eisenhower tells President Hopkins, "This is what a college should look like."

Outdoors Lovers vs. City Dwellers

The next factor is another outgrowth of the environment and Dartmouth's natural setting. If a person is interested in museums and fine theater productions, it is more likely he or she will seek out a college that is based in a city. And amongst the leading academic colleges (Harvard, Columbia, Yale, Princeton, Stanford and their similars), there are choices to be made that will provide those opportunities. But if one is attracted to the outdoors, a country setting, and related activities, Dartmouth has always had an advantage as a leading academic institution in this sort of environment. During his visit to Hanover in 1953 to speak at commencement, then President Dwight D. Eisenhower was reputed to have commented that Dartmouth's setting, its buildings, and its campus layout are what a college should be like. It would be difficult to find a better-looking campus for a bright student interested in studying close to nature and not being hemmed in by streets and large buildings. And if that student wants to spend time climbing mountains or sliding down hills in the winter on skis, the combination is as unbeatable at Dartmouth today as it was 100 years ago.

Intelligent, Leadership-oriented Students

With a reputation as a center of academic excellence since before the Revolution in 1776, Dartmouth has always attracted its share of bright, achievement-oriented students. The professors, the facilities, the setting, and the reputation among its peers have long kept Dartmouth at the top of the list for any bright student contemplating where to attend college. In the first 200 years, colleges were not rated by "top 10" guides of one sort or another. However, there were certainly opinions on which schools provided a fine education and Dartmouth had its supporters. In recent decades, Dartmouth has been evaluated consistently as one of this country's top ten academic institutions, and given its smaller student population relative to its academic competitors, this has been a result accomplished mainly by the outsized achievements of its exceptional graduates.

Since its earliest days, Dartmouth has taught and graduated some of the brightest leaders in the U.S. Many early graduates became college Presidents at other schools such as **Joseph M'Keen 1771** (Bowdoin), **Jesse Appleton 1792** (Bowdoin), **Zephaniah Swift Moore 1793** (Williams, founding President of Amherst), **Philander Chase 1796** (founding President of Kenyon and Jubilee Colleges), and **Samuel Willey 1845** (once referred to as the first citizen of California and a founder of the University of California, Berkeley); or lawyer politicians like **Daniel Webster 1801**(US Representative, US Senator; twice US Secretary of State; three times a candidate for, and arguably the most significant politician to not be elected to, the US Presidency), **Levi Woodbury 1809** (US Senator, both US Secretary of the Navy and the Treasury; US Supreme Court Justice), **Thaddeus Stevens 1814** (the most powerful member of the US House of Representatives, Chairman of Reconstruction after the Civil War), **Salmon P. Chase 1826** (the only person ever to serve as a State Governor, US Senator, a US Cabinet Secretary and Chief of the US Supreme Court); and many, many more… businessman, lawyers, doctors, educators, etc. And the qualities of these earlier Dartmouth graduates were reflected in the capabilities of the students at Dartmouth as it entered the 20th century.

The same qualities of intelligence and the ability to become great leaders were coursing through the veins of Fred Harris, Carl Shumway, **John Carleton '22, Charley Proctor '28** and all the Dartmouth skiing legends to follow. The raw material was present in the student population at Dartmouth to provide great leaders for something; and the industry of skiing became the resulting target once the skiing sport was identified as a place to be involved.

The Presence of Three Great Graduate Schools

In the building of the complex industry that makes up modern skiing, it has taken a variety of talents beyond just pure skiing abilities and the development of those abilities. Businesses require experienced, thoughtful, and imaginative leadership. Technical challenges often require engineering talents to find solutions. And the injuries of skiing are a fact of life that requires trained medical staff to handle. No other institution in the world has not only the ski history of Dartmouth College, but also three outstanding collaborative graduate schools that have been in operation throughout the development of modern skiing.

The Amos Tuck School of Business Administration was the first of its kind in the U.S. (1900). Similarly, the Thayer School of Engineering was the first professional engineering school in the U.S. (1867). And the Dartmouth Medical School (DMS) was started in 1797, becoming only the fourth such school in this country. These schools were all operating when Harris started the DOC in 1909 and they provided another resource of talent to deal with the business, engineering and medical issues of the ski industry. Today, Tuck is recognized by leading business media like the *Wall Street Journal* and London's *Financial Times* as arguably the leading business school in the world. Thayer and DMS are recognized as outstanding providers of engineering and medical education. And as is outlined throughout this book, the alumni of these schools have been frequent players in the development of modern skiing. This is another critical factor in the diversity of skills involved in skiing that have come to this role with a Dartmouth connection.

The Leadership provided by Dartmouth College Presidents

Another often overlooked factor in the establishment of skiing at Dartmouth has been the leadership provided by a number of the eminent Dartmouth Presidents from the late 19th Century to today. Few new activities take place in a substantial way on a college campus or in any organization if the top leadership is not in favor of them. In Dartmouth's skiing developments, one key ingredient has been the presence of a series of innovative and forward-thinking college Presidents. This has been a very special and critically important element of the mixture of ingredients that positioned Dartmouth for its growth as the leading institution in the development of skiing. In particular, four men encouraged many of the early events that happened during their terms of office, and sometimes outside their terms in office, to enable the Dartmouth involvement in skiing to get started and reach the point of principal leadership outlined in this book.

President William Jewett Tucker 1861 was the first of several Dartmouth Presidents to encourage modern skiing developments.

The first of these Presidents to impact the skiing activity was no doubt President **William Jewett Tucker 1861** (President from 1893 to 1909) who was a factor in Dartmouth affairs from his days as a student, his election in 1878 as a Dartmouth Trustee, leading in to his years as President, and then as President Emeritus until his death in 1926 when he was still residing in Hanover. President Tucker's leadership led to an increase in the student body from 300 to 1100, the addition of 20 major new buildings, the creation of a central heating plant, and the creative innovation of the world's first, and still viewed as a world-leading, business school, The Amos Tuck School of Business Administration. He hosted the first visit by a member of Dartmouth's namesake family from England, the 6th Earl of Dartmouth who came to lay the 1904 cornerstone for rebuilding historic Dartmouth Hall which had burned down earlier that year. Important to the skiing story, President Tucker believed in the need for every man to develop capacities within themselves. And he lived by this creed as President Woodrow Wilson, amongst a large gathering of nearly 100 of the most important College Presidents of the time at the inauguration of Tucker's successor, is reputed to have said, "President Tucker shows what the power of a single man can do." How prophetic those words were to be about one Fred Harris.

Tucker's long involvement in the local Hanover scene during the formative years of skiing had to have been a positive factor in the growth of the sport locally. He would have supported the growing level of individual initiative being shown by members of the newly formed DOC and the community involvement in Dartmouth's local ski programs. And in another side aspect, his stature amongst his US peers would have been known in England by individuals such as Arnold Lunn, a person who enjoyed association with institutions of the quality of Oxford University and Dartmouth. Lunn would recognize that Dartmouth was a college deserving international respect, and this is likely to have been another factor influencing Lunn's acceptance of Dartmouth-educated skiers in to his sphere of influence as well as being a factor in Lunn's willingness to travel to Hanover to deliver lectures in later years.

Tucker was succeeded for a relatively short—but crucial to the start of skiing—term of office by **Earnest Fox Nichols** (serving from 1909 to 1916). Nichols was a graduate of the Kansas Agricultural College (1888), a scholar, and a physics professor at both Dartmouth and Columbia University. Nichols had been involved at Dartmouth before taking on a similar faculty position at Columbia prior to answering Tucker's call to return to Hanover in the role of President. Nichols believed in the importance of broad-based scholarship to support the moral and spiritual growth of students. As an outgrowth of his belief in supporting things that broadened his student's experience, he fostered the start of the Dartmouth Outing Club and the first Dartmouth Winter Carnivals during his time of office. As noted in Chapter II, President Nichols was intensely interested in the Outing Club because he said it bred a love for out-of-doors and contributed better to a well-balanced physical development than other forms of athletics. This theme of the out-of-doors exposures being helpful to the full development of a student's potential is common both to many of these Presidents and integral to the huge, successful growth of skiing at this particular college.

The third President in this line, **Ernest Martin Hopkins '01** (President from 1916 to 1945), was another who maintained a lifelong relationship with Dartmouth and Hanover from his start as an undergrad in 1897 to his death in 1964. "Hoppy" was a man of many talents. He grew up in New Hampshire and was working in a stone quarry when he surprised his family with a decision to attend Dartmouth where he more or less stayed for the rest of his life. He was not an academic. He spent much of his life at Dartmouth, but had practical experience in his younger years and later years managing business or government organizations. He was a skilled leader and businessman. If there was a single leader who provided the glue that held together the connection between all the relevant elements of Dartmouth's role in the growth of skiing, Hoppy has a right to assert

that his position should be at the head of a long queue. First he was on or around the campus when we have indicated that most of the early ski efforts were taking place. After graduating from Dartmouth, President Jewett asked him to stay on as his clerk and then made him Secretary of the College in 1905. In this role, he organized the first meeting of what became the Class Secretaries alumni association. He both started and served as the first President of the Alumni Council. Another factor in the evolvement of the Dartmouth role in skiing was the interconnections between its alumni, something that Hoppy would have helped build. In 1954, alumni launched a program called the Alumni Award to recognize those amongst the alumni body who were active workers on behalf of the college, recognized as having success in their careers, and effective in helping others. The first recipient of this award was Hopkins.

Governor Rockefeller '30 told President Hopkins '01 at the opening ceremony for the Hopkins Center in 1962: "I came to Dartmouth because of you."

President Hopkins was a man with a wide range of contacts built up over decades of reaching out to help and participate in the world, not always an easy thing to do from Hanover, NH. He served his country in World War I as an Assistant Secretary of War and in World War II as a leader in the Office of Production and Management. President Franklin Roosevelt was a personal friend who was awarded a Dartmouth honorary degree by Hopkins years before he became President of the United States. Hopkins traveled to Europe and west to California where he met heads of state as well as actresses like Joan Bennett. His educational objective was simply to continuously evolve the idea of what an undergraduate education should encompass. He was a figure of considerable importance for many Dartmouth alumni as **Nelson Rockefeller '30**, former four-term New York State Governor and U.S. Vice President, stated at the dedication of the Hopkins Center in 1962, when he turned to the man for whom the building was named and said, "I came to Dartmouth because of you."[2]

In his long involvement with Dartmouth, Hopkins interacted with all the skiing legends from Fred Harris to great ski racers of the 1950s. He was a friend of ski-interested alumni of all sorts from **Judge McLane '07** to **Sherman Adams '20** to many more. He was there to approve the building of the Vale of Tempe Ski Jump, and the hiring of the

President Hopkins '01 at his 80th birthday party with friends; (l to r) Nelson Rockefeller '30 plus Hopkins, Judge McLane '07 (Chairman of D Trustees), President Dickey '29, and Sherman Adams '20 who all played key roles in the development of skiing (1958).

European ski coaches in the 1920s and 1930s. He would have supported the ski efforts of Dartmouth's "team" that out-skied the other US skiers in the first Winter Olympic trials in 1935 at Mt. Rainier. He would have sanctioned the monies spent in the 1930s on the Hanover Golf Course rope tow, the innovative design of the Oak Hill overhead cable ski lift, and the ski team's trip to Chile to participate in the first ski meet south of the Equator. He was a native of the region and more or less a resident of Hanover from 1897 onward, so he would have been enthusiastic about the children he encountered locally learning to ski through the efforts of Dartmouth College and its students.

And at the expense of being accused of belaboring this leadership edge, Hopkins was replaced by another long-serving President, **John Sloan Dickey '29** (1945 to 1970). Dickey was a specialist in International Affairs; he created the "Great Issues" course to expose Dartmouth students to the major problems of the domestic and international world. Is it any surprise that some of Dartmouth's greatest foreign skiing legends attended the college in Dickey's time? As has been reported earlier, one of Dickey's most famous interactions with the skiers of Dartmouth was trying to explain Dartmouth's obsession with skiing to legendary skier **Chick Igaya '57** of Japan who wrote a Foreword for this book and mentions fondly the immense personal value of his undergraduate days. It is Dickey who approved of the plans to build the Dartmouth Skiway.

And the presidential support for things involving skiing has continued. The approval of President **David T. McLaughlin '54** (1981 to 1987) was important in the 1980s for improvements to the Dartmouth Skiway that included the introduction of snowmaking. And President **James Wright** (1998 to 2009) approved further upgrades at the Skiway and provided guidance to this project in his just completed term of office. The support of these various Presidents for the sometimes difficult to come by funding for skiing activities, and their personal belief in the leadership values gained through student involvement in the DOC and other student skiing organizations, have been another critical background factor in Dartmouth's skiing history.

Philanthropic Alumni to support Growth of Ski Program

The final element in the development of skiing at Dartmouth is the role that philanthropy plays in our story. Starting with **Johnny E. Johnson 1866**, carried on by Fred Harris, and evolving through support from the Brundage family, Lowell Thomas, Jr., the McLane family, the Macomber Family, Dupré family and others have made many of the needed facilities available—from ski jumps to base lodges, uniforms and trophies, equipment, travel, snowmaking, and other advantages enjoyed by Dartmouth skiers. This has been realized partly through the skills of Dartmouth's historic leadership in soliciting support from its alumni (with its strong network of alumni, an early tradition of philanthropy, organizational skills of its Development staff), and partly thru the initiative of a few very dedicated individuals. When one considers the growth of Dartmouth skiing, it is this single element that has been absolutely necessary to enable Dartmouth skiing to sustain its distinctive leadership role throughout the history of modern skiing.

These factors of the environment, the outdoor interests of students, the individual raw intellectual and leadership talent of these students, the supportive leadership of several Presidents, and the available resources from philanthropy provided by knowledgeable skiing supporters have mixed together in ways hard to isolate, but which have been very instrumental in enabling the building of the enduring ski history that we have outlined. One net result is that Dartmouth has been getting a larger share of the type of student who just might go on to work and eventually lead organizations associated with an outdoor activity like skiing. Assuming Dartmouth provides them with lots of reasons to be enthusiastic about an ongoing involvement in skiing, the skiing industry would be the major beneficiary of a select group of contributors.

THE DEVELOPMENT OF SKI ENTHUSIASM

The Dartmouth story has many aspects to it. It is complex and on-going. Wherever there is snow, someone from the greater Dartmouth family seems to be involved there promoting and developing activities to make appropriate use of the winter environment. The earlier discussion outlined the enabling factors in the Dartmouth College situation. Even with these background factors in play, a *Passion for Skiing* would not develop without other more pragmatic activities taking place on campus to crystallize feelings of personal enthusiasm. In assessing these activities, here are a number of the specific elements that deserve special mention.

The DOC's Development of Leaders

With little question, the organization that has had the most important role in the development of skiing is the Dartmouth Outing Club, the leader amongst all US outing clubs, past and present. Born of the inspiration of a single man, Fred Harris, the DOC has gone from strength to strength for over 100 years. It was not the start of skiing at Dartmouth or skiing in the United States, but as one looks over the many stories outlined in this book, it is hard not to be impressed with both the unique leadership role the DOC has played since that first call to Dartmouth students urging them to get outside and enjoy the recreational wonders of New Hampshire in its snowy months, and the exceptional leadership training that the DOC students are exposed to during their undergraduate years.

The DOC has maintained a special role in life on the Dartmouth campus. No other organization of such substance has been largely student-run, which it still is today. Yes, there have been important full-time adult leaders from the amazing Dan Hatch to the new man in the job, Dan Nelson. They deal with much of the key decision making. But the bulk of the tasks and work involves student participation and leadership, and because of this, the DOC has had a need to develop leaders within its ranks. The opportunities for students to take charge of a task and put leadership skills into practice seem unending. The DOC has many core responsibilities: managing the training, travel, and home events of the college ski team program (possibly the only collegiate ski racing program to be conducted outside of a college's Athletic Department); supervising the hundreds of fist-year students on their pre-matriculation Freshman Trip into the White Mountains (Is there any other college in the US or elsewhere that provides such an op-

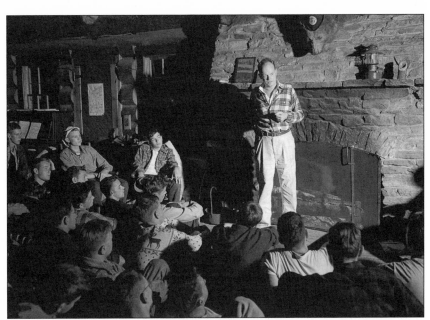

Started in 1935, the unique Dartmouth Freshman Trip has usually involved small groups of Freshman spending 2 days hiking the Appalachian Trail plus 2 days climbing or just hanging out at the Mt. Moosilauke base camp; here President Dickey '29 meets with one of the Freshman groups at the Ravine Lodge in the 1950s , an orientation task repeated several times with different small groups throughout each August and September by all Dartmouth Presidents.

portunity for self-awareness at the beginning of one's college experience?); management of the recreational opportunities at the huge Second Dartmouth Land Grant (27,000 acres of northern New Hampshire wilderness); management of a mountain (Mt. Moosilauke may only be 4,800 feet high, but it is where the history of skiing has seen so many firsts); the planning, organizing, and oversight of the most well-recognized college winter social and sporting weekend in the U.S.—the Dartmouth Winter Carnival (the source of so much of the early enthusiasm for skiing with early ski races, the fostering of ski racing for children and women, the early focus of European skiers coming to ski in the U.S., etc.); the technical support needed for ski lift design and snowmaking; and much more. Yes, the DOC deserves top billing in any analysis of skiing at Dartmouth and skiing anywhere, but it is through its training of leaders who can leave Dartmouth, enthusiastic about skiing, to venture out in to the broader ski world—and other fields of endeavor, whether skiing-related or not—that the DOC may have made its greatest impact.

None of us has the prescience to predict with confidence the challenges that the 21st century poses for Dartmouth, its graduates, and the world; but I think we can be confident that the need for competent and experienced leaders will be no less in this new century than in the last. By its very nature, the DOC trains leaders and will continue to make a positive contribution to this need whether in skiing or elsewhere.

The Creative Innovations

From the very beginning, the DOC and other Dartmouth family members have had opportunities to innovate skiing activities of all sorts. In the Hanover scene, the early creation of a Winter Field Day that quickly morphed into the Dartmouth Winter Carnival was a particularly important event as it provided a venue to create many other activities and a way for people to become familiar with, and enthusiastic for, the sport of skiing. The promotional value of simple items like Dartmouth Winter Carnival posters and various newspaper and magazine stories about this Mardi Gras of the North cannot be overlooked as a great stimulant to getting people on skis. The lasting impact of newly-introduced ski racing methods and formats and the creation of new lift techniques to enable people to move up mountain more easily were also key products of the DOC. And the early inclusion of children in the Hanover area to this new sport of skiing led to numerous leaders of skiing who did not attend Dartmouth or its graduate schools, but who nevertheless made their own impact on aspects of skiing as a direct result of this enthusiastic and broadly inclusive ski operation at the college. There is some undefined natural process that usually results in innovative people being enthusiastic about what they are doing. So the many individuals who have participated in the innovations developed in Hanover will have left this area with positive feelings about a continued involvement in something that has made them happy in some way.

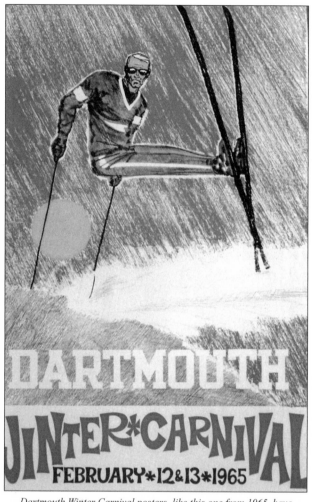

Dartmouth Winter Carnival posters, like this one from 1965, have advertised the "Mardi Gras of the North" for 100 years.

Ski Racing Success

It is hard to imagine that any institution could have had such a significant and lasting impact on recreational skiing in the U.S. without also playing a major role in ski racing. And of course, Dartmouth has played the major role in ski racing from day one—forming the first ski team; participating in the first collegiate races; establishing the major race techniques by organizing the earliest US competitions in slalom (1925 in Hanover), the modern-form downhill (1927 at Moosilauke), and the giant slalom (1937 at Tuckerman Ravine); generating the most national champion racers across the many ski disciplines; placing the most athletes and staff on US Olympic teams; etc.

Dartmouth, especially in the last 30 years or so, may not have had the best collegiate team record, winning fewer collegiate championships than in earlier decades, but it may still have had the best collection of student racers. This seems like a contradiction, but consider the continuing flow of Dartmouth national champions and the number of Dartmouth athletes on the US (and other country) Winter Olympic teams. Although not as dominant as perhaps in the 1930s or 1950s, the Dartmouth skiers are still at the front of the line in terms of the numbers of serious participants in all the disciplines.

It is not possible to easily prove a statement of Dartmouth supremacy in having the best ski talent today, but it is possible to show some factors that have led to Dartmouth's ski team results being less eminent than in prior years. First, consider that the philosophy of the Dartmouth coaches from the early days has been to encourage their

The ski racing trophies earned by Dartmouth's 2007 NCAA Ski Team Champions.

skiers to fulfill their *personal* ski objectives by skiing at higher levels than just the collegiate race circuit—even for other national teams—and to not feel constrained by an implied priority to ski for the Dartmouth team. Numerous skiers have commented on this in the pages of this book, usually with a combination of long-standing appreciation and belated awe. Also, consider the establishment in 1972 of the totally unique four-term attendance plan, the Dartmouth Plan that allows all Dartmouth students to select any of four terms to be on campus during the year. This academic calendar schedule allows student athletes, like skiers, to elect to ski in Europe or elsewhere during the winter and to attend college classes in the summer or off-season times. It also allows them to extend collegiate study beyond the normal four-year college schedule.

No other US institution—or possibly any major academic institution in the Free World— has structured its school year as Dartmouth has done. Dartmouth encourages all of its students to take regular advantage of this scheduling calendar for a variety of personal objectives, not just skiing. Therefore, many of Dartmouth's best skiers have set up school attendance calendars that take them off campus to race in other venues during the collegiate ski season (with the full support of Dartmouth ski coaches). This has resulted in numerous skiers competing at FIS or Olympic meets rather than for the college's ski team. This has perhaps not been so true at other institutions because they do not have the same coaching philosophy, can't allow the academic flexibility, or their racers—particularly foreign racers— prefer to gain a US experience. Therefore, Dartmouth is often fielding less than its best potential team—but the across-the-board quality is still so good that even the second team places well up in the competitive standings.

Scott Macartney '01 is one of the few leading racers on the current US Olympic A Team who has managed to graduate from college. He matriculated at Dartmouth in 1997 and graduated in 2004!…but he never skied for Dartmouth. He is an example of how in the past three decades, Dartmouth ski teams have rarely had the best skiers in the school competing for it. Others like **David Chodounsky '08** and **Roger Brown '04** skied for Dartmouth and then qualified for the US national ski team after graduation. **Bradley Law '02** (of Australia) and **Patrick Biggs '06** (of Canada) qualified for their national teams after starting to ski at Dartmouth. However, despite these losses, Dartmouth's coaching staff has still turned out winners or placed students high in every discipline in NCAA finals each year. In one recent five straight year stretch (2002 – 2006), five different Dartmouth skiers won the NCAA National Slalom Championship title.

Success in ski racing breeds enthusiasm for skiing just by itself. However, the way in which the college's four-semester system works together with the liberal philosophy of Dartmouth's coaches builds the best ski program for the individual and leads to an exceptionally positive feeling on the part of these skiers for both skiing and the college that sends these skiers out into the ski world with a desire to give back to both.

Outstanding Coaches

Dartmouth has been blessed with many great ski coaches. We have discussed some of the early coaches, like Prager and Schniebs, at some length. These men came to the Dartmouth campus through the foresight and active work of many individuals, from DOC founder Fred Harris to early DOC benefactor Reverend John Johnson, an 1866 Dartmouth graduate, and to many more alumni and staff over the years (e.g., **Proctor 1900, McCrillis '19, Fowler '21, Miller '24, Hatch '28, Proctor '28**, etc.). These coaches have been outstanding leaders in the development of skiing in the U.S. Their enthusiasm was catching and Dartmouth skiers caught it as well as others. Prospective skiers for Dartmouth were attracted to the school to work with these outstanding coaches. This was certainly true by the time Walter Prager's name had become familiar through his recruiting efforts for the 10th Mountain Division in WW II, his work with Olympic teams, and the exploits of his ski teams in the 1930s and 1940s.

The attraction of skiing for Dartmouth coaches has been on-going as there has been a succession of great coaches who have performed in the past 35 years, just as there was in the early days. **Anne Thomas**

Anne Thomas Donaghy '77 skied on the 1977 AIAW Championship Team.

Donaghy '77 writes that she was grateful to be a 'legacy child' and have the opportunity to know of and ski for Coach Merrill:

"I really couldn't imagine going anywhere else. Dartmouth had started a women's ski team the very first year the college went co-ed. Since Al Merrill was coaching the cross-country women, I went to Dartmouth mostly to become coached by him. He'd been a family friend of my granddad's and my father's, and some of my happiest memories of Dartmouth center around skiing with the "Silver Fox" as everyone called him. He had even helped us drive a van of furniture when my family moved from the East to Alaska in 1960. Al loved skiing, coaching, waxing, and seemingly knew everyone in the ski world, and everyone seemed to love Al. The two big cross-country ski events that I helped volunteer with every winter in Hanover area are Dartmouth's Carnival and the Silver Fox Trot which honored Al. His service to Dartmouth, heading the outdoor program, and coaching the ski team spanned many years and some of those years he was also a US National and Olympic ski coach and FIS delegate."[3]

The Dartmouth coaches of today buy in to the philosophies of their predecessors and help present Dartmouth to prospective skiers as a very special place to participate in skiing. **Peter Dodge '78**, currently Dartmouth Men's Alpine Ski Coach, outlined the philosophy of current coaches:

"I have always believed that by supporting and allowing those skiers to pursue their highest potential, and possibly never actually compete for Dartmouth, I am supporting the mission of Dartmouth College to provide and support the pursuit of excellence. To be able to provide a skier the opportunity to compete at a world-class level AND achieve a Dartmouth degree is both very rewarding and speaks well for Dartmouth."[4]

Dartmouth coaches of today are working hard at their sport all year round just like Dartmouth skiers and coaches have been doing since the 1930s. For example, Coach Peter Dodge reported in to our project this past summer from Chile where he and fellow Dartmouth coach, Christine Booker, were conducting ski seminars on slopes similar to where Ralph Miller set his speed record in 1955, and where an earlier Dartmouth ski team participated in the first races south of the equator in the late 1930s. Peter Dodge comments:

"The Dartmouth skiing tradition continues. Today I am high in the Andes, at La Parva, Chile. We are fogged and snowed in today so it is a day to finally get to some email. Life is tough in the mountains. The past 3 years, Christine Booker and I have worked with the USSA National Development System [USSA NDS] to put together a Collegiate develop camp in Chile. By working with USSA NDS, we are able to extend our training opportunities. Our camp includes two members of the team, Michael Ankeny, and Keith Moffat (from Squaw) who will be leaving a USSA project that follows our camp a week early, to matriculate at Dartmouth. They will then take advantage of the Dartmouth Plan to ski with the USSA this winter."[5]

Once again the Dartmouth coaches show their interest in advancing the skiing performance of the individual and not just in the seasonal results of the team. One may well imagine the high level of respect this builds for the Dartmouth approach and the goodwill it brings for skiing in the minds of these young skiers.

Development of Ski Skills/Interest while attending Dartmouth

A final influencing consideration is the number of individuals who leave Dartmouth having simply learned to ski while studying in Hanover. Many of these love their newfound skiing skill and look forward to making future runs on ski mountains elsewhere. Through the decades, thousands of these happy skiers have gone on to renew and improve their skiing skills on trails, glades, and open slopes throughout the world.

But there is another group of skiers who learned not only to ski, but to compete, after arriving in Hanover. Many students arrive at Dartmouth or other ski schools with serious racing results in their background. They are often recruited to display their previously learned skills on behalf of that college. Perhaps more so than is the case on most other ski school campuses, many of Dartmouth's competitive skiers have been developed by its coaches from non-racers. We have no proof, but we suspect few other college ski coaches willingly spend their time on a mission to develop ski racers out of the casual skier attending their college. They would want to spend their time rounding off and improving established skiers.

At Dartmouth, the philosophy of helping each skier, no matter at what level, to thrive is a teaching role that has been engrained since the early days when Fred Harris encouraged the Outing Club to host some

The "mighty" Hanover Golf Club hill and rope tow where so many first learned to ski.

different races and to participate in general teaching programs. This sort of unofficial Dartmouth ski racing philosophy is a step beyond the related coaching practices we have outlined earlier (i.e., encouraging good skiers to follow a path that is best for his or her individual improvement and not be caught up in the impact on team results). It is very well expressed by **Edward Williams '64** in his profile of former coach Al Merrill [Chapter XIV], where Ed credits Al with having coached somebody with no prior experience—namely, Ed himself—into a national champion and enthusiastic member of the ski community. Maybe this helps explain why so many Dartmouth skiers go on to develop different aspects of ski racing or the ski industry after college.

In Ed William's case, he was a marginal Alpine racer when he started college with little earlier experience and little expectation of being a star skier. Under Coach Al Merrill's tutelage he became one of the best Nordic racers in the U.S., winning the National 30-km Cross-Country Championships in 1963; taking first place in the cross-country event in each of the Middlebury, Williams, St Lawrence and Dartmouth Winter Carnival competitions in his senior year; and twice being named an All-American Skier. Following graduation from Dartmouth, Ed was selected to join the United States Army Biathlon Unit in Alaska. He competed in the World Biathlon Championships in 1966 (finishing as the best American) and in both the individual biathlon and relay events in the 1968 Winter Olympics (Grenoble, France). But perhaps even more important, the Merrill lessons gave Ed an enthusiasm for participating in skiing in other ways too. He was named to the US Olympic Committee in 1976 and

Ed Williams '64 was a National Champion and Olympic skier who learned all of his skills at Dartmouth.

served as Chairman of its Athletes' Advisory Council. Following graduation from law school, Ed has been an unwavering advocate of athletes' rights, including the basic right to compete, which was recognized by Congress in the passage of the Amateur Sports Act of 1978 (which Ed helped draft), now known (as amended in 1998) as the Ted Stevens Olympic and Amateur Sports Act.

This same skier enthusiasm was passed on to **Nina Cook Silitch '94** during her undergraduate days in Hanover. In the 2008/2009 season, Nina finished 13th as a racer in Ski Mountaineering in France, and she may represent the U.S. at the 2010 World Championships in Andorra. She credits coaches Cami Thompson and Ruff Patterson of the Dartmouth Cross-Country Ski Team for much of her discipline in this unusual sport which is sort of a throwback to the early days of skiing when a person had to climb the mountain before skiing down. A typical ski mountaineering race somewhat resembles the alpine stage of the Tour de France without the bike—up and down, up and down! The training plan she uses today is very similar to the principles used at Dartmouth, where she learned the importance of year-round training–something needed in ski mountaineering. Trail running and hiking were common dry-land training activities for the ski team. In college, the teams' long-distance runs on Sundays seemed endless at two or three hours. "It's hard to believe that 15 years out of college, my legs carried me across the Alps to finish 10th in the **Ultra-Trail** du **Mont-Blanc.** The race is over 103 miles with one large loop around the huge Mont Blanc massif starting in France, then south through Italy, north through Switzerland, and back west into France for the finish. Through skiing at Dartmouth, I learned teamwork, commitment and discipline, valuable traits that have encouraged me to follow my dreams"[6], says Nina.

The typical and the not-so-typical skier get educated in various ways at Dartmouth. But some of those ways can impact the wider ski world via producing a special enthusiasm for the sport within this group of Dartmouth-coached skiers. When combined with the intellectual and leadership skills to achieve results in any field that they elect to spend their time in, the possibilities are there for these individuals to become leaders in spreading the word about skiing or taking on an active role in the industry.

THE USES FOR THESE ENTHUSIASMS

In these chapters, we have highlighted the many ways that an enthusiasm for skiing has translated into positive ski-related activities by the members of the Dartmouth family. Here is a recap of some of these activities.

The Ski Club Phenomenon

The importance of ski clubs generating local enthusiasm for skiing cannot be overstated. One aspect of this was the start of the DOC and its encouragement of outing clubs in other colleges. Another was the "town and gown" mixing of locals and students in the Hanover area via the Carcajou Club and similar ski club groups. And the third was the growth of local ski clubs across the U.S. In many of these situations, an element of the Dartmouth community was involved either directly or by providing a point of contact on the needs of skiing. More than anything else, these clubs all generated further enthusiasm for skiing. Sometimes it was as simple as hosting a ski movie or singing ski songs. **Peter Caldwell '54** writes:

> "In the 1953-54 ski season, the officers of Carcajou were, Peter Caldwell '54 President and Tom Corcoran Vice-President. We had a very successful year, including sponsoring a Warren Miller film in Webster Hall with proceeds donated to the U.S. Ski Team, as I recall. We also gathered the Carcajou songs in to a 17-page Song Book with a cover designed by Shorty Chase, wife of Pete Chase, and mimeographed by my mother." [7]

Whatever the approach, the net result was usually a growth in the number of enthusiastic skiers.

The Dartmouth Members, 10th Mountain Division

It is very clear that one of the most significant factors in the development of US skiing was the more than 120 dedicated Dartmouth skiers who participated in the 10th Mountain Division in WW II. After their military service, many of them left simply wanting to stay young forever and enjoy the life they had led in the mountains. To achieve this, they became involved in the relatively new ski industry, doing things they loved. It was one of those fateful decisions that alumni, returning from war, had to make: Do I join the very early stage ski industry or what else do I do with my life? Some families no doubt discouraged their sons from joining the ski industry at that point since the future for these entrepreneurs was likely to be haphazard, financially uncertain, and very hard work. Yet the thrill of participating in this sport almost every day led to many members of the 10th finding jobs in the industry or to creating their own ski business. So just as their skiing and mountaineering skills had led them to become involved in the mountain troops, they also led them to become involved in the ski industry. And their enthusiasm, intelligence, experience and leadership led them once again to take the lead in founding and managing the various components of this new industry.

The Establishment of Ski Areas in Almost Every Part of the Country

We have devoted three chapters to documenting the substantial number of ski areas that have grown up with the involvement of members of the Dartmouth family. The number of ski areas founded, designed, or managed by Dartmouth alumni is staggering, but even more telling is the several hundred more which were developed with the technical or business assistance of Dartmouth founded/managed S-E Engineering and other Dartmouth ski area consultants. Before our research turned up the many connections in ski resort development, none of us had appreciated that Dartmouth alumni were so omnipresent as to be able to show multiple involvements in ski areas in every region of the country from the East Coast to the West Coast, from the South, up thru the Mid-Atlantic and Mid-West to the Far North of Alaska. Even with famed mountains like Vail, founded by individuals with no direct connection to the Dartmouth family, there have nonetheless been a significant number of Dartmouth people involved. In fact, the Vail case is a classic example of the indirect Dartmouth influence. Although the principal founders were not Dartmouth family members, our research clearly showed the influence of alumni like Dick Durrance I on Peter Seibert, the principal driving force of Vail. Pete worked for Durrance in Aspen and sought his advice prior to the decision to make this mountain a ski area. Pete had many Dartmouth mates in the 10th Mountain Division. **John Litchfield '39** and **Percy Rideout '40** were two of Pete's Dartmouth 10th Mountain contacts and he had worked with them at the Aspen ski instruction operations. However, even more important factors in the case of Vail were the early financial work of **Chuck Lewis '58** (later the founder of the Copper Mountain ski area) and the 25-year management of Vail Mountain by the legendary **Sarge Bill Brown**.

The Promotion of Skiing through Movies, Books and Other Means

In developing the skiing industry, one of the fundamental elements has simply been the communicating of an enthusiasm for skiing along with information on what the evolving elements of the industry were doing. As we have shown, from the very early days, Fred Harris, Carl Shumway, Jack McCrillis, Dick Durrance I and many, many others in the Dartmouth family have played a significant role in promoting the sport of skiing. Advertising, movies, magazine articles, books, and other media have been used in a variety of ways to promote the ski business. One of the most significant individuals in the ski movie business has been Warren Miller, and we are very pleased to have his personal participation in this book and his acknowledgement of some important Dartmouth alumni he has worked with over 60+ years. Our title and book theme is the "Passion for Skiing." Our communication effort has been largely about sharing with others the enthusiasm these influential individuals felt themselves, and thereby stoking the fires in people's mind to increase the likelihood of their participating one way or another in sliding over snow.

The Development of Support Industries

The ski industry involves much more than just the action taking place on ski mountains. There is a wide range of other support activities that have developed in the past 100 years to provide the substance (ski clothing, skis, housing, other sliding equipment, etc.) to enable the average skier to get ready to slide down a mountain or cross fields of snow. In our research, we were surprised at the numbers of Dartmouth alumni and family who have played a role in developing companies, serving as key employees in other companies, and providing "stuff" needed to participate in this sport. No one had looked at this aspect of skiing in detail before, and there was no information available to show how involved the Dartmouth community has been in all these support functions. At this point, we believe our research has just scratched the surface. Our word-of-mouth research campaign has led to a number of interesting stories surfacing on Dartmouth family members working in one support industry or another. However, we believe many more individuals will be found in the future who have played a similar role, and we trust our description of so many past and present contributors in this aspect of skiing will encourage more to follow this path. Skiing is a complex industry. There are many different supporting roles and many different skills required. This provides lots of future opportunities for enthusiastic ski-oriented individuals such as those coming out of the leading ski school.

The Involvement in Technical and Medical Areas

Skiing is a simple sport in many ways, but behind the actual skiing activity is a wide array of technical disciplines to properly organize Alpine and Nordic facilities. Once again, this is an area that has never been fully explored other than to recognize the work of obvious ski industry stars like **Sel Hannah '35** and **Jim Branch '52**. But when you go to school at Dartmouth and maybe spend time at the Thayer School to study engineering, you just might use your technical talent in the vicinity of ski areas. The array of Dartmouth contributions is very broad, including snowmaking, ski area configuration, lift design, and various other on-mountain technologies. The involvement of the Thayer School staff and students started right at the beginning of the Dartmouth ski story as we have highlighted earlier. Today, ski area mountain managers recognize the value of technical support to create an efficient operation, particularly with the new trend to "go green." Dartmouth engineers and technically creative types have growing opportunities as new technologies are required and applied.

John Bowler '15, a life long skier, is seen here on Dartmouth's Oak Hill J-bar. He was one of the participants of the first collegiate ski events in 1910 - 1915, and then a lifelong leader in the components of what is now the well regarded Dartmouth Medical Center.

Similarly, the field of medicine keeps growing as science finds new and better methods of treatment across a wide range of illnesses and injuries. Much of that science will find its way from national mega-facilities and research institutions to regional medical hubs and then out to hundreds of private practice physicians associated with it. As we discussed in Chapter XII, even in this area the Hanover connection between skiing and medicine has been very significant. We outlined the career work of **Dr. John P. "Jack" Bowler '15** in developing the Dartmouth Hitchcock Clinic which provides significant medical care throughout northern New England, including many communities near ski areas. Dr. Bowler was one of the participants of the first Winter Sports Day (1910), the first collegiate ski race (1914), and then held a lifetime leadership role in medicine for Hanover and northern New England as the founder/President of the Dartmouth Clinic (1927), Chairman of the Board for the Mary Hitchcock Hospital and Dean of the Dartmouth Medical School for over 30 years.

At the other end of the health care spectrum are individuals like expert skier **Dr. Amos "Bud" Little '39** who bailed out of a plane over the Colorado Rockies to treat the survivors of a B-17 that had crashed at over 10,000 feet; he saved lives using only what he could carry with him and what he could retrieve from a medical supply drop. And in the same spirit of going where the need was, recreational skier **Dr. Wylie Scott '58**, an orthopedist in California, volunteered his time and paid his own way to accompany members of the US Ski Team to out of the way ski training venues in Europe. And on the senior surgeon level, **Dr. Peter J. Millett, DMS '95** is a renowned shoulder specialist and general orthopedic surgeon who is a partner at the world famous Steadman Hawkins Clinic at the Vail Medical Center in Vail Colorado. Dr. Millett works with many sports teams, particularly the US Ski Team.

Some later medical interested individuals may have found a tie-in between skiing and medical training on the Dartmouth Ski Patrol. Some engineering students may have worked on projects to figure out some engineering trick to enable skiers to go faster. Many of these more technically oriented alumni may just have looked around for ways to combine career and personal interests and found technical or medical opportunities within the expanding communities growing up around ski areas. No one has previously recognized the extent of the Dartmouth involvement in these areas, but with the attention we have focused on it, we anticipate there will be continued growth in the number of Dartmouth technical or medical folks involved in ski communities.

The International Connections

There are many Dartmouth connections with the international environment. We have commented on a long list of examples from early foreign ski coaches to ski missions to Chile and New Zealand to Dartmouth students coming from foreign countries and much more. Sir Arnold Lunn, one of the most important contributors to building up the enthusiasm for modern skiing, was among the most productive international contacts for Dartmouth. Lunn got to know Dartmouth folks at least as early as 1922-23, meeting **John Carleton '22** when John was first skiing for Oxford University. This led to information exchanges with several other people in Hanover, and eventually to visits by Lunn to Hanover starting in November 1936 when Lund gave a talk about skiing.

Lunn also expressed his disenchantment with the Olympics. He was very negative about the value of Olympic competition because he did not like the nationalism it promoted. He was even more nega-tive about women competing in races. Lunn apparently thought that women who stayed in competitive skiing too long became "tough" and no longer feminine. This may have been a viable thought in the

John Carleton '22, one on the many stars in skiing history to grow up in Hanover, NH.

1930s, but certainly one that would stir lots of negative comments today. One might think Lunn was out of step with the Dartmouth folks since the DOC had just organized the first competitive races for women at a Dartmouth Winter Carnival the February preceding his initial visit to Hanover. However, Lunn was not alone in his thinking as the comments expressed by members of the DOC at the time showed that there were some questions within the Dartmouth community on the wisdom of women participating in ski races.

Returning to Hanover several times, Lunn mainly discussed skiing; but later, he also used these visits to express his strong opinions about the Catholic Church, another passion of Sir Arnold, whose early religious beliefs were in a much different direction. The Georgetown University Special Collections Library in Wash-ington, D.C., holds his papers, and most of those are on his views about Catholicism. His exchanges with Professor Proctor and Dan Hatch were sometimes not very friendly. Sir Arnold had strong views on subjects like amateur status, and sometimes the key Dartmouth people did not agree with him. He also knew well a number of other people in the region, like Dartmouth's ski coach Walter Prager (whom Lunn recognized as one of the greatest racers of the 1930s by awarding Walter the fabled Arlberg-Kandahar Diamond Pin in 1956) and Hannes Schneider (with whom Lunn started the A-K races in 1928). The bottom line is that Sir Arnold and his *British Ski Journal* regularly talked up the ski capabilities of the people in Hanover, NH, and at Dartmouth College, publicity which had to be helpful in positioning Hanover and Dartmouth as the early US leaders in skiing.

OTHER COMMENTS

From culling through the many comments and connections generated during the last two years of in-tensive research and three earlier years of light research, there are a few take-away thoughts that we would like to share with the reader. Perhaps these personal descriptions of individual Dartmouth experiences might make our review of the *Passion for Skiing* more real to the reader. As you read the words, think about earlier comments on the enthusiasm passed from one Dartmouth family member to the next and on to the rest of the potential ski community. Think about the role of the contribution of this nation's only mountain troops in fostering skiing activity around the world. Think about the success of Dartmouth ski coaches in encouraging their skiers to keep on developing their skills well beyond college days. Think about the great help to one's life it is to be enthusiastic and passionate about something.

Dick Blum '53 (Cleveland, OH) commented about his going to Dartmouth, skiing, and long lasting friendships:

"This is a terrific project that you are undertaking. I wish I had some great stories to contribute to your research, but I really don't. I do remember back in the Fifties and Sixties that you could never go skiing anywhere without running into Dartmouth guys. And all of the areas were run by folks who knew everybody from the Big Green. A different side of your research could be the impact that Skiing had on Dartmouth. I think that there were a lot of us (like me) who went to Hanover so we could learn to ski. Others already knew how, but wanted to keep it up. The skiing friendships that developed then have continued all of these many years".[8]

Bernt Stigum '56 (Oslo, Norway) wrote about a distant but still fresh incident of personal interaction with Walter Prager:

"You are engaged in a marvelous project, and I am sorry for not having had anything with which to contribute. I was injured in a soccer game and Walter Prager came to Dick's House and told me that it was all right if I concentrated on my studies during the winter season and kept my cross-country skis in the closet. I wondered if you have included a description of how the Dartmouth Skiway was built in 1956. Walter Prager was in charge, and I spent the summer with local workers cutting trails for him. Walter was a wonderful boss. After lunch the last day of my employment he came to my working place and insisted that I come along for a hike. We hiked to the top of the trails, sat down and marveled at the view that confronted us. Walter talked about skiing at Dartmouth and wondered if I was prepared for getting married in a few days. I am not sure I was, but Walter and the other workers gave me presents to help me start my marriage the right way. That afternoon at the Dartmouth Skiway was a memorable event for me. It is, also, an example of the human touch that Walter Prager had in his dealing with other persons...Hjertelig hilsen."[9]

Dudley "Skip" Gill '79 (Saint Louis, MO) writes about his delayed entry as an active skier:

"Although I didn't ski at Dartmouth, I ski because of Dartmouth. Back in the day (1976?!), I learned to wobble on skis — starting at the golf course and then tentatively at the Skiway. I quickly discovered that blue jeans and cotton long underwear aren't warm if they are wet from constant, direct contact with the slope. This prompted a LONG hiatus from "skiing". In the early '90s I retrieved my dust-covered skis from my parent's attic and took them in to a New England ski shop to get tuned. Little did I know that my near pristine Marker bindings with only 2 seasons of use were "antique." A couple of hundred dollars later, I emerged from the shop with new Marker bindings, a poly-pro base layer and a breathable, waterproof outer layer. Folks, I'm here to testify that technology improvements can enhance the user experience. Over the course of the next three winters I went from 10 skiing days, to 22 days, to 54 days a season. I was magically transformed from being a clueless (albeit warm and dry) newbie to a PSIA certified skiing and snowboard instructor. Since then, as a weekend instructor I've shared my passion for snow sports across the U.S., including Paoli Peaks Resort in Indiana with almost 400' of vertical."[10]

Dick Taylor '59 (Bethel, ME), a National Nordic Champion (1960) and US Olympic skier (1964, Innsbruck), provided some interesting insights on skiing and Dartmouth when he met with our chapter writer **Doug Leitch '65**. Doug's notes provided these comments:

"On the degree to which skiing influenced his decision to choose Dartmouth, Dick mentioned that he grew up in Gilford, NH, and was a peer of Penny Pitou and Marty Hall. All three were protégés of Gary Allen '40 who took them all up to ski Tuckerman's when

Dick Taylor '59 in his college days.

they were little tots and their most distinguishing features were knobby knees. He went to Laconia High School in New Hampshire and then transferred to Holderness for his last two years of high school. When it came time to select a college, he said going to Dartmouth would mean keeping skiing in his life, and he made the point that was not the same sentiment as going to Dartmouth to be on the ski team. He could have gone to other great schools like Amherst, but skiing would have soon been forgotten. His choice, as Dartmouth's poet alumnus Robert Frost '96 has written in The Road Not Taken, "made all the difference" and skiing has been his life ever since.

"On the influence of his Dartmouth ski coaches, Dick commented on both Walter Prager and Al Merrill as he was there through the transition from one to the other. He said Prager was a complete gentleman, always wore a sport coat and tie, and was extremely courteous. But what impressed Dick the most was Walt's intellectual inquisitiveness as Prager was always reading authors like T.S. Eliot. Al Merrill was instrumental in getting Dick into cross-country skiing and backed him throughout his own competitive skiing even when he over trained, burned out and did not make the Olympic team for Squaw Valley in 1960. Dick and Al continued working to achieve success for Dick, and a year later he won the National 30-K cross-country race at Andover, Maine, by five minutes. Three years later, Dick not only made, but also was captain of, the 1964 US Nordic Olympic Ski Team for Innsbruck. And as all stories should work out, the Olympic coach who benefitted from Dick's dedication was Al Merrill.

*"He had high praise for another national champion skier, **Ralph Miller, Jr. '55**. They became close friends and training buddies when Miller returned from military service for a year of post-grad at Dartmouth before entering med school. Miller got Taylor interested in going to the anatomy lab at DMS where they could examine cadavers and better understand physiology. Miller also recruited Taylor to volunteer for research on performance physiology at Mary Hitchcock Hospital. He would breathe various mixes of gases (CO_2, helium, nitrogen, etc.) while the researchers monitored his heart rate, blood O_2, etc. As a result he gained a much better understanding about what happened in training. He convinced Al Merrill to institute weight training for the ski team by explaining its advantages; Merrill had been opposed to using weights for his skiers' training before that. Dick wrote a book, No Pain, No Gain?, to express his understanding of training physiology and psychology for young athletes in endurance sports and the role of his philosophy as applied to that.*

"Dick likes to say you have to be smarter to be faster. And he applies that to the reason Dartmouth has historically been a mecca for high-performance skiers. He feels there needs to be a critical mass to attract performance peers and like-minded athletes to benefit from each other's training and ability. Dartmouth has always offered that for skiers, combined with its academic excellence. That academic piece, Dick says, is the "barb on the hook" that attracts good skiers to come to Dartmouth. They appreciate the fact that there is more to high performance than just the body, and that information comes in many forms from various sources.

"Dick was highly complementary on the role Gary Allen (and others like him) played in developing skiing in addition to the more highly visible performers like the Bradleys, Durrances and McLanes. However, he points out that there is another tier of contributors that runs underneath those names who make skiing performance possible simply for the satisfaction of their own love of the sport. He sees those folks as the givers who often don't get the recognition of what their work contributes to many of the ski world's great performers."

H. Newcomb "Newc" Eldredge '50 (Newport, NH) comments on his life-long relationship with members of the 10th Mountain Division:

*"The 10th has had a great impact on my life for over 60 years. I joined out of high school in 1943. I participated in cross-country skiing and ski jumping with an eclectic group of ski lovers. When I attended Dartmouth my two roommates were both 10th vets, and the Administration included several other 10th vets (Director of the DOC **John Rand '38**, Ski Coach Walter Prager, Admissions Officer **John Montagne '42** and **Professor Harry Bond '42**). They all played a role in my college*

*experience - DOC Winter Sports Director, ski squad, mountaineering club, and many adventures with other 10th vets. In Denver during the 1950s, I created the "Dartmouth Cup Ski Race" for high schools on the eastern slope of the Colorado Rockies with the involvement of several Dartmouth alumni, including **Larry Jump '36**, **Keith Anderson '38**, **Dick Rocker '32**, **Harry Lewis '29**, and **Dick Durrance '39** (all were 10th vets or trainers except for Lewis). I have had involvement with other 10th vets regularly over the years on ski trips from New England to Colorado during which the three regiments competed in dual slalom races on Cooper Hill (now known as SKI COOPER). It has been a great life enjoying the out of doors, the mountains, skiing and great friendships honed in time of battle."[11]*

Alan Danson '60 (Vail, CO) prepared some comments for his classmates and their 50th Reunion, and we have included a shortened version here to highlight how skiing has affected the lives of even those not directly in the industry:

"Skiing has shaped my life. I was born in Manhattan in 1939. My father, who was neither an outdoorsman nor a skier, took me to Central Park and put me on skis whenever it snowed. Trips to Bear Mountain followed. When we moved to Larchmont [NY] in 1953, I attended Mamaroneck High School and joined its ski club. We went on trips to Stowe, and when it came time, I chose Dartmouth for college because it was closer to Stowe. I joined the Dartmouth Ski Patrol and, in my senior year, got a job on the Mount Mansfield Ski Patrol. I served as a weekend patrolman in Stowe for the next 10 years, through law school at Harvard and while working on Wall Street, first as a lawyer and then as an investment banker. At the law firm, Winthrop Stimson Putnam & Roberts, I was put in charge of organizing the firm's annual ski weekend, where I met Jerry Kohlberg, a law firm client. Jerry invited me to join the corporate finance department that he ran at Bear Stearns. At Bear Stearns, again because of my skiing interest, I was asked to meet with Bob Beattie, the coach of the U.S. Ski Team, who wanted to do a public offering for a ski equipment company he owned. I moved to Mexico in 1972, and to Colorado when the Mexican economy collapsed in 1982. My wife Sylvia and I soon discovered Vail and fell in love with the mountain and the community. In 1998, we moved full time to Vail, where we have been enjoying the good life for the last 11 years. With any luck, we'll be able to call this home for the next 50 years – skiing all the way home!"[12]

Sam von Trapp '94 (Stowe, VT) commented in the latest von Trapp Family Lodge Newsletter on the family's passion for cross-country skiing:

"Everyone here is buzzing with ski equipment preparations and anticipation of our trails opening officially today. ... My family and I are excited to get out and share our passion for cross-country skiing in this beautiful destination. I'm hoping to lead a back-country tour, my father Johannes will focus on the history and ecology of our woods, and my sister Kristina will share her tips on getting out there with young children."[13]

Chik Onodera '58 (Tokyo, Japan) tells an amusing story of skiing at his favorite ski area in Japan with some friends—or ski bums, as he likes to call them. They encountered another group of elder Japanese skiers and were treated to a long discussion on how old these skiers were. Chik listened to their proud announcements hoping to learn how much longer he could expect to ski as they seemed to think they were the oldest in the room. But it worked out for Chik a bit differently and he found some new friends. In Chik's own words:

"After listening to their statements, we found out that all of them were younger than myself. Then my friend, another ski bum, one year younger than myself stood up and disclosed to the group that I was much older than all the group members which inadvertently put the group in dead silence. We felt sorry for them. However, over breakfast next morning, I was surrounded by the group of new friends who had even frequently helped me to get back onto my snow sliding gears. Sorry for my proud story, but I always think that skiing is the best venue to find out wonderful friends."[14]

Bob French '56 (Santa Fe, New Mexico) just sent us these comments on the groundbreaking traverse of the Bugaboos completed by four hardy alumni over half a century ago. For me, it says much about the adventurous spirit of the Dartmouth skiers in years past, and when one reads the stories of similar feats, such as the on-going "peak-bagging" conquests of **Tim Kelley '79**, one knows that spirit is still alive and well today.

(l to r) Bill Briggs '54, Barry Corbet '58, Sterling Neale '59, Bob French '56 holding their Head skis at the start of their traverse of the Bugaboos (1958).

Briggs first eyes the wide expanse to be crossed (left), and then checks a possible route (center); Corbet crosses the Grand Glaciers River (right).

*In June of 1958, four members of the Dartmouth Mountaineering Club—**Bill Briggs '54, Barry Corbet '58, Sterling Neale '59**, and I—set out from the Bugaboo mountains in British Columbia to attempt an approximately 100-mile ski traverse north to Rogers Pass. The route, now known as the "Grand Traverse," had never been done before, and only a few miles at either end had even been mapped. This was still mostly uncharted territory, but we felt confident we could do it. All four of us had been instructors for the Bill Briggs Ski School in Woodstock, Vermont, and later we all became professional mountaineering guides in Grand Teton National Park.*

The inspiration for the trip originated with Bill Briggs, whose plan was to combine extensive cross-country and expert downhill skiing. Our new-technology Head metal skis—generously given to us by Howard Head, and absolutely essential since a broken ski would have been disastrous given that any kind of help could have been weeks away—were outfitted with cable bindings that could be adjusted for both downhill and cross-country travel; the boots were regular climbing boots with a groove cut into the heel. Also essential were our new Kelty packs which, by holding the weight on our hips and snugly against our backs, allowed us to do the kind of extreme downhill skiing that would be required without the added danger of uncontrolled weight shifting. Equipment included our sleeping bags, mattress pads, two tents, a stove, fuel, and twelve days food, two 120-foot climbing ropes, two ice axes, and two pairs of crampons (some climbing and rappelling proved to be necessary). Still, at the start, our packs weighed an average of 43 pounds each—remarkably light, I would say, especially considering the relatively primitive nature of our equipment.

*The traverse was completed in ten days, largely because of good weather. Except for the last day, when we found ourselves enveloped in dense fog and had to navigate by compass across the Illecillewaet Glacier, the weather treated us kindly. The only way out of Rogers Pass at the time was by train. We hitched a ride in a boxcar to Golden, B.C., where we found the car that **Jim Loghry '56** had left for us. The traverse was not repeated until 1973 when it was done by another four-man team, but in the opposite direction. With the advent of guided tours, helicopter access, updated maps, satellite phones and GPS units, this has now become a popular (but still challenging) route of its kind.*

Some Heroes of this Story

The many Dartmouth members of the National Ski and Snowboard Hall of Fame (NSSHF) have already been recognized for their contributions to skiing. Within that group, we have given much ink to those of several of the most prominent members, including Fred Harris, John Carleton, Sel Hannah, Walter Prager, Dick Durrance, Bill Briggs and both Proctors, all of whom were of particular interest to us as their activities closely fit the story lines we have included. We regret that, due to practical limitations, we could not spend more time on several of the other Hall of Fame members even though all of these NSSHF folks have been major players in the development of skiing.

Gary Allen '40, for example, made significant contributions to aspects of skiing but, unfortunately, he is somewhat unrecognized today. He died just a year ago at age 91 and was still skiing in his 90th year, just like another of our departed friends, **Hermann Nunnemacher '36.** Gary was a great coach; he trained four Olympians, two of whom went to Dartmouth (**Dick Taylor '59** and **Walker T. Weed '71**). Penny Pitou, another legend of skiing, still says she owes much of her success and skiing career to Gary's coaching and mentoring; he drove her to many of her early competitions when she was still a teenager. Dick Taylor commented above on their mutual start with Gary in their earliest years on the ski slopes. Gary was the Assistant Chief of Competition and ran the show for ski jumping at Lake Placid in 1980. It apparently was Gary who insisted they install snowmaking capabilities on the 70-meter and 90-meter hills there, and without his insistence on doing that, Lake Placid would probably not have had a jumping hill for the 1980 Olympics when the weather was not friendly to their needs. He was a regular ski jumping judge and close associate of another legend of jumping, **Dave Bradley '38.** Gary was instrumental in starting the Gunstock (NH) Nordic Association and the Winnipesaukee Ski Club, rebuilding the Gunstock 70- meter ski jump hill to FIS specifications so Gunstock could host international jumping tournaments. Gary never had a high public profile like Walter Prager, Al Merrill, or many of our notables, but that was Gary's style. He was a low-profile personality who just went about doing his organizing and coaching and getting fantastic results. We salute him and the many others like him for whom we had insufficient space to include a proper summary.

There are just so many folks we owe so much to in the development of Dartmouth's skiing prowess, and through that to the skiing industry. What is perhaps not recognized as much as may be deserved are the contributions of a few special members of this group whom we feel shine as brightly as those now enshrined as Hall of Fame members and who may deserve a relook in some future year. Two of these are **Carl Shumway '13** and **Dan Hatch '28.**

Carl Shumway '13: In the two early chapters on the DOC, it was obvious to us that Carl was one of the most significant contributors to getting skiing off the ground at Dartmouth with his early adventure ski trips to Mt. Moosilauke and Tuckerman Ravine plus his leadership role in activities of the DOC. One could almost say that Carl initiated an earlier version of ski mountaineering in 1912 when he led a trip from Hanover to make the first ascent of Mt Moosilauke. He skied from Hanover to the top of Moosilauke and returned, all in two days, on equipment that must have been near impossible to control. That hike was neither as long nor as remote as some aspects of the later 1958 traverse in the Bugaboos by **Bill Briggs '54, Barry Corbet '58, Sterling Neale '59 and Bob French '56,** but it was conceivably just as testing in its day. And Carl's leadership of the 1913 first ascent/descent of Mt. Washington was in some ways as treacherous as Briggs's later adventure on the Grand Teton.

T. Gary Allen '40

Gary Allen '40, a member of the NSSHF, was a quiet, effective leader of skiing.

Walker Weed III '71 was one of Gary Allen's Olympic proteges.

Shumway's father's early financial support for the DOC was one of those moments of philanthropy that we mentioned earlier as a reason for Dartmouth's success in skiing which would not have happened without Carl encouraging his support. In Carl's later life he was constantly involved with innovative activities to promote skiing. His advertising business supported ski areas and a multitude of products for the industry. Carl was at the forefront of the ski train developments that enabled thousands to get to ski areas in the New England region, and his extraordinarily successful efforts to launch annual ski shows in Boston provided support for many different parts of the ski industry.

Dan Hatch '28: Although Dan's main period of activity was relatively short, stretching from his college days (1924-28) through his tenure as General Manager of the DOC (1929-1937), it was eventful and productive. Dan was a man of action. He worked to secure the services of Otto Schniebs in 1930 and later hired Walter Prager. These two exceptionally talented Europeans ushered in a new era of Dartmouth skiing greats. Hatch organized a new ski association to oversee college racing. We have commented on the growth of local clubs in Hanover to provide more opportunities for students to race. It is quite likely that the inspiration and make-it-happen guy was Dan Hatch. His leadership in the development of skiing at Oak Hill and his building the first overhead cable lift there confirmed that Dartmouth was the leader of this sport in North America in the 1930s. Dan saw the growing need for more ski runs and the desirability of uphill ski lifts beyond the difficult rope tow. He put together the team that contributed a remarkable technical achievement for its time. His skills were diverse. He knew to whom to turn to get things done—people like **Professor Proctor 1900, President Hopkins 1901, Bill Fowler '21, Dr. Ralph Miller '24** and others who were ready to help, but who needed leadership from a man who had a vision. Dan was that man. He interacted with many of the top names in skiing—both at Dartmouth and in the broader ski world— and had a hand in many early developments and issues such as the amateur status of skiers, the rapidly expanding business side of skiing (equipment, clothing, skiing services—lodging, transportation, area development, instruction), the hiring of the best talent for national and regional ski organizations, and the management/operation of national and international competition. Hatch's list of contributions is amazingly extensive!

A Related Subject: Mountaineering/Ski Mountaineering

This book is all about skiing achievements, but we also should remember early alpine skiing achievements required one to climb up a mountain before sliding down, and so the Dartmouth group has also featured in the allied activities of mountaineering and ski mountaineering. All of the early skiers before the 1940s had strong mountain climbing abilities. They had to or they would not have been able to climb high to make long ski runs. We celebrate **Dick Durrance I '39** for his ski prowess. His brother, **Jack Durrance '39**, is similarly revered by the mountain-climbing world. One of Dartmouth's leading mountain climbers is **Sam Silverstein '58** (a world-renowned medical research authority in his other life) who has climbed with the best. Sam believes the alumni of Harvard University have been a bigger institutional leader in mountain climbing, but that Dartmouth has also had several important leaders in this area.

"In the early days, Jack Durrance put in some outstanding routes in the Tetons and made the first ascent of Devil's Tower to lead the mountaineering pack. However, it was the ski descent by **Bill Briggs '54** of the Grand Teton that presaged the revolution in ski descents of very steep, technically demanding peaks and faces that have been witnessed in the past 25 years. The Teton descent was the most significant contemporary event in ski mountaineering. Much less imaginative souls than Brigger now routinely ski faces, gullies, and peaks thought to be unskiable in the 1950s and 1960s. Another major contribution was the ski traverse from the Bugaboos to Rogers Pass by Briggs, Barry Corbet, Bob French, and Sterling Neale.

"Dartmouth's strongest mountaineering participation was probably in the 1950s, 1960s, and 1970s with the **Peter Robinson '54** exploration of the Purcell Range in British Columbia, Canada; my own exploration of the Battle Range, Southern Selkirks, B.C., Canada in 1959 with **Fen Riley '56, Charles Plummer '59**, and **Tom Marshall '59**, Barry Corbet, **Jake Breitenbach '57,** and **Dave Dingman '58** and **Barry Bishop '53** were members of the 1963 American Mt. Everest expedition; Corbet and I were members of the 1966/67 Antarctic Expedition. **Andrew Harvard '71**, a former head of the DOC, led major US expeditions to Minya Konka (1980) in eastern Tibet [now China]; Everest East Face (1983) and North Ridge Research Ex.(1986), and participated in climbing Nanda Devi [northern India] and Dhaulaghiri [Nepal] in the 1970s. Corbet and I participated in the American Antarctic Mountaineering Expedition as cinematographer and climber. Barry Corbet's greatest accomplishment on the expedition was the first ascent of Mt. Tyree peak (15,896 ft), Antarctica's second highest summit and its most difficult from a technical mountaineering viewpoint. **David Seidman '68** and **Todd Thompson '70** participated in the Dhaulagiri expedition, on which Seidman and seven others were killed. In the Dartmouth group, Pre-WWII, Jack Durrance, and Post-WWII, Barry Corbet, Andrew Harvard, and perhaps David Seidman or Barry Bishop have been the mountaineering leaders. If he had lived, Seidman might have become the major figure."[15]

In addition to Sam's comments, we have pointed out the explorations in Alaska by **Tim Kelley '79**, the adventure trips of **Ned Gillette '67**, and the recent ski mountaineering racing of **Nina (Cook) Silitch '94** in France, each of which fits in to the area of extreme mountaineering or ski mountaineering.

CURRENT ACTIVITIES

In earlier pages, we have discussed many things that have already happened, but the ski industry did not stop yesterday; it continues to evolve, and Dartmouth participants continue to take on new assignments. For example, some recent developments that involve members of Dartmouth family at present include:

- **Selection of a new Chief Executive for the US Olympic Committee**: In early January, 2010, the U.S. Olympic Committee announced **Scott Blackmun '79** as its new CEO. Scott has a law degree from Stanford and worked as general counsel for the USOC in the late 1990s, serving briefly as the interim CEO in 2000-01. He has worked as the chief operating officer of the Anschutz Entertainment Group, and for a prominent law firm in Colorado Springs, prior to taking on this new role. **Tryg Myhren '58,** Chief of Mission for the US Paralympic Team at the 2006 Torino Olympics, and **Nina Kemppel '92, Tu '05,** four-time Winter Olympian and 18-time US Cross-Country Champion, served on the small USOC committee that made this selection.

- **National Champions**: In 2009, Dartmouth skiers won the National Slalom Championship (**David Chodounsky '08**), a National Biathalon Championship (**Susan Dunklee '08**), and a US Masters Championship (**Lisa Densmore '83** raised her amazing total of these championships to 57.)

- **New Director of Outdoor Programs and the DOC**: Dan Nelson '75 celebrated his new role by biking across the USA this past sum-

Max Cobb is now playing a key role in USOC management.

mer. We hope his 3000-mile bike ride will give him the stamina and enthusiasm to run fast in his new assignment and create some new history with a return to Downhill races at Mt. Moosilauke or similar such events.

- **The Dartmouth members of the 2010 Olympics and Paralympics**: The first Dartmouth connection in Vancouver is British Columbia **Premier Gordon Campbell '70** who helped land the Winter Games for the city of Vancouver, and will shortly welcome the world to the Canadian Province he has led for the past nine years.

A major participant in the International Olympic Committee activities in Vancouver will be the same **Chick Igaya '57** who provided a Foreword for this book and is mentioned in several of our chapters. Chick is currently the most senior IOC Vice President, and as such, will be likely to represent IOC Chairman Carrion and President Rogge at official functions and will be a likely presenter of many Olympic medals to winners. We hope he will have multiple opportunities to present medals to the Dartmouth participants.

We have noted several likely staff members of the 2010 Olympics activities in Vancouver, including **Max Saenger '88** and **Max Cobb '87** for the USOC; **John W. Peirce '68** and **Marie-Hélène Thibeault '02** for the Canadian OC; and there will be many more. **Jeff Hastings Tu '90** will provide ski jumping commentary on television.

It is too early for us to know all the Dartmouth athletes who will be skiing at the Olympics in February. **Sara Studebaker '07** and **Laura Spector '10** have just been selected for the US Biathlon team. It appears that two other serious Dartmouth contenders **Carolyn Treacy Bramante '06** and **Susan Dunklee '08** will not make the Biathlon team for 2010.

We noted that **Ben Koons '08**, a dual U.S. and New Zealand citizen, was the first New Zealander to achieve an Olympic qualifying standard in Nordic Skiing for the 2010 Winter Olympic Games via a race in Finland.

Scott Macartney '01 is a strong candidate for the US Alpine team. **Patrick Biggs (Canada), David Chodounsky '08, Paul McDonald '06, Andrew Weibrecht '09** and maybe **Tommy Ford '12** are also serious candidates for the Olympic Alpine events. We understand the World Cup Nordic team has been named and **Rosie Brennan '11, Kristina Trygstad-Saari '07, Ida Sargent '11** and **Mike Sinnott '07** were selected. These along with two other serious contenders, **Sophie Caldwell '12 and Glenn Randall '09,** are all in the running for the Olympic team.

Left: Gordon Campbell '70, Premier of the British Columbia, Canada with Barbara Ann Scott, Canada's 1st Olympic Gold in Skating (1948). Right: David Page '90's team members Boyer (left) and Rosow on the trek across Death Valley with skis in hand and Telescope Mt. in the distance! (Photo by Christian Pondella)

Dartmouth's Sam Naney '06 leads Ben Koons '08 and a third D skier in the pack of x-c racers at the 2005 UVM Winter Carnival (run on the course at the Trapp Family Lodge). Both Naney and Koons became D ski team captains.

For the Paralympics in March, **Carl Burnett '03** will be skiing on the Alpine Team and **Joe Walsh '84** will be serving as Deputy Chief of Mission.

As we are going to press, **David Page '90** of Mammoth Lakes, CA, a successful writer of outdoor stories for news media like the New York Times and an award winning guidebook writer (2009 Lowell Thomas Travel Journalism Award for his guidebook to Yosemite and Death Valley), is just publishing his astonishing account of hiking 17 miles from the bone-dry floor of Death Valley, CA, with several of his buddies--all packing trek gear and carrying their skis--up to the pristine snows that surround Telescope Mountain's 11,300-foot summit so they could carve fresh turns on slopes that have probably never been skied before. The full account, with color photos, is in the February 2010 issue of *Men's Journal*. It ties us right back to Dartmouth's long history of unique ski adventures from the first traverse from Hanover to Moosilauke early in the 20th century, the first exploration of the Bugaboos in the 1950s, and the current day exotic ski initiatives in Alaska. We hope to read of further mini-expeditions and probable first ski descents as David's travel map expands.

SUMMARY

If there is one outstanding non-academic activity for which Dartmouth College should be recognized nationally, it is skiing. That is apparent enough. But what was never precisely known—and what most of us never realized before—is the unparalleled pervasiveness of the Dartmouth connection with virtually every aspect of the American ski industry since it began. As I gained a glimmer of this early on, and as I only knew a very small amount of what has turned up in our later research, I began to sort out a plan to explore this subject broadly and to provide something more than a simple statement of a few facts. At the end of the day, this book has still ended up as a survey because as hard as we have worked to turn over every stone and find the many back-stories, the more we have understood how large this task is. In the end, we have settled with bringing you what we think is a representative sample of these contributions, but we must emphasize that it is only that: a sampling. However, in so doing, we believe we have justified the bold statement on the cover of this book: **The story of the alumni, staff and family of one small college in New England (Dartmouth College) dominating the development of modern skiing for over 100 years…. And they still are!**

This is a story that deserved to be told, and when I outlined my plan to then Dartmouth College President James Wright, he responded with personal interest—not as a skier, because he is not one—but with the eye of the historian that he is. President Wright quickly realized that perhaps Dartmouth College itself had not appreciated its own fundamental impact on this sport. His willingness to be viewed as a part of our leadership team has been helpful in encouraging others to join us in uncovering the background information we sought. As I outlined earlier in this chapter, a lot of credit for the skiing history of Dartmouth should be given to the past presidents of the institution, so it is entirely fitting that Jim Wright has been part of our team.

From an information support standpoint, the Rauner Special Collections Library has been of exceptional help. Although it does not really see the history of skiing as one of its main themes, there is an almost unlimited array of background stories and photographic evidence hiding within its walls. With the results of this book in hand and a couple of related books being published shortly, it is possible that Rauner will be more fully recognized for its role as keepers of skiing history than for some of its other roles because this history is demonstrably more important than most have previously thought.

Many others stepped up to help us with the details of this story. For example, aside from now co-hosting at CarniVAIL, the college's largest annual alumni gathering of skiers outside of Hanover, NH, the Tuck School does not often work with the contemporary ski industry, but it approved a student group thesis at our request to determine the impact of the ski business on annual U.S. GDP. As we pointed out in Chapter I, this has shown that this industry is a very large source of annual financial and employment activity for the United States. But more than any other consideration, the alumni, staff, family, and friends of Dartmouth and/or skiing have stepped up to help find the data needed to authenticate and illuminate a history that has never been assessed in this way before. We had unparalleled access to people and research data via the Internet to uncover many stories and facts—many that are not written down anywhere—and to effect the coordination needed to integrate the work of so many participants in so many parts of the country and the world. The net result, we think, is a rich history of very special contributions to a single sport by the long list of ski enthusiasts associated with this one institution, Dartmouth College.

Partly due to the passage of time and the growth of many other interests for students in winter months, skiing is no longer the dominating winter recreational interest at Dartmouth or in the local region around Hanover. These new interests run from many other amateur or professional sports to a large number of on-line or on-television alternatives to the many other non-sporting personal activities that people have access to. Many of the student interests of today did not exist until the most recent decades of our story. However, I think it still might be true that in comparison to the activities on other campuses, skiing at Dartmouth still ranks relatively high for student recreation in the winter. Life is much more complex these days than in 1909-1910 when Fred Harris was just getting things started at the newly formed DOC. For those who do participate, many develop that same passion for skiing as did students in the past.

Our research uncovered some particular elements that we thought important to highlight, including Dartmouth ski coaching philosophies for developing an athlete to his or her greatest potential, something repeated over and over as "unknowns" came to Dartmouth and were coached to collegiate, national, and international quality; the support ski team members have unstintingly given to disabled competitors who have medaled in the Paralympics again and again; the non-racing training for disabled skiers everywhere that Dartmouth alumni have committed themselves to provide; the business innovations and genius that so many enthusiastic skiers have shown to broaden or support the ski industry with new products or technological additions in the U.S. and around the world; and much more. The national—and even global—footprint in the snow by one small college in New Hampshire is unmistakable and indelible. One subtle underlying aspect of this story is a love of place—Hanover in all its seasons and the Outing Club in all its activities—that has encouraged an appreciation of environmental responsibility, a spirit of giving back to the institution that has molded its greater family, and of promoting what is a uniquely responsive network of educated men and women who find great purpose and broad satisfaction in helping others to enjoy the skiing experience and to succeed in those areas where their skills can be honed.

Running through the diverse areas of skiing interests are the qualities of Dartmouth student intelligence, leadership skills, and an enthusiasm for skiing that was developed in the ski-oriented environment of Hanover. The fact that skiing has reached the level of activity it now has can be attributed partly to a number of non-skiing elements that enabled it to grow. Importantly, credit needs to be given to the people who had the wisdom to authorize activities that encouraged the growth of skier enthusiasm for more than 100 years, a period of continuity in support of a unique activity that is rare for any institution. In our chapters, we have outlined many diverse areas of Dartmouth's impact on the ski world. In our Profile descriptions of 40 individuals or families, we have used stories that cut across the range of ways in which members of the Dartmouth community have impacted skiing, and still do. In both ways, our intention is to show the broad diversity and depth of these contributions—starting the first Outing Club and U.S. college ski team; developing the greatest Winter Carnival; creating the first slalom and downhill races; helping start ski clubs everywhere; leading the 10th Mountain Division; founding ski areas in the East and West; promoting skiing via movies, books and magazines; having the most winter sports Olympians and national champions; starting many of the first ski clothing and equipment companies; providing on mountain technical and medical leadership; and much more.

Now, it is in your hands to do with these many thoughts as you wish. It is time for me to leave this adventure and get on to new ones. As **Robert Frost, Class of 1896**, ends his poem "Stopping by Woods on a Snowy Evening," I, too, have promises to keep…before I sleep; so I must end here. In a parallel thought, we have miles to go before we can cover this whole story… In the meantime, let there never be an end to the thread of green weaving its way through this sport, and through our own individual and collective *Passion for Skiing*.

Stephen Waterhouse
February, 2010

"He will not see me stopping here
To watch his woods fill up with snow.

……………………………..
The woods are lovely, dark and deep,
But I have promises to keep,
And miles to go before I sleep,
And miles to go before I sleep."

— Robert Frost, Dartmouth Class of 1896

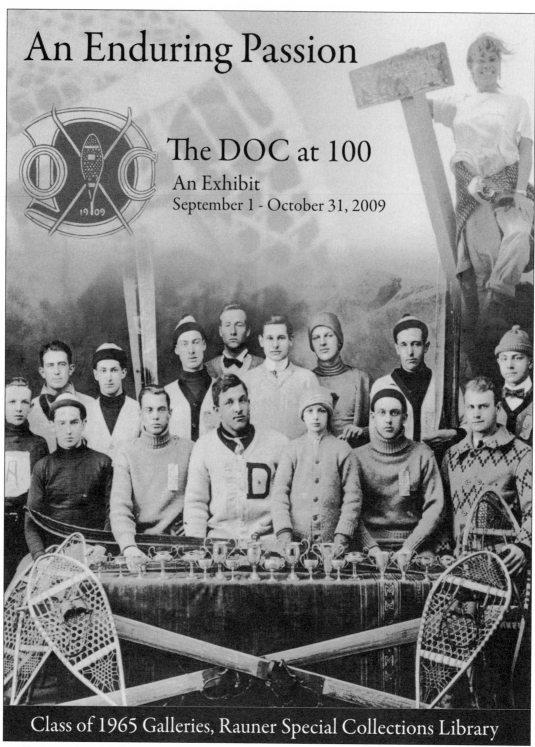

The Rauner Special Collections Library in Webster Hall used a poster with the theme of Enduring Passion to celebrate the 100th Anniversary of the DOC and to highlight a special exhibit in The 1965 Galleries. This seems to be a perfect end statement for our discussion of the Dartmouth College Passion for Skiing. (Poster created by Joshua Shaw '95.)

Chapter XVI Notes

1. Artist/Maker: Paul Starrett Sample, American, 1896-1974; Title: Nearing Home (Near the River). Object Date: not dated; Materials: Oil on canvas; Dimensions: 39 1/2 x 50 1/2 in.; Inscriptions: Signed, lower right: PAUL SAMPLE; Credit: Hood Museum of Art, Dartmouth College. Gift of Sigurnd Larmon, Class of 1914; P.974.518. 2. http://www.dartmouth.edu/~news/features/succession/hopkins.html. 3. Email from Anne Thomas Donaghy, June 5, 2009. 4. Email from Peter Dodge, November 19, 2009. 5. Ibid, September 9, 2009. 6. Email from Silich, July 2009. 7. Email from Peter Caldwell, June 30, 2009. 8. Email from Blum, November 17, 2008. 9. Email from Stigum August 30, 2009. 10. Email from Gill, June 27, 2009. 11. Email from Eldredge, November 19, 2009. 12. Email from Danson, December 30, 2009. 13. Trapp Family Lodge Newsletter, Winter 2009-10. 14. Email Onodera, Sept 1, 2009. 15. Email from Silverstein,October 1, 2009.

APPENDIX 1

U.S. NATIONAL SKI AND SNOWBOARD HALL OF FAME (NSSHF) HONORED MEMBERS - DARTMOUTH ALUMNI, STAFF, AND FAMILY

By 2009, thirty-six Dartmouth alumni and staff had been inducted into the NSSHF, comprising one of every ten of its 359 honored members. These 36, with the year of their induction, are:

Allen, Thomas Gary '40	1992	Goodrich, Nathaniel L. (Librarian)	1971
Beck, William L. '53 (and Coach)	2000	Hannah, Selden J. '35 (and Coach)	1968
Bertram, Wallace "Bunny" '31	1981	Harris, Fred H. '11	1957
Blood, Edward (Coach)	1967	Hirsch, Harold S. '29	1990
Bradley, Dr. David J. '38	1985	Igaya, Chiharu '57	1971
Bradley, Stephen J. '39	1980	Lawrence, David J. '51	1966
Branch, James R. '52, Tu '53	1994	Litchfield, John P. '39	2002
Briggs, William M. '54	2008	Little, Dr. Amos R. "Bud" '39	1965
Brown, William R. (ROTC)	1990	McCrillis, John W. '19	1966
Caldwell, John H. '50	1983	McIntyre, Elizabeth G. '87	2008
Carleton, John P. '22	1968	McLane, Malcolm '46	1973
Chivers, Howard P. '39	1973	Merrill, C. Allison (Coach)	1974
Chivers, Warren H. '38	1971	Prager, Walter (Coach)	1977
Corcoran, Tom '54	1978	Proctor, Charles A. '00 [1900]	1966
Dodge, J. Brooks '51, Th '54	1978	Proctor, Charles N. '28	1959
Durrance, Richard H. '39	1958	Rockwell, Martha (Coach)	1986
Gillette, Edward F. "Ned" '67	2000	Schniebs, Otto (Coach)	1967
Golden, Diana R '84	1997	Woods, Henry S. "Bem" '36	1966

Several other Ski and Snowboard Hall of Fame honorees are directly related to the Dartmouth family but were neither alumni nor staff themselves. We have identified 12, but there may still be others we have unintentionally overlooked.

Bradley, Dr. Harold C.	1969	Father of NSSHF members Dr. David Bradley '38 and Stephen Bradley '39.
Brown, Marilyn Cochran	1978	Mother of 3-time Dartmouth All-American and US Ski Team member Roger Brown, '04; daughter-in-law of 1948 DOC President Roger S. Brown, '45.
Hannah, Joan	1978	Daughter of NSSHF member Sel Hannah '35.
Hudson, Sally Neidlinger	1971	Daughter of Dean of the College Lloyd K. "Pudge" Neidlinger '23; twin sister of Susan Neidlinger McLane; sister-in-law of NSSHF member Malcolm McLane '46; and mother of Olympian Bill Hudson '85.
Lawrence, Andrea Mead	1958	Wife of NSSHF member Dave Lawrence '51.
Macomber, George	1973	Father of Dartmouth Ski Team members John Macomber '78, Grace Macomber Bird '81 and George "Jory" Macomber '85; All ski team captains.
Pabst, Fred	1969	Brother of Harold "Shorty" Pabst '38, rancher, mayor of Aspen, president of Aspen Meadows, and director of Aspen Skiing Company.
Robes, Ernest "Billy"	1987	Father of Dartmouth Assistant Coach Peter Robes.
Thomas, Lowell	1966	Father of Lowell Thomas, Jr., '46; grandfather of ski team captains: Anne Thomas Donaghy '77 and David Thomas '79.
Paula Kann Valar	1970	Mother of Stefanie B. Valar '76
Paul S. Valar	1985	Father of Stefanie B. Valar '76; set the Dartmouth Winter Carnival alpine racing courses for 19 years.
Witherell, Warren	1998	Father of Holly-Jill Witherell '95.

APPENDIX 2

DARTMOUTH OLYMPIANS, PARALYMPIANS, COACHES AND OFFICIALS – 1924 TO 2006

KEY: *A* – Alpine   *B* – Biathlon   *F* – Freestyle moguls   *N* – Nordic   *XC* – Cross-country

1924 (Chamonix, France)
Carleton, John B. '22 N

1928 (St. Moritz, Switzerland)
Proctor, Charles N. '28 N

1932 (Lake Placid, NY)
Competition Officials
Harris, Fred '11 – Ski Events
Proctor, Prof. Charles 1900 – Ski Jumping

1936 (Garmisch, Germany)
Chivers, Warren H. '38 N
Durrance, Richard H. '39 A
Hunter, Edgar H. Jr., '38 A
Washburn, A. Lincoln '35 A
Competition Officials
Proctor, Prof. Charles 1900 – Oly Ski Com.

1940 (Cancelled)
Bradley, David J. '38 N
Chivers, Howard P. '39 N
Chivers, Warren H '38 N
Durrance, Richard H '39 A
Hannah, Selden J. '35 N
Hillman, Harold Q. '40 A
Litchfield, John P. '39 N
Wells, Edward P. '39 A

1948 (St. Moritz, Switzerland)
Stewart, Colin C. '48 A
Coaches
Prager, Walter A

1952 (Oslo, Norway)
Beck, William L. '53 A
Caldwell, John H. '50 N
Dodge, Brooks J. '51 A
Igaya, Chiharu '57 (Japan) A
Lawrence, David J. '51 A
Competition Officials
Bradley, Stephen J. '39 – Oly Ski Com.
Little, Dr. Amos R. (Bud) Jr., '48 – Oly Ski Com.
Rand, John '38 – Oly Ski Com

1956 (Cortina, Italy)
Beck, William L. '53 A
Corcoran, Thomas A. '54 A
Dodge, Brooks J. '51 A
Igaya, Chiharu '57 (Japan) A
Miller, Ralph E. '55 A
Trembly, Charles N. '52 N
Coaches
Merrill, C. Allison N

1960 (Squaw Valley, California)
Corcoran, Thomas A. '54 A
Igaya, Chiharu '57 (Japan) A
Taylor, Richard W. '59 N
Coaches
Beck, William L. '53 A
Bradley, David J. '38 – Team Leader N
Lawrence, David '52 A
Little, Dr. Amos (Bud) R. '48 – Team Leader A
Competition Officials
McLane, Malcolm '46 – Oly Ski Com
Little, Dr. Amos (Bud) R. '48 – Oly Ski Com
Merrill, C. Allison – Chief of XC, Oly Ski Com.
Chivers, Warren '38 – Chief of Timing XC
Durrance, Richard H. '39 – Chief of Race A
Proctor, Charles '28 – Organizing Committee
Bradley, Stephen '39 – Ski Advisory Com.
Hadden, Wesley '41 – Ski Advisory Com.
Prager, Walter – Course Setter, Women's Downhill

1964 (Innsbruck, Austria)
Page, James W. '63 N
Taylor, Richard W. '59 N
Pitchford, R. Geoffrey W. '64 (Great Britain) A
Coaches
Merrill, C. Allison – Team Leader N

1968 (Grenoble, France)
Gillette, Edward F. '67 N
O'Reilly, Luke '71 (Great Britain) A
Williams, Edward G. '64 B
Coaches
Caldwell, John H. Jr., '50 N
Merrill, C. Allison – Team Leader N

1972 (Sapporo, Japan)
Berry, Scott W. '71 N
Caldwell, Timothy S. '76 N
Currier, David H. '74 A
Weed, Walker T. '71 N
Coaches
Caldwell, John H., Jr., '50 N
Competition Officials
Merrill, C. Allison – Tech Delegate XC

1976 (Innsbruck, Austria)
Caldwell, Timothy S. '76 N
Currier, David H. '74 A
Nielsen, Donald M. '75 N
Malmquist, Walter A. '78 N
Peterson, Douglas J. '75 N

1980 (Lake Placid, NY)
Caldwell, Timothy S. '76 N
Malmquist, Walter A. '78 N

Nielsen, Donald M. '74 B
Peterson, Douglas J. '75 N
Coaches
Caldwell, John H., Jr., '50 (Australia) N
Morton, John B
Page, James W. '63 N
Patterson, Robert (Ruff) N
Competition Officials
Lamb, J. Vernon, Jr., '46 – Dir. of Nordic Competitions
Merrill, C. Allison – Chief of XC
Allen Gary '40 – Ski Jumping Comp
Kendall, Thomas '72 – Ass't Chief of Protocol N

1984 (Sarajevo, Yugoslavia)
Arnold, Landis S. '82 N
Caldwell, Timothy S. '76 N
Carow, William K. '80 B
Eberle, Glen '85 B
Gaskill, Martha Hill '82 Para A
McGrane, Dennis R. '84 N
Nielsen, Donald M. '74 B
Shaw, Gale H. (Tiger) '85 A
Coaches
Patterson, Robert (Ruff) N
Page, James W. '63 – Team Leader N

1988 (Calgary, Canada)
Brosnihan, Diana Golden '84 Para A
Carow, William K. '80 B
Gaskill, Martha Hill '82 Para A
Hudson, William W. '88 A
McGrane, Dennis R. '84 N
Shaw, Gale H. (Tiger) '85 A
Thompson, Leslie H. '86 N
Walsh, Joseph F. '84 Para N
Walsh, Robert '88 Para N
Coaches
Durrance, David A
Morton, John B
Patterson, Robert (Ruff) N

1992 (Albertville, France)
Billmeier, Sarah E. '92 Para A
Forbes, Susan D. '83 N
Gaylord, William B. '90 (Great Britain) A
Harvey, Ian '90 B
Kemppel, Nina M. '92 N
McIntryre, Elizabeth G. '87 F
Puckett, Christopher C. '94 A
Truell, Michael D. '93 (Philippines) A
Thompson, Leslie H. '86 N
Walsh, Joseph F. '84 Para N
Walsh, Robert '88 Para N
Wilbrecht, Erich '84 B
Coaches
Carow, William K. '80 B
Cobb, Mathew K. '87 B
Morton, John – Team Leader B

1994 (Lillehammer, Norway)
Billmeier, Sarah E. '92 Para A
Gaylord, William B. '90 (Great Britain) A
Hoh, Ramona '02 Para (Canada) A
Kemppel, Nina M. '92 N
King, Suzanne P. '86 N
McIntyre, Elizabeth G. '87 F
Swenson, Carl J. '92 N
Thompson, Leslie H. '86 N
Walsh, Robert '88 Para N
Coaches
Cobb, Mathew K. '87 – Team Leader B
Morton, John B

1998 (Nagano, Japan)
Billmeier, Sarah E. '92 Para A
Hoh, Ramona '02 Para (Canada) A
Kemppel, Nina M. '92 N
King, Suzanne P. '86 N
McIntryre, Elizabeth G. '87 F
Walsh, Robert '88 Para N
Wooley, Stacey A. '91 B
Coaches
Cobb, Mathew K. '87 B
Derrick, Timothy K. '89 – Team Leader B
Miller, Allen '85 B

2002 (Salt Lake City, Utah)
Billmeier, Sarah E. '92 Para A
Burnett, Carl N.E. '03 Para A
Jones, Barbara E. '99 N
Kemppel, Nina M. '92 N
Macartney, Scott R. '01 A
Swenson, Carl J. '92 N
Wall, Bradley '02 (Australia) A
Coaches
McIntyre, Elizabeth G. '87 F
Competition Officials
Cobb, Mathew K. '87 – Chief of Comp. B
Kendall, Thomas '72 – Chief of Timing B
Miller, Allen '85 – Comp. Committee B
Morton, John – Chief of Course B
Saenger, Max '88 – Comp. Committee B

2006 (Turin, Italy)
Biggs, Peter R. '06 (Canada) A
Burnett, Carl N.E. '03 Para A
Konrad, Sarah K. '89 N
Ludlow, Libby A. '06 A
Macartney, Scott R. '01 A
Swenson, Carl J. '92 N
Treacy, Carolyn R. '06 B
Wall, Bradley '02 (Australia) A
Coaches
Grover, Chris '93 N
Myhren, Trygve '58 – Chief of Mission (Paralympics)
McIntyre, Elizabeth G. '87 F
Competition Officials
Cobb, Mathew K. '87 – Course Referee B
Thibeault, Marie-Helene '02 – Media Attaché (Canada)

APPENDIX 3

DARTMOUTH COLLEGIATE AND U.S. NATIONAL CHAMPIONS – 1931 TO 2009

The Dartmouth Outing Club organized the Intercollegiate Winter Sports Union in 1926, thus establishing the first organization to sponsor an annual intercollegiate championship in winter sports. The DOC also organized the first US National Downhill Skiing championships, held on the Mt. Moosilauke Carriage Road in 1933. From the time such records were kept, Dartmouth undergraduate skiers, alumni, and coaches have accumulated 243 individual championships in collegiate, national, and international competitions. (For Team Championships, see Appendix 4.)

KEY:

Events: *A - Alpine Events* *DH - Downhill* *SL - Slalom* *GS - Giant Slalom* *SG - Super Giant Slalom*
AC - Alpine Combined *N - Nordic Events* *X-C - Cross-Country* *SJ - Ski Jumping* *NC - Nordic Combined*
SM - Skimeister *FM - Freestyle Moguls* *B - Biathlon*

Collegiate Organizations: *IWSU - Intercollegiate Winter Sports Union;* *ISU - Intercollegiate Ski Union;*
NCAA - National Collegiate Athletic Association.

National Organizations: *USSA - US Ski and Snowboard Association;* *US Para - US Paralympic Skiing;*
Biathlon - US Biathlon Association.

1931	Prager, Walter (Dartmouth Coach)	Switzerland NC
1931	Mann, Thomas D. '33	IWSU A
1933	Woods, Henry S. '36	USSA DH
1934	Duncan, J. J. '40	USSA DH
1935, 1938	Hunter, Edgar H. '38	ISU SL
1936	Hannah, Seldon J. '35	ISU X-C
1937-1939	Durrance, Richard H. '39	USSA DH (3), SL(3), AC(3); Open A, ISU(7), SL, DH, X-C , SJ
1937, 1938	Chivers, Warren H. '39	USSA X-C, NC, ISU SJ, NC
1938, 1942	Chivers, Howard P. '39	USSA X-C, NC, ISU X-C, NC
1938	Meservey, Edward B. '38	USSA SL
1938	Bradley, David J. '38	USSA X-C, NC; ISU X-C
1940-1941	McLane, Charles B. '41	ISU SL
1940-1941	Skinner, Robert A. '40	ISU
1940-1942	Simpter, Roger U. '42	ISU SJ
1941	Tobin, John C. '42	ISU DH
1942	Meservey, Robert H. '43	ISU SL
1948	Stewart, Colin C. '48	ISU A
1949	Lawrence, David J. '51	USSA GS
1950, 1952	Cooke, James H. '52	ISU (2)
1953-1957	Miller, Ralph '55	USSA DH, SL(2), AC; NCAA DH, AC, SM
1954-1960	Igaya, Chiharu '57	USSA DH, SL, GS, AC(2); NCAA SL(3), AC(2), DH; Japan SL
1954-1957	Corcoran, Thomas '54	USSA SL(2), GS, AC; Canada SL, AC; Chile SL, AC; Argentina SL, AC
1958	Gebhardt, Robert '57	NCAA SL
1958	Vorse, David J.'57	NCAA AC
1958	Harwood, David S. '58	NCAA SM
1958	Smith, William E. '58	USSA DH
1960	Taylor, Richard '59	USSA X-C
1961	Bookstrom, Arthur A.'61	NCAA SM
1962, 1963	Page, James W. '63	NCAA X-C, SM(2)
1963	Williams, Edward G. '64	USSA X-C
1964	Coucheron, Per C. '68	Norway SJ
1967	Gillette, Edward F. '67	NCAA X-C
1970	Damon, Edward N. '69	NCAA SM

APPENDIX 3 CONTINUED FROM PG. 389

1973-1982	Caldwell, Timothy '76	USSA X-C(8)
1976	Cleveland, David P. '78	NCAA GS
1980	Malmquist, Walter A., II '78	USSA SJ, NC
1981	Strook, Betty '77	B
1982-1988	Shaw, Gale ("Tiger") H. '85	USSA GS(4), SG, AC(4), NCAA SL
1983-1986	Gaskill, Martha Hill '82	US Para A(3+)
1985-1987	Brosnihan, Diana Golden '84	US Para A(19)
1985, 1988	Foote, Tom J. '87	NCAA GS(2)
1986-1991	Sonnerup, Anna M. '84	B(5)
1986-1990	Walsh, Joseph F. '84	US Para X-C(7)
1986	deChamp, Miles '87	NCAA GS
1986	Thompson, Cami (Dartmouth Coach)	USSA X-C
1987	Pfosi, Eva P. '88	NCAA SL
1988	Patty, Anouk '91	NCAA GS
1988-1995	Hall, Leslie Thompson '86	USSA X-C(13)
1989	Hudson, William W. '88	USSA AC
1991-1996	Walsh, Robert G. '88	US Para X-C(19)
1991-1999	Wilbrecht, Erich '84	B(9)
1993-2000	Puckett, Christopher C. '94	USSA DH, AC(3)
1993-2001	Kemppel, Nina M. '92	USSA X-C(18)
1994-2004	Swenson, Carl J. '92	USSA X-C(11)
1995	Billmeier, Sarah '99	US Para A(15)
1996	Collins, Jennifer A '99	NCAA GS
1997	King, Suzanne '86	USSA X-C
1998	McIntyre, Elizabeth '87	USSA FM
1998	Wooley, Stacy '91	B
1998	Viele, David D. '98	NCAA GS(2)
2002	Brown, Roger G. P. '04	NCAA SL
2003	Wall, Bradley '02	NCAA SL
2004	Friedman, Byron R. '02	USSA DH, AC
2004	McDonald, Paul G. '06	NCAA SL
2004	Ludlow, Libby A. '06	USSA GS
2004	Konrad, Sarah '89	USSA X-C
2005, 2009	Chodounsky, David M. '08	USSA SL, NCAA SL
2006	Johnson, Karl A. '06	NCAA SL
2007	Randall, Glenn '09	NCAA X-C
2008	Francis, Kevin P. '06	USSA SG
2008	Spector, Laura P. '10	B
2009	Dunklee, Susan K. '08	B

APPENDIX 4

DARTMOUTH COLLEGE NATIONAL CHAMPIONSHIP SKI TEAMS

Prior to 1936, Dartmouth had a combined Winter Sports team for Figure Skating, Speed Skating, Snowshoeing and Skiing events that competed annually in the Intercollegiate Winter Sport Union (IWSU) Championships. Beginning in 1937, interested colleges established broader national championships under the auspices of the Intercollegiate Ski Union (ISU). In 1952, the National Collegiate Athletic Association (NCAA) began sponsorship of a truly national intercollegiate skiing championship. In 1976, the first Women's National Skiing Championship was sponsored by the Association for Intercollegiate Athletics for Women (AIAW). And in 1983, the NCAA added Women's Skiing and began sponsorship of a combined Men's and Women's Skiing Championship. Dartmouth Ski Teams have won at least one national championship under each format.

WINTER SPORTS

1931
Wallace Bertram '31
Lincoln R. Page '31
Maurice Whittinghill '31
James E. Flint '32
Geroge C. Sawyer '32
Morrison G. Tucker '32
William T. Dewey '33
Richard P. Goldthwaite '33
Thomas D. Mann '33
Lyman E. Wakefield '33
John D. Mahoney '34
John A. Shea '34
Otto Schniebs, Coach

1932
James E. Flint '32
Morrison G. Tucker '32
William T. Dewey '33
Richard P. Goldthwaite '33
Thomas D. Mann '33
Lyman E. Wakefield '33
Richard L. Emerson '34
Frank J. Lepreau, Jr., '34
John D. Mahoney '34
John A. Shea '34
Selden J. Hannah '35
Roy A. Kraus '35
Otto Schniebs, Coach

MEN'S SKIING

1950
Colin S. Stewart, IV '48
Tor B. Arneberg '50
Granville S. "Red" Austin '50
John Caldwell '50
J. Brooks Dodge, Jr., '51
Charles N. Trembley '52
Walter Prager, Coach

1958
Robert C. Gebhardt '57
David J. Vorse '57
David S. Harwood '58
John A. Ceeley '58
William E. Smith '58
Richard W. Taylor '59
Francis J. Noel, III '59
Don S. Peterson '59
C. Allison Merrill, Head Coach
William L. Beck '53, Alpine Coach

1976
Douglas S. Hicks '76
Arne H. Nielsen '76
Robert C. Singer '76
Christian E. Berggrav '77
R. Phillip Peck, Jr., '77
David P. Cleveland '78
Whitney L. Johnson '78
Jeffrey K. Kahl '79
Timothy F. Kelley '79
Tim G. Moerlein '79
Bryan N. Wagner '79
Robert E. Zinck, Jr., '79
James W. Page '63, Head Coach
David Durrance, Alpine Coach

WOMEN'S SKIING

1977
Anne Thomas Donaghy '77
Annie Van Curan Johnson '77
Cate Sprague Gilbane '78
Wendy Thurber Gross '78
Mary Kendall Brown '78
Harriott W. Meyer '78
Christine B. Simpson '78
Deborah H. Tarinelli '78
Caroline E. Coggeshall '80
Dale P. Breed '79
Pam Reed Merrill, Women's Coach
C. Allison Merrill, X-C Coach

MEN'S AND WOMEN'S SKIING

2007
Evan C. Weiss '06
Lindsay E. Mann '07
Michael E. Sinnott '07
Sara S. Studebaker '07
David M. Chodounsky '08
Susan K. Dunklee '08
Alexander J. Felix '08
Elsa G. Sargent '08
Michelanne Shields '08
Benjamin J. True '08
Glenn Randall '09
Hayley Jones '10
Cami Thompson, X-C Coach
Ruff Patterson, X-C Coach
Christine Booker, Alpine Coach
Peter Dodge '78, Alpine Coach

APPENDIX 5

DARTMOUTH OUTING CLUB MANAGERS – 1922 TO 2010

The DOC was founded by Fred Harris '11 in late 1909 as a student-run organization and it continues to operate mainly under student leadership today. In 1920, with the scope of annual operations and budgets growing, the DOC hired first a part-time comptroller, and then in 1929, a full-time comptroller who soon functioned as a General Manager. In 1945 the top staff person became the DOC Director. The blossoming of the environmental and outdoor movements led to the creation of the Office of Outdoor Affairs in 1970, and in 1984 the head staff position was renamed Director of the Outdoor Program Office (OPO).

NOTE: *Bold text* indicates senior staff leadership at the time.

Halsey Edgerton '22	Comptroller	1920-1922
Leslie Murch	Comptroller	1922-1925
Evan Woodward '22	Comptroller	1925-1928
James Sullivan '28	Comptroller	1928-1929
Daniel Hatch, Jr., '28	**General Manager**	**1929-1937**
Landon Rockwell '35	Assistant Manager	1935-1936
John Feth '34	Assistant Manager	1936-1937
J. Wilcox Brown '37	**General Manager**	**1937-1939**
John Rand '38	Assistant Manager	1938-1942
	DOC Director	**1942, 1945-1975**
	Outdoor Ed. And Safety	1975-1979
Hans Paschen '28	**General Manager**	**1939-1942**
Thomas Dent	**General Manager**	**1943-1945**
Merrill McLane '42	Assistant Manager	1945-1946
Richard Backus '44	Assistant Manager	1946
Robert Monahan '29	General Manager	1947-1950
Roberts French '56	Assistant Director	1959-1960
Bob Stone	Assistant Director	1960-1962
James Schwedland '48	Ed. Officer	1963-1970
C. Allison Merrill	**Director Outdoor Affairs**	**1970-1983**
Earl Jette '55A	Assistant Director	1970-1975
	DOC Director	1975-1984
	OPO Director	**1984-2000, 2008-2009**
John Donovan	Outdoor Ed. And Safety	1979-1982
Brian Kunz	Coordinator Outdoor Ed.	1984-1989
	Assistant Director	1989-2008
	Deputy Director	2008-Current
David Hooke '84	Facilities Manager	1994-1996
	Assistant Director	1996-2001
Kathleen Doherty	**OPO Director**	**2001-2002**
Julie Clemons	Assistant Director	2001-2008
Donald Cutter, Jr., '73	Facilities Manager	2001-2003
	Assistant Director	2007-Current
Geoffrey Brown	**OPO Director**	**2003**
Andrew Harvard '71	**OPO Director**	**2004-2008**
Rory Gawler '05	Program Coordinator	2008-Current
Daniel Nelson '75	**OPO Director**	**2009-Current**

APPENDIX 6

DARTMOUTH OUTING CLUB PRESIDENTS – 1910 TO 2010

Leadership of the DOC has always provided an opportunity to augment a Dartmouth academic education with one for learning to manage real-world challenges. The Club President must oversee the organization of programs and events, facilitate competitions, establish and maintain the support of faculty and administration, and, above all, promote good fellowship in the out-of-doors at Dartmouth's magnificent New England locations and beyond. Most of the DOC presidents have not been competitive skiers, but they faithfully represented the multitude of undergraduates fortunate enough to experience and appreciate the difference that skiing can make in one's life and who best understood the impact skiing has had on the character of the college. As Dartmouth's outdoor programs multiplied, a professional (i.e., salaried) staff gradually relieved DOC presidents of various responsibilities. This became increasingly necessary as the college evolved more flexible class schedules, a change which has resulted in presidents now sometimes measuring their tenures in just fractions of a year.

1910-1911	Harris, Fred '11	1950	White, David '50	1988-1989	Dillon, Kristen '89
1912	White, W. H. '12	1951	Person, Martin '51	1989-1990	Shiffman, Mark '90
1913	Shumway, Carl '13	1952	Biddle, William '52	1990-1991	Bachman, Joe '91
1914	Day, Joseph '14	1953	Leavens, Roland '53	S 1991	Kirincich, Sue '92
1915	Grills, Ben '15	1954	Perkins, Richard '54	1991-1992	Rosen, Jamie '92
1916	Hayden, Edward '16	1955	Jessup, Harlan '55	1992-1993	Allen, Jeff '93
1917	Emerson, Sumner '17	1956	French, Roberts '56	Sp – S 1993	Douple, Martha '94
1918	Tripp, Curtis '18	1957	Griffiths, Clark '57	1993-1994	Giordono, Mark '94
1919	Wilkinson, Henry '19	1958	Hart, Frederick '58	1994-1995	Barnhorst, Amy '96
1920	Adams, L. Sherman '20	1959	Adams, Samuel '59	1995-1996	Brockmeier, Pam '95
1921	Briggs, Ellis '21	1960	Huttrer, Gerald '60	S 1996	Molyneaux, Brad '98
1922	Throop, Charles '22	1961	Baum, H. James '61	1996-1997	Currier, Megan '97
1923	Bishop, H. H. '23	1962	Medrick, Fredrick '62	1997-1998	Magyar, John '98
1924	Morgan, Robert '24	1963	Davis, Peter '63	F 1998	French, Liz '99
1925	Brace, Lloyd '25	1964	Lewicki, Leroy '64	1998-1999	Berk, Ben '01
1926	Webster, Charles '26	1965	Owens, Robert '65	F 2000	Krivak-Tetley, Flora '02
1927-1928	Hatch, Daniel '28	1966	Lanfer, Steve '66	1999-2000	Dixon, Lydia '01
1929	Sanders, Richard '29	1967	Bankart, Peter '67	W 2000	Leslie, Pat '01
1930	Hatch, Winslow '30	1968	Buck, Peter '68	2000-2001	Diament Eli '02
1931	Thorn, Craig, '31	1969	Ramey, Thain '69	2001-2002	Sepulveda, Adam '02
1932	Sawyer, George '32	1970	Schwartzman, Joseph '70	Sp-S 2002	Alexander, Eleanor '04
1933	Goldthwait, Richard '33	1971	Allen, Charles '71	F 2002-W 2003	Leneis, Brad '03
1934	Allen, Donald '34	1972	Schlesinger, William '72	S 2003	Johnston, Merrick '05
1935	Rockwell, Landon '35	1973	Wood, John '73	2003-2004	Hanlon, Joe '05
1936	Niss, William '36	1974	von Loesecke, David '74	Sp-S 2004	Woodward, Jeff '06
1937	Brown, J. Willcox '37	1975	Lyons, William, '75	F 2004	Gawler, Rory '05
1938	Averill, Walter '38	1976	Hanke, Danferd '76	Sp 2005	Feld, Shara '07
1939	MacDonald, Kenneth '39	1977	Carter, Thomas '77	S 2005	MacFayden, Whitney '07
1940	Browne, Elmer '40	1978	Conte, Charles '78	W 2005	Woodward, Jeff '06
1941	McGinley, Morton '41	1979	Winkler, Mark '79	Sp-S 2006	Graham, Ada '08
1942	Bond, Harold '42	1980	Hogan , Gregg '80	F 2005-W 2006	O'Hagen, Anne '06
1943	McPherson, Alexander '44	1981	Lathrop, Rick '81	F 2006 -W 2007	MacFayden, Whitney '07
1943	Silverstein, Jr. , Leo '43	1982	Burack, Thomas '82	S 2007	Feintzeig, Jake '09
1944	Brazel, E. Quillian '47	1983	Grainger, David '83	2007-2008	Bracikowski, Phil '08
1945	Howard, Edward '47	1984	Forbes, Peter '83	2008-2009	Palmer, Andrew '10
1946	Wood, Willard '47	1985	Hardigg, Genevieve '84	Sp 2009	Vogel, Rebecca '11
1947	Backus, Richard '44	1985-1986	Keating, Chris '86	2009-2010	Flynn, Thomas '11
1948	Brown, Roger '45	1986-1987	Cobb, Max '87		
1949	Nickelsen, Richard '47	1987-1988	Murphy, Sean '88		

NOTE: *Where a single year is listed it represents the ending year of the term as president.*
ABBREVIATIONS USED: *S – Summer** Sp* *– Spring** F* *– Fall** W* *– Winter*

APPENDIX 7

DARTMOUTH COLLEGE SKI COACHES – 1916 TO 2010

The first women's ski team at Dartmouth was established in 1972; it operated as a separate entity with its own coach until 1983 when the NCAA approved a combined Men's and Women's Championship and Dartmouth unified its two separate programs under a Director of Skiing. In 2006, this time in response to an NCAA dictate limiting ski programs to two coaches per gender team, the college established four varsity Head Coaching positions—two for men and two for women—with the Director of Skiing being a supplemental function to be rotated among the four coaches. At that point, the development team became a racing club coached by a Team Manager.

Carl Paulson	Ski Jumping (Part-time)	1916
Harry Hillman	Team Coach (Also Track)	1920-1922
Anton Diettrich	Team Coach (Also Fencing)	1923-1927
Sig Steinwell	Head Coach	1927-1928
Gerry Raab	Head Coach	1928-1930
Otto Schniebs	Head Coach	1930-1936
Walter Prager	Head Coach	1936-1940, 1945-1947, 1948-1957
Percy Rideout '40	Acting Head Coach	1940-1941
Bob Meservey '43	Acting Head Coach	1941-1942
W. H. Ashley '45	Acting Head Coach	1942-1944
Sel Hannah '35	Acting Co-coach	1944-1945
Ed Blood	Acting Co-coach	1944-1945
Ja Densmore '44	Acting Head Coach	1947-1948
	Nordic Coach	1948-1951
Charlie Furrer	Alpine Assistant Coach	1953-1954
Al Merrill	Nordic Coach; Head Coach	1956-1957, 1957-1972
	Women's Cross Country	1975-1979
William Beck '53	Alpine Coach	1957-1958
George Ostler	Alpine Coach	1958-1961
Gary Vaughn	Alpine Coach	1961-1969
Robert Stone	Acting Nordic (Al Merrill absences)	1960-1964
Hermann Muckenschnabl	Alpine Coach	1969-1975
Jim Page '63	Head Coach	1972-1978
Pam (Reed) Merrill	Women's Head Coach	1972-1979
Dave Durrance	Men's Alpine Coach	1975-1978
Peter Robes	Ski Jumping Coach	1975-1978
John Morton	Men's Head Coach	1978-1983
	Director of Skiing	1983-1989
Donald Cutter, Jr., '73	Ski Jumping Coach	1978-1981
Tim Beck	Men's Alpine Coach	1978-1984
Martha Rockwell	Women's Head Coach	1979-1983
Tim Fischer	Women's Alpine Coach	1979-1987
	Women's Head Coach	1987-1989
Mark Ford	Men's Alpine Coach	1984-1989
Tim Gibbons	Women's Cross-Country	1989-1990
Robert ("Ruff") Patterson	Director of Skiing	1990-2006
	Head Men's Cross-Country Coach	2006 – Present
Cami Thompson	Women's Cross-Country Coach	1990-2006
	Director of Skiing	2006 – Present
Peter Dodge '78	Men's Alpine Coach	1990-2006
	Head Men's Alpine Coach	2006- Present
Sarah Bergstrom	Women's Alpine Coach	1990-1993
David Gregory	Women's Alpine Coach	1993-1994
Mark Schiffman '90	Women's Alpine Coach	1994-1995
Bruce Lingelbach	Women's Alpine Coach	1995-2002
Pat Purcell	Women's Alpine Coach	2002-2003
Christine Booker	Women's Alpine Coach	2003-2006
	Head Women's Alpine Coach	2006- Present

APPENDIX 8

CAPTAINS OF DARTMOUTH SKI AND WINTER SPORTS TEAMS – 1922 TO 2010

Prior to 1936, Dartmouth had a combined Winter Sports Team for Figure Skating, Speed Skating, Snowshoeing, and Skiing. In 1936, it was decided that skiing would be the only competitive winter sport recognized with a college-sponsored team. In 1972, Dartmouth became coeducational and a Women's Ski Team was started fairly soon but didn't elect its first team captain until 1975. Therefore, this Appendix is split in to three sections to reflect the various changes in ski team activities from 1922 to 2010.

WINTER SPORTS TEAM

1922	Richard Bowler '22	1928	Charles N. Proctor '28	1933	Lyman E. Wakefield Jr., '33
1924	Weston Blake '24	1929	T. Truxtun Brittan Jr., '29	1934	John A. Shea '34
1925	Thurston D. Frost '25	1930	Hermann N. Sander '30	1935	Selden J. Hannah '35
1926	Thomas B. Farwell '26	1931	Wallace Bertram '31		
1927	Charles N. Proctor '28	1932	Morrison G. Tucker '32		

SKIING - MEN

1936	Henry S. Woods '36	1966	Brian A. Beattie '66	1987	Elliot C. Harvey '87
1937	Warren H. Chivers '38	1967	Edward F. Gillette '67		Terrance C. DelliQuadri '88
1938	David J. Bradley '38	1968	Alexander Cameron '68	1988	Terrance C. DelliQuadri '88
1939	Richard H. Durrance '39	1969	Edward N. Damon '69		Mark W. Saenger '88
	Howard P. Chivers '39	1970	Charles C. Bent II '71	1989	Timothy K. Derrick '89
1940	Percy A. Rideout '40		Walker T. Weed III '71		Andrew M. Reynolds '90
1941	Charles B. McLane '41	1971	Daniel Gibson '71	1990	Andrew M. Reynolds '90
1942	Jacob R. Nunnemacher '42		Walker T. Weed III '71		Jay T. Davis '91
1943	William G. Distin '44	1972	David N. Hazelett '72	1991	Jeffrey C. Kirwood '91
1944	William H. Ashley '45		George P. Perry '72		Andrew N. Sveen '91
1945	Howard C. Hewitt '46	1973	Erik Jebsen '73	1992	Charles R. Martin '92
1946	John K. Snobble '44	1974	Donald M. Nielsen Jr., '74		Carl J. Swenson '92
1947	Philip F. Puchner '44		Richard C. Thirlby '74	1993	W. Morgan Burns Jr., '92
1948	Malcolm McLane '46	1975	Christopher D. Nice '75		Carl J. Swenson '92
1949	Wilbur I. Bull Jr., '46	1976	Craig T. Stone '76	1994	Todd H. Grover '94
1950	Tor B. Arneberg '50		Edward F. Waters '76		James D. Nohl '94
1951	Weston Blake Jr., '51	1977	David P. Cleveland '78	1995	J. Andrew Martin '96
	Colin C. Stewart IV '48		R. Phillip Peck Jr., '78		Cory H. Smith '96
1952	Frederick C. Barstow '52	1978	John D. Macomber '77	1996	Cory H. Smith '96
	Charles N. Tremblay '52		Whitney L. Johnson '78		Colter P. Leys '96
1953	J. Brooks Dodge '51	1979	David L. Thomas '79		Jeremiah K. Thompson '96
1954	Russell Cary '54		Bryan N. Wagner '79	1997	Jean- Pierre Daigneault '97
1955	John D. Bassette Jr., '55	1980	William K. Carow '80		T. Paul Stone '98
1956	Peter M. Kirby '54		Timothy S. Itin '81	1998	T. Paul Stone '98
1957	Chiharu Igaya '57	1981	Mack J. Lyons '81		David D. Viele '98
1958	David S. Harwood '58		John M. Mott '81	1999	David D. Viele '98
	William E. Smith '58	1982	Robert L. McGrath '82		T. Paul Stone '98
1959	Richard W. Taylor '59		Kirk G. Siegel '82		Andrew T. Pennock '99
1960	David J. Vorse '57	1983	Todd C. Willmert '83	2000	Stephen C. Donahue '99
	Arthur A. Bookstrom '61		Christopher G. Wise '83		Maciej B. Zwiejski '00
1961	Arthur A. Bookstrom '61	1984	Arthur S. Lussi '84	2001	Scott H. McArt '01
	James E. Delong Jr.,'61		Erich K. Wilbrecht '84		Eric D. Reinhardt '02
1962	James W. Page '63	1985	George C. Macomber '85	2002	Matthew J.Cleveland '02
1963	James W. Page '63		Christain H. Bean '85		Eric D. Reinhardt '02
1964	James W. Jacobson '64	1986	Chauncey G. Morgan '86	2003	Brayton K.Osgood '03
1965	Richard S. Durrance '65		Jon M. Underwood '86		Andrew G. Biggs '04

APPENDIX 8 CONTINUED FROM PG. 395

2004	Andrew G. Biggs '04		Karl A. Johnson '06		Benjamin J. True '08
	Andrew E. Hunter '04	2007	Michael E. Sinnott '07	2009	Benjamin M. Koons '08
2005	Eben R. Sargent '05		David M. Chodounsky '08		Ross W. Heise '09
	Erik A. Kankainen '05	2008	David M. Chodounsky '08	2010	Francis Fortin-Houle '10
2006	Samuel T. Naney '06		Alexander J. Felix '08		Patrick K. O'Brien '10

SKIING - WOMEN

1975	Mary H. Osgood '76		Susan W. Seymour '90		Katherine L. Pearson '02
	Judith Zimicki '76	1990	Amy Fulwyler '90		Erin J. Quinn-Hurst '02
1976	Mary H. Osgood '76		Susan W. Seymour '90	2002	Tracy M. Wilson '02
	Ann Van Curan Johnson '77	1991	Anouk Patty '91	2003	Susan M. Kloek '03
1977	Anne Thomas Donaghy '77		Stacey A. Wooley '91		Megan E. Ganong '03
	Mary B. Kendall '78	1992	Vanya Grandi '92	2004	Eileen D. Carey '04
1978	Mary B. Kendall '78		Allison E. Arians '93		Emily J. Chenel '04
	Wendy A. Thurber '78	1993	Sari A. Skaling '91		Emily A. Copeland '04
1979	Jeanne H. Straus '79		Amy C. Farrens '93	2005	Grace R. Crandall '06s
	Caroline E. Coggeshall '80	1994	Jane D. Eckels '94		Jessica J. Philip '05
1980	Kerstin S. Annella '80		Liza L. Kiesler '94		Alison L. Keller '02
	Kimberly A. McConaughy '80	1995	A. Heather Eliassen '95	2006	Alexandra Archer '06
1981	Anne Hallager '81		Jessica C. James '95		Jean L. Polfus '06
	Grace C. Macomber '81	1996	Nora H. Stowell '96	2007	Alexandra Archer '06
1982	Nancy Pease '82		Laura M. Turner '98		Alexandra E. Fucigna '07
	Margaret M. Singer '82	1997	Pam M. Finnerty '97		Sara S. Studebaker '07
1983	Eliza A. Deery '83		Valerie L. Wrenholt '97	2008	Elsa G. Sargent '08
	Belle O. Traver '83		Laura M. Turner '98		Michelanne Shields '08
1984	Elizabeth A. Cowles '84	1998	Gabrielle Holt '99	2009	Hayley J. Jones '10
	Anna M. Sonnerup '84		Jessica A. A. Smith '99		Christine C. Roberts '10
1985	Sarah E. Millham '85		Laura M. Turner '98		Hannah G. Dreissigacker '09
	Diana E. Shannon '85	1999	Gabrielle Holt '99		Courtney E. M. Robinson '09
1986	Kathleen A. Corcoran '87		Jennifer A. Collins '99	2010	Hayley J. Jones '10
1987	Katherine A. Maddock '87		Jessica A. A. Smith '99		Christine C. Roberts '10
	Eva P. Pfosi '88	2000	Katherine L. Pearson '02		Ida K. Sargent '11
1988	Julia Fulwyler '88		Jennifer L. Viele '00		Katherine C. Bono '10
	Lisa R. Thomas '88		Augusta B. Swift '01		
1989	Amy Fulwyler '90	2001	Augusta B. Swift '01		

APPENDIX 9

DARTMOUTH FIRSTS

Compiled by Thomas G. Washing '63

Many Dartmouth College alumni, staff, and families have been involved in the initiation of activities across the whole spectrum of recreational and competitive skiing. We have compiled here a representative listing of these firsts. Although there may be items on this list that someone might attribute to another institution where a similar activity was taking place somewhat earlier than the dates we show, we believe any such differences will be minimal and, at worst, that Dartmouth would perhaps be better listed as "one of the first." This list is not intended to defend one or two particular points, but rather to present the diverse fields of enterprise in which members of the Dartmouth community have been leaders since the early days of skiing in the United States. We do not know of any other institution that can claim a list of similar magnitude with regard to the sport of skiing.

1910 – **First US College Winter Field Day or Carnival.** Held at Dartmouth College, Hanover, NH.

1914 – **First Intercollegiate Ski Meet.** Dartmouth vs. McGill in Montreal, Canada.

1915 – **First Intercollegiate Ski Meet held in the U.S.** Hanover, NH

1916 – **The first Dartmouth alumnus to have answered the call for volunteer mountain rescue work on skis in support of the Allied Forces in World War I**, and quite possibly the first American to use skis to provide this type of aid during military conflict: Charles Dabney Horton '15. At the end of the winter of 1916, Horton became a member of the Lafayette Escadrille and flew missions for the French Air Force. He was awarded a Croix de Guerre by the French Government.

1919 – **First retail ski shop in the U.S. focused on selling skis, ski gear, bindings and ski clothing.** The Dartmouth Cooperative Society, founded by John Piane '14 in Hanover, NH. Originally called The College Bookstore. Piane developed the business as its manager before eventually buying and renaming it the Dartmouth Cooperative Society (later called the Dartmouth Co-op).

1919 – **First Person to market branded skis to retailers.** John Piane Sr. '14. Sold through the Dartmouth Co-op Ski Shop.

1921 – **First US intercollegiate ski team.** Organized at Dartmouth College with initial members Seth A. Densmore '21, R. Bowler '22, John P. Carleton '22, David W. Trainer '21, Oliver J. Frederiksen '16, and Captain Thomas H. Griffith '21.

1922 – 1957 – **First college to create and operate its own ski facilities on college property**: Dartmouth College: ski jump (1922); rope tow and J-bar lift (built in 1935). The Dartmouth Skiway, with a lodge and several lifts, opened in 1957.

1924 – **First American-born member of the US Winter Olympics team.** Ski jumper John P. Carleton '22 at Chamonix, France.

1925 – **First slalom competition in the U.S.** Held on the Dartmouth Golf Course ski hill.

1927 – **First downhill ski race in the U.S.** Organized by the Dartmouth Outing Club and run at Mount Moosilauke, NH.

1929 – **First weekly newspaper column dedicated to skiing.** "Old Man Winter," initiated by Carl Shumway '13 in the *Boston Evening Transcript.*

1930 – **First person to license and manufacture a commercial ski binding in the U.S.** John Piane '14 introduced the Kandahar-Dartmouth-Hanover Ski Binding.

1930 – **First lighted night skiing in the U.S.** Installed by the Dartmouth Outing Club on the Dartmouth Golf Course.

1931 – **First persons to initiate ski train service to New Hampshire's White Mountains.** Carl Shumway '13 and William Fowler '21 on trains originating in Boston on the Boston & Maine Railroad.

1931 – **First ski clothing designed and made in the U.S.** Harold Hirsch '29 founded the White Stag Ski Clothing company.

1931 – **First film of a downhill ski race made in the U.S.** Recorded by Jack McCrillis '19 at Mount Moosilauke, NH. The film was presented to the National Ski Association in 1932 and led to the official sanctioning of the first National Downhill; held at Mt. Moosilauke in 1933.

1933 – **First collegiate downhill ski race held in the U.S.** Mount Moosilauke, NH.

1933 – **First winner of a US National Downhill Ski Championship.** Henry S. "Bem" Woods '36 at the first NSA-sanctioned National Downhill, NH.

1934 – **First winner of a National Downhill Ski Championship held west of the Mississippi.** Joseph "Joe" Duncan '40 at Estes Park, CO.

1935 – **First consumer ski show.** The National Winter Sports Exposition and Ski Tournament launched by Carl Shumway '13 in the old Boston Garden. The event drew 42,000 people over a three-day period.

1935 – **First US college ski team to enter the National Ski Championships and Olympic Trials wearing team uniforms.** Mount Rainier, WA.

1935 – **First overhead J-Bar cable ski lift in the U.S.** Constructed at Dartmouth's Oak Hill Ski Area by the DOC and the Split Ballbearing Co. Operation began in December 1935; opened to the public in January 1936.

1937 – 1939 – **First person to win the Harriman Cup and its first (and only) three-time winner.** Dick Durrance '39, Sun Valley, ID.

1936 – **First women's intercollegiate Winter Carnival race.** Held by the DOC at the Dartmouth Golf Course ski area. Patty McLane of Smith College was the winner.

1937 – **First giant slalom competition held in the U.S.** Event organized and course set by Dick Durrance '39 and Dartmouth Ski Coach Walter Prager at Tuckerman Ravine, NH. Concomitant objective was to reduce the number of injuries typical of downhill racing by requiring periodic turns.

1937 – **First use of dynamite charges to release potential avalanches in a ski area.** Attempted by Walter Prager at Tuckerman Ravine prior to setting the course for the first US Giant Slalom race.

1938 – **First Professional Ski Patrol hired in the U.S.** Included patroller Sel Hannah '35, at Cannon Mountain, NH.

1939 – **First National Four-Event ski competition winner.** Steve Bradley, '39; at the first National Intercollegiate Four-Event (downhill, cross-country, slalom, and jumping) Championship; Sun Valley, ID.

1942 – **First soldier to enlist in the US Ski Troops.** Charles McLane '41 was the first volunteer to join the 87th Mountain Infantry Regiment. (The 87th would become part of the 10th Mountain Division shortly thereafter.).

1952 – **First Adaptive Skiing Program in the U.S. for the disabled.** Started under the leadership of Larry Jump '36 and his team at Arapahoe Basin, CO.

1952 – **First equipment designed and patented specifically for grooming ski slopes.** The Bradley Packer was invented by Steve Bradley '39, Manager of Winter Park Ski Area and was first used there in 1952. (We respectfully note that Mt. Cranmore, NH, was using standard tractors and other common mechanical equipment as early as 1941 to "groom" its slopes.)

Early 1950s – **First university course on snow avalanches.** Established by Professor John Montagne '42 and Charles Bradley (a member of the Bradley Family of Dartmouth fame) at Montana State University in Bozeman, MT.

Early 1950s – **First slope grooming conference in the U.S.** Organized by Steve Bradley '39 at Winter Park, CO. Bradley became known as the "father of slope maintenance." Groomed slopes attracted increasing numbers of novice skiers and became an important factor in popularizing the sport.

1955 – **First person to be timed at over 100 miles per hour on skis.** Ralph Miller '55 in Portillo, Chile; timed by French skiing champion Emile Allais and witnessed by future US National Alpine Champion Buddy Werner and Japanese Olympic Silver Medalist Chick Igaya '57—and a crowd of astounded international on-lookers.

1956 – **First US citizen (naturalized) to be awarded the Arlberg-Kandahar Diamond Pin.** Awarded to Walter Prager, Dartmouth ski coach. The award was given to Prager for his A-K skiing successes in the early 1930s as arguably the leading ski racer of the time and for his career Coaching contributions.

1958 – **First Person(s) to traverse the Bugaboos in British Columbia, Canada.** Bill Briggs '54, Bob French '56, Barry Corbet '58 and Sterling Neale '59 completed 100 mile traverse in 10 days.

1959 – **First (and probably only) person to secure a Small Business Administration loan to start a ski area.** Murray "Mike" Thurston '43; to develop Sunday River Ski Area, ME.

1968 – **First person to launch a multi-faceted marketing campaign for major brand names built around the image of a ski personality (Jean-Claude Killy) to the general consumer goods market.** Rick Isaacson '64, T '65.

1971 – **First descent on skis from the summit of Wyoming's Grand Teton Mountain.** Bill Briggs '54. Previously considered unskiable by experts, Briggs' feat ignited the modern extreme skiing phenomenon.

1978 – **First person to secure federally guaranteed financing for ski areas.** Investment banker Marshall Wallach '65; for Vail Mountain, CO, and Copper Mountain, CO.

1984 – **First person to complete an auction sale of a ski area.** Marshall Wallach '65 for Vail, CO.

1988 – **First person in the U.S. to invent and patent a roller ski that simulated cross-country snow skiing.** Len Johnson '56; the V2 Roller Ski (now with a 75% market share in North America).

1990 – **First human powered race winner on the Iditarod Trail, Alaska.** Tim Kelley '79 and Partner Bob Baker.

1991 – **First Snowboard Descent of the Invisible Chute of Mt. Superior** by Bill Hunt '80 on a Winterstick Swallowtail board.

2008 – **First person to "peak bag" (or summit) over 90 Alaskan peaks.** By Tim Kelley '79 who is still bagging more peaks.

APPENDIX 10

OTHER NOTABLE DARTMOUTH ACCOMPLISHMENTS IN US SKIING
A sampling of the exceptional, compiled by Thomas G. Washing '63

Dartmouth College alumni, staff, and families have often constituted the largest group in many skiing activities and/or have most frequently achieved the desired result. Collected here is a representative listing of some of the most notable accomplishments documented in this book. We cheerfully acknowledge that determining indisputably accurate numbers for some of these categories is perhaps not possible, but we also believe that those which are presented are as factual and accurate as the reasonably available resources indicate. This list, tentative and incomplete though it may be, is intended to highlight the fact that, in addition to so often being "the first" to participate, the Dartmouth family has regularly demonstrated a passion for and a considerable depth of involvement in the diverse array of activities which comprise modern skiing in the United States. We do not know of any other institution that can claim a comparable number of such achievements.

OLYMPIC SKIING AND SNOWBOARDING

Most Alumni from One College or University who have been Members of Winter Olympic Teams: 66. This number includes Olympics and Paralympics members.

Most Alumni from One College or University who have Qualified for Competitor Positions on Winter Olympic Teams: 109. Since the first Winter Olympics held in Chamonix, France, in 1924.

Most Consecutive Winter Olympics Participated in by One Athlete: 5 by Tim Caldwell '76, from 1972 (Sapporo, Japan) through 1984 (Sarajevo, Yugoslavia)

Most Medals Won by Alumni from One College or University on US Paralympic Teams: 26. Since competition began in 1984.

Most Consecutive Paralympics Participated in by One Athlete: 5 by Rob Walsh '88, from 1988 (Calgary, Canada) to 2002 (Salt Lake City, Utah)

Most Competitive Events participated in by Alumni from One College or University in Winter Olympics: 202. This number represents 159 events in Winter Olympics and 43 events in Winter Paralympics.

Most Winter Olympic Coaches from One College or University: 23.

Most* Winter Olympic Team Leaders from One College or University: 7.

Most* Alumni or Staff from One College or University to Serve as Officials of Winter Olympic Competitions: over 100. This includes officials who have served on various Olympic Games staffs and on USOC Olympic Skiing Committees.

RACING

Most Winners of National Skiing Championships (Individual and Team) from One College or University: 180. This does not include Paralympics champions.

Most Eastern Intercollegiate Ski Championships won: 29. From 1922 through 2009.

Most Alpine National Championship Ski Titles (USSANationals): 9. Gale H. ("Tiger") Shaw, III '85 and Dick Durrance '39 are tied with Bode Miller for this distinction.

Most Women's Championships Won in Cross-Country Skiing (USSA Nationals): 18. By Nina Kemppel '92, Tu '05.

Most Individual Paralympic National Championship Victories: 19. By Rob Walsh '88.

Most NCAA Individual National Championships: 6. By Chiharu ("Chick") Igaya '57.

Most NCAA Individual National Ski Titles in One Year: 3. Five athletes have achieved this feat; two are from Dartmouth: Chiharu Igaya '57 (Downhill, Alpine Combined, and Slalom) and Ralph Miller '55 (Downhill, Alpine Combined, and Skimeister).

Most Alpine Masters National Championships: 56. By Lisa Feinberg Densmore '83.

Most Dartmouth Winter Carnival Team Ski Victories by One College or University: 37. During the years 1922 through 2009.

ALSO OF NOTE

Most* Alumni from One College or University to be Involved with the Ski Infantry Troops and 10th Mountain Division during World War II: over 120. 1941-1945.

Most* US Ski Areas Founded, Developed, or Managed by Alumni from One College or University: 40. This number does not include the more than 450 ski areas in the U.S., Canada, Australia and New Zealand which received crucial lift engineering and snow-making advice and consulting from Sno-Engineering, a consulting firm founded or managed by Sel Hannah '35, James R. Branch '52, Tu '53, and Joseph Cushing '52, from 1958 through 1995.

Most* Doctors or Medical Staff at US Ski Area Communities who are Alumni of One College or University: 85 and counting.

* Cannot be established with absolute certainty due to incomplete or missing records, but no credible evidence to the contrary has been found or presented as of this writing.

APPENDIX 11

US SKI MUSEUMS AND HISTORICAL ORGANIZATIONS
by Meredith Scott '96

These historical organizations hold in public trust the history of a sport that for many is a way of life. Although only a sampling, these are among the best. We have noted some of the Dartmouth contributors.

US National Ski and Snowboard Hall of Fame and Museum, Ishpeming, MI: (**Paul Bousquet '53, Chairman of New Member Selection Committee):** The NSSHF is dedicated to the preservation and promotion of America's skiing heritage through the recognition of nationally outstanding skiers, snowboarders and ski sport builders in the USA. *www. skihall.com*

Mammoth Ski Museum, Mammoth Lake, CA: This is home to the Beekley International Collection, the largest private collection of skiing's fine art and literature. www.mammothskimuseum.org

Squaw Valley Olympic Museum and Western Winter Sports Heritage Center, Olympic Valley, CA (In progress): The museum highlights the skiing heritage of the western US and celebrates the 1960 Olympic Winter Games held here. **Linda Williams '80, Project Manager**. www.squaw.com/olympic-museum

Western SkiSport Museum, Truckee, CA: Founded by the Auburn Ski Club preserve the history of winter ski sports in the western United States. www.auburnskiclub.org

Colorado Ski Museum, Vail, CO: The Museum and Hall of Fame preserves the history of skiing and snowboarding as well as honoring individuals from Colorado's rich skiing legacy. www.skimuseum.net.

Ketchum Sun Valley Historical Society – Heritage and Ski Museum, Ketchum, ID: The Society preserves the history of the region and provide facilities to store/exhibit historical material. www.ksvhistoricalsociety.org

Ski Museum of Maine, Farmington, ME: The Ski Museum of Maine celebrates Maine's ski history and heritage; and recognize distinguished Maine skiers. www.skimuseumofmaine.org

New England Ski Museum, Franconia, NH: (**Jeff Leich '71, Executive Director**) This museum preserves a broad spectrum of ski history, particularly in New England. www.skimuseum.org

Pennsylvania Ski and Winter Sports Museum & Hall of Fame, Stroudsburg, PA: (**Alex L. "Buzz" Bensinger '44, Founder**) This museum is dedicated to preserving Pennsylvania's winter sports heritage. www.paskimuseum.org

Alf Engen Museum, Park City, UT: This is home to the Intermountain Ski Hall of Fame and, along wiht The George Eccles 2002 Olympics Museum, part of the Joe Quinney Winter Sports Center. www.engenmuseum.org

Vermont Ski Museum, Stowe, VT: (**Meredith Scott '96, Director**) The museum preserves Vermont's skiing history, and houses the Vermont Ski Museum Hall of Fame. www.engenmuseum.org

The International Skiing History Association: (**Dean Ericson '67, President**) ISHA is a not-for-profit corporation, whose mission is to preserve and advance the knowledge of ski history and to increase public awareness of the sport's heritage, particularly thru publication of Skiing Heritage magazine. The first meeting of ISHA was conducted in 1991 at the Hanover Inn, Hanover NH. www.skiinghistory.org.

INDEX

PASSION FOR SKIING

Dartmouth skiers ready to go up the mountain; what Harris started has blossomed!